CHOCKS AWAY!

CHOCKS AWAY!

ROGER A. FREEMAN

CASSELL&CO

Special edition for PAST TIMES

Cassell & Co
Wellington House, 125 Strand
London WC2R OBB

First published by Arms and Armour 1989 as
Experiences of War: The British Airman
This edition 2000

ISBN 0-304-35631-X

9 8 7 6 5 4 3 2 1

Designed and edited by DAG Publications Ltd
Printed and bound in Great Britain by
Cox & Wyman, Reading

PAST TIMES®

Contents

Acknowledgements

A full list of the contributors whose names appear adjacent to their quotations in the narrative is to be found at the end of this book. To meet the aim of this work, ranks are omitted and it is hoped that this is not seen as disrespect, for some contributors rose to high rank. The book exists solely through the interest and willingness of these contributors' co-operation, to whom I tender my sincere thanks.

Acknowledgement is also made to Michael Bowyer, David Brook, Frank Cheesman, Alan East, Eric Munday, Dave Osborne, Merle Olmsted, John Rabbetts, Nat Young; to Ian Mactaggart and George Pennick for photographic expertise, to Bruce Robertson for editorial guidance, and Jean Freeman for preparing the manuscript.

Roger A. Freeman, 1989

Introduction

The forties were a very different world – a cliché, yes; but certainly that time *was* different in many important respects. Then, British youth were more disciplined, respectful and patriotic than their counterparts half a century on. Their experience was parochial and knowledge of other nations restricted to school geography lessons. No package holidays then to sunny climes, for foreign journeying was limited by expense and difficulties of travel. The working man spent his holidays at the 'seaside' if he could afford even that luxury. Most were paid literally by the hour, which meant no wages for holiday weeks, and short weekly pay at Christmas or when Bank Holidays occurred. Pre-war life was simpler and expectations modest. No television, washing-machines, refrigerator or vacuum cleaner, advances then only within the financial reach of the better or well off.

A semi-detached house, small car and white collar job might evaluate one to 'middle class' standing, but not to the aforementioned luxuries that would one day be deemed as essentials of domestic comfort. The divisions of class were also much more pronounced, largely allied to income. A factory worker would have rented terraced accommodation in the town; perhaps two up, two down, with a sewered lavatory in the backyard. A farm labourer might enjoy a large garden, but he often lived without benefit of electricity and piped water, which had still to reach many outlying rural areas; a flush lavatory was rare in those localities. In short, the industrial and agricultural developments that gradually elevated the ordinary person to the comparative affluence of the 1980s were at an early stage. What people did not have, they did not know. Life was generally harder; daily working hours longer and Saturday morning part of the working week, domestic chores harder, with less time for leisure.

Although there was more of a 'them' and 'us' atmosphere in the British society of 1939, national patriotism was not bounded by class. The menace of Nazi Germany was met with the same determination to support King and Country in a humble cottage as in a stately mansion. A conditioning in the glories of Empire was chiefly responsible for the common belief that Britain was still the greatest nation, whose values and traditions placed it head and shoulder above the rest. So when war was declared and something had to be done about Hitler there already existed an intrinsic sense of duty. For the majority it was unthinkable not to fight for one's country. Even the slaughter on the Western Front, not yet a quarter of a century removed, could have a dampening effect on patriotism. Perhaps fathers who had experienced the bitter taste of trench warfare were not enthused to encourage sons, but most did not dissuade. The tyranny and the threat to democracy of the Nazi regime, as projected by newspaper and radio, was accepted. The citizen was ready to become a warrior once more.

In the conflict of arms known as the Second World War, military aviation has been authoritatively assessed as making a decisive contribution to the Allied victory. The United Kingdom's participation in what was commonly called the air war was on a considerable scale relative to its total war effort, almost a half of armed forces expenditure. Of this only 10 per cent was invested in the Royal Navy's largely seaborne Fleet Air Arm, while the lion's share went to the Royal Air Force, the world's first fully autonomous military flying service.

The RAF had been formed on 1 April 1918 by amalgamating the Army's Royal Flying Corps with the Navy's Royal Naval Air Service. Aviation technology, then in its infancy, led to the military value of the aeroplane being questioned by the majority of conventional force commanders and strategists. Overall, in the first decade following the Great War, the RAF was adjudged a useful adjunct to the Army and Navy, particularly handy in far-flung corners of the Empire for 'showing the Flag' and policing the natives. To those who wore its blue uniform it was a pretty nice service to be in - and great fun if you were a flier. Air power remained largely a word in the vocabulary of theorists.

The slaughter of the Great War had left a heavy scar on national attitudes. Few families did not have a member who knew the horror of the ground fighting, while every village War Memorial bore witness to the scale of the sacrifice. Another conflict of that nature was to be avoided, and, while the general outlook was not pacifist, there was a turning away from the military at many levels. It was supposed that the German population, their economy in chaos, were likewise imbued with a 'never again' outlook. Even when the National Socialists offered to restore German pride, the leaders of most other European nations did not at first see this as a threat to peace. And when they did, appeasement appears to have been the favoured ploy to buy time.

In Germany the revived military were quick to embrace technology as a means of ensuring better equipment and ordnance, not least in the air. The tool of trade of an air force was the aeroplane and with the encouragement of the Nazi hierarchy the drive to develop aircraft more advanced than those of other European neighbours was pressed with vigour. Belatedly the British and the French moved to re-equip and expand their air forces, but not with the required expediency; there was still a belief that the gathering storm would pass by. As a result, the German Luftwaffe's equipment was in many respects superior to that of the RAF when war was declared on 3 September 1939. The Luftwaffe was also better trained for its task - primarily, tactical support of the ground forces. It would take the RAF months in some respects and years in others to achieve parity. The RAF, both leaders and men, believed they were more than a match for the enemy air force and, after costly experience, this eventually proved to be the case. Because of technical and tactical weaknesses, that success was achieved with heavy loss of lives. In retrospect there appears to have been a degree of tardiness in some areas in pushing the development of new aircraft, engines, armament and equipment, for technology should have been recognized as being of major importance in achieving the superiority that would lead to victory. This is not to underestimate the difficulties of making up for years of neglect.

What then of the ordinary men and women who made up the Royal Air Force and who often did not recognize their own part in any grand strategic plan or tactical move, but carried out the orders of Command, performed their duties, and lived or died? On the pages that follow I have set out to record the experiences of some of those who survived and through their words to evoke an expression of service life during the most extensive clash of arms in history. In recounting these events, attitudes, motivations, fears, hopes and many other aspects of individual expression are revealed, helping to convey something of the feel and flavour of RAF life in those days. Only the war with Nazi Germany and its European allies is covered in this work; the RAF in the Far East is to be the subject of a later volume.

Roger A. Freeman

Sprogs

JOINING UP

'I don't want to join the Air Force
I don't want to go to war
I'd rather hang around
Piccadilly Underground
And live upon the earnings of a high-born lady. . . .'

This well-known ditty rang out in many a Royal Air Force Mess during the war years, but it did not reflect the truth. Young men did want to join the Air Force, thousands of them. Aircrew were only drawn from volunteers and there were always more men who wanted to fly than the force could absorb. The disappointed usually opted for ground duties with the hope that one day their desire to become aircrew could be realized. Not that there was a dearth of recruits for non-flying duties. The RAF was also the first choice of the majority of conscripts.

Most young men who wanted to 'do their bit' and had family traditions of the Army and Navy were understandably drawn to those services. For many others who were reasonably well educated, in particular the ex-grammar-school boys, the RAF seemed to offer more interesting prospects, a developing form of warfare dependent on the latest technology and more fitting to the intelligent. And the RAF did require a good standard of education for the majority of duties in almost every operational branch of the service. Fred Lomas has no doubts about its popularity among his school friends:

'From my secondary school over half the boys who reached military age during the war went into the RAF. There seemed much more glamour attached to flying than there was to the work of the other services. We had our own Air Training Corps squadron at the school and if you joined you were pretty sure to be accepted for the RAF when you volunteered at 18. The appeal also lay in the more personal *esprit de corps* of flying units where it was you, or you and a few other chaps, alone in one aircraft. This was something conveyed by those who had joined up at the beginning of the war and who often came back to the school when on leave. I also estimate that of those from my school who went into the RAF and flew, about 80 per cent became casualties.'

The 'adventure of flying' angle is well represented by the desire of Jim Betteridge:

'I joined because I fancied myself as Biggles. Those stories inspired a lot of young fellows to want to fly. They certainly made me air-minded and in turn had inspired me to join the Air Defence Cadet Corps, forerunner of the Air Training Corps, and Air League in 1938. The latter was an organization set up to promote British aviation when it became apparent that we were lagging behind that of other nations during the mid-thirties.'

There were, however, many and varied individual reasons for joining the 'Raf'. Not a few young men saw it as an escape from a low standard of living and poor accommodation. Eddie Wheeler:

'By 18 I had outgrown my fold-up bed located in the tiny kitchen at home, and this became more problematic as time went on – bouts of cramp became more prevalent. It was at the cinema one evening that I saw George Formby in *Something in the Air* and immediately I felt convinced that my salvation could be in joining the RAF – if only to get a bed large enough to accommodate me without doubling my knees with ensuing cramp!'

For some a choice of uniform was important. It hung on one item of clothing for Alfred Jenner:

'When war looked highly likely, if not inevitable, the patriotic thing to do was join the Territorials or a reserve organization: so I joined the RAFVR (RAF Volunteer Reserve). My choice was based on the fact that the RAF was the only one of the three services where the lower ranks wore ties. I was called the day after war was declared and spent the next few weeks at Padgate in what was known as "square bashing". Not only were there no ties but no uniforms available for my intake. Instead we drilled in the civilian clothes in which we arrived. Unfortunately, in my case this included a pair of plus-fours which were then a fashion for the well decked out young man about the provincial town. The drill sergeant thought otherwise, particularly as the elastic which was supposed to retain each leg of the garment neatly beneath the knee proved too weak for the job. One or other was frequently flapping around an ankle when we marked time or drilled at the double. His remarks became more pointed and coarse as the days went by and it was with great relief that uniforms were at last received. These turned out to be old-style twenties uniforms with a high button tunic – and no tie!'

Others who were attracted by the uniform also saw the RAF as more accommodating to their way of life. Bill Japp:

'I think I volunteered for aircrew for a host of wrong reasons. A new airfield, Edzell, had been opened in 1940 near my home and my parents became friendly with the station commander. Then, at 17 I was given the occasional flight in an Anson or Dominie and was much influenced by what I observed around the station. I liked the uniform and fancied the idea of silken wings on my breast. Then too, it appeared to offer an easier way of service; bacon and eggs for breakfast, clean sheets on your bed, more gentlemanly conduct. There was no deep reasoning behind the decision to volunteer; no fire in my belly to fly as some fellows I met claimed to have.'

Patriotism was the principal spur to volunteering for military service, although such action was sometimes encouraged by the looming presence of conscription when one might not be able to join the service of one's choice. It was known that the army claimed most conscripts, and for many young men influenced by fathers and relations who had survived the horrors of infantry trench warfare in 1914-18, the prospect was undesirable. Particularly so during the 1939-40 'phoney war' period when the stalemate of static warfare appeared to be about to repeat itself. The army was also considered the dumping ground for ignoramuses and the uncouth element of society. If you aspired to better company the RAF appeared a safer bet. This, perhaps false, but widely shared belief, sometimes found endorsement through personal experience; as in the case of John Sampson:

'I was 17 years of age and in the Home Guard. One evening in the summer of 1940 we were being taught the rudiments of bayonet fighting by a sergeant in the Coldstream Guards. We had to rush across an open piece of ground with an ancient American Springfield rifle and stick the bayonet into a sack filled with straw, shouting as loud as we could during the process. I thought I had done quite well until the sergeant bawled at me, "Don't stand there like a pregnant nun." In that instant I decided the army was not for me and volunteered for aircrew duty with the RAF.'

The desire to fly remained the principal aim of volunteers throughout hostilities, with pilot being the most sought after position. On average, of every fifteen men who applied for pilot training only one was accepted. And only 60 per cent of volunteers passed muster at aircrew selection boards. Some individuals went to great lengths to be accepted. Bob Thompson was one:

'At the beginning of the war I was working in Birmingham and decided to give up my job and fly with the RAF come what may. I went to the local recruiting office and in due course got a letter telling me to report to Padgate for an aircrew selection board. There I was confronted with a group of senior RAF officers all decked out in their best and rather intimidating. The first question asked me was: "Why do you want to take up this dangerous occupation?" Well, I wasn't very good at the King and Country lark and was absolutely floored. I didn't know what to say. The interview floundered on and at the end they said they didn't think I was suitable for flying duties but they could find me a ground place. I said, "No thank you, I've set my heart on flying." I went away absolutely desolate, the bottom had fallen out of my world. After a few days I thought I'd have another go. So I went over to Sunderland to an aunt and asked if I could give her address if I went to the local recruiting office. She agreed and so I applied and received notice of another interview, this time at Cardington. Here again I was confronted with an intimidating row of officers. However, their questions took a different line. They opened with: "You're a healthy looking fellow, how do you keep so fit?" There couldn't have been a better question for I was able to say sailing, rugger and all the sports in which the type of blokes they were looking for would indulge. I was accepted.'

Even when they liked the look of you there was still the stiff medical to get through. A sturdy young man was demolished on learning he had a minor eyesight or hearing defect that immediately took him out of the running. In a few tests one's performance during the medical could be enhanced; as in George Irving's case:

'Enlisted for flying duties as a navigator, I was instructed to attend an interview and medical at Padgate on 2 November 1940. During the interview I stressed that I would make a much better pilot than navigator and although at the age of 28 I was on the maximum age limit for acceptance for training as a pilot, they agreed to give me the opportunity subject to passing the medical. The medical was very thorough, one of the tests was blowing into a little tube to hold a mercury level on the hundred scale mark and to maintain the pressure for at least fifty seconds. Being very determined not to fail I held on until I almost blacked out. The doctor was obviously impressed because he said I held the record to date by holding for 95 seconds.'

There was another feature of all Selection Board medicals which, although simple, gave many a problem. Jim Eley:

'As was usual, I was required to give a urine sample. When I couldn't, the official said, "I expect you were like all the others and "went" before you came in." I was given a drink of water and made to stand barefoot on a cold stone slab until I could "go".'

A bar to volunteering for military service was employment in a reserved occupation. In most cases this did not apply to aircrew acceptance which brought some men into the ranks of the RAF who had previously held other ambitions. John Osborne:

'I was a sergeant in the Home Guard and fancied army service. I was dead keen to get into the Reconnaissance Corps – armoured cars and light tanks – which had just been formed when I became old enough to volunteer in 1942. So I went along to the Recruiting Office and signed up, only to have my boss call me aside a few days later to tell me he had heard from the army but was holding my reserved occupation for 12 months – we were making alkathene parts for radars. Well, I wasn't very pleased. So, knowing he could not reserve me if I volunteered and was accepted for aircrew. I took the afternoon off and did just that.'

For non-aircrew, even acceptance into the RAF and partial training did not ensure continued service in a blue uniform. In the last two years of hostilities many hundreds of recently conscripted RAF personnel were transferred to the other services for various reasons. Jim Eley:

'While taking a 12-week Morse course at Blackpool, we were told that those who obtained the required speed would be transferred to the navy which was short of trained wireless operators. Wanting to keep one foot on dry land, I purposely failed the test. However, my time in the RAF was short-lived because soon after completing training I was told I was being transferred to the army who were in dire need of W/T operators. At the Huyton transit camp I met blokes who had been with me on the original course and had been sent to the navy. Apparently the army's need became greater than the navy's so they were transferred again. In the course of nine months they had worn three different uniforms!'

On the other hand the RAF received several trained fitters and riggers from the Fleet Air Arm as the navy had too many. The RAF also recruited army personnel as aircrew for army co-operation units. Rex Croger was an artillery officer who made the transfer following an earlier and unusual association with the Air Force:

'I was looking through ACIs (Army Council Instructions) which every army officer was supposed to read, when I saw a request for commissioned artillery officers to volunteer to fly with the RAF as air gunners. I thought it sounded interesting and decided to have a go. The job entailed a course of training in air gunnery, following which I flew on a single Nickel (leaflet) raid over Lille in a Wellington on the night of 5 April 1942. Seated in the front turret, I had a box-like instrument on my knees to watch for variations of the indicator in a dial while over enemy territory. The purpose was to discover if the Germans were using a specific form of radar. I was never quite sure why Ack-Ack (anti-aircraft) officers were chosen for the task. Thereafter I was one of a few army officers sporting an air gunner's wing on my tunic. Some months after returning to my searchlight unit I saw another ACI which announced that army officers could volunteer for pilot service with the RAF in army co-operation squadrons. Evidently at that time they anticipated a pilot shortage. Having enjoyed my brief period as an air gunner I decided to apply. No doubt the previous air experience helped, for I was accepted immediately. They never transferred me to the RAF; I was just seconded, despite receiving an RAF number and taking RAF uniform and rank.'

There were, of course, adventurers, perhaps the most notable being those foreign nationals who clamoured to join; albeit that they felt the cause was just – Nazi Germany was a tyranny that had to be countered. However, the primary motivation for volunteering to fly for the British was the attraction of the 'derring-do' of the fighter pilot, as established by the air aces of the First World War twenty years before. Practically all fancied themselves in the cockpit of a Spitfire. This enthusiasm is well illustrated by the intentions of James Goodson:

'Having survived the torpedoing of the *Athenia* on her fatal western voyage soon after the outbreak of war. I eventually ended up in Glasgow. Not being very pleased with the people who had tried to confine me to the deep, I sought out a recruiting office. The recruiting sergeant was at a loss what to do when confronted by an American who wanted to join the RAF. After a telephone call to a superior he informed me that he thought it would be all right but I would have to swear allegiance to the Crown. I said that wasn't going to be a problem. He then handed me a form and proceeded to outline a few details of what was expected if I were accepted. All seemed simple until he said: "It will be three shillings a day." A quick bit of mental calculation transformed this sum into five US dollars a week. Crestfallen, I stammered, "I don't think I can afford that." He looked at me a little strangely before replying, "Well, that's what the pay will be." Of course, I didn't tell him I thought he was asking me for three shillings a day or my delight at attaining my fondest dream. To think I could join the RAF and fly a fighter plane while actually being paid for doing it! The lovable fools, they could have had my services for nothing!'

Goodson was successful and eventually joined the ranks of one of the three 'Eagle' squadrons, units specially raised to embrace the considerable number of Americans who joined the RAF. Young men from many other neutral countries also joined and flew for Britain, but not in such numbers as those from the USA to warrant special squadrons.

Initial Training

Whether you had volunteered or been conscripted, leaving the shelter of the family home to report to an RAF reception centre was, for the majority of young men and women, a step into the unknown, and one faced with concern. The experience of Don Nunn is not untypical:

'Like most 18-year-old recruits I was a bit apprehensive on first reporting to Lord's cricket ground, the London reception centre for aircrew. But it wasn't quite the awesome experience expected. Turning in my civilian belongings I got my first lesson in service dodges. As each ration book was surrendered the reception clerks slyly flipped through and removed any still valid coupons. These were obviously being secreted away for personal use. They may have eaten well but, like the rest of the intake that day, all I got was a plate of soup. Lord's was not quite the harsh regime I'd imagined. In the following days I was even able to sit in the Members' Stand and watch a game. A somewhat incongruous scene as next to we young boys in blue there was a bunch of old gents sipping G & Ts and occasionally applauding; all as if the war had never happened.'

The transition from civil to military life was a rude awakening for many youngsters, particularly girls with a refined background. Maureen Brickett found it an almost traumatic experience:

'The shock horror of my first few days in the WAAF are a lasting memory – having been educated in a Convent where Modesty was the eleventh commandment, I joined RAF Innsworth near Gloucester on November 13th 1941. Our first bitterly cold night in a Nissen hut ended with a "march" to the ablution block a hundred yards or so away in temperatures below zero – standing in the icy concrete shed faced with a long line of wash basins and only cold water and confronted with hardier types stripped naked, I nearly died with embarrassment! I don't think I really washed for a week, just kept sprinkling the talcum powder! When I eventually discovered a bath and hot water, I thought I was in heaven!!!'

Men accepted for aircrew usually spent a few days being processed; which simply meant collecting kit and an introduction to the preliminaries of military drill, while somewhere clerks found an establishment where each newcomer could be sent for initial training. Those destined for non-flying duties generally reported to one of the larger basic training establishments such as Padgate or Cardington where discipline and drill were endured for eight weeks. 'Short back and sides' removed the last vestige of civilian status, as Martin Mason discovered:

'Reporting to the recruit depot at Padgate in July 1940, I spent ten days being fitted out with uniform and having endless inoculations before being posted to a new station, RAF Kirkham, near Preston. Young men took a pride in keeping their hair trim, attending the barber every two or three weeks, but there was no opportunity for me to get a short back and sides at Padgate and Kirkham lacked a barber. The authorities were aware of the problem but had difficulty obtaining the services of a civilian barber. It wasn't until a Sunday morning that one arrived to shear us. A queue of possibly fifty new recruits soon formed. The barber, seeing the daunting task ahead, worked at prodigious speed with his electric shears so that by the time each man was clipped the tail end of the queue was still moving forward to take up the slack resulting from his move into the chair. The effect was that the queue seemed to be constantly moving forward. I, and most of the others, had the quickest haircut of our lives.'

And then there was the uniform. A recruit did not really feel part of the Air Force until he or she had donned the distinctive blue. At the start of the war a male recruit eventually received two No. 1 Dress uniforms, of which one was kept for parades and walking out – 'Best Blues'. Later, one set was replaced with a No. 2 uniform, a blue version of the army 'battledress', and this was used for everyday wear. The initial decking-out would be followed by variations as desired by different branches of the service. Ernest Thorpe had some pertinent observations on dress:

'The war "respectabilized" uniform. Before, if a girl was seen with an airman there was the comment: "Fancy that; well I never." But with dear Uncle George in uniform all this changed. As a member of the RAF Regiment from its inception, I became well aware of the importance of uniform. Uniform dictated who you saluted and who gave the order, "Right dress!"

'With our usual Air Force uniform we were first issued with peaked caps. Our sergeant referred to us as his "bus drivers". We were glad when these were discarded in favour of side caps. Some wore these at an extremely jaunty angle, presenting balancing difficulties. The Air Force pullover, very durable, was often worn in bed for warmth – and I only saw one instance of an airman wearing pyjamas persistently in the worst conditions.

'Our underpants were heavy, knee-length drawers, button-up fronts with brace loops; the male equivalent of the "passion-killers" that WAAFs were reputed to wear. For our shirts, some bought Van Heusen collars as they were smarter, softer and more comfortable; illegal, as was another practice of widening the rather narrow trouser bottoms of the "best blues". This was achieved by putting inverted Vs in the bottom of the seams, giving a slightly flared look. A civilian tailor in Hythe would carry out this work, always sounding us out on the probability of an "invasion", he being a Jew. As the alterations were frowned upon by the "powers that were", we had to take evasive action when sighting RAF Police.

'Providing one was wearing the correct uniform, smartness was encouraged. There was a practice of "stick" man. The smartest man on parade would be excused the guard. A reservist named Parker was always our "stick" man. But he was also a bit of a rebel and they eventually posted him to the Middle East.

'In 1941 I was pleased to make the transition to khaki with more comfortable battledress blouse and the blue boiler suit fatigue dress replaced with khaki denims. Later on, after being on a motor vehicle driver's course, with the usual service cussedness I was given a motor cycle. Breeches and dispatch-rider boots, waterproof jacket and leggings, were topped off by a hated crash-helmet which seemed to be made of papier mâché. How we appreciated civilian clothes when on leave!'

There were few women who were completely happy with all items of the WAAF uniform which, basically functional, gave little acknowledgement to current feminine fashions. At least the issue was plentiful, something which impressed Irene Storer:

'In 1940 there were so many of us that the supply of uniforms ran out and I was issued with two navy overalls, a navy beret and a grey raincoat with an armband. Later on I was issued with proper uniform and received the following: 4 shirts, very roomy in smooth cotton poplin, blue; 8 separate matching collars; 1 black tie; 2 air force blue serge skirts and jackets, both unlined; 2 caps; 1 cap badge; 2 pairs black flat lace-up shoes; 3 wool vests; 2 suspender belts, old-fashioned pink corset fabric about 6 inches deep; 4 bras, same fabric as suspender belts; 4 pairs heavyweight grey lisle stockings; 6 pairs wool winter knickers, black; 6 pairs wool summer knickers, grey, and 1 pair plimsolls. I had never had so many clothes in my life! The greatcoat was double-breasted with a cream woollen lining, but I did not receive one until December 1940.

'The only scope for any measure of individuality was in underwear, and as service underwear was reminiscent of 1914 these were the garments we tried to substitute – with difficulty without clothing coupons. I appreciated the bras and suspender belts, having previously had to wear an uncomfortable corselet; but the knickers were really awful! The only difference between the summer and winter ones was the colour – the winter ones being called "blackouts" after the fabric used to black out windows. A favourite practical joke was to raise a pair of blackouts on a flagpole! I continued to wear my own panties until they needed replacing, when I made some from whatever fabric was available. Petticoats were not issued, and as the serge skirts were rough, many service women made petticoats from cut down nightdresses, old evening dress fabric, or parachute silk – but one could be punished for using the latter. Service women were permitted to wear their own stockings if they were of regulation colour.'

Following reception some recruits found themselves quickly moved on to what, compared with the civilian life they had just left, were primitive conditions. Rumour, that persistent service infection, sometimes voiced a suspicion of exploitation. Albert Benest:

'After reporting to the Air Crew Reception Centre at Lord's cricket ground in London, I was sent to Ludlow in Shropshire. This was really no more than a staging camp until they had sorted out where we were to be sent for basic training. We had to live in bell-tents surrounded by mud, with which we fought a losing battle to keep it from our brand-new uniforms and equipment. It rained most of the time and to keep us occupied we were set to digging trenches which were then piped. The story that went around was that the ground was part of an estate owned by an Air Vice-Marshal who was taking advantage of the available labour to have some free drainage carried out.'

A recruit's early days in the RAF are well summed up in the experiences of James Donson who aspired to fly:

'One's memory of the early days of aircrew training is a hazy recollection of almost continuous movement from place to place – a gathering together process, a few days at one place where we got to know what a sergeant was; some perfunctory drill; inoculations, documentation; then on to somewhere a couple of hundred miles away; more documentation, then after a week or two making sure that we knew our own names and numbers. Sergeants and corporals had only ranks, they never seemed to have names; it gradually dawned on us that the fact was not surprising since, in the view of most erks, NCOs had no fathers. After what seemed an age (some three weeks) we were issued with uniforms. On then to Initial Training Wing (ITW) – yet another journey. When we arrived at our destination we found our HQ was a large comfortable seaside hotel on the Welsh coast equipped with wash-basins, baths, beds and proper loos, none of which any of us had seen since leaving home. We began to feel that at least for a time there would be respite from primitive, makeshift conditions. Life became a routine of early rising, PT, lectures, route marches and meals. Lectures on meteorology, navigation, signals, rules of the air, etc., always took place in rooms about a mile apart and we marched from one to the other in "flights" at the regulation 40 paces a minute. As yet, no one had seen an aeroplane at close quarters but we had a number of lectures on aircraft recognition, no doubt to lessen the shock when we would eventually see one.'

The rapid expansion of the RAF after the outbreak of war and the vast influx of new personnel during the early months, led to Training Command being reorganized as Flying Training and Technical Training. The pre-war facilities were swamped and the situation was met by taking over a wide variety of civilian properties, in particular hotel and holiday camp facilities in the large seaside towns. Although the rigours of 'drill' and 'bull' did not endear these early weeks of service to the participants, there were sometimes compensations. Peter Catchpole:

'One of the good things about the initial training at Blackpool was that at least once a week we were sent to the Derby Baths to swim. This vast place had been one of the pre-war attractions of Blackpool as a seaside holiday centre. About 500 air force fellows would descend on these baths at one time. Only about half had swimming-costumes or trunks, the rest swam nude. It was an eye-opener for an 18-year-old like me, who had led a fairly sheltered life before joining up, that there were so many differences in men; long fellers and short fellers, big fellers and embarrassed fellers. Guards were placed at each entrance to keep the locals out and to watch over our deposited rifles and equipment. However, we heard that the cleaning women who were supposedly kept away from the baths area while we were swimming, had made peepholes through doors and shutters and regularly enjoyed the spectacle.'

One soon learned that there was little regard for individual modesty. No problem if you had been a school boarder, but hard on those from a sheltered background or the self-conscious. There was one particular contact with the Medical Officer that no one liked. Ernest Thorpe:

'In retrospect, "flashing" to order in the "FFI" (Free From Infection) inspection was humorous, but not at the time. "When the MO comes to you, you will drop your pants." Embarrassing, degrading. I sometimes speculated inwardly as to whether the WAAFs were subjected to this ordeal.'

The conditioning programme to which all recruits were subjected had the aim of instilling discipline. Rigorous exercise, menial tasks and constant verbal persecution by the non-commissioned officers (NCOs) in charge was an unpleasant experience. One had to 'take it' for any individual who showed signs of rebelling was branded insubordinate and suffered greater indignities. The general resentment among recruits now and again produced subtle forms of retaliation. Cyril Clifford:

'My original trade was Service Police and in the winter of 1940 I was posted to No. 1 RAF Depot, Uxbridge, the home of "bull", to take a course. The police course was quite interesting and they made us feel the job was very necessary. The camp discipline, however, was very rigid and there seemed to be a senior NCO around every corner waiting to pounce on anyone who stepped off a path or had a button undone. Victims would find themselves in the cookhouse, after the day's lectures, cleaning out baking-tins, etc. Friday night was "bullshit" night when the barrack rooms were scrubbed and polished so vigorously that you could see your reflection in every surface. The Station Warrant Officer would come round inspecting, wipe his finger along the top of a door and, showing us three specks of dust, exclaim: "This place is not fit for pigs to live in!"

'The harsh regime was, understandably, resented although we had to accept it; but for a time we had our little dig at authority. There was a long path from the lecture rooms to the airmen's canteen. If someone saw an officer in the distance he would pass the word along and we would deliberately spread out in a long line so that the officer would have to return hundreds of smart salutes. After a while the authorities began to realize what was going on and we were ordered to form large squads and march between the locations.'

A more daring snub to authority is recalled by Ray Lomas:

'At University Air Squadron we progressed from basic drill to continuity drill. That is, the whole squad went through a drill routine without shouted commands for the series of movements. When the drill corporal shouted "Forward March" we carried on right the way through the routine, having memorized the changes. We reached a pretty good standard. After the UAS we all went to the Air Crew Reception Centre in London and suffered the usual chasing around new recruits had from the NCOs. Getting a bit fed-up with one particular corporal we got together and decided to bring him down a peg. The opportunity arose when we were out on the square in front of some officers. As soon as the corporal gave his first order we went into our continuity routine. It looked perfect to the watching officers but we were ignoring all the corporal's commands and putting on our own display. He was very quiet thereafter.'

An impromptu plot against the PT overseers is recounted by George Irving:

'Squads were marched down to Scarborough sea front where their sergeants could position themselves on the road above to roar out their orders. One morning it was very windy, the tide was in and the sea rough. The squad next to us was composed of "old-timers" who had been in the RAF prior to the war and had remustered for aircrew training. Their sergeant called out "Running time; begin!" so they jogged off along the sea front and appeared to be unable to hear the "About turn" order and just disappeared from sight before their rather red-faced sergeant could get down on the lower road. After calling in at a café for tea and buns, they reformed and jogged back through the town in immaculate formation. Their drill sergeant was very cross.'

Most of the haranguing from NCOs was impersonal but occasionally more direct animosity arose, usually where an individual confronted the authority of an NCO. One trainee who believed he was being singled out devised a novel way of hitting back.

James Donson:

'In order to collect fatigue parties to flatten all the food tins in which most of our rations came, the duty sergeant would find minor defects on daily inspections – like blankets not folded in creases or dust on the waste-pipe under the wash-basin and similar trifles. The occupants of the rooms in which such "unairmanlike slackness" occurred would be issued with 7-pound sledge-hammers for their evening task. One sergeant always seemed to pick on a particular trainee every time. On one occasion the trainee was prepared. When the sergeant stood over him, immaculate in his bearing and appearance, he edged a full tin of corned beef into his pile and brought down the sledge-hammer with full force on it. Smashed corned beef flew in all directions, most of it on the walls but some on the sergeant's immaculate uniform. There was an exchange of words, brief from the trainee, voluble from his tormentor.'

Later many of the sufferers came to realize that the dreaded NCOs of 'square-bashing' days had been encouraged by their superiors to behave in a hectoring fashion. An observation nicely summed-up by William Reid:

'When you were an AC Plonk doing your basic training, you always felt the PT corporals were such hard men. Yet when I met some of them later on they were really such nice fellows. You came to understand that all that shouting and discipline was a necessary part of the conditioning process so that an order was accepted without question.'

A facet of training days which few escaped was guard duty. This usually inflicted discomfort and boredom, although in Eddie Wheeler's first and only commitment to this role tedium was soon dispelled:

'A water-tower which supplied the Yatesbury camp was located on a hill surrounded by trees on the other side of the main road to Calne and was viewed as a potential target for saboteurs. Hence the necessity to mount a guard throughout 24 hours daily. My turn for guard duty on the water-tower arrived and the weather was foul, bucketting with rain, and I was assigned for night duty from 6pm to 6am next morning. The shifts were two hours on and two hours off, the rest period to be spent in a tent adjacent to the water-tower. Our Lee Enfield .303 rifles were issued by the sergeant of the guard and live ammunition seen for the first time. Two guards were to patrol round the tower, meeting each other at about 10-minute intervals. The usual challenge procedures were outlined by the sergeant. On approach to the tower persons were to be challenged: "Who goes there, friend or foe?" If no response, the challenge once again. After the second challenge if no reply, then fire!

'Patrolling at night in pouring rain – surrounded by trees – was the most soul-destroying job one can imagine. My boredom was suddenly broken by a distinct rustling in the trees. Petrified, I am sure my challenge "Who goes there?" was but a whisper. Further noises emanated from the trees – could be two or three assailants – but still no response to my next hysterical challenge. Panic-stricken at the thought of the tower being attacked during my patrol, I released the safety catch on my rifle, aimed at the area from whence the distinct noises came, and fired. There was a thump within the trees and my heart sank – "God, I've killed someone." The sound of the shot brought the other guard and the sergeant running with shouts of "Bloody hell!, what was that?" Shaking like a leaf, I was rooted to the spot while the sergeant investigated. He returned with the news that I had shot a local farmer's cow which had strayed into the trees.'

Flying Training

After basic training those who would eventually join a ground trade went to one of the technical training establishments – seven out of every ten RAF personnel. Men accepted for aircrew proceeded from an Initial Training Wing to an elementary flying training school. Here would-be pilots came face to face with the realities of taking to the air in a machine which, as in the case of Philip Knowles, temporarily tempered their enthusiasm:

'In August 1942 we arrived at No. 18 Elementary Flying Training School at Fairoaks for our first flying experience, in Tiger Moths, and to be graded for training as either Pilots or Observers. At our first meal a collection was made for a wreath for an unsuccessful student, which was very cheering. Later that evening we were paraded at the edge of the airfield for guard duties when a Tiger Moth started a take-off run downwind, careering all over the place. What fun we thought, an Instructor giving us a demonstration of crazy flying. However, the Tiger turned and started climbing at an angle which even we knew was impossible. It then stalled straight into the ground, with fatal results. The pilot was a ground-crew member who had apparently been rejected from Fleet Air Arm training and wanted to give a demonstration of his flying capabilities. Our first task was then to guard the wreck, with particular regard to the pitot head protective cover, which was still in place, thus preventing any air speed indication. For several days our landing approach was close to the wreckage – a chastening symbol.'

However keen and competent to fly, there was one problem that did not manifest itself until actually taking to the air for the first time – airsickness. An unco-operative digestive constitution put paid to several flying careers. It was a question of degree and could be conquered. Hugh Fisher had no intention of quitting:

'When I began my flight training as a Wop/AG I quickly discovered that I suffered from airsickness. My instructor sent me to the Medical Officer, who asked a few questions and told me to eat barley sugars and the problem would go away. So I did as I'd been told but on my next flight I was sick again. The Instructor wasn't very pleased and said: "Didn't I tell you to go to the MO?" When I told him I had, he said, "Well go again." So off I went. The MO said: 'Didn't you come and see me yesterday?" I told him I had and what happened. I was again told to go away and eat barley sugars but it made no difference and my instructors continued to complain. A corporal said dry bread was a cure; I never tried it. However, later on I discovered that eating dry fluffy biscuits before a flight seemed to help. It took about six weeks before my stomach finally settled down. Even then I was never really comfortable when flying, particularly if there were a lot of turbulence. Now and again I would be airsick, but I managed some 1,600 hours flying.'

There was nothing quite as exhilarating as one's first solo flight, although that did not mean acceptance as a pilot. An average one out of three failed to make the grade in the initial flying course and these men usually went on to navigation training. Not everyone had the necessary aptitude for flying an aircraft although acceptance depended very much on the instructor's judgement. Even past the first stage one could be 'washed out' at a later date as happened to Cyril Clifford:

'To avoid wastage of places on flying courses, those hoping to be pilots had to do a grading course of 12 hours' flying on Tiger Moths. I'd flown about ten-and-a-half hours' dual and was sitting in the crew room on my own when an officer instructor came in. He asked me if I had flown that day and when told I had not, he took me up. After an hour or so's instruction, including landings and take-offs, we came down for the last time and taxied to the petrol pumps. I thought we had finished for the day and awaited a verdict on my capabilities as a pilot. When the fuel tank was full the instructor got the pump attendant to swing the propeller. When the engine was running he shouted down the speaking tube: "Do one more circuit and bring it back to dispersal."

'Determined to do my best, I taxied carefully to the take-off point, did the cockpit check, looked around to see if anyone was about to land, and then turned into wind. Full power and up to 1,950 revs. Line up on something on the horizon and keep pedalling the rudder bar to keep straight. Stick forward to raise the tail then centralize. "Unstick" trim for climb and watch the airspeed. At 500 feet throttle back to 1,850 revs. At 1,100 feet level off, re-trim and throttle back to cruising revs, 1,750rpm. It was only then, on relaxing my concentration, that I realized there was no helmeted head above the front cockpit: I was on my first solo.

'I completed the circuit and made a reasonable landing with only the slightest of bumps. Having satisfied my instructors I was sent to Elementary Flying Training School in Canada, but my instrument flying was not considered good enough to allow me to continue to the next stage. However, I had the satisfaction of knowing that I had soloed in quicker time than did a number of distinguished RAF pilots.'

Instructor pilots were often older men or those 'rested' from operations. It was a demanding task, particularly at EFTS, with perhaps a score of take-offs and landings a day. And one had to be ever wary for unexpected action by students. Ian Glover of No. 14 EFTS:

'One had some strange explanations from student pilots for their actions. The most memorable occurred one beautiful, warm, sunny day when landing at Hockley Heath. This satellite to our main station at Elmdon was really nothing more than a large meadow. As we came down I asked the pupil in the rear cockpit of the Tiger Moth how he knew when to level off. "When I can smell the clover, "Sir!" came the cheeky reply.

The usual 10-week course at EFTS was followed by an advised 16- (later 20-) week advanced flying course at an SFTS (Service Flying Training School) where the aircraft types were predominantly Miles Masters or North American Harvards for single-engine training, and Airspeed Oxfords for twin tuition. Training proceeded apace, often at far from ideal locations and in poor weather, which increased the number of accidents involving neophytes. 'Near thing' incidents were experienced by the majority. The pitfalls of the trainee pilot were many. George Irving:

'My initial cross-country exercise involved laying out a course to steer from base to the Brecon Beacons and back, noting special "pin points" on the track and time over same, everything having to be logged. We had to take off at three minute intervals so I thought it would be a good idea to arrange with the pilot of the Oxford following mine to fly in loose formation to prevent us getting lost, as two heads are better than one. I arranged to take off and clear the aerodrome, then hang back a bit until he took off and caught me up, before proceeding on the allotted course together. After taking off, I cleared the 'drome and did a slow 360 degree orbit, but the other Oxford never appeared. Finally, I turned back on to the course to steer and completed the exercise on my own.

'On returning to base I reported in to my instructor for the log to be checked. About five minutes later my friend arrived and also checked in. I was just admonishing him about not joining me on the trip when the phone rang in the instructor's office. It was an enquiry from Balloon Barrage Control at Portsmouth about Oxford T1336, which had strayed into their area while the balloons were flying. My friend had taken off after me, but had set his compass on the reciprocal course and had flown into the Portsmouth area instead of to the Brecon Beacons.'

On completion of the advanced course the qualified pilot went on to an Operational Training Unit (OTU) where he flew the type, or similar type, of aircraft that he would use in an operational squadron. OTUs were linked to the respective Bomber, Fighter or Coastal Commands. After completing this final stage of training a pilot would join a squadron in the appropriate Command. Among RAF aircrew OTUs were characterized as run-down organizations, a belief nurtured through experiences while undergoing this part of their training. George Irving again:

'After ten days' leave I was posted to No. 51 OTU at Cranfield. We had both long- and short-nosed versions of the Blenheim; most of them had been seconded to Cranfield from operational squadrons. All looked very tired and jaded. The instructors were on rest from ops and, like the planes, tired and jaded. After three short trips F/O McLure, my instructor, said: "Take it up on your own and for Christ's sake don't bend it when you decide to come down, we're getting a bit short of planes." It was at this stage of my training that I realized that it was not only the Germans we would have to contend with in the war; the other, and possibly the more dangerous, would be the aircraft, their serviceability and the weather conditions. Flying was only called off when the base had to close down through fog or low cloud. It was raining heavily when I took off one night, the cloud base being at 1,000 feet and solid up to 5,000 feet. After clearing this I completed my exercise and was very relieved to get back to base as the aircraft engines felt a bit rough and the weather was deteriorating. I made my report relating to the exercise and notified the ground crew as to the state of the aircraft and the suspected "mag drop" on the engines. Returning to the crew room I met Sgt Martin Johns who was leaving to take off on a similar mission. I informed him about the weather conditions, also that if he was assigned to use the same Blenheim to give it a thorough check before taking off as it had been running rough. Half an hour after taking off he crashed and both he and his navigator were killed.'

The aircraft at OTUs may have been wanting, but so too were some of the fledgling aircrews. Exceptionally so in the incidents witnessed by Don Nunn:

'The day our crew arrived at No. 29 OTU, Bruntingthorpe, we witnessed a Wellington over-shoot and crash off the end of the runway. We learned it was the second time that week the crew had crashed while trying to land – no one was hurt. Group obviously had misgivings about these fellows and sent down a screening officer to fly with them. Off they went, only to crash again while trying to land.'

Too often OTU accidents brought tragedy, such as that witnessed by Eddie Wheeler while instructing at No. 18 OTU, Finningley:

'Standing outside the flight offices one evening, we watched as a Wellington was taking off with a pupil crew going solo for the first time. As the plane lifted off at the end of the runway, the port engine cut out and the aircraft struggled to gain height. One of the pilot instructors near me said, "For God's sake, don't turn into the dead engine!" At about 1,000 feet that is exactly what the pupil did and one officer exclaimed, "He's had it!" As the Wimpy turned, probably in the hope that he could get on to the end of the runway and land, the plane flipped on its back and dropped like a stone. There was a thud followed by an explosion and a huge pall of black smoke. Six young men with high hopes would never see their first operation. During four years of war I had witnessed so many similar instances, but one was still shaken each time it happened.'

In Bomber Command there were Heavy Conversion Units (HCUs) to ease the path to large four-engined aircraft. These also had foreboding reputations and not without cause as Gerry Hatt discovered:

'In my case I was far more apprehensive at the Con' Unit than on operations. My Halifax Heavy Conversion Unit posting was Wombleton. Having found the billet I'd been allocated, I walked in, chucked my kit bag on the bed and then noticed a bloke sitting on the next one looking miserable. In an effort to be sociable I joked: "What's the matter mate? It can't be that bad." "You're new here aren't you?" he said. "Yeah," I replied. He said: "I've done three bloody cross-country's and come back by train each time. On three consecutive trips I've baled out, ditched and crash-landed." The bloke was right. It was positively hairy there. The first time my crew went out solo we had to come back on three engines. On another occasion we all had to bale out. The chop rate was pretty high. There were probably other reasons for the high casualty rate, but the state of the aircraft was the main one in my opinion. The Halifaxes were usually old and well worn, having done a great many flying hours. Also, they were the early production models with the unstable tail unit.'

On finally reaching a squadron, training was by no means a thing of the past. To be sent on a course was almost SOP (Standard Operational Procedure) as new techniques and equipment were introduced. In the early days the training courses were often instituted to improve basic trades where weaknesses were identified, notably air-to-air gunnery. The benefit of sending a power turret gunner to practise flexible gunnery, as in Alan Drake's case, is questionable, even if no Blenheims were available – but it provided a bit of excitement:

'In October 1939 we W/Op Air Gunners were packed off from our squadron to No. 2 Armament School, Manby, to receive three weeks' air gunnery training.

The School used Fairey Battle monoplanes and Hawker Hind biplanes. The Hind had open cockpits with little protection from the icy blast of slipstream. Communication between the gunner and the pilot in front of him was usually by hand in view of the engine and air noise. The gunner's cockpit was surmounted by a Scarff ring to which was fixed the Lewis gun used for air-to-air firing at drogues. Normal procedure was for the gunner to tap the pilot on the shoulder at the commencement and cessation of firing so that the pilot knew when to hold the aircraft straight and level or when to dive or climb away. On one occasion, after I had ceased firing, I turned to tap the pilot's shoulder with the flat of my hand but somehow managed instead to give him a hefty box on the ear. He gave me one hell of a look and promptly turned the Hind over on its back. The result was sheer panic on my part trying to make sure I had secured the Dead Man's Hook to the bottom of my 'chute harness and to prevent anything loose from falling out. Not content with scaring the life out of me, I also received a rollicking from the pilot on landing before he departed, nursing his sore ear.'

The estimated aircrew demand was such that arrangements were made for training to be carried out overseas in Commonwealth countries, most notably Canada and eastern and southern Africa. This not only eased the strain on UK establishments, but offered a better environment for elementary and advanced flying training. Those who had this experience were almost universal in praise of their hosts. Tom Minta:

'The generosity and hospitality of the South Africans was something I am unlikely to forget. From our ship we were put on a train in Cape Town and sent north to Bulawayo in Rhodesia. When the train stopped at Mafeking to refuel, we found the station platform lined with trestle tables filled with cakes, fruit, lemonade and so on. The people were wonderful, they really spoiled us, took us round the town in their cars and returned us to the train when it rang its bell. This kind of hospitality was to be repeated on many occasions at the various stations in Rhodesia.'

The largest number of training establishments for RAF aircrew outside the UK were in Canada where, as in Africa, the experience was akin to an adventure holiday after the blackout and rationing of the UK. Many trainees 'never had it so good' and took advantage of the situation when about to return to the Old Country. Len Barcham:

'I did a fair amount of my training in Canada and, when qualified and commissioned, I returned to England with a certain quantity of goodies; things unobtainable in this country at that time; silk stockings, nylons, dress lengths, perfume, etc. A good proportion went to my current girl-friend who, in typical feminine fashion, became suspicious: "Have you been faithful to me?" she asked. I gave her the perfect answer – "Frequently." '

In general, the Canadians treated the British trainees royally and endured with understanding the occasional incident that put them and their property at risk. D. A. Reid was privy to one mishap that could have had nasty consequences:

'In 1944 I was sent to Canada for training, taking a course as a Bomb Aimer at No. 5 Bombing and Gunnery School, Dafoe, Saskatchewan. The usual bombing exercise had pilot plus two U/T (under training) bomb-aimers with a load of 12 practice bombs in an Anson. The bombs had a small charge, sufficient to make a bang, flash and smoke that would mark the point of impact for the aimer some 10,000 feet above. Each trainee dropped six bombs singly, taking turns.

'One night, as the Anson banked over Dafoe town to head for the target, I looked down in the nose and saw my mate, Ginger, drop the release "tit" on the floor. The bomb-release light went out as a practice bomb descended on to Dafoe town. We abandoned the exercises and returned to base; Ginger was a very worried man.

'Next morning a townsman arrived at the main gate and was taken to the CO. Presently Ginger was called to report to the Office. We all expected the worst. A little later Ginger came back grinning. The bomb had detonated just outside the bedroom window of the Dafoe man's wife. She had been in labour at the time with a doctor present. The doctor said it was the quickest delivery he'd known!'

The Canadians' most common complaint was about low flying. Unauthorized low flying was a punishable offence but the temptation was too great for many trainees; Peter Culley being one of those apprehended:

'The exhilaration of low flying was my downfall. The first reprimand came through scaring the daylights out of a repairman who was up a telegraph pole stringing wires. He, or someone, reported the number of the Fairchild Cornell I was flying from Alberta Elementary Flying Training School. My next piece of devilment was taking too close a look at an Indian reservation, for which I was also reported. My final undoing, however, was while on a three-leg solo navigational flight from my Service Flying Training School at Estevan, Saskatchewan. I had met an interesting girl who came from a small town and decided to pay her a visit. After finding the place, I thought it would be fun to take the Anson down the wide main street. I did this three times – level with the rooftops. Unfortunately, the performance was viewed by one of our instructors who happened to be on leave visiting this particular town. A couple of days after the incident I was notified by the instructor, on his return to the unit armed with aircraft number and time of the "attack" that this serious misdemeanour was a Court Martial offence. However, this officer was a great fellow and, after playing down the incident, I was allowed to re-muster to Trainee Airgunner. Following a short period of training, my career as an airgunner proved to be no problem for the next three years – as I could only fly as low as the "Skipper" decreed!'

There was an even more favoured location: the United States. Britain was offered by the US Government arrangements for pilot training, initially at civilian establishments and, after America became involved in hositilities, at a number of US military bases. William Reid was one of the early trainees:

'My flight training was done at Lancaster in the Mojave Desert. We arrived before America entered the war. Then the Japs hit Pearl Harbor and you'd have thought California was about to be invaded and the place laid waste by air raids. In those first few weeks the Californians got into a bit of a panic as if their shores were about to be invaded, yet once they decided to do things then no one could touch them. People's attitude to the military changed rapidly. At one time it wasn't everyone who would pick up an Army hitchhiker, but after Pearl Harbor the civilian population couldn't do enough for them. Then suddenly servicemen were the most important fellows around. We couldn't have had better treatment and were always being asked about the war back in Britain. When Bomber

Command flew the first thousand bomber raid you would have thought we had actually taken part in it ourselves, the way they fussed over us. When we went into town we wore our best RAF "blues" and many local people thought the albatross insignia on our shoulders were wings and that we were already pilots. Of course, we didn't disillusion them. There were always invitations. And when they said come to supper they really meant it. It wasn't said in the non-commital way we do over here. There was no lack of genuine hospitality.'

Evidently the mode of instruction varied and some pupils found certain aspects wanting. William Drinkell:

'After elementary instruction I went to the United States under the Tower's Scheme whereby RAF pilots earmarked for Coastal Command were trained by the US Navy and brought to a standard where they gained their wings. After some basic flying on Naval Aircraft Factory N3N biplanes, we went to Pensacola for an advanced course, finishing on Catalinas. The US Navy instructors never taught me to handle an aeroplane as if it were an extension of myself. Everything was by numbers, a sequence of detailed exercises. For example, you were instructed how to do a loop at such and such a speed and with precise directions. No one told you you could carry out the same manoeuvres at different speeds and using different techniques. They took me through to my wings in an efficient manner, but never taught me the love of flying. Years later, when I became an instructor, I always wanted my students to love flying first. If they did then the rest would follow easily.'

The wide open spaces and clear skies of the United States certainly provided safer flying training than in Britain but, inevitably, the pupil pilots gave their instructors some anxious moments. Stanley Ward:

'The experience of being sent across the Atlantic to undertake pilot training in Oklahoma is something I am unlikely to forget. Nor do I think one of my American instructors will forget me. We did our advanced training on Harvards – AT-6 Texans the Yanks called them. Nice aircraft; a joy to fly. Well, on this particular occasion we were taking off dual, me in the front and the instructor in the back. As we lifted off the ground I selected Gear Up but it didn't come up. Now our training was that before you select Gear Down you always closed the throttle momentarily so as to activate the warning horn. You then opened the throttle up, selected Gear Down, closed the throttle again momentarily and if there was no warning horn you knew the gear was down and locked. Anyway, we are just off the ground and I had selected Gear Up with no apparent response. So I said to the instructor: "Gear still down, Sir." He replies, "Okay, select down," meaning for me to go through the sequence again to see if the wheels would come up next time. So what do I do through force of habit? Close the throttle. No problem when you're letting down to land, but we were just off the ground and climbing towards the hangars at the end of the field. In the brief moment it took for me to realize my folly I saw the hangars suddenly loom large and several guys on the apron running for their lives. With the throttle full open again we did miss the top of the hangar but not by much. It would not be kind to repeat the instructor's comments from the back seat.'

And, of course, there were always the adventurous who broke flight regulations, as Philip Knowles recalls when at No. 1 British Flying Training School:

'On 22nd June 1943 I was flying an AT-6A (Harvard) on a night cross-country from our base at Terrell, Texas, to Shreveport, Louisiana, and back with another cadet, Alan Lamberton, in the back seat navigating. It was a lovely clear starry night and as we approached Shreveport the city lights were spread out in front of us. Everything was under such good control that I asked Alan about trying a slow roll. He agreed, so I had a go. Half-way round there was a great commotion from the rear cockpit and a terrible smell. I thought we were on fire and was relieved to get back straight and level without seeing any flames. The aircraft was behaving normally, but there were fearful curses coming over the intercom. It turned out that the rear relief tube was blocked and had been used – some time ago! When we inverted it emptied itself over Alan and his navigation board. The smell was unbelievable, even with both hoods open, and we had an hour's flight back to Terrell. That was bad enough, but what could we say to the next pair who came out to take the aircraft on a similar trip? We could not admit to night aerobatics!'

However, it was not always the pupils who were in error as John Peak found out at No. 13 SFTS:

'There was a Standard Beam Approach flight on the airfield with Harvards specially fitted with the necessary radio equipment for beam flying, and the perspex of the rear cockpit, under which the pilot having instruction on instrument flying flew, was green. The pupil wore red goggles enabling him to see the instruments – albeit with a red tinge – but looking out through the green perspex was just a black void.

'A relief airfield at Brada, 10 miles south-west of our base at North Battleford, was fitted with the beam equipment. Pupil and instructor would take off from base and fly towards Brada where the instructor handed over to the pupil who would then have to intercept the beam and turn on to the correct course to carry out an instrument approach to the airfield. While training we would not waste time by landing but would climb away for another approach. These training sessions would last for about 1½ hours and were quite mentally exhausting. On the other hand, the instructors, who each had four pupils allocated to them, used to find it rather boring. One particular instructor, whom we liked a lot, was on a rest between operational tours on Spitfires over Europe. To relieve the monotony he would start the session by taking off from base and when clear of the airfield would drop right down to zero feet and fly for several miles over the prairies before climbing up to 3,000 feet and handing over to the pupil to fly the beam. When the session was over he would again take over, return to base and do a wheel landing – as soon as the main wheels touched he would open the throttle and hurtle down the runway racing car fashion, closing the throttle just in time to turn off at the end of the runway and taxi in.

'On one occasion when we were night flying SBA, I was No. 3 to fly and while No. 2 was flying No. 1 came back to our living-quarters and warned me that the instructor had a bottle of whisky with him and had got through most of it. When I reported to the crew room, everyone was having a coffee break except our instructor who was asleep in a corner. Most instructors were briefing the next pupils to fly, but when my instructor came to he just said, "Okay, let's go."

'He had the engine running and was taxi-ing almost before I had strapped in, did a fast turn on to the runway and we were airborne! As soon as we had cleared the airfield he switched on the aircraft's landing lights, dropped right down on the "deck" and repeated his daylight performance with corn stubble flashing by inches below in the glare of the landing lights. After a while he climbed up to 3,000 feet and said, "Okay you have control, carry on doing back beam approaches." We had to get experience at back beam approaches which meant approaching the airfield from the opposite direction, where you then did not have the benefit of the outer and inner markers. This was fairly straightforward, provided other aircraft were also doing it to avoid approaching in opposite directions.

'After I had done two of these approaches, there had been no sound or comment from the front cockpit and I concluded that my instructor must be asleep and not keeping a lookout for other aircraft. The thought then struck me as to whether the others flying were also doing back beam approaches. I therefore decided to raise my red goggles so as to see outside; I had just done so when there was a loud roar and I saw the exhaust flames of what must have been another Harvard going in the opposite direction. I waggled the stick violently and a sleepy sounding voice said, "I have control." He flew back to base and did one of his racing car landings, but misjudged his braking and ran off the end of the runway amongst the scrub before returning to the perimeter track and taxi-ing in.

'The next morning all four who had flown with him were called into the flight commander's office and told that when the ground crew put the plane away in the hangar they found that a picketing hook situated beneath the wing had been torn off, together with the panel to which it was attached. He asked if we had noticed anything about our instructor's flying that night. We all replied, "No Sir." I believe he was grounded pending an inquiry, but we graduated shortly after and were soon on our way home to the UK, so I never knew the outcome.'

The Drill

Creature Comforts

Some two million men and women served with the Royal Air Force at some time during the 1939–1945 War, a large proportion of whom, at the time, considered boredom the main feature of their war. This view was not confined to the non-flying section. A reappraisal, half a century on, finds the majority declaring it to have been an experience that they would not have missed. Patriotism and duty aside, the fact remains that the result of tedium was that the individual's main occupation became personal welfare. Paramount in this situation was sustenance, for the pleasure of eating and drinking was often marred by scarcity, monotony and poor cuisine; sometimes to a point where it became almost obsessional for the deprived. For every station with a good mess, it seemed three could be found where the reverse was the case. Perhaps it was a matter of opinion or palate, but there were messes where the meals left a lasting impression. Roy Browne:

'The food at Skellingthorpe was absolutely appalling. Dreadful stuff; all slop. I think it was the cooks, not the ingredients. Some brave corporal did get up one day and voice his disgust to the Orderly Officer but things never improved. It must have ranked the worst food in the RAF.'

For Maureen Brickett it was the method of serving rather than the food that made meals so awful:

'My first breakfast in the WAAF: the enormous dining hut . . . orderlies shouting "'ats orf" . . . picking up a plate at the end of a long queue and receiving a slice of liver, a ladle of gravy, two slices of bread, a pat of butter and a spoonful of jam all piled on top of each other. Having found a place to sit and fetched my tin mug of tea from an urn marked "sweetened tea", I returned to my place to find everything a soggy mess in a sea of gravy, half cold and fast congealing, but nevertheless eating what I could because I was so cold and hungry!'

Sentiments echoed by Ernie Edwards:

'It wasn't so much the food as the way it was prepared and served that was the problem. You queued up at the counter and the mess staff came along slapping it on your plate; a bit of lukewarm mutton with lukewarm gravy and synthetic mashed spuds, all flopped together in an unappetizing mess. We got this day after day. To be fair, there must have been 500 senior NCOs in our mess. How the devil the kitchen staff coped with it all I don't know. I think the reason the meals were so poor was that the kitchen staff were overloaded with work.'

Small units, where the cooks did not have the pressure of numbers, offered better fare. The problem of poor food or poorly prepared food appears to have been more acute on large stations. This was particularly so in Bomber Command where two or three thousand personnel had to be catered for on a single station. The monotony of the meals was a common grouse – although this cannot have been John Everett's initial reaction:

'After completing training as an engine fitter I was posted to No. 102 Squadron at Topcliffe. My first meal in the Airmen's Mess was quite an experience. I sat down with a plate of sausage, cabbage and potato. Cutting into the cabbage I hit something hard and retrieved a three-inch rusting nail. Other diners were amused at my comments about cabbages having a high iron content. I wasn't, but didn't like to complain, this being my first time in the mess.'

In fairness, the problem of running kitchens and a mess on the scale demanded at most large stations was fraught with difficulties. In order to improve matters many mess administrators attempted to impose timed servings to take the load off kitchen staff and thus improve the cooking of meals. At some stations this was stringently applied as Albert Herbert relates:

'Seems that on No. 115 Squadron too many aircrews were coming into the Sergeants' Mess for meals after the appointed time period. Late meals were anathema to the Mess Sergeant, so all late meals had to be asked for by presenting a chit from the squadron adjutant. Well, the crew of a particular friend of mine came in late and behold – no meal chits. So the Mess Sergeant told them there would definitely be no meals served to them in the sergeants' mess that night. This did not please the crew who had returned from an operation and suffered debriefing, particularly my friend Val, who thundered at the Mess Sergeant: "Who the hell are you? You must have been the cook at the Last Supper!" Quick as a flash the MS replied: "Yes, I was, and Judas Iscariot had no meal chit – and he got no dinner either!"

One of the incongruous things about service life was that one might move from a station where meals were limited and lifeless to one of plenty, where cooking was excellent. At one location the 'grub' was so good it even had a soporific effect. Dennis Baxter:

'The food at No. 17 ITW Scarborough was good. Plenty of plum duff and the like and the problem arose of keeping awake at the lectures after lunch. We were given navigation lessons from a pleasant ex-schoolmaster named F/Lt Stirling. Half the class would usually nod off, but he didn't seem to worry unduly about the snoozing. Sometimes he'd drop a ruler on the floor or rap on a table to try and wake people up. He could have made it very difficult for the offenders, but as far as I am aware he never reported anyone for being asleep. His attitude was: if you want to learn you can, the choice is yours.'

At those stations where meals left much to be desired, personnel endeavoured to supplement RAF fare with refreshments from civilian sources. Thus many sought out the local cafés and restaurants in off-duty hours. In the early months of hostilities expense was the only problem, but as rationing became more severe civilian eating-places had little to offer – apart from what was 'under the counter'. Jim Double:

'In 1943 I was a member of staff at No. 10 Radio School, Carew Cheriton, South Wales. Across the road from the main gate there was a wooden building known as "Smokey Joe's", a café run by a very jovial cockney. Cooked food – bacon, eggs, sausage, etc., could always be obtained although officially rationed. However, it was not unknown when part way through a meal for the plate to be whisked away from under you, to be replaced once it was decided that a food inspector was not on the scene.

'When the liberty trucks returned from Tenby at night the café would be inundated with airmen and WAAFs getting tea, coffee or a sandwich. Cheese sandwiches were 7 pence each, rather expensive, but as Smokey pointed out, he had to have sufficient funds for any eventuality.

'One Monday morning, when off duty, I dropped in for a coffee and was asked by Smokey to help count out 100 £1 notes. He had got to attend the Magistrates' Court at Pembroke Dock, having received summonses for no less than 28 food offences! He estimated £100 should cover it. Later in the day I met him again, wearing a beaming smile, to be told: "Tell everyone to be in the Plough tonight; I will pay." '

Even the normally figure-conscious WAAFs sought to supplement their diet in civilian establishments. Maureen Brickett:

'I was stationed at RAF Turnhouse near Edinburgh, but as a Clerk Special Duties working in the Operations Room, I never actually lived on the station. We were always "people apart" and were billeted in big and usually very elegant houses which had been "taken over". Edinburgh was a land "flowing with milk and honey" compared with London. There were two restaurants in Princes Street, Mackies and MacVities, where you could eat to your heart's content at any time of the day, the most tempting and delicious savouries or pastries! I was 8 stone and 3 pounds when I joined and three months later I had put on three-and-a-half stone! One day one of the RAF flight sergeants was showing a group of "resting" pilots around Ops and laughingly pointing at me said, "There's the best TWO girls in Ops," and the nickname stuck!'

At various locations a shortage of accommodation necessitated RAF personnel being billeted with civilians. In such circumstances those involved usually dined royally, mothered by the lady of the house who was glad of the extra rations provided. Unfortunately, this was not always the case as Peter Catchpole relates:

'With the large intake of RAF trainees at Blackpool, many of us were found billets in the area. With three other fellows I was sent to a guest-house whose owner was paid by the RAF to sleep and feed us. They obviously didn't want to take servicemen and we were given a tiny little room with three bunk beds and fed on the minimum that these people could get away with. Every Saturday for dinner, without fail, we each had a small meat-pie sitting on a plate of gravy – no vegetables or anything else. The place was taking in Lancashire holidaymakers for a week's stay and while we were faced with the meat pie these civilians would sit down to a good Saturday dinner. It got so that some would take pity on us as their week wore on, and slip us food. Anyway, I think the rations allowed by the RAF were probably being used for the civilian guests. I've never wanted to eat a meat-pie since.'

On airfield sites out in the countryside, the proximity of farm and garden produce found many a Nissen hut with a cooking stove and makeshift larder for off-duty additional meals. Eggs, rabbits, game and vegetables were bought, scrounged or pinched in the nearby villages. There was always an airman from a country background who would be willing to draw a pheasant or gut a rabbit ready for the pot. Little was sacred to those feeling a bit 'peckish'. Frank Clarke:

'I was stationed at Wellesbourne Mountford, Warwickshire, on 'C' Flight Wellington IIIs at No. 22 OTU. Close to our dispersal point was an old Nissen hut used as a repair shop and for sheltering from the rain. Somehow we acquired a pet goose who became very tame and friendly with the regular members of our Flight. However, if a stranger came along the goose would go for him and chase him away. It could be quite vicious. When NAAFI time came and we were working, the goose always gave a warning call to tell us the van had arrived. It was then first in the queue to obtain a bun or some tit-bit from one of the NAAFI girls. The bird used to follow us around, coming over to the aircraft dispersal area and sitting near us while we worked. Woe betide any stranger who arrived; a guard dog could not have done a better job. We had him for about 18 months until one Christmas when, sadly, he disappeared. No doubt he ended up on someone's dinner table.'

The sources of some fare were surprising. On 2 September 1943 two Hurricane squadrons attacked with rockets the Zuid Beveland lock gates in the Dutch islands. Meeting fierce opposition, four aircraft were lost and several others damaged. One of the latter was the Hurricane of No. 137 Squadron's CO, John Wray:

'Once I thought I was out of range of fighters I settled down on course and took stock of my damage. My aircraft had been hit in a number of places; at the time I did not realize how badly. Also, I had a wound in my right arm, although I didn't find this out until after I had landed. My eye was travelling around the aircraft looking for damage when suddenly it lighted on a duck hanging by its neck close to the wing tip on the leading edge. During the operation and escape I had obviously picked it up. After landing back at base my ground crew took possession and had it that night for supper!'

When it could be passed off as a communication or training flight, aircraft were often used in the cause of enhancing a mess larder. A ploy used by Tom Minta when at Headquarters, 19 Group, Coastal Command:

'The mess made one old penny on each drink and as we were not too keen for this money to go to central messing, every now and then we had to have a party. I thought it would be nice to have some lobsters so I took a Proctor and flew down to Portreath where I knew I could buy some from local fishermen. The lobsters were put in a basket in the back of the Proctor and off I went back to Roborough. After I'd been airborne for about 15 minutes I suddenly noticed control movements unconnected with my own movements of the stick. It was the damned lobsters which had somehow escaped and were all over the floor and pulling on the wires with their claws. I flew the rest of the way just hoping one didn't get jammed in the controls.'

After food, a pint and a fag were often the means of making service life more tolerable. A limited supply of beers were available on most stations through the good offices of the NAAFI, but airmen generally preferred to get off station to the pubs for the local ale. In England most public houses were tied to a local brewery and only stocked its brews. Hence the attraction of a particular hostelry was often a case of how the beers suited the palate. True, Guinness, Bass and other special bottled beers were also available in most pubs, but the airman's pay kept him to draught 'mild', 'bitter' and the like. Beer was another commodity in short supply and publicans tended to evoke their own brand of rationing with 'under the counter' supplies for favoured customers. Thus you had your regular pub knowing continued loyalty would ensure access to the liquid reserves.

Beer was also the favoured drink with officers, a 'noggin or two' with pals in the mess was a way to spend an evening. Spirits were in even more limited supply and a luxury even on an officer's pay. Scotch became a totally 'under the counter' commodity. There were other sources if you chanced to be stationed in the right area, as Ken Campbell discovered:

'While attached to No. 489 (RNZAF) Squadron, Royal New Zealand Air Force, equipped with Hampden torpedo-bombers, I was stationed at Wick, Caithness, up in the north of Scotland. At that time Caithness was a dry county, pub-wise that is; weather-wise it was something else! Wet, wet, and wet most of the time, with lots of Scotch mist and low cloud. There was no local place – apart from the mess – for off-duty airmen to chew the fat and put the world to rights over a pint of ale. So by far the greater part of our crew's leisure time was spent tramping across the surrounding moors and heather – weather permitting. An extremely pleasant pastime too, seldom encountering another living soul, apart from the sheep who were docile enough; the epitome of quiet perfect peace.

'Out walking one rare fine day and feeling "peckish" after covering several miles, we chanced upon one of the well-scattered crofts. Hoping we would come across the occupier and be able to buy a snack of some sort, I gave a gentle knock on the door and awaited some kind being to answer my call. The portal was duly opened and a grizzly-looking old crofter appeared. "Good morning Sir," says I, "Would it be at all possible for me and my pals to buy a snack and a drink please?"

"You'll get nothing here bar a drop o' goat's milk. I've haaerd aboot ye canny Customs and Excise frae yon Edinburgh," said the sage, casting a beady eye over our uniforms.

"A glass of milk and a sandwich will do fine, thanks; but, Sir, just to put your mind at rest, we're not Excise men from Edinburgh. We are airmen from Wick RAF station taking a stroll on the moors:"

"Airmen frae Wick eh? Ye've nay been sent to spy on an old honest crofter then?"

"No, we are truly from Wick airbase."

'After much thought and careful soul-searching the old boy reached a conclusion: "Och, well noo laddies, come away in and sample a wee dram o' Hamish's special brew."

'Inside his croft, Hamish reached behind a sack of spuds and produced a bottle of his "special brew" and forthwith proceeded to pour out four very liberal tots. Raising his glass aloft Hamish, with a broad grin on his craggy face, chirped: "Lang may ye lum reek the noo airmen frae Wick." "Lang may ye lum reek, Hamish," heartily chanted three weary but contented airmen frae Wick. Lang may ye lum reek – long may your chimney smoke. What a wonderful salutation; far better than our half-hearted English "Cheers".'

While not every airman drank, there were few who did not smoke. The cigarette habit was unquestioned; smoking was the adult thing to do. A packet of Weights or Woodbines in the erk's top pocket, Players or Gold Flake were a step up the social ladder, and if you aspired to be thought a cut above the rest then it was Craven A or du Maurier. While it might be claimed to be a matter of taste, the brand price had more bearing on choice – an officer concerned with his image would never dream of smoking Weights or Woodbines. They said a cigarette put one at ease, relaxed you; few recognized the need as an addiction to nicotine. Smoking was, of course, officially never allowed on duty and this put strain on the would-be chain-smokers. Jim Swale of No. 295 Squadron recalls one desperate individual:

'Special ops meant that we had little sleep for two nights and a day, and Taffy was very young and very, very tired. After our egg (for night work), bacon and beans we felt satisfied; but not so Taffy. Taffy could not exist long without fags and there was not a single fag to be scrounged from anyone in our section at Rivenhall. Most of us preferred pipes in which we smoked Balkan Sobranie – three bob an ounce at the NAAFI. Taffy said, "I'll nip down to Kelvedon, I think I know where I can get some fags." He departed on his bike; we went to bed. Some considerable time later he had not returned. Anxiously, we went looking for him. We found him still seated on his bike and propped up against a thicket in a low ditch on the way back from Kelvedon. He was fast asleep in the hot sunshine! We also saw that there was a rectangular shape in his left-hand tunic pocket.'

Smoking around aircraft was strictly taboo, a court-martial offence. Fuel fumes pervaded most aircraft and so the fire hazard was very real. Even so, there were individuals who took the risk as they just could not do without a fag. John Everett:

'I was working on a Halifax in one of the Topcliffe hangars late one evening. Beside the aircraft I was fixing there was another Halifax and a Stirling in the hangar. The only other person around was an engineer from Handley Page who was in the other Halifax disconnecting fuel pipes. Suddenly I heard a shout and a lot of commotion and saw this chap fall out of the fuselage door with his clothes alight. I jumped down and looked for something to smother the flames. "Don't worry about me," he said, "I'll put myself out. The plane is on fire; try and put that out." I ran for the extinguisher up near the hangar doors. The thought of what would happen to three heavy bombers and the hangar made me run as fast as I could. Climbing in through the fuselage door of the Halifax I found the inside well alight. Luckily I was in time as the flames had not really taken hold of anything inflammable and I was able to use the extinguisher to put them out. I then remembered the burning man but found he had been able to smother the flames and he didn't seem harmed. He was more concerned about there being any other witnesses to this incident and was relieved when told we were the only two people in the hangar. I had no wish to get him into trouble but somehow I had to account for the fire extinguisher being emptied. For my trouble he gave me 5 shillings – a lot of money in those days – which I used to start a Post Office Savings Account for my small daughter. No wonder the engineer was anxious to keep the incident quiet; I discovered that although working with petrol and having it all over his clothes and splashed around the fuselage of the Halifax, he had actually struck a match to light up a cigarette!'

How the pleasures of alcohol and nicotine rated against the pursuit of the opposite sex was very much an individual case. RAF aircrews certainly had a reputation of being Casanovas among British services, even if there is little evidence to prove them more romantically adventurous than the army or navy men. Perhaps this reputation owes something to advertisements depicting a spruce airman, by a well-known hair-dressing, leading to the other services' quip of 'Brylcreem Boys' for the RAF. That aircrew were thought by some to be womanizers is illustrated by George Irving's encounter with a doctor:

'I was sent to the RAF hospital at Halton, near Aylesbury for tests as my eyes were rather inflamed and did not improve with the normal treatment by the MO. At Halton I was given a very thorough eye test and blood samples were taken. In fact, I told them if they took any more I would demand a blood transfusion. On the third day the ward doctor came on his rounds and said: "We haven't found your trouble yet but you're clear of VD." I told him that I wasn't in the least surprised as I didn't sleep around or go out with naughty girls. He replied: "We always test you flying types just in case."'

Perhaps the MO's attitude had been influenced by seeing something akin to the information Eddie Wheeler found displayed at Newton:

'Walking into the crew room one morning, I spotted the serviceability board bore the names of girls in Nottingham, many of them familiar to us, with details of their sex prowess, dates when they should be overlooked, whether they were married or not, and whether overnight accommodation was available. This information was updated almost on a daily basis and it needed to be consulted before embarking on any blind dates."'

On the other hand, romance most certainly flourished for many young men met their future wives while serving. A good proportion of WAAFs married airmen they knew in the Service and with whom they worked. This was to be expected. There were some unusual introductions to girls, however, like that Tony Murkowski had:

'At Andrews Field we had to do readiness duty to scramble if a flying bomb was reported. Jerry was launching them from aircraft at this time, the winter of 1944. One morning I had been stuck in the cockpit of my Mustang near the end of the runway for nearly an hour and was getting very thirsty. Then, when a "Sally Ann" van arrived at a nearby dispersal, I could see the airmen collecting big cakes and getting mugs of tea. This made me feel even more thirsty. So I called out to the ground staff mechanic who was sitting on my wing, "Go and ask that girl how about a cup of tea for the pilot." So he went across and presently this good-looking girl comes with tea in an old mug. I wanted to pay her – it was a penny a mug – but because I'm strapped in I couldn't get a hand in my pocket to get a penny. So she says, "That's all right." I say, "Okay, thanks. Let me take you out one evening to repay you." So we fix a date to meet in the town. Well, it is dark in the winter evenings, no lights because of the blackout, but I'm there and I wait and she doesn't turn up. Okay, too bad. Then I see her on the airfield a week later and ask her why she don't turn up. She says, "You never turned up!" We find that I had misunderstood her directions. We must have been waiting on opposite sides of the street and did not see each other in the dark. It ends well; we got married.'

Pay, Leave and Promotion

Next to appetite and creature comforts, pay and leave frequently occupied the mind of the airmen. A humble aircraftman (AC 2) received two shillings a day as a new recruit. His 'keep' was, of course, found by the Air Force and the pay amounted to little more than pocket-money. It allowed the purchase of a packet of cigarettes, a round of sandwiches and two pints of beer. Different grades and promotion brought better pay and there were rises as the war progressed. Aircrew received a higher rate; even so it provided less remuneration for NCOs than many war-work civilian labourers were getting. John Studd was surprised to hear a justification for this:

'I was drinking in the pub one evening when I was asked by a gentleman with an Irish accent, who said that he worked on the airfield, how much I was paid as a sergeant bomb-aimer. When I told him 15 shillings a day he said: "I get more than that – but of course it does include danger money for working on the runways."'

Pay was always meagre – roughly a third of what US servicemen of equivalent rank received when they arrived in Europe – but Albert Herbert recalls an additional source of income:

'Operational aircrew in Bomber Command could qualify for a five shillings a day leave grant from the Nuffield Fund, which could be anything from one in four to one week in eight, depending on the attrition in their squadrons. Personnel receiving awards such as the DSO, DFC and DFM, got £10 for each "gong" and another for each bar to that medal. The NCOs would keep their money, but the officers were expected to give theirs to a Benevolent Fund.'

Officers were not alone in being expected to contribute to some deserving cause. Despite their low pay, other ranks were often solicited for hand-outs, notably for some station fund, occasionally in a manner that appeared obligatory. One such instance was strongly resented by George Watts:

'As we filed out of the Watton hangar after pay parade, an officer and an NCO would be sitting at a table collecting sixpences for the sports fund. As we "erks" were working seven days a week, sports were not for us. Only officers and WAAFs had the time to use the tennis-courts and other facilities. Deciding this was not fair, on the next occasion I refused to pay. The officer immediately reprimanded me, but when I asked if that meant the levy was compulsory he declined to answer and simply took my name and number, implying that I would later be called to account for my action. Nothing more was heard of the matter and when the next pay parade came round their takings were down considerably. I had spread the word.'

More than one comparative newcomer to the Service encountered a situation where there was a suspicion of being the victim of a racket. Ray Howlett:

'Reporting to Uxbridge for posting after initial training, we were mystified when at our first payment we were charged for "barrack-room damages". None of us saw any damage or any reason for the two shillings deducted and felt like breaking a couple of chairs to get our money's worth. I wondered at the time if it was a fiddle to boost the NCO's pay!'

There were no hard and fast rules on leave for ordinary airmen. It was normal to receive a week's embarkation leave before being sent abroad to the Middle or Far East but some ground men in the UK, stationed far from their homes, were never afforded an opportunity to see their families throughout their wartime service. The majority were able to take advantage of a '48' (48-hour leave) allowed and administered by the station at which they served. There were no travel allowances for these and one had to get home and back as best one could. John Everett:

'Weekend passes and hitch-hiking have a place in wartime memories. Of the varied lifts, mine included an ambulance, a hearse and the back of an empty brick lorry which left me half choked with red brick dust at the end of the journey. We had a "Geordie" airman on the base who walked along the railway line at Thirsk and thumbed a lift by goods train to Newcastle.'

The return to camp following leave could be a fraught business if delay threatened to make one late. Ken Brotherhood was one of many who had this experience:

'Given a weekend pass, I decided to visit my girlfriend in Manchester. Leaving RAF Lindholme I travelled to Doncaster and then on to Manchester with a mate. Although we had arranged to meet at the station on Sunday and return together, my mate was nowhere to be found so I set off back alone. It was necessary to change at Wakefield and after alighting I asked a porter where to catch the train to Doncaster. Small and stocky, silver watch-chain complete with medallion spread across the front of his waistcoat, he stroked his moustache, pushed his cap to the back of his head and said, "Eh lad, tha'll have to go over t'other side." A guard was poised with green flag and whistle beside the train standing at the opposite platform, so realizing it was about to depart I dashed over the footbridge and just got aboard in time. We chugged along, stopping at various stations, but when we reached Barnsley I realized I was the only person left in the carriage. Feeling a bit concerned I called out to a female porter on the platform, "What time do we get to Doncaster?" "You won't get to Doncaster on this train," she replied. "it's going into the sidings now until morning." I think she saw my look of despair and took pity on me because after a few more questions she said: "The engine is going back to Wakefield. I'll ask the driver to give you a lift." He agreed and off I went, riding on the footplate, where I enjoyed a mug of tea and a bacon sandwich. It was also explained that when the Wakefield porter had said "the other side", he meant another station on the other side of town. Hitch-hiking on a locomotive was a novel experience and saved me from a late return to camp and the trouble that would have brought.'

Vic Holloway while stationed at Montrose was one of the less fortunate where taking leaves was concerned:

'For the four years that I was stationed in Scotland my home was in Hampshire, too far away for a 48-hour pass. We did find means of getting a longer leave though. Because of the difficulties in travelling, any man who lived in the Western Isles was allowed to count his 48-hour pass from the time he arrived at Mallaig or the Kyle of Lochalsh to board a boat, through to the time when he arrived back in those ports to go back to his station. The drill was to leave camp and go to Perth and spend a night there. Next day to catch the train to Inverness and spend a night there, then on to the Kyle in the morning. When you arrived at the ferry you had your leave chit date-stamped. Forty-eight hours were spent on Skye and you arrived back at the Kyle to have your pass stamped again to be within the allotted time. Another couple of days were taken to go via Inverness and Perth back to Montrose so that leave had been extended from 48 hours to six days. I did this with a friend on several occasions and others were pulling the same trick. Somehow the authorities never got wise as to what was going on.'

Aircrew received more generous leave, generally between postings, with at least a week after completing an operational tour. The length of leave depended very much upon the availability of personnel in a particular command to which assigned, the more so in the final 18 months of the war. In some circumstances the Air Ministry were particularly generous. Rex Croger:

'After I got my wings in Canada I returned to the UK early in 1944 and was sent on a month's leave. Just before it was up I received a letter telling me I had another month. Eventually I had four months' leave before finally being posted to an OTU. At that time there were obviously more pilots than needed.'

Another beneficiary of an extended leave was Tony Spooner, who eventually ascertained the reason why:

'Being on the staff of Admiral Pridham-Whipple, Vice-Admiral, Dover, for D-Day operations was an interesting experience, but once the Channel was secured and the "fake" invasion across the famous Straits of Dover a thing of the past, there wasn't any need for the liaison appointment. When I mentioned this to the Admiral, he promptly told me to go away on "indefinite leave".

'The possessor of a conscience has disadvantages. After several weeks of blissful leave I began to worry. "Could an Admiral send a S/Ldr on indefinite leave? Would Coastal Command be looking for me?" I duly reported back to HQCC. "Oh dear. Not another of you. I suppose you also want to get back to a squadron. You see, the trouble is that not enough of you S/Ldrs got yourselves killed during the immediate D-Day period. We reckoned on quite large numbers. How about going to Transport Command? They are looking for Air Traffic Controllers. It could get you another stripe soon." In the end, I was posted to assist a Wing Commander in HQCC and he didn't know how to occupy his hours. Apparently not enough Wing Commanders had been killed either. It was a tough war for the planners.'

The benefits of rank were obvious and there can have been few AC2s who did not aspire to eventual elevation to AC1, however lacking in ambition. Promotion not only meant better pay and privileges, but was an acknowledgement of one's standing, something to be proud of. For ground men and women attaining promotion could be a very lengthy business, whereas for aircrew it could sometimes be meteoric, the result of heavy attrition. Bill Japp:

'When four captains of No. 14 Squadron were killed in a night-flying accident in 1943, Ron Gellatly literally found himself promoted from Flying Officer to Squadron Leader overnight!'

Although a wanting necessity in many battle depleted squadrons, the elevation of an experienced NCO to commissioned officer status was not so easily achieved. Roy Wilkinson, then a Hurricane pilot of No. 3 Squadron, was one such case:

'On 15 May 1940 we were doing some low strafing (which we should not have been) when the CO was hit by an Me 110 and shot down. I managed to shoot down the 110 and by chance to blow up an ammo' lorry at the same time. By the time I got back to our base at Merville, Officer Commanding 'A' Flight, Flt Lt Walter Churchill, had received confirmation from the front line that the CO had been shot down and that I had got the Me 110 and the ammo' lorry. "So," he continued, "as the senior flight commander, I am now the CO; and you Wilky, are now 'A' Flight Commander." "I can't do that you know, Sir; I'm only a Sergeant and you've got a couple of Flight Lieutenants there." "There's a war on now," he explained, "King's Regulations are thrown out the window! I'm the boss now so do as I say. You're our top scorer by far; you are now the flight commander. I've seen Bunny Stone and the other officers and they are quite happy to fly behind you. In fact, I shall probably fly behind you too, for you to lead the squadron."

'When we were evacuated back to the UK the Air Ministry told the Boss that he could not list a sergeant as OC 'A' Flight. He replied, "I can. I've done it. I told you to make him a flight lieutenant a fortnight ago and you didn't, so he stays there." Air Ministry tried to compromise by saying, "Let him do it, but don't put him at the top of the list on squadron Daily Returns." But the CO stuck to his guns and for a couple of weeks I continued to command 'A' Flight as a sergeant pilot. Then a signal arrived and I was commissioned as a flight lieutenant back-dated to when I had taken over in France.'

Promotion enabled the bright and successful to elevate themselves to ranks above their former superiors, a situation that the latter naturally did not relish. Thus due promotion was not always quickly forthcoming if those handling 'the papers' felt their position threatened. An instance of this was encountered by Steve Challen:

'In July 1940 I was sent to No. 1 OTU at Silloth near Carlisle, along with several other recently qualified AC2 air gunners. Our course instructor was a Sergeant Air Gunner, Busby by name, who we thought had the rank because of his duty. He told us about the Air Ministry Order which was promulgated December 1939 making all qualified aircrew no lesser rank than Sergeant. This particular AMO was not to be seen on any notice-board where such things were usually posted. Was someone sitting on it? Inquiries at the Orderly Room drew a blank. Inquiries to the Station Warrant Officer produced an abrupt dismissal. A deputation from we "plonks" finally gained an audience with the adjutant who was a little "put out" but said he would look into the inquiry. The AMO was posted some days later, causing a rush to the stores to draw enough tape to provide chevrons for both sleeves. The "permanent" NCO staff in the Sergeants' Mess didn't take kindly to the invasion of these "jumped-up" volunteer aircrew. Everything had obviously been arranged for we were allocated tables apart and a "second sitting" in the dining-hall. A division was also evident in the lounge area of this wooden building. "Okay, just passing through. Life on the squadron will be better," we consoled ourselves.'

The granting of commissions, particularly after training, was a contentious subject among aircrew, with many men believing that the decision was made on your background and not solely your ability. Certainly there were instances of this as noted by George Irving:

'Prior to completing the course at Cranfield we had to attend an interview for officer selection. We had been told at the commencement of our training that the granting of commissions depended entirely on our individual efficiency during training. Of the 43 pilots who finally completed their training, only eleven were granted commissions as Pilot Officers. It was noted that all of these had been educated at public schools. We others were given the rank of Flight Sergeant.'

Experienced civilian fliers, exalted scientists, notable business executives and the like who joined the RAF were often bestowed with a rank and task which the authorities thought fitting to their status. There was a suspicion of the 'old pal's network' in some of this; the managing director of a food manufacturing concern, who had never moved out of central London, given a squadron leader's uniform was one example. Such bestowals of rank were resented by those RAF regulars and VRs who had come up the hard way – and suffered by very senior officers who experienced the lack of military formality often exhibited. Tony Spooner:

'At the outbreak of war, the large Brooklands School of Flying civil flying organization concentrated its considerable staff of flying instructors at the RAF aerodrome at Sywell, Northamptonshire. By pulling in instructors from Brooklands, Sywell, Dunsfold, etc., it had about 50 civilian instructors. On 1 September 1939 we were all put into uniform according to which RAF Reserve we served. Some curious rankings resulted with the Deputy Chief Instructor becoming Flight-Sergeant Goldsmith with dozens of RAF officers under him. We had just the one bar. This became our joint mess with officers and sergeants mixing freely; as we had done the day before.

'Duncan Davis, who part-owned the Brooklands organization, appeared as a F/Lt while his local manager appeared as Wing Commander Mackenzie. Soon we were visited by a very senior officer, Air Chief Marshal Sir John Steel. Duncan and Mac were doing their best to explain to their distinguished visitor that we were really all civilian pilots "dressed up for war". It wasn't going down too well, especially as Sir John was critical of the usual "lunch-time snort" which we were having between the morning and afternoon sessions of battling with our pupils. To appease the visitor, Duncan decided to introduce him to a well-known peace-time pilot, Ken Waller, who had figured prominently in the famous race to Australia in 1934 in the original DH Comet. Now Ken was one of those who was wearing his brand-new Sgt-pilot's uniform. He was also a languid, affable chap who called nearly everyone "Old Boy". He was glad to be introduced. He rose gracefully from his chair. "Glad to meet you, Old Boy. Now it's my turn for a round. What will it be, Old Boy?" Somehow Air Chief Marshal Sir John Steel was not impressed by his brief meeting with the renowned flying instructor.'

The disciplines imposed by rank were an accepted part of the service. In combat units the division between officers and other ranks was not so rigidly imposed, particularly in crews with a mixed complement of officers and NCOs.

Basic training establishments tended to have the most authoritarian regimes for reasons already outlined. Interestingly, the most common prejudice against officers among other ranks is that reflected by George Watts:

'As to officers, I found the fliers and regulars much easier to deal with. War service ground officers were usually pompous and arrogant being ex-solicitors, council clerks and the like. We called them Penguins (no wings and flat feet). But this also applied to several NCOs in the same mould.'

The RAF, like the other services, had its share of those bestowed with temporary commissions who used their rank belligerently and to enhance their own standing. Those officers more involved in leadership than administration were generally of a more understanding nature, but the popularity of any commanding officer really hinged on the character of the individual. A good CO could be firm yet be seen still to be a good sort, a reputation which, once established, became known throughout his command even by those who had no direct contact with him. Vic Holloway:

'The CO at Montrose was one of the Coleman family, the mustard people. A great man and popular with all of us. The winter of 1940–41 was hard with lots of snow. He had all 1,200 men on the station out on the runway marching up and down in lines until we had trampled the snow down hard so flying could be resumed. And the CO was there, tramping up and down with us until the job was done. He liked his bit of fun too. At an officers' party I once saw him stand on his head and then drink a glass of whisky while supporting himself with the other hand. Of course, as an other rank I wasn't supposed to have been around to see this.'

Station Commanders also had sufficient rank to be able often to effect retention of personnel who enhanced their domain. Mick Osborne:

'The Station Commander at Martlesham was very keen on football and when he learned I had been a keen amateur player before joining up he soon had me in the Station team. Called The Robins, we were one of the best in the district and had a lot of success against other RAF and local teams. I went to Martlesham in 1941 as a rigger on the Air Sea Rescue Flight and stayed there for over three years. I'm sure this was because the Station Commander made sure I didn't get any postings as he wanted to preserve his football team.'

The workload of commanding officers in operational units was considerable, involving them in both administration and combat leadership. Even so, many impressed their men with the attention paid to an individual's welfare. James Donson, a pilot in No. 500 Squadron, gives an example of this:

'At the beginning of April 1942 we started operations in earnest under a new CO, W/Cdr D. F. Spotswood. Under his guidance the squadron was transformed and a vast amount of work was done with a corresponding boost to morale. In the first ten days of April my crew and I flew five anti-submarine patrols each lasting some 5½ – 6 hours. On the last one I had experienced one or two sharp spasms of stomach pain, but when we reached the limit of our patrol and turned for home the pains became more frequent and intense. We sent a message by W/T and some 2½ hours later we landed, closely followed down the runway by an ambulance. The squadron MO came on board and I was taken to the local hospital and had my appendix removed the same day.

'After about a fortnight I returned to the squadron. When the station MO saw me he glanced at me from his chair and, without a word, filled in a small piece of paper and handed it to me, made a dismissive gesture with his hand and I left. After a moment or two I read the chit, which simply said, "Fit to return to duty. Height limitation 4,000 feet."

'I made my way over to the squadron offices and went into the crew room where I was cheerfully greeted by the few aircrew who were in there awaiting the time of their next take-off. After a brief rest I went in to the office of my Flight Commander and told him I was fit to fly again. "So is my dead grandmother," he replied and disappeared at once. He reappeared almost at once and said, "The CO will see you now." As I entered the CO's office he was looking at the MO's chit which I had handed to the Flight Commander. His frown became more menacing. He had bushy black eyebrows, black hair and a formidable black moustache, all of which could make him look like an approaching thunderstorm. "This piece of bumf says you are fit to fly." He then looked me up and down. "It so happens that I am about to take off for a short air test to keep my hand in, you can come with me." As he was getting up from his chair he said, "My parachute is over there," indicating a corner of the room, "Pick it up for me, I'll just get my helmet from the locker." I walked over to the other side of the room and tried to pick up the 'chute. Try as I would I could not raise it beyond knee level. "Leave it, come and sit down." He opened the door and said quietly to someone in the orderly room, "Bring two cups of tea."

'He then went on to talk to me, questioning me closely about exactly what the MO had said to me, what examination and tests he had carried out on me, etc. I told him exactly what happened. During this time the tea came in and he talked of many things and asked me a host of questions, mostly concerned with service life, including, surprisingly, how did I feel about being under the command of someone younger than myself. That few minutes told me more about him than I realized at the time – that he wanted from everyone the best that they could give and that he was determined that they should be, as far as possible, happy and comfortable in the service to give it. He ended the interview with. "By the way, I am sending you on 14 days' leave. Flight Sergeant Frewen is flying to Liverpool tomorrow with his crew to be interrogated by the Navy into a possible sub' kill. Go with him, it will cut down your journey a good deal. Call at the orderly room in the morning for your travel warrants. Doc Gordon will be back from leave when you return and we'll see how you are then." Years later, I was not surprised to learn that a new Marshal of the Royal Air Force was Sir Denis Spotswood.'

COs were also faced with restraining the exuberance of junior officers, many of whom took a delight in trying to outwit authority or engage in pranks that officially would be classed as unbecoming. Few would deliberately confront their CO in this way, but it could happen by accident. Tony Spooner:

'Few pilots could have had a more varied and interesting war than I. Yet it was due to knocking over my Commanding Officer. It was my misfortune, as I then saw it, that I happened to be a pilot/navigation instructor at the outbreak of war. Being young and foolish, I wanted a more active piloting role. However, the great need was to create pilots and navigators quickly and in large numbers. So there I was. Moreover I seemed destined to spend the entire war instructing as the school which I served (No. 2 School of General Reconnaissance) was moving to Canada. I had my sailing date. Our training airfield, Squires Gate, Blackpool, a pre-war racecourse, was narrow. It was raining "cats and dogs". My Anson had no screen wipers. As I came in to land at the end of another detail, I espied a figure walking across the airfield. To teach the miscreant a lesson, I side-slipped the Anson straight at him, only kicking on opposite rudder at the last moment. It worked a treat. The man, in an officer's raincoat, broke into a trot and slipped in the mud. The last I saw of him, he was floundering like an abandoned turtle.

'"The CO wants to see you," I was informed upon arrival. "And me him, I want to report some silly clot. . . ." The CO was about the only Wing Commander in the RAF with the ribbon of the army's Military Medal upon his tunic. During the First World War he had been, so I was told, a Regimental Sergeant-Major before transferring to the RAF or RFC. Certainly he retained an appropriate stentorian voice. So fierce was this "bark" that he had been nicknamed "Woof-Woof".

'"Come in," he roared, in response to my knock. There he stood, covered in mud. He was a Wingco, I was a freshly commissioned P/O on probation. I tried in vain to point out that it was all his own fault; how dangerous it was to walk across the landing area in pouring rain. I was off the boat immediately. I never got to Canada. Nevertheless I had a fascinating war, flying everything from Tiger Moths and Spitfires to Liberators and Dakotas; survived three tours of ops and became a liaison officer with the Navy; all due to knocking over my Commanding Officer.'

Sometimes even squadron COs were not above being intimidated by those of very high rank and position as the following anecdote from John Wray shows:

'He was an Air Chief Marshal, the Inspector General. When he visited units he always picked on one particular subject upon which he briefed himself extensively, there would be no chance that you would know more about it than he did. If you tried to pull the wool over his eyes you'd had it. He always mentioned other things first, in passing, then suddenly the question. All the time he was catching imaginary flies as he spoke; clapping his hands together here and there. Most disconcerting for those being interrogated, already sitting on the edge of their chairs.

'He arrived at my Wing and I'd got the word through underground sources that the question was to be cleanliness of aircraft. I passed this on to my anxious squadron commanders. He always flew himself, accompanied by his white-faced PA. I met them and we proceeded to the first squadron. We sat down with the squadron commander and the action started. Details of operations were sought, did they like the aeroplane, etc.? The squadron commander's voice was now high-pitched as he eagerly tried to provide what he thought was the right answer. Suddenly, "What about cleanliness of your aircraft. How do you clean them?" "With petrol, Sir." "And do you find that satisfactory?" "Oh yes Sir, its gets them very clean." "Have you ever used Gunk?" "Oh yes Sir." "And how do you find that; does it clean the aircraft better?" "Oh yes Sir, it's very good, much better than petrol." The Air Chief Marshal was now catching flies: "That's interesting," he said, "It's not yet been issued to the Service."'

If an opportunity to take advantage of authority presented itself there were always those quick to act. Any innocent new to a unit or station was fair game as Tom Minta discovered:

'After arriving at St. Eval, a brand-new Pilot Officer on my first squadron, one of the early duties assigned to me was as officer in charge of church parade. Some 150 men were mustered, and off we went behind a band to the church which was close to the perimeter track. At the church, like the good bright boy I was, I stood in front of the parade and called out: "Fall out the Roman Catholics and Jews." I walked into church with about five blokes!'

RED TAPE AND INITIATIVE

Bureaucracy is despised, chiefly because of its impersonality. The mechanics of administration engender bureaucracy and, applied to a service through which two million men and women passed in six years of war, often became impersonal and sometimes a dispenser of the irrational. It seemed that there had to be a form and a number for everything. But errors were inevitable and once entered into the system were difficult to erase. The service number bestowed on each man or woman was a typical example of this, following a clerk's slip of the pen or finger on the typewriter. Tony Spooner:

'It all started when my newly wed wife said: "Isn't your number 740827?" When I nodded she went on: "Why then do they pay me my little wifely allowance under a different number, 740824?" I examined her Allowance Book. It was all too true. There she was married to Spooner A. Sgt-pilot 740824. I was new to the Air Force but not so new as to imagine that it didn't really matter. "Suppose," I thought, "that Spooner A. Sgt-pilot 740827 went missing, would the kindly RAF then pay a pension to the wife of Spooner A. Sgt-pilot 740824?" Something told me that they wouldn't. It would be bad enough to get the chop but doubly so if my "nearest and dearest" couldn't later collect.

'Thus began a fruitless correspondence. The more letters I wrote, the worse the situation became. On one occasion, thinking that perhaps a little humour might work where logic had failed so miserably, I signed one of my letters:

Spooner A. Sgt-pilot 740824
Spooner A. Sgt-pilot 740827
Spooner A. ACII

'At an earlier stage of my life I had been an insurance wallah and had passed the exams of the Associate of the Chartered Insurance Institute. At that time being an ACII was regarded as a "good thing". Back came a letter addressed to Air Commodore Spooner A.

'Relief seemed in sight when one day my CO informed me: "Spooner, you are up for a commission tomorrow. See that you clean your buttons properly for once and report to the Board at ten hundred hours." I soon became Spooner A. Acting Pilot Officer on probation, with a number of 82848. In this exalted rank, I was even allowed to pay my own wife an allowance. My troubles were over.

'But were they? Within weeks I began again to be haunted by my *alter ego*. A "Spooner A. Acting Pilot-Officer on probation, number 82948" began to appear. Until war's end I never knew which I was. Nor do I know which one of us was demobbed after it was all over. For all I know, the other must by now be the oldest PO in the RAF; perhaps with a whacking big pension, too.'

Many are the horror stories of clerical errors and the tribulations that followed. There was another common occurrence – to judge by the number of examples encountered. A recruit would be instructed in one trade, only to be posted to take up an entirely different trade. Likewise aircrew would end up in assignments for which they had not been trained. These changes were often deliberate and of necessity as there were no personnel available at the time to fill a particular demand. There were, however, to be irritating orders which could only be the result of blind administration. Vic Holloway:

'I joined the RAF Auxiliaries in 1938 as a driver and regularly drove RAF transports before being called up about three weeks before war was declared. Then three months were spent at Locking in Somerset driving just about every type of vehicle on the station. The next thing was an order to report to Blackpool for instruction in driving motor transport!'

It frequently appeared that postings were based on the whim of some clerk rather than meeting an actual requirement. 'You felt like pawns in some giant game being played out on a map of Britain – whom shall we send where next?' was the disillusioned comment of an airman who maintains he was shifted six times in six weeks. Tony Spooner also had an experience akin to this:

'Half-a-dozen of us were posted from Squires Gate to an airfield miles from anywhere deep in the heart of East Anglia. We were to report "at once". It was November 1940 and the London *Blitz* was at its worst. This had disrupted the British rail system. Our train came to a halt at a station near Leamington. "No trains to anywhere tonight" greeted us. More for a joke than anything else we inquired where "that little train was going". It consisted of a couple of ancient carriages pulled by a small tank engine. It had steam up. "Oh him; nowhere special. Have a word with the driver. See if he can help you." The driver was helpful. He could not possibly get us to East Anglia or to London but he would agree to take us to Northampton where we all had friends, but only if we paid him a night's lodging there. It was swiftly arranged. However, just as we were marvelling at the *ad hoc* manner in which the rail system was operating, we found ourselves defeated. A larger group had outbid us and had persuaded the driver to take them to Leicester!

'How the rail system managed to operate in this way I never discovered. Nor did we discover why we had to report to Bassingbourn "at once". When we eventually did get there, about two days late, they had never heard of us. Two of us were promptly posted to Lossiemouth instead. That train journey was also quite an event. At one time about 20 of us were "seated" on the floor of the luggage van of a panting train in the highlands with one dear old soul complaining that she had a first-class ticket. At Lossie? You guessed it. They, too, had never heard of us. Also, they only trained whole crews. However, after some delay they did teach us to fly Wellingtons. Whereupon we were posted to PRU at Benson to fly Spitfires!'

There were forms for everything and even forms to acquire forms. 'Too much bumf' was an oft-aired complaint at all levels. Records were necessary but some people's requirements for paperwork could be very frustrating. Alfred Pyner was one who suffered in this way:

Above: *His Majesty King George VI in the uniform of Marshal of the Royal Air Force. (Official.)*

Right: *Billet fire escape enjoyed by Rex Croger (front) and friends while training in Canada. Note Air Gunner's brevet on Army uniform.*

AIR MINISTRY,

WHITEHALL, S.W.1.

21st July 1943

MESSAGE FROM

THE SECRETARY OF STATE FOR AIR.

You are now an airman and I am glad to welcome you into the Royal Air Force.

To have been selected for air crew training is a great distinction. The Royal Air Force demands a high standard of physical fitness and alertness from its flying crews. Relatively few attain that standard and I congratulate you on passing the stringent tests.

You are, of course, impatient to begin and you naturally ask, "When do I start?" Your order on the waiting list is determined by your age, date of attestation, and so on; and you may be sure that you will not be overlooked when your turn comes.

While waiting, go on with your present job, or if you are not in employment, get a job - if possible one which helps on the war effort.

You will want to know why you, who are so eager, should have to wait at all. I will tell you.

The Royal Air Force is a highly organised Service. In the first line are trained and experienced crews whose stirring deeds and dauntless courage daily arouse the admiration of the world. Behind those men and ready to give them immediate support are the newly-trained crews fresh from the schools. In your turn, you and other accepted candidates stand ready to fill the schools. Unless we had a good reserve of young men, like you, on which to draw, time might be lost at a critical moment and the vital flow of reinforcements would be broken.

I hope this explanation will help you to understand. The waiting period should not be a waste of time. There is much that you can do. You are very fit now or you would not have been chosen. See that you keep fit. Work hard and live temperately. Learn all you can in your spare time about the things you must know if you are to be efficient later on in the air. The more knowledge you gain now the easier it will be when you come to do your training.

In wishing you success in the Service of your choice, I would add this. The honour of the Royal Air Force is in your hands. Our country's safety and the final overthrow of the powers of evil depend upon you and your comrades. You will be given the best aircraft and armament that the factories of Britain and America can produce. Learn to use them well.

Good luck to you!

Archibald Sinclair

SECRETARY OF STATE FOR AIR.

Left: Patronizing and unctuous letter sent to those accepted for aircrew to caution against possible delay in call-up.

Right: Most WAAFs considered the cap the best piece of their uniform. The smile is Maureen Brickett's.

Right: Ernest Thorpe in dispatch rider's gear astride an Ariel motor cycle. The beret was both practical and comfortable and dispatch riders were the first RAF personnel to be issued with this headwear which, eventually, superseded the forage cap.

Left: **Left:** *Right dress! Even the girls did not escape drill. (Official)*

Right: *Ivan Mulley while at AVRC. The white cap flash was the distinctive mark of those accepted for aircrew training. Once having passed through ACRC and ITW to pilot or specialized training phase, the flash was tucked down inside the forage cap fold as an indication that one was no longer a complete sprog.*

Below: *Black on orange striped Fairey Battles used by the bombing and navigation school at Moffat, Rhodesia, 1943. (J. Heap)*

Above: *The popular Harvard (AT-6 in US terminology) advanced trainer over the Canadian wheatlands. (R. Croger)*

Left: *Pilot Officer George Irving, 29 August 1941.*

Right: *Sergeant Ken Campbell, 1942.*

Below: *The visit of King George VI to Malta in 1943 included this drive up Kingsway toward Porta accompanied by Lord Gort, VC, the island's Governor. A souvenir snap from Graham Smith's album.*

Left: *Warrant Officer John Strain. (K. Campbell)*

Right: *Corporal Irene Storer.*

Below: *Dame Laura Knight's painting of a WAAF balloon site at Coventry features Corporal Irene Storer's Flight at work securing their charge. Corporal Storer is on the right. The bed, complete with concrete blocks, is shown behind the girls. This painting hangs in the Imperial War Museum, London.*

Left: Pilot Officer Peter Thomas, first Nigerian pilot commissioned in the RAF.

Top right: *The Sergeants' Mess at Marham airfields Norfolk, 1940. Fortunate were personnel posted to inter-war built stations such as this where barracks and messes were substantial and heated. (H. Kidney)*

Right: *Jim Donson and members of his Hudson crew outside one of Stornoway's cold Nissen huts.*

Left: *Sergeant Leonard A. Johnson. After his tour in Bomber Command he returned to the United States and was commissioned in the US Navy. He lost his life while in the comparatively safe job of operating flying-*

Above: *The wreck of Fortress WP: 0 at Kinloss. There were at least twenty hits from cannon-shells and bullets on this aircraft.*

Top right: *Sergeant Mick Wood (left) and Harry Sutton (right), a picture taken at Kinloss after the crash-landing.*

Right: *Wellingtons, the workhorses of Bomber Command during the early years. These are aircraft of No. 214 Squadron at Stradishall.*

N BU

HANDLEY PAGE

Left: *Stanley Tomlinson, in centre of door nearest camera, and men of 149 Squadron pose beside Stirling OJ:K at Lakenheath. Patch forward of tail fin is the repair of battle damage sustained on 5 November 1943.*

Bottom left: *Nose decor of* 'Friday The 13th', *veteran No. 158 Squadron Halifax, when this aircraft was on display to the public at a site just off London's Oxford Street, summer 1945.*

Below: *Sergeant Steve Challen, Canadian volunteer, in 'flying togs' early 1941.*

Above: *Morgan Hewinson with other members of the crew.*

Left: *Flight Lieutenant William Reid, VC.*

'Early in 1941 I was posted to Finningley, Yorkshire. As was always the case in the Air Force, if you were a latecomer you were an outsider; those already there were entrenched in comfortable places. So I found myself an LAC in charge of the flying wing stores for a new OTU being formed to handle the Avro Manchester. We had just one example for familiarization purposes. As it always seemed to have one engine removed it never flew. This and an assortment of other types and equipment was inherited from No. 106 Squadron which provided the basis of the new unit. At Finningley the main stores was still on a peacetime footing; the war hadn't disturbed the service's love of paperwork. I was confronted with a huge pack of volumes known as the RAF Vocabulary – spare parts books for everything under the sun. There was an even bigger pile of documents which were amendments to the first heap. Vouchers had to be filled out in triplicate and unless the paperwork was correct there was an inquest on every request or movement.

'One day I had to dispatch a rogue aircraft engine to the main stores. My training was that all plug holes had to be sealed to keep muck from getting into the cylinders while in transit. As I had none of the proper bungs I screwed in some sparking plugs I found, before the engine was hoisted on to a small lorry and sent off. The main stores would not accept it as there was no voucher for the sparking plugs!

'I was angry at this bit of red tape and not very happy when someone rang up to say he had put in an order for a table for his office two or three days ago and where was it? This only added to my irritation that someone should be fussing about a table when I was up to my neck in dud engines. I turned to my helper and asked him to look up the application adding: "There's some bloody bloke here who doesn't know there's a war on!" The following morning an arm with a lot of rings on it appeared round the door and a voice said: "I do know there's a war on." It was the Wing Commander Flying. He had evidently overheard my aside. But he took it as a joke; in fact he put me up for promotion to corporal. Only they now had to supply someone for an overseas posting and, of course, last in was first out. I went to South Africa.'

There were important records, such as those covering airworthiness. Trouble could rightly result from any breaches in this respect; aircrew safety could depend upon listing the correct information. James Kernahan had good reason to remember Form 700:

'In 1941 I was a flight mechanic, airframe, at Wigtown in Scotland, a training airfield. Taking charge of an Anson one evening, I gaily signed the Form 700 (which gave the serviceability status of the aircraft) on the word of the mechanic I was relieving, that he had performed the necessary inspection. The Anson was scheduled for a cross-country to Blackpool and back that night and when the crew arrived one of them moaned that he didn't want to go as he was missing a date. I consoled him with: "That's all right, you'll be back soon, the undercarriage doesn't work." So away they went. About a quarter of an hour later the Anson appeared in the circuit, came in to land and the undercarriage collapsed!

'Having finished my six-hour shift, I was awakened in my Nissen hut by an SP and taken to the station flight office to face a number of officers. By then I had a good idea what this was all about. One of the officers asked me to repeat exactly what I had said to the aircrew member of the Anson and why. I explained that it was just a joke and that we had been told always to put on a cheerful face for aircrew for it was not desirable for any man to fly if unhappy or stressed. They accepted my explanation and there were no questions on my signing the Form 700. That was the last I heard of the incident. But it was a lesson to me on how careless words could bring trouble.'

Much of the paperwork had to do with regulations, the need to establish and maintain order. But regulations were a handy excuse for many people to take no action, a bastion against initiative. Far too often when a change was patently desirable nothing was done. Albert Heald became involved in such a situation:

'The transport at Ridgewell before the first squadron moved in was limited to a crash tender, an ambulance and a few light vehicles. We found the crash tender was fitted with a speed governor on the carburettor as an economy device, restricting the speed of the vehicle. In December 1942 No. 90 Squadron arrived, but the first Stirling to land ended up with a collapsed undercarriage on the runway. The crash tender driver set off immediately as I and others clambered aboard. We started yelling "put your foot down" although we knew the thing would only do about 30mph flat out and due to lack of acceleration it took a considerable time to reach that speed. Additionally, we had to drive halfway round the perimeter track and then down the main runway to reach the crashed aircraft. Fortunately it had not caught fire, but received a spraying of foam just in case. Ironically the position where the Stirling came to rest was almost opposite the tender's parking place, but muddy conditions prevented a short cut across the grass. It was plain that if the aircraft had burst into flames it could well have been burned out by the time it was reached. The situation was brought to the notice of our administrators, but no action was taken.

'By coincidence a similar accident occurred sometime later while I was on duty with the crash tender. As the ground was frozen rock hard we took a short cut to reach the disabled Stirling – which again did not catch fire. As the action was against regulations there was an investigation as to why we had driven over the grass as opposed to the authorized procedure of going round the perimeter track. The result was removal of the carburettor governor and the construction of a hard road to the runway to enable the tender to take the shortest route. It took someone breaking regulations to get the administrative bureaucracy to act.'

Despite a system which often mitigated against individual enterprise, the inventive and the opportunists were in evidence and their actions were at times acknowledged by their superiors. An unusual example of initiative is recalled by Philip Knowles:

'In the spring of 1944, No. 650 Squadron, based at Cark-in-Cartmel, was involved in target towing for the Army, who were firing mainly with Bofors AA guns. Our Martinets were fitted with a winch mounted with its axis horizontally across the front of the rear cockpit. The towed-target operator (TTO) used this winch to let out the flag target on a steel cable, controlling it with a brake. The cable was wound in again by a small windmill (outside the port fuselage), which could be rotated so as to face the slipstream and power the winch.

'One army unit was particularly accurate and shot away four targets in quick succession, each time requiring the cable to be wound in and let out again with the new target. In this process the winch brake overheated and caught fire. With no fire extinguisher, Corporal Hall, the TTO operator, had to make use of the nearest equivalent with which nature had endowed him. This was successful, the Martinet got back safely and Cpl. Hall was commended by Group.'

A less fortunate incident was of Ken Campbell's making:

'The hydraulics of the Blenheim Mk IV were somewhat unique. The central system allowed two separate functions to be activated; one, power to operate the undercarriage and flaps (air brakes); the second supplied power to the gunner's turret. Unfortunately, however, not all at the same time. The drill was for the skipper to select wheels and flaps for take-off. On becoming airborne and well clear of the ground, the hydraulic power was transferred to the turret and the guns were brought on stream. Back in the circuit preparatory to landing, the switch was turned to make the undercarriage and flaps live again.

'On the morning of 13 January 1941 the squadron was assigned to a daylight escort job for a bunch of Coastal Command strike aircraft heading out over the North Sea to the enemy coast. During pre-flight briefing the Wing Commander reminded crews of the opposition's latest ploy, a hazard experienced by crews reaching home base on completion of recent sorties – as if we needed reminding! – Old Adolph's fighter boys had come up with the most delightful little party piece. As our Blenheims neared base and manoeuvred into position to make the final approach prior to landing, wheels down, a brace of bloody Junkers 88s swept in from nowhere and shot the hell out of us. Couldn't do a darned thing about it – no operating turret d'ya see?

'As was the usual routine after the main briefing, a question and suggestion session followed the essential operational flying tactics and planning. At this stage I feel it is time to mention that a tiny minority of the navigator and pilot fraternity looked upon air gunners as a pretty thick mob. Most notably such views were held by the odd callow youths with oodles of egg-head qualifications and fresh out of school or college. Gunners thick? – no way!

'Back to the briefing room where the Wingco had just finished talking. I stood up, touched my forelock and half stammered: "Sir, after the skipper has committed himself to landing with wheels down and part flap would he re-select the turret and we rear-gunners could very soon put a stop to Jerry's little skylark." I swear I saw the Boss grin happily and murmur: "By God, he's got it. The sergeant at the back there has solved the whole ruddy problem." Like I say, air gunners just ain't so stupid after all.

'I was rewarded for my brilliance by being made lead gunner in a vee formation of three for the escort. The operation was highly successful and all aircraft returned to base. Undercarriages were lowered and locked, turrets re-selected. It was great, all we rear-gunners were having a ball, firing the guns like they were going out of style. The Ju 88s buggered off right sharpish. I felt mighty pleased and smug with my day's work.

'We landed. The pilots couldn't extend full flap as the system was still tied in to the turrets. All three Blenheims ploughed through the hedge at the far end of

Bircham Newton. I dodged the de-briefing. I thought the air might be pretty solid around the Operations Room area. Maybe the sergeant at the briefing room was after all inclined to be on the thick side. Even so, I don't reckon the Wingco and the rest of the boffins were over brilliant for going along with such a bloody silly wheeze in the first place.'

There were also ideas that were too daring. Or, in the case offered by John Wray, decidedly suicidal:

'My squadron commander was a man of original thought. One night we were in the crewroom listening to Lord Haw Haw when the lights went out and a series of loud bangs told us we were under attack. The hangar caught fire so we picked ourselves up and rushed in to try and rescue our rather heavy aircraft by pushing them out on to the airfield. In the morning we came down to survey the scene and were surprised to see that one of the aircraft had six feet missing from one of its wings. No one recalled us hitting the doors in our hurry to get them out of the hangar and so we went inside to see if we could find the piece of wing. We did not have to search very far for there was a big hole in the hangar floor, and when we approached it and looked down we saw an unexploded bomb lying at the bottom weighing about 500lb. We all made off at high speed with one exception, our Squadron Commander. He had suddenly been struck with an idea that, in those circumstances, would have never occurred to any other rational human being.

'He called to his retreating adjutant, a meek and mild man of a shy and retiring disposition. "Come here," he said. "Go and get some rope and some airmen; we will get this out, have it emptied, paint it red, cut a slot in it and use it as our squadron post box." The adjutant remonstrated as best he could with an individual who was used to getting his own way, but to no avail. He had just returned with a length of rope and some very reluctant airmen when, fortunately, the Bomb Disposal Squad turned up. They were absolutely livid when they saw what was about to happen and sent everybody packing.

'Our station commander was a man of few words, but each word had a telling effect. He read the Riot Act to my squadron commander, who had heard it so often before that he knew it by heart. For our squadron adjutant he reserved the unfairest of jibes: "If you want to mess about with unexploded bombs, I'll get you posted to a Bomb Disposal Unit." Needless to say, within the week we had a splendid new squadron post box – a 500lb bomb, painted red with a slot cut in it through which one posted one's letters.'

BASES AND BILLETS

Peacetime Royal Air Force establishments provided reasonably comfortable accommodation for both officers and men. Many had centrally heated quarters, spacious messes and good recreational facilities. But a goodly proportion of the RAF's 'wartime warriors' were never fortunate enough to be posted to one of these stations, and, if serving in the UK, most likely only woke to view a Nissen hut ceiling's curved corrugations. The rapid expansion programme following the outbreak of war necessitated requisitioning large country houses, seaside hotels, furniture warehouses and redundant shops for use as barracks and to provide training and operational facilities. More than 2,000 establishments ranging from small listening-posts to vast storage and maintenance depots were used by the RAF in the UK from 1939 to 1945. Of the total, well over 500 were airfields or airstrips, less than 100 of which dated from pre-war. Therefore the most likely airfield billet would be one of the prefabricated huts, perhaps wood and felt or asbestos panelled if you were lucky, but more probably a Nissen hut with damp concrete floor. The old hands, like Morgan Hewinson, knew that one had to look after oneself, addressing the situation with the following unofficial dictum:

'Basic rules for aircrew on being posted to a new station:

1. Find comfortable accommodation.
2. Find the cycle store.
3. Find the Mess.
4. Report in. In that order.'

For comparative newcomers there was often little opportunity for choice; you went where you were told. Archie Elks:

'After we had done our signals and gunnery training we were posted as Sgt WOP/AGs up to Llandwrog, North Wales. When we arrived an NCO took us across to some Nissen huts which looked absolutely awful – dripping wet with water on the floors. He said, "That's where you'll be living. These are unfit for human habitation." Always being quick to meet sarcasm with sarcasm I quipped. "All right for aircrew then." "You're dead right!" he snapped back, and stormed off.'

From 1941 most new airfields in the UK were built to handle multi-engined aircraft to a Class A standard with paved runways and roads and accommodation for 2,000 souls. Each had facilities to make it self-contained, with electric power, water and sewerage if local services failed. Each Class A airfield cost about £1 million, a prodigious sum at the time, when labourers earned 30 shillings a week and a new bungalow might be raised for £500. The airfield building programme was, at the time, the biggest civil engineering feat ever undertaken in the UK; but due primarily to haste, the quality and nature of construction left much to be desired. Material shortages found many structures still incomplete when airfields had to be occupied. Obtaining further action to get matters put right was a frequent frustration. The solution devised by one enterprising officer faced with a problem was noted by Tom Imrie:

'I think RAF Polebrook must have been put together fairly quickly as during the summer of 1941, when there were frequent thunderstorms, the camp roads – particularly in the area of Squadron Headquarters – became flooded. The station commander, Group Captain Evans-Evans was obviously getting little help from "Works and Bricks" so, ingeniously, he retrieved a rescue dinghy from one of the Forts, put in three WAAFs and floated the lot on one of the ponds which had a road below. The photographs he sent to the Air Ministry did, I believe, bring immediate results.'

Airfields were constructed the length and breadth of the land, wherever the topography was satisfactory and, in the more rugged areas, where it was not. The locations of several airfields, particularly those for Coastal Command, were very much 'last resort' where a base was needed to better the range of aircraft that would operate from it. One such was Stornoway, which left a lasting impression on Jim Donson:

'At Kyle of Lochalsh we embarked on one of MacBrayne's ferries, which still serve the islands, and arrived at Stornoway at around 1am. A lorry drive and we were at the airfield in the early hours. After a makeshift meal we were shown to our quarters. Nissen huts surrounded largely by peat bog. Unfortunately no beds or lockers had yet arrived so we were obliged to make up our bedding on the floor. Travel-weary after the tedious two-day journey from Norfolk, we fell asleep at once, to be awakened a couple of hours later by a great clamour on the iron roof of our hut. This was to be our alarm-call every morning – sea birds in great numbers trying to alight on the slippery rounded roof in a high wind. After another hour or two of fitful dozing, a knock on the door was followed by the entry of the duty sergeant announcing that he would return in half an hour to escort us to the mess for breakfast. This we thought strange. We soon learned when we joined some half-dozen other new arrivals the reason for what at first appeared to be "Nanny" treatment. All the huts were linked by narrow paths which had been built by putting tons of hardcore into the peat and it was essential to keep to the paths. This applied all over the station, roads, runways, dispersals and so on. I found often that landing on either runway was rather like landing on a jelly. Proof of this was to be seen later when the pilot of a Liberator (the only one I ever saw land there) in turning at the end of the runway to taxi back, found that one leg of the main undercarriage sank slowly through the surface causing the Liberator to come to rest on one wing. There it had to stay until the runway had been sufficiently reinforced to enable the use of jacks and cranes to liberate the Liberator!

'The weather at Stornoway was another matter. I once had the job of flying with a new pilot, both to check him out and to familiarize him with the airfield and its surroundings. His only comment after landing was, "This is supposed to be July, does it piss down like this all the time?" I assured him there was a break, lasting maybe an hour, at some time during each week.'

One advantage of the large number of airfields dotted around the UK was the presence of a ready haven should the weather turn bad. In rugged country, thick cloud often hid hills and the prudent pilot did not penetrate the murk over high ground if he could avoid it. But dropping in to land unannounced at strange places could bring hazards, as Philip Knowles discovered one stormy summer's day:

'In July 1944 ground crew members of No. 650 Squadron, target-towing at Cark-in-Cartmel, attended a course to improve aircraft servicing efficiency. Since this was measured by the number of flying hours achieved per month, the pilots were encouraged to make flights whenever possible for whatever reason. As one result of this policy I was ferrying a squadron member to Glasgow to go on leave.

'On the far side of the Solway Firth the solid cloud base came down to the sea and it was obvious that we could not get to Abbotsinch. I decided to divert to Carlisle, where my passenger could get a train. This was a grass naval airfield with Sommerfield tracking providing a form of runway. I was surprised to see large white crosses near each end of the runway, but assumed that they represented aircraft carrier limits for Fleet Air Arm training. I received no signal from the ACP hut at the downwind end of the runway, but came in anyway. Just as I touched down I saw (a) a number of men leaping up from the runway; (b) the ACP hut was a builder's hut, and (c) there were large spikes sticking up from the tracking all around us.

'Fortunately we hit neither men nor spikes, but I got a terrible dressing-down from the naval Station Commander ("Didn't you see the white crosses?"). I got another rocket on returning to Cark, as my diversion had gone unreported and my failure to arrive at Abbotsinch had set off a search operation. Not a good day.'

The proliferation of airfields also produced the trap of which Horace Nears quotes an example:

'One night a guy came back from ops and there was a little bit of cloud sitting on top of Lasham so Flying Control told him to divert to Odiham. The pilot replied that there was no need to divert him as he could see the Lasham runway clearly. Flying Control agreed to let him land and switched on the floods. They waited and waited and finally became concerned when no Mosquito arrived. Not half as concerned as the pilot of the Mosquito when he found he had landed at nearby Odiham!'

Many of the pre-war airfields were situated in areas where they could not be extended or developed to meet the requirements of operating larger and heavier aircraft. Some prestigeous aerodromes were quite primitive by later standards. Tony Spooner:

'The American had crossed the Atlantic for the first time. Pan Am had flown him to the Shannon. Here he was taken to the land airport to board a Dakota for London. After an uneventful flight, the young RAF pilot of this aircraft, having safely landed at Croydon, recently restored to its original role of "London's Airport", was about to taxi in when the American burst into the cockpit. "Well done skipper. You made it OK but what happened. . . .?" The pilot looked puzzled. "Nothing happened. We've arrived. This is London Airport. . . ." "Oh gee, my mistake. I thought that we had come down in a field!" And so, of course, they had. Croydon was nothing more than a rather bumpy grass field; devoid of any runway and with a huge hollow at one end in which a Dakota could completely disappear from view from the Tower.'

Among the pre-war airfields was one originally formed from low-lying meadows that had a peculiar distinction which Morgan Hewinson exploited:

'The airfield at the School of Air Support at Old Sarum was a very special field. It had a watch tower to one side and a "land where you please" policy. What was unusual about it was the enormous crop of mushrooms it produced. Aircraft landed only infrequently, so with a promise from the watch tower controller to warn of approaching aircraft, one would go out on to the field in the evening armed with a large bag or container to collect the next morning's breakfast. Of course, the inevitable happened. No warning from the tower. It must have made a very funny spectacle; one small dark figure in the middle of the field not knowing which way to run as the light aircraft sped towards me. I felt as a snail must when being chased by a goose.'

Oppos

Celebrities and Characters

If one performed fairly mundane duties, day in and day out, for five or six years, the highlight of service could be coming face-to-face with one of the great names in history – an occasion remembered and recounted with pride. This was the case for Desmond Jenkins:

'Being a cook was a fairly uneventful job; most of my time with the RAF was spent in kitchens. The most memorable day of my whole service was Christmas Day 1944. I had been badly burned in a kitchen accident and was rushed to the burns unit of a large hospital just outside Brussels. That morning, while sitting in a bath of saline water having my chest and arm burns treated by a medical orderly, we were informed that Field Marshal Montgomery was going to pay a visit to the hospital and I had been one of those selected to meet him. This was a great thrill for a humble LAC and I was happy to sit in my bath of warm water, particularly as there was snow outside and the day was very cold. The press men were present and while waiting for the Field Marshal one of them took my photograph. It was a couple of hours before the great man arrived but it was worth the wait and a memorable experience. With the excellent Christmas dinner that followed, washed down with a few bottles of beer, it was an enjoyable occasion, despite my burns. A few days later an aunt, who was a nurse in a military hospital outside Cardiff, happened to be looking through a copy of *The Nursing Mirror* and to her amazement saw the picture of me in the saline bath. This was the first my family learned of my accident because I had been unable to use my hands and write home.'

An audience with the great could come about by chance circumstances; such as befell Graham Smith while walking to Valletta on a bright day in early 1943:

'The hot dusty road to Malta's capital seemed its usual long hike. The prayer was always a lorry of some sort, anything on four wheels would do. Lo and behold the answer to the prayer, a gleaming car with a pennant flying on the bonnet; chauffeur-driven. Field Marshal Lord Gort, VC, Governor of the Island deigning to stop and offer a lift to a mere LAC! "Hop in my man," came the gentle-toned command. I was put at ease immediately by his general manner as he enquired how long I had been on the island and asked for my overall comments connected with my stay, which covered the dark days right through to the rapidly improving state we had reached at this juncture of the conflict. The journey into Valletta seemed but brief as the Field Marshal chatted animatedly, especially when I mentioned that my father had served under him on the Western Front during 1914–18. He almost sounded as though I could have been referring to a fellow officer – not just Corporal Smith, one of the many thousands of men under his overall command.'

Even if you were not fortunate enough to encounter the truly famous, a crossing of paths could still be a memorable experience. Len Barcham:

'While on courier work I was stranded in France on Christmas Eve 1944 when our aircraft sustained damage taxi-ing over rough ground. After a Christmas of onion sandwiches I finally scrounged a lift back to England on the 29th in an American Dakota piloted by a Lt Geiger. Our destination was Bovingdon where Geiger put up a real black. On his approach he was given many red Very lights from the runway control van which he apparently chose to ignore, having failed to notice a Liberator behind him doing its usual long low approach. The Liberator eventually had to "go around" again. When we got into flying control the reception was not friendly and I was jolly pleased I hadn't been piloting. The Liberator was Churchill's and he was in it, just returning from the Yalta Conference!'

A souvenir linked with the famous is treasured by Hugh Berry:

'When volunteers were required for cinema projectionists I was accepted as this had been my civilian occupation. Eventually I was teamed up to operate Mobile Cinema No. 12, an Austin 3-ton lorry equipped with 35mm projectors, screen, petrol generator and all equipment to make it self-contained. Our job was to visit RAF establishments behind the North African battle lines and give the boys a film show. On one occasion we were playing to wounded in a Benghazi hospital and learned that in the audience was Lady Rosalinde Tedder, wife of the Air Commander-in-Chief who later became Marshal of the RAF Lord Tedder. Afterwards she kindly signed our Completion Certificate, a form required by the authorities in Cairo to prove we had actually given a performance. Lady Tedder didn't have her glasses and inadvertently signed on the line marked Comments but added "A very good show – liked by all." The next day she flew back to Cairo, the plane crash-landed, and she was killed. I still have the carbon copy of what was probably her last signature.'

Then there were those who actually knew the famous. Sid Cottee:

'While instructing glider pilots at Weston-on-the-Green I shared a hut with a tall, well-spoken chap with black wavy hair, named Desmond Leslie. I didn't know a lot about him but he took himself off to London a lot and had a good line in civilian clothes. One morning he didn't turn up for duty until around 10 a.m. The Flight CO, Flt/Lt Ridout, a ruddy-faced, bald-headed, experienced pilot who had once flown biplanes on the Northwest Frontier, properly let Leslie have it, demanding to know why he was so late. "Matter of fact," Leslie explained in his deep, cultured voice, "I was dining with the PM at Chequers last night and when I came to leave the guards wouldn't let me out." Ridout obviously didn't take kindly to having the mickey taken out of him by one of his tug pilots. "Why the ****** ****** didn't you go back and wake Winston up and ask him what the ****** password was?" he exploded. I didn't know it at the time, but Desmond Leslie was telling the truth; he was Winston Churchill's nephew.'

During the course of hostilities many famous people who had distinguished themselves in civilian life joined the RAF. The most popular were those who had made a career in entertainment or sport, becoming well known to the public through exposure at the cinema, on the radio or in newspapers and magazines. Thus it became a point of interest to relate that you served under Richard Murdoch or that Dan Maskall was your PT instructor, although such names would probably only mean something to your contemporaries. For others there was, and remains, a certain pride in having been in close proximity to one of the RAF's own famed; men such as Guy Gibson, Douglas Bader, Leonard Cheshire, Johnny Johnson and so on. There were also those in RAF service who had distinguished themselves in the First World War or in other spheres of aviation. A few were not only renowned for their deeds, but for their eccentricities. A famous individual encountered by Tom Minta was most certainly in the latter category:

'I was posted to the Central Flying School at Upavon. Not to learn to fly but as a mechanic to look after the many different types of aircraft they had there, ranging from current service types like Spitfires and Wellingtons to the new Stirlings and Manchesters. George Stainforth, Schneider Trophy winner and world air speed record holder, was the CO of the flight responsible for writing the Handling Notes for all new aircraft. George was quite a character. He would arrive at the hangar in the morning with a Sealyham and a pet fox both on leads. There were a couple of stakes in the grass with rings to which he tethered the fox while he was on duty. George would occasionally go home in the station "Spit", taking the Sealyham with him. His arrival back on Monday morning often featured a series of low passes, upward rolls and inverted flying as he beat up the place to make sure we were fully awake. Then he would land, taxi over, get out, lift up the flap just aft of the pilot's seat – which normally held the radio – and extract a basket in which was the Sealyham. The dog was retained by four pieces of elastic from its collar to each corner of the basket. It didn't appear to suffer unduly from the aerobatics but he did tend to walk sideways for a bit when he was put on the ground.'

Tom Minta was later – while serving with No. 58 Squadron – to encounter another extraordinary character who became something of a legend:

'One morning I was in Operations waiting to be briefed, when the CO said, "Oh, Mint, I want you to take a passenger with you tonight. Wing Commander Cohen. He's from Command and wants some first hand experience." Cohen turned out to be 68 years old and a distinguished First World War airman with a DSO and MC among his medal ribbons. This was the time when the U-boats had started coming out in packs. Because of the risk of cross-fire if we happened to come on a pack we tried to arrange that there were other aircraft in the vicinity that could be directed to make an attack. On this occasion we were called in by someone else but he had been shot down by the time we got there. Cohen was on the front gun so at least we felt he had seen a bit of action. We got back to Holmsley near midnight after about an 11-hour haul, debriefed and had sandwiches in the mess. Cohen said he'd like to see me in the Ops Room at 9 next morning. After a short, sharp sleep I made for the Ops Room, still somewhat tired. Reporting that I'd been asked to be there by Wing Commander Cohen, I was told: "Oh yes, he's left a message. He's awfully sorry but he decided he'd go out with the Beaufighter boys early this morning." I was more than a little taken aback and remember thinking that I hoped I'd be as spry if I made 68.'

Lionel Cohen's intrepidity and energy were remarkable for a man of his age. Recognition of this was his DFC in 1944. At 70 he was the oldest man to receive this award. Every command had its celebrities and, it seems, there were few units without a colourful character or two. This was particularly so on operations where stress and relief continually fluctuated and the latter was expressed in unrestrained conduct. Often a man whose air discipline was exemplary would be the life and soul of the mess on the ground. Such individuals are remembered with a mixture of affection and admiration by more sober comrades who never tire of recalling connected exploits. Typical is Ken Campbell's anecdote of a squadron star:

'Warrant Officer John Strain, a No. 489 (RNZAF) Squadron pilot at Wick in 1943, seldom made an error as a skipper when airborne in his Hampden, especially during an operational flight. However, it must be said, away from the flying scene the happy-go-lucky Johnny was guilty of dropping the occasional clanger.

'Among his many activities, "J.C." (as he was widely known) took a very keen interest in, and had a good working knowledge of, all his aircraft's equipment; not merely in the cockpit but bombsights, guns, navigator's paraphernalia, radios, etc. In line with this knowledge, Johnny liked always to see his aeroplane neat and tidy, he hated clutter which could impede quick access and exit should any emergency occur. He took a look around the inside of his aircraft two or three times a week to make sure all was up to scratch. It was during one of these informal "look arounds" that Johnny was in the vicinity of the rear turret, checking that there were no gash ammunition cases lying around, when he saw he was not alone. Beyond the rear gunner's position the fuselage of the Hampden narrowed so that it was an all fours job to progress further up towards the tail. Johnny could see the rear end of a prone instrument man who was in the process of servicing the master compass, which was situated just about as far back towards the tail as one could go. The repairer was intent on the delicate job and did not appear to be aware of Johnny's presence. Never one to miss an opportunity for a laugh, Johnny quietly stretched up the fuselage and prodded the instrument bloke sharply and firmly between the buttocks. "How's that for dead centre, chum?" quipped the practical joker, as the startled technician did an abrupt about. It was Johnny's turn to be startled; the betrousered WAAF instrument specialist was not at all amused!'

COMMONWEALTH AND ALLIED MEN

The Royal Air Force became a veritable mix of nationalities as the war progressed. In addition to British stock, there were a large number of volunteers from the Empire and Commonwealth, whose countries eventually supplied the complements for whole squadrons. Airmen who escaped the occupation of their European homelands were numerous enough to be formed into units with special national associations. There were also several hundred United States citizens who volunteered for aircrew, some of whom preferred to remain in the 'Raf' after America became involved in hostilities. Finally, there were the odd volunteers from other neutral countries, mostly attracted by the adventure of combat flying.

The first Commonwealth squadron in the RAF was No. 75 which, in April 1940, was designated as a New Zealand unit to be manned mainly by aircrew of the Royal New Zealand Air Force. Other Commonwealth designated squadrons followed; predominantly Australian and Canadian, and although personnel were part of their country's own air forces, they functioned under RAF command in the UK. As there were shortages of Commonwealth personnel trained in specialist trades or aircrew duties, these squadrons always had a varying number of British nationals on strength. Conversely, men from the Commonwealth and Empire were frequently to be found in RAF units.

During the early days a 'We of the Mother country know best' attitude prevailed in many quarters within the RAF which was, understandably, irritating to those from overseas. Mick Wood was involved in one incident that smacked of this bias:

'On the cold and foggy Boxing Day morning of 1940, a bus arrived at Uxbridge with the first batch of pilots from Australia. From the headquarters building came a Wing Commander demanding to know who we were and whence we had come. Someone explained that we were 32 pilots arrived for OTU training, having reached Scotland from Canada on the previous day. "And what is that uniform you are wearing?" "The Royal Australian Air Force uniform," we replied. "Well, you can't wear that here," he snapped. With that the entire 32 of us re-boarded the bus with a scarlet-faced Wing Commander feeling much put down by this batch of insolent colonials. Presently the matter was put right. The Station Commander appeared, welcomed us all and we were taken to the mess for lunch. With hindsight the mistake was probably reasonable. At that time the RAAF issue greatcoat had been cut for use by the post-First World War airmen who occasionally went about their duties on horseback; besides which the colour of the cloth was much darker than that worn by the RAF.'

A more blatant touch of prejudice was encountered by Vincent Elmer in a reprimand he received:

'The second morning after our contingent of ground crew men arrived at Middleton St. George we were allowed to go down to the hangars to see what Wellingtons and Halifaxes were like. Our training in Canada was only on basic trades and we had never been anywhere near any operational aircraft. We were going to have to learn our job from the RAF lads as we went along. There was a No. 420 Squadron Wellington loaded with incendiaries and HE bombs parked in front of a hangar. After looking it all over with great interest from outside, I decided to explore the interior and climbed up the ladder under the nose. Fascinated by the equipment, I moved along to the bomb-bay. Here I was too inquisitive and somehow managed to set off the flotation bags which were for use in a ditching. With the hiss of air going into the bags I made a hasty retreat back to the nose. There I was confronted by an RAF Flight Sergeant who had heard the hissing and was not at all pleased. He made his contempt for Commonwealth help very plain: "God blimey. You ruddy colonials! We should send you all over to

Hitler and the Luftwaffe. You'd soon mess things up and this war would be over in a hurry." '

Such an outburst was simply the normal habit of finding a convenient reason to distance oneself from the offender. Relationships between Commonwealth airmen and their British counterparts were generally excellent – many RAF men preferred to serve with Australian or Canadian squadrons. For young men making their first overseas journey, wartime Britain and its customs took a little getting used to. Vincent Elmer again:

'British plumbing was a joke to most Americans and Canadians, but my introduction wasn't at all funny. Soon after arrival in England I took the opportunity to visit a pub. Whether it was an effect of the beer consumed I do not know, but I had an urgent need to visit the toilet. The flush system was like nothing I'd seen back home and I couldn't find a handle. Finally I figured that the chain, attached to what looked like a cistern high up the wall above the toilet, must be the flush control so I gave it a pull. Nothing happened, but as there was a bit of resistance I gave it a real hard tug. A little too hard for the chain and just about everything attached to the other end came straight out over the top of the cistern and a cascade of water with it. The landlord didn't have a very high opinion of Canadians as he strove to check the flood.'

Apart from Canadians, Australians, New Zealanders and South Africans, there were representatives from just about every country in the Empire. A darker face among air crew was not that rare. One individual endeared himself to Jim Double:

'On 1 October 1941 I was posted to No. 3 EFTS at RAF Watchfield, near Swindon, Wiltshire, and on arrival was allocated the top bed of a double bunk. It was late in the evening and I found the bottom bed was occupied by a Nigerian who was fast asleep. He proved to be a distinctive character!

'He was Peter Thomas, son of a Nigerian chief who had, I learned from Peter, sponsored several Spitfires. Peter had been passed down from many previous courses to join the new intake! It was quite normal for him to get lost regularly while solo. Strangely, he would choose to land on the only ploughed field around and across the furrows to end up on his nose! He would come trudging into the billet late at night having been fetched home yet again! When we suggested he would get washed-out, his reply was always – "My father will buy some more."

'Halfway through the course it was wound up and we were transferred to the Arnold Scheme in the USA, but Peter remained at Watchfield. This lad had trained at an English university, but still insisted, should he get into combat, the enemy would not kill him as he would turn into a wild boar! After I returned from the USA I saw a photo of Peter Thomas of Lagos, the first Nigerian to be commissioned in the RAFVR; he had got his wings. Sadly, I later learned that he had been killed in a flying accident with a Spitfire. I still keep his photo.'

Then there were the men from the occupied countries of Europe: Poles, Czechs, French, Dutch, Norwegians, Belgians, Yugoslavs and Greeks, all of whom had specially formed squadrons linked to national identity; the most numerous being the Poles with fourteen squadrons and the French close behind with twelve. Here too there was a proportion of British personnel to fill trade vacancies or to ensure the necessary liaison. Polish pilots, particularly those in fighters, had a reputation for being a wild bunch but tenacious combatants; records show they achieved considerable success. As in the case of Commonwealth personnel, several men from the occupied countries served in RAF squadrons because there was no requirement in one linked to their country; but also sometimes through choice. These individuals often endeared themselves to the British airmen. John Wray recalls a man who won his admiration;

'This was a Free French Air Force Lieutenant in one of the squadrons in my Tempest Wing. He was small in stature, unprepossessing and wore rimless spectacles. Although he spoke good English, he was of a quiet and retiring nature. None of this was surprising because he had been a master in a school in a small village in France. The outbreak of war and the subsequent battles across France, resulting in the capitulation of that country scarcely touched him. He continued to teach, considering this was his job. However, when the Germans came to his village he became so incensed by their behaviour that he escaped to England and joined de Gaulle. So, to look at he didn't really measure up to what most people considered a pilot should look like. In fact, he wasn't a particularly good fighter pilot and those who had him flying as their No. 2 had an uncomfortable feeling in the seat of their trousers!

'Now the Tempest was a great fighter aeroplane, but she did have some annoying little habits. Like most women she did not like being kept waiting. If, for example, one had to wait to take off for any length of time because other squadrons were landing or taking off then, if you were not careful when opening the throttle for take off, at best you received a shower of oil over your windscreen and at worst the engine would stop. One day our Frenchman, taking part in an operation with his squadron, had to wait for take-off while a Spitfire Wing landed. When the Tempests eventually took off, our Frenchman's engine stopped halfway down the runway. He stood on his brakes but went off the end of the runway and turned over. I rushed out with the fire tender and ambulance, though fortunately the aircraft did not go on fire. However, unlike an upturned Spitfire where a few lusty airmen under the tail could lift it up to allow the pilot to be released, the Tempest was much heavier and so we had to get a crane, all of which took time.

'When eventually we lifted the tail the Frenchman dropped out, his right hand completely severed. This had come about when, realizing he was going to turn over, he instinctively put up his right hand to protect his face. The glass screen on his gunsight cut off his hand. Without a word, he jumped to his feet and started to walk towards the ambulance. Suddenly he turned round and walked back to the aircraft, he got down on his knees and reaching inside pulled out his parachute. He stood up, threw his parachute over his shoulder and walked to the ambulance. I saw him six months later in the bar of the Park Lane Hotel, fitted with an artificial hand. It is to my eternal shame that I have forgotten the name of this little French schoolteacher with the heart of a lion.'

And then came the Yanks. Many young Americans had joined the RAF before their country found itself at war with Germany, mostly by volunteering for the RCAF. Americans turned up in every RAF command and quickly earned the respect of those with whom they flew. There was a certain amount of glamour attached to the image of Americans, as most British ideas were derived from the cinema where Hollywood dominated. A friendly, outgoing nature was the general impression left through initial contact, but the ladies sometimes had their expectations of glamour squashed. Alan Haworth:

'My skipper, Johnny Johnson, was a Texan farmer who went up to Canada early in 1941 and joined the RAF. He was a burly, good-natured guy who, being a Sergeant, was issued with boots whereas I, a Pilot Officer, had shoes. On Saturday nights when we were not flying, together we went to dances held in the upper hall of Haverhill town hall. The floor of the hall must have seen a lot of use because it was worn quite smooth, but had hard knots in the wood which protruded as bumps. During the course of those dance evenings in the summer of 1942 Johnny's feet got rather hot so he would take off his boots and dance in stocking feet. But as he was afraid his boots might be pinched if he left them in the cloakroom, he insisted on tying the laces together and wearing them round his neck while he danced. I cannot remember him making many conquests among the Haverhill belles!'

The cockpit of a fighter was the main attraction and not at a loss to recognize the political and propaganda value of letting United States' nationals fight the Luftwaffe, the Air Ministry formed three special American fighter units identified as Eagle Squadrons. These were ultimately transferred to the United States Army Air Force (USAAF) when this organization commenced operations from the UK in the summer of 1942. By this time the RAF was battlewise and prepared to act as mentor to their American cousins. The general expectancy among RAF personnel was that US airmen would be much like themselves apart from different accents. The reaction on finding that Americans had different attitudes and outlooks on many aspects of both the military and social scene brought – behind their backs – mild disdain, ridicule and even a little resentment. The new allies were welcomed, but many RAF officers reserved an opinion. The stories were many. James Donson:

'In July 1942 I was involved in flights from Stornoway to set up a navigational beam for an operation known as "Mother Hen". The purpose was revealed when one day a B-17 Fortress appeared with a dozen P-38 Lightnings in formation, soon followed by similar air reinforcements from America via Greenland and Iceland. There seemed to be little room on the airfield while the P-38s were being serviced and refuelled. It was our first meeting with any Americans and we immediately discovered that their attitude was more informal than ours in the officers' mess. One entered in full flying kit, including calf-length, red leather, high-heeled boots with spurs. He removed the bulb from a light socket, plugged in an electric razor and proceeded to shave. Those RAF officers present did their best to look unconcerned and refrained from comment in the best interests of this welcome new alliance.'

There is no doubt that Americans had their preconceived ideas about the British and were somewhat surprised by many aspects of wartime Britain. If we found their military conduct casual they were undoubtedly amazed by the antics that transformed many an RAF officers' mess as Tony Spooner observed:

'One evening in the summer of 1943 a B-17 unexpectedly dropped in at Turnberry after a flight from the USA via Greenland and Iceland. The crew were invited to stay the night. Later that evening we decided to introduce the pilot, who hadn't been in the UK before, to our particular mess game of stripping down to underpants and carrying out a circuit of the room via the chairs, tables, rafter beams, etcetera without touching the floor; made more difficult by carrying a lighted newspaper. He entered into the spirit of the game but was obviously astounded by our antics. It transpired that before leaving the States he had been briefed not to expect too much overt friendliness because of our natural reserve. Hence his repeated muttering as he went round the course of, "Heck, where's all this British reserve." '

Nevertheless, what were seen as the idiosyncracies of their new allies became the subject of many a mess anecdote in RAF establishments, often embellished to add the correct trans-Atlantic flavour. An accomplished raconteur like Hamish Mahaddie could make delightful play with an occasion he recalled:

'I was supposed to be fielding for a scratch baseball team and was put out as far away as possible so as not to interfere with the play . . . when a Fort landed at Oakington. A funny little gentleman with a baseball cap, smoking the last of a cigar, got out and approached me, stopping a few yards away. He put his hand in his battledress jacket and pulled out a very large John Wayne-type hand-held cannon, pointed it straight at me and asked: "Say Bud, do you speak English?" I replied that being a Scot there was some doubt about that. He then asked what the name of the town behind me was and I said it was Cambridge. He said: "Is that the same as Yale and Harvard?" and I said, "Good gracious, no, there is a lot of doubt about that." He then asked in which direction was Alconbury and, having got a taste for the jargon, I said: "Just go down this trail a piece for ten, maybe fifteen miles, and there you will find Alconbury." He then put away the hand-held cannon, got back in the aircraft and took off. We heard later, however, that he was very lucky because many aircraft of that squadron landed in France where they didn't speak English! But very rough old Germanic Saxon. . . .'

The American fliers were integrated into the British system of flying control and also adopted many other RAF procedures. RAF personnel acted as instructors until such time as the Americans could provide their own. Although much was new and strange, the Americans learned quickly. Inevitably, there were some individuals who were not easily led from more casual ways as Bill Japp discovered:

'When a new US B-26 Marauder Group arrived from America in 1943 the crews had to be instructed in the Flying Control and R/T procedures used in North Africa. A number of RAF Marauder pilots were assigned to fly in the right-hand seat to check out the American captains on these procedures on completion of their course. This revealed that at least one of the Americans wasn't convinced of the necessity of correct radio procedures. I was flying with a pilot who went through all the formalities for take-off correctly and was cleared to proceed in his aircraft "D-Dog". As we were going down the runway, from the B-26 behind us came the laconic inquiry to the tower control: "Say, can I follow that rollin' dawg now?" '

For some RAF stalwarts the assessed shortcomings of US airmen remained a convenient moan, just as there were those US personnel who preferred to see only the worst side of the British, but eventually there were few RAF men who did not come to acknowledge that their USAAF counterparts were making a major contribution to victory. Perhaps the relatively higher pay and the attraction British women had for Americans invoked a little jealousy, but practically every RAF man who had first-hand experience of US servicemen found them likeable. American benevolence was famous too, as Harold Southgate experienced:

'When stationed at Defford, with the Telecommunications Flying Unit (TFU) in the later stages of the war, it proved quite difficult and time-consuming to use public transport for returning to Colchester on leave. Knowing there was a USAAF base at Boxted just outside the town, I had the idea of trying to arrange for someone to fly me to Boxted in order to get home quickly. This was surprisingly easy to arrange as an experimental flight with a Lancaster. It took 45 minutes to fly to Boxted where we received immediate permission to land. My aircraft took off back to Defford while I reported to the Control Tower to be greeted warmly and asked where I was heading. Told that I was going home to Mile End, about three miles from the airfield, the Duty Officer immediately rang for transport and within minutes a jeep arrived and conveyed me to my front door. Total time less than one hour compared with the seven to nine hours if I had come by train. Never had a bad word to say against the Yanks after that!'

ATTITUDE TO SENIOR SERVICES

The air of vanity which pervaded RAF personnel, in spite of belonging to the Junior Service, was also reflected in inter-service rivalry. Predominantly good-natured, one never missed an opportunity that arose to score points off the Army or Royal Navy. Tony Spooner gives an instance:

'As was the custom, when a group of RAF officers became accustomed to a station they adopted a certain bar. It became their off-duty "drinking hole". So it was at Blackpool. The staff of the School of General Reconnaissance there adopted the Casino Bar. To our horror, we were "invaded" one night by a group of very "la-de-dah" army officers in full regimental dress. They must have been Hussars or some such judging by their colourful uniforms with much chain-mail around their young shoulders. It was too much to bear. One of our lot sidled over with a sweet, innocent expression and inquired: "Would you young gents mind settling a bet for us simple RAF folks. Which of the colliery bands do you all play for?" '

Naturally the japes were not all one way. Tony Spooner again:

'Thanks to really foul weather there was no air activity by either side over Malta on Christmas Eve 1941. The beer flowed. I had been working in close co-operation with the Fleet Air Arm squadrons at Hal Far, only a few miles from my own base at Luqa, and it was natural, when the booze was running out at Luqa, to pay them a visit to see how their booze supply was coping. Their supply seemed unending, their hospitality was generous and I was soon incapable of driving myself back to Luqa. "Not to worry, old chap. We'll put you up. . . ." The accommodation was by far the most palatial I experienced in Malta. Sheets (long forgotten around Luqa), a huge dry room, a real bed and they even supplied me with red silk pyjamas. Soon I was dead to the world and it would have taken a bulldozer to have awoken me. It was only next morning, when a startled orderly roused me to advise me that the officers were about to serve the men with their Christmas dinner, that I learned that I had spent the night in the bed, and in the pyjamas, of the Station Commander – a naval Captain. I didn't visit Hal Far again.'

The frequent use of 'pongo', 'squaddie', 'fish-head' and other such terms for soldiers and sailors underlined the slightly contemptuous view RAF 'bods' had of the sister services. On the serious side there was considerable co-operation in many spheres – the Army Co-operation and Airborne Forces squadrons which involved mixed Army/Air Force teams. Likewise Coastal Command liaised with naval establishments. There was also an interchange of personnel to fill specific needs if one service had a surfeit and another a dearth. Fleet Air Arm mechanics were used to service Stirlings in airborne squadrons. These were remembered with affection by Jim Swale of No 295 Squadron:

'A number of Fleet Air Arm lads joined our airborne operations squadrons at Harwell just before D-Day and stayed with us when we moved. Few had ever been to sea anyway. We, however, were literally "at sea" for some time, as their nautical terms kept us in a state of high amusement. The plum being, "Are you going ashore tonight?", which meant a visit to the towns and villages around Rivenhall. We called them matelots, a mixture of sarcasm and endearment I suspect. It did not really matter, for they were good lads. Two who had been warned not to ride their bikes behind Stirlings waiting for take-off clearance at the end of the runway, just ignored the warning. As they pedalled behind one of these aircraft the pilot put on full boost. The result, two matelots and two bikes blown across the airfield like paper bags, causing damage, a broken arm and multiple bruises.'

Whether Army, Navy or Air Force, there was an unspoken bond between all servicemen, past and present, as Albert Herbert discovered:

'With my "half wing" and stripes up, I passed out of Madley, No. 4 Radio School with a posting to London. I popped into the tea bar at Liverpool Street Station for a cuppa and a sandwich. When I went to pay my bill and gave the old lady behind the counter my half-crown, she said that I must be proud to be a pilot and that she hoped I'd shoot down one of those Germans for her. I didn't want to disappoint her by telling her that I was a wireless operator not a pilot, so as I picked up my change I said "I'll try" and left to catch a bus. When the conductor came round I discovered the old lady had short-changed me and I only had half the fare. Embarrassed, I explained to the conductor that I was on my way to my next posting and had nothing more in my pocket. He took what I had and gave me a wink. When I got off the bus I noticed he had a DSM and '14-18 ribbons on the breast of his jacket. Then I understood why he let me ride the whole way to my destination. "Thanks mate," I said.'

WOMEN'S AUXILIARY AIR FORCE

The Women's Auxiliary Air Force came into being as an adjunct of the Royal Air Force two months before the outbreak of war. Broadly, its purpose was to use women in a supportive role, in suitable duties where they would release men for other work. Initially these duties were few and chiefly of a domestic and clerical nature, reflecting the general male view of a woman's place in society. The supposed frailty and subordinate role of WAAFs was reflected in the Air Ministry's view that they should be paid a third less than most equivalent male ranks and receive a smaller food ration. In reality, like their male counterparts in air force blue, WAAFs came in all sorts and sizes, many with healthy appetites and not lacking in physique or physical ability. By all accounts a few were more worthy of belligerent duties than many males who had to shoulder rifles. Irene Storer encountered one such individual while training:

'In our entry was a girl of voluminous proportions and with thick, wiry vermilion hair. She turned all conversation into an argument during which she soon ran out of words and let fly with her fists which had some weight behind them! We all kept our distance if we could. From somewhere she had received a black eye over which she wore a black patch. We were all marching along past a brick wall with a line of airmen sitting on it when one of them called "Hello Nelson". She hesitated then stopped and we all thought she was going to pull the man off the wall. She changed her mind, however, and carried on marching. I suppose she reasoned that it was not worth a charge just as we were about to be posted to our sites.'

There were, apparently, misgivings among some senior RAF officers about having women in the service at all. The chief concern being that feminine charms would distract men from their duties. Certainly romances occurred but RAF personnel who served alongside WAAFs quickly came to appreciate their contribution to the war effort and thought of them first as workmates. Indeed, the general dedication and efficiency of these girls earned them considerable respect among both airmen and officers. Rex Croger's assessment of those encountered in No. 26 Squadron is not untypical:

'Most of the squadron transport was handled by three WAAF drivers; they took us to our aircraft and collected us on return. They were fine, good-looking girls. We went swimming with them in the Solent now and again. They didn't bother about costumes! But it was all decent fun; the relationship was platonic. We were all good mates.'

The pre-war morality, where the majority of British women preserved their virginity until marriage, was challenged by wartime pressures. For servicemen the knowledge that there might not be a tomorrow undermined sexual restraint. Being removed from parental influence and on stations where men predominated, some girls did engage in unguarded amorous affairs. Elsie Lewis was a WAAF Nursing Orderly who saw the result of such liaisons:

'There were a few young girls who got into trouble. Usually the new recruits who had been at boarding-school or strictly brought up. To them life in the WAAF was comparative freedom but they didn't know how to cope with it. One girl started to develop a tummy but said it was due to a gnat bite when the MO made another suggestion. When she said she hadn't been with anybody and insisted it was a gnat bite he commented to me: "All right, we'll have to wait won't we Lewis. Nine months should see who is right." An NCO was heard to murmur. "It must have been a bloody big gnat." '

Such happenings involved only a small minority; for the most part chastity prevailed. Many girls volunteering for the WAAF were young and of comparatively sheltered upbringing; even a little naîve when it came to the crude world of servicemen. While men would modify their language and conform to accepted behaviour in the presence of WAAFs, there was many a kindly joke at the girls' expense behind their backs. This example from John Wray:

'My station Equipment Officer was a well-known businessman who would shortly be returning to civil life. I was on one of my tours of the station and dropped in on him to have a chat and a cup of tea. While we were talking a knock came on his door. "Come in," he said. The door opened and in walked a young WAAF. "Please Sir, where can I get felt?" The Equipment Officer and I dared not look at one another. "Go down the passage", he said, "and speak to the Sergeant, he will help you." Once the door closed we both exploded!'

It would also be wrong to imply that the WAAF was characterized by the young and innocent. The average age was 23 years and a goodly proportion, if conscientious in their duties, were high-spirited enough to flout regulations if they thought they could get away with it. Fraternization between officers and other ranks was not encouraged and there was a certain amount of risk involved in pursuing such harmless associations as Eva Sizzey discovered:

'I was friendly with a WAAF officer and at her invitation went out for a trip to St. Ives when we had some time off. On return, a boyfriend of hers gave us a lift in an Air Force vehicle. My cycle was put on top of the roof. When we got back to Oakington and into the WAAF site, as he drove round a corner my cycle fell off right in front of our Orderly Officer's van and she ran over it. My officer friend made out the cycle was hers, while I hid down behind the back seat of the vehicle we were in. If I had been found out it would have been "jankers".'

Punishment of WAAFs was a peculiar business. Legally a girl had the right to refuse to accept punishment and could discharge herself from the service. A situation that understandably was not given prominence and was unknown to many girls. WAAFs subject to disciplinary charges usually appeared before their RAF Station Commander or his deputy. John Wray relates a skilful piece of manoeuvring when erring with a penalty:

'Mine was the only squadron on the station and so when the Station Commander was on leave I had to act as such as well. I carried out these duties, mainly, by calling in at SHQ each day to deal with any business that the adjutant had for me. One morning he said, "We have a WAAF on a charge of losing a Service bicycle." These bicycles, issued to those whose duties required them, were not supposed to be used for private purposes. Needless to say, they were. This WAAF had taken hers down to the local pub and somebody had pinched it. I sat in my office looking very formal and the young WAAF was marched in by the WAAF Flight Sergeant, accompanied by the WAAF Officer. The usual procedure of identification of the accused was followed and the charge read out. She had absolutely no defence. She had done it and the bike was lost. I gave her a reproving lecture on responsibility for public property, delivered with great pomposity. I went on to say, "This is a very serious offence and so I am going to make you pay for the cost of replacing this bicycle." This was about £4.

'She, being on about four shillings a day, burst into tears and was led sobbing from my austere presence by the Flight Sergeant and supported by the WAAF Officer. When the door closed the adjutant said, "You can't do that. You have exceeded your powers. You can only dock her a maximum of a day's pay." "Oh dear!" I said, "We had better have her back." A red-eyed WAAF was then marched back and I said to her, "I have reconsidered my decision and have decided to be lenient with you, you will pay four shillings instead of four pounds." '

The WAAF constituted more than 15 per cent of the overall personnel strength of the RAF. At peak strength in mid-1943 they numbered 181,835 of whom one in 26 was an officer. While largely a volunteer force and drawing girls from all walks of life, commissioned WAAFs tended to be middle or upper class, several with academic qualifications and, like the other women's services, among the officers one could encounter the daughters of important people. George Irving:

'I made an awful "black" one evening at Bradwell Bay. We had retired to the lounge for coffee and dinner and joined a group "chatting up" some WAAF officers, one of whom offered me a cigarette. Just as I was about to take one I noticed it was a Craven A, a type I disliked to smoke. So I apologized in what I thought was a humorous way by saying, "Thank you very much indeed but I never smoke Craven As. I think they are awful." She looked at me in rather an odd way and carried on her conversation with the others. Later, when it was time to leave to go on patrol, one of our chaps came to me and said: "You rotten bastard, just as I was doing a nice line chatting up that lovely brunette you go and offend her." Nonplussed, I asked how. She had only offered me a cigarette which I declined because it was a Craven A. Jock then told me the lady in question was Miss Carreras, whose father owned the tobacco firm producing Craven A. Next evening I was able to apologize to her for my lack of tact in refusing a cigarette. I must have been forgiven because she presented me with a full 20 packet of Craven A, saying, "It's time you stopped smoking that other rubbish; try these again."'

Whatever the background of a WAAF officer, an RAF other rank did not have to salute her unless he chose to, another reflection of prejudice in a male-orientated service. What would become identified as feminism was never really evident in the wartime WAAF, but many girls found intelligent comradeships among their WAAF associates. Irene Storer:

'One evening I went into a hut and found the girls listening to "The Brains Trust" on the wireless. I was surprised. "Come on Corporal," said one girl, "It's "The Brains Trust tonight." I sat and listened and found that they turned the programme into a discussion group cum questionnaire among themselves, with much laughter. It was amazing. A thought struck me that we could organize our own "Brains Trust", which we did, with me thinking up the material for it. It was great fun and what a lot I learned about those girls in that pleasant way. One could put up with such hard work and deprivation in living conditions when you shared it with people as sensible as those.'

As the months passed so the duties and trades in which the WAAFs predominated multiplied. By VE-Day WAAFs served in some 85 defined categories ranging through clerical, store-keeping, vehicle driving, engineering and barrage balloon handling. A vital task in which they excelled was air traffic and operational control. WAAF were to be found in most control rooms on combat, Sector and Group stations. In these duties many became very familiar with squadron loss and achievement. Another aspect of this is recalled by Maureen Brickett:

'Working in Ops was a fascinating experience – we were almost always busy and the work was varied and interesting, but of course there was a sad side to it – often groups of young and glamorous pilots would come to see "the other side of the job" during their "resting periods"; sadly on their return to flying duties many of them were shot down – what a dreadful waste it all was.'

The most physically exacting trade in which WAAFs figured was that of Balloon Operator. Not only did work on barrage balloon sites demand physical strength, it frequently meant exposure to the worst excesses of UK weather. Louise Howell:

'Being in Balloon Command was a hard but rewarding job in every way. We were a small band of twelve to each balloon, always sited on the outskirts of a town, usually in a park. We did everything ourselves, even making up the guy ropes and splicing steel cables. The times I dreaded most were periods of bad weather and high winds. On these occasions we were out most of the night, turning the nose of the balloon into wind whenever it varied. One wild night I got caught up in the tail rope and suddenly sailed ten feet into the air; not a very pleasant experience.'

During 1942 the WAAF became the major source of personnel in Balloon Command, serving in more than 40 operational squadrons at strategically important locations throughout the UK. Each balloon site was normally in the charge of a WAAF Corporal, an exacting command for what could be a dangerous job – steel cables downed many balloon operators as well as enemy aircraft. The following is Irene Storer's account of a hazardous event:

'Then came the day when, at about 12.15 I left the office to go and see how the lunch was faring. The phone rang and the LACW dashed into the kitchen calling. "Storm-bed Corporal!" "What?" said I. It was a lovely day. I told the duty cook to keep the dinner warm and ran outside. The sky was clear except for a few clouds away in the distance which were rolling together like a speeded-up film and heading for us. I called to everybody "Storm-bed!" They all dashed to their positions and we had that balloon down in double quick time, which was none too soon. I stood as near as I could to the winch driver saying, "Slow down, now speed up again," and so on. We all had our eyes glued to the balloon. Suddenly a civilian woman ran screaming on to the site and made straight for me. I couldn't have anything to do with her at all, the situation was dangerous enough as it was and anything could happen if I were distracted. The duty cook heard her and ran up and grabbed her away from me. She kept shouting "Come and shift this balloon." She was taken to the kitchen where she explained that a balloon had caught fast on her chimney pot and her house was full of smoke. The cook asked her if it was ripped, because if not then it was full of gas which could set fire if she did not go home and put her fire out. She could see it was obviously not our balloon. She went home after the cook had promised to inform HQ of her address.

'We had just finished bedding when a freak wind hit us. I made everybody sit on chairs round the balloon, each of us watching a section of it. Every time anyone saw something slip or come unhooked she dashed up and re-fixed it. The concrete blocks banged up and down on the bed making an awful din. It was over an hour before we were able to leave it in the hands of the guards and go in to partake of a belated dinner – during which we watched balloons sailing away in the air, some with sandbags hanging on them and we all thought it looked very funny. Those balloons could have come from anywhere and must have broken away before the rip-line was tied to the bed. Later we learned that ours and the one at Arboretum Park were the only ones saved in Derby. I think it was Coventry that lost every one. I was glad HQ had given us the order in good time.'

Two members of the site team had to stand guard over the balloon night and day, come fair or foul; usually the latter in the British climate. This could be a miserable task, particularly as protective clothing appeared to be available only in large sizes. Louise Howell:

'If there were small sizes for the WAAF I never saw them. Every Monday morning a lorry delivered clean overalls. When the pile was thrown out there was a scramble to find a pair to fit. Needless to say, being only 5ft 2in I always ended up with one a foot too long in the legs. As for being dressed for night guard duty, which each of us had to do, two hours on, four hours off, any German who invaded our site would have died laughing at the vision he encountered. I had to stand all the time because I couldn't sit down in all the gear I was wearing. This consisted of a pair of slacks over my pyjamas, a sweater, seamen's thick socks, that came nearly to my thighs, Wellington boots, an oilskin coat that hung down to my feet and with the sleeves turned back to my elbows, and all topped with a sou'wester hat that was so big it fell over my eyes whenever I moved. Last but not least a truncheon to take on intruders and a whistle to call for help!'

While WAAFs proved their worth in many and varied duties, they were not permitted to fly aircraft. Knowledge of this led to many aircrew being surprised in a similar way to the incident described by Frank Cheesman:

'One fine morning in mid-1942 the inmates of No. 11 (P) AFU, Condover, were agog with anticipation by the rumoured visitation of a Mosquito aircraft that very day. At this time the Mossie was largely an unknown quantity, so to speak, to the general public and even in the RAF by no means commonplace, so its appearance at this training unit was looked forward to with no little interest. Although all had heard of its achievements and capabilities, few had been fortunate enough to see one at close quarters. Now was their opportunity. Mixed with a natural curiosity about the aircraft itself was an understandable interest to see just what type of superior being the RAF considered suitable to fly this fabled aircraft. The general opinion was that only pilots of above average ability and great operational experience would qualify. With these thoughts in mind groups of airmen and WAAFs, all of whom had contrived some reason for their presence on the airfield, gathered near the expected parking spot as the Mossie seemingly hurtled round the circuit with the pilot inspecting the airfield and awaiting a "green" from the Control Tower. The critical audience noted with approval the smooth final approach and touch-down as, despite the high speed, the main wheels merged with the runway in a noiseless and smokeless union. An absolute "greaser" of a landing which seemed to bear out their view that only the best pilots were to be entrusted with such a "hot ship".

'The Mossie turned off, made for the marshaller and switched off. After a while and with the ladder in place the pilot made his exit. There first appeared a pair of bootees into which were tucked dark blue trousers. "Hell," said someone, "the Fleet Air Arm." The next forecast was, "A bloody Aussie." Both were wrong as further steps revealed a strikingly good-looking and rather shapely young lady of the ATA. Shock and confusion reigned for a few moments at this turn of events, the major sufferers being the more male chauvinists present. Among the rest discussions of a comparative nature broke out vis-a-vis the attractive lines of the Mossie and those of its driver. The latter was a comfortable winner. There ensued some chat with the pilot until some self-appointed Galahad, looking at his watch, said, "It's nearly lunchtime so we'd better check you into the Tower and then go to the Mess for a drink and meal. Sorry there's no transport but, not to worry, I'll borrow a cycle for you." "Oh no," was the dismayed reply, "that's no good. I NEVER LEARNED TO RIDE A BIKE." I think she finally made it on someone's handlebars, backstep or crossbar!'

Many excellent women pilots flew with the Air Transport Auxiliary ferrying aircraft, but the ATA was not part of the RAF. Indeed the expertise and experience of these ladies – who regularly handled a score of different types – was far in advance of the average RAF pilot. While WAAF were not permitted to fly aircraft, the need arose for flight trained nurses to accompany patients on air ambulance flights. These volunteers became the only WAAF recognized as aircrew – even if not officially classified as such. There was one crucial hurdle to acceptance, flight compatability. Muriel Anderson:

'Having volunteered to be an operating theatre assistant in the WAAF, while waiting for a posting I was sent to work as a nursing orderly at Winthorpe near Newark. As nothing more was heard, it was suggested by an MO that I might like to volunteer for air ambulance work, for which recruits were then being sought. This sounded interesting so I applied and after a week or so received orders to report for an air test. Obviously they first had to find out if I was going to be airsick.

'The appointment was on a Monday and the preceding weekend I had been out cycling in shorts and been badly bitten by mosquitoes. Allergic to the bites, my legs became so swollen I had to have injections and bandages. I was not very comfortable when arriving for my first flight and even less so when I was taken out to a Lancaster bomber and instructed to climb over and sit on the main spar. The pilot was Squadron Leader "Mickey" Martin who, although I didn't know it at the time, was one of the surviving Dam Buster pilots. We took off and headed out over the Wash. Although I felt fine, if a little nervous, the crew must have found it unusual to have a girl on board and were intent on getting a laugh out of the occasion. The undercarriage was lowered and I was told that we were about to land on a cloud. Mickey Martin's next joke was to mention that one engine on the starboard side had stopped. I looked out and saw the propeller blades were stationary, which didn't give me any concern, but the next thing I knew the other propeller on that side had been feathered. I daren't look out at the port wing. Anyway, this gave the crew a good laugh and we returned to earth safely with no signs of airsickness on my part.'

The air ambulance WAAFs were a select few who did sterling work on the continuous shuttles ferrying wounded from continental airfields back to England during the final nine months of hostilities in Europe. Muriel Anderson again:

'As a WAAF air ambulance orderly I flew regularly with crews on Nos. 512 and 575 Squadron Dakotas bringing back stretcher cases and walking wounded from the Continent. As the only members of the WAAF on regular flight duties we were, I suppose, something of a novelty but we were well accepted, if subject to a bit of leg-pulling now and again. Jimmy Edwards, the comedian, was one of the pilots I flew with and Al Bollington, the famous London organist, was another. On flights when we had no wounded aboard I used to think Bollington flew with his feet on the rudder pedals as if he were still playing an organ, the way we zig-zagged about sometimes. His favourite prank was to ask me to go back to the galley in the rear of the aircraft and get him some coffee. As soon as I got back there the Dakota would bob up and down and the coffee went all over the place. When I returned without the coffee and he complained, I politely told him where it was if he still wanted it!'

The Line

War and Ethos

When, on 3 September 1939, war was declared on Germany by Britain and France, the rank and file of the Royal Air Force were fairly confident that they could give a good account of themselves, a view generally shared by the British public. High Command, with the benefit of Intelligence reports, was not complacent, but did not fully appreciate the weaknesses of the RAF in certain areas. In fact its opponent, the Luftwaffe, not only possessed a greater number of modern aircraft, in most respects technically more advanced than the RAF's best, but had developed better operational tactics. Regular RAF airmen while dedicated, proficient and confident, were to a large degree unaware of what was stacked against them. As John Wray points out, the majority faced the unknown:

'In 1939 only those few who had been in the First World War knew what war entailed. Some, of course, had chased tribesmen in the Middle East and India, but in the main none of us had the remotest idea what it was going to be like when the shooting started. We had read books and we had seen *Wings*, *Dawn Patrol* and other films that gave one some idea but, as one was to learn later, the real thing is very different. So, when we went to France in September 1939 and were told that we were to carry out reconnaissance over Germany, it was realized that we might be about to find out. We were to go at night, an interesting thought because I had more night flying experience on the Blenheim than anybody else in the squadron, and I had ten hours. My flight commander had clocked up four hours. Added to this was the fact that our navigators had more or less been recruited off the street and sent on a short course where all their navigation was DR over the sea. Our gunners were good wireless operators, though inexperienced in the art of shooting at other aircraft. Because we couldn't operate out of our small grass airfield at night we had to go forward to Metz and take off from there. We would fly to Metz, three aircraft for each night sortie. Once there we would be briefed, and then hang around for the rest of the afternoon until it was dark. On one occasion it was a lovely sunny day and quite warm. The three crews had been briefed about a trip to Hanover, and we were all lying on the grass in the sun, our Blenheims lined neatly wingtip to wingtip *à la* peacetime. After all, this was 1939 and the war was not a month old.

'Six French Curtiss Hawks taxied out and took off in formation and climbed to about 3,000 feet. They then flew backwards and forwards across the airfield in various "pansy" formations. Although the front line was not all that far away, it could just as well have been peacetime. Their flying added a delightful buzz to the lovely summer day and helped us to relax and dream of cricket on the green and lovely popsies. The scene was enhanced when an aged Dewoitine biplane taxied out with two people in it to carry out a series of circuits and landings. What a lovely scene.

'Suddenly there was a great whoosh as if the Demon King had arrived. He had, in the form of a Me 109 going like the clappers at nought feet. Of course, none of us had seen a German aircraft before and we were frozen where we lay. We watched in fascination then with realization as the 109 started to chase the unfortunate Dewoitine around the circuit. Needless to say, the Curtiss Hawks, completely unaware of the drama that was unfolding below them, continued to fly backwards and forwards across the airfield, changing formation. After the first burst of fire the pilot of the Dewoitine realized something was amiss and he endeavoured to take avoiding action. Suddenly, he blew up in a ball of flame and crashed into the middle of the airfield. The 109 was gone. One would like to say that this all took about ten minutes, but in reality it was more like three. However, the effect on all of us was dramatic and lasting. We had seen what war was really like.'

During the early years of hostilities RAF men were frequently at a disadvantage in pursuing operations and it is much to their credit that in the circumstances they acquitted themselves so well. Although the junior service, the RAF status was elevated by the direction the conflict took. If the Royal Air Force had no meaningful public identity before 1939 it most certainly had six years later. In part this was the result of patriotic propaganda which had presented the fighter pilot as the saviour of the nation in the Battle of Britain, and the bomber crew as the resolute avengers of the *Blitz*. But there also existed an image of a gallant airman with a squashed cap at jaunty angle, handlebar moustache and silk scarf, uttering nonsenses like 'Wizard prang' and 'Piece of cake'. This caricature arose from customs and jargon created during those savage years, but it became the most distinctive of all British service types.

Although the RAF was the world's first autonomous air force, by 1939 it had few practices derived from its own traditions. Mess rituals, yes, and some indigenous slang. Mostly conduct was modelled on Army and Navy ways. After the declaration of war, customs, attitudes and language quickly developed that gave the RAF the foundations of its own folklore. The extent and colourfulness of RAF slang made it famous. While a little was inherited from other services, much was self-originated, although the sources of particular sayings are obscure. Air-to-air and air-to-ground radio communication necessitated code-words for simplification and confidentiality. Some of these terms were adopted as slang. A cautionary service publication called *Tee Em* (using the phonetic form for TM standing for Training Manual) made use of this jargon to sweeten its lesson and played a large part in its dissemination. Observers of the scene suggest that slang was heard much more extensively in fighter messes than in those of other commands.

The supposed British predeliction for understatement was to be found in its most exaggerated form in the RAF. 'Dicey dos' – dangerous situations – were commonplace in both flying and combat, and anyone who started to relate his adventures with too much enthusiasm would be told to stop 'shooting a line'. Such was the stigma of being classed a line-shooter that it became an accepted part of air force life to play down any personal experience. Presumably this attitude produced the art of pronounced understatement practised by many RAF air crew. Similarly, 'stiff upper lip', the overly calm and collected attitude portrayed by the British serviceman faced with danger, appears to have been accentuated in the RAF. Instead of getting in a 'flap' when a serious situation arose, one endeavoured to make a dismissive or humorous comment. An example of this is given by Horace Nears of No. 613 Squadron:

'The Squadron was on a stand down and a grand station piss-up had been organized in the airmen's mess. Most of us were not feeling our best when, about noon next day the Tannoy blasted forth requiring Black Section to report to the crew room immediately. That included me and, with a few of my oppos also suffering hangovers, I staggered along to the crew room where the first person we met was the Doc. He had a great box of barley sugars and said: "Here, take a handful of these, they are guaranteed to cure anything." My regular pilot didn't turn up and I was sent on the trip with a spare Squadron Leader we called The Count. Apparently it was an urgent request to clobber some SS troops down near Limoges, quite a long ride, and we had to have under-wing tanks on the Mossies. Switching fuel in tanks in flight was quite a procedure. You took off on the internal outers, emptied these and then changed to the internal inners. When these were getting low the juice was pumped out of the under-wing tanks into the internal tanks, switching back to the outers and finishing up on the inners. All went well until I was doing the last change. Twisting the cocks I felt something go loose and come away in my hand. Out came a long rod with a collar and a bit of pipe on the end. So I nudged The Count and held the thing up. "What the hell is that?" he asked. "It's one of the petrol switches," I replied. He then wanted to know what tanks we were running on. I said I didn't know because I was in the process of changing from the near empty outers to the inners, our last full tanks. So he just grins and says, "Oh well, pass me a couple of barley sugars and we'll hope it does the trick." '

If a humorous quip was the way to weather anxiety, it was also used to meet adversity and horror. The remark overheard by John Everett of No. 102 Squadron would have been considered outrageous had it not been uttered by a flier regularly exposed to the same risk of death as his subject:

'There were several crashes around the airfield and if you were one of the first on the scene the sights were grizzly. A Halifax hit a house while coming in to land, burned and exploded. On top of the rubble lay a giant's skeleton. I assume that heat had caused it to stretch. Someone said this was the pilot. A friend of his who was present at this grim scene remarked: "Well, I won't be playing cricket with him this evening." I suppose you had to adopt that sort of attitude to be able to cope with such dreadful sights.'

Minimizing one's own contribution or performance while praising a fellow comrade was a feature of British reserve in all armed forces. Because of the interdependence of aircraft crew members this attitude was particularly prevalent in the RAF. The following accounts solicited from the pilot and the navigator of a No. 90 Squadron Fortress, long after the event described and without either man knowing the other had been approached, illustrates this facet. First the pilot, Mick Woods:

'Four Fortress Is and crews from 90 Squadron went on detachment to Kinloss on 5 September 1941. The aim was to attack and destroy a German battleship then berthed in Oslo. An attempt was made on the 6th, but at that time Oslo was under ten-tenths cloud. Four aircraft set out on the 8th in a loose formation. Three of these aircraft were intercepted by Me 109s over the south-west coast and two were shot down, one crashing in Bygland and the other into the sea. The third Fortress climbed swiftly and the bombs were jettisoned. This aircraft was attacked soon after at a height of some 30,000 feet. Two engines were disabled, one of which caught fire but this went out. The aileron control was destroyed which made a turn difficult. The floor in the navigator's compartment was holed and his maps and instruments were sucked out. The fighter broke off his attack – it was suspected that his ammunition was exhausted – and came alongside before returning to his base. Previously enemy fighters had difficulty in reaching and staying at the high altitudes at which the Fortresses flew. But, fortuitously for the Luftwaffe, its only operational units with the Me 109T model, having longer wings and better altitude stability, were based in Norway.

'The navigator had memorized two radio beacon call signs on the Scottish coast and with these and the radio compass, guided the aircraft to a landfall by which time the height had dropped to 1,500 feet. The pilot then ordered the navigator and wireless operator to leave by parachute, but this was ignored with the remark, "We would rather stay with you." With one gunner dead and another severely wounded, it was decided to attempt a downwind wheels-up landing at Kinloss. The tyres were punctured and the flaps were not expected to be fully operable. At that time Kinloss was grass and the risk of fire was less there than on the sealed strip at Lossiemouth. With much firing of red Very cartridges the aircraft made a downwind approach over the bomb dump to be confronted with an OTU Whitley taking off in the opposite direction. Without flaps the aircraft floated longer than usual before settling down in a cloud of dust. The CO_2 bottles had been fired in the engine nacelles and there was no petrol fire on impact. An American Master Sergeant remarked that two hundred thousand dollars had been spread across the grass. It was thought that it was the first ever wheels-up crash landing of a Flying Fortress. The pilot recommended the navigator for a DFM for his efforts when all seemed lost. This was refused as there was not an officer witness on board at the time.'

Harry Sutton, the navigator involved:

'Mick Wood was magnificent in his handling of our shot-up Fortress, bringing it back and making a superb crash landing. No one had any idea what would happen when we hit the deck; when it was of paramount importance to get the wounded out as quickly as possible in case the whole thing went up in flames. Thus I removed a hatch aft of the cockpit and braced myself ready for the crash. The moment we "grated" down the runway, I shot out of the hatch and round to the rear of the aircraft. However, the ambulance boys, who had been following us, beat me to it. When Mick emerged and joined me his first remark was: "You had me worried for a moment, Harry. You got out so quickly I damn near ran over you!" '

In truth the individual sublimated his feelings and expressions because of an ingrained sense of duty. One was there to serve King and Country and willing to give one's life for the nation and the cause of democracy. Fellow aviators were in the same situation, faced with the same stark reality. So why make a fuss? Act matter-of-fact. One might be frightened but duty was something not to be shirked. A certain amount of pride was involved in duty too. For aircrew duty was paramount; others depended upon you whom you could not let down. An illustration of the value of this conscientiousness is given by John Wray:

'I was in a Blenheim IV squadron which hadn't had the aircraft very long. Other squadrons more experienced on the type had some nasty accidents due to one of the engines failing on take-off. At Wyton five aircrew had been killed in one day. We had already lost one pilot attempting a single-engine landing and we had had one or two instances of engines stopping in the air, although pilots had managed to start them again. I was carrying out a photographic survey of London flying at 15,000 feet. My gunner from my open cockpit days was with me in the front of the Blenheim and was bringing me up on my start points and levelling the camera, etc. He was an AC1 Fitter by trade, aged about twenty and married. I was also just past my twentieth birthday but unmarried. We were just coming to the end of one of our runs and were over Colchester when the starboard engine failed, and there was no way I could get it started again. Not trusting my port engine I decided to make an emergency landing at Eastchurch, a grass airfield.

'Landing successfully, I drew a lot of interest from the Eastchurch personnel because the Blenheim IV was still quite new. I asked the CTO if he could have my engine attended to. For an hour the engine was checked and eventually run up. Ignition switches were checked and as all seemed well I decided to carry out an air test. There then followed the dramatic scene of the 20-year-old officer saying to the 20-year-old aircraftman, "Now, I am going to carry out an air test and as anything might happen I am going alone; you are a married man and so I want you to stay on the ground." To which he replied, "Sir, it is my duty to come with you, whatever the risk." As we climbed into the cockpit I said to him, "Directly we are off the ground you pull up the undercarriage, then I can keep one hand on the control column and one on the throttles." We taxied out, opened up to full power and bounded across the grass. After the aircraft rose and the wheels came up, there was a cough and a bang as the starboard engine stopped. Had my gunner not been there to retract the undercarriage we would not have been one of the few to survive an engine failure on take-off in a Blenheim.'

Seeing others display courage and fortitude was an important factor in lifting one's own morale, particularly in an operational situation. Combat units with high morale invariably had one or two intrepid and resolute individuals who inspired the other personnel in the face of adversity. The small and intimate nature of the squadron – the RAF's basic unit – helped build that necessary spirit of determination and confidence. Even when suffering severe attrition the *esprit de corps* of many squadrons was remarkable. There were, of course, demoralized units, but in many cases the causes were other than combat misfortune. Tedium often played a major part, where personnel felt their duties made no worthwhile contribution to the war effort. This was particularly so during the early years of the conflict. John Sharman, in charge of an RAF Regiment detachment, reflects this viewpoint and identifies a personal change of attitude:

'Manston was often the first touchdown for damaged aircraft returning from ops. In consequence it had what must have been the largest aircraft cemetery in the country. Witnessing so many crashes and with nothing but setbacks and bad news from the war fronts, our gun team felt very low. Early one morning in 1942 I was awakened by a tremendous roar – the ground literally shaking. I dashed up the mound upon which my Bofors were sited and there, across the airfield outside headquarters, were about 60 Spits warming up, ready for take-off. This scene was an eye-opener and did wonders for morale. I turned to my corporal and said: "Do you know Corp, we're going to win this bloody war!" For me it was the turning-point.'

The prospect of being killed was very real. Combat losses were given in the Press and on radio. Within the service, briefings and periodic reviews would reveal the number of sorties so that an idea of the rate of attrition could be assessed. But such matters were rarely mentioned unless in light vein. However apprehensive one might be, there was an underlying belief that one would survive, it would always be the other fellow who would get 'the chop'. As a natural counter to the prospect of the dangerous trade followed, crews away from operations attempted to make life one long party; their hallmark was exuberance. Many drank liberally and engaged in wild pranks. Authority recognized this as a psychological safety-valve and was tolerant. Religion was the succour for some, although generally of a private nature. Individual demonstrations of religious faith were rarely made in public. There seemed to be an unspoken acknowledgement that one would cause embarrassment by calling on the Almighty's help before your fellows. However, those who showed deep conviction were respected, as Cyril Clifford observed:

'On a navigator's course at Portage la Prairie, Manitoba, Canada, I shared a large hut with many other students, mostly like myself, re-mustering. The first night we were preparing for bed and indulging in the usual noisy barrack-room banter when suddenly the room went quiet. One young man was kneeling by his bed with hands together saying his prayers. Most fellows pretended not to notice and quietly went on with what they were doing. One joker, however, seeking to extract some humour from the situation, shouted some ribald remarks towards the prayerful one. Those nearest to the comic shook their fists in his face and whispered threats so he shut up. The lad saying his prayers gained our immediate respect, not only for his faith but for his courage in showing it. In six years of barrack-room living it was the only time I saw anyone carry out his devotions publicly.'

For every three fatalities one man was wounded or injured. Brilliant surgery and dedicated nursing saved many lives. The fire hazard inherent in aircraft of the time meant that many survivors of crashes or airborne conflagrations were badly burned, some horrifically. The fortitude of those who faced many painful skin grafts left a lasting impression on those they encountered. John Wray:

'Arriving as a new boy, or rather, new patient at the Palace Hotel Hospital, Torquay, about lunch time, I made my way to the dining-room and there he was.

Sitting by himself, no hair on his face or head, no ears, no nose, just two holes for his eyes, two holes for his ears and the hole that was his mouth. He had two fingers missing from one hand and one from the other. I believe the worst case of burning there had been up to that time. I was so sickened by the sight that I had to leave the dining-room immediately, having no further stomach for food. But what a marvellous person he turned out be be. One soon didn't notice his burns and treated him as a normal person. He loved playing tennis and if someone hit the ball hard at him the racket would fly out of his hand because he had only three fingers left on that hand, and he would roar with laughter. He was the life and soul of any party and if at any time anybody was down in the dumps, as was likely to be the case in a hospital, he would use his enormous enthusiasm to cheer them up.

'One night he, with others, went up to the Imperial Hotel, which was occupied chiefly by rich people who had left London, and we went into the bar. So far as we were concerned there was nothing wrong with him, but two women who were sitting at a table said in a loud voice. "It's disgusting to allow somebody like that out into a public place." Before we could gather our wits a young VAD who was sitting by herself, leapt to her feet and tore into those two women, causing them to retire in disarray with red faces and very red ears. He spent his time commuting between East Grinstead and Torquay for a considerable time and I don't know what happened to him. But he taught me a thing or two about courage and humility. If anybody deserved to be restored to normality, it was him.'

How then did others – citizens of other nations – view the ethos of the wartime Royal Air Force? The habitual character and disposition evoked by those who served under the banner *per ardua ad astra*? Opinions inevitably ranged from the commendatory to the adverse via an extensive and varied middle ground of prejudice and indecisive judgements, all no doubt coloured by national outlook. Whatever views were held they were rarely expressed to RAF personnel directly. Frank Cheesman tells of a notable exception:

'Surprisingly, soon after the United States entered the war, a USAAF captain was attached to our squadron for the purpose of getting the hang of the night-fighting business in the ensuing weeks. Mel, as he became known, was a regular or "career" officer, having entered aviation by way of West Point and the US Army and had done spells of duty in Central and South American countries. It was soon evident that he was a pilot of considerable experience, having flown most of the aircraft types on the current USAAF inventory, not to mention a good quota of civilian machines. He could also speak authoritatively on such accoutrements as fan markers, radio ranges and the like, things about which the average fighter pilot did not know his As from his Ns. It was not surprising, therefore, that Mel converted readily to our Beaufighters and was shortly not only flying the beast to the manner born, but with sufficient expertise to be included on the duty rosters. A career officer he may have been, but it was obvious he was also a "professional" pilot and an avid type-hunter to boot. Any spare time found him at the ASR squadron or the Gunnery Flight cajoling them into letting him fly their Ansons, Lysanders, Defiants and – joy of joys – their Walrus. Socially he fitted in well, was quiet and clean around the house and took part in most activities except the more outrageous. Reserved by nature – one might say taciturn – he was not given to idle chat and the utterances he did make were often droll, sometimes pungent and always to the point. Like all true soldiers he had a cynical philosophy and anyone misguided enough to voice a complaint about some injustice was drily reminded, "Waal, nobody said anything about fair play!"

'Mel's transition from the fleshpots of the USA to the atmosphere of a somewhat remote and stark RAF camp must have been a traumatic experience though he showed no signs that this was so. The new environment, the unfamiliar routines and perhaps most of all the mish-mash of nationalities he was now living and working amongst were all taken in his stride as he merged readily into the set-up. The time arrived when his attachment was over and that morning he arrived at the dispersal, looking very snappy in his olive and fawn uniform, to clear his locker and say his farewells. Well-wishers from the other flight and elsewhere swelled the throng. Occasions like this were normally marked by an exchange of ribaldry and mutual expressions of a derogatory nature – the RAF way of demonstrating regard – but it seemed not quite appropriate here and a comparative hush prevailed. His luggage having been loaded, Mel got to the car door, stopped and took a long searching look over the length of the airfield. Dropping his gaze he ran his eyes along the assembled faces by now full of expectancy of a memorable pronouncement. It came. With the faintest grin and in ringing tones tinged with disbelief Mel opined, "Jesus H. Christ. If this isn't the Goddamndest air force I've ever seen!" – shut the door and was gone.'

Close Encounters

Understandably, an individual's most prominent memories of service life are those when he or she was faced with possible extinction or personal catastrophe. This did not necessarily involve a brush with the enemy, for there were risks enough in flying during wartime. Cyril Clifford:

'As a qualified navigator recently returned to Britain from Canada, I did an advanced flying course on Ansons to get used to European wartime conditions such as the blackout and the presence of balloon barrages, and to use the few navigational aids available. This took place at Llandwrog, an airfield only nine miles from Snowdon. As a safety measure we were told that if we had to descend through cloud and were approaching over the sea we should knock five minutes from the ETA and come in at low level. Conversely, if approaching from the land side we should add on five minutes to the ETA to be sure we had cleared Snowdonia. One night, coming in overland, the pilot said he could see the sea and would start descending. I said our instructions were clear and we should stick to them. So he agreed and we maintained height for another five minutes. We descended right into the airfield circuit and the pilot realized with a shock that what he thought was the sea was actually snow on the mountains! So we escaped being yet another aircraft wreck added to the large total of crashes in Snowdonia.'

Albert Benest:

'At Westcott near Aylesbury, there were a number of ATC boys who were often on the airfield trying to get flights. Because these lads would be joining the RAF when old enough we were instructed to give them encouragement whenever possible, particularly air experience. One weekend we were asked to take a few of these cadets on a cross-country, when for some reason – probably weather – this was cancelled. So as not to disappoint the cadets my pilot said he would take them up for a flight around the local area. He said that in the circumstances there would be no need for me to go along so I went off for a snooze. Around five that afternoon I walked into the officers' mess for a cup of tea to be greeted with some strange looks followed by a few exclamations. Everyone thought I was dead! I then received the bad news that the Wellington had lost its starboard wing in flight and all in the aircraft had been killed. It had been supposed that I was on board too.'

Len Barcham of No. 404 (RCAF) Squadron:

'In August 1943 we had detached from Wick to train for practice firing the rocket projectiles for which our Beaufighters had just been fitted. At the mouth of the Dornoch Firth a target had been set up out on the beach and we were doing circuits and bumps all day trying to find out the best way to aim the rockets. Normally they had HE, incendiary or armour-piercing warheads, but for these trials we were using practice concrete heads. No navigation being necessary, we had agreed to give a ground erk a flip – his first ever – putting him in the navigator's seat under the rear cupola. I was standing astride the well behind the pilot, F/O J. H. Symons, thus not strapped in at all, while calling out and checking various speeds, angles of attack, etc., while he concentrated on the target. One engine suddenly lost all its oil, seized up solid with a dreadful scream, wouldn't feather and from then on we went more or less where the Beau' took us, which happened to be downwards towards Clashmore Wood and Evelix.

'The Beau' was a very strong aircraft indeed; our expression was "built like a brick shithouse". We finished up in a clearing in the woods where the trees had been cut down to 2-foot stumps. These literally tore the Beau' to bits each time we bounced. With rockets and cannon now firing of their own accord, it was indeed something of a panic. When we eventually came to a stop, only about the first 10 feet of fuselage was left in one piece. Though badly bruised and shaken, we got out a bit smartly and looked round for our passenger. He had apparently been catapulted out before the remains of the aircraft came to a stop and we caught sight of him just disappearing over a nearby hill at a great rate of knots. I never ever set eyes on him again. Before the trip he had told us he had been accepted for flying training. It would be interesting to know if he carried on with that idea!'

George Irving of No. 406 (RCAF) Squadron:

'In May 1943 I was taking off on a normal air test, travelling down the runway at about 100mph, when, without warning, the constant speed regulator packed up on my starboard engine throwing the propeller into coarse pitch. This caused the Beaufighter to swing violently to starboard, off the runway. We raced across the grass and just got airborne in time to clear a Wellington taxi-ing across towards its bay. I then cleared the hedge and roofs of a housing estate by a few feet. Gradually gaining height, I was able to make an emergency landing on the first circuit. There were several complaints from the housing estate residents about low flying over Exeter.'

Bill Dickinson:

'My first solo trip in a Beaufighter at No. 2 OTU, Catfoss, was quite an experience. After take-off I discovered my radio was u/s. Everything else was fine so I flew around enjoying the new experience. After about three-quarters of an hour I came back to the airfield to land, noticing things were rather quiet and there was no one else in the circuit. When I touched down the aircraft swung violently, so much so that I couldn't control it. The Beau' veered off the runway, swung across the grass, hit the edge of another runway, ground looped and the undercarriage collapsed. The ambulance and fire engine came streaming out but I was only shaken and worried what was going to be said. We had been warned about the Beau's tendency to swing on take-off and landing. "I made a mess of that," I said apologetically to the first blokes to arrive. To my great relief they told me that I had a tyre burst on take-off and that this had been seen flapping about before the wheels were retracted. An instructor had taken off in another Beaufighter with the intention of communicating with me but couldn't establish radio contact. Flying had been suspended while they waited for me to come in and crash – they say ignorance is bliss!'

Roy Larkins:

'We took off from Charmy Down, near Bath, on what was supposed to be a training flight. The instructor said, "Let's forget about the exercises today. Let's take the old kite up, as high as we can." It was an Oxford aircraft and certainly not designed to fly at any great height. At 10,000 feet, or perhaps a bit more, it stopped climbing and just hung there, in the rarified air. We were very much in a "nose-up" position and although the propellers were spinning, they were not pulling us forward or up, but rather, just holding us there. The instructor was flying the aircraft and I was there, simply enjoying the ride, until I glanced along the wing. A small feather of flame was coming from the engine cowling. "Port engine's on fire," I shouted. "What shall we do?" shouted back the instructor, more for moral support than anything else because he had practised this manoeuvre many, many times. "Let's dive and hope that the wind puts it out," I replied. "At least we'll be nearer the ground that way."

'I was not frightened in the least – nothing to the apprehension I suffered when I practised this manoeuvre. Also, this was the second time that I had lost an engine, but perhaps it was the instructor's first. The aircraft dived at a speed that I had never encountered before (or since) and the sensation to the body was like that of the deepest part of the Big Dipper in a fairground. At the commencement of the dive the flame had grown a little and as we screamed earthwards it tried to grow larger still, but the wind was blowing it out. I don't know for how many seconds we were diving, but the battle between flame and wind was an absorbing one. First, the flame gained and then retreated. Then it gained again and similarly retreated. And so it went on. Luckily, just as the plane came out of its dive, the flame went out. The instructor trimmed the aircraft to fly on one engine and we went back to base. As I was not captain of the aircraft in this incident, I did not have to attend the inquiry concerned with this engine fire. I learned later that moisture on the plane at that height had frozen near to where the exhaust gases leave the engine. This restricted the flow of outgoing gases, which in turn caused the engine to overheat and eventually to catch fire. The final comment on the accident report stated, "Cause of fire . . . block of ice!" '

James Donson of No. 2 Armament Practice Camp:

'At the time of the cross-Channel invasion, June 1944, it was feared that the dispatch-rider system of communication between the stations of No. 16 Group Coastal Command and their HQ might be interrupted by enemy parachutists. To counter this risk, air delivery was ordered and our unit at Docking in Norfolk given the task of the daily round trip, landing at all the Group airfields and carrying mail to Detling in Kent from where it was transported by road to HQ at Chatham. We carried out our "Pony Express" programme, as we called it, from early June until the end of August.

'During the early weeks after the June invasion the V-1 attacks on the south-east began and increased in intensity. Balloon defences around London increased, so that we could no longer fly directly to Detling. We used a route to Watford and turned east in the area of Guildford and on to Maidstone where we made another turn and flew on to Detling. One day in a Martinet I was on the Guildford-Detling leg at about 2,000 feet, just under the cloud base, when a V-1 appeared to my right and passed at right-angles close in front of me. It all happened so quickly; I felt a blast of hot air and was rolled almost upside down. Realizing the aircraft had half rolled, I put on more throttle and continued to roll. On regaining level and stable flight I saw a mast a few feet below my starboard wing. Checking my position I found I had just missed Crowborough beacon – a tall radio mast along our normal route.'

Some 'close shaves' were nothing short of traumatic. Tom Minta:

'Because there were more pilots than needed at the time, we returned from training in South Africa to be sent down to South Cerney to keep our hand in by flying Oxfords. We had to do quite a bit of formation flying and one of the exercises involved three Oxfords in a vee formation, with each taking it in turn to be leader. The position change took place over the airfield. The drill was for No. 3 on the starboard side to move forward, No. 1 to stay where he was, while No. 2 slid along the back from the left to take up the position previously held by No. 3. One day I had been flying No. 2 and was in the process of moving across to make the change. Just as I got astern of the other two I saw them coming together. The next thing the complete tail unit of one came hurtling back and knocked my aerial off, it was that close. The Oxford which had lost its tail dropped out of sight, but the other one started to flip over right in front of me. I expected his wing to go into my belly as I tried to miss him; how it didn't I'll never know. My Oxford was holed in several places by bits of debris but all that remained of the others was a couple of smoking wrecks on the aerodrome. The instructor came out and asked how I was feeling. "Bloody awful really," was my reply. "Well get another aircraft and up you go right away," he ordered, and I did. It was sound advice.'

Being mistaken for the enemy and attacked by your own side happened on a number of occasions with tragic results. Few people could match Tony Reid's experience of this:

'On 21 December 1939 I was in a Hampden of No. 44 Squadron returning from a sortie along the coast of Norway and flying at around 1,000 feet. The weather was cloudy with a slight haze and we were supposed to come in at Lossiemouth before continuing down to our base at Waddington. Instead we made a shocking landfall, some 130 miles to the south at Dunbar. Hurricanes of

No. 111 Squadron were sent to investigate and this regular squadron saw we were Hampdens and sheered off. Not so the former auxiliaries of No. 602 Squadron who intercepted us with their Spitfires. They apparently identified us as Do 17s and attacked. Two members of our crew were shot, one fatally. The pilot managed to ditch into the approaches of the Firth of Forth where, with the other survivors, I escaped with a ducking – but it was cold! A second Hampden was also shot down but all four crew escaped without injury.

'A couple of months after recovering from this ordeal, on 3 March 1940, I was co-pilot in a Hudson of the Photographic Development Unit with an assignment to take vertical photographs from 7,000 feet of selected airfields in the south-east for the benefit of the French Air Force. The weather was perfect and our first objective after leaving Heston was Gravesend. Arriving at this location we were suddenly attacked from the rear by Hurricanes and the Hudson became a blazing inferno in seconds. I managed to bale out by squeezing through my cockpit side window, the sole survivor out of four. *Mais – c'est la guerre!* By chance, a year or so later, I met the flight leader of the three No. 32 Squadron Hurricanes that shot us down. When I asked for an explanation he insisted we had fired on them first! But our only armament was two fixed Brownings in the nose! The only theory we could evolve to explain this illusion was that our trailing aerial was glinting in the sunlight and that this was mistaken for tracer.'

Another man with Lady Luck on his shoulder was Arthur Anthony:

'Early summer 1942 found me at Ford, Sussex, a flight mechanic/engineer just out of training school. I was serving with No. 605 Squadron which had been wiped out in Java and was being re-formed as a night intruder unit flying twin-engined Douglas Havocs and Bostons. Although learning about the engineering tasks with these aircraft, I was keen to have a flight. As the pilots spent a lot of time practising interceptions it wasn't necessary for other crew members to go along, so ground men were often allowed to go in their place. I did not have to wait many days before one of the pilots said I could come on one of his training sorties. For a 19-year-old who had never been in the air before, this was a very exciting prospect. The pilot was a very energetic type and engaged in a series of climbs, dives and turns. One moment I was looking out of my position in the nose at fields, the next there was nothing to see but blue sky. It wasn't long before all this throwing about made me violently airsick; by the time we had landed and taxied back to the dispersal I was feeling dreadful. Somehow I dragged myself out of the nose compartment but accidentally pulled the emergency exit panel as I left. This didn't make me very popular as it was a tricky thing to reinstate. Then in my agony I picked up my parachute by the release handle and the whole lot spilt out on the ground. For all this I had to take a lot of stick from my mates plus having to pay one of them a half-crown to clear up the mess in the nose. "You'll never be any good for aircrew," was the cry from many of them.

'However, I was still determined and waited my chance to get airborne again. I didn't have many days to wait and this time I flew in the back compartment. The training exercise consisted of making dummy attacks on another Havoc which took evasive action. This time I managed not to part with my dinner. After landing to refuel I was all set to go up again when the pilot continued the exercise. While waiting, three Canadian soldiers appeared and wanted to know if they could have a trip up. It didn't rest with me, of course, and I advised them to see the two pilots and ask. I said I'd be quite prepared to stand down as there would be lots more chances for me to fly. The Canadians returned, all smiles, and I gave one of them my 'chute and harness. The other two flew in the second plane. Off they all went while the "Chiefy" gave instructions that I was to remain until the two Havocs returned and then refuel them. This meant I would be having a late tea. It was a beautiful afternoon so it was pleasant to while away the time lying on the grass. I'd been idly lounging there on my own for perhaps a half-hour when Chiefy came pedalling up on his bike: "Go and get your tea Anthony." "But Chiefy, you said I had . . ." He cut me short.

' "You lucky little sod! I've just had a phone message; those two Havocs have collided in mid-air and all six are dead. It happened over Banstead."

'For a few seconds I thought he was having me on; I couldn't believe it. Then the realization that this was true enveloped me in a dread sinking feeling; as if I had been responsible for those Canadians' deaths. But neither was it lost on me that if they had not come on to the airfield I would have been one of the fatalities. A morning or so later the rigger and I were doing a duty inspection on a Havoc. We pulled the port prop through and then crossed in front of the aircraft to the starboard engine prior to engine run up. As I went to get hold of a prop blade there was a loud blast of gunfire. Under the nose lay 21 ejected bullet cases. Had I moved across in front of the nose a couple of seconds later. . . . Armourers were testing the electric solenoids but were unaware that the four machine-guns were cocked. No one could tell me about luck.'

If your side didn't get you, the enemy could still make life risky on home ground. Alan Staines:

'I was called up as a Reserve in June 1944 and sent to the ACRC in Regent's Park right in the middle of London. We were billeted in blocks of flats, but at the time the Flying Bomb campaign was at its height. One Friday afternoon we were supposed to go out for rifle drill in the road by our billet in St. James's Terrace. Our corporal appeared dressed up in his best blues, which puzzled us at first. "I'll give you a quarter of an hour of my time," he confided, "and then you can go back to your billet and lie low until 4 o'clock when your next lecture is due. I'm off to meet a bird in the West End. Should someone want to know where I am, just tell them I got took ill." We were quite happy to go along with this if it got us out of drilling on a hot afternoon. We did fifteen minutes and while the Corporal crept off to see his girl, we went back to our billet, which was on the top floor of a block of flats. We were taking it easy when some of the chaps who had been out sun-bathing on the roof came hurtling down the stairs shouting that a flying-bomb, engine still running, was diving straight for us. All we could do was throw ourselves on the floor and hope. There was a hell of an explosion, a shock wave and lots of dust. When we picked ourselves up and looked out, we could see that the bomb had struck in the street outside, partly demolishing a house on the other side and caving in the lower part of our building. Three RAF chaps down below had been killed and about 30 injured, but all on the top floor escaped. It didn't take long to realize that our squad of 35 should have been marching up and down that road had our corporal not gone AWOL to see a girl. Was my life saved through a bit of illicit romance? I'm sure it was.'

It could happen that a man who had experienced several 'near things' in the course of combat operations was more impressed by traumas encountered in what should have been more peaceful surroundings. Harold Southgate, a veteran Bomber Command pilot, is unlikely to forget the occasion he went to collect his second 'gong':

'With my wife and baby daughter, I set out in my Ford 8 from Worcestershire to attend an Investiture at Buckingham Palace to receive a Bar to my DFC. The first stage of the journey, to Coulsdon in Surrey where we were staying the night, was completed without event. However, next morning when I went to start the car it would not. No joy whatsoever. Took out the plugs, pulled out this and that, tightened anything that looked as if it was loose, but still no joy. It was now getting late so the car – which had by this time been pushed down hills in an effort to generate life – was abandoned in Coulsdon High Street. A taxi was ordered and, after cleaning up as quickly as possible and suffering some anxious moments, we arrived at Buckingham Palace with just ten minutes to spare. The Investiture went without hitch and it was an honour to meet the King for the second time. It was not without problems for my wife, as the daughter in arms cried throughout the ceremony and was eventually taken in charge by Buckingham Palace staff.

'Having returned to Coulsdon by train I found, of course, that the car started first time. So we set off back to RAF Defford. Leaving Marlow up a slight incline, a small boy on a bike decided to turn right – having given no signals – just as we were overtaking. The boy managed to make it safely to the other side of the road and sped away, presumably very happy with life. We were not so fortunate as, in taking avoiding action, the Ford went up a bank, turned over on its side, ending up partly in a ditch. My wife and I were able to crawl out through a window, having passed out our daughter like a piece of luggage. Help soon arrived in the form of the police and an ambulance. A hospital check-up found we were all okay. Arrangements were made for the car to be collected and made roadworthy again while we continued the journey to Defford by train. The car was collected a month later with repair costs of £5. All quite an adventure. But I was convinced it was safer to fly.'

Bomber Types

RAF Bomber Command's campaign of wreaking destruction in the enemy homeland became a controversial issue in post-war years. With the benefit of hindsight the morality of aerial bombing, with the huge casualties and the manufacturing effort and money expended for debatable achievements, was questioned in many quarters. Judgements vary, for it remains a campaign without clear answers in several areas, particularly the true worth of destruction and disruption caused by the bombing – plus contesting these raids – had on the German war effort. With in excess of a million persons engaged in air raid defence and associated work, this alone must have imposed a heavy burden on the Reich's war economy.

The visionaries' belief that strategic bombing could defeat an enemy without need for bloody land battles was never realized. In the first instance the RAF chose to operate principally under cover of darkness, to minimize losses from enemy fighters and anti-aircraft artillery, but the development of radar devices by the Germans eventually made the night sky very dangerous. Meanwhile, the development of the long-range escort fighter was the salvation of the day bombing undertaken by the USAAF. Moreover, while night operation may have afforded the RAF bombers some protection, it also made targets more difficult to locate. During the first two years of Bomber Command's operations only a small percentage of bombs dropped fell on the targets for which they were intended. Bomber Command did not possess the technical means of accurately hitting factories and similar strategic targets of limited size in darkness. Not until the final months of the war in Europe were the equipment and technique readily available to do this work successfully.

To meet the situation whereby most bombs dropped at night were going astray, Bomber Command leaders turned to so-called 'area bombing', attacking cities to disrupt industry and communications by causing worker casualties even if war plants in the area survived. The concept that in total war the factory worker was as much a legitimate target as the soldier was not universally supported, even if the Luftwaffe had apparently tried the same tactics over Britain. 'Innocent' civilians inevitably suffered. There was, allied to this doctrine, the belief that sustained bombardment would break civilian moral and precipitate a collapse of the national economy. British morale had held in the London *Blitz*; so why should enemy morale succumb to bombing? Perhaps the instigators had been conditioned into believing the propaganda that the German was an inferior being. Only on a few occasions were Bomber Command's attacks heavy and concentrated enough to bring about a complete breakdown of order in an enemy city.

However, that Bomber Command's effort made a contribution to victory is without question. The degree is in question as is justification of the cost. A total of 55,358 aircrew are listed as killed in both operations and accidents, which is almost four-fifths of the total RAF war dead. It has been said that no other service command suffered such a high percentage of loss in the Second World War apart from the German U-boat crews. The strategy that brought such attrition to comrades has in no way mellowed the pride of survivors. To them it was duty, well performed in the face of grim odds. There is perhaps no greater camaraderie than among the men of an individual bomber crew.

AIRCRAFT, EQUIPMENT AND EXPERIENCE

In wartime aircrew were subordinate to the aircraft they flew in official reports and Press releases to newspapers and radio. It was not '5,000 men of Bomber Command attacked Essen last night' but '700 Halifaxes and Lancasters'. The bomber was the tool of trade and the hallmark of the aircrew – 'I was in Lancs . . .', 'I was a Halybag mid-upper . . .', and the like. Loyalty to the aircraft type that had seen you successfully through an operational tour was unshakeable, as demonstrated by opinions such as Bill Coote's:

'I first became associated with the Wellington bomber at 21 OTU, Moreton-in-Marsh, and from that time no other aeroplane captured my affections in quite the same way. Designed by Barnes Wallis, there can be little doubt that it was the finest British bomber taking part in World War 2. Of course there were varying opinions about its handling, stability and ability to fly on one motor, although it must be said that much depended upon the Mark of the aircraft and its engines. Naturally, the early Wellington ICs, equipped with Bristol Pegasus engines developing 1,050hp, used at Operational Training Units, did not have the same performance as the later Mk Xs, powered by Bristol Hercules developing 1,700hp, in which we operated with No. 70 Squadron in North Africa. Nevertheless, the one aspect of the Wimpy, universally acknowledged and agreed by all who flew in them, was the extraordinary strength that existed in its geodetic construction. It was unique in its ability to soak up punishment, far beyond that of any other aeroplane, and still continue to fly!

'There are numerous instances of its toughness on record, typical of that experienced by my colleague, W/O Custance, who while flying over Budapest in July 1944 collided with another aircraft, losing 10 feet off his port wing in the process! We were based at that time on Tortorella, a satellite of Foggia Main, and I remember walking over to dispersal the following morning to witness the result of the collision. I shall never understand how old Cuss managed to fly that aeroplane back to base in such a condition, since he was quite short in stature and the task must have presented him with many problems.'

Perhaps others who had a wider experience of RAF bombers would be less laudatory about the Wimpy, but the fact remains that this alone of the three medium bomber types in squadron service in September 1939 endured in operational squadron service until the end of the war, which gives an indication of its worth. The Wellington was a reliable performer, until 1942 the most numerous medium type in Bomber Command. Along with the Whitleys and Hampdens it gradually gave way to the new four-engined heavies. The first of these, the Short Stirling, was generally viewed as anything but reliable. William Drinkell on an experience while at No. 14 OTU:

'On my first solo in a Stirling I lost an engine due to oil pressure failure and had to feather. Then the Gee navigation set burnt out, filling the cockpit area with smoke. On top of that, the undercarriage wouldn't lower hydraulically and had to be wound down – 960 turns by hand of the emergency lever. Finally I made my approach only to have the rear of the aircraft shimmy as soon as the tailwheels were on the ground. I cleared the runway, notified the control tower I was going to check the tailwheels, applied the parking brake, took off my helmet and placed it on the control column, unstrapped and went back to have a look. There was a chain linking the dual tailwheels and I thought that might have broken, but the investigation didn't locate the trouble.

'So back to the cockpit to continue taxi-ing to a dispersal point. When I replaced my helmet I was told to report to the watch tower once the aircraft was parked. When I got there I was reprimanded for bad language and asked to apologise to the WAAF operators present. Not given to swearing, I was a bit taken aback. It was explained that following the request to park on the perimeter to inspect the tail wheels, our radio had continued to broadcast the intercom conversation. I realized that in placing my helmet on the control column the "Transmit" switch had been moved to "on". In my absence the bomb-aimer had asked the others what they thought of this Stirling and the rest of the crew responded in no uncertain terms, including a few cryptic comments as to what the Chief Instructor could do with it. It would have been very painful.'

George Smith was another unimpressed member of Stirling aircrew:

'A cumbersome giant, some pilots had difficulty getting the hang of the Stirling. We had several mishaps in 1651 Heavy Conversion Unit at Waterbeach. A lot of the time was spent doing night cross-countries. After one such flight we were finishing our landing roll when there was a hell of a bang and the Stirling nosed over. I cut my knee in the haste to get out of the navigator's seat. There was no fire and none of the other crew members were badly injured. Not until out of the aircraft did I discover we had collided with a steam roller! The pilot had landed too far down the runway, crossed the perimeter track and ended up in some construction work. The next night we spent two hours doing circuits and bumps at Tempsford with the same pilot. On the last bump before returning to Waterbeach the port tyre burst and the Stirling slewed off the runway and chewed up a parked Halifax with its props. Our pilot was distraught, "This is it. This is the end for me." It wasn't. He may have been unlucky enough to wreck three four-engined bombers in a few days, but the RAF weren't going to waste a trained pilot.'

The trouble remembered by Stanley Tomlinson was not – to be fair – a fault in the aircraft:

'The Stirling was a horrible aircraft to land and always having undercarriage problems. There was a spate of brake failures while I was with No. 149 Squadron and some of this was found to be due to corrosion of components. This puzzled the authorities for a while until the realization that it was due to the "nervous pee". The last thing the crew of seven did before going on an operational trip was to relieve themselves. And out on a bleak airfield where there is no cover the only substantial object to hide their modesty was a main wheel. Under this repeated shower, followed by heat generated in taxi-ing, all sorts of chemical changes occurred. We were told that the nervous pee had to be directed elsewhere.'

Nevertheless, there were many aircrew who became very fond of the Stirling, having mastered its idiosyncracies. Roy Ellis-Brown, a US national, was a veteran of 30 operations in the type:

'When I joined No. 7 Squadron they had only recently commenced operations with Stirlings. Some of the early aircraft were none too reliable and beset with mechanical problems. Then we started getting those built by Short & Harland and the Austin Motor Company with even more troubles. One of the biggest worries was the efficiency of the throttle exactor controls. The lines to the engines from the throttle controls were so long the designers decided to use an hydraulic system. Before starting engines the system had to be primed and this was achieved by pushing all four throttle levers right forward, which opened valves in the oil reservoir. Unfortunately these hydraulic lines were given to leaking like blazes at the many connections and this allowed the throttle levers to creep. As this was common it was necessary to keep a hand on the throttles during take-off – usually the Second Dicky got this job. On one occasion after take-off, as we passed 200 feet, I told my Second Dicky to set the rpm for climb. When he took his hand off the throttles all four levers shot back and the engines started to die. There was a wild scramble by both of us to push the levers forward again, but only two engines caught. Such happenings were not good for the nerves. They never really cured this problem in my time.

'The design of the undercarriage was terrible and crumpled undercarts were a frequent event. Each landing was an adventure as the airfield was not large and the Stirling was a very heavy aircraft. You didn't want to overshoot and you had to guard against swinging off. When I arrived at Oakington there were no concrete runways and it was easy to get bogged down. The drill was to taxi with the throttles well open to keep her moving. Even then you would often slip and slide. It was a worthy old bird in the air but a brute to handle on the ground.'

The Stirling was withdrawn from bomber squadrons by late 1944 and the heavy effort was carried out by Halifaxes and Lancasters. Early Halifaxes suffered hefty teething troubles, a few only becoming evident when the type was well into squadron service. Later Halifaxes had a better reputation as Derek Waterman proclaims:

'The Halifax Mk IIs with Merlin engines and triangular fins were pretty hopeless in my opinion. They had a tail imbalance at certain flight attitudes which could lead to an uncontrolled spin. Quite a few were lost this way. I only flew them during type conversion and, happily, when I reached No. 158 Squadron at Lissett they had the Mk III which was a completely different kettle of fish. The Hercules XVI radial engines were more battleworthy and enabled the Mk III to outclimb the Lanc as well as giving a faster speed in level flight. Also most Mk IIIs had the revised rectangular-shaped tail fins and rudders giving greater stability.

Apart from a rather nasty swing on take-off, that had to be guarded against – and was a characteristic of most powerful multi-engined aircraft – I found the Mk III an excellent bomber. My first trips with 158 were in several different Halifaxes, but then my crew was given a veteran which carried the nickname Friday The 13th. This embellishment was derived from the fact that the aircraft was received by the Squadron on Friday, 13 March 1944. Some of my crew may have been a bit uneasy about the name, but I wasn't particularly superstitious, having been on course Number 13 during my pilot training in America. I flew most of my tour in this aircraft, 26 trips to be precise, and apart from the flak fragments that were almost inevitably collected on visits to the Ruhr, we came out practically unscathed. Friday The 13th went on to survive 128 raids, a record for a Halifax, confirming my view that it was a marvellous aircraft.'

This again reflects the individual view of an aircraft that brought a flier through a tour of ops. Such loyalty was not expressed for the obsolescent Fairey Battle, which equipped the squadrons of No. 1 Group in the early months of hostilities. A single-engined monoplane of poor performance and light armament, it stood little chance against enemy interceptors. The Battle squadrons were decimated during the 1940 Battle of France, but the type had to continue in service until better bombers were available. Eddie Wheeler, who survived two tours totalling 66 sorties with Bomber Command, started his operations on No. 150 Squadron Battles and describes the puny effort of those days:

'Ginger took up his position as navigator in the well of the aircraft, a most unenviable position, and sorted out his route maps. Rocky, our pilot, ran up the engine to full power, checked that we were all satisfactory, and then said, "Here we go chaps, good luck." We bounded across the grass field and took off for the first of our affrays against enemy-held Europe. Of the three squadron aircraft assigned to attack Hingene airfield near Antwerp, one had to return to base within half an hour with engine trouble. My brief was to keep a listening watch on the Command frequency at half-hourly intervals for possible recalls or diversions, and at my position in the rear of the aircraft, with cupola open, to man the Vickers Gas Operated gun against possible fighter intervention. It was very cold but at the same time sweat was very evident under my flying-helmet. Many times I thought that I had sighted interceptors, but then realized it was the shadow of our own plane on the clouds. It was a constant switch from "safe" to "fire" on the VGO gun but I was determined not to be caught napping. The thoughts that went through my mind varied from, "Have the armourers correctly set the interrupter gear on the gun?" – this enabled the gunner to sweep the area of fire to the rear and quarters without shooting off the tail – to "How near is my parachute in case I need it in a hurry!" Happily, the flight in effect was "uneventful" and we dropped our four 250lb bombs on the target with 7/10ths cloud obscuring results. After we landed back at Newton. I thought, "One down and 29 to go; if they were to be as easy as this perhaps I would see my 21st birthday." Ginger emerged with his maps and logs smothered in glycol and this was to be a persistent feature on all flights; the Battle was notorious for its glycol leaks.

'Four nights later, on 29 July 1940, we were briefed to attack Waalhaven with our usual "magnificent" load of four 250lb bombs. In my anxiety to scour the sky for enemy fighters I was guilty of missing the first group broadcast cancelling the operation and instructing all aircraft to return to base. As a consequence we landed long after the other Battles. We were met by the CO, Wing Commander Hesketh, who said, "Do you know you were the only aircraft over enemy territory tonight?" Nevertheless he was glad to see our safe return and handed me my first pint of beer, which was to be the first of very, very many over ensuing years.'

Like aircraft, the navigational and bombing aids improved as the war progressed. Personal equipment too. In the early days this left much to be desired when flying in the bitter cold at 15,000 feet. Steve Challen, a gunner in No. 40 Squadron:

'Our first operational sortie scheduled for 27 December 1940, the target Le Havre, take-off 16.30. Just before we made our way out to Wellington T2515 we were issued with a flask and a bar of green foil-wrapped plain chocolate – the best ever issued! No escape aid package, benzedrine pills, silk map, no flying-boots that could be separated at the ankle leaving the bottoms looking like civilian shoes. None of these helpful items for us. I had just the stuff that was issued me at Manston a year before; Sidcot brown-padded inner suit, long silk gloves, light leather gauntlets, black sheepskin calf-length flying-boots, helmet with earphones, oxygen mask with microphone and goggles. Over the top of the Sidcot came a parachute harness suit known as the Goon Suit which had the clips to attach the chest-type 'chute. What a job to get into the turret the first few times, especially if the 'chute had been clipped up to the upper starboard curved-in side of the turret. It was easier to get in, then lean back and bring the 'chute over the top of your bulk. All this exertion usually made for heavy breathing causing the perspex to steam up, more sweat trying to clear it.

'During the next two weeks we were issued with sheepskin flying-suits that had plugs for heated gloves and boots. I could only just get my Goon Suit over the top and the zips under the chin were hard to start. Wilhelmshaven, 16 January 1941, was a try out for the gloves and boots, which seemed to get too hot. The only way to control the heat on the extremity, which was too hot, was to unplug. Not an easy thing to do, especially reaching your ankles where the connections for your boots were located. Another most important extremity was very hard to reach when you wanted to pee in that empty bottle! What a struggle, sheepskin trousered flap, parachute harness straps in the way and the centrepiece of the Goon Suit (about three to four inches wide) which came between the legs from the back up to the front under your chin where the zips connected: zipping downward making a tight fit around your legs. Not a situation for urgency! Removing your gloves to use the bottle, your hands soon became cold enough not to know when you returned them into the heated gloves whether they were hot, warm or cold. I suffered blisters on occasions through not feeling how hot the gloves had become.'

The rear-gunner's perch was the coldest and loneliest position in Wellingtons and Whitleys although few could have had such an uncomfortable operational début as Tom Imrie:

'After completing my training on Whitley Vs at No. 10 OTU, Abingdon, as a Wireless Operator/Air Gunner, I reported to No. 51 Squadron, RAF Dishforth, on 1 September 1940. I was assigned to rear turret duties for my first night operation on 9 September to bomb the naval base at Bremen. Those who knew the rear turret on the Whitley with its four Browning .303s had been suitably impressed that it was essential to make sure the double doors were securely locked before the turret was operated. This required the pulling of one door towards your back by a strap and, having got yourself into position, closing and locking the other door with your spare hand. On this first trip all seemed well until the "skipper" ordered gun testing and turret movement. I dutifully swung my turret through 45 degrees to be greeted by a loud bang – a door had opened and I was jammed with my backside out over the North Sea and my parachute out of reach in the fuselage. An unpleasant couple of hours followed while we bombed secondary targets on the Dutch coast and returned to base where I was suitably chastised. Not a good way to start one's squadron service, but perhaps a blessing in disguise. I was, from that night on, confined to the comparative comfort of the wireless operator's position adjacent to the navigator.'

Not to fully heed the directions or warnings of others is a common failing of the self-confident. Personal experience is a far more effective cautioner as Harold Southgate, a No. 50 Squadron pilot, discovered:

'Having raided Rostock on 24 April 1942 with comparative comfort and with very little opposition, another raid two nights later was regarded as "a piece of cake". Although a long trip of some four hours and on a more or less direct route, the flight to the target was uneventful. The Manchester was loaded with one 4,000lb bomb plus several canisters of incendiaries, and feeling – stupidly – rather brave, I decided to bomb from 4,000 feet, the minimum altitude from which a "cookie" could be dropped safely. Having started the bombing run, all hell was suddenly let loose from below with Flak bursting all around us and shrapnel hitting the aircraft. In an effort to avoid this surprise reception the bombing run was continued in a dive – contrary to Bomber Command's laid down procedure – and the load was eventually released from about 2,000 feet.

'Our Manchester was nearly blown out of the sky by the detonation of our own bomb plus sundry others which had been released correctly by other aircraft from far above. We took hits in several places and the controls were becoming unmanageable, particularly the rudder. Fortunately, on board for a familiarization trip was a young Flight Sergeant pilot. He really had to earn his keep on the way home, as both of us had to push hard on the rudder controls to keep the Manchester on a straight course. This was a really hard struggle for more than three hours. Approaching our base we received a priority for landing and with a great deal of effort got the Manchester down safely. It taught me two lessons: always obey orders, and never underestimate the Germans – who had completely reorganized the defence of Rostock in two days.'

The confined, noise-ridden and vision-restricted world of the bomber crew in the night sky invited error, particularly from the adventurous. Continually finding one's way with a degree of accuracy was in itself a demanding task. As the war progressed, so new electronic navigational aids, Gee, H2S, etc., gave outstanding improvements, but even then it was easy to blunder. Ivan Mulley of No 432 Squadron:

'Our first operation took place on 17 September 1944, a daylight mission to Boulogne in support of First Canadian Army who were investing the port. The aiming-point in France was at the end of a timed run on a specified heading from a defined point on the Kent coast. In Halifax aircraft the bomb-aimer operated the H2S set situated in the navigator's compartment, which was forward of the pilot's cockpit and blacked out so that readings could be taken from both the H2S set and "Gee". Both instruments had been used in our journey down England and shortly after crossing the coast in the vicinity of Clacton and while traversing the wide mouth of the Thames estuary, Walter, our bomb-aimer, moved forward from the darkened navigator's compartment to the nose in order to set up his bomb-aiming instruments. He saw the Thameside coast of Kent coming into view, and panicked, declaring he could see the French coast, and requested that bomb-doors be opened. The pilot and engineer, who had been studying the scene below with interest as we passed over the flight path of the aerial armada which was *en route* to Arnhem and the other areas in Holland, and who knew where our aircraft was flying, refused the request. Eventually Walter settled down and made a successful bombing run – on France!'

THE DEMANDS OF BATTLE

The whole Command learned lessons the hard way, but as its technique and strength improved so did the enemy's counter-measures. Losses over Germany almost doubled for a not much greater number of sorties in 1942 when, under a new commander, Air Marshal Sir Arthur Harris, a new urgency was adopted. A typical scenario for a bomber 'trip' during that year is given by Alan Haworth, a navigator with No. 214 Squadron:

'The pattern of a night raid on one of the industrial cities of the Ruhr varied little. From Stradishall to Cromer, climbing to 7,000 feet, Cromer to the Dutch coast, climbing to 15,000 feet. Avoid cities like Rotterdam where the anti-aircraft guns (flak) were formidable. I usually sought to cross the coast at the small island of Over Flakkee where, ironically, there was no Flak. As you approached the target you saw two or three independent searchlights sweeping the sky, apparently aimlessly. But let one of them catch you and you were immediately the centre of a cone of five or six. Getting out of that demanded immediate and very strenuous action of cork-screwing, weaving and diving, anything to escape those lights and their attendant guns and fighters. Many seasoned crews were known to wait around the target until the cones of searchlights were busy with some other unfortunate. During the summer nights of 1942 the German night fighters were especially menacing. A moonlit night, with vapour trails forming at the height you were flying, made you a sitting target. There was some safety in the numbers of other bombers which were around and about you but sooner or later a fighter was sure to pick on you. On three trips in July and August our Stirling was attacked and on each occasion our gunners managed to fight the enemy off claiming two destroyed and one damaged.'

With more resources, better aircraft and equipment, the number of sorties rose steadily in 1943, but so did aircraft losses and the survival rate was little improved. In 1942 on average one aircraft was missing for every 24 sorties and in 1943 one for every 27. With these odds, the chances of surviving the 30-raid tour were slim. Despite attrition, morale was generally good among aircrew, with a stoic acceptance of the situation; and while they nicknamed Harris 'Butch' – the Butcher – his leadership was accepted. An entry in the diary of Harry Quick of No. 101 Squadron reveals this confidence:

'After such a long period of inactivity, we were very glad of a visit from him on 17 Sept, to inform us that without a doubt we were winning the war, and should win the war if we could keep going as we had been doing during the last few months. It was mentioned that since April – the month of our joining the squadron – had been the best time for the RAF. Give us the planes and bombs and good weather and we will keep it up. By this visit he proved himself a grand chap, and by his reference to air-gunners' pay, being – "If I had my way you would all get £10,000 a year." '

Those aircrew who survived their tour had by then become the veterans of their station. The crew on which Ralph Harrington served as a WOP/AG, in No. 78 Squadron Halifaxes, was one in this category, and also had the unusual distinction of all members collecting the DFC or its NCO equivalent of DFM:

'Our crew must have been one of the youngest in Bomber Command. We flew all 30 ops of the tour together, except on one occasion when we had a different rear-gunner as ours was sick. We started with Milan, Italy, on 12 August 1943 and finished with Lens, Belgium, on 10 May 1944, taking in most of the tough targets during this period. At the start we were seven sergeants and by the time we finished six had become officers. We had also collected six DFCs and one DFM. The rapid promotion was the result of the misfortune of others – during hostilities our squadron had over a thousand aircrew members missing, nearly three-quarters fatalities. Our pilot started out as a sergeant and had four promotions in five months, becoming a Flight Lieutenant in January 1944.'

The belief that Bomber Command was performing a war-winning job was the chief motivating factor for aircrew. Even so, the prospect of being shot down prompted many captains of aircraft to encourage their men to practise emergency drills. William Drinkell, a No. 50 Squadron pilot, believed in being prepared and his account also highlights crew superstition:

'We had a good idea of the attrition in Bomber Command, but one believed it always happened to the other chap. Even so, you could not help thinking about your chances and taking measures to better them. My crew regularly practised dinghy drill and also clearing the aircraft on the ground. We had it down to 11 seconds from the word "go". As the captain I was the last one to leave. Before an operation you made sure you had your best bib and tucker on, clean underclothes and were well shaved. Firstly to aid escaping if shot down; secondly, to be well clad if ending up in a prison camp. There was a pecking order for climbing into our Lancaster on every raid. I was first and then the others always in the same order. Nobody decreed that this should be so, but it was adhered to rigidly, a kind of ritual I suppose. Some of the crew had personal superstitions. The mid-upper always carried a medallion that had been given him. The navigator made a point of never looking out at any target, he always drew his curtain. He had another superstitious practice: if we were going across the North Sea he wore water boots; if it was only a short crossing of the Channel he wore shoes. But he was an excellent navigator and looked after us well. The bomb-aimer always placed his

***Above:** Halifax II J-Jig of No. 35 Squadron. Fuselage letters were the usual means of reference used by RAF personnel to identify individual aircraft. The pair of letters were the unit code marking. (Megura)*

***Below:** No. 90 Squadron Stirlings on dispersal at new and muddy Ridgewell, early 1943.*

Above: *Tour-expired aircrew of Lancaster LM241, GI:Q at Mildenhall, 12 August 1944. Sitting on the Wing (l. to r.): Bernard Dye (mid-upper), Arthur Horton (pilot), Ken Monether (navigator) and Dave Parsons (flight engineer). At back: ground crew member, Jock White (wireless operator), Brian Grant (rear-gunner), Brian Gray (bomb-aimer) and the other two members of ground crew.*

Left: *Gerhard Heilig of No. 214 Squadron. Note whistle attached to left lapel of jacket, which was for use in drawing attention if disabled in a crash or parachute landing. It also served as an unofficial mark that the wearer was 'on ops'.*

Right: *Powerful, but initially troublesome Sabre engine as exposed in Typhoon SA:L of No. 486 Squadron at Raydon, early 1944. (M. Olmsted)*

Below: *A Whirlwind of No. 137 Squadron, one of only two squadrons to be fully equipped with the type.*

Right: *The immortal Spitfire came in many models. A Mark IX of No. 66 Squadron with two-stage supercharged Merlin engine, usually considered the best all-rounder.*

Right: *A clipped-wing Mark XII of No. 41 Squadron, with powerful Griffon engine. It excelled at low altitude.*

WC X

Left: *A Spitfire Mark VII of No. 154 Squadron, Merlin powered with pressurized cockpit for very high-altitude work. (M. Olmsted and P. Knowles)*

Bottom left: *A formation of Mustang IIIs of No. 309 Squadron clutching 75-US gallon 'drop tanks' which gave this excellent fighter a combat radius of more than 600 miles. Fighter pilots with ranks of Wing Commander and above were permitted to identify their personal aircraft with initials. The Mustang marked ZW is that of the Andrews Field Polish Wing CO, flown on this occasion by Tony Murkowski.*

Below: *High jinks at Biggin Hill, January 1945. Snowball fight team are, left to right: Flying Officers 'Bluey' Hargraves, 'Junior' Newell and Philip Knowles. (P. Knowles)*

Left: *More high jinks at Biggin Hill, January 1945. Flying Officer Ron Palmer and baby Austin leaving the Officers' Mess. Actually, the car had been man-handled up the steps by fellow-officers. (P. Knowles)*

Above: *George Irving (left) and his radar operator 'Wee Georgie' Millington with ground crew after bagging a Do 217 in Beaufighter VA:A.*

Below: *George Irving flying Mosquito NF 30 of No. 125 Squadron at 25,000 feet over Church Fenton, May 1945. (G. Irving)*

Left: Even the tapering rear fuselage of the Sunderland had plenty of room to move around. Note the workbench behind the navigator who is checking Dead Reckoning Compass master unit. (Official)

Right: *A Sunderland of No. 201 Squadron in Coastal Command's white dress, flying near Lough Erne, Northern Ireland. (Official)*

Below: *Flight Lieutenant Tom Minta, second from right, and the crew of No. 58 Squadron's Whitley Z-Zebra.*

Above: *Flight Lieutenant Len Barcham, second from right, and a No. 404 Squadron group beside Beaufighter EE:C at Davidstow Moor, June 1944. Deputy Squadron Leader Schoales (with white scarf) flew back from Norway on three occasions with one engine stopped.*

Top right: *A photograph taken from Beaufighter EE:Q by Flight Lieutenant Barcham shows rocket attacks on a German destroyer (just visible above tailplane) beached on D-Day plus one at Ile de Batz. The crew were trying to re-float the vessel when the Beaufighters arrived. In contrast to the usual successful report on a vessel destroyed, this one read that 'the captain went up with his ship'.*

Right: *Familiar to all who served at Shallufa, Egypt; the popular haunt of off-duty hours. (H. Kidney)*

SHALLUFA R.A.F. CINEMA

Left: *A tin can served for erks' washing-day in the Western Desert. 'Twitch', 'Hyme' and Harry Kidney (right) at Gambut, 1941.*

Below: *Desert breakfast, Libya 1941. Charlie and crew beside their No. 37 Squadron Wimpy B-Beer, serial number R1033. (H. Kidney)*

Right: *Disaster at Shallufa, 1941. A 20lb anti-personnel bomb explodes in a Wellington. (H. Kidney)*

Below right: *The new and the old. A Douglas Boston light bomber and a Vickers Valentia at Hurehada on the Red Sea. The ageing biplane was used to transport personnel around the Middle East. (H. Berry)*

Left: *Steve Challen nurses a neck wound caused by a splinter from the shell burst that blasted the tail of No. 108 Squadron's Z-Zebra. (S. Challen)*

Below: *A Marauder of No. 14 Squadron ready to roll.*

parachute pack under his thighs during the bombing run – but that was more for self-protection!'

There were many instances of an act begun that had always to be repeated. Vernon Wilkes:

'When our crew started ops the rear-gunner, Danny Driscoll, made a habit of spitting on the tail for luck before climbing aboard for a raid. No one thought much about it at first, just a bit of a joke. Then one day as we were on the peri' track just about to turn on to the runway, the brakes went on and I heard the skipper, Gordon Markes, came on intercom and ask, "Danny, did you spit on the rudder before we boarded?" "No, I forgot." "Well get out and do it now," the skipper commanded. There followed a lot of cursing from Danny but the skipper said he wasn't moving until the usual ritual had been performed. Finally Danny got out of his turret, opened the rear fuselage door, and dropped out. By this time there were ten or so other Lancs lined up behind us, no doubt wondering what our rear-gunner was doing round the tail. Flying Control must also have been concerned as we ignored their repeated "greens" to start on to the runway. Danny wasn't very happy as the slipstream from the props kept taking his spit off target. He only achieved his aim by cupping his hands and almost kissing the rudder. He then had the problem of clambering back into the aircraft as the doorway was about four feet from the ground. What with his bulky flying-clothes and slipstream blast from the engines, Danny was somewhat hot and out of breath when he finally struggled aboard. By which time the skipper, impatient to be off, had started to taxi our IQ:B on to the runway. From then on we made sure Danny always greeted the rudder before a raid. I wouldn't like to say it was responsible for getting us through 36 ops unhurt, but at the time no one was going to let him break the pattern just in case!'

Perhaps belief in acts and articles being lucky helped an individual's confidence; for even some of the most brave and intelligent airmen took comfort from a secret talisman or rite. Equally, anything that had associations with misfortune would be tagged unlucky and avoided if at all possible. This even included people. Bernard Dye:

'In 1944, when not on duty with the lads from No. 622 Squadron, I would spend many happy hours drinking and singing in the Bird 'N Hand just outside Mildenhall 'drome. Behind the bar was a very attractive young blonde, the object of much male attention. Three young officers who each fancied the girl made a pact that each in turn would take her out. Our gunnery officer was the first and soon afterwards he was shot down. The second to take her out was also shot down and so was the third. From thenceforth the young lady was known – behind her back – as "The Chop Blonde".'

Good aircrew discipline was another factor that improved the chances of survival, an immediate response to intercom messages being one facet. John Studd of No. 101 Squadron describes what could happen if one didn't get it right:

'There probably wasn't greater comradeship than that of a bomber crew. We seven depended upon one another and no one wanted to let the side down. We were drawn from all walks of life and two were Australians, including Frank our skipper. Frank was a bit of a rough diamond and quite a character, but an ice cool disciplinarian in the air. We had set procedures for instructions and requests over the intercom and it was essential that we all adhered to these: a misinterpretation might cost us our lives. Human nature being what it is, in a dicey situation apprehension could cause a lapse. When an enemy fighter was seen, the rule was for the gunner spotting it to warn the pilot in which direction to evade. We were going over Essen one night; it was on the last leg into the target and as bomb-aimer I was busy in the nose. Suddenly over the intercom I heard the gunners shout "Dive!" A fighter must have been making an overture, but we kept on our course. "Dive," the call was repeated and still no action from Frank. A third time the alarmed gunners yelled "Dive," and received the exasperated roar from Frank: "Which fuckin' way?!" He got his answer, he dived and we lived to fly another day.'

Immediate evasion manoeuvres were generally acknowledged to be the best means of escape from fighter interception. However, there could be a deterrent to such action, as Vernon Wilkes discovered:

'Our flight engineer, Ken Brotherhood, unfortunately suffered from airsickness and was frequently sick on ops. Normally he suffered in silence as he was keen to continue flying with us. This showed courage because had he so wished he could have been medically grounded. One night we were over the target with Flak and numerous searchlights when, as I was sighting the target through the bombsight, the Skipper's peeved tone came over the intercom to the crew, "If we're attacked by a fighter you've all had it! Ken's been sick on the throttles and I'm not going to touch them!" Fortunately his threat was not put to the test so once again our Lancaster returned home to Hemswell unscathed!'

In 1944 the survival position improved with a loss for every 42 sorties, with Germany remaining more dangerous with a one in 30 rate. In the final six months of hostilities the position improved to better than one in a hundred sorties. Not that this was generally known or would have been of much consolation to aircrews. They still preferred to put their trust foremost in fellow crew members; being part of a good crew gave some sense of security. Ken Doughty of No. 101 Squadron was one who recognized this:

'I was 19 and didn't think all that deeply; somebody had to go and it was me. People got killed or didn't come back, but when I started my tour in the latter part of 1944 the losses weren't that bad. Perhaps I had a cushy time on my 31 trips compared to some. To a chap of my age it was exciting and I don't ever recall worrying about getting the chop. For one thing, the fact that there were six others up there with you, each one depending on the other, made for a special kind of comradeship that gave you confidence. There were only two occasions when I was really scared. The first was when we were caught in searchlights; the black of night suddenly turning white with the expectation that any moment cannon-shells would come crashing into the 'plane. The other occasion was on take-off with a full bomb-load when, just as we reached the speed of no return, an engine faltered. The pilot had to feather the prop and there were some worrying moments wondering if we were going to clear the row of houses beyond the end of the runway. Somehow we struggled over them and gained enough height to jettison the bombs in the sea. Take-offs were always anxious.

'People who had been through some harrowing experience probably had more trouble with fear. The pilot and myself – the engineer – teamed up with five chaps who had managed to bale out of a stricken Lancaster over England. Their original pilot and engineer couldn't get out and were killed. After our first trip with them the rear-gunner went LMF; he could no longer take it. I didn't realize how the experience had affected some of the others until one night when over Germany, two engines cut out. It was only a momentary failure due to a fuel or ignition switching, perhaps no more than a second or so, but two of the crew panicked, picked up their parachutes and started for the exits.'

LMF – Lack of Moral Fibre – was the official classification for those men whose nerve broke. This could be levelled at a man who quit at the outset of his tour or a veteran of many raids succumbing through horrific experience and battle stress. The lumping together of all cases as LMF, regardless of individual circumstances, caused considerable resentment among aircrew. Little sympathy was shown for the obvious collusion that caused the break-up of Bernard Dye's original crew.

'The target was Stuttgart, our first trip. After arriving at the Lancaster we did our pre-flying checks and then smoked and chatted with the ground crew until it was time to board. As we taxied round the peri' track for take-off the two Canadians on the crew, the bomb-aimer and navigator, came on the intercom and said they had destroyed their maps and refused to fly. Our pilot called the tower and reported we had to return to our dispersal point. The Wingco was awaiting us and, after questioning, the two Canadians were arrested and taken to the guardroom. The rest of us were completely shocked by all this as we had trained well together and there had been no indication that anything like this was going to happen. Next day our crew was again on the night's "Battle Order" and the bomb-aimer and navigator were released from detention. We all ate together, attended briefing and it seemed that all was now well and we would soon be on our way. The target was again Stuttgart. As we taxied out exactly the same thing happened as on the previous night, the two men came on intercom to say they had destroyed the maps. Once back at dispersal they were both re-arrested and taken to the guardroom, eventually facing a court-martial. The last I heard they were sent to an Air Crew Correction Centre.'

If a man did not have the fortitude to face the bombers' war he would usually succumb to his fear after the first operation or so. Ralph Harrington:

'On one of the Berlin raids we were asked to take along a new pilot for his first operational trip. As was the practice with newly arrived crews, the captain flew his first as second dickey with an experienced crew. It was a fairly hairy operation but we got back safe and sound, ours being one of the first Halifaxes down. The new pilot was the first chap out of the aircraft and found himself surrounded by a group of newspaper reporters who had been sent to our airfield. They were asking him about the raid and as he seemed willing to shoot his mouth off, our crew left him to it. Next day there he was spread all over one of the national dailies with quotes of how we clobbered the target and fought our way through heavy enemy defences. A real line-shoot and it read as if he was an experienced bomber pilot rather than a rookie on his first outing. The irony of the episode was that this chap never flew another operation. He left the squadron and we never saw him again.'

Gerry Hatt recalls an instance deserving of more sympathetic treatment:

'One day I noticed that a sergeant, a much older bloke than the rest of us, about 30, was missing from our section but the rest of his crew were there. The story I was told was that on the previous night's raid they had been attacked by a fighter but got away. The pilot noticed that the mid-upper turret hadn't fired so he sent this sergeant, the flight engineer, back to have a look. When he reached the turret the gunner was sitting in his saddle but didn't answer. So the engineer unhooked the saddle and swung the gunner down. When he shone his torch in the gunner's face there wasn't one; it had taken a direct hit from a cannon-shell. You can imagine the shock and the sheer horror of such a sight. It was too much for the engineer. He was made LMF, which wasn't really fair as he'd previously done five trips and it was simply this ghastly experience that made him quit.'

There is no doubt that the stigma of LMF was considerable and one suspects that this classification was instituted with some thought of its deterrent nature. The majority, however concerned for personal safety, avoided any action that might be construed as looking for a way out by fellow airmen. Sometimes this thought would induce men to try too hard, as in the incident described by Morgan Hewinson:

'The unofficial motto of No. 9 Squadron was "There's Always Bloody Something!" And there was. One evening in the summer of 1942, our third operational trip. Sprogs then! In a Mark III Wellington we taxied to the end of the runway, revved-up and started to take off. About halfway, realizing there was something amiss with the starboard engine, braked hard and pulled up at the far end of the Honington strip. Pilot to crew: "We'll go around and have another shot at it. Our last two trips were scrubbed because of faults. They will think we don't want to go."

'The second attempt seemed to be going better, the wheels left the grass. I switched off my intercom to tune my radio for the half-hourly broadcast, then realized that something was wrong. Switched on my intercom and heard the navigator say in an urgent voice: "Jim, your starboard revs are dropping back." We were clear of married quarters and just above the trees; luckily we missed hitting them on the way down. I heard the pilot say: "Right, here we go chaps." Braced myself between the radio equipment and the back of my seat. There was a bump and violent vibration and shuddering. The radio equipment broke away from its moorings and swung around to the left with my forearm. This probably saved me serious injury, leaving me with nothing worse than a small cut above the left eye.

'The rest of the crew were leaving via the pilot's cabin. I looked back, intending to escape by the astrodome in the fuselage, but the incendiary bombs were already burning. I thought that this would be a write-off, so everything I could take would be mine! Strange how cool and mercenary one can be on these occasions. I collected my watch from its container on the table, log-book and parachute. The door between the radio operator's and pilot's cabins was jammed. A heave from my side and a kick from the other and the door came off its hinges. A climb on to the wing and we were out. A walk or run across the field and shelter behind a hayrick. By this time ammunition was exploding, pyrotechnics flying and the incendiary bombs (our load for the raid) well and truly burning, and eventually an explosion as the full petrol tanks blew up. Fire engine, ambulance and crews arrived, but any effort to extinguish the blaze would have been useless, so none was made. Later, walking into the mess, there sat the very glum looking reserve crew, old colleagues of ours from OTU, eating their "Ops" meal of bacon and egg. Everyone stood and greeted the rear-gunner and myself. The drinks flowed. This and six days survivor's leave made it all worthwhile.'

The effect of combat stress on aircrew did not go unnoticed by the ground staff who could soon distinguish the suspect malingerers. Roy Browne:

'Occasionally, when the aircrew were ready in the aircraft, an op was scrubbed for a few hours for some reason or other. The crews would then go to the flight huts the ground staff had near the dispersals. Here they'd sharp cards and play up merry hell until it was time to go. Joking and laughing, you'd think they were going to a football match rather than a possible date with death. Some of this was undoubtedly due to tension – and there was a lot of chain-smoking too. But I never saw any fear displayed. At breakfast, after a raid, you'd hear someone say, "So-and-so boomeranged last night." That meant he had abandoned the raid because of some supposed mechanical problem, a mag' drop or something. Of course, there were genuine cases but a few pilots made a habit of doubtful failures. On the other hand, I've known pilots who came back because of a mechanical fault, had it seen to and went off again, an hour behind the rest of the squadron.'

But the men who were deemed LMF were very few, a mere 0.9 per cent one study concluded. The vast majority of aircrew suppressed fear and did their job.

A Near Thing – For Some

Often the four to eight hours spent in a thundering, vibrating bomber was fraught with fatigue as much as apprehension, although most men had moments when their worst fears seemed about to be realized. There follow three examples of such experience. Harry Robinson, a No. 101 Squadron wireless operator:

'As a wireless operator in a Lancaster you were tucked down in the fuselage behind the pilot, flight engineer and navigator. Apart from on the bombing run, when it was duty to observe from the astrodome to provide another pair of eyes, you couldn't see much of what was going on. The occasional searchlight beam and the odd flash if you looked up through the canopy, but for the most part all was dark, the only illumination being the shaded lights over the radio set. You concentrated on listening out for broadcasts and only knew what was going on around through the talk of other members of the crew that could be heard on the intercom. All this against a background of constant engine roar and vibration.

'In an emergency you felt rather helpless; it was a case of sit there and take it. On one of my trips – 4 April 1945 – I was listening at the set when the gunner called out "Corkscrew! Corkscrew!" As we dived and turned with engines screaming, my log and everything loose went flying. The smell of cordite filled the cabin, I didn't know if it was from our guns or from hits we might have taken from the night fighter. Neither did I know whether we were out of control or what was going on. A few seconds of terror and confusion and then we were flying level again. I began to sort myself out and pick up the scattered equipment. I found my log under the navigator's foot. As we had been shot up the pilot decided to land at Juvincourt in France. There we found holes in the Lanc but the damage was not serious and we were able to fly home next day. At Juvincourt they had been unable to notify our station that we were safe so we were still thought missing when we arrived at Ludford Magna. I suppose after this bit of excitement for a 20-year-old I felt quite important. Until I turned in my log to the signals officer. He took one look at the print of the navigator's boot and proceeded to tell me off: "What a state to bring a log back in." My explanation was no excuse; he was making it plain that standards had to be maintained, even if you were being shot at.'

Ken Brotherhood, No. 150 Squadron flight engineer:

'We were 15 minutes from our target in the Ruhr with plenty of anti-aircraft fire and searchlight activity all around. Vernon Wilkes, the bomb-aimer, was checking his bombsight and selector switches when we heard him cry out over the intercom, "I've been hit!" Pausing just long enough to grab a portable oxygen bottle from its stowage, I leapt from my flight engineer's seat and went down into the nose. All sorts of things flashed through my mind – "How bad is he? How do I get him back up into the main cabin? Who will do the bombing?" By the time I reached him Vernon had discovered the hefty blow to the chest and back he had received was not due to enemy action but his having accidentally inflated his Mae West. The lever of his life-jacket had caught on something as he moved about in the confined nose compartment. The immediate inflation under his tight parachute harness felt like a mighty whack.'

Gerry Hatt, a No. 426 (RCAF) Squadron flight engineer:

'The Jerry night fighters could home on our H2S ground scanning radar sets so the procedure was to turn off the modulator as soon as we had bombed. As engineer, it was my job to do this. On one occasion when we were at 20,000 feet it was time to go back to the H2S set. I got myself a portable oxygen bottle and strapped it on to my parachute harness. It tended to make you top-heavy and with everything else you were like a walking teddy bear. I set off climbing over equipment and had just reached the wing spars when I heard the rear gunner open fire. Bad news, followed by being sent crashing face first on to the wing spar as the pilot put the Halifax into a dive. Although badly shaken my first aim was to get back up front to keep an eye on the fuel tank gauges. If one was holed and losing fuel the procedure was to bang all four engines on to it and use what you could before all was lost. Apart from being frightened in that I didn't know what was happening, I was trying desperately to keep my oxygen mask in place even though my face was cut and bleeding. After much effort I struggled back up front to find I was the only man in the crew still using oxygen. We were down to 2,000 feet!'

Reg Fayers of No. 76 Squadron:

'He seemed too young, a schoolboy masquerading in battledress as a sergeant-pilot, and now, for a Jolly Jape, inserting himself somehow into our company-at-arms as a Second Dicky – or conversely perhaps it was that we seven had been unconsciously aged by our fifteen trips. Anyway, he came, a stranger, with us to Mannheim one night. Next day, liking the boy, we laughed easily together, bestowed a nickname on him, played snooker in the mess, drank tea –

and prepared for Nuremberg that night. He stayed by Steve, standing watchfully by the controls, I suppose learning the bomber trade, while I kept my head down over my charts as usual, concentrating my mind, holding my water until after we'd bombed and set course for Yorkshire and eggs and bacon. I smile with hindsight's incredulity to think that, still over Germany, I should have unplugged and gone back to the Elsan down near the tail merely to pee. But, seduced by the hubris from which young men in particular suffer, I went back. I really did.

'Even as I was still back there, fiddling about, we ran into trouble. Steve started throwing the Halifax all over the sky, engines screaming as we dived and twisted about through the great night skies in a frenzy to escape the searchlights and Flak. Stumbling and crawling and being flung from North Star to Nowhere and back, I lurched in my own private chaos of gravity back up from the tail to rejoin my crew. The port inner engine was on fire and heavy Flak was still exploding all around. They had us. Still the Halifax was flung about. I stumbled against a body, prostrate in the darkness, before I reached my table and plugged back into the intercom, but it was all part of the vast bewilderment that encased us all in the confusion of attack. Skipper and engineer between them conquered the engine-fire and somehow we slowly escaped back into the relief of the straight-and-level way homeward. "Has somebody been hit, Steve?" I ventured. "Where the hell have you been, navigator?" he stormed and tore me off my well-earned strip. Soon through the intercom mush terse bulletins issued from Phil and Lew as they struggled to tend the wounded Second Dicky – until the final one. "He's gone, Steve." "Are you sure?" with some disbelief. "Yes." "OK. Back to work."

'We landed at Ford, just into Sussex. Next morning, totally subdued, we went out to inspect our aircraft. The picture was entitled 'The Morning After the Battle'. The great stricken Halifax stood nose-in-air in silent suffering on the tarmac. Inside it was drenched and spattered everywhere with the congealed life-blood of Witt, the dead schoolboy Second Dicky. He had said, "I think I've been hit, Skip . . ." and merely lowered himself away from Steve's presence. The aircraft had been pierced time and again by shrapnel but there, in the unbelievable peace of an August morning in lovely Sussex countryside, we were able to trace clearly the tragic trajectory of that single significant lump of German metal, no more than a couple of inches across, that had shot up through the bottom of the aircraft capriciously to sever the main artery in Witt's thigh. And on its way upward, we plainly saw, it had torn a neat hole in the canvas of the seat – my seat – upon which I should have dutifully been sitting had not the chance wisdom sent me back down to the aircraft to the Elsan to pee.

'As we left our desolate aircraft reflectively, we were accosted by a young sprog MO. Did we realize, he demanded, that we ought to have saved Witt's life last night? Within that first silence of our indignant anger, I kept hearing not that cruelly unnecessary lecture on the application of tourniquets – for did we not have desperate practical experience of the attempted application of tourniquets under battle conditions, which he did not – but only the sound of his leather gloves continually slapping against his own left palm. He too was very young, still "wet behind the ears", beautifully kitted-out in his brand-new Bond Street uniform, although his new cap was already pressed fashionably into an "old sweat" shape. One or two of us began to storm at him, about did he have the remotest notion what it was like up there over Saarbrucken, the chaos, the darkness, the long moments of not-knowing, of those great demons of gravity, the confusion of an aircraft on fire. He had started to apologize and cringe a bit under the fury of the crew's anger even as I deserted them all and walked off to cogitate on the odds of living or dying. If He chose to move in ways so mysterious His wonders to perform as to appear a nonsense, then I'd henceforth be placing my bets with a different bookie.'

By and large, aircrew considered Flak the most intimidating part of the German defences but, naturally, individuals' reactions varied. Freddie Brown's fears were not untypical of mid-upper gunners:

'By the time you'd seen a Flak shell explode, if you hadn't been hit then there was nothing to fear from that burst. You didn't consider the next, if there was going to be one in your vicinity; that was the unknown. Running up to a target there would be comment about the Flak from the crew up front and I'd sometimes ease the mid-upper turret round for a brief look. Often there appeared to be a solid wall of shell explosions ahead and an exclamation of "Bloody Hell!" was appropriate. It looked worse than it was as you were seeing bursts over a large area. Once amongst the barrage you saw it was actually well spread out and your chances of getting through seemed much better. Although your firepower was inferior to that of enemy fighters, being behind a pair of guns did give that "him or me" feeling. If your vigilance was good and you saw him first or he missed with his first burst, there was a chance. Searchlights gave me my greatest anxiety. On one occasion, over Essen, a big blue light found us and immediately many others caught us in a perfect cone. The vivid brightness took away what little security the turret offered, I felt exposed to the whole of the German defences; absolutely naked! I had one foot out of the turret on the step as I cowered from the blinding light. Somehow words came from my mouth telling the pilot to dive starboard through the main concentration and luckily we quickly escaped into the lovely black sky. We were free.'

The majority of Bomber Command losses were from night fighters, the fatal blast of enemy fire being the first the bomber crew knew of the enemy presence. When a night fighter approach was seen, evasive action could be taken while the rear and upper gunners engaged the interceptor in a duel. The rifle calibre machine-guns of the British bombers were no match for the heavy cannon in the German fighters; but the outcome was not always in the enemy's favour. Bernard Dye witnessed a particularly successful air battle:

'We took off in Q-Queenie at 23.48 hours, 14 June 1944, and set course for Le Havre. Cheshire had marked the target, we dropped with no problems, turned away and headed home. It was a beautiful night, clear skies, stars shining and a full moon coming up behind us. All around I could see many Lancs heading back to their bases. My thoughts turned to the bacon and eggs and the issue of rum to be enjoyed when we landed. All at once I saw a Ju 88 open up at a Lancaster on our port side. Excitedly I reported this to Arthur Horton, our pilot, with the suggestion we pull over and give the Lanc support. "No bloody fear," Arthur retorted. Of course, he was right; his duty was to get his aircraft and crew safely home. Then I saw that good shooting by the other Lanc's gunners had set the Ju 88 on fire. It broke off the attack and I watched it go into the sea below. Almost immediately a second Ju 88 appeared and started to fire at the same bomber. The gunners returned the fire and again the enemy caught fire and spun down in a mass of flames. Back at Mildenhall our Wingco, Ian Swales, was taking an interest in our debriefing when suddenly in burst an excited Flt Lt Hargraves and crew shouting that they had destroyed two enemy night-fighters. Quite a feat.'

There were other very real dangers in the Command's war. Aircraft stacked in the bomber stream heading to and from the target, each hidden from the others in a veil of darkness, except when in very close proximity. Vernon Wilkes recounts one hazard that was not an uncommon occurrence:

'We were on a night trip to Munich flying through pretty murky weather. As usual I was in my bomb-aimer's compartment keeping an eye open as we could feel the slipstreams of invisible aircraft ahead. Suddenly the alarmed voice of Ken Brotherhood, our flight engineer, came over the intercom shouting "Climb Skip!" Without hesitation the skipper pulled the nose up making the aircraft feel as if it was going to stall. I leaned forward into the transparent nose cone and saw a Lancaster pass from left to right about fifteen feet or so below our nose. It was close enough for me to distinguish the illuminated instruments in its cockpit for that fleeting moment. As I thought what a narrow escape we'd just had, there was an explosion about a quarter of a mile to starboard as the other bomber hit someone else. Two burning masses cascaded down. No one in our crew said a word about this incident until we'd bombed the target and safely landed back at Hemswell after a nine-and-a-half-hour trip. Collisions were fairly common, but this was the nearest we'd been to having one. Gordon Markes, our skipper, aged just 20, always refused to fly with George (the automatic pilot) engaged and never queried spontaneous directions given him by the crew members. If he had hesitated on this occasion our Lancaster would have been a gonner.'

Dick Enfield's experience was an even closer 'near thing':

'Our first trip to Kiel, a piece of cake. The skipper said, "If they are all like that we've got no worries." We had more worries than we wanted on our second. We were on our way to Stuttgart. Over France I was idly pushing out "Window" (anti-radar foil), sitting on the lowest of the steps from the flight deck to the bomb-aimer's position, when there was a sharp ripping sound. My immediate thought was that we'd been raked by fire from a night fighter. I bounded back up to the flight deck just in time to see a four-engine bomber going down in flames below us. From its proximity I realized it had collided with our kite. A scan of my flight engineer's instrument panel revealed the starboard inner engine oil pressure had dropped to zero. "Shut down starboard inner," I yelled to the skipper and while he closed the throttle and cut off the fuel, I moved to press the prop feathering button. At this instant the engine burst into flames which streamed back past the tailplane.

'The skipper called: "Prepare to abandon aircraft!" but at the same time decided to put the Lanc into a dive which snuffed out the fire. When he levelled off there was a definite vibration from the port side. Another look at the engineer's panel and the needles on the port engine gauges were oscillating like metronomes. It was obvious the props had been bent in the collision – our props had cut into him and his had ripped along our underside. The skipper wanted to know if we could carry on to the target. I informed him we had only one good engine and were going to need a lot of luck to get home from where we were. So he gently turned the Lanc out of the bomber stream and took a heading for home. Because of intercom noise it was apparent that one member of the crew had left his transmit switch on. The skipper called us individually but got no response from the rear gunner. Our WOP/AG was sent to investigate. After a couple of minutes he came on the intercom and said "He's gone Skip." I suppose the gunner saw the flames going by his turret, thought the aircraft was doomed and baled out. All this time we were losing altitude. The intention had been to jettison the bombs when we reached the Channel, but at 4,500 feet it was obvious we'd never make it so we had to let them go over France. At least we could now maintain height although the port engines had to be run at reduced revs.

'We made it safely to southern England where it was decided to test the undercart. When I selected "down" the port wheel didn't budge and the starboard only came halfway, enough for us to see the tyre was flapping in the breeze. As our radio was dead we decided to make for Woodbridge which had a special long runway to handle aircraft in distress. Once in the circuit a red Very cartridge was fired to signify we had an emergency and the skipper then ordered us to take up crash positions behind the wing spars. He put her down so gently we hardly felt a bump. It didn't even crack the bomb-aimer's perspex nosepiece. We got out in double-quick time but there was no fire.'

In addition to collisions, aircraft were in danger of being struck by bombs from higher aircraft – even in daylight. William Drinkell of No. 50 Squadron:

'Our daylight trip to Duren on 16 November 1944 should have been an easy trip with fighter escorts there and back. We had settled down on our run at 165 IAS, the optimum speed for a Lancaster's bomb-sight, when the rear-gunner reported another Lancaster approaching from the rear with his bomb doors open. I had a quick glance back but wasn't concerned as he would be doing the same speed as we were. I returned my attention to the instruments when the next thing there was a terrific thud and the aircraft dipped violently to the right. For a moment I thought it was going to invert. There was some frantic action at the controls and a fleeting glance at the starboard wing revealed a large hole right between the two engines and what appeared to be a trail of flame behind the wing. After hitting the feathering switch on for both engines, the crew were called and told to stand by for abandoning the aircraft. Out went the escape hatches and the draught created whipped up the strips of Window anti-radar foil we carried. It really was a dog's dinner inside the cockpit.

'Part of the drill was to take your helmet off in case you strangled yourself while baling out. Having done this, I managed to bring the aircraft level so we could jump and was about to give the order when I realized I could hold this flight altitude. So I kicked the engineer with my foot, as he was off intercom as well, and gave him the thumbs up sign when he looked round. He stopped the navigator going out and he in turn yelled back to the gunners who had the rear door open and were ready to go. Although I could keep her on an even keel I couldn't understand why we were going down so fast, then suddenly realized we still had all our bombs on board. A pull on the emergency toggle to jettison them solved that problem and stopped our descent. Then there was time to assess the damage. A 1,000-pound bomb had gone clean through the main fuel tank between the two starboard engines, fortunately missing the main spar. The escaping fuel had apparently been ignited aft of the trailing edge by engine exhaust but had not burned the wing. The mid-upper turret gunner had seen another bomb pass between the wing and the tailplane on the starboard side. We had been extremely lucky. Having lost so much altitude – we were down to around 3,000 feet – and alone with two engines out, our concern was being picked up by an enemy fighter. There was no sign of our own escort all the way home. When we landed at base our aircraft, T-Tommy, became the object of much attention. Its ground crew were horrified.'

A less fortunate episode was experienced by William Reid of No. 617 Squadron, this also on a daylight raid:

'On the last day of July 1944, 617 Squadron was sent to Rilly-la-Montage in France to block up a railway tunnel that was being used to store flying-bombs. We were to go in at 12,000 feet to obtain a precision drop with our Tallboys while a following higher formation of Lancasters was briefed to complete the job with 1,000-pounders. Just after I had dropped our bomb and was starting to turn off, there was a bang – we had been struck by bombs from an aircraft above. One knocked out our port outer engine and the other must have come down through the rear fuselage severing cables, as the control column went sloppy. What followed occurred in a few seconds of time, far quicker than it can be told. The Lanc was literally knocked down and it was beyond control. I shouted for the crew to bale out, got my parachute from the engineer and tried to force my way out of the side window despite the likelihood of going into the props. Centrifugal force made movement almost impossible and I then turned attention to the top hatch. At this moment there was an almighty crash and the aircraft broke up. The next thing I was falling free and pulling the release on the 'chute, but also keeping an iron grip on the pack as I was not sure if I had attached it to the harness properly. After the jolt of the opening I just had time to transfer my grip to the shrouds before crashing through the top branches of an oak. My next concern was the likelihood of being clobbered by a piece of the falling wreckage.

'My right hand and face had been badly cut when the cockpit disintegrated and after getting free from the 'chute a dressing was taken from the personal first-aid kit in an effort to stop the bleeding. My face also had several nasty cuts. I pushed my Mae West under a bush and did the same with a .38 revolver as I had lost the small box of ammunition carried in my hip pocket. Then I picked a way through the wood to get away from the place where I had landed, then sat down to adjust the dressing on my hand. On looking up, the barrels of three machine-guns were pointing at me. The Germans were from a nearby Flak installation and had watched my fall into the wood. Ordered to march, the crumpled tail section of my Lancaster was seen. I persuaded the guards to let me take a look. The rear-gunner was dead, half out of his turret. In another piece of wreckage lay the body of the mid-upper gunner. Neither man had a chance to use his parachute and had probably been trapped by centrifugal force as the bomber spun down. The only other member of the crew to survive was the wireless operator, who was nursing a swollen ankle when brought in by the Germans.'

William Reid was one of the nineteen Bomber Command aircrew to receive the Victoria Cross during the Second World War. This, the highest of the nation's decorations for valour, was awarded for his conduct on the night of 3/4 November 1943, when he was captain of No. 61 Squadron's Lancaster O-Orange. The following is his personal account of that operation, together with his observations on the reasons for the Award:

'We were over Holland at around 20,000 feet on our way to Düsseldorf when I received an almighty thump on my left shoulder. At the same time there was a blast of cold air and fragments of perspex peppered my face as the windscreen panels shattered. The night fighter didn't attack again – he was either driven off by the gunners or lost us when the kite started skidding around. The elevator trim had obviously been hit, but I could not get any information from the rest of the crew as the intercom was out. Eventually Jim Norris, the flight engineer, came up to me and indicated that everyone else was all right. To protect my eyes from the grains of perspex coming off the shattered windscreen I put on a pair of flying-goggles. The silk gloves I usually wore were no longer sufficient to keep my hands warm and the heavy leather pair kept in the cockpit were used to lessen the effects of the icy blast. The compass was u/s but as I could remember the briefed course changes there was no reason not to go on to the target. My shoulder was a bit sore but I wasn't really aware of any injuries at that busy time. Then, crash, we were riddled with cannon-shells and bullets again. I dived the Lancaster in an effort to evade, but the enemy fighter gave us a second burst before he lost us. My hands had been hit by shell fragments and the oxygen supply was failing. After a minute or two the flight engineer came back from the navigator's cabin and spread his arms out, meaning that Jeff was out; I didn't realize he was dead and that the wireless operator was wounded. I made signs for Norris to get me a portable oxygen bottle which I connected to my mask.

'Despite the mauling the Lancaster had received, all engines were operating satisfactorily and although we had no port elevator it was possible to keep the plane straight and level by holding the stick back hard. So I decided to continue to the target, an estimated 45 minutes' away. To turn back now and fly a reciprocal course in the midst of the bomber stream presented a high risk of collision, while without communications or compass, guessing a new course away from the bomber stream might get us hopelessly lost and make us even more vulnerable to night fighters. In my mind, continuing to the target was the right action to take. I was now becoming conscious of my wounds; blood kept trickling down my face from under my helmet. My memory of course changes was proved correct and there was no difficulty in finding the target. After Les Rolton, the bomb-aimer, released our load I used the Pole Star and moon as direction guides to help in getting home.

'As the flight progressed I began to lose my concentration and felt I might lapse into unconsciousness. Norris and Rolton had been helping with the controls all along and now that the bombs had gone Les stayed at a position where he could help hold the stick back. As the intercom had been out the bomb-aimer had been unaware that there were casualties among the crew. We received the attention of the Flak batteries before leaving the Dutch coast. After crossing the North Sea, landfall was made over Norfolk and we prepared to land at the first airfield we saw that was big enough for us to get down on. Morning mist shrouded the runway, making it difficult to see the lights, and what with the blood still getting in my eyes and my own weakened state, it required both the flight engineer and bomb-aimer to put all their strength on the control column to counter the lack of an elevator on the approach. We made it, but one leg of the undercart started to fold and we ended up on our belly about fifty yards along the runway. Only after being removed from the aircraft did I learn that our navigator had died of his wounds.

'I was carted off to hospital to have metal and perspex removed from wounds that I had not realized were so extensive. There was a hole in the left shoulder and my hands were skinned on the surface like a gravel rash. My head had a bad cut just above the hairline and my face had been peppered with perspex fragments. Minute pieces of perspex appeared on my skin for weeks afterwards whenever I shaved. While in hospital I received a visit from AVM Cochrane who commanded No. 5 Group. He was full of praise for my determination to carry on to the target and said this would be an example to others. I think they felt there were too many turn-backs on raids, and that some were not for genuine reasons. I got the impression that was why they made such a big fuss about my experience. It was not for me to say so at that time, but had I known the navigator was badly wounded – which I did not – and that there had been any hope of saving him, or if I had not felt the aircraft was still capable of reaching the target and bringing us home, then I would have turned back without hesitation. There was no intended act of bravado on my part; I did what I thought the right thing to do in the situation.'

In the winter of 1943-4 Bomber Command took some of its highest losses, largely in a sustained series of raids on Berlin. These raids were made at long range, often in severe weather, and in the face of well organized and effective defences. The losses were most grievous in squadrons equipped with Stirlings and early marks of Halifax; aircraft which could not operate with a load at the higher, safer altitudes of 20,000 feet plus where Lancasters and newer-model Halifaxes flew. These squadrons were eventually given less vulnerable work, but this simply had the effect of adding to the concentration of Luftwaffe night fighters attacking those bombers engaged in the Berlin raids. Fortunate indeed were those crews that finished a tour during this period. The combat stress involved is evident in the final mission entry of Harry Quick's diary – for the night of 2/3 December 1943 – which saw the heaviest loss of aircraft attacking the enemy capital, 41 bombers. This was also the fifth Berlin raid in two weeks:

'Number thirty, on Berlin, with the Wingco and a new 'U', on her maiden voyage; so was not feeling very happy and did not feel very happy till we got back. He seemed to have finger-trouble and, I think, it turned out the worst trip I have had. I brought back a bit of Flak in my turret that made a hole in the perspex the size of a half-crown, being deflected by an armoured stay. Bags of other holes as well as mine, two in the petrol tank, from which we lost a little fuel; a good job we had two hours' spare, as all this happened before we reached the target. We had been caught by searchlights and held for several minutes, but why we were not shot at then I fail to understand. Perhaps we were being held for a fighter which did not turn up, thank God. Met boobed with their wind direction predictions, which were all round the clock, making the navigator's job very hard and making other crews late bombing, breaking up the concentration. More fighter flares than I have seen before were evident, but no fighters seen. The moon showed up plenty of ours going in to bomb.'

LAUGHS AND SURPRISES

It would be wrong to imply that the grim statistics of the bomber airmen's war sapped youthful spirits. Indeed, the dangers faced appeared to have had the effect of accentuating play; parties were wild, pranks were many, the outrageous remembered with delight by veterans. Such famous occasions as when the adjutant of No. 101 Squadron swept down the grand staircase of the mansion serving as officers' mess to greet distinguished party guests. He was naked but for toilet roll swathed in strategic places and a tin hat on his head. A few drinks had aided this display. Perhaps a case of drink and be merry for tomorrow we die, except, as has been already noted, each individual believed it would be the other fellow and not himself. The 'who gives a damn' antics could sometimes lead to remorse, as Stanley Tomlinson of No. 149 Squadron experienced:

'At the back of our frying-pan (aircraft dispersal point) at Lakenheath – or Foresakenheath as we called it – there was a small pit and bank of earth. Before you took off for a raid the rear-gunner depressed his four .303 Brownings and fired a burst into the pit to test the guns. Behind this particular frying-pan, about 200 yards away, was a wooden hut that had been used by the Forestry Commission before the airfield was constructed. There was still pine forest beyond this side of the airfield, but the hut was now derelict and abandoned. One winter's afternoon when we were preparing to go out on a raid and I was about to test fire the guns, the mid-upper gunner calls out over the intercom: "Tomo, why don't you try and knock that soddin' window out of that old hut." He only said it for a laugh. But I was 22 years old and as silly as they come, so what the hell. Without thinking, I lined the ring-and-bead sight up on the one unbroken pane of the four frames in the hut window and let fly with a short burst – around 300 rounds I reckon. To my amazement the door flew open and a bloke belts away like I've never seen anyone run before or since. He looked as if he was wearing three overcoats, he had on a battered old hat and hanging from a belt round his middle were several tin pots. Now this really shook me I can tell you; I could not believe anybody would be in that broken-down hut. Of course there was nothing I could do, but I worried all during the trip and when we got back. After interrogation and supper I went to bed but couldn't get it out of my mind. Was there someone else in the shed who I'd killed? I couldn't sleep and eventually got up, cycled the three miles out to the frying-pan and went over to the hut. Apart from some straw and some lavatory leavings in a corner, the place was deserted. The Gentleman of the Road must have been laid out having a kip when I put all that lead through the hut a few inches over his head. I bet he never forgot it. I didn't.'

Nor were aircrew slow to exploit opportunities afforded by an operational mission to enhance their future entertainment. Harold Southgate:

'Both Nos. 50 and 617 Squadrons had selected crews for a special mission to Italy and after bombing were to fly on to land at Blida airfield near Algiers. The raid was launched on 15 July 1943. The attack on the target, a power-station at Reggio, was not very successful but we enjoyed a lovely flight out over the Alps and across the Mediterranean. We had to remain in Algiers for nine days owing to bad weather back in England. Much of the time was spent in nearby Arab markets buying things that were in short supply or unobtainable in the UK, such as wine and exotic fruit, although a good deal of the fruit went bad before it could be flown home. One bright spark in 617 Squadron decided that as they were having a mess party in the near future they would take a very, very large flagon of wine back with them. It took all the aircrew and most of the ground crew to manhandle this flagon into a Lancaster which, with the rest, was expected to bomb a target at Leghorn on the journey to England. We completed the trip without incident, but I later learned that the large flagon of wine blew up as the Lancaster carrying it was forced to increase altitude to cross the Alps. Fortunately no damage was done except to mess funds, from which a fair amount of cash was recovered to pay for the wine that had flushed out the fuselage of a Lancaster.'

Eddie Wheeler, a No. 97 Squadron WOP/AG, was another who was deprived of his investment:

'After our flak-damaged Lanc was written off on landing in North Africa, we hitched a flight back to England on another aircraft. At Gibraltar I purchased a whole bunch of bananas which were practically unheard of in the UK. As we emerged from the Lancaster at Scampton we were greeted by the Station CO and when he saw my branch of bananas he said how nice it was that I should think to bring them back. He peeled off six and handed them to me and said the remainder would be sent to the children in a local hospital. I stood dumbfounded, but then agreed totally with the CO that it was my intention to do just that! Never did taste one banana as even the six I had were entered as prizes in a raffle!'

Wisecracks in the face of adversity were a common veil for courage and concern. There were instances when verbal bravado was heard in the most surprising circumstances. John Sampson:

'During the latter part of 1944 Oboe ground stations were positioned on the Continent and, being moved forward as the Allied armies advanced, eventually provided facilities to reach as far as Berlin, although it necessitated taking the Pathfinder Mosquitoes to 34,000 feet to receive the signals. The last raid on the German capital by RAF heavy bombers was on 24/25 March 1944, but the city was subsequently bombed on many occasions by the Mosquitoes of the Light Night Striking Force, the last being on the night of 20/21 April 1945. I always seemed to miss out on the notable events, but had flown to this target the previous night with a force of 79 Mossies. Our load was four Target Indicators (T/Is). As the Germans sometimes tried to confuse the situation by using false target markers it had become the accepted procedure to announce over the VHF radio when we had made the drop. On this occasion my pilot, Derek James, DFC, called out "Pathfinder F – Freddie – Markers going down," to be greeted by a chorus from the pilots of some of the other Mossies (listening in for the signal) of "Lookie, lookie, lookie, here comes Cookie" – "cookie" being RAF slang for the 4,000-pound bomb.'

John Sampson flew with No. 105 Squadron, then part of the special Pathfinder group that marked targets for the main force of bombers. Pathfinder crews were selected from experienced men who had successfully completed a tour in bombers. Precise navigation was the foundation of good pathfinder work, but there were lapses as Alan Haworth – also of 105 – tells against himself:

'Despite having completed an operational tour on Stirlings, one of my first in Pathfinder Mosquitoes of 105 Squadron was not a distinguished piece of navigation. The target was Aachen and our task was to light the aiming-point with flares from 31,000 feet. On the way in I worked out that the wind-speed at that height was 125mph as forecast, but from north-north-west, not west as the Met boys had said. After dropping our flares and seeing the start of the raid, we were hit by Flak in the port wing. The port engine packed up and with it all the electrics and radar equipment. We had the task of returning to base in Norfolk on one engine with this considerable wind blowing against us. And instead of using new courses based on the winds I had worked out on the way to the target, I made the error of relying on those based on the Met forecast. As a result, instead of crossing the coast at Great Yarmouth, we came in over Southend. Having no electrics we were unable to send out the normal identification signal required when returning home and as a consequence the Thames Valley guns opened fire on us. Luckily they missed. I gave my pilot, Ian McPherson (who played outside-right for Arsenal before and after the war), a new course for about an hour's flying to Marham, our base. I sat back content that my job was done and started eating my currants and barley-sugars with which you were issued on each raid. The pilot was less pleased because we had lost a lot of fuel and he was scared that we would have insufficient to get us to Marham. He reached across me, tapped the fuel gauges on my side of the cockpit and said with feeling: "And what do you think we will get home on – piss?" '

While No. 8 Pathfinder Group aided bombing performance, No. 100 Group was set up late in 1943 to reduce losses by counter-measures against the enemy's defences. This work took many forms, but much was connected with the burgeoning electronics technology for detection and disruption, all highly secret. Gerhard Heilig:

'Because of my ability to speak German, I was sent to No. 100 Group which was engaged in counter-measures against enemy night defences. Flying in No. 214 Squadron Fortresses, my job was chiefly jamming. The control unit in the aircraft had a cathode-ray tube scanning the German fighter frequency band. Any transmissions would show up as blips on the screen. We would then tune our receiver to the transmission by moving a strobe spot on to it, identifying the transmission as genuine (this was where our knowledge of the language came in as the Germans were expected to come up with phoney instructions in order to divert our jammers), then tune our transmitter to the frequency and blast off with a cacophony of sound which in retrospect would put today's pop music to utter shame.

'On one of my leaves I had lunch with my father at a Czech emigrées' club in Bayswater. Among a group of his friends there was a WAAF sergeant and I made polite conversation with her. To my opening question she replied that her work was so secret that she could not even tell me where she was stationed. However, before many minutes had passed, I knew that her job was my own counterpart on the ground with 100 Group. When I started to grin, she told me indignantly that it was nothing to laugh about, it was all terribly important. She was mollified when I told her that I was in the same racket. She then told me the following story.

'Receiver operators pass Luftwaffe radio traffic to a controller who then issue co-ordinated false instructions to transmitter operators designed to cause confusion to the enemy. One night there was nothing happening whatsoever. Then the controller was roused from his torpor by repeated calls for a homing which obviously remained unanswered. Mainly in order to relieve the utter boredom he decided to give the lost sheep a course to steer to – Woodbridge airfield in Suffolk. The German pilot had been faced with the prospect of having to abandon his aircraft and was going to buy everyone concerned a beer on his safe return to base. He came down safely – to find himself a prisoner, and could hardly be expected to keep his promise to stand drinks all round. The aircraft was a Ju 88, stuffed with the latest German equipment, quite a catch for Intelligence. The capture of this aircraft was made public at the time, but not how it had all come about.'

View from the Ground

On a heavy bomber station there was an average of eight to ten ground personnel for every aircrew member. Most fitters, riggers, armourers and other specialists remained with one squadron for the duration, becoming more the squadron than the aircrew – whose association was generally only a few months, if fortunate enough to complete a tour. Ground staff personnel were often in a better position to assess morale and status of their squadron. Roy Browne reflects a mechanic's view:

'*Esprit de corps* at Skellingthorpe was very good despite the heavy losses. In the six months I served as a rigger in "B" Flight of No. 50 Squadron, four of my Lancasters went missing – and this was the final period of operations when overall losses were lower. None of these Lancs survived more than a dozen trips; one never completed any. This was W-Willie. A new crew under a sergeant pilot arriving in the squadron was given this aircraft. That afternoon, 20 March 1945, they took it out for a practice bombing over a range and that night went on their first operation – against an oil plant at Bohlen. I never saw them again. You couldn't be indifferent to losses, but in cases like this it didn't have the effect that the loss of old hands had. Unless it was your own aircraft or one from a nearby dispersal, you didn't know the night's losses until you went to breakfast. Then you'd hear another erk say "so-and-so went for a Burton last night." If it was a crew that had nearly finished a tour everyone felt a bit down. There was a Canadian crew who we got to know well. They lived in the next hut on the squadron site and when we were working and they weren't flying at night they would light the fire in our hut. Conversely, if they were on ops, when we got back from the 'drome we'd light their fire so the place would be warm when they returned. This crew completed a tour of 31 ops just as a tour was raised to 32. On 14 March 1945 they went out on number 32 with a force of 244 Lancs to hit an oil-refinery at Lutzendorf and didn't come back. Such rotten luck, really upset me; just hoped they'd all survived.'

John Everett of No. 102 Squadron expresses similar sentiments:

'Ground staff mechanics on bombers did not usually have a lot of contact with aircrew apart from when they came to check the aircraft or were going on a raid. I was an engine fitter on D-Donald, a 102 Squadron Whitley, and although the same crew usually flew this aircraft on ops there was not much opportunity to get to know any of them very well. However, one morning the pilot came out to take the plane on a test flight after engine overhaul. He asked if I would like to go on this local flight and I jumped at the opportunity. We took off with me in the 2nd pilot's seat and climbed several thousand feet and circled the Vale of York. The pilot then motioned for me to take over the controls, a great thrill. This pleasure was short-lived for the wireless operator appeared and shouted he had just received a signal that an enemy intruder aircraft was somewhere in the clouds. The pilot quickly took over again and brought the Whitley back to Topcliffe. It was nice to be appreciated in this way, for ground people rarely got a chance to fly. While one became hardened to the losses the squadron regularly sustained, it was particularly sad for me when this crew didn't come back.'

Ordnance and highly inflammable material were part of everyday life on a bomber airfield. Roy Browne again:

'The RAF did more damage at Skellingthorpe than ever the enemy did. In August 1944 a WAAF was driving a tractor towing several bomb trailers round the perimeter track when the train started to snake and the last bomb was flung off. There was a hell of an explosion as the lot went up, demolishing a nearby Lanc and killing the WAAF. On 1 February 1945 a No. 61 Squadron Lanc was taking off for a raid when the starboard outer engine cut out. The pilot got it off the ground and after flying the circuit, brought the bomber down again. There should have been no problems; his approach was okay, but he hit hard and then proceeded to run all the way down the runway, off the other end, where the undercart folded and the whole thing went up with a tremendous explosion. There was nothing much left. A little while later a Corporal was cycling round the perimeter track over a quarter of a mile away, when he saw something lying off to one side. He went over and found it was the rear-gunner, alive but in a bad state. They got him to hospital and although just about every bone in his body was fractured he recovered. What probably helped was the absence of perspex in the rear of his turret. No. 5 Group Lancasters had this panel removed as it reflected glare at night. Open to the elements it was a cold perch for the rear-gunner but in this case it saved his life. In the same month our Squadrons attacked the Dortmund-Ems Canal, but weather interfered and the kites returned with some bombs. E-Easy, with four left in the bay, taxied to a dispersal near the Repair and Inspection hangar where the crew departed and a bowser came to refuel. Half-an-hour later the Lanc suddenly exploded, killing three of the ground staff and making a mess of the hangar. A Court of Inquiry later decided the bomb doors had not been closed properly and the combination of wind speed and a heavy landing severed the wire securing the arming device of one of the half-hour delayed-action bombs.'

John Everett tells of another miraculous escape:

'One evening in the summer of 1941 a No. 102 Squadron Whitley blew up on its dispersal at Topcliffe. Presumably one of the delayed-action bombs in the bay had some fault – the aircraft had been bombed-up for a forthcoming raid. At the time of the explosion an armourer had been putting protective canvas covers over gun turrets but his remains could not be found. It was assumed he had been blown to bits. Then word came that the missing man had been found in his bed, bruised and suffering from shock but otherwise okay. Apparently, arms outstretched, he had been in the act of placing the canvas cover over the rear gun turret when the explosion occurred. The canvas caught the full force of the explosion and, acting like a parachute, deposited the shocked man a considerable distance from the wrecked Whitley. Dazed, he picked himself up and staggered back to his billet unnoticed.'

Ground staff engaged in servicing and arming aircraft frequently worked long hours, often in trying conditions. The bomber dispersal points dotted around the 3-mile perimeter track were exposed to the vagaries of the weather and mechanics often worked in wind, rain, frost or snow to prepare their charges for operations. Maintenance equipment was basic and some tasks performed would never have survived safety regulations of later years. Albert Heald can testify to this:

'There was a strong gale blowing with torrents of rain. Everyone was busy getting the kites ready as evidently good weather had been forecast come the night – which did nothing to help us. Apart from getting wet there was the usual "duff gen" going around that ops had been cancelled, when in fact they hadn't. It transpired that what had happened was that the target had been changed for some reason or another which, in turn, created extra work, particularly for the armourers who had to change the bomb load. During all the on-off duff gen that was going around the rain gradually stopped, making life a little easier. It was necessary to get to one of the engines and to do so I clambered up on to the wing of our Stirling via a trestle. As I stood up my feet slipped on the wet surface and the next moment I had slid off the wing. It must have been my lucky day, for the 18-foot drop to the ground ended on a pile of canvas engine covers. As I picked myself up, unhurt, I did not appreciate "What do you do for an encore?" and the various remarks made by my mates.'

Apart from falls there was another danger for ground staff which claimed several lives. John Everett:

'Carrying out an engine run-up with other members of the ground staff, we noticed that a wheel cover that might be damaged by the slipstream was still in place. One of the men went down to remove it. I was looking out of the pilot's window and saw this chap approach from the side and remove the guard. Then he must have forgotten himself for he suddenly started to move forward towards the propeller arc. To my horror I saw what was going to happen and dashed my hand against the throttles to cut them; the engine had been running quite fast. For a moment I dared not look out, expecting to see a bloody mess on the ground. Fortunately, my cutting the throttles and the instant change in noise had brought the bloke to his senses. He had stopped only a foot or so away from those lethal blades.'

Propeller blades became invisible when engines were running and the noise tended to have a soporific effect, making people drop their guard. Notably, there were a number of accidents through people walking into propellers in those squadrons which converted from Stirlings to Lancasters, there having been no risk with the former bomber as the blades at their lowest point were some ten feet above the ground. In Jim Swale's squadron there was a rhyme to remind one of this danger:

'On a Stirling, props a-whirling will miss your head. But on a Lanc you'll get a spank, and then you're dead.'

Sabotage of aircraft was an oft heard rumour but there were true incidents of this, albeit rare. Roy Ellis-Brown:

'Before I made any test flights in my Stirling I used to do a very thorough walk-around examining tyres, control surfaces and essential parts of the aircraft. On one occasion I climbed up on to a main wheel to take a look at the undercarriage locks. The Stirling's undercarriage weighed a ton each side, a tremendous thing that folded up in two sections; it was the only way they could get that long undercarriage into the wing. The height was necessary because of the length of the aircraft. When she was standing on both feet the cockpit was 23 feet off the ground. Well, I was up there looking around when I saw a strange wire coming down through the gear: I couldn't see where it went to or understand its purpose. So I got hold of my chief mechanic, Sgt 'Rosie' Fuller, a very fine man. I said: "Rosie, what in blazes have you got hung up here. What's this jury rig here?" He climbed up with me and said it was nothing that he had put there. I said, "Well, how about shaking this out and finding what it is. It doesn't look like part of the aircraft to me." So he said, "Okay, I'll do that." I got down while he rigged up a stand to get right beneath the wing for an examination. After several minutes he came down; his face was white. He said, "Skipper, it's a good job you looked up there," and opened his fist which held a Mills hand-grenade! "This was taped up to the struts. The wire that you saw was leading to the safety-pin. When you next retracted the undercarriage that pin was going to come out. The grenade was right under No. 6 tank which holds 481 gallons of petrol and you would have gone up in smoke."

'We were a bit perturbed about this and there was a very quiet but thorough investigation of all the Stirlings on the field. However, I had the dubious honour of being the sole recipient of this particular piece of felony; it may have been that the perpetrator didn't get around to doing any more. The first thought was an enemy saboteur, but I later learned that suspicion fell elsewhere. At the time a permanent concrete runway was being installed at Oakington and we had a large number of Irish labourers around. Labour was so short in Britain that they were bringing these Irish boys over. There was strong evidence that an IRA extremist had got in amongst them and decided it might be fun to blow up a British aircraft. We heared a search was made and one of these workmen was led away by the police. The whole episode was kept well hushed-up.'

The maintenance effort required on bombers was considerable. Many items of equipment were prone to failure, and improved versions were long in being introduced into production. There were often parts shortages which meant that make-do and mend was the usual policy. This was particularly so with second-line aircraft where wear and tear could try the patience of the gods. Martin Mason recalls a particular example:

'Being detailed for a 24-hour spell of Duty Crew with an engine fitter, our job was attending to visiting aircraft that arrived on our station at Binbrook. One of these was a Wellington which should have given us no bother as our squadron, No. 12, was equipped with this aircraft. Unlike our Wellingtons, which were Mk IIs with liquid-cooled Merlin engines, the visitor had air-cooled radials and try as we might we could not get these to start. The engine fitter was in the cockpit operating the switches while I was on the ground pushing the button on the mobile starter accumulator. After some perplexing minutes wondering why our efforts failed, my colleague noticed "Tired Tim" painted on the side of one of the engine cowlings. On the other side of the aircraft he found the engine called "Weary Willie". Comments which indicated to us that we were not the only fitters who had experienced trouble starting these.'

Fighter Types

KITES

An interest in aircraft or the desire to fly were the paramount motivations for joining the 'Raf'. If you were going to fly you wanted to be a pilot; and if successful in that aim, fighters were the first choice. The appeal of duelling in the sky in a fast interceptor held the imagination of many young men, but achieving this particular ambition was not easy. Only one in five of those gaining their wings were required for fighters and these were men who, during the various phases of training, had measured up to the medical and character assessments deemed necessary for the occupation of a fighter cockpit.

The type that most aspired to fly was the Spitfire, the beauteous and nimble craft which the public believed far superior to enemy contemporaries. In fact, the Spitfire's performance was in some important respects inferior to that of its main antagonists, the Me 109 and Fw 190, and while the later marks gave the required advantages, not until the closing months of hostilities were versions in service capable of better acceleration in a dive than the enemy types. Being able to attain higher altitude than your adversary and out-dive him were the two most advantageous factors in fighter-fighter combat during the Second World War where surprise attack and swift escape were the main tactics for success. For too long British fighter pilots had to fight at a tactical disadvantage. That they more than held their own acknowledges their tenacity and skill. The Spitfire was the chief vehicle of this achievement for it became the most numerous type in RAF squadrons. Antoni Murkowski was a Polish pilot with considerable experience in 'Spits':

'As with most pilots who had experience in different fighters, the Spitfire was a favourite. It was very manoeuvrable and enjoyable to fly. I liked the clipped wing Spit' V best as it didn't have the tendency to fly one wing down like those with the original wing design had at low altitudes. There were no aileron tabs so you had to hold the stick slightly over all the time to keep level flight at low altitudes. I never found this necessary with the clipped wing V. The Spit II could be a bit tricky until you got used to its controls. The undercarriage had to be pumped up by hand and it was awkward because the selector was on the right-hand side of the cockpit and the hand pump lever on the left. To work this you had to change hands after take-off; it was awkward. When you see a formation of Spit IIs taking off they go bobbing up and down, up and down because the pilots are all pumping away like mad. The Spit' IX gave us the extra power we needed; it was a very good kite at high altitude. Our squadron, No. 316 (Polish), got the IX when at Northolt in March 1943. It had the Merlin 63 engine, early models having an automatically engaged supercharger when you reached 18,000 feet. Sometimes, instead of engaging the engine conked. You could re-start but it was not a nice thing to happen. Once the squadron was jumped by Focke-Wulfs near Abbeville and as we were at a disadvantage we went into a slow vertical spiral climb to out-manoeuvre them. I was Tail-End Charlie following Sgt Stuka. We went up through some thin cloud at 16,000 feet and had just emerged when Stuka's engine suddenly conked – the supercharger hadn't cut in. He immediately nosed down and spun. Like a good No. 2, I followed. We came out of the cloud right into the middle of a large formation of Focke-Wulfs. They must have thought the whole Royal Air Force was attacking them for they broke away in all directions. Just like a shoal of little fish, flicking over and diving. There were only the two of us and we didn't even have time to shoot.'

Fred Pawsey was another enthusiast for the lively steed, although with some reservations about attachments it was sometimes required to carry:

'The Spitfire IX, with its slightly longer nose, was to me and everyone else who flew them the most beautiful aircraft ever. Even on the ground it epitomized the grace of a bird. However, when it had a 90-gallon overload tank slung between the undercarriage legs it was transformed into something more like a pregnant duck, making taxi-ing, take-off and flying much more difficult. On one occasion in April 1944 my squadron, No. 253, was detailed for an escort of Marauders and Mitchells bombing Rome marshalling yards. My section was top cover and the round trip from our base at Borgo Bastia, Corsica, required 90-gallon overload tanks – the first occasion we had used them. We were the last section to take off and as we were delayed coolant temperatures were high when the green was fired. I swung straight on to the runway and opened the throttle immediately.

'We had been instructed that with the 90-gallon tank extra forward pressure was required on the stick to get the tail up, but care was necessary as the pressure could cause the tyres to blow out – especially on the metal plank surfacing. As the Spitfire gathered speed I found that much more pressure had to be applied than was anticipated – I kept forward pressure on the stick but the tail wouldn't budge. Concerned, I increased the pressure. All at once the tail rose and kept rising and for one frightening moment I thought the aircraft was going to nose over. Pulling the stick back countered this tendency and the Spit eventually staggered into the air off the end of the strip. Now the nose kept rising and I could not get enough force on the stick with one hand to bring it down. The pressure of two hands prevented the oncoming loop and stall, but to add to my alarm the nose was now going down again and wanted to keep going down. Once more both hands were required to pull the nose up. This see-sawing continued three or four times until I managed to hold a more or less steady climb.

'This fight for control had been an unnerving experience for the prospect of a crash had been very real. As I went into a gentle turn I saw the rest of the section cutting corners to catch up and no doubt wondering what my strange manoeuvres were all about. As we headed for the rendezvous over Monte Cristo I asked my No. 2, Jack Finnie, to have a look at my tail unit as I felt something must be wrong. He assured me he could see nothing adrift so as we were now climbing steadily I decided to continue. Throughout the trip the nagging fear persisted that something was broken or loose and that if I entered combat and had to engage in violent manoeuvres the aircraft tail might come away. However, the escort proceeded without incident and the handling seemed to improve. In any event I was able to make a normal landing on return to base. The Engineering Officer was somewhat sceptical of my report, but the next day he called me over to the flight lines. He had two empty 90-gallon tanks lying on the ground and he asked me to try and lift each of them. The difference in weight was very obvious and it provided the explanation for my two or three minutes of take-off terror. The lighter tank had been fitted to my aircraft and was found to have too few baffles in it to prevent fuel movement. As a result that near half-ton of extra fuel had been slopping backwards and forwards accentuating each change of flight attitude. It could easily have induced a crash with almost certain death for me. The initial fault was in manufacture. Had the ground crew had previous experience of the weight of these tanks they would have queried the weight of the empty tank before fixing it to my aircraft. That was a really close shave.'

The sturdy, able, if less technically advanced, Hurricane predominated in fighter squadrons during the first two years of war and was expected to be replaced by an advanced design from the same manufacturer, Hawker. In the event, the Typhoon proved unsuitable as a fighter to contest the 109s and 190s on their own terms. George Aldridge:

'I was posted to No. 198 Squadron at Ouston while it was working-up on Typhoons in January 1943. At the time there were still a lot of problems with the aircraft which Hawker's didn't seem to know how to solve. To start with, because of the possibility of carbon monoxide fumes penetrating the cockpit from the engine compartment, we used oxygen immediately the engine was started. There were stories going around of what happened to pilots in other squadrons and I didn't have a lot of confidence in the type. Several Typhoons had lost their tails in tight turns and it was found they were coming apart at the fuselage joint where the tail section was attached. They did a bodge strengthening job, riveting patch plates all around this join. The work was carried out by an MU at Henlow. With others from our squadron I was sent to collect a batch that had been doctored and on the way home we put down at Church Fenton to refuel. When I selected "wheels-down" only one leg of the undercarriage lowered. I tried everything to budge the leg that was stuck up, but finally had to retract the other and make a wheels-up landing on the grass. While at Church Fenton, waiting for transport back to home station, a Typhoon from the resident squadron that was being brought back from Henlow also had an undercarriage leg fail to lower and was brought in with one wheel down. There were other incidences of undercarriage failure on modified Typhoons returning from Henlow. An investigation found that a WAAF with a tractor was the cause. The attaching chains she used to tow Typhoons around the Henlow grass were not taking up the strain evenly and often twisting part of the undercarriage assembly.

'The 2,200hp Napier Sabre was also troublesome. There was plenty of power but it dropped off rapidly at higher altitudes. Most of my operational flying was spent skimming over the Channel waves patrolling for hit-and-run raiders and at this height we could overtake most other aircraft we came across. Of course, the Typhoon really came into its own as a ground-attack aircraft after D-Day.'

The Typhoon certainly made good in a ground-attack role, doing sterling work supporting ground forces following the invasion of Normandy. Its successor, the Tempest, had a superior performance to most of its contemporaries at the lower altitudes and left a favourable impression on most pilots. There were two indigenous fighters that never really made the grade. The two-seat Defiant with power turret armament, based on a misguided concept of air fighting; and the Whirlwind, a beautiful single-seat twin-engined interceptor that could offer little tactical advantage over the less costly Spitfire. Nevertheless, those who flew Whirlwinds had a great fondness for the type. John Wray:

'It had a big tear-drop canopy which gave excellent all-round visibility, when others were still peering through bubble-type hoods. It was easy to fly by day and by night despite its higher than average "over the fence" speed [110 mph]. It had the big Fowler flaps which allowed one to land shorter than the Spitfire. It was faster at sea level (where we mainly operated) than any other aircraft apart from the Fw 190. However, this speed was reduced by some 20mph with bombs on. It had two very reliable Peregrine engines which were slightly hotted-up Kestrels, as used in the old Hart variants. This was very helpful in operations where one was likely to receive a hit in the engine doing low-level attacks. In a Spit or a Hurricane you'd have had it, but many times we came home on one engine. It was very manoeuvrable and in the hands of an experienced "Whirly" pilot could see off a 109 or 190 provided it weren't being flown by Galland, Nowotny or someone of that calibre.

'The Whirlwind did have some shortcomings; no fuel crossfeed for example. So, if you lost an engine you couldn't transfer the fuel from its tank to the good engine. It had drum-fed cannon with only 60 rounds per gun. However, the pilot looked straight down the guns, mounted in the nose, which was ideal for ground attack. It had the exactor system of controls for throttle and airscrew. This used oil under pressure as opposed to linkage. Both throttle and airscrew controls had to be primed from time to time. This involved going to full throttle for the power and to fully coarse for the aircrew controls. At altitude the engines were frequently getting out of synchronization and so one was constantly priming them; not always convenient if you had a 190 up your backside! However, we did not have any problems at sea level where we mainly operated. We did, however, always prime for landing in case we had to go around again, in which case one would want the engines to pick up together.

'Because there were only two squadrons, Nos. 137 and 263, few people had the chance to fly Whirlwinds. Pilots tended to go from one squadron to the other! On promotion to Flight Commander, for example. Moreover, the pilots tended to stay, unless they weren't good enough. So we had a lot of experienced Whirlwind pilots. Therefore pilot error accidents were rare. I think it is fair to say that all who flew the aeroplane for any length of time came to regard it with affection. Those of us who operated fairly extensively with it can think of occasions when, if we had been in another fighter-bomber, we would not have got back. One can remember those occasions leaving the French coast, bombs gone, throttles hard against the instrument panel, the 109s gradually dropping back. Or on a moonlight night low-level over France or Belgium, happily listening to the busy buzz of the two Peregrines and feeling much safer as a result. As one of our Canadian pilots said, "She was a great little bird".'

Of the American-designed and built fighters acquired by Britain, only one, the Mustang, was considered worthy of extensive employment in Europe. The version fitted with a US-built Merlin engine became one of the most successful fighters of the war, having all-round versatility and possessing those two essential capabilities, high-altitude performance and high diving speed. The Mustang's unique attribute for a single-engine, single-seat fighter was inbuilt fuel capacity which gave a 400-mile radius of action and made it ideal for escort duties. The early Mustangs received by the RAF had low-altitude rated Allison engines and these aircraft served in a fighter/reconnaissance role. They proved redoubtable in a war where the average life of a fighter plane was about six weeks. Rex Croger:

'Funnily enough, the first thing that I recall about the Mustang is its cigarette-lighter. I was astonished when I first saw this, but I'm told most of the early aircraft supplied to the RAF by America had this fixture. The cockpit was roomy and comfortable, far more so than contemporary British fighters. A pilot's opinion of an aircraft type must, to a large extent, be based on a comparison with other similar types he has flown. In my case the only other experience of fighters was with Hurricanes and late marks of Spitfire. Both these British types, being lighter, left one with an impression of being more manoeuvrable than the Mustang. All the same, I never found the Mustang lacking in this respect. It was fast, had no real vices that I recall, and could be flown rock-steady for photographic work. There was a speed restriction of 505mph when diving as the acceleration was surprising and pilots were warned that they could quickly get into difficulties if exceeding that figure. The Allison engine was smooth and responsive, even if it lacked power at high altitudes. This was not important in our job which, when I joined the squadron, was spotting targets for naval guns in Channel coast German strongholds, and looking for V-2 sites in Holland, all at altitudes below 5,000 feet – the ideal height to get yourself shot at by light Flak. Although I did not know it at the time, the Mustang assigned to me for the majority of my sorties, XC:Y, serial number AG361, was the 17th Mustang off the production line in 1941 and had already seen three years of service when I became its pilot. That was an exceptionally long operational life for a wartime aircraft. I flew it on the last operation undertaken by our 26 Squadron; on 12 May 1945, to check that the German gunners in Jersey had dismantled their artillery guns as ordered.'

The Few

The Battle of Britain dominates any review of Royal Air Force fighter action. This crucial victory has captured the imagination of succeeding generations of Britons. It was won by a narrow margin, and the grim reality of that time is captured here by accounts of men on the ground. William Drinkell:

'On Tuesday 12 August 1940, the ground staff of No. 266 Squadron moved south from Wittering to Eastchurch to support our Spitfires. The next morning I was up bright and early. While happily making my way to the ablutions from our wooden hut with other members of the maintenance crew, an Irish aircrafthand remarked, "See all them Ansons up there." I looked and started to run; my aircraft recognition being more accurate – they were Dorniers. Small bombs could be seen coming down so we threw ourselves on the ground as these burst quite near. Fortunately the surface was so soft the bombs penetrated deeply before exploding and there was little shrapnel. Our squadron's hangar was set on fire, but all aircraft were pushed out and only one was damaged. Other units were not so lucky, with 16 airmen killed and 48 injured and five Blenheims written off by No. 53 Squadron. The whole airfield was devastated and we were forced to move to Hornchurch next day. No. 266 was in the thick of the air fighting during the next week and we worked day and night to keep the Spitfires serviceable. Although an engine fitter, I found myself doing everything: riveting, changing wheels, harmonizing guns and many tasks I had not been trained to handle. We didn't have to be told the seriousness of the situation and Spitfires were repaired, modified and serviced one after another. The turnround of aircraft was such that we often only had time to chalk the squadron identification letters "UO" on the fuselage sides before replacements were sent into battle. On the 21st we were withdrawn to Wittering. In ten days' fighting half the squadron's pilots had become casualties, eight Spitfires had been destroyed and a dozen damaged.'

Alfred Pyner:

'In June 1940 I was sent to the small grass airfield at West Malling, formerly Maidstone Airport. It was occupied by Lysanders of No. 26 Squadron recently back from France. After a few days in general stores I was put in charge of fuel, about 50,000 gallons of aviation petrol in an underground store tank, as well as that for motor transport. Visiting aircraft were serviced with a tractor and towed bowser operated by a small group of personnel who also did duty as ground gunners. But I often had to pitch in and help them. At first things were all very peaceful, but early in August we received our first bombing which caused a few casualties and made a mess of a couple of Lysanders. From then on we had a number of bombing attacks. We began to get used to a lot of activity overhead; vapour trails, smoking aircraft and occasionally the nastiest noise of all – which seemed to fill the sky – an aircraft coming down vertically out of control. On the afternoon of 15 September I was on my way back from the fuel store when suddenly a whole crowd of aircraft came over the field, seemingly from all directions, some of them firing and in the middle was a Heinkel He 111. With the Intelligence Officer, who was coming from the other direction, I ducked down. When the row stopped we looked up to see the Heinkel on the ground no more than 50 yards away. We reached the plane as ambulances came up. One of the Germans climbed out and the ambulance people removed four more, one dead. I put out a small fire under an engine and saw that several of the fighters engaged in the fight were coming in to land. The German who had climbed out of the Heinkel was complaining bitterly in English to the Intelligence Officer about our fighters still shooting at him when he had his wheels down. Two RAF fighter pilots were arguing over who shot the Heinkel down, while six or seven Hurricanes and Spitfires stood in a cluster, a perfect target for an enemy plane that might make a strafing run. Luckily none did. I remember thinking: this is chaos, not an air force engaged in modern warfare.'

Hugh Berry of No. 249 Squadron:

'Our squadron was on a "recce". It was a beautiful sunny October afternoon in 1940 when, without warning, a crowd of Me 109s swept over North Weald dropping high-explosive bombs. I was outside the cookhouse at this time and dived for the only bit of cover that I could see nearby – a trestle-table! As one bomb struck a few yards away, I vividly remember screaming as débris rained down on top of the table. This particular bomb caught a hut, half of which was the orderly room and the other half consisted of toilets. One poor airman was actually on the throne at the time and a large piece of bomb splinter sliced him almost in half. While I was still in position under the table, Hurricanes of No. 257 Squadron were taking off to intercept. One had barely got off the deck when a bomb caught him and he pancaked only yards from me. It was a blazing wreck with ammunition going off in all directions. The Station Fire Crew eventually foamed it out and when Jerry had departed I decided to go over and have a look at what remained of the aircraft. In the cockpit, hunched over the controls, was what looked like a hunk of charred wood in the shape of a human being . . . the only relief in colour was a yellowish excretion oozing from the skull remains of that young pilot. This ghastly sight – my first corpse – made the realities of war very clear to me that day.'

THE PRIDE AND THE PITCH

Horrific sights were inevitable on the battlefield or as a result of accidents. The unexpectedly gruesome embedded itself in memory. Peter Hearne:

'In August 1944 I was at Boulmer, Northumberland, giving advanced trainee pilots the benefit of my operational experience. One day I was walking near the control tower with the station commander, Squadron Leader Stonham, when a Spitfire made a shallow dive at the runway trying, it seemed, to land. The pilot opened the throttle, retracted the undercarriage and flaps and went round again. His second attempt was also abortive and Stonham, sensing an emergency, dashed up to the control tower and established communication with the pilot. The barely coherent and agitated pilot was calmed sufficiently by the authoritative voice of the Squadron Leader who, with consummate skill, talked him down safely to a safe landing.

'The pilot taxied the Spitfire round the perimeter track and parked close to Flying Control. A crowd of curious airmen gathered round as Stonham came out of the tower and strode purposefully towards the aircraft. His annoyance that a fully trained pilot should act in this manner could be contained no longer. He mounted the wing of the Spitfire and launched into a verbal inquisition of the pilot, who was still in the cockpit. He had hardly commenced his tirade when there was a sudden stillness – an eerie silence which seemed to transmit itself to all around the aircraft. Even Stonham paused to see what was the matter. All eyes had focused on a large hole in the leading edge of the port wing, about half way down its length around which were splashes of blood. One airman moved forward, looked into the hole, stretched an arm right into the wing and pulled out a human head. The Squadron Leader's reaction was immediate and compassionate. As gently as he could he helped the pilot out of his cockpit and, with his arm around him, walked quietly to the mess. It transpired that the pilot had been authorized to perform some army co-operation, carrying out dummy low-flying attacks on soldiers training nearby. The enthusiasm of a soldier on spotting duty had taken him to the topmost spindle of a tree and this tree had been in the line of flight of an ill-judged low pass by the Spitfire.'

Attrition in fighter squadrons varied considerably, generally being highest in units engaged in ground attack where light Flak and small-arms fire had to be faced. While overall casualties were but a tenth of those suffered in bombers, it was nearer one to two when only pilots are taken into consideration. The nature of most fighter operations was such that the mood of aircrew was more eager, a 'let's go and get 'em' attitude pervaded many units. This is not to suggest that the average fighter pilot was fearless or less concerned with fate. Rather the mood of concealed apprehension engendered among bomber aircrew through having to 'sit there and take it' was not found in a fighter squadron. For the average fighter pilot fear came only in a moment of crisis and with the pace of action might not even be recognized. John Wray:

'We were the first squadron to become operational on the Hurricane IV, carrying eight 3-inch rockets with 60lb explosive heads or, as an alternative armament, two 40mm guns. We opted for the rockets as our principal armament because they were so devastating. However, we were not allowed to take the rockets overland into enemy territory because the Air Ministry wanted to keep them as a surprise for the Invasion when it came, so we were confined to attacking only shipping targets. This, of course, meant that we could not carry out "Rhubarbs", something we had enjoyed a great deal in our beloved Whirlwinds. So we kept six aircraft armed with the 40mm cannon, just for "Rhubarbs". These weapons were very accurate when correctly harmonized, and really sorted out trains. Whereas the 20mm and .303 would cause steam to rise from the punctured boiler of the engine, the 40mm blew the boiler right off.

'Four of us set off on a "Rhubarb" in an area just behind Le Touquet. The Hurricane IV had no defensive armament, the two remaining Brownings being used to "keep heads down" when attacking ground targets with our primary weapons, to which the gunsight was harmonized. Moreover, with all the weight we now carried, the poor old Hurricane, never the quickest climber, had a pretty poor rate of climb. On the instrument panel was the boost override toggle, a red knob that could be pulled out an inch or so which gave emergency boost if required. However, if you used it for more than about two minutes the engine was liable to blow up. The red toggle had a piece of wire which extended through the instrument panel to the boost control on the engine.

'We had just attacked a train when the air was suddenly full of Fw 190s. One would like to say there were a hundred, that is what it seemed, but there was probably only a squadron. We had a big turning match, the Hurricane still retaining its amazing manoeuvrability, and then one by one we managed to make cloud cover. We landed back at base individually, but more or less at the same time. As we walked in I said, "That was a dicey do, by God." A Canadian said, "I wasn't the least bit worried, I didn't see any problem." I noticed he was clutching something in his hand and asked what he was concealing. Unknown to himself, he was clutching the red toggle of the boost override, with a couple of feet of wire attached. He had pulled it right out of the instrument panel!'

Cool nerve and clear thinking in a dangerous situation enhanced survival for the fighter pilot – characteristics common to the majority of those who survived three or four years of combat flying. Such attributes are discernible in this account from Peter Hearne, a No. 65 Squadron pilot, of extracting himself from a 'spot of bother' on 8 April 1943:

'We were above cloud and in the vicinity of Brest when three Fw 190s bounced us going straight through the squadron and carrying on down through the cloud. No one was hit. We were flying Spitfire Vs, each with a 30-gallon slipper under the belly. My immediate reaction to the attack was to jettison my slipper tank and follow the Fws down. Visibility was misty below the cloud and there was difficulty in adjusting to the low light conditions after the brightness above. I looked round for my No. 2 who should have followed me, but I was on my own. Two Fw 190s were seen heading towards the French coast and I gave the rear aircraft a long steady burst at 30 degrees deflection. There appeared to be some strikes, but I knew I was somewhat out of range. Worse still, all my 20mm cannon rounds were exhausted, leaving only the .303s. About five minutes after I had turned for home, flying low, I noticed I was being chased by two Focke-Wulfs in line abreast. I opened the throttle to the gate but they still gained on me. Waiting until they were just outside effective firing range, I turned steeply to port, then came back on to my course for home. This simple manoeuvre, executed at the right moment, outwitted both aircraft and I knew then that I was not dealing with very experienced pilots. However, once again they were behind, catching me up, but this time they were in long line astern. The second man was too far behind and instead of being in position to pick me off as I turned sharply to port, he found himself head-on with me at 300 feet above the sea. Overland I would have accepted a head-on attack, but with no No. 2 to report my position if an unlucky hit put me into the sea, I quickly decided my tactics. With 300 feet to spare I had no qualms in flipping the Spitfire on to its back, righting it again as I passed underneath, to climb steeply immediately and confront the Fw wherever I found him. Possibly bemused by my manoeuvre and expecting to find me in the sea, he had tamely pulled up straight ahead and I was now behind him in perfect position to open fire. Alas, when I pressed the firing button the guns fell silent after only a few rounds. I was mortified; but had been taught an important lesson – not to waste ammunition firing out of range. I broke away and turned once more for home. After a while I knew I was no longer being followed so could relax somewhat, looking around the cockpit, checking my fuel, air speed, etc. I did not think the aircraft was travelling fast enough bearing in mind my throttle setting. I reached down for my slipper tank release toggle and pulled it again. The Spitfire seemed to leap forward and I knew then the reason those Fw 190s caught me so easily.'

The night fighter squadrons were mostly equipped with twin-engined aircraft; at first the Blenheim, then American Havocs, followed by the versatile Beaufighter and the even better Mosquito. A two-man crew was the norm, the companion being the radar operator who gazed at a cathode-ray tube screen for 'blips' and directed the pilot towards the quarry. Mostly the quarry was an enemy bomber unless sent on offensive operations to hunt Luftwaffe night fighters over enemy-held territory. Even in enemy airspace this sparring in the dark came to depend largely on electronic aids, as indicated in the account of an interception made by George Irving of No. 125 Squadron:

'When operating from Bradwell Bay we were able to use a forward ground control station near Arnhem. This unit was actually in a specially fitted-out glider which had taken part in the recent airborne landings but had fortunately landed on the Allied-held side of the Rhine. We were notified by Bomber Command of the time and place of bombing missions and would go out on the edge of the bomber stream to protect it from the attacks of German night fighters. On the night of 14 October 1944, more than a thousand bombers went to Duisburg and on the way out I made contact on several bogies which, on closer inspection, turned out to be bombers straying slightly off course. Coming into the range of the forward "glider control", called Milkway, they directed me towards a bogie which was following a Lancaster. This was probably a German night fighter under their ground control because as I closed in he suddenly dived away from the Lancaster, no doubt having been warned by his GC that he was being followed. Almost at once George found another contact at about 15,000 feet and on closing in I identified it as a German by the markings on its fuselage. But I could not identify the type. It was a twin-engine aircraft with tailplane dihedral, the engine nacelles extended behind the wings and it rather resembled a Dornier 217. I dropped back and opened fire from about 150 yards and the starboard engine exploded. My second burst hit the cockpit and wing tanks. The aircraft spiralled into a slow dive to starboard in flames while I followed it down and saw it explode on the ground.

'After watching our bombers reduce Duisburg to a huge bonfire, I turned east. George informed me he had picked up a signal on his rear-seeking radar and almost at once Milkway informed me we were being followed by a bogie, probably a German night fighter. I commenced a slow dive and orbited to port on to a reciprocal course, hoping to get a contact on the follower. Milkway then informed me that it had dived rapidly away towards Münster. Back at base, on reporting in to complete my combat report, our Intelligence Officer was unable to identify the aircraft that I had shot down. Later it was found to be a Heinkel 219, a new type recently brought into use as a night fighter. It carried a crew of three and was equipped with their latest radar and infra-red equipment designed to home on aircraft exhaust emissions. I was informed that this was the first sighting and destruction of an He 219.'

In the summer of 1944 fighter squadrons in England turned their guns on a new type of hostile invader. 'Tony' Murkowski of No. 316 (Polish) Squadron:

'We were at Coltishall on Mustangs. One evening a big team arrived from Rolls-Royce with special fuel, special oil and bits and pieces to put on our engines to give us more boost. They warn that if you run at full power for more than ten minutes the engine will be ruined and have to be changed. The fuel, of purple colour, blistered your skin if you got it on your hands. All this is to let us catch the flying-bombs that had just started to come over. First thing next morning six of us are sent to West Malling and take it in turn to be at readiness. It was one of those hot and humid days and a little bit foggy. There were no flying-bombs reported and West Malling is being inspected by a party of high-ups. When I returned from my lunch my flight commander said I was to take over Red Section on readiness so he and the others who hadn't eaten could go. I put my parachute on the wing and got myself a chair and was going to sit down near my aircraft and amuse myself by playing spit in the ring with pips and watching the cavalcade of air force VIPs. I had only just sat down when the telephone rang in the Readiness Hut. I thought it is the officers' mess wanting to know when the pilots I and my No. 2 had relieved were coming to lunch. It wasn't that, but "Red Section, Scramble!" When we got airborne, control advised: "Red Leader, Witchcraft 5 miles east of Hastings." Witchcraft was the code-name for flying-bombs at that time. I was just coming up to the coast when suddenly there was a puff of white smoke ahead, a flare fired by the Royal Observer Corps, a signal to indicate where the flying-bomb was crossing the coast. Looking down I saw it flying just below me. Well, it was a piece of cake. I opened the throttle, turned into a shallow dive to gain more speed and quickly took an accurate sighting. It hardly seemed that I had touched the firing trigger before the flying bomb exploded. The force lifted the Mustang about a thousand feet – just as if someone had given me a big kick in the arse. I heard my No. 2 say "Cor!" I had hardly time to recover from the surprise when Control came over the radio, "Good show Red Leader. You may return now to base and pancake." I say, "How do you know? I didn't tell you I shot down that thing." It was the first flying-bomb shot down by a Mustang.'

Officially frowned upon because of the general policy to encourage teamwork and not the individual, the distinction of being an 'ace' (shooting down five or more enemy aircraft) was well publicized by the contemporary Press. Those with large 'bags' were individuals with courage, skill and more than a little of what passed as luck. There were, inevitably, outstanding fighter aces for whom luck ran out and who left an indelible impression on the memories of compatriots, like the pilot John Wray recalls:

'He was a loner, much older than we his contemporaries, and much more experienced as he had been a commercial pilot before the war, flying newspapers to Paris at one time, often in bad weather. He was a devotee of Lawrence of Arabia and had his own personal reasons for hating the Germans. Few knew him well, this rather older Pilot Officer. His squadron of Defiants also had four Hurricanes which had been given to them to operate with the Turbinlite Flight. However, this particular form of night fighting had not been too successful and so the squadron commander flew one of the Hurricanes, the flight commanders the other two, and he flew the fourth. They were Hurricane IICs with four 20mm cannon. These Defiants had no radar aids, and therefore were not much use as night fighters. Although the Hurricane was also without radar it gave the pilot a rather better chance, particularly on Fighter Nights. The Pilot Officer was a law unto himself. He would take off at night, sometimes in quite nasty weather, and once airborne would clear himself with Sector Operations before switching off his R/T and disappearing into the night. Mind you, he would switch on his R/T from time to time to pick up useful information, but he did not want all the other chatter. He was a good shot and often attacked his target from the side, which was unusual in night fighting at that time. He said that one of his greatest aids was the British anti-aircraft fire. "They can't hit anything," he would say, "but their tracking is superb. When I follow a line of AA bursts I know that there is a Hun out in front."

'He would often wander about the country, using all his R/T frequencies to get information. He would land at any airfield when he was short of fuel then take off again and resume his wanderings. At times he shot down more than one aircraft in a night. In the morning he would return to base. He destroyed 14½ aircraft at night, without any onboard aids other than his R/T. All his victims crashed on land and were confirmed, except one that crashed into the Humber, missing a fishing boat by feet, so they confirmed that one. He often went out to inspect the crashed aircraft and on one occasion as he approached he had to dive for cover because of a fusillade of bullets came at him, fired from a pistol by the dying pilot. His flying clothing and equipment was German, taken from his victims. He claimed, with some justification, that it was much lighter and less cumbersome. As a Pilot Officer he was awarded the DSO, DFC and Bar, but those who knew him always feared that if he was posted to where he could operate in Continental air space he might stick his neck out too far in his keeness to get at the enemy. His half victory was awarded to him when he shot down a Ju 88 over Liverpool. In the morning, after a Defiant from the local squadron had also claimed an 88, both .303 and 20mm holes were found in the aircraft, so a half was awarded to each. He was promoted to Acting Flight Lieutenant and posted to a night intruder Hurricane squadron on the south coast. He failed to return from his first sortie. Today, when the names of those who distinguished themselves in the last war are mentioned, his is not one of them. Yet he was unique, and displayed a determination and skill that, probably, has rarely been surpassed.'

Play and Style

If RAF operational aircrew had a reputation for extreme behaviour when at play, it seems the most exuberant of all were fighter pilots. Their escapades were legion. Senior officers with appreciation of conventional military conduct attempted to bring order to these situations but appear to have fought a losing battle – and some even succumbed to the merriment, as Peter Hearne observed:

'In October 1942 my squadron, No. 65, moved up to Drem, near Edinburgh. Shortly after arriving we lost a flight commander in an accident. His replacement was a young officer wearing a DFM, which meant we would be led by an experienced operational pilot. The squadron celebrated the occasion with a party in the mess, a prestigious peacetime edifice, built to the highest specification. The party developed as I was to see such functions develop many times during the war. Always there were a few who never knew where to set a limit. Well after most people had retired for the night the festivities continued.

One chap took off his shoes and socks, placed his feet in the dead embers in the fireplace and, by using tables and chairs, was able to leave the imprint of his soles on the very high ceiling of the mess. He then autographed his masterpiece. Others followed suit. The next morning the station commander, Wing Commander Sir Archibald Hope, walked into the mess and, alerted by the disruption still in evidence, his gaze eventually settled on the smears on the ceiling. Apparently he had not hitherto encountered such desecration and was beside himself with rage. Summoning the Orderly Officer of the day to his presence, Sir Archibald ordered a detailed examination of the signatures to establish the identities of the offenders. Unhappily, the only legible signature was that of the newly appointed flight commander. Such behaviour was unheard of among officers in those parts and had to be dealt with in no uncertain terms. The only culprit identified received an immediate posting.

'Two years later I was commanding No. 19 Squadron at Peterhead and who should be the station commander but none other than Sir Archibald Hope. A big party was laid on to mark the end of hostilities and as inhibitions vanished all sorts of madness reigned. Much energy was expended in a trick called the Dooley Dive, named for its originator. This involved climbing on to the mantelpiece and jumping head-first through a burning newspaper held by assistants, to land deftly on an upturned armchair which would right itself through the momentum of the impact, leaving the performer standing on his feet. This was old hat and the merrymakers sought something special to mark the occasion. Suddenly my No. 2 in the air, Jack May, dropped his trousers and his underpants and then proceeded to rub his bare backside in the fireplace ash. The onlookers knew what assistance was required and five or six of us lifted Jack, bottom high, until he left a discernible imprint on the low ceiling of the prefabricated building that served us as a mess. Jack then called out for a pencil. He was a big boy and the strain was telling on us, but I reached out for a pencil offered by one of the other bodies heaving-to and handed it up to Jack. Jack duly scrawled 'Jack's Bum' and handed the pencil back to its owner – Wing Commander Sir Archibald Hope!'

Communal sing-songs and recitations were a common feature of RAF mess and crew room life and more than one impartial observer has opined that the subject matter was decidedly more crude in the realm of Fighter Command. Such ribaldry was often triggered as a response to a commonplace act, for example, if somebody started messing about with the fire:

'If it's warmth that you desire,
Poke your wife and not the fire.
If you lead a single life,
Poke another fellow's wife.
Poke his wife or poke your own,
BUT LEAVE THE BLOODY FIRE ALONE!'

And this was mild in comparison with many ditties which dwelled excessively on acts of excreting and fornicating. However, propriety was exercised in many circumstances; the like was never uttered if a woman were present. Bawdy ballads helped to beat boredom in the air too. Alan Drake:

'During the summer of 1940 our squadron, No. 29, was based at Wittering, Lincolnshire, and flew regular patrols out over the North Sea in Blenheim IFs. These trips were invariably uneventful and to lessen the boredom the two-man crew would frequently engage in the singing of ribald songs over the intercom. Unfortunately, on one occasion my pilot, Bill Campbell, had forgotten to switch the radio transmitter set from "Transmit". As a consequence several RAF stations in Lincolnshire were treated to our duet and no doubt many a WAAF was caused to blush. Needless to say we suffered upon our return to base.'

Unnecessary use of radio transmissions was important as enemy listening-stations could quickly fix the broadcaster's position. On the other hand, radio communication was a vital part of successful fighter operations through the passing of tactical demands and warnings of enemy presence. Towards the end R/T discipline was more lax, particularly on very long-range escort missions undertaken by Mustangs in the final months of the conflict. Bill Fleming, a No. 126 Squadron pilot, recalls some of this radio chat heard nearly 600 miles from home station:

'The longest mission I flew was to Swinemünde, a Baltic port north-east of Berlin, where the pocket battleship *Lützow* was berthed. Our Mustangs escorted eighteen Lancasters of No. 617 Squadron which, despite murderous Flak that downed one, sank the ship. We were operating not far from the Russian front and on nearing the target we picked up a ground radio station in our earphones. A female controller was speaking in what I at first presumed was the German language. However, pilots in the Polish Mustang Wing, who were operating as part of the escort, identified it as Russian and excitedly began to curse and swear in English and Polish over their radios. When a male voice replaced the female one the British response was, "Put the girl back on again." The next day the British Press reported: "Yesterday the RAF and Russians exchanged greetings over the air." Some greetings!'

The assertive nature of the fighter pilot led to a desire to establish visual identity of his profession. The squashed hat, sweater protruding below tunic, silk scarf and – of course – battledress jacket top button undone, were all part of fighter pilot display, a mark of the fraternity. To relieve a fighter pilot of his scarf – a crucial part of flying togs if a chafed neck was to be avoided – became a trophy of some distinction sought by more adventurous young women. This attraction even spread to the Continent, as Philip Knowles discovered in the course of an amusing adventure:

'On 9 April 1945 my squadron, No. 126, was part of the Mustang escort for Lancasters attacking targets in Hamburg. On the way out my engine started to fail over the Zuider Zee, so I broke off and headed for Maldeghem, near Ghent. Although running very intermittently, I was able to maintain a medium height, largely by use of the fuel priming pump. I was getting homings from Maldeghem, but could see little through the 9/10ths cloud layer at 2,000 feet, which I was reluctant to go below. When I thought I had reached Maldeghem I let down through the cloud, to find I had just overshot the airfield. On turning back, the engine stopped completely, so I asked to come in directly. As I approached on a deadstick landing I saw that the airfield, including the runway, was covered with sheep, and realized it was not Maldeghem but Ursel which, we had been warned, was now closed. However, there was no alternative and I pressed on with a wheels-down landing. Full flap, though, seemed rather ineffective and I had difficulty in slipping off surplus height. It was only after getting down – and missing the sheep – that I found an unfamiliar device limiting the movement of the flaps, which had been left in place by the previous user.

'Ursel had a single RAF officer looking after it and he was having a terrible time trying to stop everything being stolen by the local population. Already several unserviceable aircraft on the field had had their tyres cut open and the inner tubes taken, for shoe repairs, I was told. On my arrival he was doing some painting on the front of his office. When he got back, the paint and brush had gone. While he was looking around for that they took his chair as well. When waiting for transport from Maldeghem, the local Police Chief came and I was invited to go with them on a tour of all the known local thieves' premises, but nothing was found.

'The Maldeghem ground crew reckoned the Mustang needed a new engine so I returned with them by road, stopping on the way in Eekloo for refreshment. Here the girl behind the bar offered her favours in exchange for my flying-scarf, to which she had taken a fancy. It seemed a very reasonable proposition, had it not been for the waiting ground crew. After a fairly hectic night at Maldeghem, where all the drinks were free as the mess was closing, I managed to hitch a ride back to England on a Dakota. The subsequent train journey and night in London were interesting, with no money, cap, tie (all left at Bentwaters before the flight) and carrying a parachute.'

Kipper Fleet and Pickfords

WITH COASTAL

Although usually overshadowed by the actions of fighter and bomber men, the war of those whose task was defensive or offensive flight over the sea was one of great achievement. From its inception Coastal Command was given the roles of friendly shipping protection and enemy shipping harassment. As this involved a good deal of general reconnaissance, the Command was also handed photographic surveillance and meteorological flights. However, the major commitment was protecting convoys and seeking enemy submarines, work for which it was long lacking adequate numbers of aircraft with suitable endurance. Even though wanting in strength and equipment for four years, RAF coastal squadrons were ultimately credited with the destruction of more than 200 U-boats, amounting to more than two-thirds of all German and Italian submarines destroyed at sea by Allied aircraft. Additionally some 150 U-boats were damaged by Coastal Command action and many more caused to abandon their stalking of convoys because of the presence of aircraft. This contribution to victory in the so-called Battle of the Atlantic has been judged the decisive element.

Command units also sunk a considerable tonnage of enemy shipping through torpedo, rocket and bomb attack, operations where most of its own losses were suffered. For the majority of men engaged in ocean patrol, tedium was the common factor. Scanning mile after mile of ocean surface for hour after hour and sortie after sortie. Many completed a tour of 300 hours without once seeing a U-boat. The ocean-searching aircrews were considered to be 'a fairly steady lot', less given to the wild excesses of bomber and fighter types, but proud of their profession. One well-known mark of distinction of being a member of the Kipper Fleet – as Coastal Command was cheekily known in other Air Force circles – is cited by Tom Minta:

'In Coastal Command it was not unusual for flying officers to let their cap badges become tarnished. The greener the better; this being a sign of much low flying through sea spray and the hallmark of an old Atlantic hand. Almost like that old rugby chant, "Go low, boy! Go low!" '

At the outbreak of war the Command had around 400 operational aircraft of which three-quarters were Avro Ansons, a type with a 260-mile radius of action around the British Isles through being limited to a flight of four hours' duration. The only other worthy aircraft were a couple of dozen Lockheed Hudsons and a similar number of Sunderland flying-boats. The Hudson was an adaptation of an

American light passenger aircraft, but had a maximum endurance of six hours. The long-distance ranging rested with the Sunderlands which could keep aloft for 12-14 hours. This large flying-boat served Coastal Command throughout the war, although only in the closing stages were sufficient available to satisfy demand. It was a stalwart aircraft, beloved by all who flew it. James Kernahan:

'The Sunderland was probably the most spacious of all RAF operational aircraft; plenty of room to move around on the long 10 to 12 hours' flights we made on anti-sub or convoy patrols. There were two pilots, a navigator, flight engineer and assistant and also a wireless operator and assistant, the mechanics and WOs doubling as gunners. We would spend two hours in a turret and have four hours off. When you were relieved you'd go into the bomb bay where there were bunks. Even though the two engines were roaring away each side, it was only a matter of a few minutes before you were asleep; the noise was no obstacle. The Sunderland had a nice galley at the rear and we ate well, especially while flying out of West Africa when we had steaks, oranges, bananas, sweets and all those things that were never seen by the general public in the UK. The worst thing was the boredom, continually searching the ocean with your eyes until you'd lose the horizon as sea and sky became one. Even so, there was no chance of becoming disorientated as the turret had to be rotated to and fro all the time, the two bolted doors behind your back rattling away every time you turned them into the slipstream. To try and overcome the boredom I'd have a crafty smoke – which one was not supposed to do in the turret – or scribble notes with my name and address on bits of paper, forcing them out of the rear turret. Watching them flutter away I probably hoped some girl would find them and write me. None ever did!'

Despite the opportunity to catch some rest during patrol, these long flights induced weariness in all crew members. Tedium and incessant noise were paramount in this, and by the time the sortie was completed individuals were not as alert as they should have been, as evidenced in the mishap which befell Steve Challen of No. 201 Squadron:

'After a 14-hour, 15-minute patrol in our Sunderland P9606, ZM:R, we finished very tired at Invergordon. As a newcomer to the crew I had been trying to make myself useful. "Mucking in," I had been doing the odd chore about the boat. On this occasion I went forward with Biggs who usually did the mooring up to the buoy. Winding back the front turret Biggs positioned the bollards and hung the short, shaped ladder over the port side. The system used by this crew was for the pilot to approach the buoy, keeping it on his port, as slowly as possible with inner engines shut down. When the aircraft nudged the buoy Biggs would go over the side on to the ladder; hanging on with the right hand he would push a sliprope through the wire rope vertical loop on top of the buoy. The assistant would then lean over the bow to take the loose end and make a hitch on the bollards. Not an "Advised Procedure" method, especially when the guy on the ladder falls into the water because he had not fixed the ladder securely! Biggs had the foresight to have a safety rope attached to the ladder with which I pulled until I could grab the top of the ladder. Biggs then climbed the ladder and me, taking a grip of my clothes, arms, anything; up and over me into the aircraft. Back in the "saloon" he stood shivering, much to the amusement of the lads. The pilot, F/O Fleming, had his head out of the side window wondering what was going on as it was difficult to keep the aircraft nudged up to the buoy with the tide running out of the Firth. That helpful fellow, myself, fastened the ladder, quickly down, passed the sliprope through the loop, caught the loose end, up the ladder and took a hitch around the bollards, then used the boat-hook to snag the mooring pendant attached to the buoy, dropping the grommet over a bollard. Thumbs-up to Fleming and he shut down the outer engines. The rest of the mooring up could wait until the "swimmer" returned to the job.

'All this panic seemed to have taken a long time but it had actually been a few minutes. I looked at my watch. . . . No watch! Ah yes, Biggs had grabbed my wrist on his way up and over me; thank you very much Mr. Biggs. A frantic search below my feet; no sign of it. I was shattered at the loss. My aunt had presented the self-wind, waterproof, Rolex Oyster to me on my 20th birthday. I never revealed the loss to her, my feelings were that mixed. Since then I've often pondered the thought that the watch is still ticking away at the bottom of the Cromarty Firth, wound up by the action of the tide. What an advertisement for Rolex if it were found still showing the correct time!'

After innumerable trips when there was nothing important to report, contact with a U-boat was an exciting event. Too often the submarine crew were on look-out and submerged before an effective attack could be made. James Kernahan of No. 228 Squadron had reason to remember one such incident:

'Our Sunderland, M for Mother, left Pembroke Dock in the early evening of 6 July 1943 for a 12-hour anti-submarine patrol over the Bay of Biscay. It was uneventful until the sun started to brighten the sky in the east. I saw something on the sea ahead and excitedly told our Skipper, Flt Lt Gordon Lancaster, I could see a submarine. Before we could get within effective range the sub had disappeared but the Skipper decided he would conduct a square search of the area. As we were on the last leg I again caught sight of the submarine on the surface. The skipper called out "Tally Ho!" and we charged in. Sitting in the front turret I opened up with the single Vickers .303 and saw the bullets curving into the conning tower. This fire was only intended to dissuade the crew from getting to their anti-aircraft guns. While I was firing, Flt Lt Lancaster had run the bombs out on their trollies and released them, but the rear-turret gunner reported only splashes and no detonations. Disappointed, we finished our patrol and flew back to Wales. We were greeted by the Intelligence Officer who produced a manual of submarines and asked me to identify the type. I selected what I thought was similar but he said: "No, you're wrong, you attacked a British one like this," and pointed to another picture. This was a demoralizing blow but happily the Navy lads had not taken any harm through either they or us being in the wrong place at the wrong time. Had we been able to find out who the crew were, it was our intention to stand them a dinner. Sadly, Gordon Lancaster was killed in a crash in France the following year while flying Air Chief Marshal Leigh-Mallory out to the Far East, but I've always wanted to fulfil the promise to make amends.'

Accurate identification of a submarine from an aircraft was not easy, even in good conditions. Roy Larkins gives another example:

'What a Heath Robinson Outfit this is, I thought – but it works! I was a Sergeant Pilot at 61 Air School, based at George in South Africa, and on operational training to qualify as a General Reconnaissance Pilot with Coastal Command. The Station was staffed by RAF personnel at night and by South African Blue Army Air Force people during the daytime. The South African Red Army operated anywhere in the world, but their Blue Army only operated from their homes between 9am and 5.30pm, Mondays to Fridays inclusive. Thus, we had a South African pilot during the day and an RAF pilot during the night. Goodness knows what would have happened if we had been scrambled at 8am. Presumably the war would have had to wait until 9 am!

'We had about twenty Avro Ansons, each with a pilot, a pilot/navigator and a wireless operator. Our job was to "protect" the convoys as they passed between Cape Town and Durban and to discourage all enemy craft. The aircraft were not armed in any way, unless you counted the Very pistols. We would go out, to identify passing ships and to photograph neutrals and doubtfuls.

'On my very first trip I learned not to get too close to a convoy because after weeks at sea the sailors tended to fire first and to consult their identification signal manuals later. At least it proved that I was on "Active Service"! On other occasions we went out on anti-submarine patrol using the fan search method. Three, four or five aircraft set out together, each on a course 15 degrees to the right of the aircraft on its port side. In this way we fanned out over a large area. We were so slow that had an enemy submarine been on the surface, it would have heard us coming and been submerged again long before we got there. But this was part of our strategy. The German submarines used in our waters were usually of a fairly old design, needing to come to the surface every 24 hours to replenish their air supply. And so the longer we kept them submerged, the more the advantage swung in our favour. After we had passed over a suspect submarine it waited an hour and then returned to the surface for fresh air. By that time we were on our way back and, hearing us coming from a long way off, the submarine submerged again. Eventually the air in the submarine became so foul that it was forced to surface and remained there for some time taking on fresh air. And it was when we found one of these submarines sitting on the surface that we radioed base. As we had no weapons ourselves, there was at base a Hudson aircraft already bombed up and ready to take off. This Hudson droned out and was usually quite successful in damaging, if not sinking, the "sitting duck" on the surface. Yes. Truly a Heath Robinson outfit, but it worked!

'On 8 May 1944, in Anson aircraft 'O' with Sergeant Lowes as first pilot, we were out on a routine patrol over the sea-lane between Cape Town and Durban. I was the pilot/navigator and up to that moment had seen no sign of the enemy. And then it happened! There on the surface was a small plume of spray leaving a trail of bubbles behind it. The trail spread back some distance and just under the plume was a large submerged object, moving at about five knots. Quickly, I referred to my submarine identification manual and felt that the object was indeed one of the smallest versions of a German sub. The pilot and wireless operator confirmed my opinion and so we immediately radioed base, giving the position of this suspect enemy craft. Base confirmed our signal and we knew the Hudson would soon be airborne. As these signals were being exchanged, I took two or three photographs of the sub, as it proceeded steadily in an easterly direction. Just then it surfaced. It was a very large whale! Consternation reigned in the cockpit and by the time we had radioed base, informing them of our error, the Hudson was on the runway. Luckily, it was prevented from taking off. During the night my photographs were developed and the Commanding Officer readily agreed that the object did indeed closely resemble a small submarine. Later, the photos were used during identification lectures and the class usually thought they showed a U-boat.'

Many Coastal Command crews experienced being shot at by the trigger-happy sailors on the ships being shepherded. Hugh Fisher of No. 233 Squadron had good reason to be dismayed by the circumstances he relates:

'While based at Aldergrove we escorted a convoy leaving Liverpool. Our Hudson was with it for six hours, all the time keeping at the regulation distance. When it was time to leave we closed in on one of the escorts to report our departure and were immediately fired at. Not shots across the bows, but very close bursts indicating that they considered us hostile! The standard of aircraft recognition among naval gunners may have been bad, but we didn't expect them to take six hours to decide we were an enemy plane.'

From 1940 until 1942 Coastal Command received a small number of Whitley bombers with the object of providing increased cover over the Atlantic shipping lanes where most sinkings occurred. A stop-gap until more suitable types were available, the Whitley endeared itself to many pilots, one being Tom Minta of No. 58 Squadron:

'The Whitley was a fairly solid and lumbering machine. It may have been slow, but you could make the thing slide about the sky if attacked by fighters; slap on full rudder and she would skid, beautifully; and his tracer would go way out. If you could judge when the enemy pilot was going to fire you could make it very difficult for him to hit you. Mechanically they weren't too troublesome. The late versions had Rolls-Royce engines with the usual problem in that we had to run them on very weak mixture if we were after maximum range – about 7 to 8 hours' duration. As a result the cylinder liners tended to crinkle a bit which let the coolant get past in the wrong places. If your exhaust colours took a green hue you knew there was a glycol leak and it was probably time to think about going home. They flew nose down and looked like a stick of celery from the side. I became very fond of them and was quite sorry when they were retired.'

But there remained an area in mid-Atlantic that few maritime patrol aircraft could reach from either North America or the United Kingdom. Tom Minta recalls an attempt to stretch the Whitley's range:

'They said we must try to close the mid-Atlantic gap. So they put four extra fuel tanks in the Whitley's fuselage. With the extra 600 gallons of petrol it was an overload. We had a fellow on the squadron named Freddy Fox, a district officer in Africa before the war, who volunteered to undertake the first flight. He took off from St. Eval and disappeared from sight below the cliff edge. According to Freddy the Whitley kept losing height until the air was so squashed between his wings and the sea that it kept him up until he'd used enough petrol to gain some height!'

The extremely long-range Catalina flying-boat from the United States had the necessary duration, but was a type in short supply. The near ideal was the Consolidated Liberator, which although designed as a bomber, had the required range, speed and armament to make it an excellent anti-submarine aircraft. This was also manufactured in the United States and like other types from that source was generally popular with aircrews. Hugh Fisher:

'The thing about an American aircraft was that the designers did appear to have taken count that there was a crew going to fly in it. All those I flew in were reasonably comfortable and thoughtfully laid out. British aircraft were the reverse; in many, provision for a crew seemed to have been an afterthought.'

Liberators were urgently sought by many Allied air forces and Coastal Command did not really obtain the numbers it wanted until 1944. To supplement the few that entered service in 1941, Liberator bombers were sent on detachment to Coastal Command stations. Mick Wood, one of the pilots involved, tells of a trying sortie, revealing the origin of a well-known crew room tale in Coastal messes:

'Although we were part of Bomber Command in the spring of 1942, several Liberators and crews were lent to Coastal Command for the detection of submarines far out in the Atlantic. On 25 May we were airborne at roughly 0800 hrs. The first leg took us out to Rockall, the rocky outcrop in the Atlantic, and from this leg a wind was computed by the navigator. This wind was then used for navigation for the rest of the trip and, if on the homeward leg we found Rockall, the area searched could then be exactly defined for Coastal Command. The search went off in the usual way. A square search over several hundred square miles and eventually the time to return came round. In the meantime the weather had packed up and we were down to two thousand feet searching for Rockall. Failing in this search, we set course for Nutts Corner, but a diversion message was received sending us to Tiree – Nutts Corner being closed by weather. Presently Tiree also closed and we were diverted to Prestwick. *En route*, Prestwick also closed and we were further diverted to Stornaway where we touched down after some 12 hours airborne. Everyone was tired and a bit strained after several diversions. The Operations Room at Stornaway was part RAF and part Naval Western Approaches. It contained a great number of people of both sexes in both services and a number of very senior officers. It must have been a quiet time of the day, for we were debriefed with silent people all around us.

'The Intelligence Officer had his nose well into the job. The trip was recorded in great detail and every one of us was looking for an early end to this business. "On the return trip," asked this busy man, "Did you see Rockall?" "No," said the second pilot, "We saw Fuckall?" The effect in the Ops Room was magical. One very senior Naval man roared with laughter. Some of the others laughed, some blushed, some hid their faces. Best of all the Intelligence Officer went on writing. It was a spontaneous reply from a very tired and sorely tried young airman.'

Inclement weather was without doubt the principal enemy of the long-range patrol aircraft. The fronts that swept westwards over the Atlantic frequently hid home bases in the west of the UK, to say nothing of concealing high ground. Towards the tropics, the weather could be even more treacherous for the unwary. Peter Lee of No. 490 (RNZAF) Squadron:

'To patrol the Atlantic sea lanes off the west coast of Africa, West Africa Command had four Sunderland squadrons, No. 95 at Bathurst, Nos. 204 and 490 at Freetown and No. 270 at Lagos. During my tour – in the last nine months of the war – there were few U-boats in the area except the odd one in transit from Japan with a special cargo. Our biggest hazard was the weather. Coming back from an eight or ten-hour patrol in the early evening, huge tropical storms were often encountered. These would form off the mountains and extend for three or four hundred miles out from the coast. The mass could rise to 40,000 feet above sea level. Approaching this barrier in darkness was a pretty unnerving experience with the constant flashes of lightning along the line of the front. To reach base we could only go under the storm where there was usually only a few hundred feet between the sea and the base of the clouds. The trouble was that once there, the pressure readings dropped away and the altimeter reading might be several hundred feet out. In pitch-darkness it needed extra vigilance to see you didn't fly into the sea. On the other hand, if you were too high the vicious up-currents and down-currents would take the boat up and down like a yo-yo; it was impossible to fly straight and level. A French Sunderland crew from Dakar tried to penetrate too high one night and before they knew what was happening they found themselves upside down at 14,000 feet. They managed to get out of it – a bit shaken, no doubt. The weather also affected reliability. Maintenance was difficult with all the boats moored out on the river. It was either pissing down with rain or scorching hot. Our crew came back four times with one engine stopped. Sometimes the weight of rain was so heavy it was impossible to get enough lift to take off even though the mid-upper turret was removed and the fuel loads reduced to save weight.'

Several squadrons served to locate and attack blockade-runners or submarines passing through the Bay of Biscay to their bases on the French Atlantic coast. These flights had the risk of encountering Luftwaffe Ju 88s operating as long-range fighters, thus demanding extra vigil from fatigued crew men. Hugh Fisher of No. 224 Squadron:

'Sixteen-hour sorties to patrol over the Bay were laid on in November 1943; the longest I did was just coming up to 18 hours. As we were called four hours before take-off and when we got back didn't have a priority for transport, it was at least another three hours before we finally got to bed. This made rather a long day. The Liberator was a noisy aircraft and it was the noise that tired you as much as anything. We may have been young but sometimes, being awake for 24 hours, you did feel a little the worse for wear. It was always a struggle to keep awake during the final hours of the flight. We Wop/AGs used to swap round positions every couple of hours but even so, with the very bright sunlight, it used to make your eyes tingle and you would have given anything to drop off. However much you tried to remain alert the act of continually scanning sea or sky had a mesmerizing effect and the efficiency of your observation declined. That was when you could miss seeing a surface vessel or be jumped by Ju 88s.'

The enterprising discovered one way to add a little variety to these trips. Tom Minta, a No. 58 Squadron Halifax pilot:

'On long hauls down in the Bay, to break the monotony we sometimes did a circuit over the countryside along the Spanish coast. People would wave at us as we passed over at three or four hundred feet. This was quite an entertaining diversion until the beggars started shooting at us. Very unfriendly.'

Coastal Command's offensive arm originally consisted of a few squadrons of Bristol Beaufort torpedo-bombers, periodically despatched against enemy shipping along his Atlantic and North Sea coastal waters. The nature of delivering torpedoes against a target was fraught with dangers and the losses suffered were the highest for any type of RAF combat during the first three years of war. Nevertheless the Beaufort was a popular aircraft whereas a contemporary torpedo-bomber had the distinction of having the worst reputation of any aircraft in the RAF. James Donson's sentiments were not untypical of those encountering the Botha:

'One of the aircraft used at the Coastal Command navigational training station, Squire's Gate, close to Blackpool, was the Botha, probably the least successful of all would-be operational aircraft. It was designed as a torpedo-carrier but its operational endurance with full load was only a little more than twenty minutes. It was a heavy, high-wing monoplane powered, or rather underpowered, by two Perseus 850hp sleeve-valve engines, which really needed to develop double that to perform successfully. Inside it had watertight bulkheads and doors and the outside skin and doors were watertight too. Evidently the designers (if it had any) expected it to ditch quite often, which it did. One which ditched near Arklow Buoy off the coast of Ireland floated for about three weeks until it became obvious that it was not going to sink so an air-rescue launch was despatched and succeeded in towing it to within a few miles of the English shore where it sank in a storm and almost took the rescue boat with it. During one fortnight the Botha caused 27 fatalities, though one must say that fifteen of those were passengers getting off the London express which had just arrived at Blackpool station as a Botha and a Defiant collided over the station. The pilots' opinion of the Botha was summed up by a neat frieze painted round the walls of one of the crew rooms:

"My abject all sublime,
Is to make a Botha climb,
On one engine at a time. . . ."
Later, someone added in pencil, "Done it! – for two seconds." '

Ageing Hampden bombers were impressed as torpedo strike aircraft but these were more vulnerable than the Beauforts. The adaptation of Fighter Command's Beaufighter proved the most successful aircraft for this mission and several squadrons were ultimately formed to harass enemy coastal shipping. Later, air-launched rocket projectiles became the preferred ordnance. Mosquitoes were also used as coastal strike aircraft, but these could not carry torpedoes. Success in shipping strikes was in large measure dependent upon surprise. To achieve this the outward journey was made at a few feet above the waves. Len Barcham of No. 404 (RCAF) Squadron:

'Trips to Norway averaged some 300 miles each way from our base at Wick. The journey out was always done at low level, a mere fifty feet to stay below enemy radar detection. This produced a great sensation of speed as we sped over the wave tops, until sighting our target when we had to climb to 1,500 feet. Immediately one had a contrasting sensation of being about to stall and that the Beaufighter was hardly moving at all. Although this happened scores of times as we prepared for attack, I always had the same fear of stalling which I was never able to suppress. . . . Especially when operating off the Norwegian coast, a long way from home and in range of enemy single-engined fighters, we much preferred bad weather and good cloud cover. At Wick the saying was "we prefer to fly when even the seagulls are walking" – and Wick seagulls were a very large and hardy breed! During 1942 and early 1943 we usually carried a pigeon with us in the Beaufighter on our shipping strikes off the Norwegian coast. The bird was housed in a sawdust and shavings filled tin box which, being loose in the aircraft, sometimes got chucked around, particularly when we were taking violent evasive action. The bird was, of course, intended to be used should we ditch to carry our position home. On return to dispersal after an "op" we were sometimes told to release the pigeon, whereupon it invariably perched on top of the aircraft's rudder and showed no inclination to fly anywhere, not even back to its loft. We decided that "rough rides" must have upset its gyro-compass navigational system and eventually didn't think there was any real point in continuing to carry the bird. This very much upset one of our better navigators, Peter Bassett, who always said that his accuracy was due to the fact that he never gave a course to the pilot to fly until he had shown it to the pigeon who somehow indicated whether the gen was "pukka" or "duff".'

Weather reporting flights were handled night and day by Coastal Command units; sometimes they were the only aircraft airborne around the British Isles when weather conditions grounded all others. These sorties usually involved extremes of flight, as known in those days, and were not just a safe and comfortable joyride, as many envisaged. Peter Catchpole:

'Although trained in meteorology I had no flight experience and was eager to remedy this. The Met Fortresses operated out of Langham, and the crews were allowed, if so disposed, to take up fellows like myself. I finally managed to get accepted for one of these North Sea trips which proved to be an unnerving introduction to flying. A triangular course was flown, so many miles at high level, so many miles at low level, up and down as met readings were taken. All was well until the climb to 20,000 feet over the North Sea and we were told to go on oxygen. It was then discovered that there wasn't the necessary connecting piece to fit between my oxygen mask tube and the outlet on the aircraft's oxygen system. My fears of expiring from anoxia were very real even though a member of the crew told me not to worry and hold the end of my mask tube to the supply outlet. So there I sat, petrified, clasping the oxygen tube to the supply and unable to see out for two or three hours until the Fortress descended to lower altitude. Then we ran into a storm with all the turbulence that means and St. Elmo's Fire round the wings and engine cowlings. I expected the plane to fall out of the sky at any moment. When we were really low, down just above the sea, I was sent up into the nose where I was more than a little apprehensive to see there was only the large plexiglas nosepiece between me and the waves. If they are honest, I suppose most newcomers are a bit scared on their first flight. Mine was certainly a rude introduction. After a few more trips it was all "a piece of cake".'

Coastal Command also controlled a number of Air Sea Rescue squadrons in the UK with their flights deployed to give service all round the coast. Spotter and amphibian aircraft worked in conjunction with rescue launches, saving more than

6,000 airmen during hostilities. Pop Ewins flew Spitfire IIs modified to carry smoke floats and an inflatable dinghy for dropping near airmen down in the sea:

'Our squadron, No. 276, had 300 plus rescues to its credit. One of the most memorable occurred on 19 July 1944, shortly after the cross-Channel invasion. Patrolling with another Spitfire, flown by F/O Lamb, I found a number of dinghies with waving occupants and directed a Walrus to the spot. When the Walrus landed and taxied to the dinghies the crew found to their considerable surprise that the occupants were Germans – a whole U-boat crew totalling 46. The senior German officer was taken aboard the Walrus and gave the bemused crew a couple of bottles of wine as souvenirs. We saw no reason why this 46 should not be added to the Squadron total of successful rescues!'

WITH AIR TRANSPORT

Although air transportation had been a feature of RAF activity in pre-war years, albeit on a minor scale, not until the spring of 1943 was a Transport Command formed. This organization controlled RAF air transport units operating world-wide, together with those engaged in ferrying, air ambulance and airborne forces work. However, there were several units that did not come under the Command. Additionally, a small number of RAF aircrews found themselves flying air transports that were not part of the service. Ray Jones was one of these pilots:

'In January 1944 I was seconded from the RAF to BOAC [British Overseas Airways Corporation] who required crews to operate their Dakotas. It was a peculiar situation in that while being RAF officers and paid by that service, we lived a civilian life. We were not subject to any day-to-day control by the RAF, could live where we chose, and when off-duty could do as we pleased and wear civilian clothes. BOAC uniforms were the norm for flying, but in civvy street nobody recognized these, so if we wanted to pull a few birds we'd put on our RAF blues. Initially we operated from Whitchurch, near Bristol, on a service to Lisbon, every two days. Most of the passengers were diplomats. Lisbon was a spy's paradise and it was not unusual to return to your hotel room and find your case had been gone through. The trips to Portugal also gave us access to all those luxuries that were unavailable in the UK. Lufthansa crews, made up of chaps seconded from the Luftwaffe – as we were from the RAF – were often drinking in the same bars we frequented. Yet elsewhere in Europe the RAF and Luftwaffe were busy killing each other!'

By 1944 the predominant squadrons with transport associations were those trained and equipped for carrying paratroops, towing assault gliders and the re-supply of airborne forces with weapons, ammunition, fuel and food. A few of these squadrons also engaged in operations supporting the resistance forces in occupied countries, activities involving small numbers of aircraft and often drawing the full attention of enemy defences in the area. It was dangerous work, particularly in the lumbering Stirlings often employed. Ernie Edwards of No. 620 Squadron:

'As a crew we completed a full tour of 32 operations, the majority of which were the classical 38 Group ops – dropping supplies to partisans in occupied

Europe, mainly France. After the liberation of France our attention was directed to Norway. It was during one of these latter ops, near the end of our tour, that we had our biggest scare. Having completed an apparently successful drop in northern Norway, we had returned down to the south coast and crossed it somewhere near Kristiansand and out over the Skagerrak. Shortly after leaving the coast I spotted an unidentified aircraft about 1,000 yards astern. It was bright moonlight – these operations were always conducted on moonlit nights. Moments later I positively identified it as a Ju 88, thus giving rise to the eternal dilemma faced by air gunners; what next?, when we were within range of his cannons, whereas he was well outside the range of my .303 machine-guns. Another alarm was ringing in my mind. Was this one a decoy? They often hunted in pairs. In response to the skipper's anxiety I decided I could wait no longer and ordered him to turn to starboard, to the dark side of the sky. The next instant a burst of cannon-shells (which could have come from a second aircraft) crashed into us. We changed the evasive action to weaving and this the skipper maintained for the duration of the action. The ensuing battle lasted some minutes with me catching occasional glimpses of one or other of them and getting the odd burst in here and there. Although shot at several more times, we received no more hits and fortunately the hits suffered in the initial attack had not damaged anything vital. There is no way of knowing whether it was due to any success on my part that they broke off the inconclusive engagement when fuel and ammunition were unlikely to be short. In retrospect, I feel we must have been favoured by the gods in order to have survived when the odds were stacked so heavily against us, but I am conceited enough to believe that we helped ourselves in no small measure by not being taken by surprise. My personal good fortune extended further inasmuch as a cannon-shell from the first blast passed through the bottom of my turret without immobilizing or injuring me.'

In Europe there were three major airborne assaults involving RAF airborne forces support squadrons: the D-Day drops of 6 June 1944, the attempts to secure bridges at Arnhem the following September and the landings on the eastern bank of the Rhine in March 1945. Of these the Arnhem venture was the most costly, claiming 55 of the Stirlings, Halifaxes and RAF Dakotas involved. Hilary Upward:

'After the Arnhem landings the Keevil squadrons were busy over the next few days dropping supplies to the beleaguered paratroopers. I thought it would be a break from my work in Operations to fly on one of these re-supply trips and permission was obtained to go with Flt Lt Rees' crew of No. 299 Squadron. Our Stirling, X9:B, assembled as lead of a three-plane vic and set off line astern behind two other vics. Approaching the drop zone we reduced altitude to the required 800 feet. The Germans let fly with everything they had and while I couldn't hear anything over the din of our Stirling's engines, there were lots of little black puffs sailing past the cockpit windows. Looking down I saw a Stirling on the ground aflame from end to end. Sitting in the navigator's seat the thought came to my mind that it had been foolish to make this flight which I expected any moment, to be my last. We were briefed to make a climbing turn to port as soon as we had dropped our panniers. All at once I heard over the intercom, "Panniers gone" and Rees exclaimed "Bugger me!" The sky ahead was criss-crossed with tracer and exploding shells. Rees immediately pushed the control column forward and dived the aircraft. Looking back as we sped low over the Dutch countryside I saw that several other aircraft had followed our move, diving to tree-top height to escape the Flak. After what seemed an age Rees started to climb and it was a relief to find we had come through the hail of fire without a hit on our aircraft. Rees told us that three of the six aircraft ahead, including the CO's, had been shot down. In total the two Keevil squadrons lost fifteen Stirlings during the Arnhem operations with many damaged and several returning with wounded aircrew.'

Similar grim accounts can be had from most airmen who survived the airborne drop and re-supply trips to Arnhem. However, one published account was not all it appeared to be, as Ernie Edwards relates:

'When we set out for Arnhem we had a newspaper reporter on board. While going through cloud the pilot of the glider we were towing got disorientated and went out to one side causing the tow-rope to break. We were still over England, and had to abort and return to Fairford. While waiting for the crew bus to convey us to debriefing, our skipper turned to the reporter and said, "Sorry you won't get your story, old chap." The reply was, "Oh don't worry on my account. I'll get my story." Lo and behold, when the news of the operation broke in the newspapers there was his account in great detail of how he had been to Arnhem, complete with names of the crew with whom he was purported to have flown. The substituted crew were real enough as were his eye-witness details. The truth is that, like us, he never left England that day. We all had a good laugh at the cheek of the man, but I shall never understand why he thought it necessary to present his report as a personal experience when many people knew it to be a downright lie.'

Above: *Dusty Lings v. Old Sweats soccer match at Berka, North Africa, 28th November 1942. Note the varied choice of attire both off and on the field. In the desert correct uniform was a joke. (H. Kidney)*

Below: *Not a knobbly knees contest, just the mode of dress for well turned-out fighter pilots in warm climes. Like most squadrons in the MTO (Mediterranean Theatre of Operations), No. 253 (Hyderabad) Squadron had pilots from six different Commonwealth countries. Seated on the Spitfire wing are, left to right: Warrant Officer Ken Russom, Sergeant Derek Preece, Lieutenant Ronnie Briggs (SAAF), Warrant Officer Alec Day(NZ), Flight Sergeant Fred Ellis, Flying Officer H. H. Miller (Canada), Warrant Officer Alec Bowman and Flight Lieutenant Fred Pawsey.*

Above: Air crew accommodation, Italian style. The main street of No. 70 Squadron's Tortorella encampment after a winter storm. Each tent had a sunken floor covered with steel runway planking to give more headroom. A deep drainage ditch was dug all the way round the outside of the tent to prevent flooding. Heat came from an oil drum stove fed on diesel with the smoke stack running out under the base of the tent. (J. Heap)

Top right: Engine fitter at work on the engines of TH:M, one of No. 418 Squadron's most successful Mosquito VI fighters, Hurn, July 1944.

Right: Having successfully extinguished an engine fire on this crash-landed No. 21 Squadron Blenheim at Watton, station fire-fighters – some splashed with foam – are joined by a curious throng of airmen. Fighting aircraft fires was a dangerous job, often with the risk of exploding bombs and ammunition. (S. Clay)

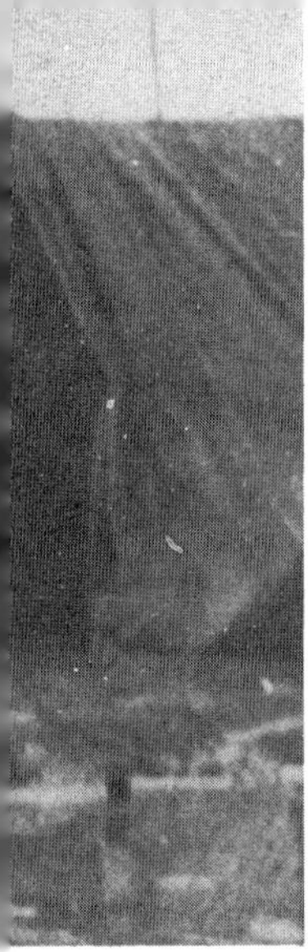

Left: *Convoy of RAF signals cabin vehicles (Crossley Type Q in foreground) on a French road in 1944. The RAF always operated many more motor vehicles than aircraft and many more vehicle types than aircraft types. (Official)*

Bottom left: *Q and K sites were given Lewis gun armament with the aim of picking off any lured low-flying enemy aircraft. Ken 'Badger' Baker mans the Cavenham Heath weapon. In the background are three realistic dummy Wellingtons made mainly of canvas and wood. (R. Howlett)*

Right: *A Sergeant pilot down in France on 5 February 1941, surrounded by his captors. Note torn right boot.*

Below: *'A' Flight, No. 277 Squadron at Martlesham Heath. An example of the traditional unit pose with all personnel assembled in front of an aircraft – in this case a Walrus amphibian. Mick Osborne is third from left, front row.*

A
HE

Top left: *The twice a day head count assembly, common to all major prison camps that held RAF PoWs. This photograph was taken at Stalag Luft I, Barth (R. Armstrong)*

Left: *Backbone of the fighter effort during the early war years was the dependable Hurricane. Outclassed by the Me 109, it was nevertheless the aircraft chiefly responsible for the RAF's success in the Battle of Britain. This is a No. 263 Squadron machine.*

Above: *Flying could be dangerous and crashes were numerous. This Mustang developed mechanical trouble on a non-operational flight and ended up in a field near Gravesend, killing the pilot, victor of many air combats and survivor of several dicey do's with the enemy.*

Below: *Two fingers for two flying-bombs brought down. Squadron Leader Antoni Murkowski climbs from a Mustang's cockpit after another successful sortie. His thirteen confirmed enemy aircraft and seven flying-bombs included the first V-1 destroyed by a Polish pilot and the last Me 262 jet.*

Above: *The Polish airmen were renowned for their prowess. This group discussing tactics on a warm spring day at Northolt are members of No. 316 'City of Warsaw' Squadron. Spitfire V in background is that of the CO, Squadron leader A. Gabszewwicz. (A Murkowski)*

Left: *Few RAF 'regulars' who commenced operations in the first month of the war were still around in May 1945. One such survivor was John Wray, a Pilot Officer flying night reconnaissance sorties over Germany in September 1939 and a Wing Commander with a Tempest Wing on the Continent in 1945.*

Right: *A commemorative cartoon featuring Goering and Hitler, made available to No. 9 Squadron crews after memorable operations. (M. Hewinson)*

Left: *Corporal Hugh Berry.*

Below: *Stirlings of Nos. 295 and 570 Squadrons assembled at Rivenhall for the launch of Rhine airborne crossing.*

Right: *Vernon Wilkes at the bombsight in Lancaster IQ:B.*

Above: *Indian fighter pilot. Pilot Officer D. A. Samant of Bombay in the cockpit of Whirlwind SF:C of No. 137 Squadron, 1943.*

Left: *The 19-year-old rear-gunner of IQ:B, Danny Driscoll, 'christening' the tail before take-off.*

Above: *Wellington crew, off-duty, at Newton, August 1941; l to r: 'Denny' Denman (AG), Eddie Wheeler (WOP/AG), Paul Carlyon (pilot), Bill Bossom (AG), 'Ginger' Thomas (navigator), and Sam Huggett (2nd pilot). The two pilots did not survive the hostilities.*

Right: *AC2 Edwin Wheeler, Yatesbury, Wiltshire, December 1939.*

Left: *Tom Wingham, complete with pin-stripe trousers in orchard of his Belgian hosts, 1944.*

Right: *The Belgian family who sheltered Tom Wingham; l to r: M. Schoofs, Jennie, Audree, Mme Schoofs and Pascal.*

Below: *Sixty-eight feet long Air/Sea Rescue High Speed Launch and crew photographed at Calshot in August 1944. (B. Robertson Collection)*

2556

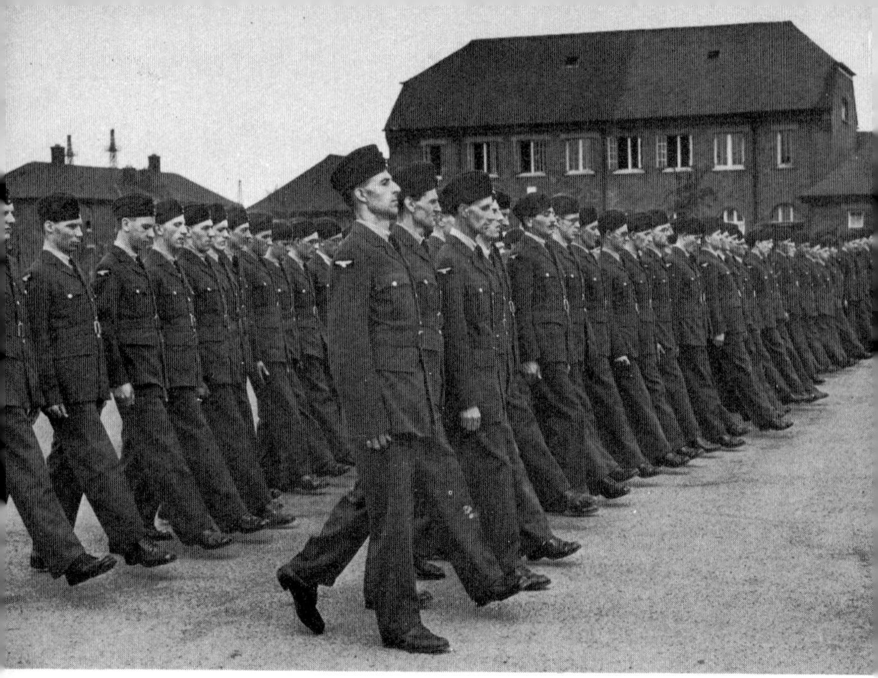

Above: *Parade ground for new recruits, 1940. It took time to get the line straight. (B. Robertson Collection)*

Below: *Few RAF airfield Watch Towers in the UK were without a strong complement of WAAF operatives by the end of hostilities. All were selected for their suitability and capability and it was just coincidence that this group, serving night operations at No 54 OTO, Charter Hall, Northumberland, have such good looks. (E. F. Cheesman)*

Round the Med

At the outbreak of war the RAF presence in the so-called Middle East consisted of some 300 largely out-dated aircraft in a score of squadrons deployed in colonies, dependancies and protectorates taking in Iraq, Aden, Jordan, Palestine, Kenya, Somalia, Egypt and the Sudan. The potential threat was Italian forces in East Africa and Libya, which eventually materialized with the declaration of war on Britain by Mussolini in June 1940. During the following nine months British and Commonwealth forces managed to eliminate the Italians in East Africa, but by that time German forces had joined their Axis partners in Libya and had also moved into the Balkans. With the then critical situation in the UK, little in the way of reinforcements and modern equipment was forthcoming from home. During 1941 the RAF fought in Greece, Crete, Libya and Egypt with mostly inferior aircraft to those of the enemy, and often with fewer numbers.

The Blenheim was the most modern warplane on hand when actions commenced. Before the end of the year, when Axis forces appeared to be about to take Egypt, some Wellingtons and Hurricanes arrived from Britain. Expansion came to depend on production from United States sources, with Boston and Maryland bombers and Tomahawk fighters arming most of the new squadrons, several manned by South African, Canadian and Australian crews. For most of 1941 and early 1942 air superiority over the Western Desert was held by the Luftwaffe's Me 109, largely due to that German fighter's superior performance over the available Allied types. Weight of numbers and improved tactics began to tell and by summer 1942 the advantage moved to the Allies and remained with them. The Allied air forces followed the armies in the North African campaigns, culminating with the German surrender in May 1943. Then on to Sicily and, in the autumn of the same year, southern Italy.

Desert Squadrons

For those RAF personnel arriving from verdant lands, a lasting impression of desert service was climate and terrain, together with the unpleasantries that went with them. William Coote:

'Of course, on first arriving on a desert squadron, it took time to get accustomed to the heat, mosquitoes, snakes, scorpions, dung-beetles, to say nothing of the Arabs! But probably the most irksome was the sand-storm. Lasting for hours, and sometimes days, the sand got everywhere. Despite the risk of being indelicate, in your mouth, eyes and ears, up your nose! You name it! It was present! To be followed often by long hours of digging out and trying to adjust to an entirely altered terrain!

The desert discomforts were borne by officers and men alike. Aircrews were known to declare that they would rather be on operations as flight brought relief. Perhaps just flippancy; but the ground staff certainly had no escape when duty called and the worst conditions prevailed. In the see-saw of advance and retreat across Libya, living and working conditions were always primitive and the enemy often too close for comfort'.

Harry Kidney was one who suddenly found he was in the front line with, for once, reason to be thankful for the harsh desert elements:

'*Circa* March 1941, a small detachment of No. 38 Squadron was based at Gambut, a grim desolate place in the Libyan desert, once occupied by the Italian Air Force. I was one of the privileged few selected to be sent there. Gambut is approximately halfway between Tobruk and Bardia, inland from the sea, with the landing-ground sited on an escarpment with wadies running down from it. Our Wimpeys [Wellingtons] were operating from here subsequent to the land forces' offensive which had come to a halt at El Agheila – some miles west of Benghazi. History shows Erwin Rommel appearing on the scene about this time and commencing to push our forces rapidly back towards Egypt. Orders came for the abandonment of Gambut and retirement eastwards to Sidi Assiz – a landing-ground near Bardia. Four armourers, my best RAF pal, Alec "Chunky" Bell, two others and myself, were instructed to remain behind after all other personnel departed, to deal with armament stores. We were assured that transport would return later to collect us. It was with more than a little apprehension that we watched our colleagues depart in the early morning.

'We completed our assignment swiftly and returned to a derelict corrugated-iron shed located at the base of the escarpment in a wadi. This was a flea-ridden Italian relic. That day our transport failed to materialize and we knew the Afrika Korps was advancing rapidly; visions of Stalags loomed. Nightfall came and our imaginations ran riot as with every slight sound we expected massive blond Aryan types to burst into our shed firing their Mausers. Our thoughts were not entirely without substance as we learned later that enemy armour did traverse the landing-ground while we were hiding in the wadi. Two factors saved us: one was the element we hated and cursed most in the desert, the Khamsin, a scorching hot, soul-destroying sandstorm which blanketed everything out of sight within a few feet. Thus obscured, the Germans had not seen our shed in the wadi. The other factor was that Rommel chose to pursue his offensive deeper in the desert leaving the coastal area for the time being which enabled our belated lorry to reach us the next day, much to our relief. We set off at speed and reached Sidi Assiz, thankful for escape; but this relief was short-lived as enemy elements were reported approaching this vicinity.

'Once again we quickly boarded our lorry and went helter-skelter for the Egyptian border, reaching Fort Capuzzo extremely fatigued. Nightfall came so we decided to rest awhile but no; as soon as we were putting our groundsheets down, again it was panic stations when we learned the enemy was close on our tail. With alacrity we boarded our lorry and continued the flight eastwards, passing the border at Sollum, by which time it was dawn. Having reached a point somewhere near Sidi Barrani, exhausted, particularly the driver, we decided to rest whatever the consequences. Happily the Axis advance was halted at the Libya/Egypt border. So, after a few hours' rest we pressed on until reaching 38 Squadron's base at Shallufa, safe, thankful and in a bedraggled state, to learn that we had been listed "missing". Lady Luck had certainly been on our side.'

Many of the Wellingtons urgently required for bombing operations in the Middle East were flown out from England, staging through Gibraltar and Malta. The refuelling stop in Malta was a hazardous business as Joe Pugh discovered:

'In 1941 I was a member of one of the crews ferrying a batch of Wellingtons out to the Middle East. At Gibraltar we were told that the trip to Malta was more dangerous than operations as the enemy usually knew when aircraft were going to land there and had fighters up from nearby Pantelleria to intercept. We took off in darkness and landed at Luqa airfield, Malta, to learn that the Wellington that had left Gib before us had been shot down. As we were carrying a Wing Commander and an Air Commodore we were given priority on refuelling and took off again after only a brief stay. Our destination in Egypt was reached without any problems, but we later learned that many of the other Wellingtons were bombed at Luqa and their crews spent the next two or three weeks filling bomb holes in the runway before they could get out of Malta.'

The ordinary airman was always kept in the dark as to the purpose behind his duties other than the cause of ultimate victory. Nevertheless, most could figure the broad line of strategy. This was not the case with those who served in the desert during the months prior to the autumn of 1942. Most were simply bewildered by events. 'We staggered from one victory-cum-disaster to another; everything always seemed to be in such a bloody muddle,' recalled one disillusioned erk. Something of the same sentiment is to be found in Australian pilot Mick Wood's account of his arrival in the Middle East:

'I was sure in 1942 that the British would ultimately win the war. They muddled with such finesse. With my No. 159 Squadron Liberator and crew we flew out of Gibraltar to Egypt in June 1942. Before we left we were shown the "hot spots" to avoid and were given strict instructions to "circle Ras El Knias" before we approached Kilo 40 to refuel. Day broke with the delta in sight and we proceeded to lose height to 1,500 feet to carry out the circling and be recognized. While still over the water and out from the coast it seemed that inland from the Cape of Ras El Knias there was a great deal of dust with hundreds of vehicles moving east. I then decided to give the recognition instructions a miss and thus proceeded directly to Kilo 40. On landing there was the usual debriefing during which the Intelligence man announced, "I say, I hope you didn't go to Ras El Knias." We confirmed that we had not. "Good thing," he said, "Rommel's troops passed there two days ago." '

As in western Europe, only the fighters and light bombers normally flew against the enemy in daylight, while the mediums and heavies (when they arrived) bombed under cover of darkness. During 1941 and 1942 Wellingtons ran regular raids on the Libyan ports used by Axis shipping to supply their forces. At that time, the Flak defences deployed around these places were claimed by old hands as fiercer than those at many German cities. Steve Challen of No. 108 Squadron had good reason to subscribe to this view:

'On 24 September 1941 we were briefed for the "milk run", Benghazi. Flight Lieutenant Vare was rather keen to make a good show of our first op in the Middle East so we stooged straight over the town. Our target was supply ships against the harbour moles and quays. There had been a few before us so all kinds of Flak was coming up, the lights making it difficult as usual to pinpoint anything. Around again. Vare decided to alter height and approach from a different direction in a shallow dive, hoping the increased speed would baffle predictors. No chance! The lights clamped on us, the multi-coloured Flak seemed draped around us. I had fired some short bursts on the first run, knowing there wasn't much chance of putting out those lights, but perhaps the bits of spent lead raining down might possibly disrupt their accuracy. This time round even lower, I fired longer, calculated squirts until my port gun jammed. The .303 calibre ammo we were using was First World War vintage. Again "No bombs gone". I stripped my Browning to find out what the stoppage was, putting the parts with names like "Rear seat retainer keeper and pin" (who thought that name up?) on the ledge where the sides and dome of the turret joined. Third time around lower and slower from a different direction which must have been right for the aiming-point because the chant began: "right, right, left a little, steady, steady, bombs gone". The same instant there was a bang, a rattle against the turret and a burnt smell. I put out my hand to feel for the breech-block bits, but felt only breeze. Then a sensation in my throat; I wanted to cough but couldn't. Putting my hand to my throat it was warm, sticky and wet. Switching on my mike I tried to report that I had been hit, but could tell there wasn't much noise coming out of me. Sergeant Gord Murray, 2nd pilot, said "Okay, Steve. Coming back". We were out over the Med by now, in no danger from that "hot spot". The turret wouldn't move with the hydraulics so I engaged the hand gear, which needed two hands to wind the handle to centralize the turret so that I could open the doors and climb out. There was quite a breeze and light shining in on the port side where fabric had been stripped off. The hydraulic pipes supplying the turret had been punctured and oil sprayed everywhere, no mistaking the smell. I thought that maybe the rudder or elevator controls might be damaged, but was unable to see as I continued along the catwalk until meeting Gord on his way back. I sat on the fold-down cot while Gord shone his torch on my damage. Not much to be done other than place a field dressing over the wound holding it in place with my hand as I lay on the cot. Chuck came back for a look as did Gibbo. Paul and Vare were busy up front as the controls were not quite right.

'With dawn coming it was light enough for me to write some questions in a little diary, like: "How big is the hole in my bloody neck?" and, "Where are you dropping me?" Wireless inquiry to base had advised landing at Fuka Main where an ambulance would be waiting. A soft touch-down at 7am. I crawled out of the mid under hatch where at one time in the design there was to have been a "dustbin" turret. While people became a little impatient I produced my little camera and insisted the occasion be recorded as I stood near the damage for snaps to be taken. Taken to 21st Medical Receiving Centre, a tented hospital in the desert, I was operated upon at about 10am by Squadron Leader Wallace, assisted by his medical orderlies. He removed a piece of Flak from my larynx.

Unbeknown to him and me, there were bits embedded in my scalp which some time later were raked out as I combed my hair.'

The light day bombers – Blenheims, Bostons, Marylands – suffered most grievously during this period, despite the presence of fighter escort over the front line. As appears common, personal experience of combat did not necessarily provide the most frightening incident for an individual during an operational tour. Bob Thompson of No. 11 Squadron had no doubts about this:

'We were recalled for some reason while the squadron's Blenheims were on army support ops. When we landed at an advanced landing-ground one of the main wheel tyres went flat and we swept round in a circle with one wingtip trailing in the sand. As soon as we came to a standstill I gathered up my maps, disconnected the camera and got up from my navigator's table in the nose and then noticed the pilot had left. Going into the cockpit and sticking my head out of the hatch in the top of the fuselage, I was surprised to see the pilot and turret gunner running away as fast as their legs would carry them. It was then I remembered the load of bombs and was not long in getting out of that hatch and belting after the others. Later it was my job to go back to the aircraft and replace the safety-pins in the bombs, which had been removed in flight. To my horror I found that some of the extension rods fitted to the nose of the bombs (so that they exploded at surface level rather than penetrate the ground) had been forced up hard against the bulkhead when we had gone down on one wingtip. These bombs might easily have exploded. The diceyest do I ever experienced.'

That one's own bombs could be more threatening than the enemy's was well known to armourers. Accidents when detonating loads, destroying aircraft and claiming lives, were by no means rare in any theatre of war. Removal of bombs from crashed aircraft was a task tackled with apprehension, particularly so if they were fitted with delayed fuses. Ted Scott:

'Our squadron was operating from a landing-ground in North Africa on anti-shipping work. About eighteen Wellingtons of No. 221 and another squadron were lined up awaiting take-off when Jerry found us and played havoc. Ten Wellingtons were destroyed and most of the others damaged. They had been loaded with bombs having delayed-action fuses timed to work within from four to twelve hours. Our Sergeant Armourer, a grand chap, came to our tent for volunteers to remove the bombs from three aircraft that, having undercarriage damage, were lop-sided. But it wasn't a case of volunteering as there were only four armourers present. Although each of us carried on as if it were just another job, I'm sure we were all dead scared. I knew that with delayed-action bombs you could not tell if the fuse capsule had broken and the delay system was already working. Each second felt like an hour as we worked on those bombs. We were lucky – and three Wellingtons were saved for repair.'

After the battle of El Alamein and the Allied invasion of French Morocco and Algeria during the autumn of 1942, the campaign to drive the Axis forces from North Africa intensified. Fresh RAF squadrons arrived, as did new aircraft and equipment. Spitfires, Beaufighters, Bisleys and improved versions of the Hurricane and Wellington. From the United States came Kittyhawks, Baltimores and Marauders. The RAF only had a single squadron of Marauders operating in the Western Desert (although five South African Air Force squadrons later used this Martin bomber in the Mediterranean area). One of the most controversial yet successful Allied warplanes, initially it had a reputation of being dangerous to fly. In view of this it is surprising that some pilots came to Marauders straight from ambling Oxfords and Ansons. Bill Japp was one:

'After my flying training in Rhodesia I went "to the war up north". Without any operational training unit experience whatsoever I was sent with three other pilots from the replacement pool to No. 14 Squadron, the only RAF squadron with the Martin Marauder, a new American twin-engined bomber. At first we flew as second pilots and once familiar with the controls advanced to the left-hand seat. My transition came at Blida, Algeria, where I started by flying a few circuits with my skipper and another experienced Marauder pilot. Then they put an unsuspecting Aussie, George, who had just joined the unit, in the second pilot's seat and told him to keep his hands on the two toggle switches of the manual pitch control mechanism and watch the rev counters in case we had a runaway prop. When the aircraft was lined up on the runway and everything checked, I opened up the throttles to the specified setting but nothing happened. The tension of the occasion probably caused me to forget that there would be a delay in response and the warnings not to advance the throttle levers further, which I did. Suddenly my seat hit me in the back and we were away like a rocket. The flight was without further incident and only after landing did I inform George that his first flight in a Marauder had been my first solo.

'At this time I knew nothing of the Marauder's reputation in America where it had an alarming accident rate. I was only aware that the aircraft had a very high wing loading and didn't suffer fools gladly. Apart from the occasional failure of the electric propeller pitch control mechanism, a known problem and one which was eventually corrected, we found nothing unusually hazardous about take-offs or landings. The high landing speed – 150mph – didn't seem exceptional simply because I had no experience of landing any other combat aircraft. The most advanced type flown in training was the Oxford and as that came in to land at about 80mph there was no comparison. When all the prescribed procedures had been carried out and you were on final approach at 150–155mph, you felt, as the runway came up to meet you, that the aircraft was on rails and would arrive at just the spot you wanted. This was about 10mph faster than advised by the Americans, but it gave that extra margin of stability and safety while really not making much visible difference to your rate of descent towards the runway. The Marauder, like all American aircraft I flew, was beautifully made and comfortable. The knobs and buttons in the cockpit were so neat and well laid out compared with most British types I later flew. However, I didn't really appreciate just how advanced and what a grand aircraft it was until the squadron returned to the UK and converted to Wellingtons.'

With Axis forces driven from Africa, relief came at last to the once beleaguered island of Malta, recipient of countless bombings over three years. The battering claimed many RAF lives, both in the air and on the ground, but Air Force personnel played a major part in the creation of the indomitable spirit that came to be Malta's hallmark. And, as Tony Spooner relates, despite the pounding, that measure of courtesy opposing combatants showed towards each other still flourished – even if his example did indulge a captive to a degree that must have left him completely nonplussed:

'It was unusual for a Ju 88 to be shot down so close to Luqa, Malta, that we could watch the parachutes open and stream downwards. The last to abandon the crippled bomber landed so close that we set forth to investigate. We arrived just in time to prevent the angry Maltese peasants from hacking him to death with their simple tools. We escorted our "prisoner" back to the large flapping tent which served as the officers' mess after the original one – and much else – had been flattened by the Luftwaffe. While someone phoned the Special Police, we were left to entertain our unexpected guest. The difficulty was that he spoke no English and we no German. "The only German I know are the words of *Lilly Marlene*," lamented one. We all knew these words. It was at an early stage of the war when this catchy tune was purely a German one. Later, Vera Lynn and other British song-birds purloined it for our use too. In Malta we were subject to ceaseless German propaganda usually introduced by this haunting refrain sung so seductively in German. With little else to listen to, we had learned the words. Accordingly, until the SPs arrived to take him away, we entertained the astonished visitor as best we could. First we had rescued him. Then we sat him down, gave him a cigarette, a beer and sang him the famous German tune in his own language. I doubt that Dr Goebbels' infamous propaganda machine had prepared him for this "greeting".'

The gleeful atmosphere so often found in a station mess or crew room in the UK was no less evident in and around whatever served a similar purpose in the desert or Mediterranean agrarian patch, as William Coote observed:

'War is not all danger, daring and decorations. Fortunately, when large numbers of men are thrown together in the services there are always the wags, wits and practical jokers. On reflection, one tends to feel thankful for them since they contributed so much at times to making long, monotonous days bearable. One regular "leg-pull" practised among aircrews flying with Nos. 70 and 37 Wellington Squadrons of 231 Wing, 205 Group in North Africa, was to suggest to new or replacement crews that they might like to freshen up with a shower after the long trip out from England. After deciding that a shower would be just what the doctor ordered, the unsuspecting pilot and crew were directed towards the far side of the airfield. Inquiries where the showers were brought the inevitable and serious response. "You've been misinformed! The only showers hereabouts are where you've just come from!"'

As pranks were adapted to the situation and location, so was 'lingo'. A rich air force vocabulary arose, far more varied than that within the home commands, due to the influx of personnel steeped in the language and expressions of many nations where they had previously trained or served. John Heap:

'In Italy and North Africa we used a lot of Arabic and 'gypo expressions in everyday conversation. As many service people had come out of India to the Middle East when things were bad, several Indian expressions were in use too. We had an exclusive squadron war-cry. It started off as something the Arab drivers used to shout to their horses on the streets of Cairo – "Hod hod!" It became our catch-phrase. If you wanted someone to get a move on you'd say "Hod, hod! you so-and-so." We even used it in the air as an identification. You'd hear people call up Control and just say "Hod hod!" Control knew immediately it was a 70 Squadron aircraft.'

ITALY AND THE BALKANS

The Allied armies met stiff resistence in their attempts to drive up the leg of Italy, eventually coming to a virtual halt in the mountains that barred the way north to Rome. The Allies dominated the skies and the Luftwaffe was never again the threat it had been during the fighting on the southern side of the Mediterranean. Farther afield it was a different matter and ranging RAF reconnaissance or attack aircraft still ran a real risk of interception. An individual's reaction to this kind of situation and what appeared to be pending termination is graphically described by Bill Japp:

'We were doing a reccy of the French Mediterranean coast in the vicinity of Cap d'Agde, of which we were very wary as we knew it had radar-controlled Flak batteries. While gingerly approaching the coast at our normal operational altitude of 50 feet, three unidentified aircraft, presumably enemy, were seen at some distance. Our pilot, Merv Hogg, immediately took the Marauder round on a reverse course, the best thing to do in such circumstances. There was always a chance that we had not been seen, but the gunners soon reported that three Me 109Gs were coming after us. Merv reduced height to about 30 feet above the waves and gave us full speed, a little over 300mph. As the 109 had only about a 50mph advantage at low altitude it was some time before they got within firing range and all the time we were drawing them out to sea. Our defensive armament consisted of a single hand-held .50 calibre gun in the tail position and twin .50s in the mid-upper power turret, not much with which to fight off the firepower bearing down on us. No member of our crew needed to be told we were in a very sticky situation. I remember seeing the sea moving just below me and thinking that in that Mediterranean I would probably end my life. All very matter-of-fact; no fear, just tension.

'One Messerschmitt positioned directly astern and the others off each wing tip to catch us if we turned. As the 109 approaching the tail came within firing range our navigator, watching from the astrodome, shouted which way to skid turn to evade. For six minutes the three 109s took turns in pumping 20 millimetres and bullets into us and although we both took turns in throwing the Marauder around she appeared to be hit on every pass. Then the good news that all three 109s had turned back, perhaps low on fuel, out of ammunition or maybe one had been hit by our gunner's fire. We didn't know. Merv Hogg, like all Canadians, was always well supplied with chewing-gum and kept a generous supply available on the throttle pedestal. I was not, and never became, a chewing-gum addict, but it seemed at the beginning of this episode that it would be beneficial for my somewhat dry mouth and I helped myself to some. It was only after the action that I felt that this gum was not very chewable and on removing all three sticks from my mouth I could see that the somewhat metallic wrapping had never been removed!

'An intercom check on the two gunners in the rear brought an okay from the mid-upper but the tail-gunner said he had a head wound. I went back along the catwalk, dodged round the mid-upper's feet, and crawled to the tail. George Senior's face was covered in blood which appeared to be coming from his head. I got a field dressing and started wiping it away but could find no wound. I then noticed a great deal of blood on one of George's hands. It took a few moments to put two and two together, but what had happened was that during the action his gun had jammed and in his desperation to clear it he had, unnoticed, cut his hand on the breech mechanism. Perspiring profusely he had then wiped the sweat from his eyes with the back of the bloody hand. The anti-climax was that finding there was no battle wound we both burst into near uncontrolled laughter, probably emotional relief at surviving a very sticky situation. Eventually I started back to the front of the aircraft looking for fuselage damage as I went. As I was passing Smithy's feet in the mid-upper again I happened to notice a neat hole through the sole of one of his boots. Engine noise made normal communication impossible so to attract his attention I thumped his leg and motioned for him to come down. When he did, I could see another neat hole in the top of the same boot. He seemed puzzled so, sitting him down in the fuselage, I removed both boot and sock. I was confronted with what looked like a miniature RAF roundel on both top and bottom of his foot; a circular red wound in the centre surrounded by a blue bruise. It was apparent that during one of our sharp evasive turns a bullet had gone clean through boot and foot but Smithy hadn't felt a thing! Only after my discovery did he start to feel any pain. Although the hydraulic system had been damaged and there were 76 holes in FK123, nothing vital had been hit. Either the enemy pilots were poor shots or our evasive action was exceptionally effective.'

Beyond Italy and the Alps, over Austria and Germany or other parts of the Balkans, it was a different matter too. The battered Luftwaffe fighter force rose by night and day to meet the intrusions of the strategic bombers and the Flak at vital installations, such as oil refineries, was murderous. Wellington and Halifax squadrons, subsequently converting to Liberators, faced similar perils as the heavies operating from England. All aircrew were volunteers, yet here and there appeared the odd individual who had second thoughts about venturing into the night sky in a bomber. John Heap:

'After crewing-up at an OTU we went to the transit camp at Almaza, near Cairo. Here you knew you were getting pretty close to the war; the next step would be a squadron in Italy or India. There were a few chaps who had become detached from crews and who had been around the place for some time. The suspicion was that they were suddenly not very keen on going to war. One individual in particular was either round the bend or trying to work his ticket. From the way he carried on this appeared to be the case. At every parade he would arrive with heavy great-coat and wrapped-up as if it were freezing when the temperature was usually up in the eighties or more and the rest of us were in shorts and light shirts in the sweltering heat. We called him "Forty Below". I've no idea what they finally did with him.'

Losses were an accepted part of operational airfield life wherever the location. A newcomer's introduction to this unpleasant fact was usually the empty bed he filled. In Italy this enlightenment could be far more stark. Alan Ackerman:

'We reached No. 40 Squadron at Foggia Main in October 1944. The first thing we asked was where do we sleep and one of the chaps took us over to a tent. There were a couple of beds that were occupied and a couple of spaces. Our guide pointed to the spaces and was about to leave as we asked where our beds were. "They become available," he said, and left. So my first few nights were spent on the tent floor. But a bed did become available quite quickly. A Flight Sergeant in one of them didn't come back from a trip and I took over.'

The most harrowing experience of losses was to see an aircraft carrying a friend explode, be consumed by fire, or suffer some other form of destruction from which there could be no escape. Usually this could only be in daylight because, for the most part on night operations, darkness cloaked identities. A loss was then only felt through the absence of a crew the next morning – or the memory of last associations before the raid. William Coote:

'It was a warm evening, just before dusk, in the early spring of 1944. The aircraft of No. 70 Squadron were lined up for take-off on Tortorella airfield in Italy while the crews relaxed on the grass, waiting instructions. Presently the R/T sets left "tuned to Control" crackled into life with orders to start engines. Immediately, everyone began making for the nose ladders to enter the Wellingtons. Next in line ahead of my aircraft was Flight Sergeant Harry Pollard's and I happened to glance in that direction. Harry's rear-gunner was entering his turret from the outside, as gunners sometimes did, and he began whistling. As I mounted the ladder there came to my hearing the first few bars of the verse to *Stardust*, Hoagy Carmichael's famous composition. The piece that runs: "And now the purple shades of twilight time, steals across the meadows. . . ." Just that: then I was inside the aircraft. Five or six hours later, after de-briefing, we sat in the mess tent having our flying breakfast. The places that Harry Pollard and his crew would have occupied were vacant. As far as I am aware they were never heard from again. Strange how particular associations persist: from then on, whenever I hear the strains of that melody, the memory of Pollard's rear-gunner climbing into his turret always seems to come to mind.'

An increasing number of operations flown from Italy involved support of Resistance and undercover organizations in eastern Europe. The longest, and usually most difficult, were to Poland, begun in the autumn of 1943 and culminating with the dropping of supplies to beleaguered patriots in Warsaw a year later. Some aircrew involved, like Leon Piechocki, were Poles:

'In the winter of 1943/44 the Polish Flight of No. 138 Squadron began flying special operations to Poland out of Brindisi, Italy. The first trip for my crew was at Easter and very emotional and sentimental it was to be over our homeland again after four years. We pushed Polish traditional painted eggs, chocolate, cigarettes and other little presents into the containers. The flight took place by the full moon with snow still on the ground. The drop from the Halifax into a forest clearing was from 500 feet. As we circled after the drop we saw a light flashing V for Victory in Morse. They were doing it by opening and shutting the door of a little cottage near the drop place. You can imagine our feelings.'

Most air aid went to Resistance movements in the Balkans, in particular Yugoslavia where Tito's peasant army made life increasingly difficult for the occupiers of their country. In June 1944 an RAF Balkan Air Force was established, using RAF, SAAF and Allied units, with the purpose of rendering assistance to the Yugoslav partisans and harassing enemy communications in that theatre of war. To co-ordinate operations, close liaison was essential, with the result that now and again RAF personnel found themselves in very strange situations. Fred Pawsey tells of one of his adventures:

'One day in July 1944, Group Captain Boyd sent for me and, after offering a glass of gin, asked whether I would go to Yugoslavia to observe and advise on the discipline and signalling necessary for successful air support. Apparently the partisans were to make an attack on a small town occupied by Germans and the Ustachi [fascist Croatians] and my squadron would give air support. "You will only need a tooth brush and a revolver," he said, "as you will only be away for about 48 hours." That night I flew in a Dakota from Brindisi across the Adriatic to an airstrip in Croatia. I sat on a sack of flour surrounded by weapons and ammunition. We landed in a remote valley, guided down by a flare path of bonfires. The speed with which the flour, ammunition and myself were off-loaded was remarkable. With equal speed wounded partisans were put into the aircraft which did not stop engines and was soon on its way back to Brindisi. Before dawn I was guided to a hillside overlooking the town to be attacked. It all looked very peaceful until the time came and the battle was fought and won with my Spitfire squadron giving air support. There were no mistakes and the jubilant partisans captured the place and took some prisoners.

'After some discussion of the battle it was time to get back to the airstrip. I was asked by my escort if I could ride a horse. My experience was limited mainly to cart-horses, but pride demanded that I say yes. Shortly afterwards three magnificent, lunging and snorting horses were brought up; none had saddles. As I stood frozen at the thought of trying to ride one, my two escorts leapt like Cossacks on to the backs of two of them and literally streaked off in clouds of dust along the track. I was obviously expected to do the same as my mount reared and lunged, eager to be off. I unfroze enough to show by signs and gestures to the partisans that they would have to help me up. As soon as I was astride, the horse was released and immediately streaked off after the others with me clinging on desperately – and I mean desperately. With every stride I was pitched one way and then another, fully expecting to end up in the dust at any moment. Almost without thinking I shouted "Whoa, whoa!" The horse evidently construed this as encouragement and went even faster. Puzzled by this disobedience it occurred to me that a Croatian horse was hardly likely to respond to English commands so I hollered "Stoy!" which I knew meant stop. To my great relief the animal came to an abrupt halt, ears pricked and quivering and obviously resentful of this command. Gingerly relaxing my arm grip around its neck I sat upright to take stock of the situation. Appreciating I was alone and that it would be very difficult to explain to partisans, let alone Germans or collaborators, my presence wearing RAF battledress and sitting on a wild horse in the middle of this occupied country, I decided it less perilous to continue. Very cautiously, making encouraging noises and with gentle heel kicks, the horse was made to walk and not gallop. In the hot sun I was soon aware that my sweating backside and legs were in most uncomfortable contact with the horse's hard and sweaty hide. This soreness became more acute with the animal's every movement along the rough track.

'Eventually I reached the airstrip where my two escorts had rejoined their friends and seemed quite unperturbed by my late arrival. There was much laughter when they realized they had to help me off the horse and even more when I indicated that I was too sore to sit down on the grass and enjoy some of the black bread they were eating. When more partisans arrived there was further hilarity and slapping of bottoms as it was explained why I was standing. How was it, they inferred, that a man could fly a Spitfire and was not able to ride a horse? Only the sudden shelling of the airstrip by advancing German tanks saved me from further friendly ridicule. Suffice to say that my 48-hour visit was somewhat extended as we fled into the hills. During the ensuing adventures great kindness was shown me, but everywhere I went my companions derived great pleasure out of recounting the tale of my sore rear-end with appropriate gesticulations.'

Another division of RAF air strength in the Mediterranean was the Coastal Air Force charged, primarily, with the disruption of enemy coastal shipping. It could be a very dangerous task, particularly in circumstances such as those remembered by Eric Myring:

'We hit the Italian coast west of Trieste, turned left and followed the coast around. As we approached Venice I saw two ships which were head-on to us, outside Venice harbour. They were some distance off, so I said to Tom Corlett, my navigator, "There are two merchant ships ahead, we'll go and prang them." Over the intercom came Tom's cool and steady voice, "They look like F-Boats to me!" I shouted back, "I know what bloody F-Boats look like, these are merchant ships, we are going to have a go at them."

' "I'm sure they're F-Boats," said Tom, but again I said that he was wrong and that we were going to attack. Now, to our Beaufighter crews F-Boats were the greatest hazard when carrying out shipping attacks. They were about the size of a corvette, very heavily armoured and their armament consisted almost entirely of short-range and medium-range anti-aircraft guns. Their role was simply that of a floating anti-aircraft platform, designed to protect shipping and shore installations from low flying aircraft. To us they were "Flak Ships", to be avoided at all cost in all but exceptional circumstances.

'I called our No. 2 over the RT, a new crew on their first op, and said, "Hello Nosey 32, this is Nosey 26. There are two merchant ships ahead, we are going to attack with rockets, follow me in." As the ships were head on to us, I had to pull over to my right, then make a sweeping turn to my left so that I could make the proper approach and attack the side of the ship. We were, of course, flying at "deck level", and when I estimated that we were the right distance from the ships, I pulled up to 1,200 feet in the usual way, then dived down on the nearest ship to me. This was the first time I had been able to get a proper look at the ship and to my horror all I could see was metal deck and what looked to me, in that split second, to be "hundreds" of guns pointing into the air! I had to make a split-second decision and decided the only thing to do was to continue my dive, fire my cannons, let go my rockets, then get away corkscrewing at low level as quickly as I could. As I have said, there were two ships, and both were F-Boats, and for some reason I cannot explain there was no reaction from the boat I attacked whereas the other F-Boat started firing at me with everything they had got, or so it appeared to me. Fortunately I was flying across their line of fire and was quickly out of range of their light gun fire, otherwise we would have been blown out of the sky.

'I was sweating like mad, wondering how I had got away with such a stupid error when a little voice came over the air, "Hello Nosey 26, this is Nosey 32. I forgot to switch on my rocket switch so I didn't fire them. Are we to go round again?" I was so shattered that rather than replying that we were not, I said, "Nosey 32, they are F-Boats. You can go round if you like, I'm going back to base!" This was terribly bad leadership on my part, but fortunately he followed me so my second lapse did not have any dire consequences. When we were out of range of the ack-ack fire we turned to port to see the result of our attack and saw that the F-Boat we had attacked was listing about 30 degrees to port. Tom, quite rightly, never let me forget the incident, frequently asking, "Do you know what an F-Boat looks like, Eric?" '

Not everyone was so fortunate in escaping the murderous fire put up by German escort vessels; and ditching was a precarious business in a Beaufighter. Eric Myring again:

'Late in the day four of our aircraft had been on a shipping strike in the northern Adriatic and one had been hit by enemy Flak and was staggering home. The pilot decided he could not maintain height and as it was too low to bale out he would have to ditch in the dark. We had all been well-rehearsed in the ditching procedure – this was necessary as all our operational flying was at low level. It was reckoned that the Beaufighter would stay afloat for a maximum of ten seconds, so everything had to be done "according to the book". Both the pilot and navigator opened their escape hoods, the pilot made a perfect ditching, they both got out on the wing taking their first-aid kit, emergency rations, local maps, local money, navigation record, etc., as well as their one-man dinghies which we all carried (and sat on). In addition the aircraft carried a large dinghy in the wing which inflated when the aircraft ditched, and this also went according to plan and within the ten seconds both aircrew, complete with their emergency supplies, were safely sitting in the large dinghy waiting for the aircraft to sink. Well, the ten seconds passed, then another ten seconds, then a minute, and still there was no sign of the kite going down. By this time they were a few yards away from the aircraft and the pilot said, "This is funny," (or words to that effect!) "I'll go and see what's happened." It was summer time, the sea was warm, so he decided to swim across, lowered himself out of the dinghy into the water and found he was standing on the sea bed! North of Foggia, on the coast there is a slim piece of land between the sea and a large lagoon. In the dark the pilot hadn't seen this, and instead of ditching in the sea was smack in the middle of the lagoon!'

The Back-Up Bods

ERKS AND OTHERS

Originally an erk was an aircraftman, fitter or rigger, but the term came to be used for other-rank members of ground staff, irrespective of trade. As there were seven non-flying personnel for every member of aircrew, erks provided the largest unofficial classification in RAF man and woman power. There were more than 300 different ground trades in the service to put aircrew, aircraft and ordnance into action. Many men and women never went near an aircraft or even an airfield, being confined throughout their service to clerical, domestic or driving duties at a depot, administrative centre or the like. But for the most part the term erk was, and still is, associated in the public's mind with the men who serviced and maintained aeroplanes with oil-stained overalls and greasy hands. Indeed, theirs was a vitally important job. Poor or faulty maintenance could precipitate disaster. Good ground crews were well aware of their responsibility and gave their very best. Even so, as in all tasks, experience taught many lessons. Fred Pawsey recounts one of his:

'In May 1940 I was the corporal in charge of the duty crew at Tangmere while the evacuation from France was in full swing. The airfield was packed with a variety of aircraft coming and going. A Blenheim landed and taxied up to the control tower. The only man aboard was the pilot, a Squadron Leader who, as he clambered out, asked me to hold his briefcase and maps, which he quickly reclaimed when his feet were on the ground. He said that he would only be gone a few minutes and instructed me to make sure the tanks were filled to the top. He soon returned, still clutching his briefcase, and wanted to know if the tanks were really full. Despite my assurances he told me to remove the filler caps again. He then got up on the wing and knelt down beside me – still holding the briefcase and maps. I expected confirmation that the tanks had been filled, but his reaction was a mild reprimand because they were not full to the brim and that more fuel could be put in each. Back came the bowser and under his supervision I slowly added a little more fuel to each tank. As he replaced the filler caps he told me that he had to fly the Blenheim to France to deliver some important items and that it was unlikely there would still be refuelling facilities available. In the circumstances every drop of fuel was vital if he were going to have any chance of making a return to England. I have often wondered what this so important mission was and about the nature of the documents in the briefcase he was not letting out of his sight.

Also if the topping-up of the tanks really did see him safely back. But the incident did teach me the need for attention to detail. Thereafter I always saw that an order for full tanks received really full tanks.'

Fred Pawsey was eventually accepted for aircrew training. Many ground crew men made this transition and became excellent pilots, their technical knowledge of airframe, engine and systems probably giving a more cautious approach to flying than found in the average pilot without this background. Another who served as a mechanic while awaiting pilot training was Tom Minta who recalls the qualms of a fitter's responsibilities at the Central Flying School:

'Like most hopefuls who were waiting to be called for aircrew training, I endeavoured to get as many flights as I could. I had acquired a parachute which I kept under the engine covers and when George Stainforth or Peter Salter came down to fly one of the aircraft I'd say, "Want any ballast, sir?" Usually they were willing to let you ride in a turret or some other out-of-the-way position and I had several trips this way. On one occasion I had just been involved in changing a hydraulic pump on a Hampden and got aboard when Peter Salter wanted to take the aircraft up. I was sitting happily in the after-turret looking around when there was a great whoosh of fine mist from the back of the engine nacelle I'd been working on. Hydraulic fluid! Peter Salter said that he was afraid the hydraulic pump had gone and that we would have to make an emergency landing at an airfield with a suitably long runway as he would have no flaps. We pumped the wheels down by hand and landed safely – he was a marvellous pilot. I thought I was for the high-jump, but when the pump was examined it proved to be nothing to do with me. All the same, I can tell you I was a very worried fellow for a time. Such an experience would be beneficial to any member of ground staff.'

The aforementioned failure was of material, but elsewhere human fallibility ensured that aircraft were lost through faulty workmanship. Often the precise cause of an aircraft accident or loss was not established, but many an erk was haunted by the thought that something he had or had not done might be a contributory factor. In general, no body of men could have been more conscientious than service and maintenance crews, frequently working until the assigned job was completed, while enduring whatever the weather could inflict for their discomfort. Much of this engineering work was difficult, tedious and sometimes exasperating – although in the example of the latter that follows Frank Clarke acknowledges much was of his own making:

'While sitting on my tool-box having a rest in our "C" Flight Nissen hut at Wellesbourne, our "Chiefy" [the Flight Sergeant] called out: "Who's on Y-Yorker?" I replied: "Me Chiefy." "Well, there's a large tear in the starboard wing. Get out there and repair it!" he ordered. I got all my gear together, fabric, thread, needles and dope and wandered over to the kite, one of our Wellington Mk IIIs which were all fabric surfaces over geodetic framework. It took me about an hour and a half to do the repair, sitting up on the main spare of the wing. Finally finished, I stood up to survey my handiwork. My foot slipped off the spar and went right through both top and underside fabric of the wing. With some apprehension I went back to the hut to tell the Flight Sergeant what had happened and that the aircraft would have to be grounded for another hour or so. Best not to repeat what he said. The Wellington should have been ready for a practice bombing sortie at 14.00 hours and it eventually took off at 16.30. I was not very popular at the time.'

MECHANICAL TRANSPORT

Motor transport occupied the attention of a section of every RAF station. Handling the heavy stuff was by no means a 'cushy job' with lorry, tractor and van drivers working round the clock to meet demand. Of those men and women recruited or called up, comparatively few had civilian licences to drive motor vehicles and in consequence there were MT driver shortages at many locations. Vic Holloway was quickly initiated into this situation:

'My first posting after initial training was to Montrose in Scotland. Four of us left Blackpool in the morning of 4 May 1940 and arrived at Montrose station at twenty to ten that night – it was just starting to get dark. We 'phoned for transport to pick us up at the station, only to be told they hadn't any drivers or transport available and we would have to walk. So we struggled up to the camp, which was about two miles out of town, and reported to the guard room. Transport were notified of our arrival and a sergeant appeared. "You're just what we wanted," he beamed at me. "There's a tractor and petrol bowser out there. I want you to take it to Edzell; they're night flying." Well, this was the first time I'd been to Scotland in my life and I had never even heard of Edzell. The sergeant said it was about twelve miles away, gave me rough directions and off I went. There were no signposts but somehow I finally found my way, arriving sometime after midnight. They certainly were short of drivers for from then on I was continually on the go, snatching a few hours sleep here and there. I discovered there were only eleven drivers to serve all the transport on Montrose and four satellites. I think it was five or six weeks before I had met all the other drivers, we were so busy.'

MT was a particularly important element of the tactical air forces, following the armies in North Africa, Italy and – after D-Day – in western Europe. RAF ground personnel moved on from location to location, now and again with reminders from the enemy. Vic Holloway:

'I was driving near St. Nicholas in a convoy of recovered vehicles which we were taking to our depot near Brussels. Looking ahead, I saw a house disappear in an explosion and two or three of our vehicles went off the road into a ditch. I was far enough back only to feel the blast. At first we were puzzled by the cause and then realized it was a V-2 rocket. Luckily none of our people were killed.

'One night in the winter of 1944-5 we were instructed to collect a fleet of lorries from a works just outside Brussels and drive them to a location that would be indicated by a Belgian guide. Every lorry that was a runner towed one that was not. Although they had all been painted up and looked quite good from the outside, it was obvious they were in poor mechanical condition. The only light on each lorry was on the back axle where it could only be seen by the driver of the following vehicle. We had no idea where we went, but it must have been near to the front lines. After parking the lorries as instructed, we were taken back to our depot. I had almost forgotten about this night when, on 8 May 1945, we drivers were sent out to these same lorries which were still where we had left them. It wasn't until we returned with these vehicles that evening that we learned the war was officially over.'

SIGNALS

With the tactical air forces went various mobile support units providing radio and radar facilities for aircraft control and headquarters communications. Mostly theirs was an unglamorous job of move, set up, wait and listen. An exception was the experience of Leonard Owens' outfit which suddenly found itself present at one notable event of liberation:

'The Allied liberation force that entered Paris on Friday 25 August 1944 is recorded as being composed of French and American troops. However, there was a British component, albeit small. I know for I was part of it. My outfit was 5285 'G' Mobile Signals Unit, attached to No. 148 Wing operating from Carpiquet airfield just west of Caen. In the early hours of 24 August we were instructed to close our W/T net and be ready to move at first light. The few hours of speculation were finally relieved by our CO, Flying Officer Baber, and the chief Intelligence Officer of 85 Group, who gave us the amazing news that we were bound for Paris whose liberation was imminent. Our presence was required with that of a Ground Control Interception unit to meet the threat of Luftwaffe retaliatory raids expected once the capital was taken. Our six vehicles, carrying the equipment plus seventeen men, set off on what was to be a circuitous route of some 200 miles. The direct route through Lisieux and Evreux was not possible as fighting was still going on nearby. Instead we went south to Le Mans to join forces with the GCI unit before turning east through Chartres, where we spent the night. The following morning we set off in the wake of a column of French Army trucks and half-tracks. Progress was slow but by mid-afternoon we were in the suburbs of the capital with the welcoming crowds lining our route becoming larger as we neared the city centre. By the Eiffel Tower a huge throng barred our way and insisted we join them in their liberation celebrations. Embraces and kisses were exchanged; with true British aplomb, all were welcomed, no matter what the sex of the donor! We joined the vast assembly of citizens in singing the *Marseillaise* to a background of small-arms fire and the occasional explosion, reminders of the mopping-up operations proceeding in the vicinity.

'Eventually we were again able to proceed to our designated site, the Longchamps racecourse. The previous occupants, a German heavy Flak battery, had evacuated the position only a few hours earlier. As we "set up shop" hundreds of sightseeing Parisians arrived to line the rails and study our form. Never were runners in any Longchamps classic scrutinised more closely than we were that day! With radar and wireless aerials and antennae erected in record time, we were prepared for enemy air activity that night but this was nil. The anticipated air strike did materialize the following night when some 150 Luftwaffe bombers swept low over the city and in the course of a half hour delivered the last and heaviest air raid Paris was to suffer. Of 1,200 casualties, 200 were fatal, while 600 buildings were damaged or destroyed. The meagre cover our GCI was able to provide had been swamped by the concentration of aircraft, added to which the topography of our site, a natural bowl surrounded by woods, made both radar and W/T reception difficult. On top of this our controllers had been unable to communicate with some of the night fighter pilots in our sector as they were employing different R/T frequencies. Morale was at low ebb following our apparent inability to even minimize the raid's effect. A move was made to a more suitable location south of the city, but the enemy never returned to challenge seriously the Ack-Ack defences that were soon in position. So the next few weeks provided several off-duty trips into the city until the higher command decided the unit could be better employed at its original assignment. These halcyon days came to be savoured in memory; none more so than that extraordinary day when Paris was liberated.'

Another branch of signals activity was the 'Y' Service which had a host of Field Units dotted about the UK and the various war zones. Broadly, their work was the interception, monitoring and reporting of enemy radio traffic. Personnel were signatories to the Official Secrets Act, but few, if any, in Field Units had the slightest idea what the reams of figures and lettered code messages heard and written down concerned or revealed. Only very occasionally could a connection be made with actual events. Graham Smith, an operator with No. 5 FU in Malta:

'On a particular 10pm to 3am watch in 1943, at a time when the Allied armies were closing the final locks on Rommel's Afrika Korps, a frenzied amount of "traffic" was found to be emanating from an enemy W/T station in Sicily. As the Malta Fighter Control VHF unit was situated in the same room, we were soon aware that the enemy messages intercepted related to swift action to dispatch and direct Beaufighters of the island's night fighter force. The coded intercepts indicated that the Germans were dispatching troops by towed gliders in order to effect a last-ditch stand in the Cape Bon area of Tunisia. The atmosphere in the ops room was somewhat electrifying as the Beaufighters caught and wrought havoc among the Ju 52 transports and their helpless gliders while in transit over the Med between Sicily and Tunisia. A few days later, Corporal Normington, one of our long-serving station personnel, "picked up" on his allocated station a whole string of German messages in plane language telling the world, as it were, that surrender to the Allied forces was taking place. Notice was given that it was the operator's final message; please advise his next of kin; followed by name, rank, serial number and, of course, "Heil Hitler" to round off this poignant transmission. Again, the amount of satisfaction gained from this was quite something for we "listeners" who normally had little excitement in our task.'

'K' AND 'Q'

Of the many and varied ground assignments within the RAF, there was one that invited the enemy to 'have a go' at you; manning dummy airfields. Known as 'K' and 'Q' sites, they were situated a few miles from a parent station, a real airfield. With dummy aircraft and/or flarepaths, the sites were intended to draw the attention of enemy bombers seeking the parent station. Of the two types 'K' airfields with dummy aircraft were for deception by day and 'Q' sites had lighting for deception at night, but the majority of 'K' sites eventually had 'Q' facilities and there were a dozen purely 'Q' sites. Some two dozen airmen under a senior NCO manned each site which was provided with a concrete shelter, substantial but not enough to survive a direct hit. Ray Howlett:

'While at a dummy airfield near Bury St. Edmunds we were down the shelter on one of our nightly air raid warnings. A stick of bombs landed on the site quite near the shelter. Two chaps were playing draughts. Above the crunch of the bombs and crash of shrapnel, one of the players was heard to say: "Not too much noise chaps, I can't concentrate on my game." Next morning, when we inspected the site, this air raid came to have a more sobering effect on us. The stick of bombs had struck in a straight line directly towards our shelter. Had there been one more bomb I doubt if any of us would have survived.'

RAF SOLDIERS

The ground defence of RAF stations received scant attention until 1939. What measures were taken between the wars were largely localized to meet special requirements, notably the formation of armoured car companies in the Middle East where indigenous populations were not always receptive to RAF policing activities. Airfield defence received more attention in the late nineteen-thirties, particularly the possibility of attack by low-flying aircraft. Even then, practical measures were largely confined to selected station personnel having additional duties, manning rifle-calibre machine-guns on airfield perimeters. The army was relied upon for heavier anti-aircraft weapon support.

After the outbreak of hostilities RAF personnel charged with manning light anti-aircraft guns were designated Ground Gunners and identified by a GG sleeve motif. With the 1940 invasion threat to the UK, Ground Gunners had the additional task of defending RAF installations against enemy paratroopers and by the end of the following year more than 65,000 RAF men were involved in some form of ground defence. In February 1942 the Ground Gunners became the basis of the newly created RAF Regiment, an organization which, both in the UK and Middle East, was charged with providing ground defence of airfields. Later, when Allied forces took the initiative, the RAF Regiment was responsible for recovering airfields previously held by the enemy, and various other tasks in support of tactical air force movements.

Airfield security remained the primary function of the RAF Regiment, with a constant guard placed at points of access and important installations, such as headquarters buildings and ordnance stores. Strict observance of a station's regulations on who should and who should not be allowed to pass was expected of guards even if intimidated by rank – of which there are several known instances. Steadfastness in such a situation certainly paid off for Fred Forsdyke:

'The road between the villages of Watton and Griston was part of the perimeter track of the airfield. The locals had Air Ministry passes so they could use the road unescorted, but anyone else had to be turned away. However, if military people or others we thought important wanted to come through, it was first necessary for the guard to consult with Gun Ops for permission to escort the persons along the road. An army staff car arrived one day, driven by an ATS officer and with a general or someone of very high rank in the back. He demanded to use the road, but the guard wouldn't let him and called me, the corporal in charge. I politely told the officer I'd first have to get permission, but that really upset him and he said he was not going to wait. So I simply told some of my men, who had come out of the hut when they heard the commotion, to man the guns. "Are you threatening me?" the officer barked. "No sir, I'm stopping you," I replied. Well, I got the permission, but as he'd given me so much hassle I set off in front of his car on my motor cycle at my pace – about 15–20mph. Later that day the same officer came past the camp on another road. He sent his aide-de-camp into the guardhouse with a message and 50 cigarettes for the corporal who wouldn't let him pass until the proper authority had been obtained.'

For many, the monotony of guard duty or manning a gun post characterized service in the RAF Regiment, particularly at isolated locations where the likelihood of a hostile approach was remote but could still not be ignored. In such circumstances, senior NCOs looked round for some means of sustaining morale. John Sharman had a novel solution:

'For many of us in the RAF Regiment the biggest problem was boredom. In my case manning a Bofors gun, four hours on and four or eight hours off, day after day. Nowhere was boredom worse than at Sullom Voe in the Shetland Isles. Close to our gun site was a deserted and dilapidated building which had been a small church. I obtained permission to use this as a recreational centre. In off-guard hours we repaired the roof, decorated the interior and constructed a stage and a bar. Beer only was obtained from the NAAFI and, with bread and cakes from local shops, plus eggs from friendly Shetlanders, we had quite a cosy place. One of my chaps painted some excellent nudes on the walls – but quite tasteful. Everything went along well until one day I was approached by the RAF padre on the main base who said, "Sergeant, I hear you've renovated the old kirk. I'd like to have a look round with a view to using it for services." Well, I was taken aback and tried to explain that I did not think the place was suitable as there were some rather revealing murals. The padre, a hearty Scot, persisted and asked to have a look round. He seemed a bit shaken when he saw the nudes. However, I suggested that we could drape the stage curtains over the walls when we had a service. He was delighted. The services were very popular with the men. The padre was a good old boy. "No sermons," he said. "What I like is a bloody good hymn. Something to raise the roof." We told him, "You name them – we'll sing 'em." And so we did.'

Airfield anti-aircraft gun emplacements had to be manned night and day, although more relaxed systems were introduced at many UK stations during the latter half of the war when the danger of air raids had lessened. Manning an open machine-gun or cannon post was not only tedious but frequently exposed gunners to most trying weather conditions. In the circumstance a little excitement was welcomed; sometimes it was not. Fred Forsdyke again:

'A 24-hour watch had to be kept by all gun crews whatever the weather. There was a terrible storm one night while I and another fellow were on duty at the Hispano cannon site near a hangar. It was raining cats and dogs and I had a need to relieve myself. Usually we had to go over to a lav by the hangar, but with the heavy downpour I didn't think a little more water would make much difference if I just went outside our sandbagged emplacement. It was an offence not to use a toilet, but no officer was likely to be out on such a foul night. So I shouted where I was going to my mate and went out of the entrance and round the blastwall. As I was standing there, out of the corner of my eye I suddenly saw a still figure watching me. If my hair could have stood on end under my steel helmet I'm sure it would have done, such was the scare I had. My first thought was that an officer had caught me out. Then, peering through the gloom, I realized the figure was the poison gas detector, a can device on top of a 5-foot pole. Relieved, I walked back round the blastwall and into the emplacement only to be knocked nearly silly with a blow to my head. It turned out the other fellow didn't hear me shout that I was just popping outside and he thought I was still in the emplacement when in the dark he saw an intruder in the entrance. He grabbed the first hefty thing available – his tin hat – and struck out with it. Not my night!'

RAF Sailors

From its formation the RAF had need of maritime vessels to use in servicing floatplanes and flying-boats. To the more than a hundred small vessels for this and associated purposes on hand by the late nineteen-thirties were added the designs known as high-speed launches. These were specifically intended for the fast rescue of airmen who parachuted into the sea or whose aircraft had crashed into 'the drink'. Further procurements established the HSLs as a major element in the Air Sea Rescue service that evolved during the early months of hostilities, and eventually came under Coastal Command control. By 1945 the RAF world-wide had more than 900 'boats', of which some 300 were manned for ASR duties. While the remainder were chiefly employed in support of flying-boats, several marine craft were used for specialized purposes such as barrage balloon launch beds and targets for estuary ranges. The success of the Air Sea Rescue launches was significant. More than 6,000 persons had been plucked from the sea around the UK and some 3,000 from the Mediterranean by the end of the war, rescues often conducted in enemy-controlled areas. Most former HSL crewmen can relate tales of the remarkable or unusual from their service experiences. The following from Ted Shute are certainly in these categories:

'During the siege of Malta we were frequently at sea picking up both British and enemy aircrews who had baled out and landed in the drink. One lovely sunny day with a calm sea, we approached a Spitfire pilot who was sitting in his dinghy awaiting our arrival. As we came alongside, one of our deckhands put out a boathook to draw the dinghy alongside. In so doing the boathook punctured the dinghy and the survivor got a ducking. When we got him on board he greeted us with a broadside of non-technical language which made it clear to us that he was not pleased at the soaking we had given him. After a while he calmed down and then we got the explanation for his displeasure at the ducking. Unbeknown to us, some of the pilots on Malta had been putting a coin into a kitty every time they went on a sortie. The kitty was to go to the first pilot who had to bale out in combat and who managed to inflate his dinghy just before ditching so that he could land in it – dry! The pilot we had just picked up had achieved a dry ditching and was looking forward to picking up a useful reward on returning to the airfield. But – we had not taken him aboard dry and so deprived him of quite a useful sum of money.

'While based at Gibraltar I was on High-Speed Rescue Launch 2583 when we were called out to a position midway between Gibraltar and the North African coast and all ships in the area had also been alerted. A Lancaster had taken off from Gibraltar on her way to England and the controls had gone so that she could not attempt to land again and the crew would have to bale out. The aircraft was flying in a wide circle over the Straits of Gibraltar and slowly losing height. We saw a number of parachutes drop on land near Algeciras, but there was still one more man to bale out.

'When the aircraft was down to less than a thousand feet it passed close to us and we could see a man sitting in the aft hatch waving. The next time the aircraft approached us it was obvious that it was on the point of ditching. At that moment the aircrew bod doubled up into a ball and rolled out of the aircraft. He hit the sea and bounced a couple of times and stopped near to a Spanish fishing-boat which picked him up. We arrived alongside within minutes and took him on board. He was somewhat shaken up but apart from that he only appeared to have a broken ankle. Apparently he did not have a parachute and so could not bale out earlier with the rest of his colleagues.'

All Air Sea Rescue crews were close-knit, self-surviving, jealous and proud of their boats. This is very evident in Cecil Featherstone's eulogy of his beloved No. 2551.

'She was one of the "whalebacks", so named because of the resemblance of the superstructure to that mammal. She was very fast, uncomfortable in a rough sea, but so very seaworthy and a great joy to us. We had experienced many trips, good and bad, and twice volunteered to go to sea when the local lifeboat reckoned it was too rough for our boat. Once, when on patrol off the Dutch coast searching for an aircrew down somewhere in a dinghy, the sea was extremely rough and a freak wave broke over us. It cleared the deck of all gear – the Carley Float, life-belts, rubber dinghies, mast aerials, searchlights – and split the superstructure. The boat was filling quickly and temporary measures were taken to try and stop the inrush. Our engines were swamped, but our two engineers worked like beavers in most difficult and very uncomfortable conditions and managed to get them restarted, a heroic effort, and slowly but surely we got back to base. We were sometimes followed back by E-Boats, mainly because we knew the way through the minefields and also because they knew that we were not carrying any armament that would be effective against them. A signal back to base and out would come the MTBs, roaring past us to do battle outside the Scroby Sands. We made many trips, some successful, some not, some in bad weather, some when the sea was glassy calm and the thrill of full speed ahead was so completely exhilarating.

'On our last trip we were some twenty miles off the Dutch coast, late June 1944; clear sky, sea fairly calm and good visibility – too good in some senses. Instructions were radioed to us to proceed to a position to pick up an American aircrew in a dinghy. On plotting this position I made it almost inside Ijmuiden harbour. After consulting with the skipper I asked the wireless operator to call back for a check. It came back exactly the same. I couldn't believe this, so asked again. I was told in no uncertain terms to get on with the job and not to disbelieve their accuracy. So it was tin hats on and in we went. German soldiers could be seen walking along the harbour walls; why they didn't fire is a mystery, but sure enough there was the dinghy with eight Americans. Over went the crash nets and all eight were hauled aboard as quickly as possible; then with the three engines flat out we headed due west. What a sigh of relief! We'd got away with it. There had been some air cover but it would seem they were running short of fuel and left before any replacement arrived. About ten minutes later down came three German aircraft and shot us up, killing three of our chaps and setting the boat on fire. There was nothing for it, we had to take to the sea. Not much was left in the way of rubber dinghies and the Carley Float was damaged. We all had Mae Wests and salvaged what we could to help our survival. The chief engineer had his knee badly shot up but the rest of us were, surprisingly, unharmed. Back came the German fighters and strafed us again but, luckily, no one was hit. We saw a lone bomber returning to England and hoped he'd seen us so that if our Mayday signal hadn't been received someone might know where we were.

'Some hours later we heard the sound of engines and only hoped they were British. They were, and the sight of two of our own HSLs was unbelievable. Sadly, our skipper had died of exhaustion and one of the Americans drowned. HSL 2551 had sunk and we had lost our skipper and three of the crew. Those of us left now knew what it was like to be on the other side of the game. When we got back to England one of the Americans insisted that I have his flying-jacket. It became my most prized souvenir.'

While manning the seaplane servicing vessels rarely incurred the risk of enemy action, manoeuvring these vessels, particularly in rough weather, was exacting work requiring considerable skill if the comparatively fragile aircraft were not to be damaged. There were lighter moments such as that recalled by Cecil Featherstone:

'While ferrying an aircrew out to a Catalina flying-boat at Oban, I witnessed an amusing incident which also illustrated the need to keep cool in all circumstances. The perspex blisters on the sides of the fuselage gave access to the Catalina, but were very vulnerable to damage from any boat coming alongside, most especially the heavy refuellers which were not the easiest of craft to manoeuvre. Such a refuelling tender was approaching the aircraft with a regular and experienced coxswain, but with a new and raw deckhand. The deckhand leaned over the bow of the refueller, boathook in hand, to pick up the mooring buoy of the aircraft in order to drop back alongside and commence refuelling. Not being very adept he leaned too far, missed the buoy and fell overboard. Some seconds later he shot upwards out of the water, boathook erect. The coxswain, still trying to keep the boat from hitting the aircraft, looked over the side and quite quietly said, "Oh come on Neptune; come back on board and do the bloody thing right!" '

Pay-Off

The Wrong Side of the Drink

'God, its cold! Where the hell are the bed-clothes? What clot's pinched them? In reaching down to pull the clothes up my hand just grasped fresh air. The bed seemed much harder than usual and my pillow seemed to have gone as well, but at least the b. . . . . had left me with the sheet I was lying on. Flat on my back I opened my eyes and gradually focused. Above me was the sky, dark but clear, with the stars just a blur. Damn! This was the first time I'd ended up in a ditch. However sloshed, I'd always managed to make it back to the billet before – but then, there always has to be a first time! Everything was so quiet. Not a sound to be heard, not a light in sight. What on earth anyway, was I doing in the middle of a field? And what were these cords doing tangled up with my arms? Groping around I gradually traced the cords which seemed to be attached to the sheet, but were also attached to the harness which was still strapped on. Then realization came. I was lying on a parachute. But how did I get here? How long it took while I gathered my senses together I'll never know. I tried to read my watch but, annoyingly, was unable to focus properly. Gradually, things became clearer. Dropping through the forward escape hatch, seeing the black bulk of the aircraft above me, pulling the rip-cord, then – nothing, till I woke up on the ground. For a while I tried to reconstruct events to convince myself that we had completed our trip and I had baled out over England on our return. But the true facts eventually came to mind. We hadn't reached the target and on our run-in to Dortmund the aircraft wing had caught fire somewhere east of Aachen and I was now the wrong side of the Channel. Action now seemed to be imperative. I must hide the chute and run. But which way? I did not know on which side of the Dutch-German border I had landed, but south-west seemed the most sensible way to go. In one movement I hit the quick-release of the harness, gathered up the parachute, jumped up to run – only to fall flat on my face. I was getting short on oxygen when I had baled out and consequently was concerned to open my parachute in case I blacked-out. We had been at 19,000 feet. Failure then to follow procedure to protect my head had resulted in the heavy clips hitting me as the parachute snapped open, so knocking me out with – if one may pun – two perfect clips to the jaw.

'Being unconscious I must have landed like a sack of potatoes and my legs and back had been jarred. The knock-out had produced concussion as a result of which my vision was blurred and this was to remain so for the next two or three weeks. However, I was alive and perhaps ignorance is bliss, for I was to find out later that I was the only member of the crew to come out without a scratch. Two were killed, one blown out of the aircraft to have a leg amputated, one with a torn thigh, but who was looked after and patched up by a sympathizer; one with a broken ankle and the other with a sprain. It seemed in retrospect that I was lucky to be knocked out.'

The foregoing is No. 76 Squadron navigator Tom Wingham's account of the realization that his Halifax had been shot down and he was in a foreign land. A parachute descent in darkness was fraught with danger as, unable to see where they were going to, many men were injured and some killed. Dick Enfield admits that he was lucky after jumping from a No. 428 (RCAF) Squadron Lancaster:

'We were at about 18,000 feet when I baled out near Bremen. All I could see were fires burning, the searchlights and Flak over the city, but where I floated down it was completely dark. There was quite a strong southerly wind and as I weighed less than 10 stones my descent took about twenty minutes. I could distinguish nothing below and had no idea when or what I was going to hit until "splash" I was underwater. As I was quite unprepared and didn't even have my feet together it was fortunate I had gone into water. I came up under the canopy but as I was a good swimmer I was able to detach myself and swim free. The water was salt so I knew I was in the sea or the estuary of the Weser. There was nothing to see but the fires and searchlights so I kicked off my boots and swam in that direction. After about a half-mile I found myself in saltings. Staggering up banks and falling down into more saltings, I finally decided to wait until light. Taking off my Mae West I lay down and went to sleep. On waking I walked along the shore and finally found a little lane leading inland. Just as I reached a bend in the lane, round the corner came a German policeman on a bike and carrying a fishing-rod. He must have had a shock because I was covered from head to foot in mud and orange sea-marker dye from the tablet attached to the Mae West. But he just rode past and said "Morgen" to which I replied "Morgen" and kept on walking. A few seconds later I heard his bike go down and a voice said "Halt!" Turning round I saw he had a revolver pointed at me so the sensible thing to do was raise my hands. He took me along until we came to a small café on the main road. The people there must have been slightly sorry for this enemy because of the mess I was in. They made me a cup of erzatz coffee and treated me well, until I was collected by Luftwaffe people.'

Arrival in enemy-held territory was preceded by the traumatic experience of escape from a stricken aircraft, a situation not lost on German interrogators who hoped to gain valuable information while captured airmen were still distressed. Stan Brooks of No. 75 (New Zealand) Squadron:

'I was the wireless operator of a Wellington shot down over Froyennes, Belgium, by ack-ack on the night of 20/21 May 1940; the very first of 193 aircraft lost by the squadron during the war, which had the second highest losses in Bomber Command. My parachute had only just opened fully before I hit the ground. Shells were exploding and machine-gun and rifle fire were going on all around and I had no idea whether I was with friend or foe. I crawled to the edge of the field hoping to find a ditch in which to hide till daylight. There didn't appear to be a ditch so I continued crawling along the edge of the field. Suddenly a brilliant light picked me out and figures ran towards me ordering "Hande Hoch!" I knew I was very much in enemy territory. After spending the night in a cottage cellar with German army types, at 8am I was put on the pillion of a BMW motor-cycle combination, guard in the sidecar, and taken on a hair-raising journey of about fifteen miles to a farm where two other members of my crew were being held prisoner. The three of us were then conveyed another twenty miles to a beautiful château where we were handed over to the Luftwaffe. Here the pilot officer who had been flying as our rear-gunner was taken up the wide staircase. After about a half-hour he returned and the Observer was taken up. The PO told me he had been interrogated by a Flak regiment major and, when my turn came, to give only name, rank and number. Eventually our Observer returned and I was taken up the stairs and into a huge room.

'The interrogating officer was seated behind a desk chatting to two young Luftwaffe pilots. As one had a bandaged leg and the other an arm in a sling, they were obviously convalescing. Both smiled at me and said, "Good Morning" in English before moving out to the balcony of the room which overlooked a lake. The interrogating officer bade me sit down and then pushed a box of 50 Players towards me. I took one and he lit it with a lighter. Then he commenced to ask me all sorts of questions to which I would give no answers other than those laid down by the International Red Cross Geneva Convention. This carried on for twenty minutes with the major becoming more annoyed and exasperated. I was not exactly pleased myself. All the time I was aware the two Luftwaffe fliers were taking a keen interest in the proceedings and from their reactions I was fairly sure they understood English. Suddenly, in his rage the major opened his desk drawer, took out a Luger and pointed it at my chest saying, "If I don't get answers to my questions I will shoot." At this point the two officers hurried in from the balcony and one pushed the major's revolver arm tight on the desk while they appeared to admonish him for his action. The major replaced the gun in the drawer and the two officers returned to the balcony.

'The questioning continued with, "We know you were the pilot of the Blenheim we shot down last night and we know the airfield you came from in England." I was a humble AC1 at the time and I then realized that as I had no flying brevet on my uniform they had assumed I was the pilot. As the Wellington exploded in the air and only three men of the crew had apparently been captured, the Germans assumed the aircraft to be a Blenheim. When I was eventually returned to the others and we had a chance to compare notes I learned their interrogation had been on similar lines. We hoped the pilots had managed to escape and the 2nd pilot, who had spent his early years in Belgium, had a good chance of going underground. Only after the war did I learn that he had been hit by ground fire while descending by parachute. Our skipper was killed in the aircraft.'

At a latter stage, most captured aircrew were processed by specially trained interrogation staff at Oberursel near Frankfurt. Dick Enfield's experience was not untypical:

'Before being sent to prison camp I went through the interrogation centre at Oberursel. For about ten days I was kept in solitary and brought out each day or so for an hour and asked questions. They knew more about the squadron than I did! When I walked into the interrogation room there was a book laid on a table in front of me with the heading 428 Squadron. The questions ranged over all sorts of subjects, but aware they might try and trick me I stuck to the usual name, rank and number and nothing else. Many of the questions about the squadron I would not have been able to answer anyway. They asked the name of the CO and while I wouldn't have told them I honestly didn't know. They tried vague threats, but chiefly seemed to be trying to wear one down. They used to shut the windows and put the heat on during the day and at night open the windows and shut the heat off. This, and the most atrocious food – black bread and weak soup – must have been all part of the treatment to break your morale. There was no contact with any other Allied airmen, but one day when I was being escorted to the toilet I found the fellow from the next cell was also being taken there. He was a Wing Commander who complained bitterly that somebody in passing had whipped his good shoes – which had to be placed outside the cell each night – and left a battered old pair in their place.'

As the war progressed and Bomber Command wrought destruction in Germany on a devastating scale, so the reception awaiting any member of aircrew who landed in the enemy homeland became more hostile. If taken prisoner by Wehrmacht and Luftwaffe personnel one was usually safe; if civilians were involved there was a grave risk of lynching. John Hart had some anxious moments with a hostile crowd:

'Our No. 156 Squadron Lancaster was hit by Flak during a daylight raid in 1945. The pilot ordered the three of us in the rear to bale out, although subsequently he was able to get the aircraft back to friendly territory. At about 1630 hours on Saturday 24 March 1945 I was a wireless operator in a 156 Squadron Lancaster approaching our target at Harpenerweg when the aircraft received substantial flak damage. The aircraft commenced to burn and the pilot ordered the crew to bale out. The navigator, mid-upper gunner and myself left by the rear door, at a height of about 17,000 feet. My parachute opened shortly after leaving the aircraft. It took an estimated thirteen minutes (at a fall rate of approximately 1,200 feet per minute) to reach the ground. The time seemed interminable. I tried spilling some air out of the chute and rotating the chute, as we had been taught during training. Yet each time I looked down the ground seemed a long way off and I seemed no nearer to it, though I knew I must be getting closer. Suddenly the ground appeared to rush up to meet me. Before I had time to brace myself the parachute swung and I landed on my back uninjured. I was in a grass field near a small town.

'Almost immediately a solitary German soldier arrived from one direction, puffing from shortness of breath as he had clearly run some distance. From other directions a collection of people were arriving. The German soldier, before advancing within ten yards, asked if I had a pistol, when I indicated that I didn't have one, he told me to put up my hands, which I did. He then approached and clouted me around the left ear. He went to repeat the action but I stuck out my left elbow and he seemed to then decide that his personal heroics were over; he was middle-aged while I was a fit 20-year-old. At the time of the German soldier's intervention the mob was continuing to grow. Among the arrivals was one in a black SS uniform who promptly clouted me in the teeth with a pistol barrel, breaking one of my upper front teeth off at the gums, and another off leaving a partial stump. Someone else gave me an almighty clout on the back of the head – I had seen someone arrive with a long-handled four-tine fork, but whether I was hit with this or another object I don't know. With the situation getting uglier by the second I realized I had to act quickly if I was to escape from the mob. I picked up my parachute and started walking towards the built-up area. The mob followed me like a flock of sheep. I had no idea where I was going, but I knew that I was moving away from a very violent atmosphere. Eventually we were going through one of the streets, with me leading everybody, when an official-looking individual arrived on a motor cycle, and the procession led by him proceeded to a local building. There I was shortly joined by my navigator, who had also absorbed a lot of physical violence and we were put into a cell together.'

There were those for whom the greater part of their RAF service was spent behind barbed wire in an enemy prison camp. By the end of hostilities more than 12,000 RAF aircrew were incarcerated in prison camps and several hundred more had been repatriated or died in captivity. Treatment was generally fair although much depended upon the administrators at individual camps. Very basic welfare became bare existence during the closing months of the war when the Germans could no longer find sufficient food to meet the required rations, and transport disruptions delayed Red Cross supplies. Enduring such privation was painful, but as one air-gunner who was confined for four years commented, 'At least I was alive whereas the rest of my crew never made it, I assume.' Morale varied from camp to camp and, understandably, depended much upon the degree of deprivation suffered by the inmates. Generally there was an extraordinary resilience and any opportunity to mock the gaolers was never passed up. 'Goon Baiting' was the term for the kind of action Dick Enfield recalls:

'At Stalag Luft VII the guards in the sentry-boxes were changed at the same time every day. The relief guards always marched up along the other side of the wire singing marching songs. A whole bunch of our people would form up in threes and when the guards arrived they would march along beside them inside the wire singing *Roll Out the Barrel* and other ditties at the top of their voices. Each group tried to out-sing the other although we probably drowned them out because of greater numbers.'

The most publicised PoW camp was Stalag Luft III at Sagan, due to the Gestapo's execution of 50 men who escaped. This dreadful act apart, the Sagan camp was reckoned by many hardened PoWs to be one of the best – until the final months of hostilities. Many famous and highly decorated airmen were incarcerated there, including the first DFC of the war, Wing Commander Stanford Tuck, and Wing Commander Braham, treble DSO, treble DFC. No. 10 Squadron navigator Kevin Murphy was particularly impressed with the high morale at Stalag Luft III, exhibited through the many and varied activities:

'The most astonishing took place in the summer of '44. Of all things, a summer fête was staged on the rugger pitch. It may have had an ulterior motive unknown to me – the "Goons" certainly thought so – but most of us took it as it seemed on the surface. Cigarettes were used as cash for the sideshows which were amazingly good. The sun shone as it probably would not have done at a real English country fête and the day was a howling success. Among the many odd characters in the camp who came into their own on this occasion was a Canadian who claimed to have been a "barker" at fairs in his home province. I teamed up with a group who proposed to engage in an Indian fire walking act. Wearing pyjamas, turbans and similar eastern looking atire, our skins were browned with a mixture of old cocoa and marg'. In full view of the guards a trough was made in the sand and this was filled with newspapers, copies of the Volkiscker Beobachter, which were then set alight. When burning nicely a member of our band, dressed as a fakir, slowly walked one leg through the flames. The guards were obviously astounded by our levity and this apparently supernatural display. Unknown to most kriegie spectators too, was the fact that the fire-proof fakir – a fighter pilot, of course – had an artificial leg of steel and plastic. I presume his covering pyjama trousers had been well soaked with water beforehand.'

Not every airman ended up in a PoW camp. More than 2,000 evaded capture and escaped to neutral countries or were secreted out of occupied Europe by escape organizations. Tom Wingham was one of the fortunate befriended and returned. Like most evaders, he is forever grateful to those who sheltered him and with enduring admiration for their bravery:

'For four months I had been hiding out in the Liège area of Belgium. A standstill order was being operated by the Escape Lines due to the chaos on the French railways caused by pre- and post-invasion bombing. The Resistance had placed me on a small farm with Monsieur Schoofs, a cattle dealer, and his delightful family. I had spent an almost idyllic July and August picking cherries, apples, plums and pears in their orchard. But now life was getting a bit tricky. The farm stood on a crossroads and in September the German Army was retreating, often sleeping and resting around the farm buildings or in the orchard. At 10am one September morning a German officer arrived and announced he was commandeering M. Schoofs' study, that there would be a small advance-party of troops just after lunch, and a large contingent billeted in the barns that night. When M. Schoofs recounted this to me I suggested that perhaps it might be a good idea for me to vacate the premises and go back to my previous safe house. M. Schoofs would have none of this; everything would be okay. Although the average German did not speak French very well, there was a risk one of them might recognize my smattering for what it was. Therefore I was to become a Flemish deaf-mute and if any queries were raised about me by the Germans my presence would be explained. Whatever happened I was to remain dumb.

'Eight of us were sitting down to the midday meal, the Schoofs and their three teenage children, a farmhand, the daily help and myself, when two German trucks drove into the courtyard. The advance-party had arrived early! The family and servants left the table and went to the outer scullery door, leaving me alone sitting at the end of the table with my back to the study door. Not my usual place, but in view of what happened next a most fortuitous change. I could hear the family laying down the law to the troops who had arrived. Then two soldiers appeared outside the living-room window fixing up a telelphone line to the study. I was conscious of their two faces pressed against the glass, the attraction being the plates of hot food on the table. They were almost drooling and I doubt whether they had seen a proper meal for some days. Suddenly they straightened up and started to busy themselves again. I realized why when the next moment the door behind me was opened and hit my chair. Fortunately the chair restricted entry, but did allow for the commandeering officer to poke his head through. He was inquiring about something to do with moving the furniture. I could see his head out of the corner of my eye over my right shoulder.

'My role as deaf-mute was about to be taxed. I decided to add an element of the village idiot to my play and flicked a few peas along the table. The door was pulled back and banged against my chair and the question repeated. I chased a few more peas round my plate and shovelled some food in my mouth. Again, the door crashed against my chair and the question put at a level that brooked no denial. However deaf I was I could not evade the movement of my chair and it seemed that nineteen weeks on the run had been in vain and would probably end with all the family being shot.

'At that point Mme. Schoofs, hearing the shouting, came back into the living-room. She was a fine, bonny and buxom woman who immediately sized up the situation, planted herself firmly in the middle of the room and let fly as possibly only a Belgian woman could. The Belgians, outwardly at least, would never show fear of the Germans and she really had a very wide range of invective about dirty Boche boots in a Belgian housewife's kitchen. He may have commandeered the study, but that gave him no rights in the rest of her house and he could take his blankety blank presence back the other side of the study door. If he had any queries, come round the proper way and ask in a civilized fashion. With that she advanced on the retreating officer, slammed the door and producing a key turned the lock.

'It was a close-run thing and after a quick conference it was decided to keep me out of the way pending arrangements to get me out. I went up to my room and waited. Within a short time my escape had been organized and I was told to be dressed and ready to leave at 2 o'clock. Nobody warned me what to expect other than that someone would collect me at that time. I was called just after 2pm and came down the back stairs into the scullery, dressed in black pin-striped trousers and black coat. My documents indicated that my name was Thomas Denis and I worked at the local coal-mine. All the family were standing in the scullery doorway which went out into the courtyard. The Schoofs girls were giggling and their parents chatting to someone standing just outside. Germans were sitting around in the courtyard, some finishing their rations, all mildly interested in the activity at the house. I was pushed through the door to greet my "wife", who proved to be a gross fat peasant woman of perhaps 35 years. With me looking all my 21 years, a more unlikely couple you never saw. There was yet more to come. A child about two-and-a-half years old was playing near the Germans and as I turned to go her Mama called out: "Now come along, get into the pram or Papa won't push you." The pushchair was put into my hands, the child strapped in and we were ready to go. With my extraordinary "wife" on my arm and pushing "my baby", we started on our way. The family stood laughing and waving us goodbye. Nobody had mentioned any release from my deaf-mute pose, so as we went past a group of soldiers I was looking over my shoulder "oo-ing" and grunting in response to the many adieus. What an exit!'

Many of the prison camps for Allied airmen were in the eastern part of the Nazi empire. When the Soviet forces advanced towards Berlin, the inmates of the camps were moved west in an attempt to prevent their liberation by the Russians. In a few instances this movement brought tragedy. Stan Brooks:

'In April 1945 a column of 2,000 PoWs was marched west from Fallingbostel when the Russians were nearing our camp. At the village school in Gresse we picked up food parcels in a distribution organized by the Swedish Red Cross. We had just settled down in a country lane to partake of our first decent meal for twelve days when six aircraft appeared in the distance. Shouts along the column warned us to keep a sharp eye on them; not too soon, for the aircraft wheeled into line astern and dived towards us. At low level they opened up with machine-guns and cannon and swept the length of we helpless PoWs. Hundreds of us jumped the hedge and ran to find cover in the fields as the aircraft, Typhoons, came in for a second attack. The leader, seeing we had scattered must have ordered the line abreast pass that followed. After this third attack I again picked myself up and started running and was then aware of pain in my left arm and upper leg. I noticed some brave RAF types standing up wearing inside-out greatcoats, the white linings hopefully signalling that we were not a marching Wehrmacht column. Perhaps this did the trick for the Typhoons broke off their fourth dive and pulled away. Confusion reigned with dead and injured scattered about. Thirty PoWs had been killed and more than sixty wounded, half seriously. Eight German guards had also been killed and several wounded. The attack took place at 10.30am and it was a couple of hours before the local population organized farm carts and transported the casualties to a cottage hospital at Boizemburg, a couple of miles away. Here I was operated on that evening for the removal of shrapnel by two German Army doctors. These two worked non-stop for several hours and the rest of the staff did a wonderful job for us.

'After surviving the British army artillery bombardment prior to their crossing the Elbe, we were liberated by a patrol from the 6th Airborne Division and eventually transported to an airfield near Luneburg Heath for an air ambulance flight to the UK. While lying on our stretchers on the tarmac, a Wing Commander with a Canadian shoulder-flash walked among us and asked how we ex-PoWs had been injured. An army type informed him in no uncertain terms of the shoot-up and the casualties which occurred. Tears immediately welled up in his eyes as he quickly walked away. He told us he had been the flight leader of the six Typhoons.'

VE-Day and Demob

On 8 May 1945 the war in Europe was officially over; Victory in Europe – VE-Day – was the tag for this occasion. Much of the war in the air had finished days and weeks before as objectives were realized. Now the ordinary chap who wore air force blue seriously began to think about 'civvy street'. But first a celebration, and knowing just how effectively aircrew could celebrate some cautioning words were voiced by wary commanders to their units. As usual, cautions had little effect; this was a very special celebration. Albert Benest of No. 75 (New Zealand) Squadron:

'On the eve of VE-Day our squadron commander called all the officers together and said something like: "Now chaps, I don't want any funny business when peace is declared. There is no need to go mad. I'm relying on you all to set a good example to the other ranks. I'm expecting your best behaviour." Well, when the end came an enormous celebration party was arranged. And who broke his leg jumping over a fire? Why, our squadron commander.'

Many wartime recruits enjoyed service life and considered making it a permanent career. Those men who wanted to go back to civilian life could not get out fast enough. However, demobilization was to be a slow process. Hugh Fisher:

'When it came to being demobbed the release date was based on an age and service group number. If you had plenty of age and years of service you had a very low number. Only wartime service counted and as I had the full six years and had been aircrew, my number was fairly low – 24. Aircrew release group numbers came up quicker than those for ground duty people. When I came out in November 1945 they were still only up to group 7 for ground staff on my station.'

Former prisoners-of-war expected preferential consideration for release in view of their unpleasant confinement, but they did not always get it. Dick Enfield:

'After liberation from PoW camp I was sent home on leave and then received orders to report to Wittering where I expected I would soon be demobbed. Instead I was told I had to undergo a Rehabilitation Course to turn us from obstructionists into complying with discipline again! There would be no demob until my age and service group number came up – in my case two years later.'

When the day finally arrived, releasees were transported to demobilization centres for 'processing'. Eddie Wheeler was in a group sent to London:

'The big hall at Olympia was a hive of activity. We received our gratuity, £75 in my case, and we proceeded to the civilian clothing hall. Scenes of hysterical laughter as suits, sports jackets, raincoats and hats of varying descriptions were tried on. After six years of nothing but service uniforms, to see all these chaps in pork-pie hats, pin-stripe suits, etc., we just could not contain ourselves but finally the NCOs in charge pushed us out to make way for the constantly arriving buses loaded with "demobs". Outside, the "spivs" were waiting to offer £25 for the complete outfits. Many "demobs" were content to accept the £25 whereupon they headed for the nearest public house with their friends and probably were flat broke by the time they reached home.'

Young men relieved from the tedium and danger of war were generally not given to assessing their RAF service in 1945, being too busy making their way through the drab period of scarcities and restrictions that characterized those immediate post-war years. Only later were they given to reflection. Whether or not the views expressed a near half-century on are true of 1945 is not easily gauged. Those questioned insist the assessment unchanged, but admit that, as so often is the case, it is all much rosier with hindsight. Don Nunn:

'If I'm completely honest my RAF service was the best thing that ever happened to me. It gave a profound sense of something worthwhile. There was never a great deal of fear; I never really dwelt on the risks involved. We were all lads together having fun and at times doing foolish things; perhaps our youth cushioned us against the real nature of the dangers faced.'

List of Contributors

Alan Ackerman
George Aldridge
Muriel Anderson (Kenworthy)
D. Arthur
G. Anthony
Leonard J. Barcham, DFC
Denis Baxter
Albert G. Benest
Hugh F. Berry
James Betteridge
Maureen D. Brickett (Bowers)
Stanley Brooks
Kenneth Brotherhood
Frederick Brown
G. Roy Browne
Kenneth Campbell
Peter Catchpole
Steve Challen
E. Frank Cheesman
Frank Clarke
Cyril H. Clifford
William V. Coote
H. H. (Sid) Cottee
Rex Croger
Peter Culley
William Dickinson
James A. Donson
James C. Double
Kenneth Doughty
Alan Drake
William G. Drinkell
Bernard Dye
H. Ernest Edwards
James Eley
Arthur H. Elks
Roy Ellis-Brown
Vincent Elmer
Richard G. Enfield
John Everett
L. C. (Pop) Ewins
Reginald J. Fayers
Cecil Featherstone
Hugh Fisher
William Fleming
Frank (Fred) Forsdyke
Ian F. Glover, AFC
James Goodson
Ralph H. Harrington, DFC
John R. Hart
Gerald D. Hatt
Alan Haworth, DFC and Bar
Albert W. Heald
John Heap
Peter J. Hearne
Gerhard Heilig
Albert Herbert
J. Morgan Hewinson
Victor Holloway
Ray Howlett
Thomas Imrie
George S. Irving
William C. Japp
Desmond Jenkins
Alfred Jenner
Raymond A. E. Jones
James Kernahan
Harold Kidney
Philip Knowles
Roy Larkins
Peter Lee
Elsie Lewis
Ronald W. Liversage, MBE

Ray Lomas
G. T. Hamish Mahaddie, DSO, DFC, AFC
Martin Mason
Tom Minta
Ivan Mulley
Antoni (Tony) Murkowski
Kevin Murphy
Eric Myring, D.F.C.
Horace Nears
Donald T. Nunn
Arthur (Mick) Osborne
John Osborne
Leonard Owens
Frederick W. Pawsey, DFC
John Peak
Leon Piechocki
Joseph Pugh
Alfred Pyner
F. H. (Harry) Quick
D. A. Reid
J. A. M. (Tony) Reid, DFM
William Reid, VC
Harry Robinson
John C. Sampson, DFC
John Sharman
C. E. (Ted) Scott
F. E. (Ted) Shute
Eva Sizzey
George Smith
Graham J. Smith
Harold Southgate, DFC and Bar
A. (Tony) Spooner, DSO, DFC*
Alan Staines
Irene Storer (Forsdyke)
John Studd
Harold I. Sutton
James F. Swale
Louise Tetley (Howell)
Robert Thompson
Ernest Thorpe
Stanley Tomlinson
Hilary Upward
Stanley Ward
Derek Waterman, DFC
George Watts
Edwin Wheeler, DFC
Vernon Wilkes
Roy Wilkinson
S. (Tom) Wingham
F. A. (Mick) Wood
John B. Wray, DFC.

*A. (Tony) Spooner is the author of *Warburton's War*, the biography of Wing Commander Adrian Warburton, the legendary photographic reconnaisance pilot.

Index

ANCHORS AWEIGH!

ANCHORS AWEIGH!

KENNETH POOLMAN

CASSELL&CO

'Not fare well,
But fare forward, voyagers.'
— T. S. Eliot, *The Dry Salvages*

Special edition for PAST TIMES

Cassell & Co
Wellington House, 125 Strand
London WC2R OBB

First published by Arms and Armour 1989 as
Experiences of War: The British Sailor
This edition 2000

ISBN 0-304-35632-8

9 8 7 6 5 4 3 2 1

Designed and edited by DAG Publications Ltd
Printed and bound in Great Britain by
Cox & Wyman, Reading

PAST TIMES®

Contents

Acknowledgements

I wish to thank the following for their invaluable help with this book:
Alan Armstrong; Tom Bailey; A. Barlow; Dennis Bond; Neville Bradpiece; Gus Britton; Jack Bryant; Chris Buist; Ivor Burston; William Capseed; Douglas J. Cole; Eric Craske; Stewart A. Crawford; Howard G. Cunningham; Lieutenant-Commander W. Curtis, RN (Rtd); Mick Dale, BEM; John E. Dodds, DSM; Lieutenant S. Donovan, MBE, RN (Rtd); G. E. Denny; Bill Earp; Lieutenant-Commander D. W. Elliott, RN (Rtd); L. W. Ellis; Peter Embleton; Lieutenant-Commander F. N. Fieldgate, RN (Rtd); Lieutenant-Commander W. S. Filer, RN (Rtd); R. G. Fletcher; S. France; G. H. Goodfellow; M. E. Grundy; F. Hall; A. C. Harman; Lieutenant W. J. Heath, RN (Rtd); Norman Hollis; Lieutenant-Commander A. Janman, RN (Rtd); W. Jeffery; Charles Jones; Lieutenant-Commander Ben Kennedy, RN (Rtd); George Knight; Denis Langdale, BA; F. Lee; W. G. Lambert, DSM; Lieutenant-Commander Richard Leggatt, RN (Rtd); H. Liddle; Lieutenant-Commander F. Longman, RN (Rtd); Lieutenant-Commander R. Lunberg, RN (Rtd); Sub-Lieutenant George MacPherson, RN (Rtd); B. Male; J. Malin; Captain A. Mathison, MN; W. McCall; Lieutenant-Commander A. J. McCulloch, RN (Rtd); George Monk; Lieutenant-Commander H. A. Monk, DSM, RN (Rtd); L. W. Nelson; Iain Nethercott, DSM, AIMEE; E. North; D. V. Oliver; Lieutenant-Commander P. Parsons, RN (Rtd); G. Penny; Lieutenant-Commander C. E. Perry, RN (Rtd); J. J. Pinkerton; Lieutenant-Commander F. C. Rice, DSM, RN (Rtd); E. S. Rickman; G. Rogers; R. R. Rowbottom; David Satherley; S. S. Saunders; Les Sayer; Jack Skeats; C. Shiels; Cliff Smith; Eric Smith; Lieutenant- Commander J. Francis Smith, RN (Rtd); Philip Spencer; Alan Todd and Mrs Roma Todd; E. W. F. Tyler; Captain W. B. Thomas, MN; Mark D. Wells; Nicola Windell; Rocky Wilkins; Phil Wilton.

Kenneth Poolman, 1989

Introduction

The two oldest items of memorabilia in my attic are a white-enamelled water dipper six inches long and one and a half inches in diameter, and a seaman's scratched and battered clasp knife with a broad blade and a spike for splicing. The first was used in my father's lifeboat to measure the water ration (half-full, twice a day) after his ship, the AMC *Salopian*, had been sunk. When George Monk, late radio officer of SS *Auditor*, called on me recently he produced an identical object, relic of his own 13-day ordeal. George was the only radio operator to pick up the SOS from my father's boat, and probably saved his life. Both men's stories are in this book, along with many others.

The 'Pusser's dirk' is mine and tells a much less dramatic story. Its spike was never used for splicing (the only thing I ever spliced was the mainbrace), though it has punched holes in many a tin of fruit, and the blade has only sharpened pencils; but it was with me in a cruiser, a minesweeper and a destroyer, where I, an HO and amateur matlow, once served with real sailors, men like Tom Bailey, who joined the 'Andrew' (Royal Navy) in the Depression for 'three square meals a day and a pair of boots', and found he liked the life; Iain Nethercott, DSM, Sea Scout, hard destroyer man and submarine sailor; Mark Wells, who went from the footplate to the saucy *Arethusa*, and felt at home; Fred Lee, who tells salty tales in the manner of the late Robb Wilton; Dennis Bond, drafted from the South-Eastern Electricity Board and the Godalming Brass Band to face *Scharnhorst*, *Gneisenau* and *Prinz Eugen*; Eric Craske, DEMS gunner from a family of fishermen and lifeboatmen, who grew to love even a 'dirty British coaster'; Bill Earp, who never saw the OK Corral but watched the mighty *Hood* blow up and shadowed *Bismarck* until revenge was exacted – and made a smashing Red Riding Hood; HO Bill McCall, who signed on for twelve; David Satherley, smooth Combined Operator who slept with a sergeant-major (female); Ernie North, who lost his heart with *Chanticleer*; 'Vic' Oliver, with us still only because none of his mines went off; Fred Hall ('From Stock Exchange to Hooligans' Navy'), who did not faint at autopsies; Alan Mathison, who never got to drive his bus but steered tramps through dangerous waters; Bill Thomas, who fought weevils in rust buckets even U-boats ignored; Jack Dodds, DSM, who survived because of where he slung his mick; Con Shiels, to whom the Andrew was home – after the sad streets of Jarrow; Bill Filer, who knew the blue altitudes and the black depths . . . and there are the flying sailors of the Fleet Air Arm, the TAGs and rating pilots, whose company I tried to join, sadly too late, matlows with the hearts of eagles.

These men, and more, tell their stories in the pages that follow. These are the tales of ordinary men at war on the sea, which brought out the best in them – the nod to the need for discipline; the love of ships, especially their own, sentimental in the best sense; the sense of duty owed to ship and self (ideally identical); to messmates and to their great loved/hated guardian, the Royal Navy, which fed them, clothed them, paid them (in many cases when no one else would) and gave them ambition, a chance of achievement; above all, perhaps, the gritty grey humour at their lot – tested, sometimes, by heartless, thoughtless treatment, incompetent leadership, worn-out weapons, hard lying and the worst of weather – 'You shouldn't have joined if you can't take a joke,' they said, and 'Roll on my twelve!'

Kenneth Poolman

Senior Service

Ganges tea is tasty, *Ganges* tea is fine,
It's good for cuts and bruises
And tastes like iodine.

Ganges bread is tasty, *Ganges* bread is fine,
A loaf fell off the table
And killed a mate of mine.

VOLUNTEERS

Wiveliscombe lies in the green Vale of Taunton Deane, Somerset. Once over the Brendon Hills to the north it is less than ten miles to the Severn Estuary, and only a short day's yomp westward to Minehead and Porlock Bay, where the river is lost in the shining Bristol Channel. The little town once bred rugby players. Members of the Hancock family, who ran the local brewery, had captained England and Wales in the 1880s, and in the 1920s the place was still a bustling market town.

The Burstons kept the New Inn, frequented by both farmhands and sailors. Young Ivor Burston, his elder brother Chris, and his friend Alfie Slocombe used to sit entranced by the salty stories of old Bill Prole who had shipped before the mast when sail was still supreme, and ex-Petty Officer Shipwright Fronde Bellew, who had gone to sea with the old ironclad Navy, and served in the dreadnought battlecruiser HMNZ *New Zealand* in the battle of Jutland. Lubricated by a steady flow of ale on the house, the teak-faced old salthorse told tales of the *Shark*, with Loftus Jones steering steadfast for the enemy though mortally wounded, of great ships blowing up, gun flashes in the mist, Von Scheer's battlecruisers looming through the smoke, and especially of Jack Cornwell, VC. A hundred jingo-jangles and doggerel verses had painted the young hero in stirring primaries. In 1927 Chris joined the Royal Marines, and was soon in the King's Hundred, an elite group. Alfie was the next to go – to the old three-decker training ship HMS *Impregnable* at 'Guz' (Devonport).

GANGES

Ivor's turn came on 2 October 1928, when he presented himself with 32 other keen lads at 126 Victoria Street, Bristol, for medical and other examinations.

Only six boys passed, including Ivor, and were given 1/6d each to sustain them on their long journey to HMS *Ganges*, the training ship at Shotley near Ipswich in Essex. The Royal Marine Recruiting Sergeant took 6d of this for 'getting you lads into the Royal Navy', and '. . . we felt honoured to pay up'. In the smoky halls of Paddington they were met by 'a gentleman in a blue serge suit and a bowler hat' who led them, not by tube, but on the top of a bus to Liverpool Street Station so that they could see the sights of London, which were a wonder to them. They felt they were already at sea, and in the City there were 'big shiny models of ships in the windows'.

They disembarked at Harwich in the dark, then were led on the double to a waiting steam pinnace with shiny brass funnel, which took them, not to a ship, but to the bottom of a long flight of steps (the famous 'Faith, Hope and Charity', as they later learned), which led to *Ganges*, a 'stone frigate' training establishment. After a bath they were shown into the 'Nozzers" (new boys') mess for a late supper of bully beef soaked in 'Alley Sloper's Sauce' and an aluminium bowl of cocoa layered with grease – the famous 'kye', which helped to keep the Navy afloat. They were kitted out and shown how to tie on the blue collar framed with three white stripes ('for Lord Nelson's three great victories – Copenhagen, where 'e "clapped 'is glass to his sightless eye", the Nile and Trafalgar), the black silk square ('black for 'is death') which folded into a narrow band to go under the collar and down into the jumper, and how to sew their names on every article of clothing. Here too they were taught how to march, and suffered various 'jabs'. Back in the main camp they became 92 Class, 35 Mess in the Short Covered Way, part of 5 Division; their Divisional Officer was Lieutenant H. W. Sharp, wicket-keeper of the Royal Navy cricket team.

They spent their days doubling between their mess (''Eave-o! 'Eave-o! 'Eave-o! Lash up and stow! Lash up and stow! Rise an' shine, the morning's fine, the sun'll burn yer bleedin' eyes out!'); on the vast parade ground for squad and rifle drill ('By the right, form Squad!'. . . 'Royal Salute, *pre*sent IPE!'); and in the classroom for seamanship – knots and splices, ship's time, shipboard duties and organization, signals and flags, the compass, navigation, Rule of the Road:

Green to green, red to red –
Perfect safety, go ahead.

Farting in gunnery class was punished by doubling up and down Laundry Hill carrying a 6in 'projjy'; there was boat work in the harbour, pulling ('raw hands and sore bums') and sailing; and plenty of sport on the playing fields of Shotley, on which a war would be won. Ivor ran long distance and played rugger with their PT Officer, Lieutenant-Commander C. A. Kershaw, the famous England scrum-half.

Dominating all their activities was The Mast, the mainmast of the old *Ganges*, a Nelsonian three-decker, whose figurehead faced all new entries at the main gate. The Mast was visible everywhere, with its three long yards and high 'tops', a symbol of those old days of 'wooden ships and iron men', when the hands hung on by their fingernails as the yards rolled above high, raging seas, and many a man, his hands frost-bitten, plunged to his death on the hard deck or in the engulfing sea, his despairing shriek drowned by the howling wind. But it was more than a symbol, it was reality for these civvy lads. The greenhorns of 92 Class were not allowed to climb higher than the first top, and they could go up through the 'Lubber's Hole' if their courage failed them at the vicious overhang of the '(Devil's) Elbow', where ratlines inclined almost horizontally over their heads out to the edge of the platform. But they had seen the ceremony of 'Manning the Mast', where the ratlines and every yard were manned by boys linking hands or hanging on the very truck of the mast, on the flat, round Button, 150 feet above the concrete parade ground. Ivor's classmate Boy Hussell tried to scramble up the last stretch of mast to the Button, lost his hold, and as he fell grabbed one of the stays, which threw him clear of the safety net to his death on the cruel parade ground.

Life on the Lower Deck of HM Navy was still harsh. The torture of the lash had disappeared, but for being found with a 'tickler' (cigarette) in his hand in the 'heads' (lavatories) at Stand-Easy Ivor was awarded twelve cuts of the cane, stretched over a vaulting horse. 'To prevent crying out you got the top of your flannel (shirt) in your teeth and bit hard.' The finger-thick cane broke Ivor's skin and, unluckily, that night was swim night in the baths on the foreshore. The sour chloride found his cuts.

One relief from the harshness of the routine was to watch the practice runs of the seaplanes of the British 1929 Schneider Trophy team, based at Felixstowe. The *Ganges* mast was one of the markers for the trial course.

MARLBOROUGH AND *MALAYA*

Suddenly training was over and Ivor went to sea. It was a proud day when, with his best suit and seaman's bone-handled knife (replaced in World War II by an all-metal, cheaper version, the spike on which was more often used to open condensed milk tins than for splicing), he embarked in the tender *Harlequin* for the battleship *Marlborough*, an old coal-burning dreadnought in the Training (and Third Battle) Squadron.

The old 'battlers' took their coal from the colliers *John* and *Francis Duncan*, or alongside the coaling wharves in the Royal Dockyards. 'Coal ship day, although hard work, was good fun,' says Ivor Burston. 'Everyone could smoke, the Marine band played stirring music, there were great vats of lime juice, from which the coal dust had to be scooped off before your mug could be filled. At the completion of coaling, usually at 1,500 or 1,750 tons, the whole ship had to be cleaned. If we won the race to get our coal in, we had cake for tea on the following Sunday – but if you couldn't fight for it you didn't get any!'

Working 'part of ship' was hard too, and much the same as it had been in Nelson's *Victory*. 'The decks were well sanded, and each boy, with a holystone in either hand, knelt down and pushed them to and fro until the whole deck was grated, when it shone really white.'

One of their trips in *Marlborough* took them to Arosa Bay, Spain, across the Bay of Biscay in some of the roughest weather there in living memory. The Fleet tug *Jenny* was sunk with all hands, destroyers took waves over the bridge and down the funnels.

In May 1930 Ivor left the old *Marlborough* for HMS *Malaya* of the *Queen Elizabeth* class, which had represented an attempt by the British Government to regain a clear lead in the naval race with Germany by introducing 15in guns before the latter had anything bigger than the 12in, with a top speed of 25 knots, practically that of the German battlecruisers, and achieved by the new oil-fired propulsion. Before Ivor joined *Malaya* all the '*QE*s' had been reconstructed, with bridge and control towers rebuilt into more massive structures, anti-torpedo bulges added to the sides, extra AA guns, and the original two funnels trunked into one big one, which gave them their distinctive appearance. Some of them were to be further rebuilt in the late 1930s.

'A very happy ship,' noted Ivor, 'under the Captain, Hugh Shipway. We excelled at Regatta, boxing, running and rugby, with Lieutenant-Commander "Nutty" Halloran, an old Irish international, being a very hard taskmaster.'

Ivor became a 'hammock boy' for Midshipmen Custance, Moore and Warmington, for 2/6d a month extra to his 8/9d a week. 'Every evening I had to sling the three middies' hammocks outside the Gunroom, then unlash them, and prepare for sleeping, laying out sheet and blankets and pillow. Each morning I had to fold up the bedding, place it in hammocks, put on the lashing, seven turns of marling hitches, and stow it in the hammock netting.'

Rough Days At Invergordon

As a Side Boy Ivor manned the gangway, 'a general dogsbody running messages for the Quartermaster'. He laughed when Midshipman Moore rammed the picket boat into the gangway at Invergordon . . . 'to my cost. The Commander was there, and Moore was placed on one lower boom shouting "I'm the middy who crashed the gangway!" and I was put on the other side, hollering "I'm the Side Boy who laughed at him!"'

Midwinter in Invergordon made this quite a harsh punishment for such a crime. It was in this bleak anchorage on the west coast of Scotland that the ratings of the Home Fleet had mutinied over the savage and senseless pay cuts proposed under the pressure of the Depression, sharpening the deep-rooted resentment at the privileges blatantly enjoyed by officers (who would suffer far less than the Lower Deck from the pay cuts) – a smouldering, sullen undertow which went back, even in 1932, in a matlow's folk memory to the mutinies at Spithead and the Nore and 'the same spirit which prevailed in 1914 as in the year 1797', and more immediately to the 'rumbling of discontent heard about the years 1916–17' (recounts Seaman Sydney Knock in his book *Clear Lower Deck*, 1932).

The Fleet at Invergordon had been prevented from sailing for 48 hours, while men like Able Seaman Len Wincott and Jack Copeman pleaded with the Admiralty to abandon the proposed cuts, which reduced the wages of the lower-paid ratings by 25 per cent from four to three shillings a day, with far smaller comparative reductions for officers. Wincott described them as 'the forerunner of tragedy, misery and immorality among the families of the Lower Deck'. Dismissed the Service he loved, Wincott joined the British Communist Party, which sent him to Soviet Russia in 1934 to run an international seamen's club in Leningrad. He spent the rest of his life, including ten years in a Stalin labour camp, in Russia, and when he died in 1984 a Royal Navy chaplain honoured his last request, via his widow, to scatter his ashes over Plymouth Sound.

UP THE STRAITS WITH THE BIG SHIPS

Ivor was soon in the Mediterranean again with the light cruiser *Calypso*, in Malta, island of 'bells and smells'; in opulent Beirut; the notorious 'Alex' (Alexandria), home of the Mediterranean Fleet; Naples, and a smoking Vesuvius; rugger in Rome for the Third Cruiser Squadron against the University; sitting near Mussolini for Italy versus Austria; back to Malta, for more Farson's beer at 2½d a half-pint, a jar of the local Ambit, 1/6d for 1½ pints; cricket, football, rugby and running – then Sliema Creek to join the destroyer *Basilisk*, on her first commission.

Ivor, now an Ordinary Seaman, youngest in his mess, was Spud Boy for the cook of the mess. They dined so much better than many of their families at home, on 'Straight Rush' (rib of beef, baked spuds, onions and vegetables), a 'Bugle' (shin of beef, carrots, celery, turnips, tomatoes and doughboys), 'Schooner on the Rocks' (joint of beef on a suet duff, with roast potatoes, fresh vegetables when in harbour), and 'Baby's Head' (individual steak and kidney pudding) at Corradino Canteen. *Basilisk* completed her commission in September 1933, and Ivor, now AB, was an established Salt, who had done a commission 'Up the Straits'.

Ship followed ship, 'big ships' and small – battleship *Barham* to Barbados and the West Indies, regattas in Scapa Flow, King George V's great Review at Spithead, the greatest assembly of naval power seen for several years. Ivor went ashore with brother Chris, now in the aircraft carrier *Furious*, cheered the King and Queen as the Royal Yacht steamed up and down the lines of warships, Dressed Overall, the flags of many nations flying. In *Queen Elizabeth*, champion ship of the Med Fleet in all sports, they just defeated HMAS *Australia* in the race for Seaman Cutters; patrolled the coast of Spain while the Civil War raged, delivering food to British embassies and consulates; cruised the Greek islands; and came home for the Coronation Review, attended by the German *Graf Spee* and the Japanese heavy cruiser *Ashigara*. Then it was marching aboard the new cruiser *Newcastle* to the Geordie tune 'Blaydon Races', and taking her to Glasgow for the World Fair.

'I was married on Boxing Day 1938 and came back to barracks to find that I had been loaned to the New Zealand Navy', complains Ivor Burston. 'The draft was a mixed blessing. The parting was hard but financially came just at the right time. My pay on marriage comprised 21/- a week as Able Seaman, with 3d a day for a Good Conduct Badge, 3d a day as a Seaman Gunner, 3d a day Kit Upkeep Allowance. I gave my wife 14/- a week, plus 7/6d a week Marriage Allowance. On secondment to the New Zealand Navy my pay was trebled, and my wife's allowance went up to £3 a week, which helped to buy a double bed, though I slept in a hammock for 18 months.' He joined HMNZS *Achilles*, a new *Leander*-class light cruiser, and as a 'Lamp trimmer' (keeping all emergency lamps in trim, in case of main electrical failure), he received another 3d a day.

'We sailed late in 1939, for the Far East, via Gib, Suez, the Red Sea (where our Walrus spotter plane crashed, a total write-off); the bazaars of Aden, Colombo, Kandy and the "Temple of the Tooth"; Singapore, where we played hockey and rugby, and beat the Raffles Hotel Select Water Polo team, who did not even give us a drink afterwards, though we made up for that in the "Happy World"; then Bali, a lotus land with silver bells, and finally Auckland, "City of Sails", on 8 May 1939.

'This watery city was warm and friendly. I called on some people from Wiveliscombe, who made me welcome. We cruised to Fiji, Samoa, the Friendly Islands, Ellice, Tonga and Pago, everywhere greeted by Hula-Hula dancers, bands, streamers and flowers, but back in Auckland we had the worst blizzards in years, and the buzz went round that war was in the wind. On 29 August the Captain cleared lower deck and told us that hostilities with Germany were expected. *Achilles* sailed for a destination and a destiny that would bring her within sight of a certain "pocket battleship" which I had last seen decked with flags at Spithead, but the only flag she would be wearing this time would be a battle ensign!'

THE NEW PRESS GANG: ESCAPEES FROM DEPRESSION

We went and joined up,
We went and joined up,
We went and joined Fred Carno's Navy,
Three meals a day,
Promotion and pay,
Number for a holystone
And scrub your life away . . .

Ivor Burston had answered a traditional call, the lure which for a century and more had made young British lads 'run away to sea' with romantic visions of tropical seas, snowy awnings, gaudy regattas and the Isles 'neath the Wind – 'Join the Navy and see the World'. But there was another tradition. A new Press Gang was active in the Britain of the 'Thirties – the pale horsemen of the Depression.

Chris Buist was born in Fife, Scotland, not far from Rosyth, the naval base, and was used to seeing warships of all kinds plying the Firth of Forth. He left school in 1933, a time when unemployment was rife all over Scotland. His father, who had fought in 'The War', was a tram-driver trying to keep four children on his meagre wages. Chris wanted to contribute to the family income. He got clothes from the Salvation Army, but there was no work anywhere. He tried the shipyards, but the only ships moving were His Majesty's. Like many other young workless men, he went to the Navy recruiting office. The only thing on offer was the Royal Marines, and Chris signed up, remembering all the yarns his uncle had spun about his Navy days in the War.

'To have food and new clothes was heaven to me. The discipline was nothing. I soon settled in, but some could not take it, and bought themselves out for £90. All I had was my 14/- a week pay, 5/- of which had to be saved for train fare to go on leave at the end of training, and we bought toilet gear, Blanco, Bluebell, etc out of what was left. With five bob a week for cleaning my mate's equipment I used to have just enough for a run ashore in Plymouth, a couple of beers at the Long Bar or the Snake Pit.'

Chris spent seven months at 'Guz', was sent to 'Pompey' (Portsmouth) for sea service training as a gunner, and then shifted to his home base, Chatham, on draft to the heavy cruiser HMS *York*, which he joined in July 1939, and sailed for the West Indies. Chris and his mates did not have very long to enjoy the rum and sunshine of their tropical paradise before war was declared, and *York* sailed flat-out for Halifax, Nova Scotia, to look after the first convoys.

In the autumn of 1938 Tom Bailey was one of the great army of unemployed, 'mother dead, father vanished into the night', walking the streets of Preston, Lancashire. 'One afternoon I found I had just enough coppers in my pocket to treat myself to the pictures. The film was "Boy from Barnardo's", in which Mickey Rooney, as a sailor boy on one of the latter's sea training ships, showed Freddie Bartholomew how to put on and tie the Royal Navy sailor's collar.' Afterwards Tom was walking home when he stopped at the Royal Navy Recruiting Office. 'If it had been the French Foreign Legion I would have still gone in.'

Tom joined the Navy, subject to having one tooth filled, and finally arrived at Guz, Royal Naval Barracks, Devonport, otherwise HMS *Drake*. He had never seen a warship before, except in the movies, but at Guz the barrack roads all sloped down to the shining sea, where grey ships of all types were to be seen, and a fresh offshore wind always blew in off the Channel.

'What a day!' he wrote. 'Joined for three square meals a day and a pair of boots. Now I've got *two* pairs!'

The 'tiddie oggies' (Cornish pasties) in the canteen were succulent and juicy, generous with the meat and potatoes, and soon Tom felt in his element. 'Squad drill and seamanship were meat and drink to me, and I devoured it all!' He was usually the one to get the class 'fell-in' ready for their PO Instructor, and he was made class leader, with the privilege of shore leave every night. He thrived on the life, passed out top of the class, and was presented with a bosun's 'call' on a silver chain. During gunnery training aboard the destroyer *Brazen* the news came in of the tragic sinking of the new submarine *Thetis*, off Liverpool. The destroyer at once landed a very thoughtful bunch of trainees and steamed back out to help rescue attempts.

After training they moved to Grenville Block and were allocated to various working parties. 'Life was good, a few bob a week spending money, good old Navy ticklers (tobacco) 1/3d a tin, a couple of bars of Pusser's Hard (soap) once a month, 3d for the barracks cinema, and of course the good old NAAFI for a cup of char and a sticky bun. I always found the food to my liking, and you could always make a meal out of a couple of plates of Pusser's soup – I have never yet come across soup to match it.' A familiar jibe at his expense was 'You're all for it, Bailey!'

'During those days a mobilizing exercise was carried out, but us youngsters didn't realize the state of the world. I was happy and courting a local girl, and that was my main concern.'

At the start of the week before war was declared, 'Clear lower deck!' was piped, and Tom fell in with the hundreds of other ratings on the parade ground. Then it was 'From here to the left – one pace forward MARCH!' 'We all wanted to go to small ships, but the "Andrew" had other plans. We were drafted to HMS *Renown*, a battlecruiser. With bags and hammocks packed we entrained at the barracks platform for Plymouth and our destiny.'

The Fleet Air Arm

Eager and ready, the crying lone flyer
Whets for the whale pathe the heart irresistibly
O'er tracks of ocean;
The Seafarer (From the Anglo-Saxon)

In 1910 Eugene Ely had flown his Curtiss biplane off a forward ramp on a US cruiser, and later landed on a platform over the fantail of a battleship. A year later Lieutenant Charles Samson, RN, was launched in a Short S.27 biplane fitted with flotation bags from the battleship HMS *Africa*. British sailors were learning to fly.

A Naval Wing of the new Royal Flying Corps was formed, and a collier was converted on the stocks into HMS *Ark Royal*, to carry ten seaplanes. Just before war broke out in 1914 the Naval Wing of the RFC broke away to become the Royal Naval Air Service. A small converted passenger/mail steamer, HMS *Engadine*, made a pioneer sortie at the battle of Jutland; another, HMS *Ben-my-Cree*, launched the first aerial torpedo attack in history, at Gallipoli, and supported the Army in Asia Minor.

Further progress was made with HMS *Campania*, an old liner fitted with a 'flying-off deck'; HMS *Furious*, a redundant 'light battlecruiser' with an 18in gun, also incorporating a 'flying-on deck'; HMS *Argus*, 14,450 tons, with the first stem-to-stem flight deck, repeated in HMS *Eagle*, 22,600 tons, a converted battleship which also featured a bridge 'island' to starboard (copied later in *Furious*); in the small, purpose-built *Hermes*, 10,950 tons, launched in 1919; and by *Furious*'s sister battlecruiser conversions *Courageous* and *Glorious*.

TELEGRAPHIST AND AIR-GUNNER

Telegraphist Jackie Heath first saw sea service in the coal-burning battleship HMS *Emperor of India*, but was then switched from the old Navy to the new with a two-and-a-half year commission in the aircraft-carrier *Eagle*. He remained in carriers, moving on to HMS *Furious*, which he had already seen in the Mediterranean when *Eagle* had operated with her and the new *Courageous* in mock strikes against other warships.

He had watched the little Fairey Flycatcher biplane fighters leap out of *Furious*'s lower hangar, and the Fairey IIIFs and Blackburn Ripon torpedo-bombers sedately sail the air.

He wrote home, 'If I'm going to be in aircraft-carriers I might as well be an air-gunner.' As a telegraphist he could volunteer for duty as a Telegraphist/Air-Gunner. In those early days TAGs were not recognized as a branch in their own right. So that they never got out of touch with their Branch, they spent no more than two years with the Fleet Air Arm, then returned to General Service as shipborne telegraphists for a year.

Telegraphist/Air Gunner was the only flying job open to ratings at that time. In April 1918 the old RNAS and RFC had amalgamated to form the Royal Air Force. Thirty per cent of FAA pilots were RAF officers, observers were naval officers, and the Navy had operational control at sea; but for sixteen years equipment, air stations and ground crews were under the neglectful direction of the Air Ministry. The FAA was regarded as a backwater for promotion. It did not receive the latest aircraft, and its personnel were generally treated as 'dirty-fingernail types'. At that time controversy raged as to whether bombers could destroy a battleship, and the carrier replace it as the capital ship of the future. The old battleship *Centurion* was used as a target, but results were not conclusive. In the USA trials favoured the aircraft, but US Army Air Corps General Billy Mitchell was court-martialled for propagating such heresy.

Jackie was accepted for AG training, spent twelve weeks at RAF Gosport on aerial telegraphy, then went to RAF Eastchurch for the Air Gunnery course. At the end of that time he was kept on for a further month to do the Bomb-Aimer course. In a Fleet exercise a combined striking force of aircraft from *Courageous*, *Furious* and *Glorious* had scored 21 hits out of a possible 32.

'You had to find the direction and speed of the wind, and on a sort of little computer put the temperature at that height, the airspeed and wind speed. That gave the speed at which your aircraft was travelling over the ground. You lay on the cockpit floor to instruct the pilot to turn left or right, in the meantime watching the red and green on your compass. When your two aircraft pointers reached the target you released a bomb and plotted it on your chart.'

When Jackie landed after his first bombing sortie, 'There was a reception committee on the tarmac. I thought "What have I done? Have I hit the Mess or something?" They asked to see my bombing chart, then told me I had broken the RAF record by dropping eight bombs in a 16-yard diameter 25 yards from the target!'

From Eastchurch he went to No 820 Squadron and *Courageous*, Flagship of the first Rear-Admiral, Aircraft-Carriers. As a Home Fleet carrier, she often exercised in the most savage Atlantic weather. While flying in a gale off the Scottish coast one of her aircraft hit a 5 ft square wooden target with a bomb from 6,000 ft. In a mock squadron torpedo attack on four new *Southampton*-class cruisers, half the 'mouldies' found their targets, while in an exercise in the Mediterranean *Glorious* scored nine hits with her strike force of fourteen TSRs (torpedo/spotter/reconnaissance aircraft). In 1936 Heath was aboard *Eagle* once again, on the China Station. War in Europe broke out just as the troopship returning him to England left Aden, and as a Leading Telegraphist he took over the ship's wireless office. He was on leave when recalled for a course on the ASV (Air-to-Surface-Vessel) version, not yet in production, of the new Radio Direction Finding (RDF), or radar, weapon.

SAILOR FIRST, AVIATOR SECOND

Norman 'Blondie' Hollis joined the Navy in 1930, becoming Boy 2C No 3987 on the books of HMS *St Vincent* ('or was that my mother's Co-Op number?').

'In 1922 my parents took over a farm, a co-operative inasmuch as Father, Mother, Brother and Sister all had their allotted jobs to do, up and about early every morning milking, feeding the animals, delivering milk twice a day, and all for one shilling a week, which was handed over to Mother. Not having a great interest in farming, and with a scarcity of other jobs when I left school, unless parents were able and prepared to pay for an apprenticeship, I answered an advertisement in the *Daily Express* for boys of 16 years of age to train in the RN as telegraphists. Mother asked me to promise her one thing. I asked her what that was, thinking that I was going to be warned off bad women and the Demon Drink, but no, all I had to promise was *not to get tattooed*!'

'Had supper on arrival,' he wrote in his diary, 'macaroni cheese, quarter of a loaf, pot of margarine and a dip – aluminium sugar bowl – of tea. (I haven't eaten macaroni cheese since.) Out of bed 0500, taught how to make up one's bed, then into Mess Room for two ship's biscuits and dip of greasy cocoa. Had thoughts of going over the wall and back home to Mum.

'12 April 1932. Joined HMS *Rodney* . . . 1,500 men and boys. We have a mess of our own and are in the charge of a PTI who has a pair of eyes tattooed on his backside! There was more gold braid aboard her than in Pusser's stores. It took ages to find your way around her, and to scrub whiter than white those acres of foredeck. When she put to sea we discovered that she had a very slow, ponderous roll, the worst sort of motion for *mal de mer*, and when she fired her broadside she smashed all the crockery in the messdecks.

'But I had a soft spot for the ugly old girl, perhaps because I was rated telegraphist aboard her, and my pay shot up to 28/- a week. "What wealth!" I wrote in my diary. "Perhaps I can afford a girlfriend!" Yes, she had her points, they didn't sing "Roll on the *Rodney* . . ." for nothing.

'From dignity to impudence. After *Rodney* I picked up the destroyer *Broke*, which had just been loaned to Gaumont British to make the film "Forever England". She was practically rebuilt with papier mâché to become "HMS *Rutland*." For a fortnight we and a couple of tugs fought the Battle of Eddystone Light. We were paid 5/- a day by the film company, who came aboard every morning with hampers bulging with food and drink which they invariably left untouched, thanks to *Broke*'s lively motion.

'After *Broke* came another of the "boats", the modern *Defender* of First Flotilla. At Singapore we exchanged her for HMS *Wren* and Captain (D) Warburton-Lee, later to win a posthumous VC in the Norwegian Campaign. We thought *Defender* was lively, but the *Wren* could stand on her bow and stern in quick succession! There was a popular Radio Music Hall song called "Red Sails in the Sunset" at the time, sung by comedienne Susette Tarri. We changed the words:

Red sails in the sunset
Out over the sea,
Out doing manoeuvres
With Warburton-Lee.

'It must have been about this time that I set my mind to getting out of boats. I'd met a telegraphist/air-gunner once in hospital. That was the life! Living at RAF stations! Flying pay of 2/6d a day! I never thought that dive-bombing, dogfighting and aerobatics could be a helluva sight rougher than *Wren* in a gale!'

Wren was half of a destroyer sub-division. Sub-Divisional Commander in *Wishart* was Lord Louis Mountbatten, and goodwill trips with him were mostly to the French and Italian Rivieras. 'Wherever we went we were followed by his private yacht with his wife and other members of his family. At Nice we were met by his Rolls with its distinctive radiator cap – a silver signalman with his flags held in the "4/6" position.'

In early August, Norman joined fourteen other budding aviators aboard HMS *Victory* to begin the telegraphy part of the new AG's course. It was a significant ship in which to begin a flier's life. Where was the link with the Old Navy? Indeed, was there a link at all? If sailors had been meant to fly . . . But it was always stressed 'A naval airman is a sailor first, an aviator second'.

Flying training was in Blackburn Sharks for radio procedure and the art of streaming and towing drogue and flag targets. 'Should you lose a target you had to borrow a bicycle and pedal around the countryside looking for it, and be prepared to pay a 5/- reward.' At RAF Northcoates in Westland Wallaces – the aircraft which had conquered Everest – they learned the intricacies of the Lewis gun, 'how to strip, rebuild and fire it'; and dogfighting, 'that is if you had remembered to operate the cocking handle on the climb to prevent it freezing'.

On 8 October 1937 he joined No 811 Squadron in *Furious*, with Swordfish, and went to Donibristle on the Firth of Forth – 'a small RAF station, beautifully maintained, a dining room with *tablecloths* on the tables, smashing food cooked and served by WAAFs' sited on a small grassy plateau overlooking Dalgety Bay, close to the Naval base at Rosyth.'

MALTA, ALEXANDRIA AND THE SPANISH CIVIL WAR

Jack Skeats was a countryman whose life was changed by the Depression. 'Aylesbury was a small market town of only 13,000 souls and as my school-leaving date approached it became apparent that there were no jobs of any kind to be found. My father had nine children of whom six were still at home. The situation was quite galling to me since I had won a scholarship to Aylesbury Grammar School, but on 18 December 1933, I joined the Royal Navy as a Boy Seaman on sixpence a day. Discipline was unreasonably harsh, the food was pitiful and I am still of the opinion that My Lords were showing the lower deck that the last had not been heard of Invergordon.

'A year later I went to sea, seventeen years of age, Boy Seaman First-Class and a fifty per cent rise to ninepence a day (old money). I took passage on the *Hood* to Gib, passing on the way *Nelson* stuck on Hamilton Bank. The Press made much of this – "History Repeats Itself", etc. At Gib I was shifted to *Ajax* for onward passage to Malta and *Revenge*, known affectionately as the "*Rev-en-gee*", which carried the Flag of the C-in-C, Med Fleet. Before long the Fleet sailed to Alexandria – gunboat diplomacy – to show our Government's disapproval of the Italians' conduct of the Abyssinian war. The Maltese disapproved also; a large part of the population depended upon our ships, partly for employment but mostly for food. All the garbage was sifted by the gasheens who kept watch at the rubbish chutes and sorted it out into food and other desirables which were then sold down at the Marsa. It may have been uneatable to us, but the poor Malts loved it and missed the Fleet no end. They felt the pinch so badly that regular collections were held to alleviate their distress. At Alex I enjoyed all the pleasures of Sister Street, the gilly-gilly boys and so on.

'There followed two commissions in the "boats" (destroyers) and I volunteered to become an Air-Gunner. It had always been my ambition to fly – as a child I was never without a model aircraft and I used to go to Hendon each year, to see the Air Show. It was then 1936 and we were soon snarled up in the Spanish War. We were in Gib when the *Jaime I*, flagship of the Spanish Navy, nosed its way up to the breakwater asking for water. The lower deck was in command, all the guardrails were missing, and we were told that the officers had been rolled up in them and thrown over the side. Life became more interesting, we did a little cloak and dagger work and evacuated some British from Huelva. A distress call was received from "Potato" Jones who was famous for shipping spuds into Spain, running the blockade. He was not alone since he had the *Scheer* for company, the German "pocket battleship".

'The situation was tense, she trained one of her turrets, we trained torpedo tubes. "Auf Wiedersehn" she said, and left. Either side bombed us at will and on one occasion, after speeding all night to rescue the survivors of the Spanish cruiser *Canarias*, we had the hell bombed out of us while slowly circling the wreckage to pull seamen out of the oily sea. A whaler lowered by one destroyer suffered an almost direct hit which killed one crew member. And it wasn't even our war. We looked a mess with vertical black bars of oil from hauling up survivors standing out against the light blue paint of the ship's side.

'Still no news of becoming an Air-Gunner. Then I was told that I had been under observation for several years as a possible officer. The truth being out, I was shipped to Pompey Barracks to commence an Upper Yardsman course. Hardly were matters on the run when I was in front of the Commodore, wondering what on earth I had done wrong. Here's me with one foot in the wardroom door and up in front of His Nibs. "Skeats," he said, "I have a piece of paper here calling you for training as an Air-Gunner, I presume you wish me to tear it up?" "No, sir," I said. He stiffened. "Are you telling me that you would sooner be an Air-Gunner than a Naval Officer?" "Yes, sir," I said. He gasped and pointed to the door.

'During flying training at Eastleigh war seemed a certainty. Ralph Richardson and Laurence Olivier appeared as pilots and I gathered Rafe's autograph in my flying logbook and "Lolly Olly's" on the back.' 'What a lovely wife he had in Vivien Leigh,' remembers Doug Cole, another TAG trainee, 'who was so very kind to many of us young lads. She walked on water as far as we were concerned.'

BECOMING A RATING PILOT

In the House of Commons the Government announced that the Fleet Air Arm was to be returned wholly to the Navy, although basic flying training would remain in RAF hands. The formal take-over was to be on 24 May 1939. One result was the publication in June 1938 of an AFO asking for volunteers to train as Rating Pilots. *Ab initio* training was in Avro Tutors at Short Brothers, Rochester, followed by No 1 FTS at Netheravon, Wiltshire, and armament training at RAF Catfoss, Yorkshire. In January 1939 the first Rating Pilots joined No 811 Squadron, 'Like the TAGs they were treated as nonentities,' says Norman Hollis, 'ringless hacks considered to lack the "moral fibre" to make a torpedo attack'.

Freddie Longman's early life was spent in Potters Bar, in those days not much more than a village, partly in Hertfordshire, partly in Middlesex, but famous as the place where the Zeppelin *L31*, shot down by Lieutenant Wulstan Tempest, RFC, in his B.E.2c on 2 October 1916, had crashed in flames. The blazing airship hit an oak tree a glancing blow as it fell, which Freddie and his pals used to go and look at, and which stands today in a garden in Tempest Avenue. He was one of five children, money was very tight, and in 1931 he joined the Lanes & National Sea Training School in Wallasey, Cheshire. 'The school trained young lads for both the RN and MN, and the competition was always on to be one of those selected for the RN.' Freddie joined *Ganges* in November 1932. From there he went to the cruiser *York* and was paid off in October 1936, an AB and Seaman Gunner.

'The *York* carried a Fairey IIIF, catapulted off and hoisted back inboard by crane. The aircrew, Lieutenant "Ting" Little (pilot), Lieutenant French (observer) and Leading Telegraphist Basil Gill, were my heroes. The highlight of my day was to be on the end of the "wing tip line" getting the aircraft back on the catapult. *The bug had bit!*'

He passed for Leading Seaman, and in the brand-new light cruiser *Southampton* became Turret Captain.

'*Southampton* carried two Walrus, two hangars and a catapult, and by now I wanted to be a pilot! After a final board during a day at sea in HMS *Courageous* during the Munich crisis and one more ship as a salthorse I was called back early from Easter leave in 1939 and sent to HMS *Pembroke*, Chatham Barracks, for flying training with No 4 Rating Pilot Course, first at Short's, Rochester, in Avro Tutors, then at No 7 FTS, Peterborough, on Hawker Harts. I won my wings in August 1939.'

In 1932 Eric Monk was at Grammar School 'with little hope of matriculating as my French was poor and one had to pass six subjects at one go, Maths, English, Science, History or Geography, Foreign Language, with Physics, Chemistry, or English Language. My family were market gardeners, lots of hard work and small returns. Just before half-term one of my form mates showed me an advertisement "Boys required for the Royal Navy".'

At 5.30p.m. on a cold wet February night in 1933 he was shivering in the fore-peak of a steam pinnace on his way to *Ganges*. On the fourth day there, as a special treat, they went swimming. 'It was still freezing, and we were ordered to put on one of a row of white canvas "duck suits" which had been hung up wet, and were frozen stiff. Non-swimmers were sent to the deep end of the pool and flung in, the others had to climb to the top board and jump in.'

The great mast held no special terrors for Eric and his mates. 'J-class yachts used to race off Shotley, and after the p.m. muster there was a race by "spare" boys for the seat on the truck. The worst part was getting from the bare pole at the top on to the button. I'm pleased to say I managed it, and clung to the lightning conductor for an hour'.

'The final event was to point and graft clews and lashings for one's hammock, the only friend you took to sea. It was decided that we were to do the rope-climbing display for the RN at the Royal Tournament. Chatham boys would then go to the cruiser *Sussex*, which was to take the Duke of Gloucester to Australia for the Melbourne Centenary on a year's exchange with HMAS *Australia*.

'We picked up the Duke at Marseilles and sailed blue summer seas to Oz. We Boy Seamen (under 18s) were invited to spend leave at the Scout Training Camp at Pennant Hills. As a result, several of us joined the Deep Sea Scouts and spent many happy evenings and days with shore-side Scouts and Cubs in Australia and also during our tour of New Zealand. We also had a happy Rover crew in the ship, and it was not long before our shipmates gave up remarking when we went ashore in Scout uniform.

'In the Solomon Islands I heard of the drive to recruit Air-Gunners, and set myself to reach the standard of 16 words per minute in Morse to qualify. At Tulagi I and other volunteers were each taken up in the ship's Osprey floatplane by Lieutenant Evans (later Admiral Sir Charles Evans) which gave me a vivid memory of the island, its bright green coconut palms, brilliant white coral beaches and pale blue shallows darkening to tropical blue deep water further out, basins of coral alive with sharks. That was my first flight.

'Back in the UK I transferred to the even newer Rating Pilot course. On my first exercise I was lucky to fly early in the day, and the target was into sun. As I opened fire I could see the sun glinting on my bullets going down so I ignored my gunsight and "hosepiped" my bullets into the target. I often wondered if my score of 68 out of 100 helped selection as a fighter pilot.

'We qualified as deck-landers aboard *Courageous*. Each pilot did 30 landings, and Jack Hadley finished up in front of the bridge, tail up, nose down, port wheel in the range-finder seat, and the fin broke the glass screen of the compass platform. This was the end of training and Jack and I were sent to No 800 Squadron, *Ark Royal*. We joined the "*Ark*" at Portland only to find that 800 were at Worthy Down changing their Ospreys and Nimrods for Skua fighter/dive-bombers, the first monoplanes for the Navy. A bird book I consulted described the Skua as a gull which folded its wings and dived into the sea.

'The working-up period soon went by and towards the end of June 1939 we were the RN Display Squadron at the opening of Birmingham and Derby Airports, after which we moved to Lympne for leave in early August. War seemed imminent.'

Ron Lunberg would never have settled to a land-lubber's settled existence. Many years later, when he could look back on his life in the Navy as 'the absolute fulfilment of a career to the extent that I enjoyed even the black spots', failing School Certificate seemed to have been fate. There was no work to be had on Merseyside in 1931, but there was still employment at sea. He signed on as Pantry Boy aboard the freighter SS *Aquila*.

For 12/6d a week he slaved from 0445 in the forenoon to eleven at night, with one stand-easy of two hours every other day. 'I was fed and that was about all.' He found out that a probationary Writer (clerk) in the RN received 17/6d a week on joining and 25/- at the end of six months' training, and after just six weeks in the Merchant Navy he made the switch, and signed up for twelve years. He was in HMS *Vernon* after training when he read AFO 848/38 calling for Rating Pilots.

'To me the AFO was electrifying!' He applied instantly and his name was forwarded, subject to passing the ET2 exam. With his strong motivation, this proved easier than School Certificate, and in May 1938 he reported to RAF Leuchars in Scotland with the nineteen others, including Eric Monk, on Course No. 41.

'We looked forward to exercising a lead when we were in a position to do so. In Rating Pilots this was frowned upon. Commissioned aircrew generally treated us as equals as far as flying went but there were one or two who did not approve of us until we showed a good degree of competence and skill. Unfortunately I was involved in a flying accident on what was almost my first flight as a newly qualified pilot.

'I had joined the cruiser *Glasgow* in place of a lieutenant pilot to fly one of her Walruses. With sister ship *Southampton* we were escorting King George VI and Queen Elizabeth to Canada. I had never been catapulted in charge of a Walrus, and had never made the normal seaplane touch-down in the "slick" of a ship's wake as she turned, when *Glasgow* was ordered by *Southampton* to "Exercise slick landing with junior pilot". *Glasgow* queried the wisdom of the order but the SO in *Southampton* insisted. So off I went.

'The first touch-down, after three dummy runs, was so much of a resounding *crunch* that I decided to go round again. After all, it was fairly choppy. The next attempt resembled the first but I decided to stay down. This time the starboard wing float broke off and the aircraft cartwheeled with the starboard wing in the water. The TAG who had come with me, to hook on to the crane when hoisted inboard, and I were picked up after about 10 minutes but he died on board of shock. You can imagine how I felt!'

Merchantmen to Militarymen

There's steam on the capstan,
Smoke in the stack,
The boys on the fo'c'sle are hauling in slack,
We're slipping the buoy now, the ocean to plough,
I wonder, my darling, who's loving you now . . .
HMS *Keith*, 1939

Other boys had begun life at sea in the Merchant Navy with more luck in their first ship than Ron Lunberg. It was not surprising that a boy brought up in Hull should go to sea. Alan Mathison's stepfather was a steward in the Bell Line, his grandfather a ship's carpenter in various tramp steamers, though on leaving school at 14 he became an errand boy on 5/- a week for a shipping chemist supplying medical items to ships for their medical cabinets as required by the Merchant Shipping Acts. 'The contents of a ship's medical cabinet were meagre in those days – a few rolls of bandages, a bottle of iodine, Black Draught for constipation, Cough Linctus, tins of Stabichlor for purifying doubtful "fresh" drinking water, jars of zinc ointment for scratches and abrasions, a jar of mercurial ointment for "crabs", aspirin, toothache tincture, and a couple of lances for boils.' Alan's job got him cycling down to various ships in Hull Docks, and his interest in the sea really started then. As a joiner's labourer at Brigham & Cowan's ship repair yard he talked to sailors about their voyages. 'It was then that I decided that I would like to go to sea and see for myself all "Those faraway places with strange-sounding names, far away over the sea". My parents knew somebody in a Ship Agency office, and he got me a job in a tanker as an Ordinary Seaman in April 1932.

'The *Saranac* was owned by the then Anglo-American Oil Company (later the Standard Oil Company, and finally Esso). She was at that time the world's largest tanker, at about 17,000 tons deadweight. After three years as Deck Boy and Ordinary Seaman, I qualified for Able Seaman and joined *Saranac*'s sister ship *Cadillac*, but I did not see eye to eye with the Chief Officer, who was a slave-driver, and I was logged, for the first and only time in what was to be 45 years at sea, for "swearing at the Chief Officer", which appeared in my Discharge Book as the only blemish in 96 separate voyages.'

After only two voyages in *Cadillac*, he was in several ships as AB, the last prior to the outbreak of war being the worst, the *Llandilo*, a Cardiff-owned tramp:

'The diet was almost a starvation one, the seaman and fireman were treated like dirt, and you only had running fresh water if you ran along the deck to the engine room for a bucket of hot water from the condenser hotwell, and even that was rationed if the duty engineer felt bloody-minded.

'In March 1939 I decided enough was enough and found myself a job ashore. I became seasonal bus conductor with the East Yorkshire Motor Company, which lasted until the start of hostilities, when the Ministry of Transport ordered me to report for seagoing duties as I was registered as a seaman. "Failure to report", they said, "will result in your being re-classified for service in the Armed Forces," and no doubt they meant the Royal Navy.

'I had every respect for the Royal Navy, but the two seagoing duties are poles apart, and besides it is better the Devil you know. On reporting to the Shipping Federation I was asked to volunteer for a course in gunnery run by the RN at the closed-down Earl's Shipyard. Being full of jingoistic ideas, I jumped at the chance to learn to hit back at the enemy. The course only lasted twelve days, and from later experience I realized that twelve days was as good as useless, especially when the gun crews of German submarines and raiders were probably the best trained in the world at the outbreak of the war. Immediately I came out of the gunnery school I was sent to Barry to join a ship called the *Stangrant*, which I did on 28 October 1939, an AB with an additional 6d (2½p) per day for my gunnery certificate.'

Mark Wells had started his seagoing career in the Merchant Navy. Born in Dover, when his father's business moved them to Leeds he spent all his holidays back at Dover with his grandparents. A distant relative was the Radio Officer on the Southern Railway steamer *Canterbury*. Mark wandered all round the docks all day looking at ships, and met *Canterbury* when she came in. 'At the age of ten I knew I just had to go to sea. All and sundry tried to talk me out of it but it fell on deaf ears. I drew ships at school on the back of exam papers. I guess I just loved ships.'

At 13 he joined the old wooden wall TS *Arethusa* at Greenhithe on the Thames, and from her got the job as deck boy with the Federal Steamship Company, part of the New Zealand Shipping Company, joining the former German SS *Cambridge*, bound for Auckland, New Zealand. 'I was going to sea!'

Mark saw a lot of sea, and chipped a lot of paint. They were three weeks in the Pacific without sighting another ship. In New Zealand waters they went round both islands unloading, then round again loading up. 'I found in my travels that seeing places was fine yet I was always glad when we were at sea. Somehow I never ever tired of it. I loved the sound of the engines clanking away, the solitude of wide-open seas, and us on a little island, as it were, desperately trying to maintain 15 knots or so.

'Back home again it was bad news – the ship was to lay up. It was a bad time for shipping. We paid off at Falmouth, and I noticed in the River Fal ships, ships and more ships, even liners, all rusting away, with no work. Up in London I walked the docks looking for vacancy signs on gangways, though it was usually "No Hands Wanted". Then one day I was offered a steward's assistant's job on MV *Orari* at Falmouth, loading for Australia. My duties consisted of endless washing up. After we had finished picking up cargo from coastal ports I told the

Chief Steward this wasn't for me and said good-bye to *Orari*. She was a nice ship and I loved the luxury of sheets and bedding. In the *Cambridge* you had one blanket, a mattress and a pillow and that was it, no radio, nothing, yet somehow we were a happy, contented crowd.

'Work of any kind was hard to get. I sold and delivered papers and other odd jobs, and worked in a factory, hating it, still pounding the docks at week-ends. Railways had always been another love of mine. Someone in the family remembered this and got me a job in the Locomotive Department at King's Cross, and there I started my days cleaning and training for the footplate. By the time 1938 came round I was well established on the footplate and I felt the exhilaration that I had at sea, and must say I enjoyed the footplate life and thereafter never bothered to go to the docks looking for work, though I often went to see the ships, went aboard many of them and enjoyed the seafaring chit-chat. It was still a part of me, deep down.

'1938 brought Munich. If there was going to be a war I would have to be at sea, and I registered. But by October 1939 I had heard nothing so I went to the nearest Recruiting Station and registered for the RN.

'At HMS *Royal Arthur*, Skegness, the uniform was very familiar to me, and I showed the others how it was worn. In time fancy "eye-shooting" bows appeared on caps, copying mine, U-fronts on jumpers, concertina trousers, bell bottoms. The old Chief said, "Well, you *look* like sailors, even if you aren't."

'When it came to choose which branch we wanted to go into, somehow I didn't feel I'd be happy in anything but the Engine Room Branch, it seemed right for me, leaving railway engines – I did know something of steam. Also down below you work in a small team. It's more confined than any other branch. I was surprised at how few had the same idea. Most of them wanted to be seamen, signallers, cooks.

'I was shipped off to Chatham, which I found the most depressing place I had ever been in. The training really was basic, no talk of damage control, emergency procedures, even what a ship was like. It was there that I saw my first naval ship close-up. It didn't impress me like the old P & O liners and Cunarders. Still, it was after all a war machine, not meant to be a thing of beauty. After end-of-course leave I was given a draft chit to HMS *Arethusa* – my second *Arethusa* – a modern light cruiser.

'She looked so small after a merchant ship. There was only a handful of stokers, mostly regulars. Two RNR men had been at Jutland. But they were all friendly, and we settled in. There were two boiler rooms, A and B, each with two POs, one in charge, one a watertender, and two stokers. I was in B. We were shown how to flash the burners and how to change them. Everything seemed to be run by the POs and Chiefs, with ERAs the background of the Engineering Department, in contrast to the Merchant Navy, where the Engineers were always there and for the most part did most of the work. It puzzled me why so many men were required to do anything. Even on deck it took so many more than the five forward and five aft in a 16,000-ton merchantman.

'We sailed, and started our watchkeeping, four hours on, eight hours off. At sea you could wear whatever you wished, more or less, but in the Engine Room it was underpants and a boiler suit, and a sweater if you went on deck, never a cap. Upper deck men called us "dustmen", and we called them "dabtoes", "shell pushers", "crab wallahs" or "gorillas". They seemed to think we were a little below them.'

Sea Scouts Go To Sea

Iain Nethercott from Canvey Island in the mouth of the Thames was one of the few Grammar School boys to enter the Royal Navy pre-war as a 'common-sailor'. He had been in the Sea Scouts from the age of eleven, and both his uncles owned old yachts on which Iain spent 'a lot of time, energy and skin off my hands'.

'In those days Sea Scouts used ex-naval Montague whalers for sailing and pulling, and old naval picket boats with petrol engines fitted to replace the old steam engines. By the age of 12 you were expected to know all the boat drill and how to pull an oar for at least a couple of hours. All the lads were mad keen on the sea in those days. They were a rough and ready crowd from working-class homes, quite a few with their dads on the river in tugs and barges. We learnt the International Code, semaphore, Morse light signalling, buoys and lights, fog signals, with hours of rope work and splicing in the winter evenings, and by the age of 14 we were fully conversant with the arts of boats and sailing. Most of the boys joined the Navy as Boy Seamen or Boy Signalmen, going to either *Ganges* or *Wildfire*, although quite a few of my friends went to sea in the Merchant Navy, mostly with the old Orient line.

'Every year at Easter all the Sea Scouts on the Thames went to a big meet at Cookham, near Richmond, up the river. As we sailed up the river from Barking with two naval pinnaces towing whalers and gigs right the way down the line to dinghies and kayaks, we used to meet up with the lads from Sheerness, Southend, Leigh, Gravesend and Tilbury, Purfleet and Rainham, and so on up-river with all the Central London troops, and then the posh lads from Putney, Mortlake and Chiswick.

'At Cookham we used to camp in bell tents in the river meadows, and over the week-end we battled it out at whaler racing and canoeing. At night we sat in our thousands round a huge camp fire singing till about two in the morning, and believe me the songs we sang in those days were not the ones sung at the "Gang Show". "The Harlot of Jerusalem" and "Nobby Hall" were good examples, although we all knew the old sailing ship shanties like "Blow the Man Down" and "Shenandoah" and all the others.

'Yes, in those days our boy sailors were dead keen and very easily satisfied. All that was needed was an old boat to muck about in, plenty of sausages cooked on the stove and plenty of sea or river to swim in. They were probably the happiest days of my life, and for most of my companions. It was a good thing they were, because within ten years most of them were dead.'

Iain joined the Navy and early in 1939 came back from a commission in the Mediterranean in the destroyer *Hotspur*, 'browner than Alexander'.

'The barracks was no rest home for seamen then, but full of Gestapo in belts and gaiters and whistles looking for deserters from Coaling Party. They whistled, bellowed at you and sang out "What are we, then?" It was best to keep your reply simple. "Football Party" was a good answer. For patrolling two-ringers, "Anti-gas Fumigation Party" or "Hygiene Manipulative Yeoman, sir!" were recommended, probably confusing the poor man, who would bellow "Well, put your cap on straight, then!" But all this palaver grew wearing. I decided to blend into the landscape. No one ever notices a man pushing a broom. And no one would do the job from choice, would he? Every day I worked my way slowly round the barracks, free as the birds of the air. But it was all very boring and ridiculous, and I longed to get back to sea.

'In July the Reservists were called up and I got my longed-for draft chit. It was to HMS *Keith*, a flotilla leader of the "B" Class destroyers, then in Reserve at Chatham. The Reservists, bewildered tobacconists and hotel doormen, were kitted out, inoculated, vaccinated, those with teeth given corned dog sandwiches and an apple and many mugs of Pusser's bromided tea, and we were all sent on our way rejoicing to the Dockyard, found our ships, sorted out our messes and settled in. I did well, I was an Iron Deck man and bowman in the motor boat. Lovely! And I found a good slinging billet up by the paint shop.

'*Keith* was similar to *Hotspur*, though five years newer, one of the Admiralty-type Destroyer Leaders (others were *Kempenfelt* and *Duncan*) included in the 1928 Estimates; keel laid October 1929, launched 10 July 1930, completed 9 June 1931 by White's of Cowes, Isle of Wight, the oldest builder to the Navy.

'There were certain domestic improvements – a bathroom about 12 ft by 8 ft with six basins for 130 men. No taps, no water. You took your precious personal bucket (also used for dhobi-ing) along the Iron Deck, filled it at the freshwater pump, proceeded to the leeward side doors of the coal-fired gallery, and begged a bucket of "hotters" in exchange for your bucket of cold, hoping the chef was in a good mood. If the weather was rough, and Chiefie presiding over a great sliding mass of Straight Rushes, potmesses (Irish Stew), and Pusser's peas leaping out all over his boots, he was not sympathetic to the toiletry needs of a hairy-arsed AB.

'My Action Station was No 2 (trainer) of the Port 2-pounder pom-pom. This made sense as I had shown no aptitude for gunnery (*far* too noisy), and had never seen a pom-pom before. Ours must have been used in the Boer War. The belts holding the shells were made of canvas, which swelled up in seawater and heat and jammed the old cannon, whereupon one clouted the breech with a sodding great mallet, supplied for the purpose. The gunlayer was as ignorant as I was, and the Gunner's Mate not interested in our little gun. His love lay in his 4.7s, the TS (Transmitting Station) and the Director. Our weapon was fitted with two ring sights, calibrated for 100-knot aircraft – Stukas, Heinkels and Ju 88s would of course slow down for us!

'The ship was sailed to Weymouth in August for the King's Review – an antiquarian collection of "V" and "W"-class destroyers, Great War vintage, old "C" and "D"-class light cruisers, and a heterogeneous gaggle of ancient battleships including Jellicoe's old coal-burning *Iron Duke*, de-militarized.

'We polished up all our brightwork – then painted over it, fitted warheads to the torpedoes, put ready-use ammo in the shell racks near the guns, unshipped and landed the Captain's furniture and chintz curtains, took on board a ton of Pusser's peas and two crates of Ally Sloper's Sauce, and HMS *Keith* was ready for war.

'On 3 September at about 1130 in the forenoon we sailed, leading our ancient flotilla of Vs and Ws out to sea from Plymouth Sound for a sweep up the Welsh coast looking for any U-boats already in position there.'

Bill Thomas began his seafaring career as an Ordinary Seaman in the coastal steamer *Avon Gwilli*, sailing out of Llanelli in August 1932 with coal for Continental ports and bringing back general cargoes to the UK. In November of that year he was apprenticed to the Cardiff tramp ship company Evan Thomas Radcliffe on world-wide voyages in the steamship *Vera Radcliffe*.

'Conditions in tramps were tough in those days; there were still sailing ships around, and our senior officers were all ex-windjammer men who insisted on treating us in the traditions of sail. Fresh meat stores were kept in an ice chest on deck, the contents of which melted as soon as we hit the tropics, a week out from the UK. From there on, until our next port of call our only fresh meat was "Weevil", picked out of our morning Burgoo (a sort of porridge). Our staple diet became salt beef and pork, which was quite tasty, much preferable to the rotting remains of fresh meat which the steward always tried to give us.'

In 1936 he qualified for a Second Mate's ticket and served in the Llanelli pilotage service until 1938, when he went back to sea as Mate in coasters. Aboard the steamer *Stronsa Firth*, taking a cargo of ammunition from Saltash to Loch Swine in Scotland, he heard Mr Chamberlain declare over the radio that Britain was at war with Germany.

To War at Sea

When I went down to Devonport
My face was cold as slate,
They gave me a number for my name
As I went through the barrack gate.
Charles Causley, Signalman HMS *Glory*

In the early hours of Wednesday, 30 August 1939, the draft for HMS *Renown* arrived at Portsmouth Station. 'There was a lot of skylarking unloading the kit from the train and on to lorries,' Tom Bailey noted, 'then away to the dockyard to join my first ship!

'What a sight! Thirty-odd thousand tons, six 15-inch guns and twenty 4.5s plus pom-poms and machine-guns!

'"Pick up your hammocks and turn in anywhere!" was the order, then after Reveille we had kippers for breakfast! We had kippers for breakfast *every* Wednesday all the time I was on board *Renown*.

'Frantic hours of work then, storing and ammunitioning ship and the wonderful experience of buying a packet of Duty Free Woodbines for 4½d!' Tom, who had joined for 'three square meals a day and a pair of boots', was well pleased with life, though like most of his messmates he had really wanted a small ship, a dashing destroyer for preference. The significance of all this urgent labour was lost on them. 'Us youngsters didn't realize the state of the world.'

They were at sea heading north when the signal came in: 'Fuse all shell. Ship all warheads'.

'When we left Pompey on Saturday evening, 3rd September, my first duty was SSO Messenger.' Later that evening Tom carried a sealed envelope to the Captain, little knowing that it contained the disturbing news of the sinking, 250 miles west of Ireland, of the 13,581-ton Donaldson liner *Athenia*, bound for Montreal with 1,400 people on board, by a German submarine, with heavy loss of life, including many women and children. After Divisions on Sunday the Admiralty made the war at sea official with the terse: 'Commence hostilities with Germany'.

The torpedoing of *Athenia* revealed that U-boats had taken up war stations before the event. For the old Reservists it was *déja vu*. Once before the U-boats had almost beaten the Royal Navy and almost starved Britain into surrender. In fact, there were no more than ten German submarines at sea as yet, but there was a big building programme. The German surface fleet was also far inferior in numbers to that of the old Imperial German Navy, and to the 1939 British Fleet, but most of the latter's ships were ageing relics of the Great War, whereas Hitler's warships were all modern: the three 11in Panzerschiffe, called 'pocket battleships' in Britain, *Deutschland*, *Graf Spee* and *Scheer*; two powerful, fast battlecruisers, *Scharnhorst* and *Gneisenau*; three new 8in heavy cruisers; with two huge 50,000-ton battleships, *Bismarck* and *Tirpitz*, under construction, not to mention the revival of another potent First World War weapon, the armed merchantman commerce raider, with her fast speed and hidden guns. All these sea wolves were to be unleashed on Allied merchantmen.

THE SINKING OF *COURAGEOUS*

When all the Royal Navy's ships in reserve had been reactivated and crewed, there was still a serious shortage, particularly of cruisers, which was not helped by the early loss of an important unit of the Fleet.

'In order to bridge the gap', records Winston Churchill, 'of two or three weeks between the outbreak of war and the completion of our auxiliary anti-U-boat flotillas, we had decided to use the aircraft-carriers with some freedom in helping to bring in the unarmed, unorganized, and unconvoyed traffic which was then approaching our shores in large numbers.'

One night, in very dirty weather, the new destroyer leader HMS *Kelly*, commanded by Captain (D) Lord Louis Mountbatten, was investigating a possible submarine contact off Land's End when an SOS came into her wireless office from the carrier *Courageous*. Aboard the carrier, in No 821 Squadron, was PO Tel/AG A.G. 'Murgy' Brown. 'There was no "phoney war" as far as the Navy was concerned – Admiral Dönitz and his U-boats saw to that. *Courageous* sailed from Plymouth with a destroyer escort, and started operations in the Western Approaches right away. Our Skipper was "Salt Horse", not an aviator (though he had a lot of time for aircrew) and the ship's company were mostly RNR, some very senior citizens among them, who should have been ashore, digging their allotments.

'We were flying day and night anti-submarine patrols, and one night, in poor visibility, one of our aircraft returning from patrol missed the ship – they flew right overhead, turned back and failed to see us. The Skipper had to make a difficult decision: accept the loss of his aircraft and crew, or break W/T silence (to give them a bearing) and fire a star shell, giving our position away. He chose to try to save the crew – without success – and the Germans had us pegged. About 8p.m., on 17 September, two torpedoes from Otto Schuhart's persistent *U-29* hit us on the port side, and we keeled over. I was below, having a shave when it happened. Dropping everything, except my precious Rolls razor, I made my way to the upper hangar. The lower hangar was on fire, and a young Marine hangar sentry was operating the sprinkler system and trying to lower the fire curtain. "Bit too late for that, now, Royal," I said. "She's going soon," and grabbing two Mae Wests from the nearest aircraft I chucked one to him and told him to follow me up top. "No," he said, "I must wait until the Sergeant tells me to leave." And he stood fast. I've always admired the Marines, and never more so than at that moment.

'On deck, I helped a seaman hack a Carley float loose, and after a struggle we managed to drop it into the sea – and it was promptly seized by a group of swimmers and paddled away. I slid down the ship's side, hitting every ring bolt with my backside on the way, and into the water. Looking up as I drifted past the stern, a huge propeller ticking over a few feet from my head, I saw a Marine officer calmly smoking a fag as he ditched his confidential books over the side, before diving in. Suddenly a huge wall of water loomed up, higher than the ship's side, and I went under. When I eventually surfaced, lungs bursting, *Courageous* had gone – taking more than 500 of her company with her.

'The destroyers, including *Kelly*, were bustling around by now, dropping depth-charges all over the place; no joke for those of us in the drink – it was like being kicked by an elephant when they went off. I swam towards one of the destroyers, but never seemed to get any nearer. It was dusk by now, and I'd nearly had it, when I spotted a merchantman nearby, an old tramp bound for Liverpool from Sierra Leone. I made for her and managed to reach her as darkness fell. I was a good swimmer, and surprised that I was so exhausted – until I realized that I hadn't inflated my Mae West! Apart from being frozen stiff, I was all right, but others, who had seemed OK in the water, had first-degree burns – and begged to be put back when they had been pulled out.'

At midnight the tramp steamer's passengers were transferred to the destroyer *Inglefield*, which had come alongside, looking for survivors. 'We then searched the area until morning,' says Murgy Brown, 'picking up a few bodies, and continued patrolling for another two days before we were put ashore at Plymouth. Some survivors had been picked up by an American liner, and been given the full VIP treatment by the passengers – fitted out with civvies, hob-nobbing with film stars, and all set for a run ashore in the USA. They got a shock when Mountbatten turned up and took them aboard!'

In *Kelly*'s crowded Sick Bay 'Poultice Mixer' PO Sick Berth 'Tiffy' Bert Male made his patients as comfortable as possible. 'They were all exhausted, and had bad burns, lacerations, shock, and internal damage from gulping the oil.' One man, a stoker, was carried below to Gordon Rogers' mess. 'He had slid down the ship's side when she had heeled over and the barnacles had torn his back and his buttocks and hands and he was in a very bad way. The gash bucket in the mess was full of tealeaves and scrapings off our supper plates. When the poor sod saw the bucket he fell on his knees and stuck his hands all torn and bloody right into it. "Don't do that, old matey," I said, and tried to pull him back, "you'll get blood poisoning or something." "I don't give a shit," he said, "it's cool, cool, cool". . . When I looked closer I saw that he was pissed as a newt. The Yanks had poured a bottle of whisky into him, and they had given them thick blankets and warm clothes.'

For Murgy Brown it was back to *Daedalus*, and fourteen days' survivor's leave. 'My wife was waiting at the gate – she had been waiting there for days. All too soon our leave was over. We were lined up for a pep talk by Admiral Bell Davies, VC. "Cheer up, lads," he said enthusiastically. "The sea is His, He made it . . ." ". . . and He can keep it," muttered someone behind me. My sentiments exactly.'

For Tom Bailey in *Renown* and the other big ship matlows, 'Scapa Flow was a time of exercises, AA control and Damage Control, days at sea and plenty in harbour, working party ashore helping to build the new canteen'.

'What a time! Take your tin mug ashore to drink your beer, a mess kettle for enough pints to take back for your mates. And still kippers for breakfast every Wednesday!'

NORTHERN PATROL

As well as defending British seaborne trade against German submarines and surface raiders, the Navy had the important job of blockading Germany by stopping her merchant ships, of which there were many scattered round the globe, from reaching the Fatherland. Old 'C' and 'D'-class light cruisers, and occasionally one of the most modern ships, had revived the World War I Northern Patrol, which stretched a thin net from John O'Groats to Greenland, but they were too few, and the 'C's and 'D's were 'showing the flag' ships, not intended for the wild weather of these seas. There were too many gaps in the net.

These were to be filled, as in World War I, by Armed Merchant Cruisers (AMCs) – liners and cargo/passenger ships with a fair turn of speed, armed with old 6in guns, crewed by Merchant Navy sailors on the special T124 articles (known in the RN as 'rockies'), officered mainly by Royal Naval Reserve Merchant Navy men ('cargo-shifters'), and commanded by Royal Navy captains brought out of retirement – some of it enforced by the pruning 'Geddes Axe' of the Depression. Their job was Contraband Control, the stopping and searching of ships suspected of being disguised German blockade runners. They were meant to take on German raiders.

On 29 September the first AMCs steamed into Scapa Flow. The Admiralty had previously earmarked 50 of these ships for conversion in time of war, when they had reckoned they would be 75 regular cruisers short for their commitments. Ships were 'stiffened' to take the weight and operating stresses of 6in and 4in guns, pedestals and mountings.

On 26 August the Royal Mail Line's big 22,098-ton *Asturias* had steamed up Southampton Water fresh from a Mediterranean luxury cruise, disembarked her passengers with brusque haste, and cast off for Belfast and a change of role. Young Geoffrey Penny had been a shipping clerk in the City, and now found himself 'to my amazement' a paymaster sub-lieutenant RNR in an Armed Merchant Cruiser fitting out for war.

'*Asturias* was stripped of most of her rich fittings. Dockyard mateys took away all the lovely mahogany and walnut furniture from the saloons, lounges and smokerooms, the golden wickerwork chairs and beautifully carved cedarwood tables from the Winter Garden, which was so bright and sunny, done out in the Spanish style. The First-Class Smokeroom was to be the new Wardroom, and the Grinling Gibbons carvings there were not touched, likewise the marble Adam fireplace in what was to be the Anteroom to the Wardroom.

'The ship's big forward funnel was sliced off at deck level with oxy-acetylene torches, then lifted in one piece by a giant crane on to the dockside, and we were fitted with eight old 6in guns, some smaller ones, searchlights and a primitive fire control system. The only ack-ack guns we had at first were two Great War Lewis machine-guns, which jammed when they were tested.

'When the conversion work was finished, the dockyard foreman said to me, "We've made a nice mess of your beautiful ship" – some of the truest words ever spoken. Our sister ship, *Alcantara*, got the same treatment at Southampton.'

One of the older generation serving in AMCs was 50-year-old Bert Poolman from Bath, Somerset – my father. He had spent most of his life close to water – river, sea and ocean. As a young man in the long, golden Edwardian summers, he had rowed on the Avon, won cups and medals in regattas, competing against the heavyweight farmers' crews from Evesham, while apprenticed to the firm of Stothert & Pitt, crane-makers. As a Territorial he was sent to France in 1914 but with his engineering experience was released to work on submarine trials from Newcastle-on-Tyne, which he found 'a bloomin' sight more dangerous than the trenches', in spite of the experience of having his old boyhood friend literally blown to pieces as he handed him a dixie of stew on the dugout steps.

Watching the big ships come and go from high up on a gantry while installing cranes in Southampton Docks had given him – to lace the Romany blood he had inherited from his mother – a longing for ocean travel which his experiences in submarines had not killed, and after the war he went into the Merchant Navy as an engineer, serving in 'dodgy old tramps' like *Bosworth* ('We used to have bets on which half we'd be in when she broke in two'), and graduated to the Bibby cargo liners *Somersetshire* and *Dorsetshire*. Beached in the Depression, with a wife and son to feed, he suffered the harshness of the dole, the indignities of the Means Test, but eventually got an engineering maintenance job with the pork butchers Spears of Bath. But his heart was still away at sea. He taught me to swim and row on the near-derelict stretch of green, tree-lined river which he himself had once adorned as a young lithe oarsman, took me on paddle steamers in the holidays at Weston-super-Mare ('Weston-super-Mud') or Weymouth, where we collected warship photographs.

Just before the Second World War started we both went aboard the destroyers *Fortune* and *Firedrake*, moored just downstream from the old Bristol Bridge. My father talked earnestly to an engine room artificer of impending war, as they gazed down into the grease-green pits of the huge pistons in the engine room. When war did come, he got the train to London on the very first day of hostilities, and came home a Sub-Lieutenant (E), RNR. Too old to sign T124 articles, he had been let in on a 'gentleman's agreement', and a few days later my mother and I saw him off in his darkened train at the Midland Station for Birkenhead, on the Mersey, and the Armed Merchant Cruiser HMS *Salopian*. Appropriately for him, the ship had originally been the Bibby liner *Shropshire*, loading in August 1939 for Rangoon and Colombo, but the county nickname 'Salop' had been used to manufacture a new name to avoid confusion with the County-class heavy cruiser HMS *Shropshire*.

When my father saw her she too had suffered a sea-change. 'The first thing I noticed was that she had lost two of the four masts that had made the old Bibby boats stand out. She'd had her black hull, white upperworks and pink funnel all daubed over a dirty grey. She looked proper down in the mouth. The men call her "Sloppy Anne". There is a sprinkling of RN ratings (captains of guns, gunlayers, key men), and the Captain is Sir John Alleyn, Bart., RN. He was a Great War hero (navigator of *Vindictive* at Zeebrugge) and is a re-tread like me and we hit it off being in the same age group.

'The ship is ballasted with pig-iron and her holds and 'tween decks are filled with thousands of empty 15 to 50gal sealed oil drums for extra buoyancy in case we are "tinfished", though I don't think they would make much difference. The guns stick out like great lumps.'

Asturias, Aurania, California, Chitral, Rawalpindi, Salopian, Scotstoun and *Transylvania* were the first AMCs to reach the Flow. 'We were surprised to find such a huge area of water with all kinds of warships dotted about,' wrote Geoff Penny, 'all blinking away with signals and a great number of ships' boats all going the rounds.

'We in *Asturias* are quite green in RN procedures. It is my job to make sure that the ship's company is properly clothed to face patrols up beyond the Arctic Circle. The ship's stores, which had been one of the first-class passenger suites on C Deck, sells thick vests and longjohns, shirts and shoes, sheets and hussifs, and I have managed to "borrow" heavy fur coats, seaboot stockings, leather seaboots (much prized) and oilskins from the naval stores in Kirkwall.

'None of us are sufficiently worked up to go on patrol, and it is too rough outside the Flow to make a start; in fact it has been too bad *inside* to take on stores.'

The AMCs were trapped in Scapa, and the old 'C' and 'D'-class light cruisers of the 7th and 12th Cruiser Squadrons continued to maintain the Northern Patrol, 'straining our rivets', described Roy Coles, a young ERA in *Diomede*, 'and old engines in mountainous seas, with lookouts peering through snowstorms and driving sleet, boats, booms, bridge screens and guardrails smashed, lifelines permanently rigged on the upper deck, broken messtraps washing about in six inches of water below decks, and no way of keeping dry, even with oilskins over our hammocks, or shaving without serious risk of cutting your throat. High seas made it impossible to man the guns.'

On 2 October there was a flurry of excitement in the Flow. During the First Dog Watch the Commander-in-Chief hoisted a flag signal, addressed to *Ark Royal* and *Renown*, ordering them to raise steam for full speed by 1800. On the previous day survivors from the steamer *Clement* had reached the South American coast and reported that their ship had been sunk by the pocket battleship *Admiral Scheer* on 30 September. The Admiralty immediately organized a number of hunting groups to track her down, of which *Ark Royal* and *Renown* formed one – Force K.

The stranded AMCs were badly needed to plug the Denmark Strait gap, between Iceland and Greenland, where low fuel endurance made it impossible for the old cruisers to patrol. Through this gap homeward-bound German merchantmen and contraband neutrals were sailing with impunity, except when the odd modern Home Fleet cruiser could be released. But even the new *Sheffield* could only spend two days there, though *Belfast* bagged the German Hamburg-Sud-

Amerika Line's cargo/passenger liner *Cap Norte*, disguised as a Swede, on 9 October.

It was the time of the 'Phoney War', a muddled period of uncertainty when signals like the following were exchanged:

Admiralty to Destroyer X: 'Proceed with all despatch'
Destroyer X to Admiralty: 'Request destination'
Admiralty to Destroyer X: 'Aden repeat Aden'
Destroyer X to Admiralty: 'Am at Aden'

'A very eerie, cold and stormy time,' noted young *Salopian* boarding officer Bill Jeffery, in the Flow, 'chaotic, uncertain, anxious and bewildering'. It was desolate aboard the big, gutted liners, cavorting at their cables. 'Vast areas of the ship are just open spaces where scores of passenger cabins have been torn out. Meals are eaten amidst piles of the old furniture.

'At least we were safe inside the "impregnable" Flow, or thought we were. Various gates, nets and booms kept submarines out, and German bombers, with no aircraft-carriers to transport them across the North Sea, could not reach us . . .'

But just after one o'clock in the dark hours of the middle watch on 14 October they were all awakened by the deep underwater explosions of torpedoes. 'The impossible had happened, there were U-boats in the Flow.' Soon all the sleeping ships were awake, 'up-anchoring and zigzagging round the Flow in near-panic'.

Oberleutnant-zur-See Günther Prien – the 'Bull of Scapa' – had found a weakness in the defences at Kirk Sound, crabbed his *U47* inside, and got out through the same hole, leaving behind the 29,150-ton battleship *Royal Oak* capsized at her anchorage after four torpedo hits, with the loss of 830 men. If he had made his daring move twenty-four hours later he would have found no way in. The hole at Kirk Sound was known to the Admiralty, and a blockship was to be sunk there the very next day.

All the big ships were ordered to sea out of harm's way. There were no immediate repetitions of the sinking, but four days later two squadrons of Junkers Ju 88s flew over the anchorage and bombed those ships still there, hitting Jellicoe's old *Iron Duke*, doing duty as a base ship and floating coastal defence battery; she was damaged underwater by near misses and had to be towed into shallow water and beached.

The nine AMCs which had gathered in the Flow had left the day before, 17 October, passing a patch of oil below which the submerged tomb of *Royal Oak* lay. 'It could so easily have been one of us,' reflected Geoff Penny. *Rawalpindi*, *Scotstoun* and *Transylvania* had managed, not without difficulties and hold-ups, to complete their working-up, and were despatched at once to the Denmark Strait. *Asturias*, *Aurania*, *California*, *Chitral* and *Salopian*, although not properly worked up, were allocated mostly to more southerly patrols, with *Asturias* taking a convoy across to Halifax, Nova Scotia.

There was frequent trouble with the old guns, some of which had been made in 1898. *Rawalpindi*'s 6in were 1901 and 1909 models, allowed to rust for decades, with bores, pivots and mountings worn by firing in the First World

War, and even when the Gunner's Party and the engineers managed to get moving parts to move, 'proper maintenance is impossible,' reported Petty Officer Shipwright Peter Winiatt of *Rawalpindi*.

'On the open decks the mechanisms (and the crews) are exposed to the severity of the weather. Water penetrates the moving parts, and some of the guns can only be trained with the help of two or three of the gun's crew pushing on the barrel.'

On 21 October a ship brought in to Kirkwall the crew of the Norwegian *Lorentz W. Hansen* with the news that the latter had been sunk by *Deutschland*. This confirmed the suspicion that there was more than one pocket battleship at large. On 22 October the German raider captured the American SS *City of Flint*.

Meanwhile the weather was the worst enemy. *Scotstoun*'s four forward guns were unworkable sculptures of frozen spray, gales cut her speed and ice stove in her forepeak, though she still managed to apprehend *Eilbek* of Hamburg. *Laurentic*'s guns jammed, her boats were holed. On 12 November the Norwegian *Tvirfjord* was brought into Kirkwall for examination, and her captain told the Contraband Control boarding officer that on 4 November they had been stopped by *Deutschland* 700 miles west of Ireland – he had forborne to radio the information for fear of reprisals by the Germans. On 20 November *Chitral*, after gun practice on an iceberg, caught the clumsily disguised German SS *Bertha Fisser*. 'This ship – no good,' said her captain when taken aboard the AMC, 'Our big ships come tomorrow. They take us away.'

The weather was so rough on the night of 21 November that *Chitral*'s boarding boat, returning from the scuttled German SS *Tenerife*, could not be re-hoisted. *Laurentic* did not even try to board the '*Flora* of Amsterdam' (actually the Hamburg-Amerika Line's *Antiochia*) and sank her with gunfire.

Also patrolling in the freezing northern waters was the 'saucy *Arethusa*'. 'Once in the Arctic,' says Mark Wells, 'we were told to wear the heavy-duty clothes issued, and no one was to undress, so we slept just as we were for duties below. It got very cold, the condensation dripped from the overhead pipes and bulkheads, everywhere was damp and cold.

'It was a joy to be on watch in the boiler room. However, as we worked in air pressure there were huge fans up top which spun round at 15,000 revs and sucked in the freezing air. At one stage there were icicles hanging down from them a foot long – and this was in the boiler room! At one stage there was ice all round the ship, when I went up top, and the ship was almost stopped. There was no wind and the sea quite calm, and I couldn't get over the silence everywhere, punctuated by the odd crunch of ice. As I tried to sleep off-watch, every half hour or so the speakers would wake me with "Port watch stand by to fend off ice aft" or some such thing, and so it went on!'

First Taste of Action

She's a tiddley ship, o'er the ocean she'll flit,
She sails it by night and by day,
And when she's in motion she's the pride of the ocean,
You can't see her arsehole for spray.

Side, side, *Achilles'* ship's side,
Jimmy looks on it with pride –
He'd have a blue fit if he saw someone spit
On the side of *Achilles'* ship's side!

CRUISER *ACHILLES*

The ancient Maori name for New Zealand is Tiritiri o te Moana – The Gift of the Sea. Her two islands lie like a division of ships in the blue South Pacific, and she is an ocean trader, relying heavily on the sea for her prosperity. The present-day Maoris' ancestors came to Tiritiri in great oceangoing canoes with names like *Tainui, Te Arawa, Aotea, Takitimu, Tokomaru* in 1350 from Tahiti and the Marquesas. For four centuries the sea god Tangaroa protected them from the greed of white plunderers, helping them to repulse Abel Tasman in the Jade Sea; but rapacious whalers and sealers swindled, robbed, kidnapped and abused the Maoris, aided by escaped convicts from Australia, decimated them with their European diseases, and sold them guns to accelerate their decline by inter-tribal war. There was some retaliation: in 1809 everyone aboard the ship *Boyd* was killed and eaten. But the Bay of Islands north of Auckland became an important trade centre for flax, wood, European-introduced potatoes and maize, and ship-victualling. 'The Gift of the Sea' was grabbed eagerly for its equitable climate, lush grasslands, virgin commercial potential and wide open spaces, backed by grand mountains and warmed by hot springs from the centre of the earth. Colonization was secured by the Maori wars and by the time the novelist Trollope visited her shores, New Zealand considered herself to be, he thought, 'the cream of the British Empire'.

Colony became Dominion, and sent over 100,000 men overseas in World War I, who suffered 58,000 casualties, including 17,000 dead – greater than Belgium, the central battlefield, with a population six times greater. New Zealand paid £1,698,224 for the honour of having a battlecruiser of her own, HMS *New Zealand*, which took part in all the big North Sea actions, sank the cruiser *Köln* at

Heligoland, finished off the battlecruiser *Blücher* at Dogger Bank, and swamped the enemy's rate of fire at Jutland, scoring many hits on the German battle-cruisers. HMS *Dunedin* joined the New Zealand Division, followed by her sister ship *Diomede* on 21 January 1926. In February 1936 she went home and secured at Sheerness astern of her replacement, the new *Leander*-class light cruiser *Achilles*, 7,030 tons (9,740 fully loaded), and armed with eight 6in guns in four turrets.

Sparker Jack Harker from Governors Bay, Lyttelton Harbour, was one of the New Zealand ratings who moved their gear over to the new ship. He had inherited a love of the sea from his father 'who sailed before the mast for 21 years and never set foot on a steamship'. After the cramped old *Diomede, Achilles* was 'unforgettable; no longer stooped under low deckheads, we stood straight and looked up at a wealth of overhead space. Individual lockers took all our kit with room for more; mess-tables spread expansively, clean and new. We felt we'd boarded the *Queen Mary* . . . The W/T department had an operating room 'as large as *Diomede*'s complete outfit!'

For the next two years they cruised the sunny South Pacific, fighting mock battles with a force of elderly V-and-W destroyers led by HMASS *Canberra* and *Sydney*. *Achilles'* sparkers kept a listening watch for missing Amelia Earhart's plane, picked up a weak, despairing SOS, and searched in vain for her as long as fuel would allow.

Just before Christmas 1938 they berthed at Tahiti, and were soon wondering how Bligh had managed to get *anyone* back aboard the *Bounty*. 'Night warmed to the tempo of the tamure; smoke, beer and champagne dispersed caution; sailors whisked barefooted pretty young vahines out into the parks off Rue Pomare and Rue de Jeanne d'Arc.' It was also a temporary farewell to the Pacific; they were on their way back to England.

At Portsmouth they saw cranes hovering like vultures over *Hood*, fitting more (but not enough) armour, and other cruisers and battleships being modernized, before the New Zealanders went off for a return visit to 'The Big Smoke'. When they returned they found new faces on the messdecks. Their Imperial quota had been replaced by new hands, of whom Lamptrimmer Ivor Burston from Wiveliscombe was one.

In late February 1939 *Archilles* rolled her way to New Zealand again. Kiwi Pete Trant from Christchurch joined as telegraphist/air-gunner for the Walrus, only to get the blame when the aircraft's pick-up from the water went wrong, and it sank.

They arrived in Auckland on 8 May and tied up alongside the Naval Base at Devonport, NZ, some 13,000 miles from Devonport, England. 'Some journey!' wrote Ivor in his diary. One of his first calls ashore was on the Hatswells, from Wiveliscombe, who made him most welcome, as did some friends of T.V. Pearse, the Wiveliscombe solicitor.

As events in Europe went from fraught to frightening, *Achilles* took the Governor-General of New Zealand, Lord Galway, for an island cruise, with the hands betting on the colour of his daughter's panties, trying discretely to observe her true colours as she negotiated ladders.

The ship continued to be hard on aircraft. Her new Walrus was launched to overfly Aitutaki and its cheering islanders; it returned to *Achilles* and made a good slick landing. Pete Trant climbed up on the centre-section while craneman Jackie Alder swung the grab down for Pete to clamp through the lifting eye . . . but the grab didn't grab, the plane was dragged on its side by the tricing wires, and capsized, taking Pete down with it. A huge air bubble shot him to the surface, to see the rescue whaler punch a hole in the 'Shagbat's' hull, and finally sink her by tearing a long gash in the wing.

From leave they were urgently recalled to store ship. Bunting-tosser Colin Malcolm 'drew money from a Devonport bank and paid all debts . . . drank in the "Mon Desir" with the old crowd . . . went down to the old home and broke down when our cat "Old Fat" came running out to see me . . .'

On Tuesday, 29 August, *Achilles* left to join the West Indies Squadron, commanded by Commodore Harwood in sister ship *Ajax*. As she left, Colin Malcolm used the 18 in searchlight to say good-bye to his Auckland girl friends, and wondered when, or if, he would see them again. Imperial Lamplighter Ivor Burston did the rounds of his charges. They might be needing them soon.

As they were battling rough seas on the way to Balboa, Telegraphist Neville Milburn, from Bradford, Yorkshire, England, received the signal: 'Britain has declared war against Germany'.

Their destination was changed to Valparaiso, Chile, to patrol the west coast of South America, looking after British ships, and looking for German vessels trying to sneak homewards, most of them hugging the neutral harbours until they saw what the situation was like at sea. At Valparaiso two German merchantmen, *Dresden* and *Dusseldorf*, were marking time. All foreign ships there were bound by the laws of neutrality, but for *Achilles* the rules were stretched, and she was allowed to fill to capacity with 1,385 tons of Chilean crude, and stuff her stores with Argentine beef, greens and spuds. Her departure was spectacular, with her Marine band in white topees, uniforms of blue, gold and red, playing them out with 'Heart of Oak'. This was partly to entertain the Chileans, partly for the watching captains of *Dresden* and *Dusseldorf*.

In Chilean ports German crews jeered them. They passed the spot off Cape Coronel where Craddock's old cruisers *Good Hope* and *Monmouth* had gone down in 1914 before the guns of Von Spee's earlier *Scharnhorst* and *Gneisenau*; but they saw no Germans at sea, and were handicapped by their lack of an aircraft. At night on 18 September they heard of the loss of *Courageous*.

On 30 September the British steamer *Clement* was sunk by a German pocket battleship which identified herself as the *Admiral Scheer*, 70 miles off Pernambuco, Brazil. Like the *Deutschland*, she had obviously taken up her war station before the actual outbreak. Survivors reported her when they reached the Brazilian coast. *Achilles* was ordered south, to round the Horn and refuel in the Falklands. Her sailors were reluctant to leave the local girls, who were 'very free with love,' Jack Harker says. Some men drank with German cadets off the training barque *Priwall*, at the German cafe 'Neptune's Bar', and saluted 'the dead already' when they were told that a U-boat waited for them outside the harbour – when they left on Friday the 13th. Ivor Burston remembers how 'The flagship of the Chilean Navy, *Almirante Latorre* (the Royal Navy's old battleship *Canada*), signalled when *Achilles* left "Goodbye to the millionaire love ship".'

Battle Of The River Plate

On 22 October *Achilles* was lying in bright sunshine in Port Stanley harbour. The German raider had sunk the tramp *Newton Beach*, freighters *Ashlea* and *Huntsman* off Ascension Island. The next day *Achilles* cruised north and met the heavy cruiser *Exeter* off the River Plate; the latter then went south for a rest, and County-class *Cumberland* took her place. An owl which had perched on *Achilles*' mainyard was killed by an albatross, which the men took as a bad omen. New Zealand coders howled with rage when they translated a signal promising only a 9d per day rise in pay instead of the promised 3/-. 'Miserable bastards!' was the mildest comment.

On 10 November *Achilles* entered Rio de Janeiro, the men bored with endless drills. Two of them deserted, and another was found dazed minus his wallet. The ship returned to the Falklands to refuel, with *Cumberland* and *Exeter* watching the Plate. A buzz went round, correct for once, that a pocket battleship calling herself *Graf Spee* was in the Indian Ocean. The Admiralty deliberated. *Two* pocket battleships south of Capricorn? The German had stopped a small tanker, *Africa Shell*, found her empty, and sunk her. *Achilles*' men worked off their frustrations in sport, 'resulting in hockey-stick shin-bruises and deck abrasions, black eyes from low-flying chucks'. Off Natal *Achilles* was identified by planes as the pocket battleship she was hunting, and was then ordered south at full speed to Montevideo. A raider had sunk the *Doric Star*, the frozen meat ship *Tairoa* and the freighter *Streonshalh* on the Cape Town–England route. On 10 December *Achilles* rendezvoused with Commodore Harwood in *Ajax*, and on the 12th *Exeter* joined them off the Plate, where Harwood was convinced one of the raiders was heading.

The sun had just risen when on the 13th the alarm rattlers sounded for Action Stations. 'Everyone fell out of their hammocks and grabbed their clothes and scurried away to their Stations,' recalls Ivor Burston, his own station being on the 0.5 in gun on the bridge.

AB 'Pusser' Hill was No 6 on P2 4 in AA. 'More bloody evolutions!' He watched the geyser of spray flung up by a shell. 'Blimey, that's a bit near for a throw-off. Christ, it's the bloody *Scheer*!'

To loud Kiwi cheers the New Zealand ensign soared to the peak.

Captain Parry had his binoculars on the unmistakable shape of a pocket battleship's control tower. 'Open out to four cables from *Ajax*, Pilot, and keep loose formation. Weave when she fires.' The three cruisers diverged so as to split '*Scheer*'s gunnery, as . . .

. . . the German gunlayers stationed
Brisk at their intricate batteries – guns and men both trained
To a hair in accuracy, aimed at a pitiless end –
Fired, and the smoke rolled forth over the unimpassioned
Face of a day where nothing certain but death remained.

'Scheer' also had the 'Seetakt' gunnery radar set, one of the first German warships fitted with this 50 cm type, while the British ships had none, and had to make do with the old optical range-finding system.

The German concentrated on *Exeter*, which had opened fire and straddled *'Scheer'*. A screaming 11 in salvo landed close aboard, splinters killing most of *Exeter*'s torpedo tube crew. 'B' turret took a direct hit, which knocked it out and killed its crew and most on the bridge, also destroying engine-room communications. Wounded, Captain 'Hooky' Bell dragged himself to the after control position. *Exeter* hit *'Scheer'* near her funnel, and hit again. *'Scheer'* made smoke and altered course.

Achilles went to full speed and opened fire. An 11 in shell dropped in her wake, 100 yards off, as the Panzerschiff engaged the two light cruisers. *Achilles'* guns began to overheat, jammed on recoil. 'Gunners with heavy boots' kicked the breeches, and they slid forward. 'What a lovely ship the *'Scheer'* is', thought Commissioned Gunner Watt irrelevantly as she came for them through the early morning sun. Six columns of black smoke rose between *Ajax* and *Achilles*. In 'A' turret Bill McKenzie said, 'Lads, you are now closer to the enemy than anyone else on board'. Gunlayer Stacey said, 'I can think of places I'd rather be'.

*'Scheer'*s 5.9s have the range now, shells swish overhead. *Exeter* draws the German's fire away from the two lighter ships, and once more takes heavy punishment. The 6-inchers strafe her, she hesitates, then replies. Men in *Achilles* can see her hull waver like a thundersheet from near-misses. Old hands joke to steady the younger ones – 'Blimey, I bin done – but I was done *first*!'

Exeter is a mass of smoke and flame, her aerials fall. The *Leanders* lay a saturation barrage. *Ajax* launches her Seafox seaplane. *'Scheer'* turns on *Achilles*. Near-misses fling red-hot splinters at her. In the W/T office Neville Milburg is hit, collapses; alongside him Frank Stennett's head is bloody. Milburn coughs and dies. Marine Sergeant Trimble sits in Control, rigid and deadly pale, badly hurt, glasses still on the enemy. The sightsetter sits dead at his wheel, young OD Rogers takes his place, to control range correction for all turrets, and immediately obtains hits. AB Harry Beesley on P1 4 in says, 'Come on, Ian, get behind the bloody gun before we catch those bloody splinters'. OD Ian Grant coughs as a steel splinter kills him. Harry carries a wounded man out of danger. Captain Parry hangs on to the binnacle, legs torn and bloody; his continued manoeuvring saves the ship.

The two light cruisers make smoke, then double back through it, guns blazing. In the boiler rooms the stokers are deafened already by the roar of forced-draught fans. Are those distant booms ours or theirs? *Ajax* is hit aft, knocking out 'X' and 'Y' turrets, killing their crews. *Exeter* has only 'Y' turret left, makes to ram the enemy, who eludes her, making smoke. Below, damage control parties cut holes to free men trapped by fire. The sea pours in through a great hole on the waterline below the fo'c'sle. *Exeter* lists, down by the bow. *'Scheer'* steers towards her to finish her off. The *Leanders* distract her again with their popguns; she swings both turrets to engage them, only five miles off.

'Attack with torpedoes!' *Ajax* hoists. As she fires hers, she is hit aft, and 'X' and 'Y' turrets fall silent. *'Scheer'* combs the tracks as an *Achilles* salvo falls along her upperworks. She in turn swings and fires torpedoes, but Lewin and Kearney in the Seafox spot them, alert *Ajax*. A hoist in her 'B' turret jams. Men replace it with a human chain.

In *Achilles'* turrets, still all on the line, something strange is happening. Their crews work almost joyously as they swing loaded trays towards open breeches, ram 100-pound shells up the barrel, shove in heavy cordite bags – men like Mexican Bandidos with belts of firing tubes round their waists clip them into the gun. The air grows hotter. The men fight their guns almost naked, drenched with sweat. This clamorous metal box becomes detached from normal time, the action is like some highly charged rite, though it is only ordinary men doing their jobs. They push and heave and grin at one another, knowing that any second might bring black oblivion to this almost hysterical euphoria . . . *Load! Ram! Correct for aim! Fire! Load! Ram!* . . .

If it's hot in the turrets, it's hell in the boiler rooms. Furnaces roar, fans howl. At any time a shell from '*Scheer*' could turn this hellish place into a flaming, scalding horror . . .

Worried about shell shortage, Harwood decides to break off and shadow till nightfall, then go in with torpedoes. In black funnel smoke he turns east.

'*Scheer*' does not follow. She too has had enough, for now, but a parting salvo near-misses *Ajax*, her maintopmast and aerials fall. The German steams west at reduced speed towards the Plate, a black hump in the sun. *Exeter*, an 18-knot shambles, is ordered to the Falklands. *Cumberland* abandons her refit to replace her.

Just after 10 a.m. *Achilles* noses within range of the enemy. Instantly bright flashes twinkle on the black hump and 11 in shells splash athwart the cruiser's bows. Exhausted men taking a breather on the upper deck drag themselves below, where young Milt Hill of P2 gun sits in his desolate, ruined messdeck, thinking 'We're bloody lucky. We could have been the *Exeter*.' *Achilles* drops hastily back again. Surgeons Pittar and Hunter turn back to their patients.

The pocket battleship suddenly transmits, giving the call-sign 'DTGS'. The duty coder says 'She's not *Scheer*, she's the bloody *Graf Spee*!' His announcement is met with indifference, but under the green domes of the Admiralty the First Sea Lord once again speculates: '*Graf Spee* as well? Where is *Scheer*? Or is this just one raider sowing confusion?' While he deliberates his aide brings another signal reporting Harwood's order to *Exeter* to leave the battle. What happens if *Graf Spee* re-engages? With 'X' turret out, 'Y' jammed, one 'B' gun useless, *Ajax* has only three 6 in working . . .

Achilles sights another ship to starboard. In a gun-happy daze lookouts identify her as a *Hipper*-class cruiser . . . then the sun picks out the bulk of a merchantman . . . A great sigh rises from the cruiser's decks.

Three hours pass. Damage-control parties clear away debris, restore communications. If *Graf Spee* comes out again, *Achilles* will have to take the weight. Harwood edges them closer, torpedoes cleared away, but the German captain has read his mind. A salvo straddles *Ajax*. She makes smoke and drops back.

In the dying sun *Graf Spee* stands out sharp against the land, where car headlights flash. *Ajax* steers to cut off the German if she should suddenly alter course to escape between the sandbanks. *Achilles* clings to her, raising great muddy following waves in the shallows. *Graf Spee* suddenly opens up, shells drop close. *Achilles* replies, and starts a fire aboard the German. On the New Zealander's bridge Torpedo Officer Davis Goff, former boy seaman, urges Captain Parry to get in 'close enough' to let loose his 'kippers'.

He will never get the chance. *Graf Spee* enters Montevideo, and Harwood takes his battered light cruisers out to patrol the mouth of the Plate. *Cumberland*, the nearest support, races up from Port Stanley. *Ark Royal* and *Renown*, Counties *Shropshire* and *Dorsetshire*, light cruiser *Neptune* and three destroyers converge. Force K had called at Rio, where, says Tom Bailey, 'in *Renown* we spent a whole day scraping the barnacles off the waterline, while being buzzed by a tiny aeroplane, a Pou du Ciel (the midget "Flying Flea", popular just before the war). The Skipper did not think it worth while manning the guns! And there were still kippers for breakfast on Wednesdays!'

Four days go by, *Cumberland* arrives. Then from the snooping Seafox comes the signal: '*Spee* is blowing herself up!'

It is over. There has been only one pocket battleship at large in Harwood's parish, and now she is gone, scuttled by the Führer's orders. Captain Langsdorff shoots himself. In *Achilles* Lamplighter Ivor Burston, who has had no chance of getting his little 0.5 into action, records 'The sad job of preparing our dead for burial at sea was being completed, and when all was ready we "Cleared Lower Deck" and paid our last tributes to our pals . . .'

The cruises of the two Panzerschiffe, particularly that of *Spee*, had disrupted the movements of Allied shipping in the Atlantic, and made the positional chart in the Admiralty out of date.

PRESUMED SUNK BY *GRAF SPEE*

Former Hull shipping chemist's errand boy, tankers' decky learner, tramp steamer AB and East Yorks Motor Company bus conductor Alan Mathison had joined the steamer *Stangrant* on 28 October 1939 as an AB with an extra 6d (2½p) per day for his hastily acquired 'as good as useless' Merchant Navy gunnery certificate, and was yet again disappointed in his ship.

'The *Stangrant* turned out to be a wreck of a ship, which should never have been allowed to sail in the state she was in. Her engines and boilers were worn out, though her hull was sound enough. It was only on the third attempt to sail from Barry for Santos, Brazil, with a full cargo of coal that she managed to get to Milford Haven for an outward-bound convoy. But she could not even keep up the speed of a slow convoy, and ultimately we were given instructions from the Commodore of the convey to *proceed alone* to Rendezvous X, some 1,000 miles out in the North Atlantic, thence to proceed as conditions allowed towards our destination.

'It is interesting to note that despite the wartime slogan "Careless talk costs lives", it was the dockers at Barry who told us where we were bound. That was not an isolated case. I found on several occasions later that the dockers in Britain could tell the crews of ships where they were going, when it was all supposed to be hush-hush.

'The convoy steamed away from us, and when they had finally disappeared over the horizon, we felt very, very alone. Hardly a day passed without the ship having to stop for some fault or other in the engine room, many of the stoppages being for several hours, during which we were a sitting duck for any enemy sub or raider that should be around. Our guardian angel must have been with us on that passage; in the 32 days it took us to reach Santos we only had two incidents which put the wind up us. Of course we were a darkened ship at night, and one particular night, fine but cloudy, we saw silhouetted against a very low moon, just above the horizon to the west of us, a warship, which we later found out was the *Graf Spee*. As we were down-moon from her, against the dark horizon to the east, she apparently did not sight us. She was steaming to the south at a high speed from the way she quickly passed the moon's face. Had she spotted us that would have been our lot.

'I had expected that gun drills would have been the order of the day, but each time I asked the Chief Officer if we could hold a gun practice, the reply was that there was work to be done on deck. It would appear that deck work was more important than training to defend your ship and the lives of the crew should the occasion arise. Personally, I would have held a gun practice every day, weather permitting, so that in the event of us having to defend the ship, we could at least have put up a stiff opposition against a submarine.

'The only other person we had aboard who knew anything about a 4in gun was a retired ex-Royal Marine, who had volunteered for service in merchant ships for the duration of the war. He was in fact in charge of the gun party, as the gunlayer, and I was the trainer. My job was to train the gun on target, open and close the breech, insert the firing cartridge.

'The rest of the gun crew had to be made up from the other Able Seamen. Prior to leading the gun to fire a practice round, we went through the procedure, giving precise instructions as to what each man was to do – one man to pass the shell to the loader, and then help to ram it into the breech, one man to take the cordite charge from the case and pass it to the loader and ram it into the breech, whereon when they were clear, I would close the breech-block and train on to the target.

'The stupid seaman who was to pass the cordite charge decided that he needed a cigarette and promptly lit one while he was bent down over the open full cordite charge case. Sparks were flying in the wind, from his cigarette. I just happened to look round and see him cradling a charge to his chest, the end of which was about an inch away from the glowing cigarette end. I screamed at him "Put that f★★★★★g fag out you stupid bastard!" Needless to say, he was not very chuffed at my outburst and asked me who the hell I thought I was, or as he put it, "I'm only an AB, same as you."

'I was not an expert at explosives, but I did know that at each end of the cordite charge there was a gunpowder bag, and I also know that gunpowder can be ignited by a cigarette. Had that charge touched his cigarette, I dread to think what the consequences would have been to all of us on that gun platform. And that was the one and only gun practice we had while I was in the ship. With friends like that, who needed an enemy!

Right: *Ivor Burston from Wiveliscombe, Somerset, as an Able Seaman aboard the battleship* Barham *in 1937.*

Below: *'Stand clear of the vent in rear!' – Royal Navy Boy Seamen training on a 6in gun pre-1939.*

***Left:** 'Manning the Mast' at HMS* Ganges, *a true test of courage for the boys of the 'stone frigate'.*

***Below:** HMS* Marlborough, *a battleship of the Training (and Third Battle) Squadron in the 1920s.*

__Right:__ Christ Buist went from dole to drafting office, to the Royal Marines, to Chatham, to the heavy cruiser HMS York *in the 'Hungry Thirties', and was with her in the West Indies when war broke out.*

__Below:__ The Parade Ground, HMS Pembroke, *the Royal Naval Barracks at Chatham, Kent.*

***Above:** HMS* York *at St Lucia, West Indies, 1938, presents a typical picture of 'showing the flag' in times of peace – gangway down, snow-white awnings rigged in the sun.*

***Left:** Harry Liddle from Yorkshire intended to go farming in Australia, but the Navy advertised for telegraphists and he went to HMS* Impregnable *to train. He humped coal and scrubbed icy decks in bare feet in the old* Marlborough, *then the new* Nelson, *and* Warspite *in the Med, before becoming a TAG.*

Above: *The destroyer* Wren *in calm seas, acting as 'crash boat' for the new aircraft carrier* Ark Royal.

Below: *After* Wren, *the 'Re-ven-gee' (HMS* Revenge*) was like serving ashore. This class of battleship was originally designed to burn coal.* Revenge*'s sister* Royal Oak *was torpedoed by* U47 *and sunk in Scapa Flow.*

Left: *Watcher of the skies. Born in Potter's Bar – Zeppelin country – Freddie Longman was a gunner bitten by the flying bug while in the 'wing tip line' of HMS* York*'s catapult Walrus. Here he has reached Petty Officer Airman rank.*

Below: *Many rating pilots flew Walrus amphibians from catapults. Here HMS* Suffolk *recovers her Walrus. Perched precariously on the top wing centre-section, the TAG is waiting to hook the aircraft on to the crane grab. One slip and he could fall into the scything propeller blades.*

Above: *Students of No 41 Course for Rating Pilots, Royal Navy, 1938, at 'Practice Camp', West Freugh. Left to right: Kimber, Morrelec, Richards, Rice, Lunberg, Clark.*

Below: *No 41 Rating Pilot Course graduates selected for fighters. Left to right: Clark, Monk, Sabey, Kimber, Hadley. Eric Monk won two DSMs, and commanded a Corsair fighter squadron as a Lieutenant-Commander aged 23. Sabey was also commissioned, having flown Fulmar intruder patrols from Malta over Sicilian airfields at night.*

Left: *Doug Cole and Bill Crowther. Crowther was later lost with HMS* Fidelity, *the only Q-ship in World War II to carry an aircraft.*

Right: *Mark Wells 'just loved ships'. Beached in the Depression, he got a job with the railway, on the footplate, and 'felt the exhilaration that I had at sea'. Here* (near right) *he is in the cab of LNER No 4797, a 'Green Arrow' V2-class mixed traffic loco ('Super engines they were too'). War took him back to sea, to the cruiser* Arethusa *and the sloop* Bridgewater (far right).

Below: *HMS* Renown. *This picture shows the beautiful lines of the battlecruiser after her final reconstruction.*

4797

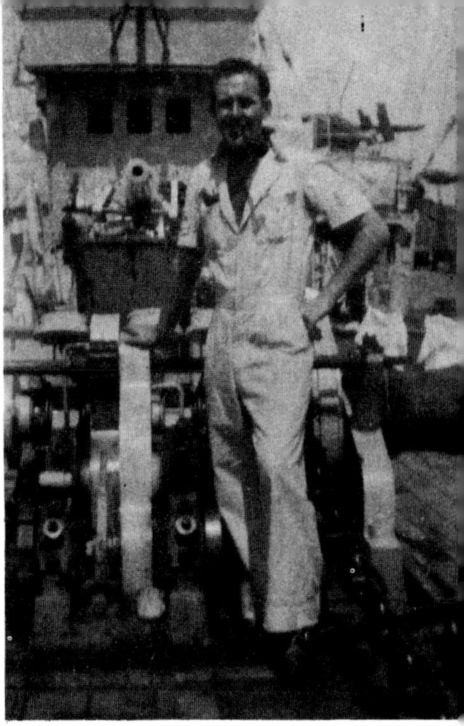

HEROES ALL OF THEM. R.I.P. GONE BUT NOT FORGOTTEN.
IN SORROWFUL AND PROUD REMEMBRANCE OF THE GALLANT 518 OFFICERS AND MEN OF THE ROYAL NAVY, ROYAL MARINES, ROYAL AIR FORCE, FLEET AIR ARM, ROYAL FLEET RESERVE, AND PENSIONERS OF H.M.S. COURAGEOUS WHO WERE DROWNED BY THE SINKING OF THEIR SHIP BY A GERMAN SUBMARINE ON SUNDAY SEPTEMBER 17TH 1939.

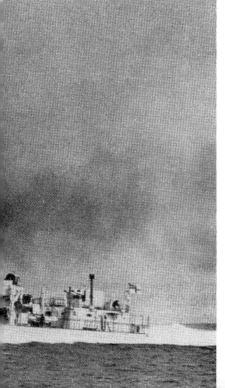

Top left: *HMS* Courageous, *with sister 'light battlecruisers'* Furious *and* Glorious, *was converted into an aircraft-carrier in the 1920s, and her squadron pioneered flight deck procedures and dive-bombing. She was torpedoed and sunk by a U-boat in the first month of World War II.*

Left: *HMS* Kelly, *the late Earl Mountbatten's famous World War II destroyer command.* Kelly *was sunk by Stukas off Crete in the Mediterranean, having survived a torpedoing in the North Sea.*

Above: *Workhorses of the Northern Patrol were the armed merchant cruisers, with their elderly 6in guns, some of Boer War vintage. Here a gun's crew closes up in Icelandic waters aboard* Asturias. *The gun has no shield, and has therefore probably come from the secondary battery of a defunct old battleship.*

Left: *New Zealand 'sparker' Jack Harker found* Achilles *'unforgettable' in her spacious accommodation, big wireless operating room and new elecrical equipment.*

Below: *The new* Achilles, *a* Leander*-class light cruiser, seen in the Panama Canal in 1938.*

Bottom: *'Crossing the Line' party aboard HMS* Achilles.

The Battle of the River Plate. Boredom with endless drills was cured by hot action against Graf Spee. *First* Exeter, *then* Ajax, *lost firepower after hits by* Spee's *11in shells, and* Achilles *bore the brunt, losing men to a steel splinter storm.*

Above: Achilles *men take a breather while her hot, blackened forward 6in guns cool down during a lull in the battle.*

Below: Graf Spee *burns after being scuttled on the Führer's orders in the River Plate. The sight broke Captain Langsdorff's heart, and he shot himself.*

Above: *The Flotilla Leader HMS* Keith *in which 'reluctant gunner' Iain Nethercott served.*

Left: *Group by 'A' gun, HMS* Keith, *March 1940. Most of these men (left to right: Wallis, Addington, Wadey, 'Scottie', Tongue and the ship's Chef) were killed at Dunkirk.*

***Right:** OD, 1940. Young Mick Dale, ex-prep school boy, Chesire Regiment drummer boy and the Territorial gunner, jointed the Fleet Air Arm as a TAG, and was called 'traitor' for it by the Army.*

***Below:** The German battlecruiser* Gneisenau *was, like her sister* Scharnhorst, *a battlecruiser, armed with only 11in guns, and designed mainly for convoy attack. The two ships were no match, even together, for the battleship* Duke of York, *which sank* Scharnhorst *in December 1943.*

***Bottom:** The Blackburn Skua two-seat fighter/dive-bomber was the FAA's first all-metal and monoplane aircraft. It did good work in the hands of pilots like PO Eric Monk, DSM and Bar, and was the first Allied machine to shoot down an enemy aircraft in World War II. Skuas sank the German cruiser* Königsberg. *Behind the Skua is a Vought-Sikorsky Chesapeake.*

Above: *On 10 April 1940 Captain Warburton-Lee, RN, took five destroyers into Narvik harbour, northern Norway, where he discovered ten German destroyers of superior gun power. He lost his ship, HMS* Hardy, *and his own life, but sank or disabled three of the enemy. Here, men of HMS* Havock *stand in front of 'X' gun aft, with the hole made in the gunshield by flying debris in the battle visible. All wear huge grins of relief at being in one of the ships that got away.*

Below: *Light cruiser HMS* Glasgow *was active in the Norwegian Campaign, landing troops, evacuating King Haakon, his country's gold reserves, and members of his government.*

Bottom: *The aircraft-carrier HMS* Furious *flew her Swordfish to the limits of their performance, their crews' endurance and her own, in support of the Allied landings in Norway, until relieved by* Ark Royal. *Here the old carrier takes it green, in company with* Renown.

'On reaching Santos, we were informed that we had been given up as missing, presumed sunk by *Graf Spee*, as we were over a week late arriving there. After discharge of the coal cargo, we sailed down to the River Plate to Montevideo, and there in the river was the wreck of the scuttled *Spee*, still smouldering.'

DODGING THE U-BOATS

Second Mate Bill Thomas, used to the rougher realms of Merchant Navy life in tramp steamers – 'weevils in the burgoo, 'roaches in the milk' – as AB and apprentice, delivered *Stronsa Firth*'s sensitive cargo of shells and depth-charges at the secret MN hideaway of Loch Swine in north-west Scotland immediately after the outbreak of war.

'We were supposed to lie at our destination at anchor, to await naval vessels replenishing their magazines from us after a major battle with the enemy. There were five or six of us, large ships and small, lying off the village of Taviallic. As there was no naval battle in the vicinity, I became bored with the daily routine of picking blackberries and assisting the cook in the gruesome business of slitting the throats of mountain sheep. Both these activities were designed to brighten up our menu. Seeking more interesting work, I travelled home, later to join a Cardiff tramp as Third Mate.

'As convoys had not been properly organized at that time and as our engines had a tendency to break down, we sailed across the North Atlantic on our own. Without meeting the enemy, we tied up safely at Houston, Texas, to load a cargo of scrap iron for Glasgow. When I enquired at the Post Office about the price of an airmail stamp to the UK, I was surrounded by customers who wanted to know how I had travelled to Houston without getting bumped off by German submarines. As this was Texas, I decided to give my audience a line of their own bull. I became enthusiastic as I described my hair-raising escapes from packs of U-boats and completed the story by giving an impression of Errol Flynn emerging from the grasp of Captain Morgan's pirates. To my surprise, my listeners were spellbound, and they competed with each other for the honour of entertaining me during my stay in port.

'I came near to paying for my duplicity en route to Glasgow, when one of those U-boats surfaced half a mile away and her officers watched us through binoculars. We had stopped as usual to effect engine repairs and as we had not yet been issued with a gun, we prepared to abandon ship. The submarine suddenly dived and was seen no more, no torpedo came our way, and when our engine restarted we continued the voyage.'

The Little Ships

We're the little ships that Churchill clean forgot
And goodness knows we didn't ask a lot,
A few more spells of leave would do us all a lot of good,
We haven't got the comforts of the *Rodney* or the *Hood*,
When it comes to week-end leave there's none for us –
We're always shoving off to do our stuff.
Now the other ships get swingtime,
All we get is f*****g sea-time,
We're the little ships that Churchill clean forgot.

THE COLLISION OF *BARHAM* AND *DUCHESS*

Fred Harman was a counter hand in a wet fish shop in Clacton in 1939. He had lived near the sea all his life without ever thinking of making it a career, other than through its products; unlike his best pal, Roy Ralmer, who was mad keen to join the Navy, and 'he twisted my brain'. At the recruitment exam Fred passed, Roy failed. 'Good lad,' said the Recruiting Petty Officer, 'that's another half a dollar for me'. In initial training much was made of a matlow's need to be able to swim, and life was made a misery for an oppo of his who could not. 'He was drafted to the *Hood*, and if he had been the best swimmer in the world it would have done him no good!'

Fred himself went to *Barham*, a *Queen Elizabeth*-class 'battlewagon' lying in Alexandria at the beginning of August. Fred was put initially on 4in AA guns with automatic breeches ('I'd never seen anything like them at Whale Island'), and ended up on a 6in in the port battery. When war came, Captain 'Hooky' Walker, later to command a task force in the hunting down of the last Japanese warships in the East Indies, informed them that they were off to join the Home Fleet at Greenock, as the 'Med' looked like being quiet.

Barham was with the Fleet off the Orkneys at 0427 in the morning watch on 12 December, carrying out the usual zigzag, with the destroyer *Duchess* on her port side, when a change of course to starboard was given. Instead of waiting for the executive signal, *Duchess* turned straight across the battler's bows and was struck amidships.

'A shudder went through *Barham*. I had just come off the middle watch and was having a cup of kye and a smoke before turning in.'

In *Duchess* Lancashire lad Jack Dodds, a former cruiser man, late of 'Whited Sepulchres' *Cumberland* and *Kent*, had also just come off the graveyard watch and was in his hammock aft of the messdecks in the canteen flat – the passageway from the messdecks on to the upper deck at the break of the fo'c'sle. 'A position', says Dodds, 'which I have always believed saved my life. The *Barham* hit us with such a loud crash that I was sure that we had either hit a mine or been torpedoed. I leapt out and dragged my mate out of his hammock as I ran for the upper deck.

'The lights were still on so I could see where I was going and what I was doing. Just inside the break of the fo'c'sle we had the coal bunker (we had not been changed to oil fires) and as I passed this I was aware of the coal falling out just behind me. By the time I reached the deck the ship was heeling over to port. I saw a couple of lads climbing over the guardrails so I ducked under the motor boat and joined them. By then the poor old *Duchess* was lying right over on her side, so we just walked down the ship's side. By the time I reached the bilge keel she gave a lurch and turned turtle, lying completely upside down.'

Fred Harman in *Barham* had 'rushed up on deck when we heard our engines put hard astern. Everyone on deck thought we had hit a submarine. All you could see was the upturned hull with the Asdic dome, which in the darkness looked like a conning-tower. It drifted down our starboard side and a few of her crew stepped off the hull on to our starboard 6in gun deck.'

One of these was Jack Dodds. 'By this time *Barham* had heaved to, and we were lying alongside, all sorts of lights were shining down on us. Some lines, which turned out to be hammock lashings taken from the midshipmen's hammocks, were thrown to us. No way could we climb up these as they were too small to hold on to, so we secured them to the Asdic dome, which was standing up like a big bollard. On these lines we all five of us swung across hand over hand, to drop down into the arms of the Chief G.I. and so on up on to the *Barham*. We were taken into the after screen and given a tot of rum – well, I call it a tot, it was a cupful, and a Pusser's cup in those days was a half-pint measure. I have often wondered if I was supposed to drink it all or not, but I did, and this is probably the reason why I can't remember anything till later on that morning when I woke up in one of the WO's cabins.'

Most of Jack's mates were still trapped inside the doomed destroyer or struggling in the black choppy waters. 'The screams of men in the freezing water and others with their faces at portholes not big enough to get through was terrible. She drifted just astern of us and then her depth-charges exploded. After that all was dead silent, no one could believe what had happened. When we went ashore in Greenock no one wanted to talk to us, as if it was our fault.'

A total of 117 men were lost out of 140 in *Duchess*. After leave Jack Dodds was drafted to HMS *Havock*, and was 'a wee bit worried for a while about joining another destroyer. But I soon got over that, and soon settled down in a very happy ship!' Another destroyer followed, HMS *Tyrian*, which took him East.

KEITH TO THE RESCUE

For nine months the destroyer *Keith* put in week after week of seatime, voyaging from mid-Atlantic to Cherbourg, up the Channel to Dover and Harwich . . .

> We're cold, hard and hungry, nothing to eat,
> No winter clothing, no boots on our feet.

Our hammocks are soaking, the messdecks awash,
We're living on potmess and biscuits and hash.

'We did our share', says Iain Nethercott, reluctant gunner (too noisy) at his jam-happy pom-pom, 'of picking up burnt and dying merchant mariners in the Atlantic, and such things as attempting to save the survivors of the *Gipsy*, blown in half by a magnetic mine in the Harwich approaches on a black and snowy night, with half her crew trapped in the fo'c'sle and no escape through the scuttles, which were too small, and all the gun hand-ups jammed . . .

'We were inspected by poor, sick George VI at Dover when we were leader of the Dover Patrol. We came in with the dawn one freezing morning in January 1940, and we were bustled out on to the Prince of Wales pier, still in seaboots and oilskins, and standing in a blinding snowstorm while this poor chap walked down our ranks!'

They lost two blades off their port propeller on Devil's Point, Plymouth, at 2a.m. in a snowstorm, crept back to the Dockyard 'and then had the satisfying thought of dockyard mateys being turned out of their beds at 3a.m. to get us into drydock. Unfortunately they couldn't work without a tiddey oggie inside them, and it was nearer six o'clock before we were on the chocks.'

'And so into Harwich, not before time,
Twenty more sea days and a gutfull of brine,
Let's get down the messdeck and drink up our tots,
We're sailing at seven and I'm on First Watch.'

'The only leave we normally had was 48 hours' boiler-cleaning leave to each watch alternately, occasionally evening leave till 10p.m. if we came in before 6p.m.; but we had to watch the ship from any pub we were in, and a black flag and a gun fired got us back in a panic. A Pusser's oilskin didn't keep out the terrible temperatures of that first war winter, we had no lammy coats or gloves (they went to the battlewagons swinging round the buoy at Scapa). The only heat in the seamen's mess came from the "fish and chip shop", the steam capstan engine sited on the seamen's messdeck on the older destroyers, with removable wooden covers but because of leaky joints always leaking steam into the messdeck accompanied by hissing and bubbling noises. It was a good place to crash down when off watch, always warm, but wet.'

Once, faced with towing a merchantman broken down in mid-Atlantic, they passed the towing strop round the mounting of 'Y' gun, the only thing which might take an 8,000-ton strain. At about 2 knots they struggled homewards, with one-hour tricks at the wheel, 'as the ship was a cow to steer with this dead weight veering all over the ocean, astern'. The 3½in towing wire was hanging by one thread when they got in, and the strain had started the gun mounting, but two years later Iain received £37 salvage money – 'a fortune for me'.

There were small comedies:

Keith to *Shikhari* (in full Atlantic gale): 'I can see your dome.'

Shikhari to *Keith*: 'Don't be so indelicate!'

At the beginning of May they were lying at Sheerness with a dozen other destroyers and the light cruisers *Arethusa* and *Galatea*. On the 10th Hitler invaded France.

Things grew rapidly worse across the Channel. On 23 May Boulogne was in imminent danger as the panzers had almost reached the coast. The destroyer *Verity* was acting as guard ship in the harbour there, and another V and W, *Vimiera*, was lying off the port. Two battalions of Irish and Welsh Guards, hastily shipped over from Wellington Barracks, were holding the town, while a big demolition party had been sent from Chatham to destroy the docks.

Keith led four of her V-and-Ws and arrived off the port in the late afternoon. In the roadstead were five French destroyers, all firing at the wooded heights to the south of the town. Fire was being returned from the shore but there were no clear targets for the British ships' 4.7s.

'The Skipper took us up the channel to the harbour, with *Vimy* astern, and *Vimiera* at the entrance to maintain visual signal contact with the rest of the flotilla. As we sailed in, a wood on the port side of the channel came alive with rifle and machine-gun fire. The bullets were whistling and pinging on the Iron Deck. Looking at the heights behind the wood, several German columns could be seen moving down towards the town. We opened up with HE at about 3,000 yards and started scoring hits immediately. Jimmy Wallis, my gunlayer, suddenly spotted several files of German infantrymen taking up position on the boulevard on the north side of the harbour. He gave me a yell and I spotted them immediately and brought the gun round. We gave them several long bursts, and brought down the portico of a hotel behind them. By now we were coming up to the centre of the harbour and had to turn to bring the ship port-side on to the Quai Chantzy.

'We were under a lot of small arms fire, mostly machine-guns, and were taking casualties. As we came alongside the jetty and made fast it was a scene of indescribable chaos. Hundreds of soldiers who appeared to be in a blind panic immediately rushed the ship. Lots of them were drunk, very few had rifles. The Skipper up on the bridge was going crackers. He ordered the torpedomen armed with rifles and bayonets and the Gunner T to "Clear all that rabble off the ship!"

'There were dozens of wounded on stretchers on the jetty and from where I was on the gun I could see them being trampled on by other soldiers who were staggering about with wine bottles. Although the Skipper refused to take off any of the French civilians who pleaded with him from the jetty, we took aboard a large party of French schoolgirls in the care of several nuns. These were stowed away on the messdecks, as the wardroom was full of dead and wounded!

'In the middle of all this activity we spotted a German Storch plane which flew over the hills and towards the harbour. The ships outside opened up on it but the pilot flew on and suddenly dropped a white flare. From then on all hell broke loose. Hundreds of German troops came pouring over the heights on both sides. We came under terrific fire and trench mortar bombs started dropping on the jetty and then on to the port side of our Iron Deck by the break of the fo'c'sle. My gunlayer was hit in the chest; the loading numbers put shell dressings on him and took him below. I took over the gun, as a large force of Stukas had appeared overhead and had just started their dives. Their bombs fell over the jetty and right alongside the ship, killing our sentries on the jetty. I got a long burst on one and blew away most of his nose, and he crashed into the harbour.

'The Captain had been shot dead on the bridge and they carried him down and put him alongside the CO of the Chatham demolition party who had been killed earlier. I had been hit in the shoulder by some of the splinters from the Iron Deck, and had been well clouted in the face with lumps of concrete from the bombs on the jetty, so I was bleeding like a pig and swearing like hell.

'Guardsmen on the jetty were repulsing an attack from motor-cycle troops, and when the dust had cleared a bit on the jetty I managed to sweep along a line of these bikes, and then blew down a dockyard crane from which I'm pretty sure the German machine-gunners who had killed the Skipper were firing. The *Vimy* next to us was in a bad way. Like us, her decks were full of dead and wounded soldiers. Her Captain was also dead on the bridge. It was a bright and sunny afternoon. A good afternoon to die.

'The *Whitshed* came steaming into harbour, her Skipper directing the guns on to targets with a hand megaphone. It was Lieutenant-Commander Conder, a man of character, who was now Senior Officer. Our First Lieutenant, who had been wounded, took over the ship. *Whitshed* signalled us and the *Vimy* to cast off and proceed to Dover with our troops, while he called in *Vimiera*, leaving *Wild Swan* and *Venomous* outside as back-up.

'*Whitshed* was engaging tanks on her port side, so on the way out we joined in as we had the guns in local control, with the TS hit. Both pom-poms were jammed and the OA and his assistant were frantically working on them. In those days rifles and cutlasses were provided at all guns, so we opened the boxes of 0.303 and carried on with rifles. There were loads of targets as German infantry were everywhere, so everyone on the upper deck including the more warlike of our soldiers kept up a barrage of rifle fire until we had passed out of the harbour mouth. We'd have used those cutlasses too.'

Iain went below and had a piece of shrapnel removed by an Army doctor.

'It hadn't penetrated very deep and after a good wash and a tot of neaters I was back in business. Off the Varne lightship we stopped engines, and the ship's company assembled on the upper deck. It was sunset, Jimmy read the Burial Service and we lowered the Captain, followed by the other captain, into the sea, to be followed by the others. It was very sad, and whenever I sail over the waters today I always pay my respects to my old shipmates.

'They sent us to Chatham Dockyard as the ship looked like a colander and all the boats were riddled with rifle bullets and shrapnel and needed changing. We were there for two days. They whipped out our old pom-poms and replaced them with two new ones with articulated belts. They removed our after set of tubes and put in a 3in HA gun. The worst of the holes were welded up, but they didn't have time to repair all the bullet holes in the funnels and upperworks. Mind you, we got *two nights* undisturbed sleep in our hammocks and we all managed to slip ashore and sink a few pints.

'We sailed down the river to Sheerness on the third day under the command of a new skipper, Captain Berthon, and with replacements for our dead and wounded. I had been made permanent gunlayer on the new port pom-pom, and the First Lieutenant had called me down to the Wardroom and let me know that I should put in for Leading Seaman. I couldn't believe, it, I was only just nineteen. I could see the war was going to improve my chances of promotion beyond my wildest dreams. The trick was obviously going to be how to stay alive to take advantage of these new conditions.

'We loaded up with extra ammunition at Dover. I met my first HOs on the messdeck. They were ODs who had been sent as replacements and the poor little chaps hadn't got a clue, they really thought that they were on a pleasure cruise. They didn't live the week out. Our new Skipper cleared lower deck and gave us a Noël Coward-type speech, and thus fortified, we sailed for Dunkirk.

'The earlier part of the evacuation, as far as we observed, was reasonably simple, as most ships, which included the big cross-Channel ferries, could get alongside the mole, and it was a simple case of troops marching down the mole and on to the ships without getting their feet wet. The drawback was that the German long-range artillery kept opening up on the mole and the harbour. Up the coast towards Nieuport they had an artillery spotter balloon which was obviously ranging the guns on to the targets. In my opinion we could have spared a few Spitfires to upset this little game. In the event, except for a Coastal Command Hudson, which was shot down on the beach, I never saw any RAF planes during the whole time I was out there.

'We carried back our load of troops in this way for a few trips, being fired on from the coast on a few occasions during the time when we ran parallel to the coast in the swept channel. I must admit that it looked very fearsome over there. The oil storage tanks were burning and the pall of black smoke covered the whole area for miles. The German planes spent most of their time bombing the beaches, though every now and then we were attacked. My new gun worked perfectly, but we had to economize on ammunition.

'On about our fourth day we were taken off evacuating troops and carried out bombardments of the German-held coast, shooting up tanks and other transport and infantry. We came under heavier and heavier air attack. At night we crept along in the main channel well to the east of the beaches, looking for E-boats which were infiltrating the evacuation fleet. One of them had sunk *Wakeful* with terrific loss of life.

'We were closed up at Action Stations all the time, and were existing on corned beef sandwiches and cups of tea. We catnapped on the guns but were getting more and more tired and especially at night it was getting hard to concentrate. The harbour was closed now with sunken ships, the big ships had gone for good, most of the modern destroyers had been withdrawn, and the soldiers were being taken off the beaches at night using small boats, and taken out to the old V-and-W destroyers and Fleet sweepers . . .'

Oars in the darkness, rowlocks, shadowy shapes
Of boats that searched. We heard a seaman's hail,
Then we swam out, and struggled with our gear,
Clutching the looming gunwales. Strong hands pulled,
And we were in and heaving with the rest,
Until at last they turned. The dark oars dipped,
The laden craft crept slowly out to sea,
To where in silence lay the English ships.

'We had by now been taken over by an admiral, Admiral Wake-Walker, who was in charge of the beach operations out there. As dawn came up on the "Glorious First Of June" we were cruising slowly in the roadstead off Dunkirk flying our Admiral's flag and our battle ensigns. We were very tired after days and nights without sleep, tired right through to our bones. The continuous bombing and artillery fire flung at us had made us all very jumpy, and the sight of so many ships bombed and sunk and all the bodies floating around, made us more and more depressed. An MTB came alongside and told us that the cross-Channel ferries had all sailed for Southampton, as the crews refused to sail to the beaches any more, and reported the buzz that *Verity*, one of our flotilla, had practically mutinied and was now moored at Dover and wouldn't sail. The news cheered us up no end.

'As dawn came up we were lying off Bray Dunes in company with *Basilisk* and some Fleet sweepers. At about 8 a.m. I spotted a large formation of Stukas coming up from the south. Most of them went round with the 3 in firing at them, out of range of our guns. Suddenly they dived from ahead, up-sun. I was firing long bursts at the first one, who pulled out just over the bridge and I saw his bomb come away, then another and another. We had full helm on and it was difficult to keep the gun trained. I thought that the bombs were going to hit the stern but they seemed to fall in the water right under our tail. The ship reared up and kept swinging, steering jammed. I saw the next formation of planes starting their dive, just as the ship straightened up. I got a long burst in on the second plane and carried on firing as he shot overhead and I blew all the wireless aerials down. I could see one bomb coming straight for the ship. It went down the after funnel and exploded down in the boiler-room. Clouds of smoke and steam poured out of the engine and boiler rooms and the ship slowed to a stop and started to list to port. An MTB came alongside and took off the Admiral, and shortly afterwards the Captain ordered "Abandon Ship". The Carley rafts were launched and most men were jumping into the water and hanging on to the rafts. The port whaler was lowered and filled with wounded, and everybody started making for the *Skipjack* and *Salamander*, which were steaming close to us. The *Basilisk* had just been sunk, I could see her going down to starboard.

'The Stukas came back and once again we got the gun into action, although the list on the ship made it difficult. I suddenly spotted several Messerschmitts flying low towards us and managed to open up on them. They opened fire on our survivors and seemed to be killing everyone in the water around the whaler. The sea around them was red with blood and I could hear the shouts and screams from where I was.

'Another wave of Stukas came diving down on us and I couldn't elevate the gun high enough to range on them because of the list. We were badly hit in the engine room and she carried on listing. Bomb splinters had killed several of our loading numbers on the gun deck, and it was time to sort them out. I noticed that *Skipjack* out to port had been hit and suddenly she turned over with all the soldiers on board thrown into the sea, but a Stuka had come down in the sea, and I wondered whether I had got him or whether it was the *Skipjack*'s gunners. Several small boats and a large tug, *St Abbs*, were alongside the starboard bow taking off the wounded and some of the soldiers. There were only two of us left on the gun deck; all the dead were piled up in the corner by the ready-use lockers. There was only myself and Paddy Dunbar, the trainer of the starboard gun, left.

'The ship was wallowing deep now and listing well to port. The cox'n saw us from the signal deck and gave us a yell to abandon ship, so we went up on to the fo'c'sle and helped to get the last of the wounded on to *St Abbs*.

'Eventually she pulled away. By then I thought my *Keith* would turn over any second, but it wasn't necessary as suddenly more Stukas appeared and dived on her. The bombs landed all over her and she just rolled over and sank. The *St Abbs* was pottering around picking up survivors of the *Skipjack* so I went up for'ard where someone had got a jar full of rum. I managed a tot, and a few minutes later a Stuka hit us with a stick of bombs. I was blown clean into the water, and bobbed up in my whaler's lifejacket, looking for the ship. She had gone. There didn't seem to be many survivors, and I felt myself going east with the tide. The water was very cold but there was no oil on the surface. There was an old merchantman lying bombed ahead of me, so I made a big effort and eventually caught a dangling boat's fall, worked my way along her side and climbed up a rope ladder on to her well deck. There was soon a crowd of about a dozen on board, including Captain Berthon. We were rummaging around when we were suddenly attacked by bombers. When they'd gone we found plenty of tinned food in the galley and had a feast of tinned salmon and some tinned rice pudding.

'The Skipper had examined one of the lifeboats which was still on the falls, and decided that we could use her to row back to England. We stocked her with corned beef and tins of pears and plenty of water. I rummaged around in the after locker and came up with the boat's sails. We couldn't find the mast or any spar that would suffice, but I told the Skipper that I could easily use two oars and rig up a jury rig. I hadn't been a Canvey Island Sea Scout for nothing! However, while I was working on this, a small motor lighter with a naval crew passed by in the deep water channel. After much yelling they noticed us and came alongside, and sailed on down the coast back towards Dunkirk with all of us on board, and transferred us to a Sheerness cement carrier, which took us home.

'I was bloody annoyed, after all that work.'

Lighting Up The Channel

If the RAF was not in evidence over the cratered and body-strewn beaches, the Fleet Air Arm was.

The urgent evacuation did not stop at dusk, but continued all through the night. To prevent U-boats from getting through to the rescue fleet in the friendly darkness, someone was required to hang a string of lights down the Channel in the night sky. The request went out for Navy air-gunners who could work a drogue winch.

TAG Jackie Heath of *Emperor of India, Eagle, Furious* and late lamented *Courageous*, star bomb-aimer, was one of those who volunteered. They were flown to Detling in Kent and he was told that his job was to 'light the Channel north of Dunkirk' so that U-boats attempting to interfere with the retreat there could be bombed. The process entailed letting the drogue out to 500ft, with a stopper at a certain distance along the wire. A specially treated flare was then sent down the wire, and the jerk when it reached the stopper detonated the flare, which burned for about ten minutes as it was towed along; then another flare was put on the wire, and the routine repeated. 'It wasn't the Blackpool Illuminations, but it stopped Dönitz from destroying an errand of mercy.'

Norwegian Waters

Norway's a shadow; sullen the cliffs at midnight,
Stagnant the streams. Stare out beyond those fisted
Rocks; whose features stung by disease and hatred
Now rise from the mother sea, the moth-winged silence;
What calm, what certainty?
Great cities crumble, ocean to ocean cries,
All falls.

Recruits entered *Ganges*, Guz, Chatham, *St Vincent* and Eastleigh in a steady stream through the early months of 1939, to be turned into seamen, stokers, flying sailors, Sick Bay tiffies, Jack Dusties, submariners and Marine seaborne soldiers – the Regulars, the 12- and 22-year men who would take the weight in the first weeks and months of war, and pass on their knowledge and example to the green HOs who were to flood through the barrack gates.

NEW CARRIER *ARK ROYAL*

In the spring of 1939 Geoff Denny joined the Sussex Division of the RNVR at Hove, and thereafter drove down from his home in Horsham twice a week on drill nights.

'It was a reaction to the Government booklet issued to arouse the patriotic enthusiasm of suitably aged young men to join the reserve forces. I thought that my modest facility to read and send Morse and semaphore would be of use in the Signals Branch of the Royal Navy. I felt very proud of the round cap, and bell-bottoms, and enjoyed the elementary seamanship, including bends and hitches, which I was also able to cope with easily as a result of my years in the Boy Scouts, and the dreaded swimming test in a duck suit held no terrors for me as I was a county league water polo player. Inevitably, at the end of August the buff envelope dropped through my letter box. Within a couple of hours I had packed my kitbag, said goodbye to my parents, handed in the key to the office safe, and was on my way to help the Navy sort out Hitler.

'It was a beautiful golden August morning as the train took me through the achingly familiar Sussex countryside to Pompey to swell the ranks of all the other Reservists who had been activated. They didn't lose much time in deciding that I was urgently wanted at sea. On the boat across from Scrabster to Scapa Flow we looked in the turbulent waters of Pentland Firth for U-boats but got into the great anchorage safely and awaited the arrival of the Home Fleet. The next afternoon we had the unforgettable sight of the *Nelson*, *Rodney*, cruisers, and destroyers coming in to anchor. When they had all dropped their hooks, we, 40 RNVRs from the Clyde, Sussex and Ulster Divisions, were taken in a drifter to join our ship – the great new carrier HMS *Ark Royal*.'

The new carrier was not everyone's idea of maritime beauty. As she began her sea trials in 1938, she had made the signal to a nearby destroyer: 'How do I look?' The 'ocean greyhound' replied: 'Go back to Loch Ness'.

'The immense size was quite staggering when viewed from the waterline – seven decks up to a flight deck 800 feet long with two hangars carrying 72 aircraft, fighters and bombers.' She cost £3,000,000 and the contract lightened the weight of the Depression at Cammell Laird's on Merseyside.

The new all-welded system of construction used in *Ark Royal* led to some murmurs of 'jerrybuilding', and Lady Maud Hoare, wife of the First Sea Lord, Sir Samuel, took four attempts to smash the bottle of champagne against her bows at launching – traditionally a bad omen – but when the crack No 820 Squadron landed their Swordfish aboard '*Ark*' for the first time on 12 January 1939 they found her big deck welcoming. 'A change from *Courageous*,' according to one rating pilot, 'which was not the easiest carrier to work from – you had to do a round-down creep or the airflow over the stern came at you like a waterfall and the hot gases from the funnel could whisk you up just when you wanted to sink down'.

There was trouble with No 803 Squadron's brand-new Blackburn Skua fighter/dive-bombers. They were the first all-metal monoplanes in the FAA, with mod cons like dive flaps, two-pitch airscrews and retracting undercarriages, but their engines were under-powered and light, and had been shifted further forward than intended, unbalancing the machine. 'Bloody hell, this *is* an old tank!' said PO Brian Seymour, No 803's Senior TAG, after his first flight in the CO's L2873.

Geoff Denny's VR 40, the first non-active service ratings to join the '*Ark*', had been given a pierhead jump specifically for flight deck duties and to release the existing rangers back to their duties as pom-pom crews.

'We spent the first few days finding our sea legs, being seasick, exploring the ship and learning our duties from the Flight Deck Officer, the "batsman". We were allocated jobs as chockmen, on the signal booms, manning the fire-fighting equipment, besides working part of ship as appropriate. When there was no night flying we had the privilege of an "all-night in" with no middle watches, but on the other hand had to get used to a very early start to get the first aircraft range off an hour or so before dawn. When we were in the South Atlantic from October 1939 to February 1940 this was no great handicap, and the sight of the tropical dawn breaking over a calm ocean is a very pleasant memory, but at the end of November, we started a patrol in the "Roaring Forties" south of the Cape. Here, in a bleak and foggy sea, it was too rough to fly and we were glad to get back to sunnier areas.

'*Ark Royal* was a happy ship, and I like to think that the ranging parties soon became an efficient team. When the aircraft landed, the job was to get the hook disconnected so that the plane could taxi up to the forward end of the flight deck beyond the crash barrier as fast as possible. This involved two wind-buffeted rangers hanging on to the wingtips.

'We had one Skua miss the arrester wires and skid over the bows, one Swordfish broke up on the catapult as it was being launched, and its depth-charges exploded under the ship, causing a bit of a panic.'

HUNTING THE DORNIER

One of the untypical moves in the relationship between officers and men in the '*Ark*' was the commonsense announcement by junior commissioned flying officers that they would rather be led by experienced rating pilots than lead themselves.

When the Fleet, with *Ark Royal*, was at sea on the early morning of 26 September the Luftwaffe sent out a flight of Dornier Do 18 flying-boats to shadow the carrier and the battleships. 'Unfortunately', says the then PO Monk, 'the C-in-C allowed the Dorniers to fly round the Fleet, and for a long time only one was attacked'.

Lieutenant McEwan, with the Senior TAG of No 803 Squadron, Petty Officer Brian Seymour, who did not normally pair off, were the crew involved. Seymour had been 'busy right up to the last minute organizing the other TAGs and myself. A TAG's work was never done, even at the best of times, let alone in this mad rush. I was responsible for getting all the information on the positions of ships in the vicinity, the call-signs and codes of the day, and for looking after the observers' gear. It was also my job to maintain my wireless set in first-class working condition – if it failed in the air, the TAG was on the bridge in front of the Captain when he got down. That was as well as manning the aft-mounted Lewis gun, of course. And there was no special hot meal laid on for us before a patrol, like the commissioned aircrew had. The Admiralty knew as much about flying as Nelson did – with slightly less excuse'.

They took off and strained their eyes through the mist and murk. Suddenly they sighted a dark, mottled shape low on the water, indistinct because of the clever camouflage in blue, green and grey – but definitely a Dornier. McEwan opened up with his four forward-firing Brownings, then Seymour raked the German with his Lewis, with the Dornier firing back all the time. After a second attack the Dornier went down and flopped into the water like a shotgunned duck. The Germans broke out their rubber dinghy, and the flying-boat sank. It was the first enemy aircraft of the war to be shot down by any Allied force. It was also the '*Ark*'s' first aircraft victory, and for the officers there was a Black Velvet party.

'Later', Monk reports, 'Lieutenant Finch-Noyes, Lieutenant Spurway and myself were allowed off but we were limited to only one attack each on our Dornier 18. I was last to attack and the Dornier's slipstream was visible on the sea so I ignored my reflector sight and watched my bullets from the four machine-guns making ducks and drakes all over the Hun. He must have been riddled like a colander but his "fans" kept turning and I often wondered if he reached home. That was my first action and very disappointing too. After landing on, I went out on to the lower weather deck to walk down to the mess for a late lunch. That was the instant the bombs from Leutnant Francke's Heinkel exploded alongside the port side. I was drenched and wondered why one bomb made black smoke and the other white.'

The upthrust of water from the huge 2,000-pounder completely obscured the '*Ark*' from Francke's sight. Later in the day German aircraft mistook the British Second Cruiser Squadron for the whole fleet, could not locate the carrier, and reported her sunk. When the '*Ark*' returned to Scapa an all too familiar voice was heard over the broadcasting system:

> '*Gar*many calling . . . *Gar*many calling . . .'
> It was Lord Haw-Haw, the Irishman William Joyce.
> 'Where is the *Ark Royal*?'

The question was repeated throughout the following weeks by Goebbels' propaganda ministry. He sank *Ark Royal* every day, like some venomous Walter Mitty. Newspapers printed the episode in red, Goering decorated Francke with the Iron Cross. Even after Captain Allan G. Kirk, United States Naval Attaché in London, had visited the carrier and reported to Washington 'No ship was hit by the bombs during that attack and no casualties received', Germany went on demanding 'the truth about the *Ark Royal*'.

Francke contemplated suicide, and for Geoff Denny 'The subsequent propaganda and refutation did much to make us the *Daily Mirror* ship for the rest of *Ark*'s life – in competition, of course, with Mountbatten's *Kelly*. When I later appeared before a CW (commission) selection board in Portsmouth I was asked about the efficiency of the Navy in general. I replied that I thought the Fleet Air Arm the strike force of the future, and that naval gunnery left something to be desired as witness all the Home Fleet failing to hit one Heinkel. I was not recommended.'

FLYING WITH THE FAMOUS

With No 803 Squadron, which was moved to the air station at Wick, then just a field on the east coast of Scotland a few miles from John O'Groats, was TAG Alan Todd. Alan had intended joining the RAF as an apprentice but succumbed to the 'life of sea and air at the same time' promised on a Fleet Air Arm recruiting poster. The boring round of training at *Ganges* was not what he had signed on for. 'Where's the flying part', he naively asked, though he was an athlete and the dreaded mast presented no problem. He asked the same question when scrubbing the decks of the old coal-burning *Iron Duke*, though he had been pleased to be selected for the Boys Gun's Crew from *Ganges* for the Royal Tournament. He remained 'in a shanghaied state of mind' aboard the old battler for six months, and was then drafted to HMS *Barham*, aboard which he saw his first aircraft, a Swordfish on floats. He was only an OD but put in for Air-Gunner. Part of his training took place in the back seat of a Shark flown by Lieutenant (A) Ralph Richardson, who drove his beloved Harley-Davidson motor-bike well enough, but, according to Alan Todd, such notables 'were not the Navy's best pilots. They were really the products of the pre-war civil flying schools, which were gentlemen's clubs. Things like oil pressure gauges, temperature gauges meant little to them'.

Alan was flying with the future theatrical knight one forenoon when the engine suddenly burst into flames. Richardson crash-landed the aircraft just outside the village of Hursley near Winchester. 'The kite went up on its nose, burning merrily. I ended up under the pilot's seat, head-first, out stone-cold. I remember coming to, and someone was urging me "Get out of here quick!" I thought I was in my billet and people were shaking me – *Why don't they leave me alone and let me get on with my kip!* I could smell burning – *Good, the stove's on* . . . Then I did a double-take . . . *Christ, we're on fire!* I was out of that plane like a jack-rabbit. It didn't put me off flying, it just made you think. I wrote in my diary "Well, it isn't all a bed of roses, this!"' Shortly afterwards Alan received a letter from Richardson. Richardson crashed twice more, the second crash killing the trainee TAG, and shortly after that both Richardson and another actor, Lieutenant (A) Laurence Olivier, were returned to the world of Show Business, where it was felt that they could be of greater value to the British public.

After training, Alan joined No 803 Squadron at Hatson – 'in theory the fighter defence of Scapa Flow. That was the biggest laugh ever. The Skua was called a "fighter-bomber", but in fact was neither. It did not have the proper engine, its Bristol Perseus sleeve-valve job being grossly underpowered. The RAF had all that was going in those days, the Navy got what was left. If it had had the proper uprated Perseus it would have been a faster and better fighter, with a better bomb load.

'Two days later, 12 April, my mother's birthday, I was shot down over Bergen. We went across the hogwash to attack general shipping, and in the dive we caught one. The engine just faded away, we heaved ourselves over a small hill and went straight down into the fjord at 100–120 knots, just slithered along the calm water and came to an almighty splashy stop. We got the dinghy out of the tail stowage and got ashore. We made our way to a little house, where the family dried us off, then their local Dr Hansen took us down to the fjord to the US tanker *Flying Fish*, but they threw us off as soon as they found out who we were, fearing the hostility of the Germans. The Skipper said, "Give yourselves up. They'll look after you."

'Ashore again, we stumbled along a little track we'd found and bumped into the doctor again, on his rounds. He was taken aback but led us to a little lodge in the woods belonging to Nurse Emma, a little old lady who hid us for several days until the hunt died down, then arranged for a boat to take us up the coast. We were then handed on from person to person, crossed a fjord to Aalesund, and after four weeks' tracking caught up with the evacuation, and I recognized men and marines off the old *Barham*, dug in there to hold off the German Army. A coastal steamer took us back to Scapa, where we found out that the Squadron had been practically wiped out.'

The '*Ark*' was recalled urgently from Alexandria. She was loaded up with incendiary bombs in the Clyde, landed some Swordfish in exchange for more

Skuas and their turreted version, the Roc, and set off for the Arctic Circle to provide fighter cover for the Allied forces landed in Norway to resist the German invasion. There she was joined by *Glorious* from the Mediterranean.

LONG ODDS FOR *RENOWN*

Also patrolling Norwegian waters was *Renown*, watching for *Scharnhorst* and *Gneisenau*, which had been reported out. Ordered to lay the mess table one day, young Tom Bailey told his Leading Hand 'If you want the sodding table laid you're the best bastard to do it!' 'Bastard' was a mild word in the Andrew, but insubordination was not tolerated. Given 14 days' Number Elevens (doubling round the deck with a 6in shell), the Chief Quartermaster 'gave me a piece of advice which I have passed on to many a young sailor – "If ever you feel like saying things you will be sorry for to a senior, go forward to the heads and call him all the names under the sun, just make sure nobody hears you." Commander Terry added "Keep that sort of language for the Germans," so when, on the morning of 9 April when we engaged the *Scharnhorst* and *Gneisenau* off the Lofoten Islands, and I had been woken from a lovely sleep on the deck of the wheelhouse, with shells falling all round the ship, I used a few choice words and the Commander reminded me of my punishment I said, "I'm only doing what you told me, sir"!'

It was Captain (D) Warburton-Lee in HMS *Hardy* with the Second Destroyer Flotilla who first fell in with the German warships; then *Renown* engaged them at extreme range, in spite of poor visibility and high seas, and made several direct hits on *Gneisenau*. In the teeth of the appalling weather the destroyers struggled to keep up, and Petty Officer Neal in *Hardy* watched the whole dramatic battle.

'Suddenly, out of a blinding snowstorm, came *Scharnhorst* and *Gneisenau*. We cleared for action. Then we saw *Renown*. She was a splendid sight and in hot pursuit of the enemy. At 4.10a.m. we engaged *Scharnhorst*. We played our part alongside *Renown*. We blazed away at both enemy ships in a sea that tossed us about savagely. It was so rough that eventually we had to drop out of the action with all our accompanying destroyers – *Hunter*, *Hostile*, *Hotspur* and *Havock*.

'They were thrilling moments while they lasted. Every man was on his toes. The *Scharnhorst* straddled us with "bricks", and our part of the sea was hot for a time.

'*Renown* kept firing away. It was possible to see her shells hitting *Gneisenau*. Every hit brought a cheer. For a time it was like being in a ringside seat and seeing your fancy pummelling his opponent.

'One particular salvo from *Renown* will live forever in our memory. It put paid to one of *Gneisenau*'s after guns, which had been devastating. It tore it out as clean as if it was a surgical operation. There was a huge splash, a flash of colour, and a gun that had just fired four salvos in succession packed up.' Petty Officer Ted Baggley became *Hardy*'s unofficial commentator. 'Glasses to his eyes, he outdid Howard Marshall [a BBC commentator of the time]. We cheer his words: "A salvo from *Renown* within only a hundred yards of *Gneisenau* . . . An ominous column of smoke rises amidships . . ."' The battlecruiser ran for the cover of the snowstorm, but 'details of the pasting given the *Gneisenau* were supplied to us in a manner that leaves no room for doubt. We saw a deal of wreckage come floating past us – kitbags, lifebelts and paravanes, all of German origin . . . Like a beaten dog she ran for cover. The snowstorm hid her in time'. *Scharnhorst* also screened her with smoke.

Tom Bailey, in his first action, was getting to know himself. 'I did not feel afraid, excited, yes, as telegraph operator in the upper conning tower, helping with tricks at the wheel in rotation, living on soup and corned-dog sandwiches, which the rough weather did not put me off. I was discovering that the rougher it was the happier I seemed to be. *Renown*'s 15in were belching fire and smoke. Suddenly just ahead of us there was a flash and a puff of smoke, and shrapnel flew. We were hit several times, one 11in "projjy" entering the half-deck, but fortunately not exploding. Either due to a near-miss or an extra-big wave I was thrown against the bulkhead, and the welded screws that held the channel plate for all the electrical cables pierced the back of my neck (I still have the scars to this day), but I still managed to shout encouragement to the guns' crews.

'While steaming at 30 knots the starboard anti-torpedo blister had been ripped open. Down on the messdeck they cheered every wave that hit the ship's side, hoping for more damage so that we could get more leave. Once again there was no fear, though if the ship's side had been stove in we would all have been drowned. In other actions, in the Med when attacked by low-flying bombers, I felt just the same, dodging behind a flimsy canvas screen, feeling confidently "If he can't see me he can't hurt me." It was all so distant, you were never face to face with the enemy.

'I have seen fear in the eyes of young U-boat survivors bobbing in the water with just their heads showing, and the absolute panic if we had to leave them until it was safe to pick them up.

'I must confess that I had one great fear, of losing my sight. Loss of arms or legs I think I could have coped with, but blindness – never.

'Then I might never have seen the beauty of the sea, both at its wildest and at its calmest, the beautiful hands of Siamese dancers, the facade of the rock temple in rose–red Petra – or the mutilation of the child beggars of India, all the squalor in the world.

'Today I saw the daffodils in bloom at the roadside, on my way to the Backworth Bowling Club, where I am Chairman.'

'We Are Going Into Narvik'

With the German heavy forces driven off, Captain Warburton-Lee made his historic signal: 'We are going into Narvik.' There the Germans were digging in and throwing up defences, and he decided, in the belief that his five destroyers would be engaging six German destroyers (in fact there were ten), to sink as many of them as he could, shell the defences and destroy German transports there.

Neal recalls: 'Though the average age of our men was little more than twenty, all were keen as mustard.

'After traversing only a short distance we pick up a Norwegian pilot who speaks very good English . . . "What is the strength of the Germans in the fjord?" we ask. "I would not go up there unless I had three times your force."

'Nevertheless, at one o'clock the next morning, the 10th, we take up action stations as the flotilla creeps into the mouth of the fjord in pitch darkness.

'Again a blinding snowstorm. We miss an ice-floe. Tea is handed round to us. We gulp it down. There is rum in it! It keeps us warm.

'At 4.10 a.m. we are right up to Narvik. The first vessel we sight is registered at Hartlepool. We slew round to face the harbour and shore batteries which are tucked away to the north side of the fjord. We slew to port. On our starboard side is a German destroyer at the narrow neck, and we fire a torpedo.

'It hits! God, what a hit! Up she goes out of the water. She has no future but the scrap heap. Must have hit the magazine. Then a firework as her ammo goes off. Every gun we have is banging away. We send the nearest German merchantman to the bottom with another torpedo. We smash three destroyers and at least seven merchantmen. Men at the guns are slipping about in the thickening snow.

'We have just fired two torpedoes into the pier, timbers fly into the sky, when from an arm of the fjord come three more German destroyers. Two more appear on the horizon. We are straddled between them.

'An enemy salvo hits the TS. L/S Cockayne and Scouser Whearty fall, Whearty cries out "I can't reach the fire gong!" Our Captain has gone down, mortally wounded. I take over the for'ard guns. No 2's layer hails me. Crash! The gun is blown up, No 2 is dead; so are four of the crew: Hunt, gun captain; Lang, layer; Hay, tray worker; and Edwards – who has just asked me if he can take the place of a wounded man. At No 1, OD Watson is killed, my legs are splintered, I smack a bandage on. Most of the guns are mangled heaps, smashed by the enemy's big 13 cwt shells. The bridge is gone, the wheelhouse, the main steampipe. A scalding jet at 300 pounds per square inch is let loose.

'Lieutenant Stanning, apparently the only officer left alive, is going to ram one of the enemy. He gives the order. The coxswain is killed at the wheel. Young Smale takes over. But there's no steam, and the wheel is locked fast to port.

'CRUNCH! We are on the beach, and being machine-gunned. Now *Hunter* is hit. She turns right over at full speed and sinks.

'The shore proper is about 50 yards off. Out of the corner of my eye I see a movement where the bridge used to be. It is the Captain, barely alive. We put a lifebelt on him to float him ashore. "Swim, lads, swim!" he says faintly.

'It is 6.15 a.m. as we abandon ship, and I prepare to leave the wonderful little lady we all love so – love her even now, battered and broken. I am now pretty weak, but I shin down a rope over the side. The cold water revives me. I just make the beach.'

Dawn Raid On Bergen

That evening Nos 800, 801 and 803 Skua squadrons at Hatston were briefed for a dawn attack on a German cruiser in Bergen.

'None of us had ever flown with a 500-pound bomb and the trip was near our endurance limit,' says Eric Monk. 'Final note at briefing was, "If you have less than 60gal of fuel after the attack, fly on to Sweden, destroy your Skua and try to get back." Not a very good sleeping draught. I went to bed shortly after briefing and my chum Ron Lunberg came along to wish me luck in the morning.

'The shake at 0300 was a relief but the thick corned-beef sandwiches we were offered at briefing remained untouched. Going out to the aircraft I had mixed feelings and wondered if my kite would fail to start. It was then I found out that once I was strapped into my familiar L2934 it was just another flight, no more worries. All was ready, bomb on, safety-pin for my bomb in my pocket in case it was not dropped, Colt .45 in my flying overall pocket alongside the compass, and L2934 started up first cartridge. Warm up the engine, check boost and revs, throttle back to check the magnetoes and check that the tanks are full. Lieutenant Finch-Noyes moved out, followed by Lieutenant Spurway, and I followed on behind. It was a fine morning as we climbed up to 16,000ft, heater on, and doing 140 knots. Eventually the coast came into sight, the sun was up, the sky blue, the hills topped with snow, lower down the pine trees and then the water of the fjord. Wonderful, except that there was a war on.

'Naturally, I was tail-end Charlie of the sixteen Skuas and as I stall-turned to enter my dive the shell bursts covered Bergen like a black lace curtain. The *Königsberg* had been damaged by the Norwegian coast batteries but there were still quite a lot of shell bursts on the way down. Steady on the target, offset turret, no mistaking the *Köln*-class cruiser, 5,000ft, check bomb is armed, 3,000ft and release, down to sea-level, weaving away down the fjord, 80gal indicated in the tanks, then out to sea into formation for the two-hour flog back to Hatston. We checked for signs of oil or fuel leaking on any of the aircraft in the sub-flight, and kept a constant check on my oil pressure. The leader's observer "zobbed" (Morse code by waving hand) "Report fuel remaining." Reply: "75".

"I was feeling rather hungry now. Two hours later we landed at Hatston with almost empty tanks and taxied in feeling tired but elated. On the way to the mess I passed the Captain who asked if I was ready to go again and I am pleased to remember that I replied "Not till I've had my breakfast."

'Two days later we did go again and Petty Officer Gardner failed to return, but he sailed into Kirkwall Bay two weeks later in a "borrowed" boat and still had a small bottle of Pusser's rum in his pocket. When the Captain sent to see him in the afternoon, the rum was in his tum and the Captain had to wait till next day. These raids continued for quite a time with Nos 800, 801 and 803 Squadrons taking part. I went on the first three but then *Ark* came back from training in the Mediterranean with *Glorious* and my squadron embarked.'

WARSPITE ENTERS THE FRAY

Warburton-Lee's five ships had sunk or disabled three German destroyers of superior gun power off Narvik but had lost *Hardy* and *Hunter*, and the enemy still dominated the Narvik fjords, with seven destroyers still operational there. Three days after this action, a much stronger British force was sent in to remedy the situation. Leading nine destroyers, including the new large Fleet destroyers *Bedouin*, *Punjabi*, *Eskimo* and *Cossack* of the Tribal class, and *Kimberley*, was Admiral Whitworth in the recently updated and reconstructed *Queen Elizabeth*-class battleship *Warspite*.

Petty Officer Pilot Rice and Observer Lieutenant-Commander W. L. M. Brown were briefed by Admiral Whitworth, the Captain of *Warspite*, Victor Crutchley, VC, and Commander Currie to:

(1) carry out a general reconnaissance for the squadron advancing on Ofotfjord, 'with particular reference to the presence of German warships inside the fjords, the movements of German forces, and the positions of shore batteries',

(2) bomb 'any suitable targets'.

Ben Rice, late of Colchester Technical College and a local Redwing Aircraft apprenticeship, which had ended when the firm went bust in 1932, leaving him jobless, had followed the trend and joined the RN at *Ganges*. He served in the destroyer *Brilliant* at Gibraltar until he was sent home to join No 41 Rating Pilot Course, on which he trained with Eric Monk. In his diary was the entry 'First solo! Wonderful!'

With Leading Naval Airman Maurice Pacey as TAG, they were launched in drizzly weather at 1152hrs on Friday, 13 April 1940, in *Warspite*'s Swordfish floatplane L9767 ('Lorna'), carrying two 250lb high-explosive, two 100lb anti-submarine and eight 40lb anti-personnel bombs.

Kapitänleutnant Schulz's brand-new Type IXB 1,051/1,178-ton, U-boat *U-64* had had her trials curtailed to supplement the defending naval forces at Narvik. She was on the surface at the top of Herjansfjord near Bjerkrik when the Swordfish crew sighted her. Rice selected his two anti-submarine bombs, put the 'Stringbag' into a dive and released the bombs at 200ft. 'I couldn't see the bombs fall as we pulled out, but Pacey saw the starboard bomb fall close alongside and the port one hit just abaft the conning tower; the U-boat was already sinking when I could see her again. She hit us in the tail with one shot. I think it was from her 37mm gun.' There were 36 survivors from the U-boat.

At 1226 a German destroyer appeared out of the mist to port; she was immediately engaged by *Icarus*, *Bedouin*, *Punjabi* and *Cossack*, and turned back into the mist. Shortly afterwards a second enemy destroyer loomed up to starboard and opened fire, followed by another, to be met by rapid fire from the British destroyers and 15in shells from *Warspite*.

Minutes before the British force came abreast of Ballanger Bay on the south side of Ofotfjord, Pacey in the Swordfish signalled that an enemy destroyer was lurking in the Bay. *Icarus* sighted and engaged her at 1307, joined by three Tribals. The German fought fiercely but in eight minutes was ablaze, her last gun silenced by *Warspite*. More enemy destroyers came up, fire was shifted to them, and a running fight developed. Rice in the Swordfish sighted a Heinkel, which kept well clear of them. At 1330 Fleet Air Arm aircraft from *Furious* bombed Narvik harbour, as *Warspite* prepared to bombard coastal fortifications. Four surviving enemy destroyers, one badly damaged, fled up Rombaksfjord, where they were attacked and destroyed.

Rice landed alongside *Warspite*, which had stopped off Narvik at 1600, and was hoisted in. Eight German destroyers were sunk during the action. Rice's

U-boat was the first German submarine to be sunk from the air in World War II. Rice was awarded the DSM, Brown the DSC, and Pacey a Mention in Despatches.

FIGHTER PATROLS

The Germans advanced on Trondheim in central Norway, and small Allied forces were landed at Namsos to the north-east and Aandalsnes to the south-west. The only protection they had from Luftwaffe planes – Messerschmitt Me 109s and Me 110s in great numbers – were two squadrons, Nos 816 and 818, of Swordfish from *Furious*. 'No fighters,' says Jack Skeats, the countryman from Aylesbury, ex '*Rev-en-gee*', who had turned down the chance of a commission to fly as a TAG, 'and only four 4.7s to fire ineffectively at the aircraft that flew just above their range of 10,000 ft and bombed at will'.

The Swordfish's first operation was a torpedo attack on shipping in Trondheim Fjord. '816 and 818 gaily left *Furious*, flying just above sea-level (flying at sea-level tends to rip off the undercarriage), passing over some skerries where the families came out to cheer and wave. We felt good although I for one had only a hazy idea what we were about. Air-gunners were not allowed to attend briefings – after all, we were only passengers. The approach to Trondheim was made at low height, with a short encounter with a flak ship and then a slow climb to top the mountains that surround the harbour and slide down the other side on our bottoms to the harbour itself and smite the Hun.

'Alas, the Hun was a damn sight smarter than we were and had left three days earlier, leaving lots of Swordfish sculling around without a target. Not dismayed, we proceeded to seek out a lone German destroyer making its way up a neighbouring, narrow fjord flanked by pines. The approach was made by side-slipping down over the pines, levelling out and then pressing the button after sighting. I am not quite sure of the pecking order but several kites preceded us in dropping their "tin-fish" and as we reached our drop position the bed of the sea came up to greet us in one big gout of sand and spume. And then another and yet another right underneath us flying as low as we dared. *Damn fine gunners, these Germans*, I thought before realization struck me. The depth of water was such that the torpedoes of the aircraft in front of us were blowing up on sandbanks in the fjord. Nevertheless, I saw at least two plumes of water rise up at the stern of the target and two hits were accredited.

'Back home to Mother who turned out to be Mother Hubbard. The mess-deck was empty when I reached it, lunch time was long gone and the cupboard was as bare as a baby's elbow. Cold and hungry I made my way to the Main Galley and did my Oliver Twist bit. The Chief Cook had obviously not read his Dickens, and said with deep emotion and great sympathy "Serves you bloody well right. You should have been here when the meal was served."'

The old *Furious* and her aircrews almost burned themselves out with the tremendous pressure of operations. Her machinery badly needed rest and repair. None too soon *Ark Royal* and *Glorious* relieved her, but even their four Skua/Roc squadrons and four Swordfish squadrons could not hope to keep the Luftwaffe at bay. 'With our strictly limited number of aircraft,' says Eric Monk, now in the '*Ark*', 'inferior in quality to the 109s and 110s we met, our only advantage was that we had dive brakes and we came to the conclusion that our only real hope was to wait until the enemy opened fire and was closing rapidly, dive down with dive brakes out and full rudder to left or right to offset the line of sight. The enemy fire should pass to one side and he should rapidly overshoot – immediately pull in dive brakes and try to get a shot in as the enemy pulled up for a further attack. Not much comfort, but the best we could think of.' In the Falklands War Sea Harrier V/STOL fighters used similar tactics ('viffing') against faster Argentine aircraft, with the vectored-thrust jets in place of dive brakes.

The Skuas battled with Ju 88s, Dornier Do 17s, Heinkel He 111s, Me 109s and 110s, and shot down at least 20. For the flight deck rangers, Geoff Denny recalls, 'the land of the midnight sun was one long greyness with persistent cloud cover. As it never really got dark we were operating right round the clock and being bombed intermittently, almost permanently at action stations, and at one time we were almost ready to drop from having been without sleep for 52 hours'.

EVACUATION

At Namsos the cruiser *Glasgow* landed troops and her whole stock of depth-charges for blowing up bridges. She then returned to Rosyth to embark 22,000 men, who were landed at Molde and Aandalsnes on 23 April. *Glasgow*'s Walrus was seconded to Wing-Commander R. L. R. Atcherley of Schneider Trophy fame, who had been detailed to find airfields for RAF fighters. Together they set up three airfields, Skaanland, Bardufoss and Laksely; TAG Leading Naval Airman Hunt from the Walrus crew was decorated in the field by the Navy C-in-C, the Earl of Cork and Orrery, for services performed when setting up the last-named field.

As the Germans pushed relentlessly north from Trondheim, the Allies tried to keep a beachhead open round Narvik, and captured the iron ore port on 28 May, but Narvik and Harstad were bombed heavily, and there was no hope of sending more aircraft to the area as the situation in France was desperate and had priority. The 800-mile link between Narvik and Britain – longer if a detour was made to avoid the Luftwaffe flying from Norwegian airfields – was too long and difficult to hold, and it was decided to evacuate the whole of Norway.

Arethusa was sitting in Scapa between patrols when she was suddenly sent to Molde to evacuate the British troops there, braving bombing attacks as she threaded the fjord. 'It was better below in the boiler room or engine room,' Mark Wells found. 'There were always things to do or keep an eye on, and there was little time to ponder over what might be happening.' The soldiers climbed on board. 'It was a sad sight to see the weary faces.'

Five 'Shagbats' (nickname for the Walrus) were embarked in *Glorious*, which was in the offing. The surviving RAF Gladiator fighters also flew aboard her, although they had no arrester hooks; but it was decided to abandon the Hurricanes of No 46 Squadron, RAF, taking it for granted that these fast modern fighters could not get down safely on a carrier's deck. Their pilots had other ideas. They proposed at least trying a dart at the deck. They had no deck-landing experience, but enlisted the help of Lieutenant Johnny Ievers and his *Glasgow* Walrus crew. Ievers gave each pilot some elementary deck landing instruction before leading them out to the carrier, their tyres partially deflated to help them stick to the deck. The Walrus then flew round *Glorious*, monitoring each Hurricane as it came in to land. All fifteen fighters landed safely with plenty of deck to spare, but when Ievers himself made to put down he was waved off and told that the carrier was fully loaded, so he diverted to *Ark Royal*, some 30 miles away.

This probably saved his and his crew's lives. With two escorting destroyers *Glorious* was sent south independently of the other returning forces because of her comparatively low fuel endurance. She had five Swordfish embarked (the last of which, pilot Charles Lamb, TAG Doug Hemingway, both of whom survived *Glorious*, was also the last FAA aircraft ever to land aboard her) in addition to her mixed load of fighters; but they had been at full stretch for days and no reconnaissance patrols were ordered by Captain D'Oyly-Hughes. Thus *Scharnhorst* and *Gneisenau* caught *Glorious* unawares, disabled her before she could launch any aircraft, and sank her with ease. One of her brave escorting destroyers, *Acasta*, hit *Scharnhorst* with a torpedo and forced the enemy to return to Trondheim, thus removing what might have been a serious threat to a returning convoy 200 miles to the north-east which had had to sail without battleship escort. On 11 June 38 survivors from *Glorious* and one from *Acasta* were picked up by a Norwegian fishing boat.

Two days later in *Ark Royal* the Skua squadrons got ready to attack *Scharnhorst* and *Gneisenau* in Trondheim harbour, and any other shipping found there. As Eric Monk relates, 'Nine aircraft from 803 Squadron and six from 800 took part, briefed to act as fighter cover. About half way to the anchorage from the coast we were attacked by Me 110s and Al Spurway and I put our theory to the test. We neither of us claimed a victory although I know I hit my 110 still with the 500lb bomb on the rack, and we were the only ones of 800 Squadron to get back to *Ark*.'

Hostilities Only

I tell you naught for your comfort,
Yea, naught for your desire,
Save that the sky grows darker yet
And the sea rises higher.

When the Luftwaffe failed to destroy RAF Fighter Command, as Goering had promised Hitler, and the Battle of Britain had been won, the war moved into the grim Atlantic and the wide-open coastal waters of the British Isles, with easy targets at sea for the Luftwaffe working from captured French airfields, and Befehlshaber der U-boote's submarines from Brittany and Biscay ports.

GLASGOW AND *IMOGEN*

When the balloon went up, TAG Norman 'Blondie' Hollis was instructing fledgling Air-Gunners and Air Observers in Morse at Pompey Barracks. 'But in June I went to Lee-on-Solent and before I had time to settle in I was on my way to join 700 Squadron, HMS *Glasgow* Flight, and about to form a relationship with a Walrus, with neither the pilot nor observers very exeperienced. The cruiser was in dry dock, having suffered from a very near-miss off Norway.'

When *Glasgow* left to rejoin the Fleet she had aboard both her Walruses for the first time since 1939, with the second aircraft and PO Pilot Ron Lunberg and his crew joining shortly after leaving port.

On 19 July *Glasgow*, with three other cruisers and eight destroyers, was closing Scapa in thick fog after a search for enemy minesweepers off the Norwegian coast. She was making a fourth attempt to get into the Flow when, says Lunberg, 'a red light appeared close under her port bow, materializing into the destroyer *Inglefield*, which shot past, missing us by inches. As *Inglefield* disappeared into the fog, another destroyer, *Imogen*, appeared across our bows. Glasgow smashed into her at a combined speed of 34 knots, laying her hull open from bow to forward boiler room and spilling thousands of gallons of blazing oil fuel into the sea'.

As *Glasgow* lost way Captain Hickling ordered the forward magazine flooded to forestall an explosion from the burning oil, while Commander Cuthbert was down in the waist organizing his precious stock of Carley floats into a makeshift pontoon bridge between the ships. In this way 120 officers and men were saved, the casualties totalling some 20 men who had been in the for'ard messdeck. *Glasgow* managed to free herself from the clutching destroyer; violent helm alterations and full astern power finally brought her clear. As she limped away, the destroyer exploded in a column of searing flame as the fire reached the magazines. *Glasgow* limped back into Scapa with a 60 ft gash in her bows some 6 ft above the waterline.

Glasgow returned to dry dock, and her two Walruses were sent to Sullom Voe on the western Scottish coast to join more Walri belonging to damaged ships and a squadron of Short Sunderland flying-boats of RAF Coastal Command. The amphibious Walrus machines suffered the indignity of being moored to a buoy. 'The camp at Sullom Voe', recollects Norman Hollis, 'was a shocker, built on a bog, and though the RAF Squadronaires dance band visited us there, there was absolutely nothing to do. Even beer was in short supply, and when fresh supplies arrived we rarely had the money to buy it. The weather was usually atrocious, and to fly became a pleasure. Our time was spent on anti-submarine patrols on the east side of the Shetlands and these usually ended uncompleted because of the weather. We would usually take a basket of pigeons to be released at the furthest point of our patrol. When the weather was really bad most of the air-gunners would not release them and waited until we were nearly back at base.'

LEND LEASE *LINCOLN*

Iain Nethercott and other survivors of the destroyer *Keith* spent a short time in hospital after Dunkirk and their harrowing experiences there. After recovering, Iain qualified as a seaman torpedoman and returned to Chatham. Here, he complains that he 'slunk into the Barrack Guard and when on duty with my trusty musket guarded the entrance to an underground teleprinter tunnel in the grounds of the C-in-C, The Nore, at the end of his vegetable garden. I rather feel that my job was more ceremonial than functional. I was fully booted and spurred, with tin hat, 100 rounds of ball, 18 in bayonet, water bottle, gas mask, etc, with others to repel any hawkers or canvassers, and to give a butt salute to anyone but the C-in-C, who merited a Present Arms. Just what I was supposed to do if a battalion of German paratroopers were to drop on this complex I don't really know – fire off my 100, then, if still surviving, chuck the C-in-C's spuds at them!

'At this time the Luftwaffe was intermittently bombing Chatham, and a small bomb fell on the stone steps outside Nelson Block and knocked off the one outstretched arm from the giant figurehead of the renowned admiral and flung it across the terrace where it killed a Chief Cook – at least, that's how the buzz went, but there were so many Chief Cooks lurking in Chatham at that time that it would probably have gone unnoticed. Kipling wrote,

> 'And Ye take mine honour from me
> If Ye take away the sea.'

That could be the song of the Barrack Stanchion, only they're always too thick to think of it that way.

'On the Parade Ground at the Gunnery School stood an old World War I tank, "Old Bill", which had seen action, manned by a Naval Brigade crew, at

Arras in Flanders, many years before. In the prevailing panic, the Captain of the Gunnery School had the petrol engines of this relic restored to running order, the guns were overhauled, and eventually, to the cheers of the multitude and amidst clouds of black smoke, the old veteran clanked its way along the terrace and took up a strategic position behind the Main Gate, with its guns pointing up the Dockyard Road.

'Meanwhile, large numbers of matlows were marched down to the football field every day to practise grenade-throwing under the tuition of belted and gaitered GIs. No one had actually seen a real grenade. They were assumed to weigh about seven pounds, so baskets of round stones were provided to simulate live Mills bombs. Long lines of sailors spent many weary hours that summer stepping forward by numbers, removing imaginary safety pins, and flinging imaginary bombs at imaginary Germans. The senior officers in charge of the defence of the barracks always assumed that the Germans would assault from the Main Gate, and all trenches and defence lines were sited on that principle. The panzers would proceed down the Dockyard Road to the Main Gate, which would immediately be closed by the duty RPOs. Should the Gate be breached, our naval tank would then open fire and proceed toward the enemy armour, followed by serried ranks of matlows flinging salvoes of seven-pound bricks. The Master-at-Arms and Regulating Staff would also be in attendance to take the cards of anyone needing a haircut.

'Meanwhile the above-mentioned MAA requested my presence in the Drill Shed together with my bag and hammock, cap box and Ditty Box at 1600 one fine day in October. The draft was given only a Steaming Party number, though everybody knew that we were going across to Yankeeland to pick up some of those ancient destroyers that President Roosevelt was dumping on us in an attempt to get rid of Winston's ever-outstretched hand, and the smell of those terrible cigars.

'When we fell in, what a shock! *About 80 per cent of my crew were HOs.* Now, I had nothing against HOs but I was used to destroyers where everyone knew his job and had years of training behind them. This crowd of poor green little sods had done a few weeks in a holiday camp at Skegness, learned to salute an officer, do a bit of squad drill, wear a naval uniform, and were then sent off to war at sea. Some had never seen a warship in their lives.

'We were given a bag meal to last us 24 hours and marched down to special trains in the dockyard, completely surrounded by military police. The HOs scoffed their meal straight away. I didn't like the look of all this security. We travelled all night and eventually arrived at Liverpool, where the train ran right down to the pierhead. Shorewards stood row upon row of MPs.

'Alongside were a couple of troopers. Ours was *Duchess of Atholl*, a CPR liner of ancient vintage. We were fell in on the jetty, and eventually finished up down in the bowels of the ship.

'We sailed for Halifax that night in a fast convoy with no escort. I spent most of the week playing Crown and Anchor down in the saloon where a CPR steward was making his fortune cleaning out the young RAF sergeants going to Canada to qualify as pilots.

'When we tied up at Halifax and before we were allowed ashore, any English money we had must be changed into Canadian currency, as you could buy genuine English pound notes for about a dollar ashore on the black market. The Germans had captured the BEF bankroll in France, found they couldn't change it through the normal channels, so had to sell it off cheap in the USA and Canada. We were sternly warned that anyone caught with any British currency would be locked up for life.

'We were billeted underneath a grandstand at a racetrack renamed HMS *Stadacona II*. It was bloody cold with no proper heating. Halifax ashore was a dead loss. It was a dry city. However, I took some of the HOs up Barrington Street, where a city cop told us the way to a speakeasy. The whisky there was real rotgut, probably wood alcohol, at a dollar a shot.

'Eventually we were marched down to the harbour as separate crews and saw our future ships for the first time.

'They lay alongside in trots of three, our four-pipers, all with American steaming crews aboard. My first opinion was that they were top-heavy. The four pipe-like funnels (which gave them their US nicknames of "four-pipers" or "four-stackers") gave them an old-fashioned look rather like French destroyers of the First War. The fo'c'sle looked too low and the bow gun would obviously be submerged in heavy weather. The torpedo tubes were mounted in four sets of three at the ships' sides, not centrally as in British ships. As a torpedoman I could envisage the tubes trained outboard. The firing seat would be about twelve feet out beyond the ship's side, and in anything of a sea would be submerged. Still – "Never look a gift-horse in the mouth."'

Thanks to pre-war naval treaties the Royal Navy had begun World War II with 184 destroyers, far too few for its wartime commitments, and after a year of hostilities this total had sunk to 171, as the completion of new ships (21) had not kept pace with the heavy losses (34). Of the 171, many were under repair or in urgent need of it. Seventeen had been seriously damaged in the Norwegian Campaign, sixteen in the Dunkirk operations. The entry of Italy into the war in June 1940 drained off more destroyers into the reconstituted Mediterranean Fleet. Mr Churchill asked President Roosevelt for the speedy loan of warships to defend Allied convoys. On 3 September 1940, first anniversary of the outbreak of war, the first step was taken with an agreement to lend 50 old destroyers to Britain in exchange for 99-year leases on naval and air bases in Newfoundland, Bermuda, the Bahamas, Jamaica, St Lucia, Antigua, Trinidad and British Guiana. The first eight reached Halifax, Nova Scotia, on 6 September 1940 and on the 9th were formally handed over to the Royal Navy. All were renamed after towns, villages or districts in Britain.

These narrow boats, with their straight, flush-decked slope from stem to stern, were not without grace and character. Iain Nethercott's draft to HMS *Lincoln* (ex-USS *Yarnall*) spent about three days going aboard daily and working with the American ratings to get acquainted with all the unfamiliar gear: 'I think most of them were shocked at the quality of our seamen, most of whom were undersized, dirty, ill-equipped and completely ignorant of the working of a destroyer.

'The Americans had stocked up the ships' stores with the finest of tinned foods, things not normally seen on British destroyers with their good old diet of Pusser's peas, Straight Rush, Oosh and Potmess. Now we saw giant cans of tomato juice and grapefruit juice, tinned lobster and crawfish and a big fridge full of steaks. Not for the Yankee "gobs" the old beef screen on the Iron Deck, with Tanky hacking away at that long-dead camel. They never tasted the delights of herrings in Ally Sloper's Sauce, and the secrets of the Naval Sausage Mk1, the constitutents of which had been passed from one Chief Cook in Jago's Mansions to another down the centuries.'

The destroyers were old, but alleged to have been refitted. They had been scrupulously cleaned and, with typical American generosity, fully stored. There were full outfits of ammunition – shells, torpedoes, depth-charges; high-powered binoculars for officers and lookouts; sextants, chronometers, parallel rulers and dividers for navigation; ample stocks of paint and cordage; a typewriter, paper, envelopes, pencil sharpeners, pencils and ink in each ship's office; messtraps of silver and good new china. Store-rooms were fully stocked with provisions, including spiced tinned ham, tinned sausages and corn.

'However, all the wonderful scran was not for us matlows. As soon as the Yanks had lowered the Stars and Stripes and marched away, the special new food was removed, some to the wardroom, and normal RN rations stowed on board.

'We had a young Active Service First Lieutenant who was a good, sensible chap, but with the exception of the Engineer Lieutenant all the other officers were RNVR, who although dead-keen, were as green as grass, needing a good skipper to help and encourage them.

'I had been made a killick although I was only 19. As a torpedoman I was more interested in the depth-charges than the torpedoes, as we were unlikely ever to use them against the *Bismarck* – which God forbid. Whenever we dropped depth-charges set shallow, the contact breakers flew off, and the ship was plunged into darkness. In the end we jammed them on with wooden wedges.

'The Canadian Red Cross had sent crates of comforts to the ships, and we each became the proud owners of Canadian lumberjackets in various tartans, and flat leather caps with ear flaps. The Skipper came aboard one morning and found his ship manned by a multi-coloured apparently civilian crew. Poor old Jimmy! He took the rub for that. We were told that the jackets could only be worn at sea during the night watches. The caps were collected and sent back. Back to our thin No 3s for the Canadian Winter.'

The handful of regulars found the ship strange to get used to. The whole design, layout and internal arrangements were different from British. The Captain and officers had their wardroom and cabins in the fore part of the ship, beneath the bridge, instead of aft. The seamen lived on a large messdeck under the officers' quarters, and the stokers right aft. The messdecks were fitted with two- or three-tiered bunks.

Eventually *Lincoln*, with *Ludlow* and *Leamington*, sailed for St John's, Newfoundland.

'Once clear of the land we found that the ship would roll on damp grass. When I did my first trick on the wheel (there were initially only about six of us Active Service ratings who could take the wheel), I discovered she was a cow to steer with any sort of sea on the bow. She would drift off in a flash, and carried a permanent 5° of port wheel.

'Once she started to really roll, my poor little HO Jack-my-Hearties collapsed in heaps down below, most of them too seasick to go on watch. Jimmy tried to keep some sort of order, but as the weather got worse, so the ship's routine gradually fell apart.

'Our messdeck in the fo'c'sle was under the wardroom, we were practically at water level with two steep ladders leading to the welldeck abaft the bridge. The scuttles and deadlights were screwed down as far as possible, but during twenty years on reserve all the rubber rings on the portholes had perished, and they were some of the things that the Yanks had *not* refitted. As we were on the waterline, as she rolled and pitched, every scuttle squirted great jets of salt water, right alongside the bunks. And the screw-down covers in our messdecks which covered some fuel tanks started to leak, so the deck was swimming in fuel oil and about a foot of seawater raging around.

'As more and more of our lads crawled into their bunks and couldn't do any watches, we lashed them in so that they just rolled within their bunks and spewed into the raging torrent on the deck. For the rest of us there was no food, as the cook was prostrate and the galley was flooded, but some of the stokers managed to get the oiled-fired galley stove going, so we had some hot kye.

'I honestly thought the ship would turn over. One roll was 57° and she kept laying over and was very slow to come back.

'There were only a few of us steering, and the POs helped out. The bridge and wheelhouse were all in one, with glass windows. The steering wheel was about three feet in diameter and needed two men to hold it, as the wheel movements were transferred to the steering engine in the tiller flat by means of wires running the full length of the upper deck. On the wheel it was impossible to steer within 20° of our course, and time and time again the quartermasters were flung off the wheel, with the ship nearly broaching to.

'The Captain got the wind up as one crisis after another hit us. All sorts of minor things were going wrong. One wave took the motor boat away and wrecked the davits. One engine had to be stopped as the bearings overheated when the stern kept lifting out of the water. The engine room hatches were stoved in in places, and the ship was making water.

'None of these things was too critical, but as one calamity after the other was reported to the Captain he gradually fell apart. In the end he went to his cabin with serious stomach pains, and Jimmy took over. We kept plugging away and eventually crept into St John's. I was starving, having lived on corned beef and kye for days. Being killick of the mess, I booted my prostrate sailors out of their bunks, we bailed out, and I made them scrub the mess till it shone. They thought I was a right bastard but I was determined that they should become real sailors and start pulling their weight. From then on aboard that ship we gradually moulded those lads, *Ganges*-fashion, into real seamen.

'The Skipper, coming alongside at Guz, had a flaming row with the Engineer Officer on the bridge, and the next day disappeared from the ship, never to be seen again. We got a new two-ring Skipper appointed, and I knew him from the past as he had been Jimmy on the *Hasty*, and ran a very tight ship.

'These lads of ours were a real mixed bunch, mostly from the Midlands. I was the youngest in the mess and in charge of them. It didn't worry me as I was six feet tall and weighed fifteen stone, and in those days I could sort out any man. I had a solicitor and a schoolmaster in the mess, also a burglar from Darlington, but as the months went by they all learned how to put the dinner up to the galley and how to put Babies' Heads in the potmess; in fact they became real destroyer matlows. I and the other killicks used to teach them wire splicing and fancy ropework in the dog watches, and in harbour at Londonderry we used to take them away in the whalers and teach them to sail. Some of them became CW candidates and eventually officers.'

For the next three years ships of the 50 'four-pipers' of the RN saw service with some of the most heavily attacked convoys. For a time *Lincoln* saw nothing much but monotonous trudging to and fro across the North Atlantic. Iain Nethercott began to feel restless. 'I was getting more and more fed up with convoy work – jogging along as flank escort on a 7-knot convoy was bloody boring. My first destroyer in the war had been the old *Keith*, which had been in very hot action off Holland, in the battle of Boulogne, and finally carrying the Admiral at Dunkirk, when we were sunk. I wanted to get back into the action, so I went and volunteered for submarines. Christ, you'd think I was bloody all for it, wouldn't you?'

On 6 April 1941 HMS *Lincoln* made one of the most dramatic and brilliantly executed rescues of the war when she took off 121 men in heavy weather from the Armed Merchant Cruiser HMS *Cormorin*, which had caught fire.

FOUR-FUNNELLED *SHERWOOD*

Fred Lee from Bradford had what he saw as a narrow escape from the 'four-pipers'. When war began he was a junior in hospital administration, and a member of the Sea Cadet Corps, very well read on seamanship, and fascinated by his father Tancy Lee's stories of the Navy in the Great War. His other heroes were a big ex-Commissioned Gunner they had in the Sea Cadets 'with a voice like the sound of the guns, six-foot odd, with a black cane with a silver handle, and he was *God*', and there was Tosh Nichol, retired Chief Gunner's Mate, 'an all-rounder, a *real* sailor, sixty-seven or -eight, he'd put the gloves on and take anyone on, five-foot-seven, built like an ox', and veteran Spike Sullivan 'who could take a 3-inch manila and splice it without a marlin spike'.

Even with this background Lee was twice almost sent into the Army, but finally made it to HMS *Raleigh*, a training camp at Tor Point, Plymouth, so new that Fred's draft helped to build it, wheeling cartloads of bricks, window frames and doors about. But there was Scrumpy and doughnuts and tiddie oggies in the canteen. Someone pointed to one of the matlows, 'Know who that is? That's Robert Newton – the actor!' 'Never heard of him,' said Fred.

Then their training began. Their Petty Officer instructor was a typical old Guz rating. 'This is 'ow yer doos it,' was his favourite expression. Fred waited impatiently for the end of the course, and a draft to something glamorous at sea.

He endured the 'Wakey, wakey, rise and shine' ('even when it was pouring down with bloody rain'), Chiefie Fenton ('like a screaming harlot up and down the Parade Ground'), the preponderance of ex-policemen in the mess ('I think they were the bane of the Service, the coppers, they had an attitude, oh, I don't know, of . . . law enforcement, I don't know what you'd call it, like the screws in the prisons . . . If you don't trust a copper outside you won't trust him inside, will you?'), though there was 'a real variety of types, teachers, bus drivers, dockyard mateys, and one bloke played for Everton . . .

'There were no real problems where food was concerned. I hated porridge, all my life I hated porridge, till I went to *Raleigh*, and then when it came round every morning I suppose . . . the cold weather, and the time of day – 7 o'clock in the morning, in the nice steaming galley and the dining hall . . . everybody ate the porridge and there was the usual stiff sausage and the solid fried eggs and screwed-up bacon – like concrete, some of it, but it was all eaten! The only problem was the 2/6d a day, not worth a lot even in those days, 15/- a week pay from a job at £2 a week – and you were supposed to make an allotment out of that . . . and there was the shelters, you couldn't sleep in the shelters for the bloody Welsh, they were always singing, and always "She'll Be Coming Round the Mountain" or "Cwm Rhondda". And ashore, in the cinema it might be flashed up on the screen for blokes to return to their ship – in the middle of a film! And outside you'd see all the ships, well, not the ships themselves, but those blue masthead lights all going down the river, in the dark . . . The seamanship, that was either boring or fascinating. For me it was fascinating, I couldn't get enough of it to fill my appetite . . .'

After the course Fred chose HMS *Pembroke*, Chatham Barracks, as his depot. On his first night there he slept, or tried to sleep, in the infamous Tunnel, supposedly an air-raid shelter but actually holding an overflow of 35,000 men every night, 'stinking and snoring'. Then he was summoned to the Drafting Office:

'You've got a draft.'
'What to?'
'HMS *Sherwood*.'
'What is it?'
'It's a destroyer.'

(I thought *great, this is it, a couple of months in the Navy and I'm off to a destroyer already!*)

'Where is it?'

'It's at Portsmouth. You'll be there tomorrow.'

'And we went to Portsmouth, and the bombs were falling all round the Guildhall and everywhere else that night and we slept in the Barracks. The next morning we went round to HMS *Sherwood*, and to my horror it was one of those four-funnellers that Churchill had scrounged from the Yanks. And I was ready that day to give it back to the Yanks. I wandered about, and instead of having the binnacle and the wheel, and the telegraph, it was . . . it resembled one of our trams that used to run around Bradford. Levers – Half-Back 2, Back 2, Forward 3 . . . oh I thought *God, I don't want this*, and then I went up around the guns, *and they were painted solid*, they were *thick* in paint, absolutely useless, they had to be cleaned, I knew that as soon as I looked at 'em, and I felt, well, this is not Fred's cup of tea, it's time to be moving . . . And, miracles of miracles, the First Lieutenant of the *Sherwood* said, "We've had too big a draft. We only wanted 11, and they've sent us 22".

'So I stepped forward in the front rank ready to go back to Chatham. I'd rather have the bombs than go to sea in the *Sherwood*.

'Eventually I went to the *Glasgow* as a foretopman. The meals in the *Glasgow* were superb, no complaints about the food in the *Glasgow*. We had fresh bread, we had a bakehouse, there was a bakehouse in the waist. We had rolls, could never get enough rolls, and the eggs were fried a bit better than in Chatham Barracks. You could always go and get a glass of lime juice, it was free . . . Another thing about the *Glasgow* was the cinema, we had plenty of films, and the favourite films were Popeye or Donald Duck, and it's amazing to think that all those grown men, on the brink of death, could turn to things like Popeye and Donald Duck . . .'

Geoff Shaw was called up during the school holidays in December 1940, having already volunteered for the Navy.

'I had all the usual schoolboy interests as a child – cars, locos, aircraft, but mainly ships, and warships were my favourites. In 1939 we managed to fit in a day's visit to Portsmouth – it was wonderful to see all those grey ships.

'When it came to choosing a career I wanted to go in for architecture, but I couldn't face two more years at school for Higher School Certificate and University, and my parents were too hard up for an apprenticeship, and when the time came when I had to make a definite decision, with the country at war, I thought of those salty ships and a life in the open air, and I volunteered for the Andrew. I was 15.

'I was judged intelligent enough to be a signalman, a "bunting-tosser", and when I actually got a draft to a ship called *Adventure* I was excited. HMS *Adventure* turned out to be, not a dashing destroyer, but an old cruiser/minelayer, built in 1924. The accent was on the mines. Money had been saved on the armament (four 4.7in AA guns) to carry 320 of them, and the main deck looked like a train ferry's, clear down each side save for the rails on which the mines ran to the two dropping ports aft.

'As a bunting I much preferred being outdoors to being cooped up down below as others were. Felt a damn sight safer, anyway – if that torpedo did hit us we always felt that we stood a better chance of survival. And it was so much more interesting to be there in the centre of things, to see everything that was going on, to be up to date as to what was going to happen and often to be amongst the first to know it. Being a small branch there was always more chumminess, and we mixed with the officers to a greater extent than did other ratings except perhaps stewards. We got to know them and they got to know us. Our Captain at one time was R. G. Bowes-Lyon, the Queen's cousin and a true gentleman. On the bridge he was just as likely to make some casual remark to me about nothing special – a lowly bunting – as to one of the officers.

'This business of being outdoors was lovely in fine weather – the thrill of being up there on the bridge or the flag deck of a ship at speed and to watch the bow waves slipping past, to see the first sight of that mast bobbing about miles away on the horizon (and hoping that it was friendly), to watch the other ships in company heaving all over the place.

'But in bad weather it wasn't quite so nice – a wild gale, rain belting down, spray blowing right back over the bridge, with you standing there soaking wet for four hours, ice floes in sight to port and bitterly cold (and the Chief Yeoman would never let us wear gloves on the flag deck on the grounds that it would impede our hoisting of flags). Always tired, aching with the effort to stand upright *and* keep a good lookout and no chance to sit down to rest weary bones – then off watch and below, only to find the messdeck with three inches of dirty seawater swilling about.

'And conditions could sometimes be unpleasant even in good weather. I once spent the whole afternoon watch on the bridge of a destroyer doing 20 knots with a wind coming from dead astern at a speed of about 20¼. The top of the funnel was exactly level with the bridge and we spent four hours breathing in the noxious fumes that came from the boilers and clung about us all the time, coughing and spluttering . . . and being up there on the bridge in thick fog, so thick that you couldn't see "A" gun or the water. You seemed to be floating along in nothingness.

'And doing cable flags – a difficult task, standing right there in the eyes of the ship as we weighed or anchored and indicating by hand flags the number of shackles of cable outboard, whether the anchor was up and down or aweigh – especially worrisome when anchoring, with the chain rushing out like a dangerous, demented snake . . .

'Always watchkeeping, unlike most others who (Quartermasters apart) could look forward to a full night's sleep when in harbour. Even when in dry dock we were on telephone watch.

'At sea – the need for eternal vigilance and smartness in order to see things before anyone else, and to answer or repeat the flagship's signals almost before she had hoisted them. In fact a bunting's life at sea was divided into two sharply different ways. When the ship was sailing independently there was little to do other than act as extra lookouts and report the occasional signals that came by W/T. But when sailing with the squadron it was a different thing entirely and things could be very hectic with flag-hoisting, and signalling by light, and the need to be always alert – always someone keeping an eye on the flagship and others watching the other ships. Buntings may have been a bit superfluous when sailing independently, but when in company with other ships there were often occasions when there didn't seem to be enough of us.

'In company with other ships and at night this non-stop vigilance became even more important. When in more dangerous waters we always used a "heather" light for signalling – a small cylindrical thing about four inches long and an inch in diameter which clipped on top of your binoculars and thus pointed in the same direction as did the binoculars. It gave a very faint blue light, and was operated by a little trigger which was pressed up and down. The trouble was that the light was too faint to be seen by the naked eye when another ship was transmitting, so there *always* had to be someone staring at the flagship through binoculars just in case she should send an urgent manoeuvring signal (this, by the way, being in pre-R/T days). It was a considerable strain, and whoever was keeping lookout had to be relieved quite frequently.

'We operated with the squadron (a minelaying squadron) for some months and became very efficient at flag signalling, getting to know almost when to expect signals and knowing all the routine flag signals and special communication instructions off by heart.

'We were then detached from the squadron and given different duties which entailed us always sailing independently for several more months with very little work for the buntings to do. Perhaps this resulted in a little rustiness developing with regards to flag signalling, perhaps it lulled us into a state of euphoria.

'Then one day, horror of horrors, we were ordered to sea with a fleet – Force H, no less, which at that time consisted of *Nelson*, *Rodney* and *Formidable*. And up on the bridge of the *Nelson* was a Very Important Admiral, and on its flagdeck was a Very Important Signal Bosun. Not only that but we had to sail as leading ship of the destroyer screen – though what use a rickety old minelayer who shook herself to pieces at 26 knots was as a destroyer I don't know.

'Great panic at once ensued. After all those independently routed trips with little for us to do we realized that we would suddenly have to justify those crossed flags on our arms, especially as one of our duties entailed repeating the flagship's signals for the benefit of the other eight destroyers in the screen. Everyone started frantically swotting up in the hours before sailing. Never had so many buntings been seen so assiduously studying so many signal books as then. And even then we had no knowledge of any of the local orders or peculiarities of signalling routine that ships which regularly operated together were apt to use. One slip-up and, great shame, the *Nelson* would have our pendants at the dip quicker than that. So we all sailed with crossed fingers. Luckily all went off all right and we eventually arrived at Gib without having made one silly mistake.

'Pendants at the dip – a reprimand, a mark of shame, a public telling-off. If a ship slipped up in its signalling procedure, then one of the other ships, usually the flagship, would display that ship's pendants hoisted at the dip and in conjunction with no other flags. Thus everyone on the bridge of every ship in the fleet knew at once that HMS So-and-so had made a bloomer. It was the ultimate in public degradation.

'One thing to be avoided was losing your halliards – usually caused by a combination of keenness and carelessness when the chappie whose job it was to hoist the flags did so rather too quickly and before the others had had time to clip on all the flags. The flag signal would then go up, perhaps incomplete, but always not clipped on to the halliard at its bottom end. There was thus no means of hauling it down again afterwards – and the hauling down of a flag signal was its executive signal. One day the flagship, *Southern Prince*, did this and was left with a long stream of flags, attached to the halliards at the head (the top) but not the tack (the bottom), blowing out horizontally astern. We all had a good laugh and considered hoisting her pendants at the dip but refrained from doing so in case the admiral was offended. On board the flagship they tried desperately to recover the flags, allowing them to blow out farther and farther astern by easing the halliards – but the wind was so strong that they would *not* drop to the deck and they just stayed up there, trailing horizontally, till they were way out over the funnel. How they managed to get them down in the end I can't remember. Perhaps some poor bloke had to go aloft.'

ROUGH-RIDING *ROXBOROUGH*

No incident in the grim Battle of the Atlantic surpassed what happened to HMS *Roxborough* (ex-USS *Foote*) during the night of 14/15 January 1943, when she was about 300 miles south of Cape Farewell, Greenland. There she met some of the worst Atlantic weather within living memory. A huge sea ripped open the bridge, crushing the Captain's cabin on the upper deck level under the bridge, and killing the Captain, Lieutenant-Commander A. C. Price. Ten others were also trapped in the upper bridge, all injured and caught in the mass of twisted steel, with seas still breaking over them; among them was the First Lieutenant, Lieutenant G. Osborne, RNVR.

Twenty-three-year-old Lieutenant G. M. Greenwood, RCNVR, the senior surviving able-bodied officer, stumbled from his bunk through ankle-deep water in the wardroom to the upper deck to find the ship completely out of control and smashing into the heavy seas. He took command, got her into secondary steering, turned her round away from the pounding seas to give the rescue party on the bridge a chance to work, and headed for Newfoundland.

The ship's doctor, Surgeon Lieutenant James Watt, RNVR, worked for seventeen hours under nightmare conditions in an emergency operating theatre in the stokers' mess, under lights rigged by torpedomen, and with his instruments in canned goods cartons screwed down to the table. Steadied by an assistant against the violent roll of the ship, he performed nine emergency operations, set compound fractures, and worked on shock cases. The First Lieutenant died on the operating table, but all the other injured men recovered.

'. . . BOILER GO BANG. . .'

It is a wonder that some of the smaller vessels could survive at all in those raging seas. The corvettes were the most roughly handled of the escorts. 'Have just seen down your funnel' signalled one of these little ships to another, 'Fire is burning brightly'. When another corvette, damaged in a gale, left the convoy to return to repairs, Senior Officer, Escort, signalled 'Hope you find necessary facilities in Belfast.' The battered corvette replied 'Hope I find Belfast.' When she finally made base she signalled 'Am tied up to No. 5 Berth,' to receive the stinging reply 'Shoe laces are tied up, HM ships are secured.' In another hard blow one old V-and-W destroyer made to another, lying dismasted, 'How come?' The hulk replied 'Scraping under very low cloud.' Minesweepers HMS *Prompt* and HMS *Jason*, which were completed, launched and commissioned on the same day, and attached to the same group, were always competitors. As *Prompt* settled in the water, decks awash, after hitting an acoustic mine, she signalled to her rival 'First again.'

As the war went on, Allied escorts joined the Battle of the Atlantic, to their cost. 'Can go no more,' signalled a Free French destroyer, 'Boiler go bang'. A fellow national in a Sea Hurricane radioed: 'Engine no good. I jump.' A US destroyer, unused to the British signal code, hoisted the Church pennant next to the Interrogative flag. When questioned as to the meaning, she signalled 'God, where am I?'

Convoy in 'E-boat Alley'

Oh I wonder, yes I wonder –
Did the Jaunty make a blunder
When he sent this draft chit round for me?

Song of the Barrack Stanchion

Battling against U-boats and the Luftwaffe were the forgotten small ships of the East Coast convoys in 'E-boat Alley'. This was in one way a harder fight, as the screaming Stukas could find them easily from their southern Norwegian, Danish and home airfields.

Attack From All Quarters

Dennis Bond of Godalming, Surrey, had served an apprenticeship as a wireman with the then Mid-Southern Utility Company (now the South-Eastern Electricity Board), and played in the Godalming Borough Brass Band – until he was called up in October 1940. He chose the Navy as most of his friends had gone into the RN. One was a Royal Marine bandsman lost in *Hood*; another former sounding-brass man was lost with the destroyer *Greyhound*.

He trained at a holiday camp on Hayling Island, Hampshire, and at *St Vincent* at Gosport for electrical brushing-up before beginning a busman's holiday as a wireman, RN – wishing he were blowing a bright brass horn in the Marine Band which played every Sunday morning at Divisions. They were set a 'trade test' which consisted of wiping a lead joint on two pieces of lead pipe – plumber's work. But someone found a load of finished tests in a dump, and they all passed, and before he knew it he was on draft to a ship called HMS *Whitshed* which, initially, as no one seemed to know anything about her, he thought must be another stone frigate. Then an elderly Chief told him that she was an old V-and-W destroyer, but where she was and what she was doing he did not know. He had not heard of the old ship's bravura dash into Boulogne harbour to support Iain Nethercott's old and bold *Keith*, when she had exchanged salvoes with panzers, point-blank.

The Drafting Office sent Dennis to Parkeston Quay, Harwich, where he was told to report to HMS *Badger*, an old hulk used for accommodation purposes. He reported to the regulating PO there, and was told that *Whitshed* was out on E-boat patrol. He took shore leave in the town that evening and 'met some of the other lads on the patrol who soon filled me in on the life, which looked anything but rosy, and the prospects of survival, which seemed poor!' About three o'clock the next afternoon he was told that the motor boat from *Whitshed* was alongside the quay waiting for him.

'After a rather choppy trip across the harbour we came alongside the *Whitshed*, and this didn't look at all like the recruiting posters of ships of the Royal Navy – dull grey, streaks of rust, dabs of red lead in places. As all electrical work in the RN came under the torpedo branch, I reported to the Chief Torpedo Gunner's Mate, a time-expired friendly man, who took me along to my messdeck, where I met a strange mixture of ratings – a PO cook, leading torpedo operator, PO Jack Dusty, leading supply assistant, leading seaman and two seaman torpedomen. There was a strange smell – damp clothes, food, fuel oil, hair cream. But they turned out to be a great bunch of lads who went out of their way to make me feel one of them. I had no trouble sleeping that night, although the hammocks were slung so close together that when the ship moved at her moorings we all swayed together.

'In the morning it was the familiar "Wakey, wakey, lash up and stow!" Washing was six basins for 150 men, a major operation, and some washed in a bucket on deck, but I was pleased to learn that for this kind of inconvenience we got 1/- a day "hard-lying money".

'After dinner the Tannoy blared: "The ship is under sailing orders. Last mail will go ashore at 1700 hours. Special sea dutymen to their stations 1830." The Chief came down and told me my duties – Depth Charge Party at Cruising Stations, which meant being on the stern and, if required, to set the depth-charges with the special key and do any electrical work necessary; meanwhile, action station on the bridge, telephone to all guns' crews and lookouts, and man the tubes if torpedo action was called for.

'Exactly at 1830 the call came: "Close all X and Y openings. Close all deadlights and scuttles. Special sea dutymen to your stations for leaving harbour." All other hands fell in in Navy blues lined up aft as we passed the other ships.

'The water got choppier. We were very near the boom defence and the open sea. (How will I react if we hit trouble? Will I do what I was trained to do, or will I just panic?) Then the guns' crews were testing the gun-firing circuits, firing blanks. I had to go and check all the navigation lights, which took my mind offf things. I rushed to the bridge. "Manning the phones, sir!" I checked on the position of the alarm rattler, which was also in my charge.

'Behind us, reassuringly, steamed two other escorts. When we sighted the convoy they were covered in a smokey haze, and looked funny with barrage balloons over them. The signalman took a message by Aldis lamp from the senior escort. He replied, the lamp clacked away, the vent fans roared, the ship creaked, the sea hissed. We were ordered to take up the rear position, which nobody likes. We ran down the side of the convoy, looking up at the tall sides of the ships. They seemed to want to crush us. We made a wide sweep into position, then began the monotony of holding our speed down to that of the slow merchant ships – up and down, up and down, just the clacking of the signal lamp now and again broke the monotony.

'One of the lads appeared, "Kye's up!" Hot Navy chocolate and corned dog sandwiches. A banquet!

'The sea was rising, we were doing the corkscrew antic so common to the old V-and-Ws.

'Suddenly the whole scene was lit up, like day.

'The port lookout shouted, "Escort firing starshell to port!"

'The OOW shouted at me, "Action stations!" I shouted it into the phone, pressed the alarm rattler and heard the distant ringing below. The whole ship erupted as men rushed to their action stations. Then came the calls in my phone. "A Gun closed up, cleared away . . . B Gun closed, cleared way, X Gun . . ." I heard the clang of shells being slammed into breeches . . . A Gun ready . . . B Gun ready . . . 12-pounder AA Guns ready . . . pom-pom ready . . .

'The Captain shouted to me "Escort leader has sighted E-boats! Tell all lookouts to be alert!" I thought – *This is not real . . . What am I doing here? I'm just an electrician, working for the Mid-Southern Utility . . .*

'Then the orders for me to pass to the guns' crews came thick and fast, I didn't have time to think about me . . .

'A lookout shouted "E-boats astern!"

'"Hard-a-port!" from the Skipper . . .

'The whole ship heeled over, I slithered across the bridge, the pencils and protractors fell off the chart table, from below came the sound of breaking. "There go our crocks," said the signalman.

'A new noise joined the rest – the ping, ping-pinging of the Asdics.

'"A and Y Guns load with starshell!" I repeated it.

'"A and Y Guns stand by!" "Guns" fingered the Gun Fire bell.

'"A and Y Guns FIRE!"

'Whoosh . . . It sounded like an express going through a station. The whole area lit up again.

'"All guns load with HE!"

'I repeated it and realized that I was not really frightened because everyone else seemed so cool and calm and some of it must have rubbed off on me.

'"E-boat bearing Red five-o!"

'"Independent fire when each gun bears!"

'The salvo rattled the bridge, the ship recoiled as if kicked. We could see the E-boat like a small white line. All the escorts were having a go. The noise was terrific. Tracers were everywhere, red, green, like fireworks.

'"Check, check, check" to the gun crews. The E-boat had turned away.

'Things returned to normal. I took stock of myself. I was keyed up, my heart was beating fast, yes, *but I hadn't panicked*. The main thing was how everyone worked together. Believe me, this does have a calming influence.

'It was 3.30 in the morning by then. I was not allowed below to my mess, because of the danger of mines, so I wandered into the seamen's mess and scrounged a cup of kye and a sandwich. Now – where to sleep? I found a small gap between the torpedo tubes and the engine room exhaust fan, pulled my duffle coat round me, my oilskin on top of me and tried to sleep. But I just lay there looking at the stars, watching the masthead going from side to side.

'The watch changed again. I climbed the ladders to the bridge again. It was peaceful, I looked at the lines of ships as we jogged along. The sky was empty save for a few clouds.

'But above was the Stuka's eerie cry. Like Tennyson's *Eagle* –

> Ring'd with the azure world, he stands.
> The wrinkled sea beneath him crawls;
> He watches from his mountain walls,
> And like a thunderbolt he falls.

'"Aircraft bearing dead ahead!". . . . The dull thumps of explosions . . . The pom-pom really does go *pom-pom-pom*. Planes were coming down either flank of the convoy. Now they were at masthead height and everyone was having a go at them. They were after the biggest merchantman and were too close for comfort. The E-boats were not too bad, but planes are the worst . . . they were coming straight for us! They were firing at us!

'"Heads down, lads", said the Skipper calmly. The plane zoomed over us, his bomb fell, and missed . . . We had put him off his aim!

'The action, short and sharp, was over. That was *really* frightening. One of the ships had been hit, but no casualties. "We got off lucky", said the signalman.

'We delivered the ships, stayed one night at Immingham and were to take another convoy back the next day.

'After a good night's sleep we were ready, but the Germans had dropped mines in the estuary so we had to wait till the sweepers had cleared a channel.

'Things looked a lot more peaceful. I was off-watch, and the weather was so lovely that I went to the quarterdeck and lay down in the sun. We were in the outer lane, going south, which meant even more vigilance was needed. I passed a pleasant afternoon on the phones. Everyone was dreading the night, but after dusk action stations, when most aircraft attacks occurred, all passed quietly. I took two hours off watch to get my tea. It was about eight o'clock and very difficult light when the sea and sky all looks one, and every gull looks like a plane. But all seemed quiet. At ten round came the kye and sandwiches. All was well with the world.

'"Ship on fire starboard side!"

'"Northbound convoy under attack!" They were passing inside us, and we didn't know where the attack was coming from.

'"Echo bearing starboard one hundred and closing . . ." The Asdic had a contact . . . U-boat?

'"Depth Charge Party close up!" *That was me!*

'My relief appeared and grabbed the phone. I scrambled aft, heart thumping, to the throwers, where the Chief TI was waiting. He gave me the key. "Shallow settings."

'The pin-ping-ping-ping was getting louder . . . The target was closing.

'*Whitshed* had formed the established pattern with the two other escorts – one ahead, one to port of us. Somewhere in between the U-boat.

'The Torpedo Officer fingered the DC firing button.

'"Fire charges!"

'I removed the pin and two charges rolled down the rails over the stern while two were shot from the throwers to either hand. The sea boiled and there came the most horrific explosion; the sea cascaded into the air, the ship shook, the funnel rattled, showers of soot fell, deck plates in the engine room were lifted by the blast. Then the sea subsided and the Asdic reported a lost contact. Whether we got the U-boat or not we never knew, but it did not bother us again that trip, and we did have a lovely fry-up that night with all the dead and stunned fish floating on the surface.'

TAKING ON *SCHARNHORST*

After his safe return to Harwich Dennis went ashore straight to the Salvation Army hostel and booked a bed for the night. There he had a nice hot bath, went to the pictures and then back to the 'Sally A' to sleep.

'I didn't get much sleep though as there was an air raid, and I missed the cool, calm faces of the gunners, the nonchalant but precise way the officers controlled the situation, and wished I was back aboard the old *Whitshed*. When I got back in the morning, the smell in the messdeck was cosy and familiar. I was home.'This pattern of life went on, five days out, three days in, unless the E-boats were pretty active and we had to leave in a hurry.

'One day came the order: "Change all torpedoes and re-ammunition with armour-piercing shells!"

'Something big was in the wind. We couldn't find out what, but were kept busy all through the night, taking out the old torpedoes, replacing them with new, filling them up with oil and water, like you'd service a car for a long journey . . .

'Then came the order: "Ships will prepare for sea immediately."

'All the preparations started for leaving harbour. Once through the boom the speakers came to life:

'"This is the Captain speaking. You will all no doubt be wondering why all the preparations over the last few hours have taken place. Well, now I will tell you. We have been informed that a large German surface force comprising *Scharnhorst*, *Gneisenau* and *Prinz Eugen*, plus a destroyer escort and also aircraft cover, has broken out from Brest and is making its way up the English Channel, so we and the other five destroyers you see with us will attempt to stop them. The task will be difficult, because of the large air escort, but I know that you will all do your best. Good luck to you all."

'"And good-bye," said someone. "It was nice knowing you." "Bloody sauce!" said the LTO. "Up the bloody Channel! What do they think we are – f★★★★★g stamps?" There was a lot of muttering from the lads. Everyone was thinking: Well, this is it, what we never thought would really happen – a torpedo attack . . . against the bloody *Scharnhorst* and *Gneisenau* . . . I couldn't take it in. Then I looked at all the lovely countryside we were passing on our way out of the estuary . . . Will I be seeing this again? I really never noticed it before. I was really nervous then. After all, we *were* a very old ship.

'"Man the torpedo tubes." We were told to strap ourselves to the tubes, with the lashings provided. I thought this was to stop us from deserting the tubes, but I found out the real reason later.

'We did several exercises to see how fast we could turn the tubes from port to starboard, and as they had to be turned by hand it was quite exhausting. We plodded on. Our radar picked up heavy vessels ahead plus aircraft.

'To cap it all, down came the fog, the sort you sometimes get at sea – one minute clear, the next in a fog bank, so we now relied on our radar a lot. We carried on. Suddenly the mist lifted and I saw them, and my heart stopped. They looked like the Houses of Parliament. Then they started firing their 11 in guns against our 4 in.

'"Prepare for torpedo attack. Train to starboard." It was hard labour trying to turn the tubes with the ship heeling right over and going at full speed. The racing water came up to my knees, and now I knew what the lashings were for. Without them we would have been washed away.

'"Stand by to fire tubes . . . *Fire one . . . Fire two . . . Fire three.*"

'"All torpedoes running, sir."

'All this time shells were falling round us. We saw the poor old Swordfish planes getting shot out of the sky. They were no match for Messerschmitts, but still they carried on.

'After firing all our fish the inclination was to turn away, but that was an open invitation to get blasted to pieces. Then fortune smiled on us. Down came the mist again. We turned away. I thought, with a bit of luck they'll be busy with the other destroyers.

'Then as if in rebuke of my unworthy thoughts, down came the Stukas through the thinning mist. They really were something, screaming down with that awful siren they had, wailing . . . It made my hair stand on end.

'The Skipper was laying right back on the bridge with his binoculars to his eyes and as a plane came screaming down and the bomb left its belly he ordered sharply "Hard-a-port!" or "Hard-a-starboard!" and the bomb near-missed us alongside. This happened several times, until at long last we were clear, though *Worcester* did get hit, and there were casualties, and one of the other old warriors broke down. None of us hit the Germans, which we blamed on the mist, and they got clear away.

'After this the convoy plod went on much as before, until one day in March 1942. We were escorting a convoy and as usual were the tail-end Charlie. I had just come off watch and was sitting supping a cup of tea when there was an almighty Bang, the ship went right over on her side and out went all the lights. I came out of the upper messdeck and found that I was going uphill. I saw the Torpedo Officer. He said, "We've hit a mine. Go into the engine room and try to put on the electrical circuit-breakers – they've jumped off – and we must have them to keep the guns firing."

'The prospect of going down below in a listing ship didn't appeal to me at all. When I got below it was chaos. One generator was useless. The Chief Stoker said he could keep one running, but as this meant that the switchboard couldn't handle the load, we had to turn off all electrical circuits except the gun-firing circuits. This we did, and I wedged up the circuit-breaker to make sure it didn't drop off when we needed to fire the guns, as we were now a sitting target for aircraft. The mine had gone off under the stern, which meant that the depth-charges had to be made safe and all the primers removed. The compartment where the spare charges were stored was now under a lot of fuel oil where one of the fuel tanks had ruptured.

'We were then informed that a tug with an escort was coming to tow us to the dockyard at Chatham, and so began a long wait. We were attacked several times from the air, but these were not pressed home too hard as we could give a good account of ourselves with the guns still working. It was pretty awful lying stopped where we could just see the beach at Great Yarmouth, with very little to eat as fuel oil had got everywhere, even into the lockers where our clothes were. One thing we were pleased about was that we had fighter cover. Every now and then the Spitties would fly over us.

'The tug arrived and took us in tow, and it seemed ages until we got to Chatham dockyard. We were then given seven days' leave, and while at home I received a telegram to say that the ship would pay off at the termination of my leave. We went back to Chatham and put her into dry dock, and then we could see that the poor old *Whitshed* had broken her back.'

After the struggle to reach Montevideo the decrepit old tramp *Stangrant* went up-river and loaded a full cargo of grain for Hull – Third Mate and former bus conductor Alan Mathison's home town, but fate did not intend him to see the lights of home just yet. At Pernambuco, Brazil, Alan was put ashore with typhoid; he spent three months in hospital there and was shipped home as a Distressed British Seaman in the Booth Line's *Crispin*, of Liverpool, which was later converted into a Q-ship. While recuperating at home he was able to study for his Second Mate's certificate. The Dunkirk débâcle occurred, and his brother joined him, his ship, the *Leo*, having been sunk off the beaches by German bombers. He passed for Second Mate in October, and was passed fit for sea service, although some misguided drafting officer obviously thought that he still needed further non-operational time – and sent him to the Fleet Ammunition Supply Vessel *Aire* at Scapa Flow, as Third Officer.

Aire had been commandeered from the Associated Humber Lines (Ellermans, Wilson and London Midland Railway Company), and was permanently moored at a buoy in Scapa, only leaving the buoy when a warship needed ammunition.

'We had on board every type of shell from the 15 in armour-piercing variety down to 0.303 in bullets. We also had on board several technicians who used to examine any faulty ammunition returned to us. Their job was to render the dodgy ammo safe for transportation back to the munitions factory at Fort William, and as far as I was concerned they could keep it. I didn't see much action while I was there, except when there was an air attack; then the air was so full of shrapnel that it was dangerous even to go out on the open deck, the air being full of exploding shells.

'After about nine months I was transferred to the *Rother*, another of the Company's ships, and spent a year on her running up and down from Leith to London with frozen meat, passing through E-boat Alley twice a week. As we had passenger accommodation we were always the Commodore's ship, and in consequence were never attacked, the Germans being wise enough never to attack the leading ships of the convoy, but always picking on the rear ships first. In misty weather we could hear the E-boats rev up their engines as we approached the swept channel – the cunning buggers used to tie up to the channel buoys waiting for a convoy to pass through. Woe betide any ship which went outside the swept channel! It was well and truly mined. I saw several ships come to grief that way. On one voyage up to Iceland with stores for the British forces stationed there, in the 24-hour daylight of their mid-summer, submarines were the things to fear, and we had to dodge a whole field of floating mines sown by a U-boat. By that time I had passed for First Mate, and was transferred to the SS *Fort Livingstone*, a ship loading in Hull with Army supplies for Monty's troops in North Africa – munitions, food, tanks, Bren-carriers and other hardware, and a new theatre of war opened its doors to me.'

DEMS In Action

Eric James Craske came from a seafaring family par excellence of Sheringham, Norfolk. His father was a fisherman and lifeboatman, his uncle a Lieutenant RN, and his three brothers served in RN and MN ships. In 1940 there was a great and growing call for gunners to serve on merchant vessels – the DEMS (Defensively Equipped Merchant Ships) unit – and Eric James chose this unique type of sea service. He joined in Hull and was rushed down to Guz.

'The confusion had to be seen to be believed. The barracks was packed, and no one seemed to know just what we were supposed to be. Well, we were packed off again back to Hull for training on 12-pounder and 4in guns by a Royal Marine sergeant whose voice could be heard all over the city. After a hurried course we cut our teeth on coasters down E-boat Alley.

'The MN needed us badly, and I was dumped at Dundee aboard the SS *Kyle Castle*, 845 tons, general cargo (lost off Granville, 8 March 1945), one of the small coasters offloading from large freighters to carry goods down the "Alley", and lived in the luxury of a small caboose or hut built on the boat deck specially for us next to the spud locker! Do you know how we did our dhobi-ing in those cockleshells? Hammocks we tied to the guardrail, let 'em trail in the ship's wash (excuse the pun) and they would come up snowy-white. Smalls we put in a bucket of cold water, bribed a stoker with a roll-me-own and he'd put it under a steam pipe tap and, Hey Presto! you've got a bucket of hot laundry! Then rig a clothes line up on the boatdeck and dry it – you couldn't do that on the *KG V*! And going ashore – we'd put a ten-bob note in our sock for emergencies (came in useful in Alex). Not much trouble from Jerry, except a scare off Middlesbrough from a Ju 88, but he flew straight by us, didn't want to know, not worth bothering about.

'We were discharging in Woolwich Docks when two of us were given the usual DEMS pierhead jump down to Falmouth for the MV *Oud Beyerland*, a small Dutch oil-carrier, very neat and tidy like all Dutch ships, to proceed in convoy west and round into the Western Approaches for Milford Haven oil terminal for crude oil. Well, the convoy rounded North Foreland and went through the channel in the clear, round Land's End and north-east for the Bristol Channel, hugging the coast before darting across the Channel to the Haven. So far, so good, we thought. But oh, no, out of the sun, as usual, they came, I don't know how many. I was below, my mate had already opened fire with the Lewis before I got there, the Dutch cook handing him fresh magazines. I had to run from our quarters right aft to them on the fo'c'sle. Before I could reach them the plane dropped a 250-pounder, a near miss, but the blast flung me against a bollard, and killed my mate at the gun. It was an international affair, the Dutch cook swearing in his horrible language at a Jerry plane, and a Free French tug coming up to tow us in. And my mate lying dead on the deck. I should have been with him, that's all I could think of. To make things worse, I knew his wife and parents back in Hull – What do I say to them? They had welcomed me into their homes when I couldn't get home. I had to go to the funeral – Will they look at me and think "Why not you? Why our boy?" Well, if they felt it they didn't show it. I have one consolation. After the war I traced his brother, still in Hull, and we write to each other. But, it's against all reason, I still feel that guilt. I should have been there, by his side, not that brave Dutch cocoa bosun.

'It was a quick-change scene, in DEMS. From the Dutch oiler I went to the *Cetus*, a Norwegian freighter, 4,500 tons, escaped from Bergen on the fall of Norway. I joined her at Hull, one of four gunners, with two Lewis guns – and I'd have taken on the bloody *Bismarck*, any day, the way I felt, after the funeral. Only the Master could speak English, and we had a real ding-dong over where to site the Lewises, settled by the DEM PO who put us aboard, pointing out the fouled anchors on his sleeve – "The Lewises go *there*, and *there* – right?" There was no further argument, and we sailed empty to Oban to join a convoy for the New World. Then those in high places realized that we had no gun on the poop deck, so it was back to Hull, and there we were split up, with me and one other going to an unknown ship in the Tyne. There we loaded our bags and hammocks into a truck. "Ah, yes," said the driver, "*Birker Force*, you two." I said "What's that?" He grinned. "A ship."

'He dropped us at the coal hoist. Who was it said "Dirty British coaster with a salt-caked smokestack"? He must have seen the SS *Birker Force*, about 1,100 tons of coal-dust-caked collier. A coal-dusted mate showed us to our readymade coal-dusted "cabin" next to the chain locker. It was going to be a nice, quiet place, and was already tastefully coal-decorated inside, with the black diamonds still thundering down into the holds. A coaster then wasn't victualled like a deepsea vessel. We were issued with ration books, just like civvies, only ours had more coupons. If the cook was so inclined we could use a small place on the small cooker in the small galley. We closed the portholes, but the dust still got in. We wondered if bangers and mash and coal dust would do our insides a heap of good. A coaster is built for maximum cargo, minimum crew space. After loading, the crew went to work with hoses, and we saw the true colour of our ship – black.

'We formed convoy at the mouth of the Tyne ("The Tyne, the Tyne, the *coal*y Tyne, the Queen of *al* the rivers" the Geordies say. How right they are – about the coal, anyway.) We were bound, not for the Rio Grande or the Isles 'Neath the Wind, but for Beckton Gas Works, London. It was my first taste of

E-boat Alley. Off the Humber we saw the results of the work of the Luftwaffe, E-boats, U-boats, mines – masts poking up out of the water, marked by a mass of wreck buoys. More masts off my home town (I wonder what Dad's doing? I'm glad he can't see me).

'It was four hours on, four hours off – but not for long. Off Yarmouth they came out of the sun again. The armed trawler escort let fly with her 12-pounder, everybody firing every which way. Then they were gone. Then the Thames Estuary, more masts, funnels, bell buoys. We tied up at the gasworks, and the DEMS contingent got ashore as quickly as possible and vanished towards the Big Smoke before the great coal dust shower could hit us.

'I did four trips in the *Birker Force* up and down to the Tyne, and, do you know, you can actually get to like a little coal carrier, if you love ships. It wasn't always the Jerries that bothered us. Our first run back to Geordieland looked like being quiet, no Luftwaffe, no E-boats, but when we got abeam of my old coast the nor'easter hit us, and being a light ship we (and the others) rolled something awful. When you're in a swept channel and have to keep station, the Old Man can't put her nose into it.'

However, if Eric thought that local weather was bad, he found the North Atlantic something else again. Two days out from New York for Liverpool he recorded in his diary:

'We can feel the change in the weather now (Father used to say "Watch the white tops, boy, they'll tell you"). The little corvettes roll and the wind is getting up. Duffle coats and wool jumpers now, boys. The bosun and his mate are checking the deck cargoes. Then the first one comes over the bows. The old *Clan Ronald* has deep well decks, the water rushes down and through the scuppers.

'Now it really hits us. It's quite dark now, and when you see the bosun's crew rigging life lines you really begin to get the shakes . . . Can barely see the *Irene Dupont* now . . . Gunlayer has traversed the gun so the shield will give a bit of cover . . . God, I've never seen the size of these breakers! The gunlayer tightens the wing nuts on the ready-use ammo locker – Won't need them!

'The hand crank phone to the bridge is near the lockers. It rings. It's the Old Man . . . "Abandon the poop and get to your quarters . . . The convoy is to scatter . . . Get to your quarters . . ." That's a laugh – our quarters are on the boat deck. If you leave the poop you have to go along that well deck, already awash, and up a ladder to the main deck, then up to the boat deck. There's no catwalk like on a tanker . . . (Well, Dad, you had some rough seas in that old Sheringham lifeboat . . . Were you scared?)

'The Third Mate has somehow got to the poop . . . "You'll have to go back by the shaft tunnel. Follow me." We go down the small hatchway under the poop along the tunnel into the engine room . . . Someone says, "*This*'ll keep the U-boats down!" The comedian says, "Yes, and we'll soon be joining 'em!"

'Two days of this weather. All the rafts lost. The bosun says, "Skipper's taken over the wheel, put her nose into it." We just about have sea-way. When things calm down a bit we return to the poop. The Third Mate comes along. "What a blow!" he says. Twenty-nine Clan Line ships were lost in the war. 3,935 DEMS gunners died. But I'd rather face a sub attack than that terrible North Atlantic storm. There was such *fury* in those *huge* seas . . . They still haunt my dreams.'

'One battleship in sight'

Suddenly around me
   The Gunnery Jacks all spoke
Their terrible words of gunpowder
   And sentences of smoke

SALOPIAN TORPEDOED

The Armed Merchant Cruiser HMS *Salopian* served for a time on the Freetown run, and was then transferred to the Halifax Escort Force. Losses among these substitute cruisers, with their slow speed, lack of armour, ancient guns and conspicuous bulk, had been high. Apart from the loss of *Rawalpindi*, sunk by *Scharnhorst* and *Gneisenau*, and *Jervis Bay*, sunk by *Scheer* in a brave and successful defence of her convoy, nine AMCs had been destroyed by U-boat torpedo – *Carinthia*, *Scotstoun*, *Andania*, *Transylvania*, *Dunvegan Castle*; and *Laurentic* and *Patroclus* within hours of each other by U-boat ace Otto 'The Silent' Kretschmer in his *U99*, with its famous Golden Horseshoe badge; and *Forfar*; with *Voltaire* sunk by the guns of the German armed merchant raider *Thor*, which had been twice beaten off, by AMCs *Alcantara* and *Carnarvon Castle*, but got away.

On 12 May 1941 *Salopian* handed over her slow convoy from Halifax on the western edge of the submarine danger zone to a destroyer escort. She then turned west and headed back for Halifax at 15 knots.

Just before first light on the following morning, at about 3.30a.m., the officer of the watch sighted a submarine on the surface, sounded Action Stations, increased to full speed and put the helm hard over to turn away. Almost immediately the ship was struck by two torpedoes on the starboard side, one near the bow, and one at the position of the bulkhead between Nos 3 and 4 holds, which fractured many engine room pipes and stopped the main engines, brought down all the wireless aerials and shattered the starboard lifeboat. A third 'tinfish' was too much for the bilge pumps, and an Advance Party left the ship in the remaining boats, leaving the Retard Party, which included the Captain, gun crews and damage control parties.

The U-boat surfaced and *Salopian*'s guns opened fire, which only triggered off another torpedo hit. The Captain ordered Abandon Ship.

Engineer Sub-Lieutenant Bert Poolman – whom we last saw being seen off by wife and son to join *Salopian*, at the darkened Midland Railway Station in peaceful Bath; who had served on the Western Front and in submarines in World War I, and was not one to panic easily – 'Saw no signs of fear or urgency among the ship's company. A lot of men were going back down to their cabins to grab rabbits and personal nick-nacks, and I thought I'd go down as well and retrieve a few things.' Nervous at the thought of keeping a watch in the engine room again, he had quickly found, like Kennedy of *Rawalpindi*, that 'it has all come back'.

He was a popular man on board, and had struck up a friendship with the Captain, Sir John Alleyne – 'Two old retreads together', as he put it. On his silver wedding anniversary the members of the wardroom had presented him with an elegant silver inscribed salver, and it was this that he especially wanted to save. He picked this up, all his pipes, tobacco and watches, a carton of cigarettes, and his gas mask bag, which had long since ceased to contain a gas mask, and was usually full of chocolate for his wife and son – in fact he was known as 'The Chocolate Sailor'.

'Once down there, I thought "Blowed if I'm going to let the fishes have my best uniform!" and changed into it.' His absence on deck had been noted, and a young fellow engineer hurried below to find him. 'For Christ's sake Bert', he shouted, 'the bloody ship's going down!' The older man said casually, 'Oh, she won't go just yet.' Up top, he climbed into the boat, clutching his precious salver.

With the wireless aerials down, no message had been sent out, but at 0830 a signal 'AMC torpedoed', giving their position, was transmitted on the old Board of Trade emergency set, which had a range of only 50–100 miles, in the motor boat.

George Monk was Second Radio Officer of the Ocean Transport and Trading Group's MN *Empire Confidence*, which was returning to the UK from Vancouver; she had been held back at Halifax from joining the next convoy because the ship had passenger accommodation and was considered suitable for the Commodore of the following one. On 4 May the Convoy Commodore, a retired Commodore RN, arrived aboard with his staff, and on 6 May *Empire Confidence* left for her anchorage in Bedford Basin. The convoy formed up and sailed in the afternoon.

On 13 May George 'came off morning watch at 0800, and returned at 0830 to relieve my Chief for breakfast. At about 0835 I heard signals on 500kcs, but they were unreadable, due to interference. When this cleared I received this message: "AMC *Salopian* Torpedoed. In lifeboats. Position 59.04N 38.15W. PSE. QSP."

'I waited for a repeat but heard nothing more. However, the vital part of the message was the position. It was dead ahead of the convoy and under 100 miles away.

'As soon as the Commodore had examined the message, signals were exchanged between him and the Senior Officer, Escorts. None of them had received the message, so SOE requested details for immediate transmission to C-in-C Western Approaches. Obviously, it was vital that other ships in the vicinity were warned of U-boat activity, and rescue of *Salopian*'s crew had to be organized. *Empire Confidence* had no HF gear to make this signal.

'By 0900 the Commodore had alerted the convoy to the emergency course it would have to make. Turning a convoy of 50-plus ships in nine columns through

Eastleigh November 23.39

my dear Todd,

I was extremely
leased to hear today that
u have not broken
nything after all. I very
uch hope that this is
rue, and that you are,
nd are feeling all right.

e were very lucky and
ery unlucky too. If we had
ad a few feet more
ight we would have
ade the brown ploughed
eld on top of the hill, and
ight have got nothing worse
han very muddy feet.

I congratulate you
ery much indeed in keeping
r head so well under rather
fficult conditions, and I
pe you will be back with us

before long

yours very sincerely

Ralph Richardson

***Previous page:** The apologetic letter which Lieutenant (A) Ralph Richardson sent to Alan Todd following their crash-landing in a Shark outside the village of Hursky near Winchester.*

***Left:** L/S Nethercott mans a Hotchkiss AA gun aboard HMS* Lincoln. *(ex-USS* Yarnall)

***Right:** Some of* Lincoln's *HOs share a food parcel – the original stocks of American food were mostly appropriated for the wardroom galley.*

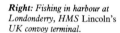

***Left:** AB Walt Hardman on HMS* Lincoln's *port torpedo tubes.*

***Right:** Fishing in harbour at Londonderry, HMS* Lincoln's *UK convoy terminal.*

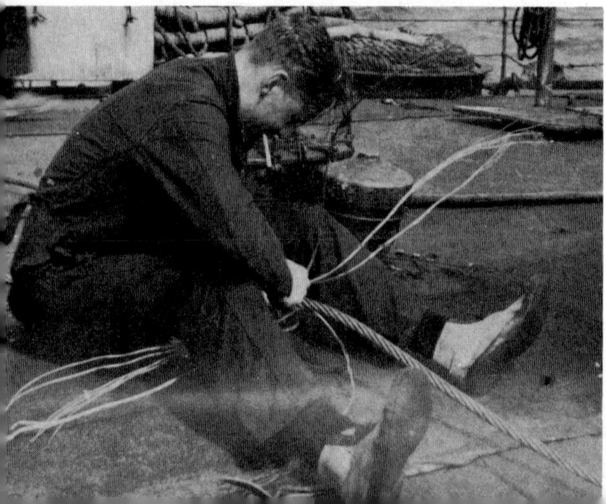

Left: Lincoln's *Active Service veterans taught their green HOs splicing in the dog watches.*

CORNED BEEF
CORNED BEEF

Left: *Dennis Bond (ex-apprentice wireman, Godalming Borough Brass Bandsman) asked of the screaming Stukas 'How will I react?' – and was answered.*

To Dennis Bond HM destroyer Whitshed, *Admiralty Modified W class, built 1918, 'didn't look at all like the recruiting posters' – but she had been to Dunkirk, and she took on* Scharnhorst *and* Gneisenau, *as a change from dodging dive-bombers in 'E-boat Alley'.*

Left: *Wiremen making fishing nets. (M. Collins, D. Bond)*

Top right: *Hauling up the whaler.*

Right: *Torpedo party, with Stuka suntans. (D. Bond bottom right)*

Left: *The author's father, Sub-Lieutenant (E) B. Poolman, RNR, who served aboard HMS* Salopian.

Right: *Ride-a-cock-gun aboard* Suffolk.

Left: *Bill Earp joined the Navy to escape 'a world of poverty'. Here he is quite an old salt, a gunner with a three-year Good Conduct stripe and the white tape of a Naval marriage to a 'Dorothy', who replaced HMS* Suffolk *in his affections – almost.*

Right: *A sea wolf if never very far from Bill Earp's* Suffolk *'Red Riding Hood' as she goes to get the rations for Granny and is sent on her way rejoicing after meeting Aladdin, in the ship's unorthodox pantomime, written by Bill, who took off Cole Porter in a duet with the Commander.*

Left: *The elegant battlecruiser HMS* Hood, *which between the wars had symbolized the whole Royal Navy in ports all round the world.*

Below: *HMS* Alcantara, *armed merchant cruiser.*

Below right: Alcantara*'s FAA contingent, Durban, 1942. Aircrew are (middle row, left to right): PO Stan Brown (observer); Sub-Lieutenant (A) Hosegood, RNVR (pilot); Sub-Lieutenant (A) Wilson, RNVR (observer); PO Freddie Longman, RN (pilot). The two rating pilots were not allowed to fly together and were never briefed before a patrol.*

Left: *Ken Illingworth from Bradford wanted a sleek destroyer, and not a tramp in E-boat Alley; but in the MAC-ship* Acavus *'the aircraft made a difference in my life'.*

Below: *Escort carriers, merchantmen wholly converted to warships, were spacious below decks, especially those built in the USA. Forty-two of these ships were loaned to the Royal Navy.*

Right: *Manning the AA guns on the escort-carrier HMS* Battler. *Note the narrow bridge 'island' and the three Swordfish ranged on the flight deck.*

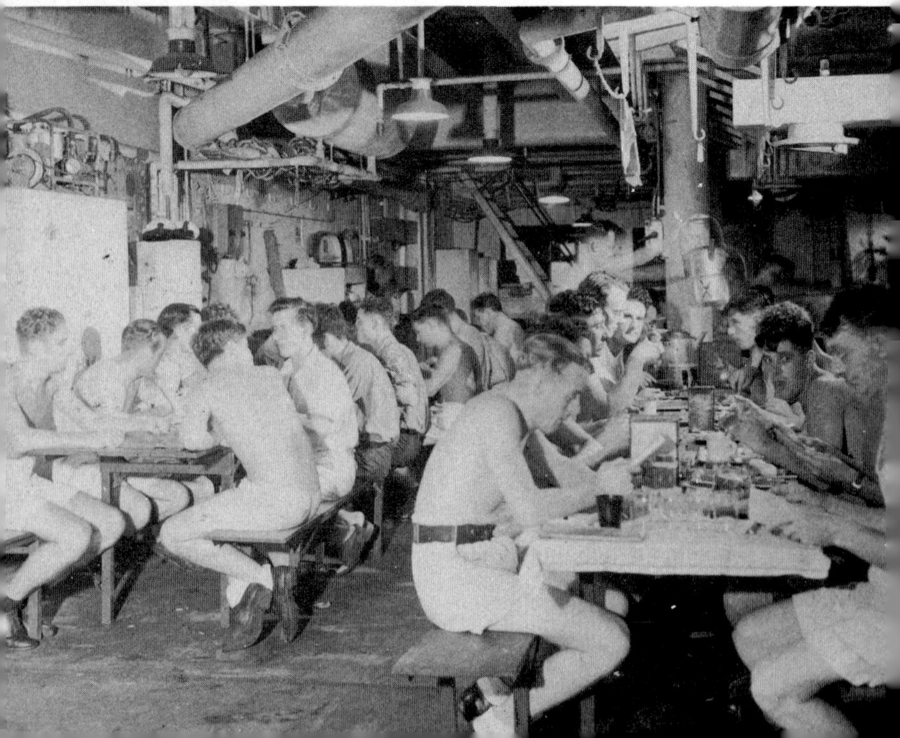

Left: Mick Dale, now a Chief PO, commanded the TAGs of Vindex*'s famous No 825 Squadron. Mick was Tag in Squadron Co Freddie Sheffield's aircraft when it sank* U765 *in the Atlantic, but in his excitement forgot to photograph the event.*

***Right:** The Air Headquarters team in* Vindex*, supplemented by three Air Artificers from No 825 Squadron, invented many effective pieces of hardware, under the command of Lieutenant Molineaux, RNVR. Here among others are Chief PO Charlie Waldram (third from left, back row), armourer Norman Pickup (second from left, back row) and Bill McCall (extreme right, second row).*

***Below right:** Young aircrew are debriefed after a sortie by Commander (Operations).*

Left: Armourers at work on a Fulmar.

Below and top right: *Carrier flight decks allowed far better recreation than other warships. Deck hockey on a US-built escort carrier (note the wooden planked deck). Snowball fighting on* Vindex's *flight deck in northern waters.*

Below right: *Russian sailors are entertained by* Vindex *Air Headquarters staff at the Murmansk terminal of one of her Russian convoy runs.*

Left: *Combined Operator. Isle of Wighter David Satherley wanted 'a sleek destroyer' – and got Combined Operations, but found that 'It was still Navy,' and was proud to wear the badge.*

Below: *The new crew of HM* LCI 127 *were delighted that she 'looked like a real ship', and behaved like one in a hairy crossing from Burmuda to Gibraltar. Note the 'eye-shooting' cap tally bows of real Jack-my-Hearties and the lowered gangway ramp (one of a pair port and starboard from which the troops went ashore).*

60° is not an easy task, but when the manoeuvres were completed we proceeded at maximum speed, away from the boats.

'I was the only operator to receive the lifeboat's SOS on my Marconi receiver, which had a crystal control on 500 kcs, because the lifeboat's transmitter (with a maximum range of 100 miles) was luckily spot-on our listening frequency. None of our officers knew of the *Salopian* by name (not realizing that it was a comparatively recent made-up one). In fact the "SOS" was suspect, the "PSE" (Please) "QSP" not being the normal format for a distress transmission. It was thought that a U-boat, knowing of the approach of a large convoy, had transmitted it on a lifeboat-type transmitter, hoping that radio silence would be broken and give him a D/F bearing. However, our convoy proceeded eastwards without further incident.'

Meanwhile, in *Salopian*'s boats they saw the U-boat's periscope cutting through the water close by them, then there was an explosion in *Salopian* where another torpedo struck her. 'The old ship rocked but still sat there like a duck', Bert Poolman thought. Then yet another tinfish hit her, and she broke in half, both halves stood on end and disappeared together in less than a minute.

The boats and Carley floats drifted for two days. They were all rationed to half a biscuit, an inch-sized cube of corned beef and two half-measures of a small white-enamelled water dipper per day.

'There was nothing to cut up the bully beef on properly,' Bert Poolman remembered after the war, 'only my blessed tray and they used that'. The tray is now in my possession, as is the dipper, and still bears the knife scratches on the back – it is not polished as often as it should be.

On the morning of 15 May Captain Alleyne despatched the motor boat to steer as far south as fuel would permit in the hope of sighting a convoy which he believed was on its way from Halifax. Just as he was losing sight of the boats astern, Lieutenant-Commander Peate in the motor boat sighted a destroyer right ahead. She had also seen them, and soon picked up the survivors. The boat's feeble SOS, picked up so luckily by George Monk in *Empire Confidence*, had been relayed to C-in-C Western Approaches in Liverpool via the Cypher Officer on duty, Second Officer Sheila Isherwood – Bert Poolman's niece. Anxiously she waited for news of survivors, unable to tell the family anything. Destroyers were sent to make an anti-submarine sweep in the area of the attack and look for *Salopian*'s boats. HMS *Icarus*, her fuel running low, was on the last leg of her final broad sweep when she sighted them. She took the survivors to Iceland, and by the time she got there she was down to 12 knots to conserve fuel. Captain Alleyne told his men that he wanted them to march off the ship smartly, and not 'shuffle off like a flock of sheep', as survivors usually did. *Salopian*'s barber gave them all a haircut, and they did their best to look like conquering heroes. Peake spoke to them before they disembarked: 'Men, although we're all very sorry to have lost our ship, don't forget – it will only take 18 months to build another, but it has taken 18 years to build the youngest man here.'

THE *BISMARCK* BATTLE

By this time a far more dangerous predator had been let loose in the North Atlantic.

'The reason I joined the Royal Navy was quite simple and clear-cut,' says Bill Earp. 'I wanted to get out of the environment that kept me and my kind in a world of poverty and low-paid factory work. I had heard many tales about the Navy from my father who served in it from 1917 to 1922, and I resolved to follow in his footsteps as soon as I was old enough to join, which I did, via the Recruitment Office in Birmingham. I found myself in that first cold winter of the war at HMS *St George*, the former Cunningham's Holiday Camp, just outside Douglas, Isle of Man. Training was tough but no tougher than civvy life for me, and, after all, I now had things of my own that had previously been denied to me . . . clothes that fitted, ample food and a chance to be part of something better than factory life, underwear, pyjamas, toothbrush and toothpaste.'

It was not until February 1941 that Bill was fully trained and then, with the other boys, he was drafted to HMS *Suffolk*, a County-class cruiser docked at Glasgow. 'In just over twelve months I had changed my life from a scruffy little factory boy to Boy Seaman on a cruiser – not much you could say, but to me it was. I had discovered a world I never knew existed.

'*Suffolk* towered above us like a huge steel fortress when we boys joined her lying alongside at Glasgow. Our messdeck was right above "A" turret magazine, and the barbette of the turret was in the centre of the mess. On the port side of the messdeck was a small partitioned caboose which was the domain of our betters, the Petty Officers in charge of us, two men completely opposite in appearance and personality. One was a three-badge veteran, like matlow poet Charles Causley's Chief. . . .

. . . older than the naval side of British history . . .
His narrow forehead ruffled by the Jutland wind . . .

. . . always with a melancholy look on his face, tall and lean and a worrier, looking for trouble round every corner, known (behind his back) as "The Dripper", his pet hatred being dripping taps. The other PO was quite a different kind of Pusser's Prefect, a fully fledged Physical Training Instructor, and I *mean* fully fledged, all muscle and some 15 stone, face bearing the marks and scars of a long pugilistic career . . . "If any of yew boys fink yew can come the old sailor wiv me then yew can fink agin, cawse if yew do I'll unship your f★★★★n' 'ead!"

'None of us boys realized just how privileged we were. We had joined just in time to meet the *Bismarck*.

'Even though it was 47 years ago I can still remember most of the things that happened in that caper. From fear I passed to relief (that we were alive) to disbelief (that it had happened at all). My memories are of being extremely cold, tired, hungry and apprehensive, of men trying to make jokes to hide their fear, nervously fingering one's inflatable lifebelt (Mae West), casually inspecting nearby Carley floats, and above all the waiting for something to happen. My Action Station was at Port 1 twin 4in AA gun as a loading number, and I consequently had time to observe the action, as this was very definitely a case for Main Armament, aided, for the first time in a sea battle, by radar, then known as RDF.'

Suffolk, patrolling the Denmark Strait within RAF distance of the ice edge on a line running north-east and south-west, was the first ship of the Home Fleet to sight *Bismarck*, but neither of her radars was responsible. 'One of our Port 1 4in AA gun's crew, Alf "Ginger" Newell, was the duty lookout who first spotted and reported the *Bismarck* and *Prinz Eugen*, and for this received a well-deserved DSM, as did AB Tinkler, our senior radar operator.'

Newell sighted the great battleship at 1922hrs on 23 May at a range of seven miles, which was dangerously close to her eight new 15in guns for *Suffolk*; but the British cruiser was able to turn back into the mist unseen, and Tinkler then picked up *Bismarck* on the 284 gunnery-ranging RDF.

Norfolk, patrolling about 15 miles abeam of *Suffolk*, inshore, with her fixed-beam RDF, hurried to get into contact with the enemy, and also sighted her (at 2032) before obtaining an echo. When she did she was closer still, and *Bismarck* fired on her but she too managed to disengage. For the next 10 hours the two Counties shadowed the German, reporting her position to Admiral Holland, who was steaming up with *Hood*, *Prince of Wales* and six destroyers to engage the enemy. The C-in-C hoped that this force 'may head them off and force them to turn back to the southward'. In spite of the bad visibility prevailing during that anxious night, Holland in *Hood* imposed a rigid radio and radar silence on his group, but at 2 o'clock on the morning of the 24th the cruisers lost touch with the enemy, and he asked *Prince of Wales* to use her 284 set to search an arc for *Bismarck*. When told that this radar would not bear, he refused permission to use the 281, which could pick up an aircraft at 20,000ft from 100 miles, a battleship at 11 miles, and find a range within about 30 yards. Perhaps the Admiral had not made himself acquainted with these potentialities of his new weapon. Tinkler knew, but he was only an Able Seaman, and he was never asked.

At 0535 on 24 May Holland sighted *Bismarck* at 17 miles' range, much further away than his radar, 284 or 281, could have reported her. *Hood* opened fire first, at 26,500 yards, followed almost at once by *Prince of Wales* – and both German ships.

Contrary to popular misconception, of the four nations which developed radar before the Second World War, Britain was the last. Experiments in Germany to develop a radar rangefinder began in 1933, and in 1936 'Seetakt' sets were at sea in *Graf Spee*, the cruiser *Königsberg* and the torpedo boat *G10*, and ranges of 17km were recorded on a large ship, 8km on a cruiser. *Bismarck*'s Seetakt, mounted in front of the main armament director, was principally a rangefinder but had good directional properties as well; it could also be used for warning of the approach of ships. Although it could not spot the fall of shot, *Bismarck* used it to make already superb gunnery even more accurate. *Prince of Wales* got no results from her 284 or 281, her first salvo fell 1,000 yards short, and she took six salvoes to cross the target. But *Bismarck*'s first salvo, perfect for range, fell just ahead of *Hood*; her third salvo hit the great battlecruiser and penetrated a magazine. At 0615 *Norfolk* signalled: 'Hood blown up.'

With little to do, AA gunner Bill Earp 'had a grandstand view of the first action, and I, who was doing a spell as lookout, saw the pall of smoke that rose as the *Hood* was sunk. At the time I did not know who had been hit but learned later when it was broadcast over the ship's Tannoy.

'How our hearts sank and how the news made us more edgy, but even so more determined to avenge *Hood*.' *Prince of Wales* was also badly damaged and forced to turn away under smoke, signalling: 'Bridge out of action. "Y" turret out of action.'

But she had hit *Bismarck*, which was trailing oil. By now British radar had picked up the enemy again, and *Suffolk*, *Norfolk* and *Prince of Wales* continued to shadow her, with Tinkler on *Suffolk*'s 284 mainly responsible for keeping contact, 'until *Bismarck* turned and fired on us. We fired back and took evasive action under a smoke screen. I saw their first salvo straddle us and thought like many others that the next one would have our name on it, but mercifully we were safe in the smoke screen while *Prince of Wales* and *Norfolk* fired back. All this enabled *Prince Eugen* to make her escape.' (The latter was following orders from *Bismarck* to oil from a supply ship and 'engage in cruiser warfare independently'.)

At 2056 *Bismarck* signalled Group West: 'Impossible shake off enemy owing to radar. Proceeding directly to Brest owing to fuel situation.'

Meanwhile, the C-in-C aboard *King George V* with the rest of the Home Fleet was steaming to intercept, and detached *Victorious*, a brand-new carrier, to launch her aircraft, although they were not properly worked-up with her, to try to slow *Bismarck* down.

Just after midnight on 25 May one Swordfish fitted with ASV MkII found her and scored one hit but failed to reduce her speed. Three hours later *Bismarck* altered course south-east, just at the moment when *Suffolk* was turning on to the outward leg of her zigzag, with her radar at that point temporarily out of touch with the enemy. When *Suffolk* swung back on course *Bismarck* was gone from Tinkler's A-scope. *Suffolk* was sent to search to the westward, unaware of the German's change of course, and of course could not find her, nor could any of the hunting ships.

Five fruitless hours later Group West signalled *Bismarck*: 'Last enemy contact report 0213. We have impression contact has been lost.'

An hour later Admiral Raeder, C-in-C of the German Navy, signalled to Admiral Lutjens: 'Heartiest congratulations on your birthday. May you continue to be equally successful in this coming year.'

Five hours later Hitler himself added his best wishes, and *Ark Royal* and *Sheffield* were heading for *Bismarck* to give her a birthday present.

British Direction Finding stations had picked up the *Bismarck* – Group West exchange of signals, and although British cryptographers could not break the code, the position indicated that she was making for France. At 1015 on the 26th *Suffolk* left the scene of the main action under orders to search for the enemy supply ships *Belchen* and *Lothringen*. At 1030 a Coastal Command Catalina flying-boat with ASV MkII signalled: 'One battleship in sight.'

Sheffield was sent on ahead to supplement the shadowing aircraft. At 1115 an *Ark Royal* search Swordfish with ASV signalled: 'One battleship in sight.'

At 1746 the chagrined CO of the Swordfish squadron reported: '11 torpedoes fired at Sheffield.' Thankfully he was able to qualify this with: 'No hits.' However, one aircraft did hit *Sheffield*, but the torpedo was a dud. She signalled to the cruiser: 'Sorry for the kipper.'

At 1954 *Bismarck* was attacked by a second striking force from *Ark Royal*, and at 2015 the German ship reported: 'Ship no longer manoeuvrable. Torpedo hit aft.'

A damaged rudder was sending her round in circles. Destroyers *Zulu*, *Maori* and *Cossack* attacked her with torpedoes, claiming two hits. At 0351 the Führer signalled *Bismarck*'s Gunnery Officer the award of the Knight's Cross 'for the sinking of the battlecruiser *Hood*', but it was a last breakfast for him, and for *Bismarck*. Her destruction was completed by *Rodney*, *King George VI*, and finally by torpedoes from the cruiser *Dorsetshire*. *Suffolk* had no luck hunting the German supply ships, and headed for Newfoundland, low on fuel.

LIFEBOAT TO ST VINCENT

Bert Poolman, survivor from *Salopian*, travelled down to London in the train with the young midshipman, one of only three survivors, from the tragic *Hood*, and realized his own good luck in being alive. *Bismarck* had been sunk, but he thought what might have happened if she had got among the ships of a convoy – 'my blood ran cold'. In fact, at Liverpool they had thought for a time that *Salopian* had run across the path of *Bismarck*, which would have meant another, and swifter *Rawalpindi* or *Jervis Bay*. Bert arrived home, and the first thing he noticed when he walked into the sitting room was the new model I had made of *Hood*, and set on brackets on the wall. 'She's down, son,' he said, 'along with the old *Salopian*.' I stared at the model. I couldn't believe it. My safe little world of models had just crumbled, and a gust of cold Atlantic wind blew across my face.

George Monk was on leave when he saw in his *Daily Mail* the announcement: 'The Admiralty regrets that AMC *Salopian* (Captain Sir John Alleyne) has been sunk by enemy action.'

He was 'gratified to see this report, as it confirmed that the distress signal I had received was genuine. I think that *U98* (Kapitänleutnant Gysae), the submarine that had sunk the *Salopian*, was positioned (with possibly one or two other boats) to intercept the convoy. The unfortunate *Salopian* was seen first and torpedoed. Through her SOS she enabled our convoy to take appropriate action and escape. It could have been a different story if *Salopian* had not been ordered back to Halifax.'

What George could not foresee was that he himself would soon be involved in an adventure more fraught than that of *Salopian*'s crew . . .

'On 13 June 1941 I joined the SS *Auditor* (T & J Harrison, 5,444 tons, Captain E. Bennett). We sailed from the Royal Albert Docks London on 15 June for Capetown, Durban and Indian ports, fully loaded with general cargo and Army stores.

'At Southend we joined a northbound convoy, calling first at Methil before passing round the north of Scotland to Oban. Sailing northward our convoy had just passed Flamborough Head when the ship ahead – a motor ship of Ellerman's – set off an acoustic mine which exploded just under our bows. Fortunately for us the mine was lying in deep water, and although it gave us a severe hammering, it did not damage the hull or the engines. At that time, merchant ships in East Coast convoys were provided with an anti-aircraft balloon; one was delivered to us at Southend and we would fly it to Methil. It was flown just above the top of the foremast, and let out several hundred feet when an air attack was imminent from a large drum attached to a cargo winch, but when the mine exploded, the shaking was so severe it loosened the winch controls, and the balloon rose, literally, to the end of its tether. The Commodore signalled "Stop playing with your balloon."'

The coastal convoy arrived at Oban on 20 June, and the ocean convoy – of some 40 ships – sailed the next day. A week later it dispersed, and the merchantmen then sailed independently to their destinations. Naval Control at Oban had given the Master a route which was to take *Auditor* due south to the Brazilian coast, then across the South Atlantic to Capetown, to steer us away from the U-boat danger area.

'On 4 July – just as the moon was setting, about 2 a.m. – she was torpedoed by *U123* (Kapitän Leutnant Hardegen). A violent explosion near No 4 hold on the port side destroyed No 4 lifeboat. I was asleep at the time the torpedo hit. I quickly put on my clothes and grabbed my "hammer bag" and lifejacket. Making my way to the radio office, which was on the boat deck aft of the funnel, I found my Chief was already there and had started sending our distress message: "SSSS SSSS SSSS *Auditor*. 25.47N 28.23W. Torpedoed."

'The emergency spark transmitter was being used, as the ship's power supply had been lost. The radio office had emergency lighting, but I could see that it was a shambles. Fortunately the emergency transmitter was in working order and the aerial intact. My Chief called out, "Get the lifeboat transmitter into No 1 boat – I'll carry on here." I left and made my way to No 1 boat station under the bridge.

'When I got to the boat deck I saw Captain Bennett who had dressed in his shore clothes (he was worried about being taken prisoner by the U-boat). He called, "Go and get your Chief – she's going fast." I lowered the emergency transmitter into No 1 boat. By this time – about 7 minutes after the explosion – my eyes had become accustomed to the darkness, and it was a clear night with stars shining brightly, I was able to move around the ship easily. When I got to the radio office I found that my Chief was still transmitting our distress signal. He asked me to get his coat from his room which was on a lower deck. This I did, and when I got there I could hear the sea pouring into the engine room below, just like the sound of a large waterfall. On returning to the radio office, we checked that the code books had been thrown overboard, and then made our way to the bridge deck.

'The only lifeboat still alongside was No 1 – the Captain's. I went down the rope ladder, followed by my Chief and the Captain. The boat rope was cut, and we pulled away. When about 80 yards off, and about 15 minutes after the torpedo hit, the *Auditor*'s bow rose up until vertical, then she sank slowly into the Cape

Verde Basin – some 3,000 fathoms below. Besides wreckage floating around, all that was left of a fine ship were a number of large crates (deck cargo), and the three boats.

'A little later the sound of diesels was heard. It was the *U123* cruising around. Obviously, Hardegen wanted to make sure that *Auditor* had sunk; he did not contact us.

'There were 23 survivors in the Captain's boat, including the Chief Engineer, Chief Steward, Third Officer, Chief Radio Officer (my Chief), myself, one AB, one Gunner and fifteen Lascars. Nothing could be done until daylight, except to keep in touch with the other two boats. As our boat was leaking it was necessary to bail continuously.

'At sunrise on Friday, stocks were taken of our provisions and these were found to be: 1½ kegs of water (about 9 gallons), 1 case of small tins of condensed milk, and a large quantity of hard ship's biscuits. The daily ration was: ½ dipper of water (3 fluid ounces), 1 spoonful of condensed milk, 1 biscuit. Later the three boats closed. As we were in the zone of the north-east trade winds, there was a stiff breeze blowing, with a choppy sea. It was difficult for the boats to keep together, and they were riding to sea anchors.

'A decision had to be made – what lands or islands should we make for, bearing in mind the prevailing winds and currents. We had no Atlantic charts, the only navigational aid in each boat being a compass. For many years prior to the war, I used to buy a pocket Shipping Diary; when in London in December 1940 I got one for 1941, and had it in my coat. Many times in the past I had seen a couple of pages giving the latitude and longitude of ports, and when I looked at this section it gave the co-ordinates for St Vincent – the port of the Cape Verde Islands. As I had my pay book as well, I was able to draw a chart and lay off a course to St Vincent which was 580 miles SSE of our present position. With this information, these islands were the obvious choice for a landfall, and so the officers worked out a course for each boat to steer. The estimated time for the voyage was 11 to 12 days. However, a factor which greatly influenced the decision was – the islands were mountainous. Captain Bennett had visited St Vincent many years ago, and remembered that these mountains were very high, around 6,000 ft to 9,000 ft, and therefore could be seen from a great distance, perhaps 40 miles or more. If they had been low-lying the decision would have been, no doubt, to set course for the NE coast of South America – some 1,700 miles distant with a voyage of around 21+ days. At the Ocean Convoy Conference in Oban, the Naval Control Officer had advised all Masters, "If you are sunk and your distress message and position has been sent and acknowledged, then do not attempt any long distance lifeboat voyage. There is always a naval vessel within 2 days' sailing distance from your position – so just WAIT – and you will be rescued." My Chief, who was with Captain Bennett at the conference, confirmed that this was the instruction given.

'So we waited, through Friday and Saturday, drifting westwards. Captain Bennett was adamant that we must wait, as it was a Naval Control instruction. By Saturday evening the officers "rebelled" and said that as our provisions were limited "Let's get sailing." So it was agreed that if no ship had been sighted by Sunday morning, the boats would set sail independently for St Vincent. During these two days the lifeboat transmitter was used to send distress messages at regular times.

'Early Sunday morning the sea anchors were hauled in and each boat set sail. By sunset the Chief Officer's boat was well ahead, and the Second Officer's boat was hull-down astern of us. The NE trade winds were blowing steadily, and our speed was estimated at 2½ to 3 knots. The boat was sailing well, but a good lookout could only be maintained when we rode the crest of the swell.

'By Monday morning the other boats were out of sight. It was fine weather, and during the day it became very warm; some of the crew were already suffering from sun-burn. At night it was very cold. As the boat was still taking in water it was essential to bail frequently, but during the day we would sit with our feet in water in the hope that our bodies might absorb some moisture this way. Steering the boat was the main task of Captain Bennett and the Third Officer; occasionally the other officers would relieve them. Steering at night was difficult as there was no light in the compass. Lifejacket lights were used to check the course, but mainly we steered by the moon and stars.

'During the next three days the weather was fine with fleecy clouds and a strong breeze. At times the sea became choppy, which reduced our speed. When in the valley of a swell, one could look up at the sides of it and see many varieties of fish swimming above the level of the boat. In this area the sea was a marvellous colour and so clear but, of course, undrinkable.

'On Friday – the 8th day – the Master estimated that at dawn we had made some 300 miles since setting sail. It was cloudy, and during the morning there was a light rain shower. The inside cover of the transmitter was used to collect some of the spots of rain, and was licked dry. Thirst was a great problem and Captain Bennett increased our water ration to two half-dippers a day. On this basis our stocks should last for another seven days. If our present speed could be maintained, one of the islands should be sighted before the water was exhausted. Ship's biscuits provided for lifeboat use were a disaster, being so dry and hard that no one could eat them. The only food that could be eaten was condensed milk, and the ration of this was increased to two spoonfuls a day. Unfortunately, the Third Officer, who was unwell when we took to the boats, became delirious.

'Monday – 11th day. During the previous three days the weather had been good, and fortunately we had remained in the zone of the NE trades, which enabled us to maintain a steady speed in spite of the heavy swell. Captain Bennett estimated that by dawn we had sailed about 550 miles, an average speed of 2½ knots. As we were obviously getting near the islands, we again transmitted distress signals at regular times. In the late afternoon a bird was sighted. Land must be near.

'Tuesday – 12th day. It was cloudy, and the men who were on lookout at dawn thought that there was a grey smudge on the horizon on our port beam. Could it be land? If so, then we were 40 or more miles off course. The effects of wind and current must have been greater than was estimated. This smudge was watched by all of us for at least half an hour to see if there was any movement – like a cloud. It did not move – so it must be one of the islands. The course was now altered to east-north-east, and we met headwinds, which meant frequent tacking. This gave us problems straight away; the sea was choppy with quite a swell running. The heel of the mast broke shortly after the course had been altered. It was repaired but broke again in the forenoon and afternoon. On all occasions it was repaired to the best of our ability, but with no tools available – except a knife – it was difficult to make a good job. Due to the stiff breeze the boat was getting a severe pounding, but luckily the mast stays held. When tacking we shipped a lot of water, and so it was all hands to bailing. Headway was made, and as the day wore on the island became larger, but at sunset we were still some 20 miles from it.

'Wednesday – 13th day. I was at the tiller for the first watch; the light of a lighthouse was seen and this helped in maintaining a course, but the wind was dropping as we came into the lee of the island. Later, when about 8 miles from the shore, the Master said "Hold her there." It was not wise to get too close to the shore until we could see what it was like. When dawn broke we could make out the layout of the island. It looked very menacing. The steep rocky cliffs came down to the sea, with no place to land. As the sun rose behind the mountains it began to get very warm, and the wind dropped completely. It was now time to get out the oars and row, and as the cliffs looked less steep to the south, that was the way we headed. Every man took turn at the oars, but it was hot and very tiring, particularly as we had not eaten anything substantial for almost thirteen days. After rowing for three hours there appeared some colours on the mountain side, and these turned out to be small houses. A little later we saw two boats making for us; they had brought out two carafes of fresh water. How good it tasted! The boats – manned by fishermen – took our ropes and towed us for the last two miles to the village of Tarrafal on the island of Santo Antao!'

SING FOR YOUR SUPPER

There was little respite for the overworked cruisers and destroyers of the Home Fleet, but in the summer of 1942 *Suffolk*, whose Able Seaman Tinkler had been solely responsible for holding *Bismarck* in the hunters' net, was sent to the Tyne for repairs, which meant leave.

'This was great for morale,' says gunner Bill Earp, 'but had one drawback – one needed money to enjoy the run ashore, and Naval pay for junior ratings was hardly adequate to ensure liquidity both financially and alcoholically. However, the Lord provides and helps them that help themselves. One of my oppos was the Padre's Comforts Fund Stores Sweeper and had access to its contents – an Aladdin's Cave of Navy blue knitted garments supplied by the good women of Britain. There was no shortage of customers, the dockyard mateys took all we could supply, socks, gloves, scarves, at one and sixpence a pair, each sale equal to at least three halves of best bitter. When we were back at sea the Padre was at a loss to understand why we had so few socks, gloves and scarves but so many balaclavas.

'Another method of raising funds was my natural ability for mimicry. As a member of the ship's concert party, I had the chance to improve my repertoire and put it to good use in the talent competitions in the pubs round the dock area. My impressions of Churchill, Roosevelt and Hitler always went down well. One of my oppos was my manager, who organized my turns in the pubs which did this sort of thing, and also led the applause, which almost every time ensured that I got a money prize. He also organized the share-out of the prize money, and the beer it could buy for our little band of mates.

'Not all enterprises were successful however. One unfortunate rating was caught red-handed sneaking through the dockyard with a large side of bacon slung over his shoulder en route to making a sale. He was sentenced to 90 days' detention for his pains, and as well as I can remember the side of bacon was charged with breaking out of ship and was sentenced to provide wardroom breakfast for a week.

'Spare blankets were also a good commodity for sale, and many of them found their way on to dockyard mateys' beds. Tinned food was a popular item. Removing it from the stores was a work of art. If dockyard workmen were required to work in these stores, then it was customary to provide a sentry to supervise this, and he would tip off his oppo who would go down to the stores with a half-full bucket of dirty water and place a few tins of food in the bucket, which raised the level of the water and at the same time concealed the tins in question. If asked what he had been doing he would say that he had been sent down to mop up some water that was on the stores deck.'

In the ship's pantomime Bill and the Commander performed a version of Cole Porter's 'You're the Top', rewritten by Bill:

You're the Top, you're a real old Caulker,
You're the Top, you're a Matthew Walker,
You're a Forward Guy, a Thimble Eye, in rope,
You're a Chain Check Stopper, a Wash Deck Locker,
You're Pusser's Soap,
You're the Top, you're the Hook-a-Cockbill,
You're the trial of the whole damn Watch Bill,
You're a Leatherneck on the Quarter Deck with Band,
You're a Jaunty's Runner, a Dagger Gunner,
You're Duty Hand. etc . . .
But if, Baby, I'm the Fo'c'sle, you're the Top!

THE MEDITERRANEAN SHUTTLE

The old *Adventure* kept up a shuttle between Mediterranean ports. Bunting-tosser Geoff Shaw made occasional entries in his diary:

'Jan 1943. A Beaufighter, flying past us, crashed into the sea. The whaler was sent away to see if we could recover any bodies with me, as duty signalman, in it. There were plenty of bits of wreckage floating about including a complete wheel and we did find one body which the subby and I pulled inboard. It was in quite a state. Upper body still wearing tunic (he was a sergeant pilot), lower body from waist down completely skinned so that all his muscles and ligaments were showing, and head cut off. The subby covered it with his duffle coat and told me to send to the ship, "Have recovered one decapitated body. Am continuing search." Somehow I managed, though standing in a heaving boat, one foot on each side of the body, trying to keep my balance and trying to keep out of the way of the cox'n and stroke oar; wasn't at all like sending semaphore in the relative comfort of the drill shed at the training ship. Eventually we went back to the ship where I found to my consternation that instead of being hoisted back on to the ship with the whaler, I had to climb a flaming rope, trying to clutch my hand flags in one hand because the Chief Yeoman would have played up hell if I had dropped them in the 'oggin.'

'April 10th 1943. On our way back from Gib, shadowed by a Focke-Wulf all forenoon which left us at lunch time, having reported our position to U-boats ahead. To avoid the U-boats the skipper decided to alter course but in towards the Bay of Biscay rather than the obvious move of out into the Atlantic. As a result, later that afternoon, we sighted a ship at about seventeen miles which, when we closed it, turned out to be a blockade-breaker. She eventually scuttled herself and we captured the crew. The irony was that we only managed to get that ship through trying to avoid trouble, while had we sailed at our proper time – twelve hours earlier – we would have missed her completely. (The skipper had asked, and received, permission for us to spend the night in Gib so that one watch of the lads could have a run ashore.) The blockade-breaker had come all the way from Japan, across the Pacific and Atlantic Oceans without being seen. They must then have been just a few hours' sailing time from the German naval bases in western France. How galling it must have been to them that after all that long trip they were captured by a rickety old ship that was only trying to dodge U-boats and that the next morning, instead of packing their suitcases to go home on leave, they should find themselves en route to a PoW camp.'

Wings at Sea

Young Joseph Soap to the war has gone,
In a Stringbag you will find him,
A big propeller clonking round in front,
And his O and his TAG behind him,
Chorus: R/Ps, D/Cs, RATOG too,
Were all made to confuse us,
We're only waiting for our demob suit,
Which no one can refuse us!

A WALRUS AND THE *ALBATROSS*

In December 1941 Mick Dale, who had struggled through a TAG's course and, with Alan Todd, flown in the hands of Lieutenants (A) L. Olivier and R. Richardson, RNVR, joined No 710 Squadron to fly in 'Walri' from the seaplane-carrier *Albatross*, based at Freetown, West Africa . . .

The land of the violet lightning and the
  thunderstorms of sheet iron,
The hills, rich and bursting with the
  brown and orange of Gauguin . . .

with periods at RNAS Hastings nearby, then just a few huts and a dirt track, and spent 'half our time there flying, the other half laid out with malaria . . .'

'We flew daily anti-submarine patrols from the harbour, with an occasional sortie in a Swordfish up the coast to Conakry to see if any subs were alongside.' *Albatross* had been built in Australia for the Royal Australian Navy in which she served from 1928 until transferred to the RN in September 1938. Although originally fitted with a catapult she now operated her Walrus by lowering them over the side on a crane for take-off from the water. As a TAG, Mick Dale's job was 'to sit on the top wing and unshackle the Walrus when we were in the water, then climb down inside, ready for take-off. Once airborne we maintained radio contact with the ship and looked out for U-boats, etc. On our return we taxied up to the ship, and the TAG climbed back on to the top wing and hooked on again to the ship's crane. If we missed we had to go round and try again. With the prop spinning round a few inches from our heads, this could be a slightly dodgy operation!

'We were once beaten up by one of our own subs. I never found out what exactly happened, but there was an almighty bang, our prop disintegrated, and we had to ditch. The sub had taken a pot-shot at us, but nothing was said officially.

'On another occasion we flew into a tropical squall and had to come down and beach the aircraft on a tropical island. It was two rain-lashed days – without Dorothy Lamour – before we could take off again. A couple more times we came down, out of fuel or gremlin-struck, and had to be ignominiously towed back to Freetown by corvettes or merchant ships – I got rather a reputation as a Jonah after a while.'

In January 1941 a 'Sub Attack' signal was picked up by *Albatross*. The routine dawn patrol aircraft was contacted but was unable to divert to the position, 110 miles west of Freetown, for lack of fuel, so Lieutenant Cheeseman, with PO Knowles as Observer and Dale as TAG, was 'rousted out in a hurry', observes the latter, 'and we took off to see if we could find out what was going on.

'We searched the area and eventually spotted men in the water, some swimming, some hanging on to rafts or floating debris – all that remained of the SS *Eummaeus*, which had been torpedoed. We chucked our inflatable dinghy out of the after hatch, radioed our position and circled around for a while. Then we spotted an empty lifeboat a mile or so away from the men in the water. We landed, in a heavy swell, secured the lifeboat, and towed it back to the main group of survivors.

'The Walrus by now was a bit battered, and there was no chance of taking off, so we did what we could to help the survivors until two trawlers arrived to pick them up. One of them took us in tow, and we had quite a rough ride back! We'd been "adrift" for about 22 hours. Lieutenant Cheeseman was awarded an MBE, and, for some reason, I got a BEM, though I really hadn't done anything to deserve it.'

A rating pilot in *Albatross*, ex-Writer Jack Francis Smith, was afterwards commissioned, and landed an unusual job, especially for a new sub-lieutenant, of vetting pilots who had been grounded for various reasons, some of them for 'Lack of Moral Fibre' (the dreaded LMF, which was stamped all over the sufferer's papers, and of which the FAA sometimes made very free). He flew with them, 'discussed at length what had gone wrong, and was required to recommend their future employment,' in liaison with the Air Medical School.

AMC Flights

Some AMCs were refitted and armed with catapults to operate aircraft. HMSs *Canton* and *Pretoria Castle* were each equipped in the summer of 1941 with two Fairey Seafox seaplanes – the type which had served so well at the Battle of the River Plate, flying from *Ajax*. Each ship's Flight included two pilots, two observers and some eight maintenance ratings under an air artificer, all from the Fleet Air Arm.

PO Pilot Doug Elliott in *Pretoria Castle* had been educated at the City of Bath School, passed his Higher School Certificate and tried to get into banking or insurance, but it was 1932, and eventually he joined the Navy. In China with the gunboat *Cockchafer* he read the Rating Pilot AFO, and after training at Short's and at Netheravon won his RAF wings in April 1939.

This was followed by purely Naval Aviation training, during which any rating pilot who failed any of the qualifications was sent right back to General Service, while an officer was allowed a re-scrub. This was potentially a stupid and scandalous waste of an expensive flying course; the father of one 'dipped' rating pilot contacted his MP, who complained at high level, with the result that shortly afterwards a dipped candidate was given the option of joining the RAF, where several of them achieved Squadron-Leader status and above.

In *Pretoria Castle*, says Doug, 'not once was I ever called aft for a briefing, which was held in the officers' quarters somewhere. I never had a clear picture of any operation I was on, the time of the attack, the Mean Line of Advance of the ship, or anything. The best I could hope for was to scribble any information I could squeeze out of the observer on my knee pad'. His accommodation, however, was above his station. 'For a petty officer to have a large ship-side cabin (with a scuttle), hot and cold running water, and capacious wardrobe, was unheard of, and many destroyer captains would gladly have swapped cabins with me.'

Other AMCs were equipped with aircraft during refit, including the South American Station stalwarts *Alcantara*, *Asturias*, *Carnarvon Castle* and *Queen of Bermuda*.

Freddie Longman from Potter's Bar, who had got his rating pilot's wings just before war broke out, was drafted to the *Alcantara*.

'I shared a cabin with my oppo, the PO observer, and we had our own bathroom attached. But AMCs were divided ships. The engine room staff, stewards and one or two others were MN, serving under the T124X scheme, which basically gave them twice as much pay as similar RN rates. The wardroom steward received danger money for being at sea in a war zone. We didn't. This anomaly did not make for a happy ship.

'We also had, as I think most other AMCs did, a CO brought back from retirement to captain the ship. During the whole time I was on board *Alcantara* I never met him.

'The ship's company were never told *anything*, like where we were going or why we suddenly went to Action Stations and then stood down. We only heard buzzes.

'Many senior naval aviators were very much against the rating pilot scheme ever starting, and many rules and regulations were drawn up to make sure that the rating pilot was kept in his place. Wings, for instance, were at first worn on the right arm as a non-substantive badge by Leading Air and Petty Officer Air Pilots. When made Chief their wings were moved to the right cuff. PO pilots were not allowed in TBR squadrons as it was considered that they were not qualified to make tactical decisions.' (Petty Officer Pilot Charles Wines, the only rating pilot to drop a torpedo in action, on an anti-shipping strike from Malta, saw a memorandum stating that the Lower Deck aviators lacked 'the moral fibre' to make a close torpedo attack.)

'In the RN,' Longman continues, 'the senior officer in an aircrew was always the Captain of the Aircraft. Therefore in AMCs, where two RNVR sub-lieutenants and two POs were the aircrew for the two aircraft, the subby pilot always flew with the PO observer. I was treated by my observer in the same way as the coxswain of the motor boat. My job, when the aircraft was required for A/S patrol or anything else, was to go on deck, carry out a pre-flight inspection of the aircraft, make sure the bomb load was correct, make sure the Catapult Officer knew the all-up weight, discuss with the senior maintenance rating any snags, sign the 700 and we were ready.

'In the meantime my observer had been up to the bridge for a briefing and met report, and then came down to the aircraft to take charge. I had no idea where we were going or what we had to do until I got the first course to steer, and my "O" gave me no further information.' On all flights, like Doug Elliott, Longman 'took the precaution of jotting down on my knee-pad courses steered, time on each course and my own estimate of wind-speed and direction, plus the last course I had seen the ship on, and estimated speed. If my "O" were killed on a flight, my only hope of survival was a quick look at my jottings and a guess at a course back to the ship. Our only communication was by W/T, and of course all the radio gear was in the back cockpit out of my reach. I was never invited to the bridge for a briefing or after a flight for a de-briefing. Only in fighter squadrons with Skuas did a PO pilot and a PO or LA TAG fly as a crew.'

Alcantara had returned to Britain after her refit at Newport News, Virginia, when her catapult was installed, and resumed her old South Atlantic patrol work.

The 7,160-ton Liberty Ship *George Clymer* was a few hundred miles from Ascension Island on 30 May 1942, when her main shaft broke down. She sent out an SOS. Ascension had no aircraft available, and C-in-C South Atlantic sent *Alcantara*.

George Clymer drifted. At 2000hrs she was hit by a torpedo from the disguised raider *Michel*'s special motor boat *Esau*. *Alcantara* arrived at 4 o'clock that afternoon and got her towing hawser out, but *Clymer*'s deckload of wooden railway sleepers and tractors for Iran made her an almost impossible tow. The AMC struggled on for a week, awaiting instructions from the Admiralty, and eventually orders came to sink *Clymer*.

The Seafox had first crack, on 11 June. 'I scored two direct hits,' reported Freddie Longman, 'but my little 100lb bombs made no impression, just exploded on her deck cargo of thick wooden sleepers. We next carried out a shoot with our main armament of very ancient 6in guns, but I don't think the shells even scarred her. The next bright idea was to depth-charge her, so we steamed at our best speed of about 15 knots as close as we dared and fired two DCs from our port throwers over towards her. I wouldn't like to guess whether they dropped nearer us or her, but she did shudder and turn upside down, so now we had about three inches of black keel sticking above the water, kept afloat very efficiently by wooden railway sleepers, and this is how we left her, while aboard *Alcantara* the engine room staff were going mad, as we had blown the port stern gland.'

LOST FROM *INDOMITABLE*

The ocean was a wide and lonely place. In October 1942 TAG Ben Kennedy was working up with No 800 Squadron in the Fleet carrier *Indomitable* in mid-Atlantic when the Fulmar he was in ran out of fuel.

'Sub-Lieutenant Lucas brought her down beautifully in the trough of a 20-foot breaking Atlantic swell. As she tipped I grabbed the Very pistol and compass, and together we struck out for the dinghy which had successfully inflated automatically. As we settled in, the other aircraft flew very low overhead and made off. They were not seen again.

'The first impression was of absolute silence except for the breaking waves. To give myself something to do I set up a lookout routine – an all-round sweep from the crests of waves followed by a rest period. I was very wet, of course, and tired, but I do not remember being particularly cold. After dark I dozed, and dreamed of home, girls, rescue by U-boat – but never that the ship was looking for us. I was not afraid – I don't know why – just very lonely and hungry. Mike was very still and quiet. A fish flapped into the dinghy. Very stupidly I threw it back over the side.

'The following day the sea moderated a little and the sun came out – I became desperately hungry and opened the ration pack to find it empty except for a tin of condensed milk, which was academic as we had nothing to open it with. During the afternoon I heard an aircraft but didn't see it. Later it came back – an Albacore – I fired my Verys and very nearly shot myself. The aircraft seemed to pass over but in fact had seen us and, maintaining radio silence, had flown back to the ship to tell them. On its return it flew so low over us its trailing aerial nearly hit us. We were picked up two hours later by the ship's seaboat.

'This incident changed my attitude to flying. Not at first, but gradually I became fearful of losing sight of the ship, and then of flying itself. It took more courage to own up to this than I possessed, so I suffered for the duration of my flying career. Still do, for that matter.'

MAC SHIPS

Ken Illingworth started as a clerk in the Electricity Department at the Town Hall in Bradford, Yorkshire, and worked there for three years before he joined the Andrew. He was a keen sportsman, a well-known figure on the soccer and cricket fields, the track and at swimming galas. He always spent most of the family holidays wandering around the port area, and went on pleasure cruises and fishing trips in small vessels. He loved a choppy sea, often to be met off Flamborough Head. He was a natural for a seagoing life, and it was not long after war broke out that he found himself a Convoy Signalman. This was a disappointment at the time – sailor Ken had always seen himself on the signal deck of a sleek and rugged convoy destroyer. But winter at Butlin's, Skegness, 1941–2, was bitter, producing chilblains on hands and feet, and he was glad to get to sea (vowing never to go to a holiday camp when he returned to civilian life, a promise he has kept faithfully – no Hi-di-Hi! for the Illingworths).

He was drafted to East Coast convoys based at Southend, where he managed to get in some cricket, made possible by bat-and-ball fanatic Lieutenant-Commander Gurney Braithwaite (later an MP), 'who did a U turn when the buzz came to his ears that RN cricketers could count on being permanent at breezy Southend – and promptly got the whole cricket team drafted to Liverpool for disposal'.

Hoping wistfully for a change from merchant ships, Ken was drafted to the MV *Acavus*. Learning that she was a tanker of the Anglo-Saxon Petroleum Company, he became confused when told that she was also something called a Merchant Aircraft Carrier. This was a type of ship, tanker or grainer, quite distinct from the Escort or 'Woolworth' carrier (which was wholly converted to a carrier); the MAC ship carried its original cargo, plus a flight deck and three or four Swordish.

'We still flew the Red Duster, but we could be a fighting ship if needed. I joined her at Falmouth, where she was still being converted, and we sailed with our first convoy in October 1943.

'The aircraft made a difference to my life, with all the excitement of take-offs and landings, which were a bit like the old Hendon air shows to us. We cheered the old "Stringbags" as they lumbered into the air, always perilously close to the bows, and our hearts were with them as they disappeared into the cloudy sky on their weary, lonely patrols over the endless ocean. Other MAC ships saw some action, or their planes did, in duels with U-boats, with the slow old Swordfish usually getting the worst of it, as at this time the German subs bristled with guns to fight it out on the surface.

'We never sank a U-boat, never even saw one, but we kept a lot of heads down. No convoy with a MAC in it ever lost a ship. When *Acavus* was converted, sword into ploughshare, back into her old form she gave good service as the *Iacra*, running to the Persian Gulf, and was actually the last of the old Anglo-Saxon (by then the Shell Company) tankers to go to the knacker's yard, being scrapped in 1963.'

The ex-merchant escort carriers, which flew the White Ensign, saw service all over the world, from Murmansk to Okinawa.

INVENTIVE *VINDEX*

Bill McCall remembers clearly how the sirens sounding over Edinburgh on Sunday, 3 September 1939, 'threw everyone into a bit of a panic'.

'The war, of course, had been expected, and my friends and I had discussed it in great detail, and I had decided that the Navy appealed to me as being about the furthest from what I was doing as an apprentice sheet metal worker in a factory. After a long wait I was accepted and told that as a sheet metal worker I could be an Air Fitter (Airframe) in the Fleet Air Arm. I hadn't a clue what that meant, but I was eager to do my bit and off I went to Guz Barracks, much to the surprise and alarm of my parents, as I had not told them about joining the Andrew. After they had recovered I think they were very proud of me. My employer was none too pleased but he couldn't say anything without looking unpatriotic, and I became FX77206.

'After the shock of square-bashing I started to enjoy the life. At that stage I remember a small man in some sort of uniform with a somewhat short neck coming to inspect us, as we were a novelty, the first of the volunteers. Somebody said, "That's Winston", which it was, in his Trinity House costume. I came to like the life so much that I transferred from HO to Active Service, and signed on for twelve. Everyone thought I was mad, but it turned out to be the best decision I ever made. I was promoted to Aircraft Artificer, and after five months with No 836 Squadron, Maydown, Northern Ireland, which supplied all the Swordfish to the MACs, I got my first sea draft, to the escort carrier *Vindex*.

'Most of the RN escort carriers were on loan from the Yanks, but *Vindex* was one of the five converted in the UK. The British conversions were very different from the American. The Yankee boats had short, wide flight decks of Oregon pine, *Vindex*'s was long and narrow and made of steel. They (the American ships) had a lot of openings in the sides of the hangar, whereas ours was a closed box forming a strength girder. They might have been all right for the Pacific, but we were built for the rough Atlantic and the Norwegian and Barents Sea, where we worked until VE-Day.

'I looked after the Stringbags and the Sea Hurricane fighters of the famous 825 Squadron, which had attacked the *Bismarck* – in which our Commander (F), Percy "Press-on" Gick had flown.

'*Vindex* became famous in the FAA for her technical inventions. The flight deck had to be lit, but not too brightly. I was detailed to produce about 40 shades to allow a slit of light to penetrate on to the flight deck. One of the T124X Engineering Officers laid a cable with lamp bulb sockets down each side of the deck. I then made a series of shades approximately one foot wide which were hinged to allow bulbs to be changed but also allowed about one to two inches of light on the deck, which, with the deck coaming, it was reckoned could not be seen by the enemy even when the deck rolled. The system was successful and gave the pilots a little assistance.'

Chief PO Charlie Waldram, in charge of the electrical staff, put together a pair of illuminated 'bats' to aid night landing, based on some electrical conduit, reflectors from the lighting in the 'heads', and an aircraft dimmer switch; and he and armourer Norman Pickup fitted an illuminated target disc on the windscreen of each Swordfish to help the pilot aim the aircraft in the dark. Another useful mod they made was a repositioning of all the switches in the Swordfish cockpits from the starboard side to the front, to avoid finger trouble.

Serving in No 825 Squadron aboard *Vindex* was a familiar character, Mick Dale, now a Chief PO and in charge of all the squadron's TAGs, his face still yellow from the malaria he had contracted in *Albatross* at Freetown. He had joined No 825 at Thorney Island in January 1943 as a newly made-up Temporary Acting Petty Officer, and it was quite an ordeal for him. 'Not only was I in charge of other TAGs for the first time, but this particular outfit was already famous for the Channel affair, and, to make my ride even rougher, my TAGs made no secret of the fact that they missed my predecessor, the famous Les "Ginger" Sayer, who had flown with Percy Gick against the *Bismarck*.'

Had he but known it, Les Sayer had himself had a tricky time to begin with. A diary entry of his reads: 'So now I am PO I/C TAGS 825 Sqdn HMS *Ark Royal* . . . most of the TAGs are wartime conscripts or volunteers – I find I have a chemist, an insurance agent, a gas meter collector, a window cleaner, a gentleman

Scottish farmer. Lt-Cdr Esmonde is the CO. He doesn't talk a lot, even less to the TAGs. But he supports me to the hilt in whatever I decide to be right for TAGs, and I have already made up my mind that the old naval disciplines are not going to get the best out of these raw recruits who have come from all walks of life . . .' Later he was able to write, 'We have quickly become a team, with a degree of trust in each other which I found very rewarding.'

'Odious comparisons soon faded,' Mick Dale later reported. He 'struck up a close friendship with Dave Todd,' Ginger Sayer's 'gentleman Scottish farmer', 'whose big, clumsy-looking hands could tie the most intricate trout flies,' and with Londoner Joe Palmer, 'a breezy character who was wont to give officers a friendly hug and a "Wotcher, mate!"'

At 2048 on 24 April 1944 *Vindex* weighed from Moville, Northern Ireland, for operations in the Atlantic against U-boats.

At 0518 on the 28th the Asdic operator in the sloop *Bickerton* reported 'Contact firm, classified submarine', and the sloops began an attack with a 26-charge pattern. As the last charge was exploding, the 750-ton *U765* broke surface half a mile away and wallowed, engines stopped. The hunters could see 'the twisted, buckled plating of the U-boat's conning tower', and the three sloops opened up on the enemy.

Sheffield, Vallely and Dale saw the U-boat about a mile on their port beam. Sheffield opened up to full throttle and turned his Swordfish towards her. At 100 yards he dived to attack through mingled fire from the escorts and a weak defensive fire from the U-boat's ack-ack, which nevertheless damaged his centre-section and starboard mainplane.

Coming down at 120 knots on the submarine's port bow, he released his DCs at 75 feet. Dale 'saw them straddle the conning tower, 40 feet apart, one exploding under the conning tower, one close to the U-boat's starboard quarter, just abaft the conning tower. Some 30–45 seconds later the sub broke in two, bow and stern each rising to 45 degrees, and the two halves sank, leaving a dozen survivors in the sea. Two of them waved at us as we flew low over them.'

Swordfish 'V' landed aboard *Vindex* at 6.43. 'As the flight deck man released the deck hook from the arrester wire, Commander (O) Stovin-Bradford rushed across to the aircraft and asked me for my camera, and a man from the photographic section stood by to rush the film down below for developing. I had to tell him that in the excitement of the action I had completely forgotten all about taking pictures for evidence . . .'

‘A Hunting We Will Go’

In the Atlantic the U-boats were getting a hammering. ‘The Brits were getting cheeky these days. You couldn’t feel safe anywhere, not even inside our own approach buoys,’ says Lothar-Günther Buchheim in *Das Boot* (The Boat). Anyone who served in the corvettes, taut sloops, sweepers or CVEs (escort carriers), ‘the little ships that Churchill clean forgot’, in the steep Atlantic stream, the freezing runs to Russia or the angry North Sea, when a ship would stand on her screws and roll her decks under, can call himself a sailor. But even smaller vessels were now braving the rough northern seas.

Combined Operation

David Satherley was an Isle of Wighter, ‘so ships of the pre-war fleet coming and going round Spithead and the Solent were well known to me, plus my sister married a Chief Shipwright, and I spent my holidays in Pompey and knew the dockyard and Pompey-based warships as well as teenagers today know pop stars. My favourite reading was the lives of Drake and Nelson, so you can say I was a hopeless case. I wanted to be a boy seaman at HMS *St Vincent* but my parents insisted on a trade. I was indentured to a printer’s and publisher’s at Cowes, and sat at a desk overlooking the Solent miserably watching destroyers and subs sailing by and “Stringbag” Swordfish from Lee-on-Solent dropping dummy torpedoes. War is a terrible thing but I actually did cartwheels when it began as I saw now nothing could stop my joining the Navy.

‘I was informed that as we did work for flying-boat makers Saunders-Roe and J. S. White, shipbuilders, I was in a Reserved Occupation. J. S. White had built a long string of destroyers for the Navy . . . *Vampire, Vortigern, Westcott, Winchelsea, Forester* and *Fury, Keith* and *Kempenfelt, Impulsive, Intrepid, Jersey* and *Kingston* . . . the names still roll off my mind . . . and I wanted to *sail* in one of them . . .

‘So like many a boy before me I ran away to sea, volunteering as a seaman and being accepted. Once I had sent a postcard telling them where I was, and the police had been informed I was no longer missing, my parents were delighted for me. My father had served four years in the Sussex Regiment, First World War, two older brothers were regular RAF and Wellington bomber sergeant pilots, and two other brothers were Territorials in the splendidly named Princess Beatrice’s Isle of Wight Rifles. If I hadn’t tried to join up I think my father would have disowned me!

'I was trained at the new HMS *Collingwood* stone frigate, and felt at home when the instructor pensioners yarned about Jutland and HMS *Lion* and the *Warrior* and Jack Cornwell. I still dreamed of a draft to one of White's sleek destroyers, and nearly heartbroken I was when I drew something called Combined Operations, then in its infancy, and went to Troon, Ayrshire, to serve on barge-like Tank Landing Craft. I thought the only time we'd go to sea whould be to land tanks when the invasion of Europe took place, which, from the state we were in, wouldn't be for years.

'I need not have worried. The Combined Ops life was great. It was still Navy, and the TLCs (later LCTs) were fun to serve in with small crews. While our Fleet counterparts were convoying to Malta, etc, we put in at ports around Scotland and the North of England, and even, when the Combined Ops fleet was extended to Landing Craft, Flak, and Landing Craft, Guns, escorted East Coast convoys and saw action between invasion exercises. Meantime we sloped off ashore in our tiddley suits, a new Combined Ops badge on the cuff of our left sleeves, and wowed the girls in dance halls from Aberdeen to Middlesbrough.

'All this came to a stop when we sailed south and loaded with tanks for a rather testing morning at Dieppe. The Germans knew we were coming. The Second LCT Flotilla beached and was annihilated, as were the tanks they carried. Others waiting to go into the cauldron were ordered to the "Waiting Pool", to see if further landings were at all possible in the appalling circumstances. My LCT had been rigged as a hospital-plus-rescue craft, and there were smaller craft coming off the beaches with wounded, under heavy fire from the batteries ashore and plenty of air activity. Towards noon we were ordered home in a mixed convoy, well protected overhead by our fighters, though some of them got shot down by trigger-happy gunners who had spent a morning not calculated to improve the nerves. I resigned myself to not surviving the war if all landings were going to be like this. But tremendous lessons were learned. Apart from more and better landing craft, with gunns, rockets, etc, at Normandy every Allied aircraft had three wide white stripes painted on their wings and fuselages (as an afterthought, overnight) to stop happy gunners blasting them.

'So I had gone "overseas", and was to go further. The new sleek LCIs (Landing Craft, Infantry) were being built in the States, and there I went on the *Queen Elizabeth* – bit of a change from an LCT, and joined *LCI(L) 127*, building at Quincy, Massachusetts, near Boston. It was great fun for us, autumn 1942, seeing lights again and being invited to High School dances, where the pupils were about our own age and there we were in Royal Navy uniforms, old salts, with a Croix de Guerre and Mentions, chatting up girls right out of a Mickey Rooney "Andy Hardy" film. When we sailed it was to join the North African landings, via New York, Norfolk, Bermuda and Gib, all good landfalls – but with an awful lot of deep sea in between!

'Skipper of one of these was actor Peter Bull, crossing the Atlantic in company with another LCI captained by Alec Guinness. He called his autobiographical record of this little adventure *To Sea in a Sieve*. I can think of no better title.

'Of the eighteen crew of *LCI 127*, three of us had been to sea before (not counting the outward pleasure cruise in the *Queen*). We had a subby RNVR skipper of the ancient age of 24. The average age of our crew was 19, three of the ODs being 16. We were delighted with our LCI, which looked like a "real" ship, with four Oerlikon guns and bunks for 200 troops.

'On leaving Bermuda with our flotilla, plus a rescue tug for the Atlantic voyage, heavy seas stayed with us the whole three weeks of the trip. Every night after dusk the convoy would scatter – unintentionally, and at dawn there we'd be in an empty ocean. A rendezvous point had been agreed, however, and then we'd either sail like crazy to catch up, or circle about until other LCIs showed up. One night in a storm we ran into a huge convoy of massive ships heading the other way and had a terrifying time dodging being run down and rammed, Skipper very calm, though only a subby then. I strained my eyes like never before. One monster missed us by inches. My diary reads "Of course no cooking on our galley stove, so sandwiches our lot. Very proud we all made it to Gib, hairy and filthy, but there. Got spotted by a circling Focke-Wulf and went to action stations for first time for *127*, but too far away to fire at."

'The Skipper, then Sub-Lieutenant H. John, RNVR (later awarded the MBE), showed at this early stage in command that he was a calm man in all situations, and a very good skipper who interfered with the lives of his crew as little as was necessary. We would do anything for him, and he, as proved on many occasions, would do anything for us. First Lieutenants came and went (we carried just two officers) as they qualified to be Landing Craft captains. Even I was offered CW candidate training but was quite happy as I was.'

Hunters And Hunted

Hunting in the North Atlantic was Captain Walker's crack 2nd Escort (Support) Group, HMS *Starling* (Captain D), *Woodpecker, Wild Goose, Woodcock* and *Magpie*. In *Woodpecker* as a brand-new Asdic Submarine Detector III was Tom Bailey, man of *Renown*. He had joined the Bird-class sloop when she was still only a job number at Denny's, Dumbarton, Scotland, and since then she had played an important part in Walker's outstanding success. They operated from Gladstone Dock at Liverpool. When entering or leaving harbour *Starling* would play 'A Hunting We Will Go' over the Tannoy, and *Woodpecker* 'The Woody Woodpecker's Song', made famous by the Andrews Sisters.

'We woke up to that tune, turned in at night to it. Sometimes the Sisters even called us to Action Stations, "And certain stars shot madly from their spheres to hear the seamaids' music." We were a famous, crack team, but a lot of the spirit went out of us when Captain Walker died of a heart attack, brought on by the strain of his ceaseless drive to scourge the U-boats.'

Perhaps their most unforgettable fight was the 15-hour running hunt and gun battle ending in the ramming and destruction of *U473* on 5 May 1944, after which *Starling* signalled: 'Cease firing. Gosh, what a lovely battle.'

Another small ship which did her bit in the Atlantic was the sloop *Chanticleer*. The name baffled Ernie North when he was given the draft. He was another ex-*Rev-en-gee* – 'A happy ship', he remembers. He had also served in *Hood* ('Even in peacetime hopelessly overcrowded'), and felt that 'a new modern ship for me was overdue'. '*Chanticleer*?' said one messmate, 'Free French carrier, isn't she?' 'No,' said another, 'Frog submarine'. He didn't find out until he arrived at William Denny's at Dumbarton with the remainder of the draft, and there she was, 'A neat little sloop, *U05*. Not exactly a fleet greyhound, but well armed, and capable of handing out a terrific wallop down aft in the sub-hunting season. I liked her from the start. The officers were a great lot, and my particular messmates a grand bunch. The seaman POs knew their job, and soon trained up their branch, 40 per cent of whom had never been to sea before.'

'In the spring of 1943 a section of our hunting group waited at Oban for the weather to clear to escort a huge capital floating dock to replace one sunk in Grand Harbour, Malta. The go-ahead was given and we were told that fine weather could be expected. Out in the Atlantic we were hit by a hurricane with really mountainous seas. The dock broke free from its tugs and was spinning round like a matchbox. We thought it would sink at any moment.

'The seas were so bad no one could turn for fear of broaching. The upper deck got smashed up, and depth-charges broke loose on the quarterdeck. In securing them, two men went over the side and were lost. No rescue or search was possible, not being able to turn, and it lowered our spirits for the rest of the trip.

'After about twenty months in commission we took a convoy from Argentia in Newfoundland back to the UK, during which we were detached to join a convoy coming up from Gib. It was mid-November, and we all thought that a bit of sun would be just the job, and what nice people they were back in the Liver Buildings!

'We joined the convoy in the forenoon watch, somewhere near the Azores. It was a glorious morning but we were told that German aircraft and subs were around. About 1220 I went down to the mess, had my tot and my dinner, when there was the sound of DCs in the distance. The ship altered course and increased speed, and the submarine alarm went almost at once.

'As we had done literally hundreds of times before, everyone rushed to their action stations, hatches were closed, fans and ventilators shut, and within one minute *Chanticleer* was ready to defend her convoy.

'My action station was as Officer of the Quarters on the two foremost twin 4 in mountings. The guns' crews told me that a sub had been sighted astern of the convoy by those already closed up . . . A quick check around the mountings to make sure they had the right ammo, range and deflection dials at zero, everything ready to open fire . . . We could hear the HSD searching for the U-boat, and the voice of the Skipper ordering the sectors to be swept by the Asdics.

'Orders came a bit quicker now. "Follow Director. Load, Load, Load!" All guns were loaded, and the gunlayers and trainers followed their dial pointers. We started our run in on the submerged U-boat, and we could plainly hear the echoes right down to the HSD's "Instantaneous echo!" A shallow pattern had been ordered, and the Gunner, normally on "X" gun, had already moved on down the quarterdeck to take charge of the Depth-Charge Party, and as I neared "X" gun the first charges were exploding astern.

'At this point, with a tremendous roar, the whole quarterdeck seemed to disintegrate upwards in a jumbled mass, and a wave of pressure and heat hit me. The ship shuddered horribly and rolled to port, then slowly came upright, moving most unnaturally. We had been well and truly fished. I thought – A helluva lot of people have just died.

'The young depth-charge telephone number was sitting on the deck by the starboard screen, his phones still on his head, looking in a bad way – the only man left alive on the quarterdeck. The ship's rudder, which weighed between 30 and 50 tons, had flown up into the air, and had come down like a great butcher's cleaver and was knifed into the upper deck a few feet from the lad on the phones. Both after Oerlikon power mountings and all the upper deck had gone and the cabins and offices below were open to the sky and sea. The prop shafts were hanging out of the wreckage, and loose depth-charges were hanging in various positions.

'I returned to the guns up for'ard. The upper deck was littered with debris from aft, and there were huge ridges and rents athwartships round the funnel. In various places there were also the more horrible remains of our late messmates. A young officer was found alive, just, in the wreckage of the cabin flat aft, but he died within minutes.

'The ship was fairly steady but was well down aft, and we were lucky in that the weather was kind. All the boats were holed and some of the Carley rafts damaged but the Damage Control Party amidships and the engine room staff were shoring up the bulkhead between the engine room and the boiler room. At the guns we remained closed up. The remains of one of the Oerlikons was on the fo'c'sle, and we ditched that and a lot of other wreckage over the side. Soon after I returned to the mounting we picked up another U-boat bearing on our starboard bow. A Sunderland then flew overhead and circled the ship, and asked if they could take pictures. They were brusquely told to go and look for the U-boats that were going to slap another fish into us.

'One of our chummy ships in the Group, HMS *Crane*, then came up to assist us, and we prepared to abandon ship, *Crane* being asked to sink us by gunfire. The men were advised not to go between decks as she might decide to leave us at any moment, but someone decided that we needed some fags, and cartons of Churchman's No 1s appeared on the upper deck from the canteen. Our canteen manager, also a dear messmate, was dead, and if the ship was to be sunk, who was there to complain?

'While the *Crane* was waiting for us another torpedo was fired, and she attacked an echo at least once. She was obviously in danger and moved off again.

'The Skipper told us that a tug was on its way to see if it could help. A frenzy of lightening ship was taking place. Everything that was ditchable was ditched. Everything that was unscrewable was unscrewed and thrown overboard. I, God knows why, decided to cut down a stubby little mast with a saw. We had only about three or four bodies available to bury, and a short service was held and we committed our very dear shipmates to the deep. There were over 30 killed in all, and on a small ship with a very close-knit set of officers and men it was a crushing blow. Not all small ships reached the happy state of understanding we had. For them it was

> Farewell, Aggie Weston's, the barracks at Guz,
> Hang my tiddley suit on the door,
> I'm sewn up neat in a canvas sheet
> And I won't be home no more.'

Hooligans' Navy

Each man waiting was two men,
The man with Paybook and number,
A rank and duty, Sick Berth

Tiffy, Torpedoman, Tanky
And Stoker, and another man inside
With a healthy fear for his own skin.
Alan Ross, Sub-Lieutenant RNVR

Mines In The Mud

Dennis 'Vic' Oliver from Basingstoke, Hampshire, worked for John I. Thornycroft, and in his teens joined the Air Training Corps to train as a Ground Staff Motor Mechanic, but when registering for call-up on impulse he chose the Navy. His technical ability became clear and, after initial training at HMS *Collingwood*, Fareham, and short spells at HMS *Excellent* and in the cruiser *Jamaica*, he was drafted to HMS *Vernon* to work on magnetic and acoustic mines, partly in counter-measures against enemy mines, but with a special job involving a new sonic underwater buoy for marking a passage through a minefield on D-Day. This work was carried out mostly in the mining trials area off Stokes Bay, west of Portsmouth. From there Dennis was moved to the Old Pier, Weston-super-Mare, Somerset, chosen 'because it was tucked away from town and out of sight of inquisitive locals, with the second highest tide in the world – ideal for trials'.

Here, under Admiral Casement, a team of 'engineers, inventors, physicists and various ranks and ratings down to the common OD' worked enthusiastically together, for the most part regardless of rank. Mines, acoustic or magnetic, for investigation and trials would arrive from Gosport, 'be checked over and set, then loaded at Weston Airport on to a Lancaster bomber which would fly to the target area at Langford Grounds, a large sandbank uncovered at low tide but at high tide with some 40–45 ft of water over it, to drop on the target already indicated by direction and wind direction arrows, with a Naval photographer filming it.'

'Meanwhile another party had set out with a skiff, pennants and marker buoys. After walking a mile across fields to the shore nearest the target, as the tide ebbed four ratings rowed across to the sandbank, now being uncovered, and three men set off across it with a strop, pennant and buoy on each shoulder, looking for the mines. When you came across one you sat across it, placed the strop round the centre, shackled the pennant to the strop, stretched it out and fastened the marker buoy to the end; then trudged off to look for the next one. It was like quicksand there, and you had to keep moving. If you were lucky you located all the mines dropped before the tide turned. Next morning you sailed at high tide in our wooden-hulled MFV (Motor Fishing Vessel) and an old car ferry to find the marker buoys and recover the mine for examination.

'One important job was the development of a small mine which could be dropped by aircraft in the canals of Germany. For this we had the use of a Boston night-fighter/bomber, which would come tearing along the coast spewing out these mines, some of which hit the water and flew up again, like playing "ducks and drakes" with pebbles on a pond. Then we would go down in a lorry at low tide and race the flow, trying to dig them out.

'Owing to the unsociable hours we had to work, we were glad of some rest at the end of the day, or a run ashore, and there was no barracks routine, it was all work, and everybody mucked in, ratings and officers alike. We once turned up for a mine recovery job well sloshed on farmhouse-brewed cider from a generous farmer, obviously not fit for wandering about on the mud flats, and the officers simply turned to and did it themselves, with nothing said, then took us all into the Royal Pier Hotel to celebrate one officer's birthday.' This treatment was far removed from the divisive snobbery separating wardroom from fo'c'sle in many situations.

THE BIG ONE: NORMANDY

In contrast to the victims of the Depression who had joined the Navy for 'three square meals a day', HO Fred Hall had been part of a totally different strand of English social history. Fred came from a comfortable middle-class home in Balham, South London, his father a hard-working jobber in the Stock Exchange in the City of London. In 1932, when Fred was eight, they bought their first motor car, a 1928 Singer 8 four-door saloon costing £15, which was the start of an annual fortnight's seaside holiday at Littlehampton, Sussex, 'common now but not then', where they always stayed at 65 Arundel Road, a private boarding house owned by Mrs Barnes, an elderly widow. 'We would see about four or five other cars. Once past Purley you were on safari into the unknown.'

Mrs Barnes had three sons, the eldest a Petty Officer in HMS *Hood*. At Navy Week in August 1933 Fred and his father spent a day at Portsmouth aboard the great battlecruiser as guests of PO Barnes, with dinner and tea and a complete guided tour of the whole ship. It needed another whole day to visit the battleships *Nelson* and *Warspite*, and the carrier *Courageous*. 'What a contrast to today's Navy Days! In those days you could spend the whole week there and still only see about a quarter of the ships. There were usually one or two battlecruisers, four battleships, a dozen cruisers, about 30 destroyers, and perhaps 30 or 40 lesser craft, plus one or two aircraft-carriers.'

Hall Senior enjoyed these annual Naval visits as much as young Fred. He had served in the Harwich Patrol in the Great War, in the destroyers *Ullswater*,

Lennox, *Sharpshooter* and *Swallow*; his eldest brother Fred, a gunlayer in Q-ships, had been killed three weeks before the Armistice; an uncle had served in the engine room in battleships; and Fred's great-great-grandfather was Admiral Sir Charles Popham of the famous Royal Naval family. In 1936 Mr Hall moved the family out to a new house at Morden in Surrey, which had been a small village until the Underground reached it in 1926; the house was one of two just completed on an unmade road in a semi-built estate, and they were the first occupants, pioneers in new suburbia. Fred joined the 12th Morden Boy Scouts.

In September 1938, time of the Munich crisis, all members of the 12th Morden Scouts aged 14 and above were enrolled as auxiliary members of the ARP (Air Raid Precautions) service. In August 1939 they became permanent part-time members as cyclist messengers, and were given training in first aid, anti-gas precautions and simple fire-fighting.

With the eruption of the Blitz in September duties rose to four or five evenings a week and all-night during air-raids. 'This continued for 57 consecutive nights. I had left school in March and was working as an office boy at 6/- a week for stockbrokers A. Miller & Company in Pinners Hall in the City. With the fires raging along the river, an average day began with an uncertain journey by bus and tube to the office, varied by raids, working hours interrupted by at least two hours in the shelters underneath the old Stock Exchange building, home by 7 p.m., duty till about 4.30 a.m., home, an hour's kip, then off to the City again. Then Balham Station was bombed and it took three hours to the office, by devious routes through bomb damage.

'One morning I was crossing London Bridge when out of the murk from Tower Bridge roared a Heinkel 111 and dropped three bombs in the river. The packed bridge cleared in record time, the four-minute mile being broken, I'm sure, many times over. Another time I was on the top of a bus passing Clapham Common when the whole AA battery there (eight 4.7 in guns) opened up and blew out all the windows on the bus. On another bus I found myself directing a new driver from the top deck by banging my feet on the floor (one for left, two for right).

'This form of civvy Active Service gradually eased up as the Blitz fizzled out, and in early 1943 I realized that most of my colleagues and friends had joined HM Forces, and I volunteered, so that I could enter the Service of my choice – the Navy, of course.

'I did my basic training at HMS *Glendower*, Pwhelli, North Wales, by courtesy of Billy Butlin, at the end of which I was offered a choice of: Steward, Writer, Coder, Supply and Stores or Sick Berth Attendant. As I had enjoyed my first-aid training in both the Scouts and ARP, I opted for the latter, and became a PSBA (Probationary Sick Berth Attendant). I was passed fit and able and sent to HMS *Pembroke*, RNB Chatham, and slung my hammock in the sweaty, foetid underground tunnel, shortly afterwards going thankfully to the RN Hospital, Gillingham, Kent, for my medical training – eight pleasant months of lectures, demonstrations and practical work.

'After a fortnight my class was marched into the mortuary to witness two post-mortems. One man fainted and others went a bit green, and a dinner of fat pork finished off a few more. This apparently was a calculated way of weeding out the unsuitables, and several men were reallocated to the Stoker Branch. Shortly after qualifying, I was drafted to HMS *Westcliff* for transfer to the Combined Operations branch, that they used to call the "Hooligans' Navy", then to HMS *Mylodon*, Oulton Broad, Lowestoft, a Combined Ops base. D-Day was near, and it was unarmed combat, small arms firing (Tommy guns, Stens included), and a crash Commando course, with me, as a medico, humping a 56lb first-aid valise on my back the whole time. I was never so fit again.

'And I went to sea for the first time in the Service, as a new member of the 8th LCT Flotilla in the Flotilla Leader *LCT 7040*, for intensive sea manoeuvres and practice beachings.

'On the Glorious First of June the 8th Flotilla left Lowestoft and sailed south, reaching Southampton Water two days later and tying up amongst hundreds of other landing craft.

'Late on the night of the 5th, having earlier loaded Sherman tanks and a contingent of Pongoes, we headed out into the Channel, arriving off the coast of France the next morning. We beached and discharged the tanks, which took some time owing to beach obstacles. I was told to report to the Beachmaster ashore, and there I found some other SBAs. The craft carrying the Royal Army Medical Corps party had not arrived, and we were to fill in for them – temporarily. The "temporarily" became seven days . . .

'Noise, smoke, dust and death . . . Salvoes from *Warspite* and *Ramillies* tearing overhead like hurtling express trains . . . a strong smell of burning . . .'

Anchored off the beach-head was Alan Mathison's SS *Romney*. 'After nine months swinging round the buoy in Scapa Flow in the ammunition ship *Aire*, waiting for a carelessly thrown fag-end to send her sky-high at any moment, followed by a year on the meat run through E-boat Alley, I had been glad to go deepsea again.

'I sailed from Hull in the SS *Fort Livingstone* for North Africa in October 1943. We went to Loch Ewe for convoy and on sailing from there were joined by ships from Liverpool and Glasgow also bound for the Med. The night all the ships joined up was in early November and it was a dirty night, blowing more than half a gale with a big sea running.

'About 7p.m. I turned-in, more or less fully dressed except for boots. I had the "graveyard" watch – midnight to 4a.m. I'd only been asleep about an hour when I heard the alarm bells chattering, I jumped off my bunk and was putting my seaboots on when there was the most unholy crash and the ship suddenly started to heel over to starboard. I grabbed my lifejacket and dashed out on deck and up on to the bridge. I thought – this is it, we have been torpedoed. When I got into the wheelhouse a most amazing sight met my eyes. There on our port side was a fully loaded inward-bound tanker (high octane spirit) stuck in our No 1 hold, and we had gone down by the head until our foredeck was awash. The tanker extricated himself by going astern. By this time it looked as though we might founder, and the Master signalled for assistance to stand by in case we had to abandon ship. They sent us an armed trawler to stand by and escort us back to Londonderry. Several ships were badly damaged that night, all because some fool in the routing office of the Admiralty had routed an inward-bound fully loaded convoy on the exact same route as the outward-bound convoy. The result was that about 140 ships got mixed up in that affair. I know one of them was towed into Londonderry with a broken back, a write-off.

'We spent two weeks in Londonderry while Naval divers put temporary repair plates over the hole in our side to enable us to get across to Glasgow to discharge our cargo. The damage to the *Fort Livingstone* was so bad that they had to completely rebuild the forward section of the ship. I left her when she went into drydock in Cardiff for repairs.

'The next ship I joined was the *Romney*, after she had docked in Hull from a 27-month voyage, which had earned her a "Mention in Dispatches" from Field Marshal Montgomery for her service in the North African campaign. She had loaded a cargo in New York for North Africa, a cargo of such importance that she was routed not across the Atlantic, but down through the Panama Canal, down the west coast of South America, through the Magellan Straits, across the South Atlantic to Capetown, up the East African coast into the Red Sea, and finally into the Med, that passage having taken 127 days, which I can vouch for, having read the scrap logbook for that passage after I had joined her. There was a rather poignant entry at the end of that logbook, entered by whom I do not know. It simply said, "End of voyage, thank God". After being away for that length of time at sea during the war, I can fully appreciate the feelings of the person who wrote it. I sailed in the *Romney* to the beachhead at Normandy during the landings there. Our position at anchorage was in the "Sword" sector, nearest to the guns at Cherbourg. We were frequently fired on by those guns, especially if the MTBs on the "Trout line", as it was called, let up on the smoke they were supposed to keep going to stop the German gunners getting our range.

'One day they did just that, for some reason or other, and in seconds the Germans had our range and dropped shells right abeam of our ship only yards from us. We had to up-anchor and get out as fast as we could before one of them landed on us. We made it safely away, but the *Iddesleigh*, one of Tatums' ships, was not so lucky; they got her and killed several of her crew and she became a total loss. We did two runs to the beachhead from Hull with supplies. The second time Jerry nearly had us. Their one-man subs had placed an acoustic mine under our stern during the night. In the morning when the LCT alongside us switched on his generator, the mine exploded and virtually lifted our stern out of the water. We survived and so did the LCT, but I saw the *Fort Lac La Rounge* get a torpedo from a one-man sub. It killed about 150 soldiers sleeping in her 'tween decks when it exploded, and badly damaged the ship, putting her out of commission for a long time.'

Fred Lee, now a Leading Hand, paid off *Glasgow* when she berthed at Hartlepool for a refit, and returned to 'HM Hellhole' at Chatham. He was not pleased to be given a draft to Combined Operations.

'I'm not going to Combined Ops, I'm a *seaman*!'

'Well now you're a *seaman* in Combined Ops!'

LST 364 was just back from Anzio. 'If I said they were bomb-happy that's the least I could say . . . I asked them what they were doing now. "We're getting kitted out and ready for the next invasion . . ." The Skipper was an RNR two-and-half ringer, a Merchant Navy officer but one of those ambitious types, and the more damage he could do on the other side the better.

'We started loading and unloading and getting ready to go to Normandy, well, we didn't *know* where we were going actually but we had a good idea. We went down to Portsmouth and loaded up with Canadians, and lorries, and we had a few tanks, and we went and lay out in the Solent, and on the eve of 6 June everything started moving, all those concrete piers and dock walls that they landed on; it all moved down the Solent towards the sea. They were there ahead of us, we left that night, and this RNR Skipper of ours was shouting and bawling at everyone to get out of the way, he wanted to get on the beach. We sailed up and down Piccadilly Circus, as they called it, and when we got there it was four o'clock. There were some LCPs running around putting ropes round bodies that were in the sea and towing them ashore. We had to wait until the tide next day, so we emptied and made off, to make many trips to the beach.

'The first thing to aggravate us were the destroyers and MLs, they were nipping up and down with smoke cans, making smoke everywhere, protecting us and suffocating us. The most horrific of all were the German bombers coming over in the dark, and underneath them came the Dakotas going the other way, and people were firing at the bombers and bringing down Dakotas, and that was a terrible thing to endure, to watch the Dakotas crashing in the sea. What bloody fools gave that order? They even used their Aldis lamps signalling to us and they still got shot down, and were still using their Aldis lamps when they crashed into the sea. There was just a big flash and everything disappeared. So that was D-Day.

'Then we ran on the beach, and we had a walk round ashore, helping the troops to get ashore. We couldn't get off. We got all the stuff out of the tank space, scrubbed it out, and laid tables out. We carried about five surgeons, and the wounded were already coming back into the LST, so as the tide came in we hauled off and the surgeons were operating. As we were having our tea these bods kept coming up from the tank space bringing cloths. What the hell had they got in the cloths? Then it dawned on us. While we were eating they were coming through with bits of legs, bits of arms . . . By Christ, it put everybody off their tea! Then we got to see some of the blokes and went round giving them fags. Most of the casualties were burns, they'd been trapped in tanks, by flame-throwers . . . They were covered in picric gauze or whatever they were treating them for burns with.

'It was certainly a nasty affair and we came back to Portsmouth and unloaded that lot as fast as the Old Man could get the thing going; he wanted to get back again and wait for another load. He travelled so fast and did so many trips that he came back one day as a commander and within the next few months he came back as Captain of LSTs at Tilbury . . . all between June and December. He was a magnificent man, though a bloody nuisance. He had a French wife that he shut up in a tower in Ryde. I went across to tell him he was wanted about half-past three one morning and I caught the flak. He said "You haven't scrubbed this bloody boat out!" At four o'clock in the bloody morning!'

The cruiser/minelayer *Adventure* lay off the French coast, acting as a repair ship for landing craft and coastal forces. Bunting-tosser Geoff Shaw recorded the high drama of the invasion in his diary:

'Early June 1944. – Off the French coast. Day and, mostly, night attacks by FW 190s and Ju 88s, sometimes bombing, sometimes minelaying. Gunfire, noise, explosions, smoke screens, constant Action Stations. Bombardments of shore by battleships, cruisers, rocket craft. Return fire from ashore. Parachutes seen descending from Flying Fortress, Spitfires and Mustangs. Mines exploding. All very hectic.

'Monday, 19 June. – Weather deteriorating. Visibility bad. Gale warning. Set anchor watch and raised steam. Weather worsening rapidly. Several ships dragging anchor during forenoon including *Bulolo* (trooper, ex-AMC), *Thysville*. Numerous small craft in trouble. Trawler *Colsay* and coaster *Eldridge* driven aground. We were flooded with requests for help but could do nothing – all we could do to save ourselves. Several ships drifting out of control.

1830 – warning of attack by glider bombs.

2030 – tug went to help *Colsay*, towed her clear.

2140 – landing craft out of control passed down our starboard side.

'Tuesday, 20 June. – Mine exploded nearby. *LCT 947* reported being mined, having casualties, engine out of order, anchor lost, in trouble. Unable to help.

0215 – explosions nearby. Shellfire?

0235 – *LCT 947* reported breaking up fast.

0330 – Air-raid warning red.

0550 – Abandoned coaster flying distress signals drifted past.

0650 – Coaster ran aground.

0655 – Air-raid warning red.

'Wednesday, 21 June.

1100 – Moved berth. LSTs ordered to land cargoes and accept all risks. Weather still wild. *Eldridge* reloaded, anchored in deep water.

1700 – *Eldridge* drifting on to US merchant vessel. US MV got under way. Tug managed to hold *Eldridge*. US MV drifting on to *Adventure*. *Adventure* berth again. Destroyer *Fury* mined, taken in tow and brought alongside *Despatch*.

'Thursday, 22 June. – *Fury* broken adrift, drifted past us, driven aground on rocks west of Cap Manvieux. Countless craft of all kinds high and dry along beach stretching out of sight in both directions – some damaged, some upside-down, some on one side, some on or against each other, some completely wrecked.

p.m. Weather beginning to improve. Counted 355 Fortresses flying overhead with Mustangs and Lightnings.

2000 – Fortresses on return journey. Wing broke off one at root, some crew members baled out. *Adventure*, *Frobisher* (cruiser) and *Thysville* returned to berths held before gale.'

This was a record of the 'Great Gale'. After that the scene off the Normandy beaches returned to normal . . .

'Friday, 23 June. – Air-raids last night. Plane shot down nearby. Large number of mines dropped during dark hours. Heavy gunfire to SE. Spitfires overhead. Mine exploded off starboard bow.

1900 – Destroyer *Glisdale* mined, towed to "Mulberry".

2115 – Landing craft mined, sunk.
2230 – Cruiser *Scylla* mined E23 berth.

'Saturday, 24 June. – More air-raids. More mines and bombs. Another plane shot down.
0655 – Trawler *Lord Austin* mined C17 berth, sunk.
0730 – Destroyer *Swift* mined, sinking.
0735 – *MT41* (US MV) K14 berth, mined, sunk.
0930 – *Fort Norfolk* mined.
1700 – LCVP blew up on mine, close to starboard, nothing left.
Evening – can still see bows of *MT41* showing above water.
2320 – *Nith* hit by bomb, casualties, towed to UK.
2340 – Near miss by bombs or mines.

'Sunday, 25 June.
0045 – Cruiser *Arethusa* mined, slight damage.
Over 40 Landing Craft inshore, discharging. Over 140 craft of all types wrecked on beach. Coaster upside-down to starboard. *MT41* bows still visible to seaward. *Fury* still aground on rocks. Several mines exploded during day. *Rodney* and a cruiser bombarding to eastward.
0914 – *Empire Roseberry* close by to port, approaching anchorage.
0915 – *Empire Roseberry* exploded mine.
0916 – *Empire Roseberry* split in two.
0919 – both parts sank, just a few heads left bobbing about in the water between the two parts. Went down in four minutes.
Orion bombarding
ML sunk by mine. MMS damaged by mine. MT mined and sunk
Heavy artillery heard.

'Wednesday, 28 June. – Sinking MT ship towed in, down by stern, decks awash aft.
Adventure shifted berth to a point near artificial harbour
2300 – *Maid of Orleans* mined, badly damaged.

'Thursday, 29 June. –
0050 – *Maid of Orleans* sank. Three more MTs mined and sunk.
No more potatoes left.

'Friday, 30 June. – Entered artificial harbour 1000 and made fast, stern to sunken blockship *Alynbank*, bows to buoy.

'Thursday, 6 July. – Fifty midget submarines reported to be in or near area, all ships in first degree of readiness. Frigate *Trollope* torpedoed a.m., towed stern-first into artificial harbour during afternoon and beached, whole ship forward of funnel blown away. Operation 'Alert Three' at 0716, 1121, 1347, 1455.

'Friday, 7 July. – *Rodney* bombarding. Two more mines went off nearby. Midget sub scares 0410 to 0800, 0930 to 1400. LCVTs dropping charges round harbour. Lancaster crashed, two casualties brought on board.

'Saturday, 8 July. – More air-raids last night. Ju 88 and night fighter shot down. Three more midget sub scares during day.

'Sunday, 9 July. – *Dragon*, cruiser, hit by torpedo or mined, towed inshore. Four midget sub scares. Usual air-raids.'

Also on the beaches of Normandy for 'The Big One' was David Satherley's by now rusty *LCI 127*. 'On landing our troops, airborne soldiers they didn't have enough gliders for, we struck an underwater obstacle some forty yards from the beach, which was being washed by quite big waves after the previous few days' poor weather. Fortified with a large gin from the skipper, I swam towards shore with a heaving line, resting about halfway there on the turret of a sunken tank (the pennant stuck above water). On the beach (with the help of some beach party and RM Commandos), I hauled in a 4in manila hawser and made it fast to the wrecked railings on the prom, coming under fire from a church steeple. I and another sailor who had swum ashore to join me then pulled together several dead men to cower down behind as the bullets were hitting the pebbly beach around us. However, our soldiers, laden with bicycles, mortars, ammo, rifles, were finding it hard to get ashore by the rope. Several floundered in the sea, so I could not but help go in and drag them out, though warned the beach could be mined. For this deed, done on the spur of the moment, I was recommended for the DSM but had to settle for a Mention.

'Even with a hole, hastily patched, we made some dozen trips to the beachhead before (in July) we were in danger of slowly sinking. We were towed to, of all places, Fishbourne Creek, Isle of Wight, for repair, a fourpenny bus ride from my parents' house. The skipper told me to disappear, and for the next six weeks I lived at home. My brother Ed (away in North Africa in the Long-Range Desert Group) had a splendid civvy suit which I wore for the whole of that time; once desperate to get into bell-bottoms, now chuffed to be a "civvy". At the local dances I was often told by squaddies to "join up", which I didn't mind at all in a superior sort of way and didn't even mention I was a serving sailor, enjoying the private joke. Every Friday night a good dance was held at the local Albany Barracks (now part of Parkhurst Prison), where rookie soldiers were in training, 18-year-old conscripts. Here I received the worst insults.

'A trestle table had been set up to serve drinks, etc, and while waiting to be served I was studiously ignored by the ATS girls at the makeshift counter. The local Newport girls knew who I was, of course, so such treatment didn't affect my standing with them and I enjoyed the dances. The only person present in a suit, I did stand out like a sore thumb, however. Waiting to be served one evening, I was faced by a woman in her thirties with laurel leaves and crown on her sleeves, a company sergeant-major of ATS, no less. She asked me how old I was (I was twenty) and why I wasn't in uniform, a healthy young man. I mentioned war work and asked how old was she, and would she care to dance? All pretty sneaky of me, I agree, and later that evening she (having refused the offer of a dance) actually came up to me and took my hand, pressing a white feather into it, the sort of little fluffy one that comes out of a pillow. I thought such things had gone out with the First World War! Still I suppose I'd asked for it.

'The following Friday I went to the dance in uniform, with half-a-dozen mates from *LCI 127*, having informed them what a good evening it provided (as it did), with good 40s music, plenty of girls, both service and civilian, to chat up. We breezed in like a blue cloud, all with ridiculously wide bell-bottoms; tiddly "eye-shooting" bows on our cap ribbons that covered our eyes; wide "U" fronts; scrubbed, almost white jean collars: gold badges and a good variety of medal ribbons (the then 1939–43 Star with the North Africa rosette had recently been issued to us, plus, pretty good for the size of ship and small crew, we had a DSM, BEM, and two oak leaves for Mentions, and thought ourselves no end of tarry Jacks). This invasion was not welcomed by the Army recruits in their stiff new battledress and big boots.

'Remarks flew, one of ours being that "the only *crack* troops in the barracks were the ATS" and soon a little squaring-up took place with the threat of a punch-up. The ATS sergeant-major, recognizing me and telling me what she thought of me, asked us to leave. This we did on my suggestion, and my mates went off to the pubs of Cowes. I stayed, had drinks with the sergeant-major over the situation being resolved, continuing the session in her private cubicle in a Nissen hut. During the night she plucked a white feather from the pillow and gave it to me to hand back to her for services rendered. I had to sneak out before Reveille, the back way across football fields and into Parkhurst Forest, pondering the fact that I had slept with a sergeant-major.'

Air-Sea Rescue

Back in Lowestoft, as there were no more landings contemplated in the immediate future, SBA Fred Hall was sent on loan to Coastal and Patrol Forces, and a hectic eight months began, working from HMS *Mantis* at Lowestoft, HMS *Midge* at Great Yarmouth, and RNSQ (RN Sick Quarters) there.

'From *Mantis* I did night operations with MTB/MGB flotillas operating off the Dutch coast, hunting enemy coastal convoys and E-boats. These flotillas did not normally carry SBAs. I was always aboard the flotilla leader at sea, and got into various actions, carried out at 40 knots plus, mostly in the *Fairmile* D-class "Dogboats", and anyone hurt in one of these boats was my responsibility. I would transfer from one boat to another in pitch darkness with both of them heaving up and down about twelve feet. Once I ended up in the hoggin in a night fight.

'With 90 per cent of crew RNR or RNVR and HO, discipline in the boats was very relaxed. Once ashore, all of us, officers and ratings together, marched to the nearest pub in our white sea jerseys, sea boots and white seaboot stockings. The boss was always "Skipper", never "Sir". At sea, when not required as a doc, I was extra lookout on the bridge. The Captain, usually a peacetime trawler skipper and a superb seaman, gave orders by hand signals and "Left a bit" or "Steer that way", "Slow down a little", etc. At 40 knots there was no time for RN formalities. Conditions were cramped, luxuries unknown, though we were only at sea for 12 hours each patrol. You sailed with your knees bent to cushion the continuous *thump, thump, thump,* as you bounced from wave to wave, and for a couple of days back ashore I couldn't carry a pint a few feet without spilling some.

'Other ops I was often involved in were the rescues of ditched airmen, carried out by *Fairmile* B-type RMLs (Rescue Motor Launches). Again I was only aboard for operations, and was involved in many, my clients exclusively men of the "Mighty Eighth", the US 8th Air Force, stationed widely over East Anglia. Every day the Fortresses and Liberators of the 8th were over NW Germany, returning over the North Sea and crossing the coast between Cromer to the north and Harwich to the south.

'During the forenoon we could see hundreds of aircraft crossing the coast and heading out over the North Sea, which would prepare us for the afternoon's operations, though nothing was said. Shortly after noon I would be ordered to report to RMLX, lying at the quayside in the River Yare, where I would make a careful check of my medical equipment, kept in a special deckhouse aft large enough to accommodate four stretchers on racks.

'About six boats would leave, and once clear of the river mouth proceed at cruising speed (12 knots) to a given position some 25 to 30 miles offshore. There were also three or four RAF air/sea-rescue launches out as well, though I never saw any of them as they covered the area south of us. There would be about eighteen vessels out in all, radiating from Great Yarmouth like the spokes of a wheel. Once at the designated spot it was heave to and just wait, engine ticking over. Every man available was on the upper deck on lookout – the Luftwaffe loved sitting ducks, and most boats had only a 2-pounder for'ard and a couple of light MGs aft.

'Sometimes we hung about idly until about 5 p.m., then went home. Mostly, the first sign of a job would be Sparks rushing to the bridge with a signal that an aircraft had ditched, with the position given. Engines went to Full Ahead (20 knots), everyone keen-eyed for survivors, sometimes in small life rafts, sometimes just heads bobbing in the water, on one occasion the plane itself, still afloat. Overhead Forts and Liberators struggled home, props feathered, great jagged holes in fuselages, trailing smoke.

'As soon as a sighting was made, nets were flung over the side, and the seamen got ready to lift the survivors on board. This was delicate, as we could not know if a man was injured or not. Once we picked up nine men, the other three having died in the aircraft. Once they were aboard I found that two were badly injured, three suffering from partial drowning and immersion, the other four relatively unscathed. I told my three seaman assistants to look after the three half-drowned airmen, while I tended the badly injured men, whom we put on stretchers right away. While the boat went flat-out for base I dressed their wounds and burns, stitching where required and putting splints on broken limbs, with the Skipper radioing base with details of their condition and our ETA so that the injured could be transferred straight away by naval ambulances to our sick quarters for immediate attention, while the others were given dry, warm clothes and refreshment (usually alcoholic – rum or brandy) while awaiting transport back to their airfields.

'This work I found very rewarding in itself, and I was many times invited to USAAF bases for generous hospitality, but my biggest reward came at a time of billeting problems when I was accommodated for six wonderful weeks in the ATS quarters in Great Yarmouth, one bloke amongst 350 females, and the first time in nearly two years that I had a proper bed with sheets – and tea in the morning! What luxury!'

The Mediterranean

We hold, in our pockets, no comfortable return ticket:
Only the future, gaping like some hideous fable.
The antique Mediterranean of history and Alexander,
The rattling galley and the young Greek captains
Are swept up and piled
Under the table.

Charles Causley: *Conversations in Gibraltar*

CHASING *VITTORIO VENETO*

Illustrious, badly damaged by Stukas, left the Mediterranean for repair in the USA. *Formidable* relieved her. On 27 March 1941 she joined the Fleet at sea to follow up a report of three Italian cruisers in the Ionian Sea. The next morning Swordfish from the carrier reported three enemy cruisers and four destroyers south of the west end of Crete, steering south-east, while Cunningham's cruisers sighted three enemy 8 in cruisers to the northwards. Out-gunned, out-ranged and slower, they retired towards the battleships. The enemy cruisers turned away, having succeeded in luring the British cruisers towards the big guns of the battleship *Vittorio Veneto*, steaming down from the north. Swordfish sent from *Formidable* to attack the enemy cruisers sighted *Vittorio Veneto* and attacked her, turning her back. The chase was on, with the Italians having the speed advantage.

Warspite was now flagship of the Mediterranean Fleet, with Swordfish floatplane 'Lorna' and two of her crew from the epic Narvik sortie. PO Ben Rice was still her pilot, Maurice Pacey her TAG, but Brown had been promoted Commander and had left the ship, to be replaced by the Fleet Observer, Lieutenant-Commander A. S. Bolt, DSC. At 1215 'Lorna' was launched as Action Observation, her duties to obtain a visual link between the two fleets and report on the tactical situation.

Bolt reported that the Italian Fleet showed no signs of pressing on to the south-east after the Fleet Air Arm torpedo attack. By that time he was worried about his fuel state. 'The endurance of my aircraft was about 4¾ hours, though we had on occasion achieved 5 hours under favourable circumstances. My routine reports of fuel state evoked no response from HMS *Warspite*, until I reported only 15 minutes of fuel remaining. Suda Bay was over one hour's flying away, so a decision had to be made to recover or destroy the aircraft although the Fleet was in hot pursuit of the *Vittorio Veneto*, having been slowed as we thought by a torpedo hit from an aircraft from *Formidable*.' (The ship hit and slowed down was actually the heavy cruiser *Pola*.) 'My aircraft was ordered to alight ahead of the *Warspite* in the grain of the Fleet. With the crane swung out on the starboard side, the plan was to hook on as the ship steamed up to overtake the aircraft, taxi-ing on a parallel course.

'The sea was calm and my pilot, PO Rice, made a good landing about two cables ahead of the ship, turned on to a parallel course and taxied at about 10 knots with the ship coming up fast astern. We had never practised this method of recovering and were a good deal disturbed by the bow wave. However, I was able to con PO Rice to a position under the grab hook and Lieutenant-Commander Copeman, with whom I had a good understanding in the recovery operation, hoisted us quickly clear of the water as soon as I gave the hooked-on signal. The aircraft was put on the catapult and refuelled while I went to say my piece on the Admiral's bridge. The ship lost only one mile through the water during the recovery and I do not believe she was doing less than 18 knots through the water at any moment during the operation.' *Formidable*'s second torpedo strike had been led by Lieutenant-Commander Dalyell-Stead, with Observer Cooke and TAG Blenkhorn, all of whom were killed.

At 5.45p.m., less than an hour after they had been recovered, Bolt and Rice were catapulted again, with PO Pacey as their TAG. 'The last thing I did', said the latter, 'before take-off was to grab three flame floats as I realized that we were going to have to alight at night on the open sea with no organized flare-path.'

Bolt sighted the *Vittoria Veneto* at 6.20p.m., and Pace made their first report by W/T direct to Alexandria W/T Station at a distance of some 400 miles. 'We had', says Bolt, 'carried out a great deal of practice with this station during dawn anti-submarine patrols from Alexandria and it was very satisfying that PO Pacey was able to clear some dozen Operational Immediate messages in a matter of minutes'. These were repeated to Malta and Gibraltar and received immediately in Whitehall, so that the Admiralty had them nearly as soon as the C-in-C in *Warspite*. These reports told Winston Churchill that the enemy was still some 50 miles ahead of Cunningham, making a speed of 12–15 knots on a course of 300°, which meant that the British Fleet had an advantage of some 7–10 knots. The chasing destroyers anticipated going in with torpedoes, and *Formidable* had high hopes of a dusk torpedo attack. The Italian Admiral could see eight of her Swordfish circling astern of him in the dying sun.

At 7.50 Bolt was relieved and ordered to return to Suda Bay. 'The night was clear and moonless and I expected that the alighting on the water without a flare path would present my pilot with some difficulty. Suda Bay was steep too and narrow, and with all shore lights blacked out was not the sort of place to take liberties with on a very dark night. The entrance to the harbour was protected by two booms watched by patrol craft. As the sea was calm I decided that we could land outside the harbour and, after doing a low-level run, to put down a line of flame floats, we turned and made a good landing. PO Rice deserves great credit for this achievement as we were landing towards the shore, it was pitch dark and there was no suspicion of any horizon. Furthermore, as there was a shortage of spares we had surrendered our instrument flying panel to the carrier squadron and the aircraft was fitted only with a primitive turn and bank indicator. We identified ourselves to the patrol vessel on the boom and then proceeded to taxi into harbour – a distance of about 5 miles, which seemed interminable. The Aldis lamp was most useful as a headlight and eventually we met a motor boat which guided us to a mooring for the night. I went to HMS *York* and reported to Captain Portal and it was on board that ship that I heard reports of our night action.' (The Italians had in the end lost three cruisers, but the *Vittorio Veneto* returned to port.)

'*York* had been attacked by explosive motor boats a few days earlier and I shared Captain Portal's regret that his wine store had been flooded. We had been airborne for more than eight hours and had had an exciting and eventful day. However, we were used to night and dawn flying operations and, though the aircraft was not radar-equipped, the open cockpit of the Swordfish enabled us to do many things which were impossible from an enclosed cockpit. Above all, as a crew, we had been together for more than a year and were able to rely on a competent maintenance team which kept the aircraft serviceable through all difficulties with a minimum of shore support.'

YORK'S WAR

It was in HMS *York* that we left Scottish AB Chris Buist steaming flat-out for Halifax from the sunny West Indies on the outbreak of war. With one of her three 8in turrets still out of action she escorted a convoy to Britain. In the Norwegian Campaign Chris spent all his time down in the 8in magazine supplying cordite to 'B' turret, and was there again on 12 October 1940 when *York*, covering an eastbound convoy from Malta, sank the Italian destroyer *Artigliere*, one of the three which had attempted to intercept the convoy; the other two were destroyed by *Ajax*. In the early part of 1941 *York* was in various actions in the Mediterranean, and on 25 March during the Allied retreat from Greece entered Suda Bay, Crete, for topping up with oil. Following closely in her wake so that the ship's Asdic would not pick them up was an Italian 'explosive motor boat'.

'I was below decks when we heard these engines revving outside in the Bay. We fuelled from the oiler and there was this bump followed by a mighty bang and a flash of flame right through our messdeck. The ship lifted up in the air, then down with a crash, all the lights and power went dead and it was black as Hell. We went up on to the fo'c'sle where all the rest of the ship's company were assembling. The ship was pulled on to the beach bows-on. As the quarterdeck was under water we lost all our stores, rum, etc. We were real chokka, I can tell you.' It was estimated that five months would be needed to render her fit for towing, but from 22 April there were incessant air attacks on the ship and she was further damaged. She was finally abandoned on 22 May, two days after the Germans had begun their assault on Crete.

While they unloaded the ship her crew lived in Army tents, ashore. 'About three weeks after the ship was hit I was unloading one of the cutters when the Germans came out of the sun with bombs and machine-guns blazing. I dodged behind a rock but a bullet grazed my steel helmet. After the raid I was shaking like a leaf, my nerves were shattered, so I was sent to the Army Hospital up in the hills.

'When the buzz went round we were getting off the island, the Colonel in the hospital said that all those who wished should try to escape to Egypt. I and several Army chaps left the hospital and made our way over the hills to a little cove where we knew we might find a boat. We pinched a Greek caique and set out for Egypt after several attempts to get the old diesel engine to work. We ran out of fuel half-way there and floated around until we saw a destroyer in the distance, which came alongside with her guns trained on us, but we were picked up and taken to Egypt.'

Malta Strikes Back

Look! Malta spun on the sea, shaping to sight
Fragilely as a promise, framed by metal
And the deft handling of airmanship.
Nudge. Nod. That's there all right. A petal
Yellow, all veined with green in the sea's hard
Flooring of other elements, of timeless running.
Malta, upon the blood-invested water, cactus, nettle-
Leafed, old prickle guard.

John Pudney

TARGET LIBYA

When on 16 October 1939 twelve Heinkels and Dorniers attacked the Forth Bridge and ships below, it was finally decided that Donibristle was no place for a training squadron, so Nos 767 and 769 Squadrons were moved by stages to the French military airfield at Polyvestre, in the south of France, with HQ at Hyères, four miles away; they continued working with the old carrier *Argus*, which carried on the deck-landing part of the syllabus just off the French coast. Trainees were mainly junior officers of the new RN (A) Branch, the RNVR (A) Branch, with some RN rating pilots. On *Argus* a pupil made one supervised landing in a Tiger Moth, then soloed in a Swordfish. This continued until 10 June 1940 when Italy entered the war. The next morning Italian fighters strafed Polyvestre, and it was time for the trainees to leave. Before they did so the instructors staged a token raid on Genoa, using improvised bombs made from 12 in shells. On the morning of the 18th they received the signal: 'Fly to England via Bordeaux but if fog precludes proceed to Bône'.

On ringing Bordeaux for a weather report, they were answered in German, so that night in the light from burning equipment on the airfield eighteen Swordfish, manned by instructors and pupils, took off for North Africa, and arrived at Bône 4 hours 20 minutes later, almost out of fuel. There they waited for further orders from Whitehall, and on 20 June the CO, Lieutenant-Commander Howie, sent for rating pilots Charles Wines and Freddie Parr and said, 'I've been ordered to form a front-line squadron to go to Malta. I've been told to take ten officer pilots, but I'm taking you two as well.' Six aircraft flew west to Gibraltar, twelve to Hal Far airfield on Malta. From there, as No 830 Squadron, they began a long, stubborn assault on Axis convoys carrying supplies and men from Italy to North Africa and also on Tripoli, the receiving port.

It was Tripoli again on 18 March 1941. Just before midnight nine Swordfish took off, two of them flown by POs Wines and Parr. The weather across to Africa was good, with some low cloud as they neared the target. Bomb flashes from the attacks by six RAF Wellingtons guided them to the target, and five aircraft dropped mines off the harbour entrance.

It was Wines' job to divert guns on the harbour mole from attacking the mine-droppers. 'When I arrived over the harbour I couldn't believe the sight below me. There were no searchlights, but the whole place seemed covered with exploding fireworks, as guns of all descriptions blazed away, their glowing trajectories converging on the centre of the harbour.' Wines, like most rating pilots, felt he was always on test in combat. The Lower Deck aviators were not intended for operations at all, but shortage of officer pilots had given them the chance to prove themselves, at first in fighters only. Now Frankie Howie had given him and Freddie Parr an opening as bombers, and he had proved to be the squadron's best. But he had to keep up his reputation.

He turned inland away from the lethal pyrotechnic display and, gliding back from the desert with his engine off, dropped a bomb straight across a seaplane hangar near the eastern mole, and saw a whoosh of fire behind him. The bomb destroyed the hangar and the nine seaplanes inside it, as well as a fuel storage dump. But he climbed again and looked for further targets.

Through the Gosport speaking tube TAG Nat Gould heard him yell, 'Look at that beautiful ship in the middle of the harbour – I'm going after it!'

From 4,000 ft Wines threw the 'Stringbag' into a near-vertical dive. Gold hung on grimly. Something big hit him in the stomach. He gasped with pain and thought 'I've been hit!' Then he saw that a spare drum of ammunition, resting on the gun ring, had slipped off and hit him. He hooked his arm over the side of the aircraft, heaved himself up and looked down over the nose of the plunging Swordfish. 'The sight nearly made my heart stop. It was like daylight, tracer racing up from all directions, swishing and cracking. Right below us the ship looked enormous. I clung on as we straddled her with our remaining bombs. I heard them all explode, then we were turning away. Charles threw the aircraft about in evasive action, the ack-ack ceased, and we were clear.'

Wines and Parr really thought that progress was being made when Howie said to them, 'You will go down to Kalafrana and carry out a torpedo course.' Rating pilots in a first-line torpedo squadron! What happened to the 'Lack of moral fibre'? What next – an invitation to briefings, perhaps? It was not a popular decision among some of the true-blue 'Darts' in 830. 'A torpedo costs £1,500, you know,' one of them said to Wines dubiously.

Down in Kalafrana Bay, Wines performed reasonably well in practice, but Freddie Parr dropped his first tinfish much too close to the Range Commander's boat and had its crew running about like frightened rabbits as it practically scraped the side, then carried on into the Bay. Out there three flying-boats were moored, a Sunderland, a Catalina and a French aircraft. The torpedo raced straight for the Sunderland and was almost on it when it turned to starboard and headed across the Bay towards the Catalina. The Swordfish turned in tight circles above, Parr and his passenger, Nat Gold, watching its progress in fascinated horror. It nearly touched the hull of the Catalina, then veered away again and made for the French flying-boat. As it approached the aircraft it gradually lost speed and finally stopped with a gentle nudge of the hull.

Captives In The Sahara

At 3.33p.m. on 12 April 1941 Squadron-Leader Whiteley's RAF Maryland reported a convoy of five merchantmen escorted by three destroyers south-west of the island of Pantelleria. One Swordfish went off first with flares to search for and shadow the reported ships. Behind him the CO led five torpedo-droppers, including Charles Wines, with L/NA Edwards as his TAG, and Freddie Parr as the dive-bomber.

At 6.20p.m. the shadower saw them – one merchantman of about 8,000 tons and four of 6,000–7,000 tons, escorted by three zigzagging destroyers and one smaller craft. At 8p.m., when the shadower thought the striking force must be near, he dropped a flare ahead of the convoy. Another flare in the empty moonlit sky was answered by a soaring Very light to the south-east. At 8.37 the aircraft of the striking force had the enemy ahead of them in the path of the moon, and against the light of more flares dropped down for their attacks against heavy and accurate flak.

Wines came in second, at what he thought was the right height, and let go his torpedo, becoming as he did so the first and only RN rating pilot ever to drop a torpedo in anger – the anger, in fact, considerable when he realized he had missed. In fact he had held on too long. As he cleared the target ship his Swordfish was hit continually and he was covered in oil. He flew on, heading towards the beach at Hammammet. Edwards got off a hasty signal to say that they were forced-landing, which was picked up in a mutilated state by Howie's aircraft. Then the Swordfish hit the sand – where in future years British tourists, including Wines himself and his family, would recline in their Ambre Solaire skins – ploughed across the wide beach and jarred to a stop. Vichy French police came running out to meet them. An Inspector said, 'There is an English lady in Hammammet. Perhaps you would like to see her?' and they were taken to Miramar, the big house owned by the Hensons, an American expatriate and his English wife, who gave them dinner before the police finally took them away to captivity.

Meanwhile the others had made their attacks. TAG Alan Todd hung on as his pilot, Sub-Lieutenant Dawson, dropped his fish amidst 'some very smelly flak. Then the engine stopped. I thought: It's Norway all over again. We hit the water short of the shore, splashed our way on to the beach and were picked up by gendarmes.' After a few weeks in the local Prisa Prison Camp at Aumale, where they met Wines and Edwards, they were transferred to the big camp at Laghouat, deep in the desert in Algeria.

There they met about two dozen RAF fighter pilots who had ditched when trying to reach Malta from a carrier and run out of fuel or had pump trouble. 'Rations in the camp were Latin – pasta in olive oil, and bap-type loaves, harsh wine from the bottom of the vat, which would stain the floor as well as any varnish if you spilled any. There was not much in the way of recreation, though

Charles Wines organized some boxing. Hardly any Red Cross parcels made their way across the Sahara. There was constant talk of escape, though we were 300 miles down in the desert, and all efforts to do so failed, as bounty-hunting Arabs simply waited at all the water holes to collect their 1,000 francs a head.' A tunnel was dug, and about 30 of the men headed north with the vague plan of wandering along the coast until they found a fishing boat to sail to Gibraltar. It was a 'Catch 22' dream. They were out for four days, then armed Arabs picked them up. After a while men from the destroyer *Havock*, which had gone aground, joined them (including Jack Dodds, who had worried that joining another destroyer would be bad joss after his narrow escape from the rammed *Duchess*). With them were the survivors from the destroyer *Legion*, whom they had previously rescued, and survivors from the cruiser *Manchester* also came in. They were all released after the successful Allied landings in North Africa, and made their way to Gib.

MALTA CONVOYS

Stoker and former engine driver Mark Wells saw plenty of action in Mediterranean convoys in the cruiser *Arethusa*.

'So began the Malta Convoys. It was the end of sailing right through the Med to Suez. That could not be done with such superior air power on both sides of the sea. We were committed solely to Malta convoy work, from the Gibraltar end, with Force H, made up of fast ships like *Ark Royal* and *Renown*, and the minelayer *Manxman*, which, it was said, could do 40 knots.

'We ourselves had not suffered much so far in the way of air attacks. Now, as Admiral Somerville said, we were going "To taste the quality of the ice-cream." Italian ice-cream was palatable, but the German variety was bitter. Sixteen hours into our first operation a spotter plane was seen, and a few hours afterwards the sky was full of "bandits". Bombs rained down everywhere. On rare dashes up on deck the blue sky was full of tracers. Once a gunner waved me to get down, I looked up and right overhead was this bomber. He near-missed us, thanks to the Skipper's skill at throwing the helm hard over just as the bombs left the aircraft.

'It was Action Stations most of the time. We struggled to get some sort of hasty meal in the lulls, but the respite was always short-lived and always the alarm went, and we sang "There's a bomber overhead" to the notes of the bugle which sounded the alarm to make it clear that this was an air-raid. Down below we plodded on with our duties as the raid went on. If only the 6 in or 4 in were firing, trouble was a little way off yet. When you heard the Oerlikons and pom-poms the bombers were getting closer to the ship. Then you would wait for the crunch of the bombs, some right alongside. More speed would be called for, the ship would heel right over, the revolutions telegraphs would clang "Ting Ting Ting" as the pointer dropped for lower revs.

'We were very tired and all over the place men lay on deck, sleeping in the shade, out of the sun. It was very hot. Once I was sleeping on the upper deck not far from the ship's gangway, lying in just a boiler suit and with my head on my lifebelt. I awoke to the sound of a bosun's whistle which meant someone important was coming aboard. I nodded off again as did others lying in the shade, but woke suddenly as someone tripped over my foot. I looked dazedly to see who it might be, and was horrified to see the Admiral, Sir James himself, standing there. I scrambled to my feet, but he said, "Don't get up, you'll need all the rest you can get. I'm sorry I woke you." So I lay down again and went off.

'Malta was being starved out, not only of food but ammunition and fuel for the few aircraft defending it. One day at Gib we started to load ammo and aviation spirit. The boxes of aviation cans were stacked on the upper deck aft, as high as the gun turret, with hoses laid over the top directing a steady flow of water over the cargo. Ammo was crammed into every available space below, alleyways, locker rooms, bathrooms, we became a floating ammunition dump.

'We were told of the utmost importance of this convoy, which included *Manxman* in the lead, *Arethusa*, and the cruiser *Euryalus* and one other cruiser. This was to be a make or break effort, made at high speed, in line ahead. We left in the dark (we had never left in the dark before) to give us a good start. The second night at sea I was in the engine room when there was a sudden thump right under the keel, followed by a few small rumbles. It wasn't an explosion. We looked at each other, puzzled. Then we learned that *Manxman* had struck an Italian submarine pretty well dead centre as she lay on the surface in the dark charging batteries. There was no question of stopping, our convoy was too vital for that. We sailed into Grand Harbour, Valletta, to cheering thousands of Maltese. At last a convoy had got through, and unscathed. *Manxman* still had part of the submarine she had hit hanging round the bows. The main body of the sub had rolled over under our keel and then under the following cruiser with no time to come to the surface again. We all wondered what the return trip would be like, but we reached Gib safely, where all the crews lined decks and gave us three cheers. We dry-docked for a quick check of the hull after many near-misses, and had a bit added to the rudder to make us a bit quicker in the turn.

'After this series of convoys it was decided to try convoys also from the Suez end of the Med, and it wasn't long before we were rounding Africa, via Freetown, Capetown, Mombasa and Aden and up to Suez and Port Said. There we saw the cruiser *Orion* and a couple of destroyers. There were precious few ships left here at the eastern end of the Med. A few convoys were attempted but so intense was the bombing that they were turned back, destroyers running out of ammunition, one with none left at all.

'Admiral Vian – Vian of the *Cossack* – took over in the Eastern Med, with his flag in the cruiser *Cleopatra* (appropriate in her Egyptian base), and we set sail with her to bombard Rhodes island. Back in Alex the boss had us hard at it, exercising damage control and abandoning ship – with us all jumping into the harbour – and cutting down the time to go to Action Stations. If a gunner was having a bath when the alarm sounded, said Vian, he would dash to his post just as he was. "These practice routines are for your survival," he said. "There are only two kinds of people out here – the quick and the dead." Another convoy was arranged, and we put to sea.

'On the third day we had fought off the bombers and were settling down slowly for what we hoped would be a quiet night. I had just relieved my opposite number as Leading Stoker in the engine room. I did my usual check round and came back to the Control Platform. It was about 1809. There was a sudden huge explosion and the ship listed over to port, sloping down for'ard as well.

'We had been hit by a torpedo somewhere below the bridge area, and the fore deck was awash on one side. There was a big fire forward of No 7 boiler room. By the merest chance the sea had got into the forward magazine before the flash, but our shipmates had suffered serious losses, a whole detachment of Marines, many seamen. There were many serious burns, and many died afterwards from shock. Many stokers off watch also died, including the man I had just relieved. The flash had flown right down one side of the upper deck and no one in its path there had survived. Boats crashed to the deck, their falls burned through, trapping others. The air was black with smoke for a long time and was sucked down the vents. The worst smell of all was the smell of human flesh.

'The night dragged on, portable pumps working frantically. At dawn we were rolling about, engines slowly turning. We tried to steam stern-first but we would never have reached Alex that way. Eventually the destroyer *Petard* arrived and towed us in, with the tow rope breaking over and over again, and we were harassed by bombers. Those of the dead who could be found were buried at sea. Every able-bodied man, led by the First Lieutenant, turned to to move the anchor cables by hand to the stern to get it down in the water a little. Down below there was only the stokers' messdeck bulkhead holding back the sea. It was shored up but the pressure behind it was terrific, and it bulged out like a bow. The messdeck itself was awash with oil, some of the tables still with cheese and pickles on them. We lost all our clothes.

'The trip to Alex took about three days and we lived on the odd sandwich and one or two good tots of rum. We comforted our burned and wounded mates as best we could, but some were unrecognizable. When we got in we were put into lorries, and spent the night in King Farouk's stables. I remember seeing the Captain being helped along the deck with most of his clothes burned off, badly burned and in obvious pain in legs and arms. One thing always remains in my mind, the quietness over the ship. No shouting, just a quietness. Just the odd senior rank calling "Lend a hand here, anyone able" and such like. We were sent to a transit camp on the edge of the desert somewhere. A PO met us and said, "There's a pile of tents over there. Grab one and pitch it somewhere."

'We had no money so we walked into Alex and saw some senior officer who arranged cash for us, and we paid a final visit to the old ship. I asked if anyone knew what was to happen to us. My two friends thought it would be the UK. Me, I really didn't care where as long as I got a ship. I hated being stuck on land even though it was an easy-going life where we were. You came and went as you pleased and no one asked where you were going, so we strolled out each day and made our way to the first cafe that had steak, eggs and chips. Love for the sea was strong inside me, as ever. None of us, strangely enough, ever mentioned the old ship. It wasn't until after the war that I realized that I never spoke of the happenings in *Arethusa*. I mention this because in civvy life people can't wait to tell you about some drama or other. Was it the same in the Army or Air Force? *Arethusa* was the only casualty in the convoy, and it was the first convoy from the Eastern end of the Med to reach Malta for many, many months.

Beneath the Waves

The ships destroy us above
And ensnare us beneath,
We arise, we lie down and we move
In the belly of death.

However terrifying the rage of a high sea can be, the dangers in its depths are more spine-chilling – nameless terrors of darkness, shadows of childhood fears. When I arrived in Malta as an Ordinary Seaman we were quartered in Verdala Barracks under a big half-Maltese leading hand who was also a diver. Under the sun-bleached colonnade on the edge of the small parade ground we used to sit and listen to his tales of the deep.

'Mate of mine,' he told us, 'big, tough bastard, just before he went down he says "Don't forget – one tug on the line, bring me up nice and slow, I don't want no bends. Two tugs – haul me up faster than that! That means I'm in trouble!" Well, down he goes, and after a couple of minutes there suddenly comes this terrific tugging on the line – not one, not two, but a whole lot of panicky jerks! We hauls him up at the double, and, you won't believe this, when he went down he had thick, jet-black hair – and when he come up it was *white* . . . and he never spoke another word . . . What had he seen down there, eh? Just think about it.'

'Have *you* ever seen anything really horrible down there, Hookey?' someone would say – anything to delay a return to square-bashing. 'Ah, now,' he would say darkly, 'there's things *I* can't even talk about . . .' 'What about octopuses, Hookey, and giant squids? And manta rays, and barracudas?' 'Hold on, hold on, my sons, or I shall think you're taking the piss! Octopuses? Nothing to 'em. If you ever meets an oc-toe-puss down there, and he grabs you, don't panic, stay cool. Before he can finish you off proper, he has to sort of spring off, to get his full strength, like, before he finally crushes you . . .' '*Reculer pour mieux sauter*' murmured a dipped CW . . . '*that's* when you whip our your old Pusser's dirk, and stick it right in his optic – he's only got one, and that'll put him right off you!' We sat there in the still air, mind-boggled.

Dangers of the Deep

From the light cruiser *Curacoa*, Bill Filer, ex-Barnado's Boy from the Watts Naval Training School, went in 1937 to HMS *Excellent* to qualify as a Diver III, but in the same year the Rating Pilot AFO came out and he volunteered, winning his wings in 1939. By the beginning of war someone in the Admiralty had thought better of the Rating Pilot scheme, and Bill was one of those returned to General Service against their wishes, which in his case meant dropping back from PO to Leading Seaman. Others similarly treated transferred to the RAF and obtained comparatively accelerated promotion. But Bill still had his non-substantive qualification, and in 1941 found himself in the battleship *Queen Elizabeth* at Alexandria as an L/S Diver.

While he was there the ammunition ship *Churukka* was sabotaged and scuttled at her moorings. The ship contained the only 15 in bombardment shells available to Admiral Cunningham, which, in view of Rommel's close proximity, made this a serious situation, and the C-in-C ordered a 24-hour continuous operation by divers of the Fleet to recover the shells so urgently needed to stem the Afrika Korps' progress in the desert.

'The holds of the *Churukka* were packed to capacity with the 15 in shells, each one weighing a ton, with the grab for picking them up of a similar weight. The first problem was that they were packed so close together that it was impossible to get the grab on them, and it needed considerable seamanship using strops and tackles and a lot of muscle to coax a shell into a position where the grab could be properly fixed on it – all this to be accomplished using the old helmet-type diving equipment with its limited mobility. Nevertheless it had to be done, and we got on with it.

'There were four holds packed with the urgently needed monsters, and a diving team worked one hold, six hours on, six hours off. From this system developed what turned out to be a somewhat unhealthy Fleet Regatta type competition, with each team of divers from the different ships trying to outdo the others in the number of shells recovered in a 6-hour session.

'This brought about Problem No 2. In their eagerness to outdo one another the divers took the easiest way out and grabbed the shells lying in the centre of the holds, which could be reasonably accurately plumbed by the crane. This was all right to start with but eventually resulted in the diver standing at the bottom of the hold with shells towering above him to his right and left in a V formation. The worst of this situation was that the uppermost shells which then had to be removed were well and truly hidden, tucked away under the coaming of the hatches, hard up against the ship's sides, and in no way could the grab be positioned to extricate them directly.

'Thus it was, on one never-to-be-forgotten morning about 0400 that I was struggling with these problems in the after hold when I was instructed over the intercom to return to the surface immediately. "Why?" I ask. "Don't argue" says Bill Scudder, and with a CPO Light Heavyweight Boxing Champion you didn't. Something traumatic was clearly afoot.

'I spindled my way back up to the surface to learn the worst. A Chief Electrical Artificer was trapped down below in No 2 hold which was being worked by the team from the destroyer depot ship HMS *Woolwich*, and his surface support team could neither communicate with him nor pull him up to the surface. Without bothering about our normal check tests, I was dropped down swiftly to find and recover the missing diver.

***Above:** Sick Berth Attendant Fred Hall went from the London Stock Exchange to LCTs and the Dunkirk beaches on D-Day, and on to the bouncing 40-knot Fairmile D MTB/MGBs in the North Sea seen here.*

***Below left:** In Ceylon (Sri Lanka) Fred Hall also drove ambulances.*

***Below right:** A maturing SBA Fred Hall before Dunkirk.*

072

Left: **Catapult Swordfish did good work in the Mediterranean flying from battleships of Admiral Cunningham's Fleet. This one belonged to** Barham **Flight.**

Renown*'s war:*

Right: *PT on a sunny day.*

Below left: *Under fire.*

Below right: *PO Shaw was* Renown*'s cartoonist.*

"POOR OLE BERT'S TAKIN' IT 'ARD."
"YEAH! 'E LEFT 'IS TOT ON THE MESS TABLE"

Left: *The* Ark *in rough weather.*

Below left: *Swordfish dropping a torpedo.*

Right: *TAG Alan Todd among the dry stone walls of Malta.*

Above: *Fleet Air Arm prisoners of war, Laghouat Camp, Algeria, December 1941.*

Left: *Bored with destroyer life in the Atlantic, L/S Ian Nethercott transferred to the Submarine Service. Here he is (exreme right) with three other* Tactician *ratings in Algiers.*

Top right: *HMS* Tactician *and ship's company. LTO Nethercott (extreme left, back row) looks, as he was, very young to be a Leading Seaman and LTO (Leading Torpedo Operator). The boat's Jolly Roger shows her to have made two sinkings at this stage, conducted two successful gun actions, and mounted five 'cloak and dagger' operations.*

Right: *There's no end to it! Cleaning out HMS* Suffolk's *8in guns.*

Left: *HMS* Antares, *Fleet Minesweeper, in Grand Harbour, Valletta, Malta. The author spent some amusing months in her as an OD (Radar), working for hostile Yugoslav partisans, paying off with a bang in Tunis.*

Men of Antares*:*

Below: *Killicks – Charlie Jones (Leading Wireman), L/S Liversedge (back, middle), Jock Campbell (L/Tel).*

Right: *Chris the Asdic.*

Below right: *Oppos ashore – AB Gear (left), AB K. Poolman.*

Above: *HMS* Kimberley *receives the surrender of all German troops on Rhodes. General Wagner came alongside while the General's aide saluted the Führer.*

Below: *HMS* Nelson, *in which 'Scribe' Cliff Smith found himself at Action Stations deep down in the 6in shell room.*

NELSON.
COPYRIGHT

Above: *Ghost ship, or a new* Marie Celeste. *HMS* Kimberley *returned home, too tired for the Japanese war, and moored at Dartmouth. The entire ship's company was ordered below for the photograph.*

Below: *The 'fore-ends' (crew's quarters) of a British submarine.*

Right: *HMS* Illustrious. *From her decks was launched the Swordfish torpedo attack which crippled half the Italian Fleet in Taranto Harbour, 11 November 1940.*

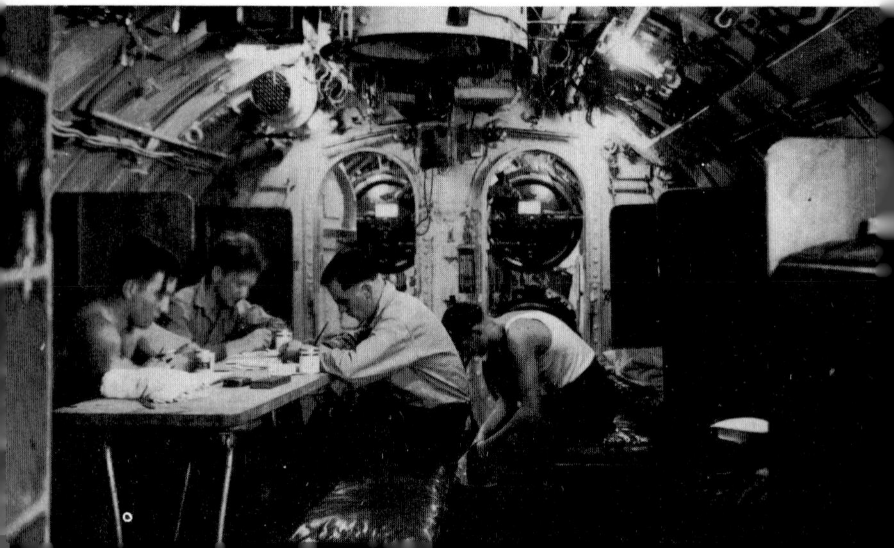

G50

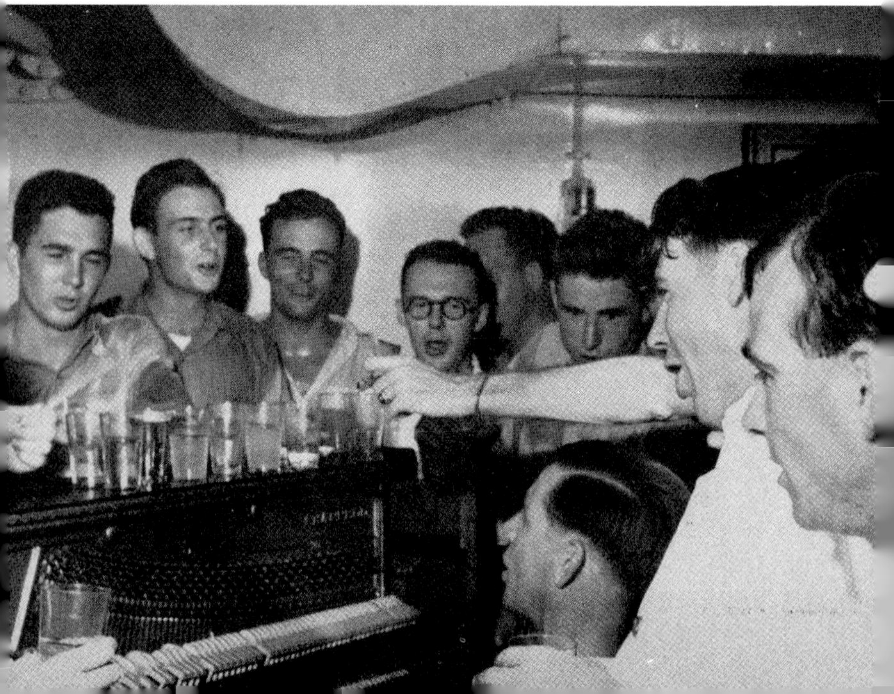

Left: *White Flight of No 1833 Corsair Squadron in* Illustrious. *Left to right: Londoner Reggie Shaw, Colonial Gordon Aitken, New Zealand Neil Brynildsen, and Flight leader, later Squadron CO, Norman Hanson.*

Below left: *'Hurrah for the next man that dies!'* Illustrious *entertains USS* Saratoga*'s air group, China Bay, Ceylon (Sri Lanka), 31 March 1944. Norman Hanson, a Gilbert and Sullivan buff, is at the piano.*

Above: *USS* Saratoga *joins the British Eastern Fleet. The huge smokestack made her and her sister* Lexington *unmistakable.*

Right: *Eric Rickman, pre-war Art School graduate, and his Avenger crew aboard* Illustrious, *March 1945. Left to right: L/A Barfoot, TAG; Sub-Lt John Rendle, RNVR, Observer; Sub-Lt Rickman, RNVR, Pilot (N).*

Above: 'Kamikaze' – *A Japanese 'suicide' plane dives on a carrier in the Pacific.*

Left: *Royal Navy Chief Petty Officer Tom Bailey joined the RN for 'three square meals a day and a pair of boots' – and found much more.*

'Down in the flooded hold I gathered up his air hose and "breast rope" communications cable, which led me to a very sad sight. There was the diver, with a ton-weight 15 in shell right across his chest, the weight of which had driven him back so hard that the nose of a shell immediately behind him had penetrated his helmet. He was trapped, drowned and dead when I reached him. Although I had never met him, a diver was a diver and not just somebody else, so understandably I had a second or so of grief. You can't wipe your eyes inside a copper helmet, so I set about relieving my feelings by getting "Steve" to the surface as soon as possible just in case he had an outside chance of survival.

'First I had to remove the 15 in shell off his chest, which, with topside co-operation, I did as expeditiously and tenderly as possible, following which I extricated him from the shell penetrating his helmet, through which the sea had entered. Drowning like that must have been a terrible experience, while still conscious. I still shudder at the thought. With signals to my surface support team, he was carefully hauled to the surface in his waterlogged tomb, with me guiding his body clear of the numerous obstructions which are always there in any wreck.

'His untimely death was unofficially ascribed, by us divers, to the fact that he had not succeeded in getting the grab secured to the shell correctly so that when the shell had been lifted some six feet clear of the water it fell out of the grab and landed up on the diver's chest. The shell which had opened up his helmet and drowned him had let the water in at some 15–20 psi. It didn't take long to drown him, but instant death in action would have been so much kinder. He just had to lie there, pinned down, and wait until he drowned. What a horrible way to go! We also felt that someone who was a top-class artificer should not have been used on this type of job, where seamanship and muscle were essential and not exactly commensurate with a "Tiffy's" skills. Also our team exercised a discipline whereby prior to a shell being hoisted clear of the water, we made sure that the diver had taken cover under the hatch coaming. Had the *Woolwich* team followed this rule the tragic loss of life would have been avoided.'

SUBMARINE SERVICE

British submarines played a big part in Mediterranean operations. New, smaller boats of the 'U' and 'T' classes took over from the old 'O', 'P' and 'R' classes which had been so out of place in these shallow waters. In the new *Tactician* (P314) was ex-Canvey Island Sea Scout, late of destroyers *Keith* and four-piper *Lincoln*, Iain Nethercott. Chock-a-block with the grinding monotony of Atlantic convoys, he had volunteered for the Submarine Service. After a course in 'demolitions, torpedoes, electrics, mines and other peaceful pursuits', at 'H Majesty's Girls School, Roedean', he 'abandoned gymslip, hockey stick and tiara' and reported to Ford Blockhouse, HMS *Dolphin*, feeling rich with an extra 6d a day, and positively plutocratic when he received his submarine pay of 2/- a day. From Roedean it was 'a mile down the social scale' to the former reformatory of HMS *Elfin*, the submarine base at Blyth, Northumberland, for operational training, which consisted of day runs to sea in the old *L23*, doing every job in the boat, grateful for a duty-free canteen and beer at 2d a pint. *Thunderbolt*, formerly the tragic *Thetis*, was alongside, back from the Med.

Finally qualified, Iain was drafted to the Clyde Flotilla at Rothesay, running from the old *Cyclops*, a coal-burning depot ship. 'The Flotilla consisted of the remainder of the old H-boats, built in 1917–18, the *Otway* and a couple of old American boats – "State Express" and "The Reluctant Dragon", so called because she often refused to dive.' They operated out of Campbelltown, Londonderry, Tobermory and Rothesay, acting as clockwork mice in training the escort groups and new ships in Asdic attacks. 'I joined *H43* as LTO, in charge of all the electrics and main batteries – and the motor room, from which the main motors were controlled when dived. This was the life! I had two AB LTOs under me and we made a good little team.'

'There was only one bunk on board, and that was the Skipper's. We kipped on cushions on the deck. We had a crew of about twenty and three officers. Our First Lieutenant was RNR, a former entertainments officer with the Orient Line, an Adonis who had a way with women, and chased them with every opportunity, though married to a red-haired virago who followed the boat around like a bloodhound. We had a succession of captains, all lieutenants who had just passed the CO's course and were getting a taste of command. One was Menzies, the Menzies of Menzies, the clan chief, uncomfortable in Tobermory and Ardrishaig among the fierce Campbells, and dubious of me as I was born in Caithness and am a member of the Gunn Clan, who used to fight alongside the Mackays, hereditary enemies of the Menzies, but a good captain. I made a good submarine brooch for him out of a silver spoon and gave him some of my tot, which he repaid with whisky in the wardroom.

'We spent a lot of time at Londonderry, where we had two narrow scrapes with American "cans" in training, which came zooming in as we surfaced, intent on ramming practice, and we scrounged a huge Stars and Stripes ensign and lashed it all round the conning tower to show the next lot we were friendly. An Aussie navigator gave us some scary moments too, when he tried to trim the boat, and sent her plunging down at 60°, thankfully straight into mud – it could have been rock. The coxswain was highly indignant as he climbed back up out of the periscope well. Another bind (literally) was our toilet, the contents of which had to be blown outboard by low-pressure air, but owing to faulty valves sometimes blew back and covered you with confusion. I once had to save our Jimmy from a vengeful husband from a Free Norwegian sub by holding him off at the gangway with a burst from a Tommy gun, like in *The Godfather*.

'But my Scottish holiday came to an end and suddenly I was available for world tours or sunshine cruises. What I got was the T-class *Tactician*, *P134*, being built at Barrow. I was glad to see some familiar faces aboard – Jack Coss, gunlayer off *Rorqual*, Les Etichnap, Killick fore-endman off *Unbeaten*, Ian Dunbar, PO LTO off *Unison*, and lots more. I was in good company. Our Skipper was Lieutenant-Commander Mainwaring off *Unruly*, who had just got a bar to his DSO. We could expect some action.

'At Barrow we lived in lodgings in the town, and went down to the dockyard every day to watch everything being put in place, though we spent more time in the pub. The super T-boats were well designed, though their diesels were never as good as the German engines. The boat was fitted with eleven tubes (six internal with reloads, and five external – two for'ard, two midships and one in the tail). The latter five were all mine, in addition to my motor room job, the TI owned all the others. In harbour I and my crew used to pull all the fish out, reload, check the horizontal and vertical rudders and the gyros, charge up with air, then strip down the pistols and detonators. When the Skipper scored a hit with one of *my* fish, it went off with a bang!

'Mainwaring went sick, and we got a new skipper, Lieutenant-Commander Collett from *Unique*, a great friend of the incomparable Wanklyn, and a good skipper who understood submariners. During the two years aboard the boat, from commissioning to paying-off, we had no defaulters and no real trouble. We all knew that in an operational boat any punishment would send us back to General Service, the worst disgrace the Admiralty could think up. Ashore we were a wild bunch, but naval authorities in all the ports abroad kept well clear of stirring up trouble with submarine crews.

'We were in good company at Barrow and later at Dunoon. *P313* was just ahead of us, and her crew mutinied, refusing to sail under the number 13. The Admiralty gave her new pennants – *P339* – and she sailed. *P311* had been sunk off Italy, and after she had gone they called her *Tutankhamen*. *Traveller* had also been lost with all hands, and we were due for the Med.

'First we did a shake-down patrol from HMS *Forth* up to Norway. The weather was terrible, tremendous seas, hurricane winds and about 20° below freezing. God knows what we were looking for – the Germans weren't daft enough to put to sea in weather like that. Conditions on the conning tower were so appalling that the skipper decided that all seamen should help do lookout duties, which included a one-hour spell for me. Although wearing many sweaters and trousers with an Ursula suit over all, within five minutes you were saturated. We wore safety belts with steel chains and dog clips to hold on to the rails on the inside of the cab as we were totally submerged in huge waves half the time. One great roller of hundreds of tons wrenched away my handholds and crushed me against the Vickers gun stand. I felt three ribs crack before my head came clear of the water. The cox'n strapped me up later. A new U-class submarine was on the next billet to us, and when we both withdrew from patrol and worked our way to Lerwick, she sailed into the harbour with all her conning tower gone, together with her gun. We returned to *Forth* at Dunoon, and eventually sailed for the Med, where we did our first patrol in the Gulf of Lions, with *Taurus* in the next billet.

'Here we made our first sinking, and ran up our Jolly Roger, but when we came up to fight a gun action with an auxiliary schooner the gun seized up. We returned to Algiers and our depot ship *Maidstone* to find that Tubby Linton, VC, and his *Turbulent* had gone, *Thunderbolt*, with all my mates, had gone, *Splendid* and *Sahib* were missing. It was a bad week for subs. The only good part of it for me was my flannelling my way through my PO's board and being rated up.

'We carried on with patrols from Algiers up the west coast of Italy and Sicily, and built up our sinkings, though counter-attacks by the Italian frigates were very accurate.

'Once we had sunk a merchant ship in convoy and were being attacked by three escorts. We were down at 200 ft with everything shut off for depth-charging, and at Silent Routine. Some of the depth-charge patterns were so close that you could hear the "click" of the pistols just before the charge exploded.

'One string of charges exploded just over the boat, and one right over the engine room hatch. I was on the switches in the motor room. Poor old Shiner Wright, the Chief Tiffy, was standing under the hatch, which had its strongbacks fitted. The explosion and consequent implosion sheared the hatch clips right off and it lifted momentarily. About a ton of water shot in, most of it on poor old Shiner, who wasn't used to sudden baths in his own engine room.

'When the Germans surrendered in North Africa we were based at Malta doing patrols up the eastern coast of Italy and Yugoslavia. We had all swapped cigarettes for Afrika Korps uniforms with the Eighth Army, stuck our badges on them, and the King must have had a shock when he saw us all lined up on the casing as he passed by in review on a cruiser. Except for going up to the Palace for my DSM, I hadn't seen him since Dover in 1939.

'As an LTO, after an attack I used to be very busy with my crew, first replacing all the shattered electric light bulbs, then checking the main batteries. The cells in a submarine's batteries stood about 4 ft high and held about 30 gal of acid each. On a T-boat they were split into three batteries of 112 cells each, which gave a total voltage of 240–350. They were strapped together with six large lead straps and bolts in a voltage-increasing configuration in the separate battery tanks inside the floor spaces between the control room and the torpedo stowage compartment. The floor boards in all the messes and wardroom were, in effect, the steel tops to the tanks, and had to be lifted up to examine the cells underneath, which lay with the straps only 18 in below the tank tops. Unfortunately, a lot of the cells lay underneath steel cross-sections between the messes and the gangway and could only be sighted by lying flat on the top of the battery and picking out the tops of the cells with a torch. Once a month every cell had to be topped up, just like a car battery, with about 3 gal of distilled water, and the boat was always in a state of complete chaos while this was being done.

'After a depth-charge attack it was always possible that some cells might have been cracked. Me and my crew would have to sight every single cell in all three batteries to check that the acid level was up over the plates. If the cell casing had cracked, the acid ran away into the bottom of the tank and the cell became dead, but still in circuit, with the danger of it catching fire during charging.

'Consequently, having sorted out the numbers of the cracked cells, I would have to draw up a cutting-out plan, to disconnect the dead cells and to pass cutting-out straps over the tops on to the next good cells. The final result gave a reduced voltage but a safe one. The problem was that the cutting-out straps were as thick as your arm and working underneath the steel floorboards and lying flat on the battery straps meant that an LTO had the full voltage of the battery passing through him, especially when his overalls were soaked in sweat and acid. Every time he moved, his arse came up against the steel deckhead and he got a huge kick of about 250 volts and several million amps. No wonder we LTOs had curly hair! I've put my freedom from rheumatism in my advancing years down to the fact that my body has been so highly charged.

'We, together with all available submarines, were sent to patrol off the Italian naval ports during the Sicilian invasion, and were then routed, after *Maidstone* was sunk, to the Eighth Flotilla at Beirut. Here we lived ashore, when not on watch aboard, in an old French colonial barracks, full of fleas. All the other boats were here, *Trooper, Taurus, Tally Ho* and the rest of the boys. In addition, Captain (S) had commandeered a first-class hotel and its staff up at Aley in the mountains of Lebanon, a luxury resort run by submarine cox'n "Brigham" Young, who had set himself up as the local potentate. Here we all went after a patrol, to go skiing up in the mountains and join in the night life. Good French wines, beautiful girls – and willing. Paradise.

'Down in the harbour was a Greek submarine depot ship together with a brood of half-a-dozen Greek submarines, crews on full pay and provisions. They never went to sea. The Admiralty guessed that they would immediately return to Greece and join the Germans. The town was dangerous for matlows, some of whom had been knifed and slung into the sewers, to appear in the harbour after a few days. Ashore, I always carried a revolver, an Italian Beretta, and a Commando knife. The place was full of disillusioned Arabs, who had expected to be liberated now that the Vichy French had been so soundly beaten, but the only scraps we got into were with the French Foreign Legion. Down in the harbour a 10ft-high fence topped with barbed wire protected the sub pens, guarded by the King's African Rifles, who did not hesitate to shoot any Arab who tossed one of their home-made cocoa tin bombs over the wire. At night the boats were enclosed in a floating boom, patrolled by two matlows in a small rowing boat who dropped made-up 1-pound demolition charges over the side every quarter of an hour.

'Every day a huge queue of ragged little Arab children used to form up outside the warehouse gate, overseen by a big fat brutal Arab who kicked and clouted these poor little waifs and sent them on board the boats for work. Our cox'n, "Fearless Fred" Fleming, would then pass the kids on to the various messes where they were immediately stuffed full of bread and jam, and given a little bit of dhobi-ing to do.

'We were very close to *Trooper*'s crew, and used to have wonderful sing-songs with them in our bar down in the French barracks. She was due to go home to pay off very soon, and we knew that we were going east. We were all operating up the Aegean now, but since the Italian surrender targets were getting short. We came in from one patrol on which we could find only caiques to sink and do a few shore bombardments.

'*Trooper* was due in a few days later, just after dawn. Down on the jetty Captain (S) had the usual welcome ready, the long tables laid out on the quay with dozens of Arab servants bringing on more and more beautiful food and fruit.

'All was ready. We were up on the casing to exchange our usual rude remarks with her crew. Captain (S) was pacing the jetty with the base staff.

'We waited and waited, but she never came home. The Arabs ate the feast, and we went back down the boat. *Taurus* had slipped and sailed for Port Said, and a week later we followed through the Canal and from Aden took the long road to Colombo.'

Beachhead Sicily

Roll on the *Rodney*,
Nelson, Renown,
This one/two/three/four-funnelled bastard
Is getting me down.

SCRIBES AT SALERNO

Naval Writer Cliff Smith in *Nelson* fancied himself as 'a devil-may-care Jack-my-Hearty manning an Oerlikon gun', even though 'We Writers and Supply blokes were kidded that we were non-combatants. This was far from the truth. My action station down in the 6in shell room lugging projectiles weighing 90 to 100 pounds was no sinecure, and being in the bowels of the ship battened down wasn't very pleasant. However, after nine months at sea, surviving a torpedoing during Malta Convoy "Halberd", and repairs and refit, I was transferred to the 4.7in supply party, a vast improvement on my last station. At least I could smell fresh air.

'However, it wasn't that much of an improvement. During other convoys in the Med, particularly the big "Pedestal" of August 1942, we all experienced some hair-raising moments. Jerry's dive-bombers were heart-stopping. It was frightening when the Air Defence Officer up on the bridge reported some 20 Junkers 88s approaching the ship. I'm sorry to have to say how relieved I was when they ignored us but dive-bombed the carrier *Indomitable*, astern to starboard. I went on the 4.7in gun platform and saw a pall of smoke issuing from one of her gun turrets which was hanging over the side. Prior to this drama I remember hearing what I thought were depth-charges being dropped, but it turned out that HMS *Eagle* had been torpedoed and I saw her go down in about five minutes.

'We just had to take it, until the tide turned in 1943 when we invaded Sicily. I well remember when the old *Nelson* escorted a huge convoy of ships, stretching as far as the eye could see, 10 July 1943. My oppo and I were off duty on the upper deck watching this remarkable armada. "Musso is in for a shock," he said, and so it proved. *Nelson* was flagship for the invasion forces, which successfully put our armies ashore. I didn't know that my best pal was among those Pongoes, and was killed on the beaches which we were attacking. I remember him every Armistice Day, and all the other brave lads who died. Later during the battle for Sicily we and sister *Rodney* were pounding hell out of some 11in shore batteries commanding the Straits of Messina, and all we could think about was how much damage our great 16in shells were doing to our own messdecks. When we were stood down we rushed below, to find every piece of crockery shattered, and chaos everywhere.

'The final engagement in the Italian campaign as far as I was concerned was the Salerno landing on the eve of my birthday. A buzz went round the messdecks that Italy had surrendered and we thought we would have no opposition. How wrong we were! That evening and night of 8/9 September 1943 was the most harrowing experience I'd had during my service. *Nelson* was in the bay to soften up the defences with her big guns, but Jerry, who had withdrawn into the Alban hills inland, threw everything but the kitchen sink back at us. Our own AA guns were working overtime and we slaved to provide the guns of all calibres with ammo. After a hectic hour or so the guns were firing faster than we could supply them, and the Gunnery Officer ordered the hatches to be opened so that ammo could be drawn straight from the magazine. This meant that there was a lift shaft from the main deck down to the magazine and any flashback or shell hit could blow us all to kingdom come. We didn't need urging on, and wasn't I glad to see the last pom-pom ammo box come up!

'One of the proudest days on board ship was in Grand Harbour, Valletta, Malta, when the surrender of the Italian Fleet was taken by General Eisenhower. Mind you, a lot of us felt a bit mad when the Italian Head of Staff, Field Marshal Badoglio, was also allowed to inspect *Nelson*'s Royal Marines. I suppose it was a common courtesy, and the Italians were now our allies, but the niceties were a bit overdone in the eyes of the Lower Deck, and most of Jolly Jack's comments were unprintable. Not that 90 per cent of us even saw the ceremony – we were banished to the depths where we could not see or be seen or blow raspberries.'

Combined Ops Isle of Wighter Dave Satherley was also at the Sicilian beaches in his beloved, now battered *LCI 127*.

'We landed our troops at Cape Passaro at dawn on invasion day, then went back to Malta for more troops. On passage back to Sicily we were ordered to proceed to Syracuse harbour as word was that the port had been captured; and we, with some LCIs and LCTs, plus a Fleet 'sweeper, headed there, passing a merchant convoy and escort under heavy air attack by extremely brave and determined Jerries, attacking mast-high, passing over our small group of landing craft low enough to see the pilots clearly. As our troop spaces were packed, plus the deck crowded with squaddies, we left them alone and they ignored us on their way to the fat prizes. An ammo ship actually blew to pieces and debris crashed around us, a piece striking my hand as I stood in the Oerlikon pit gripping the gun handles, cutting my wrist and bleeding.

'Then, as we were about to enter Syracuse harbour, an Italian sub surfaced in the harbour mouth, trying to make it to base, no doubt. It was immediately fired on and the Fleet 'sweeper's forward 4in struck the conning tower. *127*, being only yards away, went alongside, and AB Wiggy Bennett and myself jumped aboard, armed with Lanchester sub-machine-guns (posh Sten guns), and he stayed in the conning tower while I went down below to take the surrender. This was not so brave as it seems as many Eytie crew had come on deck from various hatches with white handkerchiefs, sheets, etc. First thing I saw was a young man's head and shoulders on the first "level" on the ladder going down, the rest of him had been blown away. The sub was the *Bronzo*, and the crew received me like a hero, offering cigarettes and lovely peaches. The sub was filthy, as were the crew. At that moment German aircraft appeared and machine-gunned and bombed us, and not exactly wishing to go down with a sunken sub I beat the Eyties *easily* getting the hell up the ladder to the conning tower. There Wiggy was kneeling and firing his Lanchester at an aircraft, and as my head came out the hatch his bullets missed my skull by inches.

'We took the sub in tow and entered the harbour, then went alongside the Hotel Salvatore Firenze, where our troops climbed over the guardrails to join the fight instead of wading ashore. The hotel was being looted by dozens of Sicilian peasants who were tossing sheets and pillows, clothes, mattresses and anything else to their friends below, while our Oerlikons were blasting away at Jerry aircraft passing overhead! When things quietened we nipped across the quay and investigated the hotel ourselves, liberating hundreds of dinner plates to save the washing-up problem that had brought us to punch-ups in the past. They lasted till after D-Day over a year later. I also got a Harold Lloyd straw hat which I wore with pride, and we stood to the guns in harbour with a grand selection of hats: an Italian general's worn by Wiggy, Taffy Jones in a lady's hat that would have done for Ascot, a top hat worn by Eddie Gunn, bowlers, fedoras – for the posh hotel had rooms vacated in a hurry, the wardrobes still full of clothes. I saw one Sicilian stumbing from a toilet bleeding badly, having pulled the chain and set off a booby trap. The local people certainly risked life and limb to get at some goodies.

'Wiggy and I, as gunners, were then ordered ashore into town as hordes of Italian soldiers with the inevitable suitcases were trying to surrender and getting in the way of our lads getting at Jerry. So for three days we "captured" hundreds and marched them to the railway station, which served as a gathering point. At night Wiggy and I kipped where we could, begged food, dodged shells, bombs and bullets, and enjoyed ourselves as only British matelots do when getting a spell ashore. We actually slept one night in a rather fancy brothel which had a courtyard, paying with cigarettes. Oh, and Montgomery spoke to me, asking if I were with a rifle regiment, as I had on shorts and black (Navy issue) stockings.

'We raided the Italian (Adriatic) mainland and Yugoslavia, based in Barletta, doing the run to Vis and Yugo creeks, mainly with supplies and Special Service troops, returning with wounded partisans, from October 1943 to April 1944 with occasional runs back to the other (Naples) side of Italy for landings. Our matey ship on the Yugo runs was *LCI(L) 124*, captained by Lieutenant Alec Guinness (now the famous actor). Number *124* was wrecked in a storm on a trip to Yugo and we picked up the crew. Otherwise, with the collapse of Italy and many Allied PoWs, roaming about, we often took agents behind the lines up the Adriatic coast and returned days later hoping to find British escaped prisoners waiting on the assigned beach. We never did, just plenty of Italian men and women wanting to be taken south, and the women were *very* appreciative for being rescued, so much so that we hid four of the best-looking young ones in the mess-deck for a week after returning to Barletta harbour!

'After landing troops at Termoli, up the Adriatic leg of Italy, we were attacked by a couple of Dorniers. A cannon shell blasted a rum jar in our tiny store, and Leading Stoker Gilbey, rum bosun and fully paid-up alcoholic, reckoned that the blast could easily have destroyed the other nineteen jars, which were wicker-covered stone jars. These were duly smashed with a hammer and replaced when we returned to Malta, leaving us with a surfeit of rum which we sold, greatly watered down, to US Navy landing craft we often tied up alongside. Even then we had rum in every kettle, saucepan, dixie, overflowing from lockers. Christmas 1943 was such a "rum" do that the turkey we had been supplied with was still on the messdeck table days later, cooked and untouched. Talk about cold turkey.

'In May 1944 we sailed for home and the D-Day Normandy invasion, our great little flat-bottomed LCI doing her stuff again, a record, I think, you can match with any Fleet ship, albeit we were the "Hooligan's Navy". Later, I saw *127* at Singapore. She's probably now in the Taiwan Navy or some such!'

Me and Mine

Now you take the port side
And I'll take the starboard,
We'll both paint the ship's side together,
And when Jimmy comes along
We will sing the same old song –
Thank Christ we didn't join up forever!

When I passed the Pillars of Hercules in 1944 aboard the troopship *Volendam* as one of a draft of Ordinary Seamen for Malta, not only had 'The antique Mediterranean of history and Alexander, The rattling galley and the young Greek captains' been 'swept up and piled under the table', but Malta and Matapan, Oran and Algiers, Sirte and Salerno and many young British matlows had joined them in the dust of history. All that was really left of the war was the mopping-up.

As we steamed on for Malta, Africa was distant in mist to starboard. Yellow Malta – 'Isle of honey' to the ancients, 'Island of bells and smells' to Jolly Jack – rose out of the sea like a railway buffet rock cake. After a short stay, with heart-pounding visits to The Gut of evil legend, The Egyptian Queen and Lucky Wheel, Caruana's Bar, where the distant heroes of 'Faith, Hope and Charity' once drank, I got a draft to a ship called *Antares*. The only *Antares* I knew was a red but feebly glowing star out in distant space – which was where this unknown ship might as well have been, as no one knew anything about her except that she was not a stone frigate and was believed to be somewhere in the Tyrrhenian Sea.

A Mast To Climb

To Naples I went, aboard the light cruiser *Black Prince*. As dusk came on I kipped on the upper deck with bag and hammock. I dropped off but woke up almost at once, shivering. Some men of the draft had lit up. Their fag ends glowed like campfires in the dark. I got up, strolled around the humming, vibrating ship, spoke to one or two of the men on the guns, scrounged a cup of kye from the galley. The cruiser steamed on through the night, seemingly invulnerable, a symbol in steel of irresistible power, though now and again the oily, supple sea would suddenly punch her thin, bare flanks, and the whole great structure would jump and quiver, suddenly turned to a jelly of mad atoms, rivets jarring and dancing in their holes, the skin of metal trembling as if under the whip, a ripple running right through the ship.

I stretched out again and watched the masthead as it rolled in drunken parabolas from star to star. One star did a formal dance with the lofty truck, like someone trying to fix a silver doll to the top of a swaying Christmas tree with its roots in water . . . 'And a star to steer her by' . . . The ship became a rocket in space, revolving eternally in fixed orbit, and darkness rushing past. I thought of that other mast . . . I was a *Ganges* boy, too, I had had to face that daunting ascent. The mast had been the first thing I noticed when I jumped down out of the draft truck. The mast was manned, and right at the top, balanced on the swaying Button, a boy was standing, semaphoring into the empty sky. What was he sending – his name, so that the world would notice him? Then came that fateful forenoon, when we had to make our own attempt on Everest . . .

We lined up facing the lower shrouds, three at a time.

'All right,' sang out old Harry Brown, 'First three – up you go!'

Well, the first stretch wasn't so bad, no harder than shinning up a rope ladder in the school gym, though the shrouds tapered as you rose, until you reached the point of decision, The Elbow. There, the shrouds disappeared backwards over your head out to the edge of the maintop. Of course, you could simply carry straight on and go up through the Lubber's Hole, but both old Harry, who had been in the Boxer Rebellion, and could still go up and over like a chamois, and the ancient CPO Duckmanton, whom we called the Squadron-Leader, for some reason, both these Ancient Mariners had let it be known that *their* class was expected to go over The Elbow, like *real* sailors.

I rather prided myself on my head for heights, on the strength of some rock-climbing in Cheddar Gorge, but this was worse than the overhang in the 'Easy' Knight's Climb, or even the 'Severe' Pinnacle Bay.

Then, with a panicky lunge, the lad to my right scrambled straight on up through the Lubber's Hole.

I stared after him. It was an ugly performance. A new feeling surged up in me, a boiling flood of anger at my own weakness. I took one hand away and grasped the ratlines which soared away dizzily over my head. I shifted my other hand, then my feet, and started to climb, upwards and outwards.

I seemed to be climbing forever, under the roof of the maintop. Then all of a sudden I could see daylight and the edge of the platform. Then I was reaching over the edge, gripping the thin brass rail running round just inboard of the rim. A few heaves and I was sitting on the edge, dangling my legs, looking down at the blank white faces, feeling good. In fact, so euphoric did I feel that when it came to coming down the other side I hung by one hand from the rail for a few giddy seconds before tucking my feet in and scrambling down, and old Harry's whispered 'Good lad' was music to my ears.

It never occurred to me to climb further, let alone right up to the Button. Perhaps I knew my limitations, even then. I dreamed about the mast often afterwards . . . I was back on that tall, grim tower, symbol of strength, of iron manhood, swaying with all its great spars and sails through a lashing gale, but holding firm with the massive fortitude of the Royal Navy, and suddenly I was falling, down towards that surging, howling sea, slipping, screaming . . .

I woke up sweating and trembling. Around me the scene had changed. Moonlight had broken through, silver on the sea. I went and looked down at the rushing foam as the ship shouldered forward into a wide world to be explored . . .

NINEVEH IN NAPLES

Naples was a Nineveh in late 1944, a babel of sound and lights, roaring Jeeps and soaring voices, where little *raggazzi* pimped for their clean, virgin, schoolmistress sisters, and sold rotten apples in paper cornets. We were quartered in an old castle, the Fort Dell'Ovo, down on the seafront, sleeping in the dungeons on a damp stone floor, where I quickly developed tonsillitis and was whisked off to the big white 52nd General Hospital on the hills above that famous bay. There I had a fortnight of eating melons, followed by another two weeks' recuperation on the island of Ischia, where I became happily up-homers with the Lollo look-alike who owned the small trattoria near the rest camp. Big eats, Jack, steak and chips and vino every day. *La dolce vita, bella fanciula.* My oppo there was a tall, stooped, hollow-cheeked stoker who looked like one of the living dead from a Bela Lugosi film. Once a Chief, he confided in me that he had had 22 doses of the clap . . . 'I've been out here five years, but I can't go home, not like I am . . .'

Back in Napoli I found that all my kit was gone, bought some more from shops with a 'casual', flogged the lot in a little cafe on the Via Roma, not far from the old Royal Palace, which was now a huge NAAFI, with facilities unheard of before by Jack-my-Hearty. In the wine bar was a swarthy waitress who stroked my hand as she served me . . . 'Cor!' said the Cadaver, 'The old green light! You're in there, mate. Fill yer boots!' I heard that you could even have art lessons, and had just turned into the art studio when there was a power cut. I stood rooted to the spot and when the juice came back I was standing facing a slim, dark girl, who turned out to be Tullia Matania, daughter of the famous artist. Under her guidance I brushed up my drawing, and once persuaded Tullia to use the wine-bar Sophia as a model, and there I was in heaven with lead in my pencil . . .

Another rare treat which Naples had to offer was a trip out to Pompeii, by lorry from The Palace every morning. The Cadaver knew the barrack guards, who were all from his old ship and let us come and go as we pleased, and I took the lorry every morning, to visit with the Vettii brothers, laze in their atrium, study the naughty frescoes, shout Shakespeare (I didn't know any Aeschylus) in the theatre, studying the positions on the walls of the brothel, still instructive though faded. One sunny morning I was sitting counting lizards in the Forum and listening to *L'Après-Midi d'un Faun* in my head when an Aussie voice said, 'Hey mate, how do you do this house of the Tragic Poet?' Quite without thinking I said, 'Straight down the Forum, under the Arch of Caligula, first left and it's the fourth house on the right. You can't miss it.' It was as if I was in Bath, my home town, directing some tourist to the Roman Baths or Sham Castle.

I nearly got caught. I returned to the 'Fort of The Egg' one day to find that the Tannoy had been asking for me all morning. My draft to the distant *Antares* had come through and in short time I was on passage to Taranto, this time in the huge, empty *Queen of Bermuda*, just six of us matlows in the whole of that floating hotel. We berthed at Taranto in the dark, and I was rushed off in a jeep to HMS *Antares*, lying alongside, gangway light glowing.

COMING OF AGE ABOARD *ANTARES*

She turned out to be a Fleet minesweeper of the *Algerine* class, built by Montreal Shipyards in 1943; one funnel, one 4in gun for'ard in a shield like a telephone box, and all her real business gear aft on the quarter (or sweeping)-deck: huge drums of wire for sweeping contact mines or shiny black electrical flex for the magnetic variety, 'kites' for holding the sweep wires at the required depths, Dan buoys for marking a swept channel. The radar was my concern – one Type 271 10cm surface warning set, with the old vertical handle (very useful to hang a bucket on) to turn the aerials and the old A-scope screen with horizontal trace. Back in RDF training at Douglas, Isle of Man, we had been told that the 271 could detect a surfaced U-boat at 8,000 yards, thanks to a fiendish device invented at Birmingham University called the Strapped Magnetron. There were still one or two U-boats in the Med, and I had no desire to be the hero who picked one up. The set was sited at the rear of the compass platform, with its distinctive 'lantern' containing the scanner above.

The next morning *Antares* and the other ships of the 19th Minesweeping Flotilla left Taranto and steered round the heel of Italy into the Adriatic and some very nasty choppy seas, which had us corkscrewing all the way up to Ancona, a God-forsaken wasteland of a place with one sordid cafe in a sea of mud and ruins. From here we were to sortie across to Yugoslavia to sweep the Hun mines laid all along the coast.

There, within easy range of German 12in guns ashore, our ships would sweep in echelon. The Radar Party consisted of myself and AB Johnny Hayes, a large genial youth who had been studying for the priesthood when war broke out; later young OD Brothers was added. Johnny and I formed a kite block team on the sweeping deck as well. The 'kite', which really looked like a boxkite in steel, had to be fixed by a block on to the sweep wire, which had the cutters attached. While one man swung out backwards over the ship's wake holding up the kite block, his team mate reached over from the stern and clamped the block on to the sweep wire. The kite was then streamed, and slid down the wire to its selected depth. We had some good weather, and then the sweeping deck was a fun place to be. I took boxing lessons from Leading Stoker Lightowler, a former Navy champion. But it could also be a highly dangerous place. Old hands could tell if there was too much tension in the sweep wire, first from the change of pitch in the perpetual humming sound which it gave off, then by sitting on the wire, bouncing up and down as it transmitted danger signals. When it seemed at breaking point he would leap off . . . 'Take cover!'. . . and everyone rushed forward to find shelter from the lashing, berserk wire which would leap over the stern, its jagged end looking for a matlow's tender body, or wrapping round him and cutting him in two. This never happened while I was aboard *Antares*, but we had one or two false alarms.

Another potentially dangerous job was to hold the wire with sinkers attached which also held the wires down. This had to be wound round the holder's forearm and released extra smartly when the weights were streamed, or he either got dragged overboard into the foaming wake or lost his arm. I was doing this job one day when the First Lieutenant, who was also Sweeping Officer, neglected to tell me he was streaming the weights, and I just got rid of the wire, which was doing a boa constrictor on me, before I was smashed against the after rails prior to serious injury and probably worse. I have often pondered on that little episode. I did not get along with Jimmy, who was known as 'Tojo', from a physical resemblance, but then neither did anyone else. I expect his mother loved him. He liked to keep me on the set, reporting the positions of the other sweepers in broad daylight, when radar's magic all-seeing eye was really redundant.

The ship was Canadian-built and quite comfortable. Most seamen slept in the lower messdeck, which was battened down and no-go during operations, when a mine or torpedo could have turned it into a graveyard; some, including myself, slung our hammocks in the upper messdeck, over the dining tables. There was one officer (who shall be nameless, as I don't fancy seeing him in court) who had the habit of wandering round at night (we were usually tied up by nightfall), peering and groping in men's hammocks, and I was cautioned to turn in with my hand wrapped round some form of weapon to repel boarders. The galley opened on to our upper messdeck, and food was usually hot and plenty, potmess being very popular. I have always loved my grub, and I became known as the ship's gannet. Anyone who left any of his meal always scraped if off on to my plate automatically. My particular oppos were Johnny Hayes, Chris the Asdic, and Ray Sadler, a rather bitter dipped CW candidate, who spent most of his off-watch time on a correspondence course on architecture.

I came of age, which in the Navy was 20, aboard *Antares*, and was able to draw my tot of Nelson's Blood at last, though I had been enjoying 'sippers' for some time as the price for small favours like the loan of a station card for a run ashore or a sub till pay day. It was 'grog' of course, watered rum, but very welcome as dished out by Scouse Palfrey. I was given the traditional ceremony, which included sippers from all the rummies in the mess. I passed out in the course of this orgy, and was lashed into my hammock and slung in the Lower Power Room. When I woke up with all the machinery thrashing round me, I thought I was in some sort of technological hell.

Sometimes home-coming to Ancona was less than warm, like the bitter winter night when we clawed our way in through a literally blinding snowstorm, Aldis lamps blazing, butting again and again into the boom before creeping into the harbour and crashing into our trot mate, the scruffy *Arcturus*. Once in it was cosy enough. The lads soon settled down, and the foul air of the lower messdeck was once again loud with 'Mazaire-a-vair', 'Crafty miz', 'Stick', 'Bust', and 'I'll go a bundle'. Jumper Cross would get out his guitar and try once more with his truck-driver's hands to pluck a recognizable tune from the sullen catgut. Ray Sadler thumbed his *Life of Christopher Wren*; myself my notebook, well filled by now with examples of the priceless lower deck argot and the occasional poem. While based on Ancona we fed a deserter from the Queen's Regiment who lived in the centre of a huge American Spam dump left behind by Mark Clark's overfed doughboys; he tapped on the scuttle every night with a sack of tins in exchange for white bread, bacon, butter and anything the cook would spare. Where are you now? Did they shoot you after all? Other 'rabbits' were brought aboard by the Radar Mechanic, an ex-policeman who had nothing to do on board, as the set never broke down, and had become ship's posty. His mail sack was always full.

YUGOSLAVIAN CAPERS

We received no more thanks from the Yugoslavs for our services in freeing their coasts of mines than did our lads on Russian convoys from the citizens of Murmansk and Archangel. They were all Tito people, not the Fascists of Mihailovic, and they did not like to see us ashore. Split was the nearest port, its streets so full of 'partisans' you wondered who was fighting the Germans. Offering a cigarette to a youthful *partijani* I was angrily stopped by a beautiful girl in uniform, and was about to object when I realized that, like the Venus de Milo, *she had no arms*. What damp and the vandals had needed centuries to do, a German grenade had accomplished in ten seconds. Johnny and I were invited to the home of a former professor of English and his two daughters, who wept when they confessed that they had only acorn coffee and black bread to give us, and two cabbages to take back to the ship.

More usually we tied up at a fishing village just north of Split called Kastel Sucurac. On our first stay there one watch went ashore, and I was climbing the ridge above the village when I heard a 'ping' quite close by, which sounded like a bullet to me. And so it was. No one had told us that the Germany Army had vacated the place only two hours before we arrived. While there we heard a buzz that a certain partisan leader had designs on the ship. The Skipper, a rotund, jolly Dart, took this seriously enough to ride with only two easily slipped wires – and me with a Sten gun (no bullets) on bridge watch. Irish Paddy said, 'If they pinched the f★★★★★g ship you'd never notice.' The lads got their own back on our sullen allies in a spectacular way. On the hills above the village stood the huge sign TITO in white letters. As we steamed away and left the golden shore of Kastel Sucurac (hopefully forever), the final 'O' was conspicuous by its absence.

We oftened wondered idly why the German shore batteries never fired on us, as we were a gaggle of sitting ducks, and put it down to their not wanting to ruin a good thing for themselves, having lived the *dolce vita* for years in something like a big Butlin's – with vino. Then, one day, the inevitable happened.

We were carrying out an orthodox Oropesa sweep in echelon, and the fine, sunny day had been marked by a phenomenon – our revered flotilla leader HMS *Rinaldo*, had actually appeared to lead us. Where she got to on the bad days we had no idea, but we hardly ever saw her.

Anyway, there she was, just ahead of *Antares*, on our port bow, sweeps out, float bobbing, every bit as if she knew what she was doing, when suddenly she swung away off course. A few minutes later aboard *Antares* there was an almighty bang . . . and the ship's 1,000 tons leapt into the air. Below, in the upper messdeck the cook was showing some of us one of his vast collection of dirty postcards. He thought the wrath of God had hit him and dropped the pictures all over the deck. We all thought it was a shell which those moribund batteries had at last decided to throw at us, and waited, suspended in horror, for the next round, which would surely blow us all to hell among the Chief Stokers.

None came, but a leading wireman staggered across the for'ard door, his face bleeding – as it turned out, from being hit by an attaché case falling on him. We rushed on deck, and the first person we saw was the Buffer, an unpopular man, blood streaming from his mouth and down his white shirt front. 'Buffs, Buffs,' we cried in our grief, 'What have you done?' He opened his mouth just long enough to snarl, 'I bit me f★★★★★g tongue!'

This rather set the tone of the whole drama. We had, mercifully, not been hit by a shell, but by a mine which our leader had put up – and had then got out of the way quicker than shit through a goose, instead of moving over to cover us from the rest of the assumed minefield. The mine was an 'O' type, the smallest in Doenitz's armoury, not big enough to sink us, but big enough to bite a big hole out of the bottom of the ship, and all the NAAFI stores fell out, which for some reason made the Canteen Manager very happy.

I reached my action station on the bridge just in time to pick up the buzzing phone and hear one Ordinary Seaman Metcalfe (of whom more later) report, from right aft, 'Mine exploded for'ard sir.' I repeated this to the Captain, who by now had reached the bridge and was giving a crisp series of orders which showed plainly that he, at least, knew exactly what he was doing. He listened gravely and said, 'That man is sucking up for promotion.'

Everyone was shaken, except the Captain, who was delighted at the blessed relief from the boredom of being all dressed up with nowhere much to go. The worst injury was a broken leg, and we slowly made our way down to Malta, with myself and young Brothers doing watch-and-watch in the absence of Johnny, suffering from bottled tot.

As we manoeuvred to approach our berth we contrived to go astern into the cliffs below Bighi Hospital, which did no significant damage to Malta but did *Antares*' already shaken structure no good at all. In Dockyard Creek we moored astern of the huge American light cruiser *Savannah*, and came in for some up-to-date movies on her quarter-deck, not to mention loads of tinned food from her cornucopia of goodies. She had just come in from the States, and Jack returned her kindness by exchanging for her lovely US dollars a sackful of counterfeit lire which had been dumped on us in Italy, but which the Yankee gobs and grunts seemed eager to collect, as they were heading up that way. After the dockyard men had taken a cursory look at our damage, we set sail for Ferryville, North Africa, praying fervently that we never, ever, met the *Savannah* again.

Destination Ferryville

Steaming slowly up the narrow canal to Ferryville, we eventually berthed. That night the starboard watch went ashore – and did not come back. We sat around well into the small hours speculating on what could have happened. Then, about half-past three, a very agitated and distraught Metcalfe, OD – the one who told the Captain all about the mine – struggled up the gangplank, with a truly epic story to tell . . .

'We all go into this knocking shop, see? There's a lot of French matlows in there, and we have to take our turn. Then some bloke rushes in and tells us the Patrol is outside. Them Frog dabtoes is very friendly and lend us bits of their uniforms, see? We're all sitting there trying to look French and that, and a dirty big PO of the Patrol comes in. He goes all round us, looking us up and down, and stops in front of Palfrey (the Rum bosun, a small, thin Scouser) – 'he's got one of them flat hats with a red pom-pom on, and says, "Well, *you* don't look French!" An' Palfrey says, "Well, I f★★★★n' am!" An' they cop the lot, except me, I dodged out the door at the back . . .'

Bit by bit the rest of the story came out, how starboard watch carried out a fighting retreat towards the ship, reminiscent at least of Moore's men at Corunna, with Leading Stoker Lightowler outdoing Leonidas of Sparta and Roland at Roncevalles rolled into one bringing up the fighting rearguard, but going down at last to heavy reinforcements of the local gendarmerie and being dragged off to 'le clink', where they still were, sad, sore and homesick.

When Metcalfe repeated his story in the wardroom, it was reported by the officers' steward that the Skipper laughed right through the dog watches. Collecting his battered lads from the local Chateau d'If with the promise of dire punishment for all – and a special example to be made of the valiant Lightowler – he led them back up the gangplank still grinning all over his face, gave out a few minor restrictions of leave – which didn't mean much in Ferryville anyway – and sentenced Lightowler to tend bar at the ship's dance.

Leaving a Care and Maintenance Party behind, the rest of us took passage in the floating slum of an 'Allied' Italian destroyer to Malta, and I was drafted to HMS *Kimberley*, a survivor of Mountbatten's *Kelly* class, a Med fixture known as 'Cunningham's Taxi'.

Kimberley's beat was the Dodecanese Islands, still German-occupied. Here we patrolled uneventfully, except for a bombardment of Rhodes with our 4.7 in popguns, cut short when the somnolent Germans fired back with their 12 in, and we left in a hurry.

We were back in a short time to receive the German surrender by their General Wagner. He stumped red-faced up the ladder, followed by his aide, a Goebbels look-alike, who gave us a stiff-arm Sieg Heil job. There was a growl from the lads, and the Skipper waved them brusquely below, following which we steamed through the harbour entrance once bestridden by the Colossus, and gave the new Governor, Archbishop Makarios, a 21-gun salute as he sailed in, black beard blowing in the wind.

The Eastern Fleet

Come to the Spare Crew, make no delay,
Come to the Spare Crew – two bob a day,
Sweeping up the messdecks, nothing else to do,
Come to the Spare Crew, do.
Joyful, joyful, joyful we will be
When the boats are shoving off to sea,
We'll be sweeping up the messdecks,
F★★k-all else in view,
Come to the Spare Crew, do.

HEAT AND THE RISING SUN

In Trincomalee harbour, Ceylon, in the trot alongside the submarine depot ship HMS *Wu Chang*, an old Chinese river steamer, was Iain Nethercott in *Tactician*, which had made the trip from Beirut.

'*Taurus* had left on patrol down to the upper parts of the Molucca Straits. It was the monsoon season. Filthy greeny-black skies and sheets of warm rain. We went on patrol. As we pushed on south it got hotter and hotter in the boat, and more and more humid. The only thing to wear was a towel round one's waist, and nothing else. When dived, the temperature went up to 120°–130°, and we just streamed with sweat. First of all it was prickly heat and sweat rash. The skin peeled off between our legs and from under our arms. We had no air-conditioning in these older T-boats, but Vickers had fitted us with a wonderful specimen of technological ingenuity called a Dehumidifier. Although this box of tricks used many precious amps from my battery, the Skipper decided to try it out. After a lot of work the Outside ERA got it going. It made a tremendous din, and after a couple of hours' running when dived it had wrenched about two pints of dirty water out of the atmosphere. We never used it again.

'Conditions on board after a few weeks at sea were appalling. The food was all wrong. The bread had turned to green mould after a few days, so the cook had to bake bread every night. The flour was full of weevils and had to be sieved before use. We had jars of salt tablets and "Sunshine Pills" (Vitamin C) in all the messes. For a long time these had been mistrusted by Jolly Jack, as someone had spread the buzz that they dampened his sexual ardour, like *Ganges* bromide; then it got around that in fact they had just the opposite effect, and were swallowed by the handful. I've often wondered when they'll start to work.

'Water was very short, only to be used for drinking and cleaning your teeth, and the Chief Stoker had it turned off most of the time. The boat was infested with rats and cockroaches, and before long most of us had a dose of crabs, and as we had nothing on board for that kind of trouble we tried white spirit, with its ensuing rash.

'The waters we were operating in were smooth and oily, with countless uncharted mudbanks and small islands which at night looked just like ships. The Japanese were active but the targets were not really worth all the effort. The American subs in the Pacific were getting all the good targets, and only in Sabang, Penang and Singapore, all naval bases, was anything happening.

'We finally withdrew from patrol and headed for Trinco. Thirty miles out we were escorted in by *Eritrea*, an Italian naval sloop which a few months earlier had been fighting us. This time we went alongside *Adamant*, a spotless, gleaming brand-new depot ship which, till we tied up alongside her, had never seen a submarine, having been operating bloody cruisers off the East African coast. She was all brass and bugle calls, and her paintwork shone in the sunshine. We soon changed all that when we scraped alongside in our dark-green and rust-red motley, the officer of the day and attendant side-boy with telescope glaring down at us. The splinter holes we had received in the Med had never been patched up, we had our Jolly Roger up, and the casing party made an effort and lined up in their Afrika Korps uniforms. The *Adamant* shower tied us up and just left us. No welcome, no mail, it was uncanny.

'I wandered up the gangway, wearing only my pair of greasy khaki shorts, with six weeks' beard, crabby and filthy-dirty. As I crossed the immaculate well-deck to look for their duty ERA to get the shore leads down our conning tower and belted on, I was pulled up short by a hysterical shriek. An immaculate, overfed little subby was yelling at me. I drifted over and received a king-sized bollocking for the state I was in . . . "Why aren't you in the rig of the day? Look at the mess you're making! Stand to attention! Get your hair cut!" etc, etc. I strolled back on board *Tactician* leaving my trail of greasy footprints over his white deck.

'The Coxswain tried to calm me down with a tot. The Skipper was next door entering up all the lies in the log before going inboard, heard me doing this tremendous toot and came in to ask me why I wasn't my usual smiling self. I gave him both barrels . . . Rig of the day – when all my kit was somewhere between Beirut and Colombo, and probably lost forever? And a shampoo and set was difficult on a patrol submarine, and short of jumping over the side with a giant bar of salt-water soap and bathing every night of the week, how the bloody hell do you keep clean – especially when you've been crawling about under the engines to repair the ballast pump? Etc, etc . . . Cocoa Bill – so called because anyone in the boat who made up a mug of kye at night found the Skipper at his elbow asking for a cup – had an evil sense of humour, told me to stop my almighty drip, took me to the wardroom where we both had a whisky, and away we went up the gangway. The Skipper sought out my little commissioned friend and explained to him very forcibly that submarine crews at sea did not spend their time sitting on deckchairs on the casing drinking Martinis.'

'For month after month,' says Nethercott, speaking for all the East Indies Fleet submarines, 'we carried on patrolling, sinking Marus in the Straits of Malacca, and many junks, with Japs in the water trying to kill any Malays swimming towards us, spies and raiding parties, picking up half-clad men from the jungle. We laid mines at dawn off Singapore, creeping right in under their patrols. We could fight a gun battle in our sleep. We were harried by small Jap sub-chasers, which at times were very persistent. We even had to surface one night, having been kept down overlong, till we were literally blue in the face and gasping for breath, and take on the chaser in a gun action. It was a short but bloody action in which they all finished up dead. *Stonehenge* and *Stratagem* had gone by then, and most of *Stratagem*'s crew had been executed.

'D-Day in Europe came and went, our boat was getting more and more cranky, all our batteries suffered from sulphation, the Engineer Officer was nearly in tears over the state of the main engines, the stern glands had slow leaks, the rifling of the gun barrel was worn smooth, and, worst of all, we were getting overtired. With one or two exceptions we still had the original crew from Barrow, and it was now the middle of 1944.

'The terrible heat in the boat, especially down on the Equator, gradually made us more and more ill. We lay on rush mats now, as we found that we stuck to the locker cushions when we lay on them. We wore sarongs made out of curtain material, the Skipper sporting the gaudiest. He allowed the stokers up on the conning tower at night in pairs, but nothing could really be done. At night when we were forced down in the middle of a battery charge, the engines were red-hot and the batteries overheated.

'All ventilation had to be switched off as we were hunted, and wave after wave of terrific heat built up round you. Men collapsed with heat stroke, but nothing could be done for them till we were able to open up the hatch again and vent the boat. We took a naval surgeon lieutenant to sea on one patrol to report on conditions. He collapsed in the second week and nearly died in his bunk. The temperature was 140°, beyond which they reckoned men couldn't survive. We did.

'At night when we were on the surface we had our dinner and our rum. We left most of the dinner but drank the rum. The gash buckets were always slopping over with all the dinners chucked into them. These buckets had to be hauled up the conning tower at night using a hook rope, and ditched over the leeward side of the bridge. When the boat was rolling the buckets collided with the sides of the tower on their upward journey and often half the contents finished up either in the tower or in the Control Room beneath. Once the klaxon sounded off in the middle of this operation. The gash party up top and the two lookouts leapt for the conning tower hatch as she started to dive, with about 30 swilling gash buckets lined up under the Control Room ladder. The Skipper and Jimmy were dancing around in the Control Room, leaping in and out of buckets while all of us who had to run the length of the boat to get to our Diving Stations got caught up in the general mêlée, skidding around on spud peelings and lumps of fat as the boat plunged down.

'On one patrol we were so desperately hot and sick that the Skipper took us out 20 miles from the coast and allowed "Hands to bathe", twenty at a time at 0300 in the morning, cheerfully telling us that he would dive and leave us if he was surprised by a patrol boat. It was wonderful until one of our ABs got bitten in the leg by a barracuda and let out a yell of "Shark!" We cleared the water in about ten seconds.

'Once we sailed to rendezvous at a creek in the jungle on the Malayan coast to pick up a spy who had been landed by *Telemachus*. The Skipper had checked it through the periscope during the day, and we crept inshore that night and waited for the light signal so that our SBS folboat men could creep in and fetch the agent. We got light signals all right, but they were coming from the wrong place and were not correct. While the Skipper was thinking we suddenly spotted a Jap patrol boat coming round the headland. We opened fire with the 4in and charged out to sea and dived away out of it. The spy had been captured and tortured and the whole thing was a trap.

'When we sailed on patrol from Trincomalee we used to fill the boat up with green tropical fruit which was hung in every available space except the Engine Room, Control Room and Motor Room. Looking through the boat into the fore-ends looked like the Tropical House at Kew Gardens. The trouble was that it all went rotten after a couple of days, and made the ship stink more than ever. 'Admiral "Slim" Somerville came aboard just before we went on a particularly hazardous patrol and gave us a boost-up speech and walked through the boat. When he arrived in my Motor Room and looked aft into the stokers' mess, all he saw was a mass of greenery, with one of the killick stokers stark naked looking for his seagoing sarong. "Like Tarzan of the bloody apes," said the Admiral.

'One thing about the life was that you never knew till you got to sea who you were likely to find in the mess or fore-ends. You would stroll up to the torpedo stowage compartment and in the dim red patrol lighting you would find a gang of Chinese cut-throats cleaning their guns, or strange parties of Aussie soldiers with dozens of packs of explosives and Tommy guns. We had Chinese spies in the mess; half of whom probably fought against us later on in the Malayan troubles. Men we picked up from the jungle were sometimes dying of fever, some were wounded, and we carried no medical aid other than the cox'n had, who had done a week's course at Haslar Hospital. Intelligence back in Ceylon were very eager to get hold of some live Japs, and two captains, Red McKenzie (Rufus) and the Black McKenzie were in competition to get one. They never succeeded, though not for want of trying – a great relief to us as the idea of one of those fanatics on board, possibly getting loose, and pulling every valve and lever in sight before we could recapture him, filled us with dread.

'The Japanese submarines operating out of Penang, on the Malacca coast of Malaya, were committing terrible atrocities on merchant ship crews, many of whom were ordered out of their lifeboats and hacked to death on the submarine casing. *Taurus* had sunk *I.8*, a big ocean-going submarine which had sunk an Allied merchantman, killed the crew and thrown some of them back into their lifeboats. The Captain had survived – with his hands chopped off. Yes, we were definitely after those bastards.'

UNDERWATER RESCUE

'We were detailed off at the end of one patrol to be crash boat off Sabang, Sumatra, to cover an Anglo-American carrier raid on the port. *Saratoga* was operating with *Illustrious* in a dawn dive-bombing attack on the oil tanks and other military targets.

'We surfaced off Sabang about 10 minutes before zero hour and patrolled slowly in towards the harbour, trimmed down. The Skipper had detailed Frankie Mustard, a killick stoker, and me as swimming party, as we were the best underwater swimmers in the boat. Just as dawn broke we heard the roar of aircraft coming in from seaward, Hellcats and Wildcats. In a flash they were over the port. We blew the boat right up and speeded up, and sailed in towards the harbour. A section of three American fighters flew alongside at sea height covering us. The whole harbour area was alive with explosions, the bombing was very accurate. Suddenly the first shells from the shore batteries arrived, and the Skipper started weaving the boat about.

'A patrol boat appeared inshore, coming out of the harbour towards us. The Skipper yelled "Up with the guns' crews!" and "Break out the Ensign!" to Scouse, the bunting-tosser. The 4 in opened up as we sailed in towards the shore. Our three aircraft were shouting to us and each other over the R/T and streaked towards the patrol boat and riddled it with fire. It stopped, and under another attack, caught fire. A Hellcat was down in the water close-in, and Air Escort and others were calling us on R/T while others circled the downed plane.

'We steamed as fast as we could towards the sinking aircraft, and the shore batteries were getting very close (afterwards the starboard lookout swore that one shell went between the periscope standards). The plane had practically sunk now, with only its tail showing. As we smashed alongside, Frankie and I jumped in from the starboard ballast tank and swam down. We could see the pilot inside, desperately trying to open the canopy, and it seemed to have flooded up inside. I tried pulling the canopy back but it wouldn't shift, when suddenly Frankie, who was on the other side, found an emergency release lever of some kind and we pulled the canopy back. The chap was OK and had already undone his webbing. We dragged him out and swam up with him. McNally of the casing party dived in and grabbed him, and he was dragged aboard. Our air escort gave us the all-clear and we dived away and made for the open sea.

'After a bit of medical attention our friend was walking around the boat. He was a US Navy officer, and I don't think he had ever seen anything like our boat and crew. We must have looked like pirates to him, with our scruffy beards and sweaty bodies, and the last time they had seen a sarong was on Dottie Lamour; but he was friendly enough, as we all knew that if we hadn't picked him up he would have been dragged ashore and executed.

'When we came into Trinco a few days later we had our flier up on the bridge to show him off, and the whole Task Force cheered ship. The *Saratoga* was dressed overall for us, and as we made fast alongside *Adamant* we were invaded by dozens of American launches full of boxes of cigars, crates of Coke, ice-cream and cameramen. They completely ignored the *Adamant*'s protocol and swarmed aboard and were down in the boat snapping us in every conceivable position. Eventually I managed to get aboard *Adamant* and got my hot bath and shave.

'That night we were all invited aboard *Saratoga* for films and big eats. Their Admiral had Frankie Mustard and me out in the front and gave a big speech personally thanking the Skipper. Some time afterwards Captain 'S' sent for me and told me that the Americans had wanted to give some of us a medal, but that the Admiralty had declined the offer, stating that we were only doing our job. This was true.

'We had a succession of young lieutenants and subbies sent to the boat for patrols to give our chaps a break. We had Aussies, New Zealanders, South Africans and Rhodesians. One very pink and proper South African subby came to the boat in immaculate whites to join us for a patrol. After a couple of weeks, like the rest of us he got a huge dose of crabs. He came along to Fred the Coxswain for advice. He'd never even heard of crabs and was appalled. Fred was in one of his funny moods and told him to go to the wardroom, take his shorts down and squat over a bucket of water. The human crab, he said, was a strange creature that suffers from dizziness. It would see its reflection in the water moving about, get giddy and fall off into the bucket and drown. The Springbok swallowed all this, went along to the wardroom, where everyone was turned in, and squatted down over his bucket. The Skipper came out of his box and caught him at it, laughed his head off and told him the Coxswain was taking the mickey. He explained that the proper treatment was to rub in a mixture of rum and sand. The crabs got drunk on the rum and threw rocks at each other until they were all dead.

'At Trinco the number of surface warships grew bigger every time we came in. It got crowded ashore. The Fleet canteen was built of thatch, with just Australian canned beer and long tables. The Aussies set fire to it and destroyed it, and that was that. We were still sent up into the hills to recuperate, but it was bloody boring.

'At long last we were told – one more patrol and we were going home. *Adamant* and her T-boats were sailing for Fremantle in Aussie, to be followed by *Maidstone* and the "S" boats. All submarines were to come under American command and work up in the islands.

'*Taurus* sailed for home on one engine, and we went on our last patrol. It was a difficult one. How many of our submarines had been sunk on their last patrol due to their crews being overstressed and suffering from fatigue? Wanklin's *Upholder* may well have gone that way. However, we made it, although most of us were at the Skipper's elbow almost willing him to be cautious and not take any chances.

'When we arrived back off patrol we just couldn't take it in. We were going home! In submarines you never thought beyond the next patrol. Personally, I never thought that I would survive, and now, with a bit of luck, I was going to live.'

Illustrious Goes East

Death is not an adventure for those
who stand face to face with it.
Erich Maria Remarque

Here they were, a veteran ship, but with, for the most part, an untried air group whose principal experience so far was of crash after crash, of doubt and death. They were young, the youngest only schoolboys, none of them yet masters of their temperamental machines, their new leader only a 'Temporary' VR with no combat experience. Most were newly trained men from the US Navy's Miami Fighter School, young men from all parts of the Empire, with different backgrounds and accents: 'Bash' Munnock, a tough ex-Marine from Middlesbrough; Johnny Baker, a big husky Canuck; Gordon Aitken, a colonial public schoolboy born in Ceylon, where his father, a planter, still lived; Eric Rogers, very young and very noisy, from Birmingham; Neil Brynildsen, a quiet New Zealander . . . all ordinary young men.

ENTER *SARATOGA*

Admiral Nimitz, USN, Allied Naval C-in-C in the Pacific, wanted operations mounted against the East Indies which would be both directly damaging to the Japanese war effort and draw men and material away from the Pacific, where his great offensive was in full swing. The first of these targets was to be Sabang, an island close to the northern tip of Sumatra, where oil storage tanks, an airfield and a submarine base were concentrated. HMS *Illustrious* was to mount an attack on these, in co-operations with the USS *Saratoga*.

The two veteran carriers met on a bright blue day in the Eastern Indian Ocean, *Illustrious* bringing with her Taranto, Salerno and the Malta convoys; the great *Saratoga*, the glory of Guadalcanal and the Solomons, Rabaul and the Gilberts and Marshalls. She and her prancing destroyers *Fanning, Dunlap* and *Cummings* came up with *Illustrious* at 1145 on the morning of 27 March 1944. Admiral Moody flew to *Saratoga* in a Barracuda, which caused one US pilot to comment 'Gee, the British'll be inventing airplanes any day now.' '*Sara*' sent over her Air Group Commander, 'Jumping Joe' Clifton, to lead tactfully the inexperienced British air group into practice for Sabang. In Jumping Joe's group some of the lads recognized a number of their former instructors from Miami Fighter School. There were big gin parties, with Norman Hanson, 1833 Squadron's VR

Co, at the piano; although PO Mechanician Con Shiels from Tyneside complains that the attitude of the officers, in the otherwise reasonably democratic regime which prevailed generally in *Illustrious*, showed itself when 'all cooling machinery for the rest of the ship was shut off so that they could have ice in their drinks – and we were in the Indian Ocean!' The Americans greatly improved British creature comforts, offering the use of their washing machines, cartons of Lucky Strike or Camels, T-bone steaks, Mom's Apple Pie – all free.

Sabang was scheduled for 12 April. Specific targets were the huge oil storage tanks, the airfield, tankers, supply ships and submarines in the harbour, as well as the radar station and power station and sundry targets in the town, the whole to be co-ordinated by a hovering Jumping Joe in his Hellcat, while the rest of the Fleet bombarded from seaward. It was the Corsair boys' first real op. They were excited, as before an important rugger match, but death was not in their eager minds.

'We sailed early in the morning,' says Leading Wireman Dennis Bond in *Queen Elizabeth*. 'The sea was lovely and blue and we had the company of flying fish. We steamed east for a couple of days, the Fleet looking splendid spread over a wide area of sea, with *Illustrious* on the horizon. But the heat below was stifling. Then came "Hands to Action Stations!" We had arrived. The shore didn't look very far away. It was funny to think of the Japs so close. I went down to my action station with the Leading Stoker, and, boy, was it hot down there! We sat down near the switchboard and tried to make ourselves as comfortable as we possibly could under the circumstances. Then over the intercom we heard the order "Fire when guns come on target", a routine by now as familiar as it had been in the *Whitshed*. But the next thing that happened was not at all familiar. With a gigantic roar we let go a 15 in broadside. The whole ship sank down on the recoil, and we below decks could hear the water gurgling up the side as the ship was pushed down.'

Meanwhile *Illustrious*'s Corsairs and Barracudas had taken off. As they approached the target Sabang came up, 'a little green tropical island rising from the silver water against the silken curtain of the pale-blue early-morning sky', wrote Norman Hanson. 'When the first dirty black mushroom of flak began to blossom silently above the island it seemed like sacrilege.'

No fighters came up to meet them. They nosed over and went down with the 'Barras'. '*Now*, Hans!' said Forde crisply over the R/T, and the Corsairs shot ahead. Norman, in the lead, 'aimed at gun flashes appearing above the leading-edge of the wings, too excited to notice details!' They joined up again. There was a barrage of chatter on the R/T. Norman gleaned from it that Jumping Joe's wingman, Dale 'Klondike' Kahn, had been shot down in the sea. 'He must be saved!' shouted Joe. Down below, HMS *Tactician* had seen the Hellcat go down and headed straight for it. Four Hellcats strafed an awkward shore battery into silence, the submarine reached the sinking plane and after a brave and successful rescue act, *Tactician* headed seawards and submerged.

The next targets were Jap installations near Surabaya. *Saratoga*'s Dauntlesses hit the oil refinery at Wonokromo, *Illustrious*'s planes the Braat Works, the biggest engineering unit in the Indies.

The raid was a success, and '*Sara*' departed for the Pacific. In July aircraft from *Illustrious* beat up Port Blair, South Andaman Island, a big staging post for Jap forces in Burma, and its airfield, where tiny figures tried to out-run the 'Whistling Death', as the Japs called the Corsair. Yammering 0.5s tore into parked planes, setting them off like giant fireworks. Young Londoner Reggie Shaw raced down the side of the field, knocking petrol bowsers into blazing wreckage. Then it was the radar station on Mount Harriet, target for their AP and incendiary. 'Watch that bastard with the machine-gun up on the mast!' shouted Norman.

The cruiser *Suffolk* – *Bismarck*'s bloodhound – was blasting away with her 8 in guns when a Seafire came in low on their starboard side. 'We could see he was in trouble,' says Bill Earp, still on his 4 in AA gun, 'but the destroyer on our beam began firing at the poor bugger, who was obviously trying to ditch alongside the ship firing on him. In spite of all this, the pilot got out as he hit the water and was hauled aboard the destroyer safely. We all cheered like mad but what was said when he got aboard is not hard to guess. It was unfortunate that in the heat of battle Seafires and "Zeros" tended to look alike, and it took a lot of self-control to hold fire until the order was given.'

Vian had them exercising on Christmas Day. Says Norman Hanson, 'One of our guys missed the wires and slammed his Corsair into the barrier, covering the deck with flaming oil and petrol. A fierce wind swept this aft. The kid in the cockpit jumped out on to the wing but instead of jumping down for'ard, where he would have been safe, leapt off the trailing-edge right into the fire, with sleeves and trousers rolled up and no mask or goggles – strictly against instuctions – and suffered massive third-degree burns.'

In January 1945 they struck the refineries of Pladjoe and Soenei Gerong at Palembang in south-east Sumatra.

Norman's Flight flew into a circus of 'Tojo' and 'Oscar' fighters over Pladjoe, and when they returned to the ship they were all weary, nerves shot, reflexes ragged.

Norman came in to land: 'Wheels and hook down, on to the downwind leg at 500 feet. Flaps down . . . Christ! She's not slowing down. I've been hit . . . But Bats is signalling "Roger". . . Fast let-down on to the deck . . . Suddenly the ship is blotted out (another Corsair cuts in ahead of him). Stall . . . the sea races at me, a great blinding crash . . . The world goes black . . . I come to – underwater . . . *I'm drowning* . . . hanging upside-down in my harness . . . scrabble with one gloved hand . . . There's a narrow opening between hood and windscreen . . . Somehow I rip the harness off and drag myself out through the gap. Looking up I see the lighter green water near the surface . . . A violent jerk to get free and reach that wonderful light, so near, half-drowned, gagging and swallowing water, remembering to blow up my Mae West with the CO_2 bottle . . . burst up into blinding sunlight . . .

'I lie back in the water gasping for breath, choking on salt water every time a wave swamps me . . . I see a smoke float which the ship has dropped, about 300 yards away . . . It's burning well but I can't make it . . . No thought of sharks or of getting rid of my revolver or jungle machete – no use here . . . Then, unspeakable delight, there's a destroyer coming up . . .'

AVENGER BLUES

'Three days later', recorded Sub-lieutenant (A) Eric Rickman, RNVR, of *Illustrious*'s No 854 Avenger Squadron, 'Admiral Vian came aboard to talk to the aircrews. He said that Pladjoe had been extensively damaged, and was considered out of action. That left Soenei Gerong, next door, and we were to attack each dawn until that too was destroyed. He returned to *Indomitable*. We pilots studied the model refinery Intelligence had provided, our Flight of six being allocated the pumping-house, which brought up the oil, a pin-point target about as big as the average semi.'

Eric, who shared piano duty in the frequent evening singsongs with Norman Hanson, had completed three years of art school training before being called up, and had successfully sat the entrance exam to the Royal College of Art – 'to be followed up if we won, and if I survived the war'. Eric had also been interested in aircraft 'from the age of eight, but since my father came from Cowes, and his father had sailed the world in a two-masted schooner, plus an uncle of mine was a PO, RN, I opted for the Fleet Air Arm rather than the RAF'.

Pladjoe was comparatively trouble-free, in spite of the forest of balloons surrounding it from 2,000–6,000ft.

'Next day, about 0445, we approached Soenei Gerong at 12,000ft. I could see the target ahead and the balloons, then the CO called "Line astern – go!" and we dropped back to 100-yard intervals. I had just opened the bomb-bay doors when Vick, my TAG, called on the intercom "There's an Oscar on our tail!" "Open fire then!" I shouted. I heard Vick's Browning chattering, the target was coming up just ahead, slightly to port, just right. "Gun's jammed, Skip . . .' Vick's voice was tense. "Well, unjam it fast, you twit!" I screamed, tension showing. "Never mind, I'm going down now." The refinery was almost below me, and as I trimmed the Avenger for the dive and put the stick forward, I could see the three aircraft ahead of me, and the balloons, and . . . yes, there was the pump-house, just like the model.

'Luckily the Oscar broke off. We were now below balloon height, and I could see one particular balloon cable between us and the pump-house, almost vertically below. Charlie will go round it I thought . . . but he didn't – to my horror, he hit the cable with his port wing, shearing off two-thirds of it as clean as a whistle, the rest of the Avenger going into a vicious one-wing spin, blowing up on impact seconds later.

'The Senior Pilot, Gerry Connolly, rounded the cable and was making his attack, and behind him and just ahead of me was Roland Armstrong. I could hardly believe my eyes when he hit the same cable, just as the CO had done, with exactly the same result. I felt sick and angry – how could they not have seen that cable? . . .

'Time to bomb . . . I jinked round the cable . . . The target was obliterated in a huge rising smoke cloud, black with flashes of flame in it. I pressed the button, started pulling out, realized I couldn't avoid the smoke cloud, so went straight into it. The Avenger bucked in the turbulence, and emerged from the smoke on its side at 500ft. I levelled out, went down to tree-top height, and headed round for the coast, blasting away with my front guns at horn-locator sites, lorries, huts, anything worth firing at. Approaching the coast I started to climb, looking round as I did so for Jap fighters – none. Then I saw another Avenger, away down to starboard. It looked all right, wasn't trailing smoke or anything, but as I watched it I realized it was in a shallow dive, and it blew up as it hit the sea. Result of attack – 18 direct hits. We did not need another dawn at Palembang.'

The next day they refuelled at sea and steamed for Fremantle and the Pacific. Australia did its best for them – movies, night clubs, bars and bathing beaches, two dozen oysters for lunch swilled down with champagne at five bob a bottle. Vian himself was seen with a big blonde in a night club. They were all chasing the golden hour, as the future sidled stealthily closer.

Deadly Sakishimas

Some replacement pilots joined the ship and they put to sea – just in time for Operation 'Iceberg'. This was the invasion of Okinawa. As Task Force 57, the BPF (British Pacific Fleet) would be part of Admiral Ray Spruance's Fifth Fleet in this grim task – a small unit compared with Admiral Marc Mitscher's famous Fast Carrier Force, Task Force 58.

From China to Okinawa itself was a chain of airfield stepping-stones formed by Formosa and the Sakishima Islands. When the attack on Okinawa began they would try to fly in planes from this chain of airfields. It was the job of the British carriers to stop them. 'They've given us the dirty work,' said Vian privately.

On 11 March 1945, with the carriers in the Solomon Sea, Hanson wrote in his diary: 'Scenery wonderful; the islands vary from massive outcrops of rock to green, flat reefs with lovely golden sands. Just like a fairy tale.'

Manus, the great fleet anchorage in the mouth of the Bismarck Sea, dispelled the image. Says Con Shiels, PO Mechanician in *Illustrious*, 'The Yankee matlows called the place "the asshole of the world" and quite rightly. I had to queue up at the RN canteen for one bottle of beer, though when I was made up to Chief I would be invited to the USN canteen, where we were given a book of tickets which entitled us to 20 beers. I still have one of those books, empty, of course.'

On the night of the 14th the four British carriers crossed the Equator, and on the 20th entered Ulithi lagoon, the US Pacific Fleet's main advanced base, a great, smooth stretch of blue water enclosed by rough, rocky atolls. On the 23rd the assault on Okinawa began.

Three days later they took station 100 miles south of the Sakishimas, and their part of 'Iceberg' began. Logbooks recorded: 'Strike on Sakishima Gunto: airfields.'

For the first time of many they flung themselves down from the eye of the bright, hot sun upon those criss-cross runways, deadly with thick ack-ack – and returned several planes and aircrew short. Runways were blasted out of action, aircraft shot up on the ground.

The next day they went to Ishigaki, the boot-shaped island with the fiercest flak of all. Eric Rickman sat in his Avenger, ready for take-off. This was not a day to be celebrating his birthday. 'Rick', said the voice of John his observer in his headphones, 'have you looked out to starboard?' 'I turned my head. The orange sun was just clear of the horizon, and scattered clouds in the east caused the sun's rays to form a huge radial pattern in the sky, like a celestial Japanese flag! Some omen!'

'However, the raid on Ishigaki was straightforward, apart from the flak, which even as we had approached at 12,000 ft had been smack-on for height, and too close for comfort. It seemed the nearer one got to Japan itself, the more accurate the flak became. Not surprising, perhaps.

'Next day, Hirara airfield on Miyako Jima. I got two direct hits on the radio station, and saw the large wireless mast collapse. Away at tree-top height as usual, I made for the rendezvous area, climbing. "Do you know where we are, Johnnie?" I asked.

"Near enough. How's our petrol?"

"It's OK."

"And how's the starboard aileron?"

I'd forgotten about that. Light flak had removed half of it, but it seemed to work all right, but for how long?

"Seems OK. Call the ship."

'We reported, and flew back to *Illustrious*. A mile away the ship called us. "Stay clear, we're being attacked by Kamikazes." I glanced at the petrol gauge – enough for half an hour, perhaps more. Fifteen minutes later we landed on.

'Two Fireflies, carrying a larger dinghy, had been sent to find Notts, without success. Hours later a submarine just happened to surface a few hundred yards from his dinghy. It was, I am happy to say, American.'

Now the pattern was – strike and rest, strike and rest, blast craters in the airstrips, then come back when the Japs had filled them in – on and on in a hazy chain of hard action and reaction, with losses mounting and men getting steadily more and more weary and twitched: '. . . bags of flying all day. Wrote a few letters tonight. *Bloody* tired.' . . . so that every deck landing became a thing of jarring nerves and churning guts.

KAMIKAZE

Then the pattern changed, and there was a new word for fear – 'Kamikaze'. It meant 'Divine Wind', a reference to the great storm that smashed 4,000 Mongol ships which had come to invade Japan in 1281. It was also known as 'Tokko', the 'Special Attack Force', created by Vice-Admiral Takijiro Ohnishi in October 1944 to combat the mounting force of the American offensive. 'In my opinion', said Ohnishi, 'this can be accomplished by crash-diving on the carrier flight decks with Zero fighters carrying 250 kg bombs.' This was of course a suicide mission. 'It is better to die with honour than to live without honour,' said Kamikaze pilot Lieutenant Yuko Sehi. From the battle of Leyte Gulf onwards it was a major weapon. US Navy carriers had 'soft' flight decks of Oregon pine, and many were knocked out, as well as destroyer radar pickets.

At half-past seven on the morning of April Fool's Day 1945 a 'Divine Wind' hit the BPF when a 'Zero' struck *Indefatigable*'s bridge island. There was some damage but she was operational again in the afternoon. Meanwhile the destroyer HMS *Ulster* took a 'Kamikaze' right through her Iron Deck and into her boiler room. Then a 'Deadly Johnson', as the British matlows called the suicider, to deflate some of its mystique, scraped *Victorious*'s bows.

Five days later it was the turn of *Illustrious*. 'We heard in the engine room', says Charlie Shiels, 'through the Tannoy, the Commander, who always kept us informed of what was going on up top, warning us that a "Kamikaze" suicide plane was coming straight for us. It was my fifth wedding anniversary, and I kept saying "Please God, not today, don't kill me today. Tomorrow if you must, but please, not today!" It would have hurt my wife enough to have me killed, but on our wedding anniversary it would have made it much worse.'

The gunners had seen him coming, diving towards the for'ard part of the ship. He may have been following the usual 'Tokko' practice of aiming for the forward lift. Whatever he had in mind, the Bofors gunners changed it for him, knocking him about so much that he exploded over the side.

He left some souvenirs behind. His starboard wing had actually crashed into the bridge about nine feet away from Captain Lambe, and pieces of plane and pilot were scattered over the flight deck. Bob Ellison bent down and dazedly picked up two eyeballs and a piece of skull. He was looking stupidly at them when New Zealander Don Hadman of 1830 Squadron dashed up and grabbed the piece of skull from his hand . . . 'That's my mascot from now on!' Don was carrying his mascot when he took off and stopped the breath of the next 'Divine Wind' to appear over the Fleet; then, with bitter irony, returning alone, badly shot-up, he was fired on by his own gunners in mistake for a 'Kamikaze'. A Seafire on the tail of a 'Deadly Johnson' was hit by the barrage intended for the Jap and shot to bits.

At Okinawa the 'Kamikazes' inflicted the greatest losses ever suffered by the US Navy in a single battle, killing almost 5,000 men.

Shutting Up Shop

On 13 July there were two strikes on Formosa. By now nothing Japanese was to be seen in the sky over their airfields, and nothing visible intact on the ground. On the 14th somebody stuck their head round Norman Hanson's door and shouted, 'Wakey, wakey, get up and look what's on our starboard bow!'

It was *Formidable*, fresh out from England – their relief. Every man, HO or Regular, aboard felt the great, unimaginable lift of spirit. 'The Admiralty thought we had had enough,' says Con Shiels, 'which I could not deny, and sent us home.' 'We simply shut up shop,' said Norman Hanson.

The other 'cast-iron carriers' of TF57 carried on digging holes in the Ryuku runways, with trips to the replenishment areas 'Cootie', 'Midge' or 'Mosquito' on 10, 14, 18 and 22 May, when the US escort carrier *Sangamon*'s TU.52.1.3

relieved them. After Okinawa finally fell, the Allied Fleet prepared for Operation 'Olympic' – the invasion of Japan. On 17 July the BPF joined Halsey's Third Fleet off Tokyo for strikes on the area and ships in the Inland Sea, and was refuelling again on 6/7 August when the BBC and Sydney Radio reported the atom bomb attack on Hiroshima. On the 9th the second atom bomb was dropped on Nagasaki, and the Japanese sued for peace.

Warrant Officer Alf Barlow in the escort carrier HMS *Stalker* relates, 'After many fruitless exercises and operations we were at the surrender of Singapore when the Jap generals were (as thought) going to commit suicide after seeing Mountbatten at the big parade, but of course they did not. I remember our Lieutenant-Commander (Flying) and the COs of squadrons having great difficulty in getting a flying programme to take effect after the Jap surrender. Our young, keen RNVR pilots were most reluctant to fly in peacetime; the interest in flying evaporated completely as they considered it a waste of time.'

Eric Rickman, the former art student turned Avenger pilot, considered staying in the Service, 'having much enjoyed most aspects of my four and a half years service. But I had found, in common with many FAA personnel, that the higher echelons in the Navy tended to be unimaginative, and lacking in individuality, consequently this was not for me.' Most regulars were put ashore so that HOs with low demob numbers could sail the now redundant ships home.

Also serving in *Stalker* was Tom Bailey, now a PO, who had joined in far-off days for 'three square meals a day', and discovered that he loved the Navy. Today, from his house outside Newcastle-on-Tyne he writes, 'God Bless all my old shipmates, God Bless all our present Servicemen, especially Navy – we may not have the biggest navy, but we have still got the best.'

Birds of a Feather: The Wrens

This book is about sailors – *men* who fought at sea (or loafed ashore) – but it cannot be thought in any sense complete without mentioning the *women* who made this possible, the Women's Royal Naval Service, the WRNS, the Wrens.

We never knew much about them – they were dismissed as officers' perks – and most matlows never got beyond the stage of admiring them as sex objects, of which we were so cruelly starved. Indeed, my own immediate memory of them is of attending gramophone recitals of classical music at *Ganges*. These genteel happenings were thought to be the proper pastimes for ladies in blue, and hairy matlows willingly endured a Beethoven quartet, even a blast of Bartok, just to be near them. I had a cousin in the Wrens who, as a Second Officer, referred to Fleet Air Arm pilots, whose ranks I was then desperate to join, as the 'dirty-fingernailed type'. I have never seen or spoken to her since. There was also the vague idea that Wren boats' crews were the cream, all debs and hockey-playing Honourables (Wren officers being all grammar school girls). The reality took some time to appreciate.

The wartime Director of the WRNS, Dame Vera Laughton Matthews, identified three stages in the appreciation of her 'gels'. 'First, the shock period; one admits that it must have been a shock, and many were the seafaring ancestors who were said to have turned in their graves. To the same period belongs the "Every nice girl loves a sailor" attitude on the part of the matelots (and Vivian Ellis's "Up with the lark and to bed with a Wren").

'Then came the period of astonished admiration: the Wrens were a success – in fact they were Wonderful. They could work hard . . . they could do not only the jobs expected of women, but all kinds of technical and mechanical work; they could run boats in the black-out and when it was blowing half a gale; they were calm and cheerful under bombing and shelling ("Deserving of the highest praise", said C-in-C Portsmouth in 1940). Next came the stage which is the greatest compliment of all – we were taken for granted. More and more Wrens just fit into the picture and are an integral part of that wonderful organization which is the Royal Navy . . . On D-Day there were WRNS Signal Officers and Duty Officers; Wrens received and sent wireless messages to the ships; they coded signals and plotted ships – the greatest plot ever; they serviced sea-craft and aircraft and guns and torpedoes; they saw that Jack got his mail, that his pay was in order and that he left shore well fed; they transported supplies and medical stores and ammunition to the ships.'

Today no one should be surprised that girls could run tenders, picket boats, mail boats, hospital boats, boarding drifters and skimming dishes, ceremoniously twirl a boathook and belay a rope with the best foretopman in the Fleet. It was certainly the most romantic category of women's wartime service (Monsarrat's heroine in *The Cruel Sea* dies, pregnant, in a boating accident), but entailed a tough seamanship training after a Probationer Wren had completed the General Service Training – knots and splices, swabbing decks, elementary navigation, boxing the compass, climbing ropes (in trousers of course), and leaping in and out of boats without falling in the water. Their less glamorous sisters in Motor Transport handled staff cars, supply vans, draft lorries, boat trailer tractors.

Wren Wireless Telegraphists and Visual Signallers needed a quick brain and good powers of concentration – to read and transmit by Morse buzzer, Aldis lamp or flags as fast and fluently as in a chat with the hairdresser or dishing the dirt with the girls. Wrens intercepted Morse commentaries on naval battles, the tense, terse reports from a beleaguered convoy, or sometimes the news of a husband's or brother's loss – to be kept secret from family for long, cruel weeks. V/S Wrens were closer to the ships, wagging urgent flags like racecourse tictac men from gyrating boarding craft, passing sailing instructions for take-off; Wren W/T spoke to test pilots, and received their calm relays of disaster.

The Masters of many a convoy of US Henry Kaiser Liberty ships lying-to off an English shore after battling Atlantic gales, wallowing deep-laden with urgent cargoes, gaped astonished as a young woman with blue rings on her sleeve climbed nimbly up the swaying Jacob's Ladder with complex orders which she proceeded to explain patiently in detail. Boarding Officer was the only commission most Boats' Crew Wrens would accept, as the only one which could give them the movement of a ship beneath their feet and the salty tang of spindrift.

Fleet Air Arm Wrens measured the arcana of wind speed and direction by theodolite and pilot balloon, the plotting of the weather on the 'actuals' board, rearmed guns, repaired airframes, serviced engines and radios. Some packed parachutes – 'I'd rather a woman did it than some dozey matlow,' said one Seafire pilot. Wren 'torpedomen' worked on the electrics of tinfish and depth-charges. Some griped that they were not allowed to *fly* the aircraft – fast fighters, bombers, even sleepy Swordfish. The Women's Auxiliary Air Force did, didn't they? The lucky, or crafty, ones got to test equipment in the air. Others did the same things for ships, wielding the acetylene torch, forging chain cable links, straightening bent davits, re-planking stove-in ships' boats; operated lathes and milling machines, polished lenses for submarine periscopes, qualified as riggers (how many seamen could make an apple-ring fender?).

Base of the pyramid were the Housekeepers, doing the jobs men knew they could do – the cooks and stewards, in galleys big and small, making hot meals for exhausted men just in from the Battle of the Atlantic; survivors gaunt from days in open boats; for new entries, many with the thin, starved look of poverty about them; packing rations for night-fighting ML men ('What is it tonight? We had *grapes* with the last lot . . .'). Wrens were much preferred to male stewards ('A bit like home'). Wrens learned hairdressing and made careers of it after demob.

Wren Stores Assistants handed out books and bell-bottoms, nuts and bolts, even the sacred rum ration. Wrens of the Fleet Mail Service channelled those longed-for letters to matlows ashore and afloat, took them out to them at anchor – and wrote some of the replies.

In spring 1941 the first Wrens went overseas to the East, to SEAC; others went to Normandy; many were lost in transit at sea.

Men *and* women won the war. After all, 'ODs? I've spit em!' but Wrens? 'Our lives would be misery without them', said Flag Officer, Dover.

Epilogue

'Memories . . . the *tiredness*, a continuous and overwhelming tiredness I have never known since. Even in harbour . . .

'But it was at its worst at sea, exaggerated then by the discomfort, the constant motion, the conscious physical effort of even standing upright at times – all this going on for day after day after day. And how the last few minutes of a night watch dragged by. It's 0345 and you're coming towards the end of a tiring middle watch – and going down below to shake your reliefs. Down all those ladders, through all those hatches, along all those flats and passageways, dodging over hammocks, stepping over sleepers in semi-darkness and in thick fog, then right down to the forward lower messdeck, with still-sleeping, half-awake, half-dressed, weary figures everywhere, then off back to the bridge to finish off the watch, trying hard not to give in to tiredness (not yet anyway). But I sometimes weakened – so tired that I couldn't resist the temptation to sit down, just for a few seconds, on one of the stools on the upper seamen's messdeck just to rest aching bones and muscles. And in that few seconds I have fallen asleep, only to be quickly awakened with a jerk as my elbow slipped off the mess table or I fell off the stool.

'And so back to the bridge, hoping that your reliefs really are awake and that they will put in a timely appearance. And then, glory be – they appear . . .

'Sleep . . . A hammock was a lovely, comfortable bed – snug and reasonably warm in spite of one blanket only. The pillow a rolled up jersey. All hammocks jammed together, and the ever-present muttering and movements of people coming and going underneath or alongside you – a late card school, men going on watch, returning from shore leave, sometimes bumping into you but in spite of it all you slept well – and in spite, too, of the joker who would wake you up in the middle of the night and ask "What time is it?"

'Sleep at sea was different – in fact that is just about all one did at sea (other than duties and meals, etc) where you would be so utterly tired and weary that very often one just slumped on to a bench or a table or in the hammock netting, fully clothed, and fell asleep within seconds. Many never slung their hammocks at sea. It *was* a hard life, at sea in wartime – even ignoring the ever-present danger from the enemy. Two watches (sometimes three if you were lucky), the endless heaving motion of the ship pitching and rolling, the coldness, the rain and the gales, the seasickness, the sea blowing inboard and soaking everyone even up on the bridge, the eternal tiredness from lack of sleep and effort of doing nothing more than putting up with your living conditions. And then, at last, going off watch for that precious sleep, only to find the messdeck swilling in seawater as it had been for days, thanks to leaking seams and inefficient ventilators and Atlantic weather . . . all this for day after day after day, months on end, till a spell in dock brought relief – and the sight of those molly-coddled dockyard maties swarming onboard to "work", to repair your ship by spending half their time playing poker in the forward clothing store hidden away from the foreman. These, the men who mostly lived safely at home in houses that stayed still, who slept all night in comfortable beds without the ever-present possibility of a torpedo and who awoke fully refreshed next morning and ready to spend half the next day loafing. We resented them.

'And so – hurry below to the blessed relief of your hammock or to slump, fully clothed, on to the mess stool or the table or even the deck – if it is not swilling in three inches of seawater. Only to be awakened a couple of hours later for dawn action stations which lasts just long enough for it not to be worthwhile turning in again.

'In spite of the dangers and the tiredness and the physical discomfort and everything else, if you look at it one way it could be said that we were thoroughly molly-coddled. All you had to do was do your job properly (and you were trained for that), and keep the messdeck clean and your place of work. And that was all. No rent, no rates to pay. No maintenance or repairs to see to – if that electric light bulb, or this fan, or that heater stopped working, someone came along (eventually) and saw to it, for nothing. All your food was provided free, in bigger ships without even the necessity for you to make a decision as to what colour shirt or tie or suit to buy next time you needed new clothing – those decisions were all made for you. No need to worry about money – you could spend the whole lot on drink ashore, knowing that you would manage to live without starving till next pay day. No fear of redundancies, of the firm going bankrupt or being taken over. Plenty of companionship, plenty of card games on the messdecks on evenings onboard, free cinema shows, free postage for letters (and free French-letters if you wanted them), free medical treament, free trips to all those wonderful and exotic places in the Mediterranean and the east, free heating, free lighting, the advantage of living only a few yards from your place of work. I could go on and on. Put that way, what a cushy way of life it seems to have been. Yet I don't suppose that, quite understandably, any man who ever went to sea in wartime ever thought that he was being molly-coddled. We would have thrown a dozen fits if anyone had ever suggested that to us.

'Really of course, sailors were in far more danger than were the majority of airmen and soldiers.

'Most airmen spent their war being in very little danger at all back at their airfields. Only those who flew on ops were in danger (though, obviously in *great* danger) and then only for a few hours at a time.

'Same with the Army. Only the fighting men – infantry, tank corps, etc – were in danger, and that was only when there was actual fighting taking place. And it's surprising how often, during the war, there was very little actual fighting taking place.

'All the higher-ups in both services – Group Captains, Colonels and above – usually stayed somewhere at the back in a place of comparative safety.

'But in the Navy *everyone* went into action – cooks, stewards, writers, marine, bandsmen, supply assistants, admirals, the whole lot shared the dangers equally. And there were quite a few admirals killed in action. Nor was it only in a battle that there was danger. At *any* moment throughout all the hours and days and weeks that ships spent at sea there could be that torpedo on its way towards you, that mine ahead of you, those bombers suddenly appearing from over the horizon – almost non-stop from the beginning to the end of the war the sailor, from boy to admiral, lived in danger!'

List of Contributors

Edward Baggley
Thomas Bailey
Alfred Barlow
A. S. Bolt
Dennis Bond
A. G. 'Murgy' Brown
Christopher Buist
Christopher Burston
Ivor Burston
Jack Copeman
Eric Craske
Michael Dale
Geoffrey Denny
Jack Dodds
William Earp
Douglas Ellliot
William Filer
S. France
Frederick Hall
Norman Hanson
Jack Harker
William Harman
Jackie Heath
'Pusser' Hill
Norman 'Blondie' Hollis
C. P. O. Hunt
Kenneth Illingworth
William Jeffery
Ben Kennedy
Dame Vera Laughton Matthews
Frederick Lee
Frederick Longman
Ronald Lunberg
William McCall
B. S. McEwan
Colin Malcolm
Burt Male
Alan Mathison
Neville Milburn
Eric Monk
George Monk
C. P. O. Neal
Iain Nethercott
Ernest North
Dennis 'Vic' Oliver
Maurice Pacey
Geoffrey Penny
Bert Poolman
Kenneth Poolman
Ben Rice
Sir Ralph Richardson
Eric Rickman
David Satherley
Leslie 'Ginger' Sayer
Brian Seymour
Geoff Shaw
Con Shiels
Jack Skeats
Alfred Slocombe
Christopher Smith
Jack Smith
William Thomas
Alan Todd
Peter Trant
Mark Wells
Len Wincott
Charles Wines

Index

SHOULDER ARMS!

SHOULDER ARMS!

JAMES LUCAS

CASSELL&CO

It is with joy that I dedicate this book to my beloved wife, Traude, as the representative of those uncomplaining heroines, the Army wives. To her and to all those who 'followed the drum', goes my love, gratitude and admiration for the sacrifices she and they made, on behalf of us, the men of the British Army.

Special edition for PAST TIMES

Cassell & Co
Wellington House, 125 Strand
London WC2R OBB

First published by Arms and Armour 1989 as
Experiences of War: The British Soldier
This edition 2000

ISBN 0-304-35633-6

9 8 7 6 5 4 3 2 1

Designed and edited by DAG Publications Ltd
Printed and bound in Great Britain by
Cox & Wyman, Reading

PAST TIMES®

Contents

Acknowledgements

'Before the War' – that phrase which identifies my generation – I can recall only three anniversaries which were commemorated nationally: Armistice Day, Guy Fawkes' Day and Empire Day. The British people did not celebrate any particular year, although within the folk consciousness there were certain, unforgettable dates as, for example, 1066 and 1745.

Since the war the impact of those commemorative days has been diminished. Empire Day has been abolished; the people's celebration of Guy Fawkes' Day has been channelled into joyless, municipally run firework displays and Armistice Day has been converted to Remembrance Sunday. In place of our national days the United Nations has produced international years and we are encouraged to observe those bland occasions. To the mass of the British people they go uncelebrated because they lack national, emotional appeal.

As substitutes for our national days and, in addition to the UN-designated years, it seems we are now to be given national years to commemorate. In 1988, for example, we were invited to remember the anniversaries of the sinking of the Armada and of the Glorious Revolution. If national years are indeed to be the trend, then a year which deserves to be commemorated is 1989, and the 50th anniversary of that fateful year in which Great Britain went to war with Germany. The Second World War, which began in Europe to combat Nazi aggression, spread to become a world-wide conflict. To win that struggle against the forces of evil demanded the total commitment of the best elements of our nation for almost six years.

Arms and Armour Press, decided to commemorate the watershed year 1939, by producing three volumes of reminiscences. One to cover each of the fighting services. It was my great fortune to be contracted to write the Army volume. The publisher's brief directed me to obtain from ex-soldiers anecdotes and stories connected with their life in the Service. As a first step I contacted regimental comrades and ex-service friends. They, in turn, got into touch with other former soldiers. In the second stage of the operation letters were written to regimental and corps journals asking their readers to help. The excellent response from these sources resulted in an extensive correspondence and that mass of new evidence was added to material already in my possession; the product of research on earlier books. Out of that mass of material this book has been produced.

The greatest number of those who contributed were men who had gained something from their time in the Army; others gave the viewpoint of men who resented the loss of the years they had spent in uniform.

This is a book dealing with the British Army and is confined to the men of these islands who served as Regular, Territorial or conscript soldiers. Consequently, I did not invite contributions from men who had served in the Dominion, Imperial or Colonial Forces. Nor, since the Army is, or was, essentially a male preserve, have I sought any memories from those who were in the Women's Services.

During the preparation of this book I have gained a great number of new friends. To all who contibuted go my most sincere thanks for sharing the memories they have kept, unpublished, for five decades. To one particular comrade go my chief thanks; Roy Cooke, a former Alleyn's schoolboy, who enlisted in November 1939, served in Africa, Sicily and Italy and was twice wounded. Through Roy's active help contributions came in from men in his wide circle of friends and made my work easier. I am grateful also to the officers of the Department of Documents at the Imperial War Museum and to the editors of regimental, corps and ex-service journals for their assistance. Also to the Public Record Office and to the Commonwealth War Graves Commission. Thanks also go to the editorial and lay-out team: David, Beryl and Tony, as well as to Sheila and Mandy, my agents. Nor must I forget to acknowledge the research work carried out by Claire, Victoria and Gary Shaw.

James Lucas, 1989

Introduction

The long history of the British Army and the victories it has gained across the centuries might, one would suppose, have given it in the nation's consciousness a prestige to rank with its sister services. This is not so. Consider how the public sees the three services. The image of the Royal Navy is of jolly Jack Tar, with a parrot on his shoulder, a girl in every port and free and easy with his money. The Royal Air Force image seen by most British people is of a laughing, daredevil fighter pilot, taking off to 'bag' a few Huns before breakfast. The images of McCudden, Ball, Mannock and 'Billy' Bishop of the Great War and of Bader, 'Ginger' Lacey, Stanford-Tuck and Peter Townsend of the Second World War are the enduring ones. The First of the Few is now the folk memory of the Royal Air Force.

And the Army? The thin red line topped with steel is perhaps, the only positive image that the general public has. That memory of the Crimean War is overlaid with less attractive ones including the use of the military in the so-called Peterloo massacre, where cavalry were used to maintain the peace because there was no police force. Political activists relish the myth of troops being sent to shoot down striking Welsh miners in the troubled years before the First World War – even though this did not take place. There is a newspaper reporter's dictum that says: if you can print either the truth or a story, choose the story. Critics apply that dictum as often as possible to the Army. They point to the losses of the Great War as evidence of incompetent generalship or bad strategy, but are unable to suggest alternative ways of conducting a battle or fighting a war. The Army, almost from the date of its establishment, has had a poor reputation, and yet it was for most of its life made up of volunteers; men who did not have to be taken by the 'Press Gang' as many sailors were. Regrettably, Wellington, the great military commander, encouraged civilian misconceptions when he said that the mass of the Army had enlisted for the drink. That slur was accepted and was absorbed into the national consciousness, projecting an image of shiftless, work-shy layabouts who would make pigs of themselves in the drink – the sole reason for their enlistment.

The projected image was cherished while the true picture of devoted service was ignored. The belief that men would join up for adventure, love of country or to better themselves through promotion was not accepted by the civilian masses. The Army was held to be a red-coated drunken rabble, drilled into becoming unthinking robots, incapable of reasoned thought and at best semi-literate. The Army's response to its detractors was unhelpful. Aware of civilian hostility the service grew introspective and self-protective. It was a masculine society where self-praise was considered to be ungentlemanly, where modesty was held to be a virtue and the Army made no effort to publicize its positive features or the deeds it had performed.

Lloyd George vilified the Army by expressing the belief that it was made up of cannon-fodder officered by incompetents. Aneurin Bevan expressed the same sentiments during the Second World War. The distortions which they and their like spread are still not dispelled. Yet millions of men alive today are proud to have served in an army which was led to victory in two world wars against foreign hosts dedicated to the military ethos; enemy armies which had been lavishly equipped and which had been commanded by Generals who had been trained for years. Seen from that fresh perspective, the men of the British Army and their leaders were hardly the lions lead by donkeys of popular, political calumny or the hack newspaper reporter's dictum.

Fifty years ago the then Prime Minister, Neville Chamberlain, announced that Great Britain was at war with Germany. The sons of the men who had held the Ypres salient and who had turned the Somme, in Ludendorff's words, into 'the bloody grave of the German Army', were taking up the new challenge. The scions of the men of Gallipoli, of Passchendaele and of Mons had, in their turn, to face the might of an army which their fathers had thought to be defeated and destroyed two decades earlier. More than that; they also fought and defeated two other enemy hosts; those of Italy and Japan.

The following pages are about the British soldiers who fought in the Second World War. In 1939, before the war began, an Act had been passed authorizing, for the first time in modern British history, the calling up in peacetime of men for the armed forces. Thus, to the traditional two-strata military body of full-time Regular and part-time Territorial soldiers was added a third; conscripts who served in every theatre of operations.

The text is made up chiefly of the stories of those who have much to tell but who have, hitherto, been denied a wider audience than their own immediate circle of family and friends. This is therefore a catalogue of memories; not all of battle and death, although these are the most vivid in the mind of former soldiers. The anecdotes are of other situations; of service conditions, of food and of weapons; what the soldier thought of his enemies and of his allies. It is a frequent complaint that my generation uses the war as its only reference point. This is true but hardly surprising because that conflict wrought the most profound changes in our lives. What happened to us as individuals during the war has to be the stuff of our conversations for, as a result of our years of service, we gathered experiences that could never have been gained in several civilian lifetimes.

This then, is the story of the British Army – our Army – as told by the men who served in it.

James Lucas

'Gone for a soldier'

Voluntary Enlistment and Conscription

During the years before the Second World War those who volunteered for the Army, whether on a Regular engagement or as Territorial soldiers, did not all come from one social class, though it is true that most came from the working class which formed the mass of the population. Neither were they one particular type of man, but ranged intellectually from semi-literates to academics. Nor were the reasons for their enlistment the same. Very few of my correspondents said they joined because they wished to serve King and Country. There must be many who did enlist for just that reason, but who would not admit to it either out of modesty or the fear of ridicule, for flag-waving is no part of the British character. Rather than reveal their true emotion they preferred to advance some other, but less elevating motive. The Newmark brothers, for example, claim they volunteered to pursue a hobby. John Newmark:

'My brother George and I were born in Beckenham and decided that it was only right and proper that we should join a Kentish regiment. The 1st Battalion The Queen's Own Royal West Kent Regiment was stationed in India and not only did my brother and I share the same hobby – bird-watching – but we had a common ambition – to visit India. Neither of us had the money to buy a passage. To join the Army, we decided would provide the solution. We decided that only one of us would enlist and the other would follow if service life was agreeable. We tossed a coin. If it came down heads I would join and if it came down tails George would enlist. It came down tails. George became 6342645 Private Newmark G. and spent six months training at the Depot in Maidstone.'

Trevor Parnacott enlisted in the Artists' Rifles, a crack Territorial Army unit, in order to play football. His enthusiasm was shared, so he later found out, by others who were not in the British Army.

'During the advance to Cap Bon, five years after departing to Vincent Square to join the TA, Harry Peacock and myself had a sudden confrontation with a fair-haired German officer. He was an absolute model of the Aryan Hun. Standing to attention he was crying badly with kit and arms laid out immaculately in front of him. I asked him, at Tommy-gun point, "Are you a Nazi?" "Yes, Sir." I asked him why he had joined the Nazis, to which he replied, "Because I wanted to play football." '

Some men felt so compelling an urge to enlist that they walked miles to the nearest town to find a recruiting office. One of these was Jack Brewin, whose service took him to Dieppe, Algiers, Sicily and the D-Day beaches:

'I joined at the age of 17 years and walked a distance of 10 miles from my Derbyshire village to the recruiting office in the County town. I gave my age as 18 in order to enlist and enraged my father on return home when I told him of my action. However, by the time I received notice to join the Depot, I think both my parents were a little proud of me and gave me their blessing.'

Should anyone think that I exaggerated in claiming that intellectuals also served in the ranks, I can quote Charles Morrison, formerly of the Yeomanry and then of the Intelligence Corps, as one of many University graduates who served in the ranks:

'I had been in OCTU when at school and carried on when I went up to University. Mine was not a family with a great military tradition, but both my mother's and father's sides had lost men in the first German War, all of them serving as volunteers in the Army. I saw my OCTU service as a need to keep faith with my relatives. I graduated late in 1937, and found a job in a small market town in Leicestershire. For social reasons I decided to join the TA. The choice of units was restricted to either a company of the Territorial battalion of the County Regiment or else a squadron in the local yeomanry. I became a trooper and I must say our dress was splendid and we wore it at every social function. There was, at that time, a big recruiting drive under way for the TA and a smart uniform jacket with chain mail shoulder-pieces, overalls with coloured leg stripes and clattering spurs all had a great pulling power. The unit began to train up to war standard, but well before it had reached that standard I had been detached and was posted as a corporal to an Intelligence unit. This came about because I had a Degree in modern foreign languages.'

Donald Featherstone was one of the many who volunteered as soon as possible after the outbreak of war:

'Conditioned throughout boyhood by father and uncle's fearful saga of the horrors of World War One trench-warfare, when World War Two broke out I was determined to avoid the infantry and thus Monday morning (4 September 1939) found me queuing outside a Royal Air Force recruiting office. With little to offer I was inevitably rejected and on the following day the Royal Navy displayed the same good sense by showing me off HMS *President* on London's Embankment. On Wednesday, heart hardened to mother's plea to wait and see if they call you up, my target was the Army Recruiting Office at the Drill Hall in Horn Lane, Acton. Business wasn't good that day and I was the sole recruit to be medically examined, attested, given the Shilling and a railway warrant with directions on getting to the Depot at Bovington in Dorset. The train did not arrive at Wool station until about 0300 hrs on a very dark night and the two odd miles to the camp made it a fearful affair for a Londoner used to streets with lights. I toiled on and was then scared out of my wits by the sentry's challenge at the Cologne Road guardroom. There I met my second sergeant of the day and slept on the floor under a single blanket. The Recruiting Sergeant's promise of a black beret was a "come on" – being RAC we were not entitled to such headgear!'

Thomas Burden, who joined the Territorial Army before the war broke out, had another reason for wanting to join up:

'It was in 1938, that a big drive was made to get men to join the Terriers. None of us was all that keen, but then talk started about joining the ARP and the

AFS. It is funny that there seemed to be a straight choice – either the Army or the Civil Defence. I lived at that time in Hoxton and worked in the Aldgate area. All the Jewish boys seemed to join the Civil Defence or the Auxiliary Fire Service. We said that they only joined those so they could stay at home in their jobs if the war came. The men [the soldiers] would go out to fight. None of us wanted to be thought of as a dodger; so we did not join the Civil Defence or the AFS, but the TA. One of my mates was already in the KRs [the King's Royal Rifle Corps] and he had got some of his friends to join him. To cut the story short I joined because most of my mates had. One of the things that encouraged us was that we got paid for drills, we were taught to drive, we had a canteen with prices cheaper than pub prices, we had a uniform to wear and the Army was becoming popular again so we could always get a girl. I misremember now what we thought about war coming. Well it did and we went overseas to France where I got put in the bag in May 1940. I left home in the summer of 1939 and did not get back again until the summer of 1945. Six years was a long time out of a life and I spent most of that time behind barbed wire.'

Others had compulsions stronger than patriotism, love or sport or the influence of friends. The uniform that Kipling described as 'starvation cheap' was another, but more bitter, inducement to take the King's Shilling in peacetime. There was mass unemployment and an unemployed, single man, living at home was an economic burden on his family. The Army would give him three meals a day, work to do and put money in his pocket at the end of the week. Not a lot of money but, with careful budgeting, the thrifty man could send a little cash home. And once a soldier knew the ropes and was out of barracks in the early afternoon, he could obtain casual labour which would bring him in extra cash. To others, service life offered the chance of adventure, of a life beyond the monotony of 'civvy street'. The chance of foreign travel, at a time when a day trip to Calais was a wild ambition, was another lure. There were some whose ambitions did not aspire to such heights. For them the ideal was to stay in the UK at the Depot and to become a permanent member of Depot Company. Henry Jackson recalls:

'I was called up in the spring of 1942, and went to the regimental Depot for training. What I saw there opened my eyes to the way the Army was run. The Depot Company was typical; they were the biggest rogues unhung. They were nearly all time-serving soldiers with years and years of service. You could tell this by the inverted stripes they wore on the left forearm. One stripe was awarded for three years' service, two for five, three for seven and four for twelve. Included on the strength of Depot Company were the sportsmen; those who were good at boxing or football and who would keep up the regiment's reputation in the Army championships. So if you were a good boxer you were in Depot Company and stayed there, living like a fighting-cock and with only a few duties to do. I never knew a Depot Company man to stand guard or do a picket. If some keen sergeant tried to get them on to fatigues they could produce documentary proof that they were medically unfit, incapable of carrying out the duty. So they never did much.

'Nearly all of them had a regular little job which they did inside barracks and which they had been doing, in some cases, for years. Something light, not too hard; like watering the grass strip in front of the Company office or cutting the grass of that strip. There were some who had been excused wearing boots, some who were not allowed to climb ladders, some who were not allowed to bend down. Complaints!! you name them, they had them or had had them. And yet they were as hard as nails and very fit. Depot Company won nearly every sporting event it went in for in the competitions which were run. Those certified crocks would run like weasels, climb like monkeys and never seemed to be out of breath – and yet they all smoked like chimneys, usually freemans [other people's cigarettes]. Once you were on Depot Company you were made. In peacetime it must have been a doddle – but in wartime with rationing it was a lovely little earner. They flogged the rations and could always find casual labour for their mates who wanted to do it. There was a shortage of men, you see, in wartime. The Depot Company Mafia could get you a cushy number outside the camp, like in a little café making sandwiches; somewhere out of sight of the regimental police or other trouble-makers. They knew every lonely widow who needed a bit of male companionship and if there was a window-cleaning round going spare – they knew someone who could fill it.'

There was one group, however, whose inclusion diminished the military in the eyes of the public. In many English magistrates' courts the prisoner in the dock was offered either the choice of enlistment or a prison sentence. I stressed the word English because from correspondence it is clear that the Army was held in higher esteem in Scotland, Wales and Ulster, and that magistrates in those parts of the Kingdom would not have demeaned the Army in that way. The attitude that the service is the natural repository for the rogues and ne'er-do-wells of society still prevails in England; many people today express the opinion that football hooligans should be put into the Army.

The final path to soldiering was compulsion. The phenomenon of peacetime conscription, if one excepts the Press Gang, was not one familiar to the British people. It had been hard enough to introduce conscription in the middle years of the First World War. In the late 1930s government plans for its introduction in peacetime would be certain to meet with hostility and obstruction. Aware of this opposition the government of the day proceeded with caution. In January 1939, the War Minister, Hore-Belisha, announced a national services appeal, inviting men to enlist. The appeal had the support of the Labour and Liberal parties only because they saw it as an alternative to full conscription. The response to the National Service appeal was poor. Plans were made to double in size the Territorial Army and although this was a popular move what the Army needed was a mass of well-trained men, *before* war broke out. Relying upon appeals would not bring in the numbers needed to fight a major war.

Accordingly, on 26 April 1939, a bill was laid before the House of Commons to provide for a 6-month period of military training for men aged between 20 and 21. After that period there would be a liability for a period of 3½ years in the Territorial Army. As a concession, that period of conscript service with the Territorial Army would be limited to Home Defence of the United Kingdom. The War Minister believed that the scheme would bring in 200,000 men to the services in the first year of operation and more than three-quarters of a million men within three years. In effect, by the end of December 1939, 727,000 men had been registered for the services and 4,320,000 by the end of 1941. That was the peak of British manpower resources and thereafter the numbers already in uniform or available for conscription diminished. Efforts to redress the balance by altering the age limits brought amendments to the National Service (Armed Forces) Acts. The lower age limit had already been reduced to 18, and the upper one raised, first, to 41 years and by an amendment brought in during 1941, to 51. There was strong competition between the armed forces and industry for the available manpower resources. In an effort to resolve the problem there was conscription of women to the services or for war work and of young men of military age to work in the mines, 'Bevin Boys'. More than sixteen million men and women were registered for non-military national service during the Second World War of whom 21,800 were conscripted for work in the pits. Yet, at a time when every person was needed to win the war, the country still allowed thousands of men to evade military service on the unprovable grounds that their conscience would not allow them to fight and could permit other men, eligible for call up, to escape from a beleaguered Britain and to go to America. William Summers:

'I often wonder how those dodgers feel now at having betrayed their country. They were nearly all of them from the so-called intellectual, educated classes. The working-class man stood no chance at all of dodging the column, but those others did and it seems to me that they were helped. How could they live with themselves knowing that in the United Kingdom women were being called up and that women and children were being blown to bits in the air raids baffles me. The worst thing is that when they came back after the war they got the plum jobs, often in entertainment or in the universities because the forces were so slow in releasing the men who should have had those jobs.'

The path of the conscript was a simple one. On attaining the age of 18 every male – eventually every male and female – was required to register at the local Labour Exchange. There were announcements in the newspapers so that nobody could be ignorant of the fact that they were required to register. With registration completed there was a wait of about two to three weeks before notification arrived of the medical examination. If you passed this impersonal examination you received your formal letter of conscription together with a rail warrant from the local station to the assigned barracks.

All new intakes were received on Thursdays. At the barrack gate a regimental policeman would direct the recruits to a blanket-covered table behind which sat several NCOs.

'One of these handed out a strip of paper bearing a number. This was your personal identification number – unique to you. You had to remember it because without it you did not exist. Another corporal told you to which platoon you had been assigned and a lance-corporal escorted you to your new home. The huts were called spiders. A spider consisted of a central section holding the ablutions and lavatories. On either side of the central section, so as to form the letter "H," was a sleeping-hut each holding about 30 men. I think we had a corporal in our barrack-room. The sergeant had a small cubicle of his own in the other sleeping-room. The corporal who was in charge of our room showed each man his bed space, told us to put down our civilian attaché case and to come back to the other hut where the sergeant was waiting. When the whole platoon of the new intake had gathered the sergeant and the NCOs showed us the webbing equipment and how the various pieces fitted together. The most important thing we were told on that first evening was that the colour of the blanco we had to buy to keep the equipment clean, was known as "khaki green No. 3" and that "Soldier's Friend" was the best thing to clean brasses. There was a song which we sang in Depot to the tune of *It's foolish but it's fun.* The words were: "If the Germans should invade this land, our bloody mob will make a stand with a block of blanco in each hand, 'cos bullshit baffles brains." How true it was. All the stories we had heard in civvy street that brasses were to be dulled in this war turned out to be so much eyewash. In our mob we polished all our brasses.

'We were marched down to our first meal. Not in the cookhouse but in the shed that we were later to find out was the 25-yard indoor range. That first meal included tea and doorstep sandwiches as well as bully beef fritters. Cutlery was provided for that meal only. We were later issued with our own knife, fork and spoon. After the meal we were marched back to the spider and then, late in the evening, to the stores where pieces of uniform and equipment were issued at breakneck speed. We just about got back to the spider, loaded down with clothing, webbing, boots and kitbag when we were given half-an-hour to lights out. The Army's day was ending and so was our first day in the Army.'

All intakes reported on Thursday because the TAB and Tet Tox inoculations which were given on Friday morning made the recruits unfit for duty for 48 hours. Thus the Army would lose only a weekend – not that it was empty time:

'We felt like death warmed up for those two days and were given an easy time. That is to say we learned how to put the webbing together, how to make up a bed and had a hut cleaning task apportioned. My task was to keep the window sills free from dust. Others had to blacklead the two stoves in our barrack-room. Some had other dusting tasks and some cleaned windows. Every task had to be done every day and done properly first time round. On that first day we were issued with our rifles. There was a great deal of pointing the rifle and shouting bang, bang you're dead, until the Sergeant shouted at us not to be so adjectively childish. He told us it was a "crime", the army's term that covers everything from dirty buttons to murder, to point a rifle at anyone. We were to learn the bitterness of that lesson when one of our intake was shot dead in just such an accident on the 400-yard range.

'The Commanding Officer gave us a talk in the gymnasium and we were given some sort of intelligence tests by an NCO; I think a sergeant. On the basis of matching what looked like wallpaper patterns we were each selected for special training as transport drivers, Bren Gun carrier drivers, mortarmen, fitters, or radio mechanics. Once we got over the TAB, Tet Tox jabs and I think, vaccination, work began in earnest. About that. For some reason a number of men did not want the vaccination to take and put alcohol on the scratches, but they couldn't say why they didn't want it to take. During the first day we were paraded before our Company Commander and our platoon commanders. We were then "processed". This meant that the Company Commander interviewed each man, with all the others listening to the conversation. What had you done in civilian life, who was your next of kin, had you previous military experience –

Home Guard or Cadet Force? Questions like that, intending to make a preliminary selection of those who had had some sort of discipline and those who had not. We were given our AB 64s, Parts I and 2. [The part one was the soldier's identity document recording among other things courses passed and decorations awarded. Part 2 was the pay book, recording monies received.] The officer then asked each of us how much money from our weekly pay we wished to have sent home to our next of kin as allotment. I think the service paid the equivalent sum so the more you sent home, the more the next of kin received. That first day was filled with talks, lectures, tests and a guided tour round the barracks, including a stop off to hear a bugler sound all the bugle calls. For the first week or two the only ones that concerned us most were Reveille, Lights Out and the Fire Call.'

The transition from recruit to half-trained soldier began and ended on the barrack square. Daily inspections and 'crimings' for seemingly trivial offences were part of each drill parade. The ubiquitous term used in the Brigade of Guards was 'idle'. One could be idle on parade, idle in charge of a Bren gun, idle while riding a bicycle – the permutations were endless. Ex-Sergeant Ramsden:

'I never ceased to be amazed at how many men could not match their foot and arm movements. When a normal person walks his right arm swings forward together with his left leg and vice versa. Those kack-handed ones swung left leg and left arm at the same time. It took a long time for some of them to learn how to march properly. Only one man in my experience never learned. I think he was slightly mental. He also had a bad curvature of the spine. He should not have been in the service at all. As the recruits learned the basic drills it was noticeable how more confident they became, both in themselves and as members of a group. Competition between the huts became very keen.'

At the end of six or eight weeks the recruits were no longer raw. A new batch of rookies had come in and the 6-week 'veterans' could go on to special training. Depending upon the arm of service this might be as little as 12 weeks or as long as twenty. Ex-Lance-Corporal Tony Marshall of the Royal Tank Regiment knew that the training would be intense:

'But then, we had been told it would be. In our training camp we learned to do every job in the tank crew. I do not know if this was something done only in our unit or whether it was usual throughout the RTR. In addition to my basic job as the driver I had to learn gunnery and wireless procedures. The driver's job involved a task system. Every day a special check was made on some different part of the vehicle in addition to the standard checks. One day it would be electrics, then the fuel system, hatches, internal fittings, tracks and pins, and so on. We checked everything. Then the sergeant checked what we had done and then the Squadron Commander. It was drilled into us that in battle our very lives depended upon everything in the vehicle working properly.'

Charles Ridley of the Inniskilling Fusiliers described the transition from recruit to a battalion:

'Late in 1942, I was posted from Depot to our Holding Battalion. This was the last stage as a rookie before going on to an active service battalion. I think that in each [infantry] regiment the 7th or 70th Battalions were holding battalions. While I was with ours a new drill was brought in. This was called battle drill and was supposed to make infantry tactics into a standard drill. If I remember right a

Section would stand in single file and each man would shout out what his task was. It went something like "(I am the) Section Commander, No. 1 on the Bren, No. 2 on the Bren, No. 1 Rifleman, No. 2 Rifleman, No. 1 Bomber, No. 2 Bomber, No. 3 and No. 4 Rifleman, 2 i/c of the Section. At that time the EY rifle was done away with and we used the 2-inch mortar. [The EY rifle projected Mills bombs from a cup discharger. The longer range of the projected grenade meant that the bombs were fitted with longer fuzes than the standard 4-second ones.] I cannot remember whether each section had a 2-inch mortar or whether it was one per platoon. After we had named our duties in the section, the platoon commander would indicate the section's objective – say a blockhouse. He would tell us we were under fire and we would all shout out, "Down, Crawl, Observe, Fire." The section corporal would signal with his arm to tell the Bren gun team to move to one flank. Some of the riflemen would move to the other flank. Then we pretended to give covering fire and the bombers would run and pretend to drop grenades into the firing slits of the enemy blockhouse. The whole time that this little action was taking place each man would shout out what he was doing. "I am firing my rifle," "I am moving to a flank to give covering fire," "I am throwing hand-grenades" and so on. From section drills we did platoon drills and then did them by company. Then there were battalion ones, but I do not think that we shouted out what we were doing on the company or battalion stunts.'

From holding battalion the next step was to an active service one. That unit would be part of a division training for overseas service. At that level the emphasis was on route-marching. Most divisions were moved to Scotland where the low mountainous country gave the commanders experience in solving tactical problems and the empty countryside was excellent for training. In time Commanding Officers would receive orders to line the road for a visit by a 'Mr. Lion'. This was one of the pseudonyms for HM the King who visited each Division before it went overseas. Often Mr. Lion would visit individual battalions in training. Divisional Commanders would visit battalions and give little speeches emphasizing the division's splendid training and its keen cutting-edge. Not many Generals talked about the thrill of battle or knocking the Hun for six, although Montgomery did. A great many divisional commanders had fought as regimental officers in the Great War and in France during the 1940 campaign. They realized that war was not a cricket match.

In a flurry of embarkation leaves and with the departure of the advance parties the units would prepare to march out. Their departure might – or might not – be marked by the local civilian population. The 1st Battalion of the Queen's Own was fortunate:

'We left Hawick in Roxburghshire at about 6.30 in the morning. As the battalion swung out of the park where it had been billeted in huts, we were all surprised to see the pavements crowded with people. The population of Hawick had come to see us off to war. Even now I cannot think of that morning without feeling choked. In addition to the ordinary civilians there was the local British Legion branch with its flag, as well as old soldiers with the medals of the First War on their chests, some medals showed service in South Africa at the turn of the century. The Boy Scouts, Girl Guides, Church Lads Brigade and the Civil

Defence – they were all there on parade on that bitterly cold March morning. I remember Hawick, and this goes for the whole battalion; we remember Hawick with the deepest affection.'

Then it was the special troop train and the vast echoing sheds of the embarkation port, often Liverpool. Inside the cavernous halls there would be a controlled confusion of Staff officers and their inevitable lists. Prowling about would be sinister Red Caps, there to ensure, perhaps, that there were no last-minute desertions. Then followed hours of waiting, sitting on a kitbag until the time came to file up the steep gangplank and burdened with kit to edge along the narrow passageways of a ship that smelt of warm oil, vomit and stale food. Down staircases into the hold. There the hammocks would be slung and kit stowed. Then the sudden throbbing of engines and a slight rocking brought a rush to the decks. The handful of civilians walking their dogs in the twilight did not wave back at us. They were probably blasé – how many troop ships had they seen sail on the tide?

Late in the evening the ship would sail out into open water joining other troop transports and the inevitable destroyer escorts rushing about, fussing and giving out the even more inevitable, mysterious high-pitched, peep, peep, peep signals. Eventually, the engines which had been stilled would begin to throb again and the convoy, only part of a larger one, began its voyage. The group of ships steamed quickly away from land. Soon it was only a dark line on the horizon. Blighty was behind. Ahead lay death or glory. 'The British Army', in Fred Jarvis's words, 'was doing what it had always done. Getting ready to fight in someone else's country.'

Soldiering In Blighty

These days we live in a world of constant, day-long entertainment and it is hard to imagine, and nearly as hard to recall, a Britain where the cinema, the radio and the gramophone and not the televison were the principal vehicles of mass entertainment. There was a greater dependence, then, by the public upon staged events: circuses, Tattoos and parades in which the Army played a significant, sometimes prominent role. The Aldershot Tattoo, the highspot of the summer season, as Bertram Mills Circus was the highspot of the winter, was recalled by one former soldier, A. Withey. He pointed out that in the 1930s an Act of Parliament laid down that Tattoo performers, rehearsing or acting for a period of seven days, should receive the same rate of pay as a professional actor. The Tattoos lasted more than seven days in rehearsal and performance-time, but the thrifty government clerks avoided paying soldiers the amount required by law by making Tuesday a rest day. In lieu of full payment the soldier performers were given a single 1/- (5p) canteen voucher. Withey, who recalled that particular example of service thriftiness, also remembered one Tattoo when:

'We were doing the PT display. Someone at HQ had the bright idea of bringing in the Regimental Employed, i.e., cooks, batmen, horse transport men, storemen, etc. Now training had been going on for about eight weeks and no orders were given on parade, only the beat of the drum. You can imagine the chaos when about sixty of us [new ones] joined the parade on the barrack square. We all got took off the display next day.'

Another Tattoo memory is that of Jacky Allen who saw the display, not as a soldier, but as a child, courtesy of the old London County Council:

'This took place in daylight of course and was very overwhelming to us little kids. I remember the marching and the bands and how we all joined in singing when the tune was familiar. I don't think any of us really understood too much about which battles were being fought, but we were overawed by the number of soldiers dashing about all over the place. The thing I have never forgotten and never will was one soldier lying on the ground pretending to be dead, saying to another squaddie similarly "laid out" – "I didn't join the bleeding army for this." When I got home and told my Mother I had seen the "bleeding Army" I got a whack round the ear. I was only going to say that I couldn't see why they were called that as they weren't bleeding.'

In those days, one-day outings were the only holiday for many people. Not until they joined the Army did they see anything else but pavements and buildings. One of them, Corporal Arthur Pickford was grateful to the service:

'My most enduring memory of soldiering was to be in the countryside. It was only a short route march out of barracks and we were in the open countryside. Before the war, as a child, we had day trips to places like Epping Forest or Theydon Bois. We envied the children who were evacuated at the outbreak of war because they would be out in the country all the time while we had to stay in London. I was not evacuated as I was coming up to school-leaving age when war broke out. We left school at 14 in those days. We marched from the barracks until we reached the Downs and there we did tactical exercises and things that taught us soldiering. One thing I really enjoyed was doing the various crawls; all training for close combat and hand-to-hand fighting. We took haversack lunches with us and the cookhouse would send up big dixies of tea. I don't think I was ever as happy in my life as when I was a young soldier on the hills above Boxley. I was sent on a signaller's course once to Eastbourne and for the first time in my life I saw the sea from the Downs outside Eastbourne. I shall never forget it. In my service I saw lots of sights in foreign countries and had some good times. But nothing was ever as good as the first months after I was called up and was doing my training in Kent and Sussex.'

The Newmark twins, pre-war Regular soldiers, confused their superiors as John's account shows:

'In pre-war days soldiers were not permitted to wear civilian clothes for the first two years of their Army life. When George was posted to Aldershot at the end of his training he naturally wore uniform. Not long afterwards I turned up at the gates of the Depot intending to enlist. I was wearing civilian clothes. As I passed through the gates a regimental policeman on duty stopped me. "Hallo, Newmark," he called out, "What are you doing back here? You were posted to Aldershot, weren't you?" I realized at once that the policeman had mistaken me for George, but I was given no chance to explain. He fired another question in menacing tones, "Why are you wearing civilian clothes?" "Young man," I replied, "do you expect me to come here with nothing on?" The policeman, a lance-corporal, was furious. How dare a private soldier address him as "young man". "Consider yourself a soldier under open arrest, Newmark." "I'll consider it," I replied, enjoying myself enormously. The corporal began to turn purple. "Make that close arrest!" he yelled, moving forward and intending to take me to the guardroom. At this explosive point an officer appeared on the scene. He was clearly expecting me for he shook hands and said, "Ah, you've arrived. My goodness, you really do look like your brother. The War Office told me you were on your way. Are you twins by any chance?" "Yes, Sir, we are identical twins," I told him and glanced at the now very embarrassed policeman. "Lots of people mistake us for one another, but we are quite used to it after twenty years." The policeman withdrew quickly, unaware that he would be the first of a long line of military gentlemen who were to be confused and confounded by the Newmark brothers over a period of several years.

'At the end of my six months' training at Maidstone Depot I was posted to Aldershot and reunited with my brother George. We discussed the prospects of joining 1st Battalion in India and soon discovered that drafts of men were posted overseas at intervals. Volunteers for an overseas posting were always in demand and we had no hesitation in volunteering. Nevertheless, it was the best part of two years before we actually went. In the meantime we played our part in the day to day pursuits of the army. We polished boots, cleaned rifles, went on route marches, practised on the rifle range, stood guard and suffered kit inspections, all for the princely sum of fourteen shillings [70 pence] a week. As in all walks of life, sometimes one or the other of us found himself in trouble. When either of us found himself lining up on parade with the other defaulters it was the Provost Sergeant, poor soul, who suffered. He never knew for sure which twin was which, but he never gave up trying to convince both us and himself that he could tell us apart. It was rumoured that we shared our punishments. If one of us was given seven days' confined to barracks, he would do the first four days and his brother would step in and do the other three. As far as we were concerned it was no rumour; it was the truth. Sometimes we varied our tactics by standing in for each other on alternate days, or two days at a time. There was the occasion when, for example, I was sentenced to seven days' detention and the Provost Sergeant took the bull by the horns. He issued a direct challenge. "Now then, Newmark," he bellowed, "Don't try and fool me because I can tell you two apart even if nobody else can. So just watch your step and don't try swopping over with your brother. If I find you swopping over, you'll find yourself on another charge, so watch it." Poor Provost Sergeant. We had already swopped over. He was talking to the wrong one. What little hair he had soon turned grey – then fell out.'

Bert Stubbings recalled the years immediately preceding the war:

'The bugle call, Retreat, was sounded in the middle of the afternoon, whereupon all parades and fatigues ceased for the day, unless you were on jankers. Puttees and ammo boots could be discarded in favour of plimsolls and after all of four or five hours of light drill, the weary warrior could throw himself into his flea trap and the more hyperactive bods would be exorted to " . . . well get into bed or out of barracks". Would that this were the perpetual life of the peacetime soldier. Chances were that battalion orders that night would order you to parade the next morning in FSMO [Field Service Marching Order], after collecting haversack rations at the 6am breakfast. Thereby, you would know that there was a distinct possibility that you were unlikely to see your bed again for a couple of days. This is why the squaddy is so fond of his kip-machine; there are so many absences – and absence makes the heart . . . During those days away you were either going to chase a fictitious enemy across the Downs or have a nice long route march. The pre-Hore Belisha route march is something that will never be seen again. No slinking along the hedgerows in separate sections. Their Whitehall Lordships, in those days, had not heard of Bleriot or Alcock and Brown, consequently, we marched boldly along the open highway in column of fours, each Company led by its equestrian commander. I remember in my Company, one made a point of not being in leading files of the column. Our Company horse was rather sensitive internally and marching behind a flatulant horse is something to be avoided.'

Recruit training, particularly in the first months of the war, was as rigorous as it had been in peacetime as George Webb found. He came from a family of soldiers; his father and elder brother had all served with the Grenadier Guards. Despite the alternative attractions of driving a railway engine or joining the Ministry, George Webb chose to follow his father and enlisted into the Grenadiers in April 1939.

'The training was so severe I wondered at the time whether or not I would "make it", being a country bumpkin, whereas the majority of my squad mates were nearly all hardened city or town types. Part of the training was more like torture, but I came through well above average. I can well remember our first shooting practice, with a .22 rifle. We all had to contribute a penny, which was almost like gold-dust those days, to a pool and the best shot scooped the pool. Well, when our detail got the order to load, then fire, the next chap let drive almost straightaway and the crack or explosion caused me to lose aim and by the time I regained my aim there was a melodious array of all sorts of noises going on around me. I was certainly relieved to hear the command "Ease springs!" When our targets were checked by the squad instructor, the air was most violently blue. It transpired that the recruit lying next to me had fired on my target. He was immediately disqualified and I was promoted the winner, by virtue of having the highest score. Now whether it was my own shots or those of the other chap, I will never know, but it was the only time I won anything at shooting.'

The multitude of Army rules and regulations guaranteed that a soldier would fall foul of one of them at least once. There was one charge which if all else failed could be used to bring a conviction. This was 'conduct prejudicial to military order and good discipline'. Under that all-embracing charge guilt was almost certain and to be guilty meant days confined to barracks answering the 'Jankers' bugle call, the words of the tune being: 'You can be a defaulter as long as you like, so long as you answer the call.' Immediately after Reveille the 'criminal' would have to parade in front of the Provost Sergeant and would be required to return whenever the bugle blew 'Jankers'. Punishment awarded by the Company Commander might be as severe as extra drills, wearing FSMO, or as light as scrubbing out the officers' mess. This was a doddle and usually brought with it a buckshee supper and beer surreptitiously supplied by sympathetic officers. The Guards regiments, being special, had a more ferocious system than other units of the Army. George Webb recalls:

'When one was on a charge, the charge was read out, usually by the Orderly Sergeant in Waiting. One had to say to the officer, "I thank you, Sir, for leave to speak." When that was granted by the officer hearing the case, you could explain the circumstances. However good your defence was you always came away with some sort of punishment; extra drills, CB or extra fatigues. One very educated Guardsman when on a charge was given permission to speak and said, "I am afraid the Sergeant-Major was suffering from a misapprehension, Sir." The Sergeant-Major, not knowing what misapprehension meant, when asked by the officer hearing the charge if it was correct, said "Sir" [implying consent], and the case was dismissed. There were ways of beating the system, of course. In 1941, at Louth in Lincolnshire, we were billeted in an old house, some of us were upstairs and some downstairs. Well, the officer inspecting always started his kit inspections upstairs. After he had finished in the first bedroom, all manner of things; pull-throughs, knives, forks and spoons came through a hole in the ceiling which enabled the Guardsmen on the ground floor to say, "Laundry at the wash, otherwise kit all present, Sir."

Young recruits were always hungry. Despite the regular and large meals which they received, the open air, physical exercises and their developing muscles demanded even more food than the Army would supply. The low pay made it impossible for the ordinary soldier to eat out regularly. The solution was to get FUT – 'Feet under the Table' was the euphemism given to those lucky enough to have a family whom they could visit in their off-duty hours and from whom a meal could be expected. The farther north one went the greater the hospitality, and in Scotland with fresh salmon, venison and pheasant, the lucky lad with his feet under the table lived well and usually on food he had never eaten before. It was a new experience for young soldiers. Despite the most severe rationing and the fact that FUT seemed not to be found south of Watford, there were still opportunities for free snacks. Sunday evening in Maidstone, and for all I know in other towns, too, it was possible to have three teas. The qualification was to be fleet of foot. At about 5 in the evening there were tea and sandwiches in a small mission hall down near the cinema. To sing a few hymns and to listen to the stories of the Welsh clergyman in charge was a small price to pay for stacks of sandwiches and tea. After the last hymn, there was a sharp trot up the hill and into the main street where tea and sandwiches were to be had in another church hall for another session of hymn singing. The last stop was in the Methodist Hall just off Week Street where there was time to relax and enjoy the singing, the sandwiches and tea, because by now it was too late to get to any other 'free issue'. It was not gluttony, just hunger.

Ex-Gunner Wileman was first sent to No. 1 Holding Unit at Laindon in Essex and after retraining was posted to 387th Heavy Anti-Aircraft Battery near Chatham in Kent.

'To begin with the guns were 3.7in. In a heavy barrage the shells, which stood 5ft long from base to nose, got very heavy. When the gun was being fired in an upright position they had to be punched up by hand on which a leather glove was fitted. Life was not all hard work. One day I was ordered to do stoker's work in the cookhouse and, always eager to please, I warmed up the coal-fired, hot water systems so well that hot water came from cold and hot taps alike. I was picked, together with several other men, to attend a course on the Spigot mortar and the new-type Bakelite grenades. I also learned to drive a Guy 15cwt truck, although I was already a proficient driver in my own right having been continually driving since 1934. The mortar course turned into a hair-raising affair. We picked men were to teach young officers how to use the above-named items although we had a CSM with us. It was his job to inform the officer of the procedure to be followed. One morning I was out with my officer using an old tank as a target [for the Spigot mortar] and all went well at first. I explained that should the mortar bomb fail to explode he was under no circumstances to touch it. He told me quite curtly that he was not taking orders from a bloody Gunner and when one did fail to detonate he kicked it. The explosion blew his foot off. After that incident I was returned to my unit to face a General Court Martial, but was exonerated.

'By this time we had been converted to using 4.5in heavy AA guns, beautiful weapons although, of course, weapons of death. Concrete emplacements were built round them. I was now a Quadrant Elevation layer and a Bearing layer. However, should one get caught late going on duty after the alarm had sounded, one had to act as ammunition runner. This happened to me one night. My bed was next to the alarm bell which was the size of a dinner plate. I never heard the alarm and only woke when the guns opened fire. I hurried into my clothes, rushed up to the gun position and as I entered the emplacement the gun fired. The large cartridge case came out and hit the wall about the thickness of a fag paper from me. If I had been only a few seconds later I would not be writing this now. When I got to the gun, visibly shaking, I found that we had a misfire. The procedure for a misfire was to attempt to fire the shell three more times. Then the order "unload" was given and the unfortunate runner (me) had to catch the 6ft shell as it came out of the breach. It was a fuzed and fixed shell which might explode at any second. My task was to run with that dangerous shell for a distance of 100 yards, lay it on the ground and get back to the gun. I reckon I did a mile a minute sprint. Never again was I late for a shoot out.'

Late for a shoot out, Gunner Wileman, may not have been again, but a disregard of orders brought him detention.

'At the Holding Unit to which I was sent after Dunkirk, I was made the Captain's driver and part of my duties was to go into Laindon village and collect the mail for the unit and also for the ATS who were on our site. One ATS girl, named Olive, pestered me to let her drive the Austin, open-top coupé. One day I let her and that was the day that the Brigadier was walking up the hill for a snap inspection.'

From Close Arrest Wileman passed via a Court-Martial into a Detention Barracks and his description gives an idea of how military prisons were run:

'One day the Staff Sergeant had we prisoners running round the parade ground in Full Fighting Gear in mid-July (in the days when we had good summers). We ran for two hours nonstop and then I flaked out. I was carted off to the camp hospital where the MO asked me how I came to be in the state I was.

I told him and next morning there was a heavy tread of boots coming into the hospital and it was the entire camp staff. They were lined up from one end to the other. The MO came in and stood by my bed. He then addressed them with these words: "Through your stupidity this man is now confined to hospital. If such a thing occurs again while I am MO of this camp I will have all of you from the RSM down demoted and sent to a place that is well known to all of us. He meant Barlinnie, the most dreaded Glasshouse. In Detention breakfast was chunks of bread and butter with bromide-laden tea [mythical] to stop the lads getting sexy. The polishing we had to do was mad. The broomheads and handles, the tables and legs had to be made white like driven snow and all brown lines had to be polished with brown, navy issue soap. All metalwork – dustpans, etc., had to shine like silver, but not with metal polish but with a bathbrick, a soft stone used at that time. I was given a latrine bucket as a punishment because the screw said I had not cleaned the corner of one of my buckles on my small pack. I refused to scour that latrine bucket on health grounds. The cookhouse staff in the detention barracks was made up from inmates and they couldn't cook cold water. Cabbage we called boiled gas-capes, for that is what it looked like. I know one thing. I never made a misdemeanour after that.'

According to Trooper Talbot, detention in the United Kingdom was a fearful thing. Somehow overseas it seemed less terrible, probably because of the sunshine:

'I was in the nick in the UK (at Fort Darland) at the time that two screws there kicked a swaddie to death. It was said that he was suffering from TB and couldn't do the drills they demanded. They were court-martialled and sent out of the UK and to Italy. They didn't go to a glasshouse out there though, but were put in some other unit. I reckon that every solder in Italy was looking for that pair of bastards to fill them in, but they were not found, so far as I know. I also did time in the nick near Naples and by comparison with Fort Darland it was a doddle.'

During the war there were many parades and processions: war weapons week, aid to Russia week, Spitfire week and a great number of similar occasions for which the Army produced marching contingents. One memory of what should have been a solemn event was recalled by John Eardley, who was in the second stage of his recruit training during the winter of 1942:

'In late November our CO died and all normal parades were stopped so that we could prepare for his funeral with full military honours. All the recruit squads were tested by the RSM to find those who were best at slow-marching. That group was given intensive instruction in how to march in slow time carrying their arms reversed. Other recruits who were good at rifle drill, I was one of these, were chosen to line the route in the graveyard between the gate and the grave. We had to rest on our arms reversed, a very imposing drill movement. One thing about that is that the muzzle of the rifle should in fact stick in the ground, but the Army naturally doesn't want its guns dirty, so the muzzle was rested on the left boot. The whole contingent was taken by truck to the village where the CO lived. The parade went off well and then there was food and drink for all. The officers went up to the Colonel's house; the sergeants of the bearer-party and the marching detachment as well as us in the graveyard detail, were entertained in the village hall. There was plenty to eat and lashings of drink. You can guess it was a very merry group which came back from burying the Colonel and we all agreed we had a marvellous time. It made a change from our normal routine.'

SOLDIERING OVERSEAS

The duties of a British soldier in peacetime were chiefly confined to garrison duties and/or minor campaigns in Britain's overseas possessions. Infantry regiments had two battalions, one of which would normally be serving overseas while the other was in the United Kingdom. At the end of a certain number of years the UK-based unit would go out to relieve the overseas battalion which returned to carry out home duties in Britain. It was not unknown, for both Regular battalions of an infantry regiment to be on overseas postings at the same time. The Line cavalry, the Royal Artillery and the Royal Tank Regiment were among the arms of service which had no second Line. A unit from those non-infantry arms would go overseas and when their tour of duty was completed would be replaced in the foreign station by a fresh formation. Although there were small British military garrisons in the Caribbean, it was usually to a station east of Gibraltar that a British unit would be posted. There were Army garrisons in those places which were naval bases or which had once been coaling-stations, including Malta, Cyprus, Egypt, Aden and Somaliland, all stepping-stones on the short sea route to the Far East. There was also a long sea route, round the Cape, whose stations included the Gold Coast, Simonstown in South Africa and Zanzibar. According to J. Rowlands, RA:

'Egypt and the bases in the Med were really glorified transit camps in which the outgoing unit would become acclimatized to the heat and living standards of the East. The home-coming battalions would also acclimatize themselves in the Med to the coolness of that area and would make sort of island-hopping progress towards Gibraltar and finally, Blighty.'

Sam Staples, RTR:

'The recruit in barracks in the UK heard a lot from the old soldiers about life in India and could not get out there fast enough to sample the things he had heard about. For most of the rookies this was their first experience of a foreign country and, really, you either loved India or you hated it. There was no half-measure. Either the East got you or it made you sick with the misery all around you.'

H. Penrose, a Gunner, was one who had heard the East a'calling:

'When I was young I heard a song about the road to Mandalay and wanted to see that road for myself. I saw it and stayed in Burma for years. Looking back it may have been the Burmese women that kept me there after the regiment's first tour of duty was expired. My unit moved on to Hong Kong, I think it was. I asked for a transfer to the new artillery regiment that was going to relieve us and it was granted. I did nearly ten years in Burma, including peacetime and wartime service. I loved the place and the people. Like little flowers they were.'

Another man who when he went East heard the call and stayed for years, was the late 'Nobby' Esplin. He sailed for India in 1904 and returned in 1938. With

34 years of unbroken foreign service, he set a record in the modern British Army which will now never be broken.

There exists among many British people a longing for the romance and the majesty of the East. Jack Kelly of the Royal Fusiliers found that:

'The truth was a world away from that. Of course, as a white man in India you were someone of importance. You were looked upon by the Indians as powerfully rich. The natives were so poor that even a Private's pay was unbelievable wealth to them and they did their best to get some of our wages for themselves. As for the luxury of India – luxury turned out to be a stinking hot, bug-infested barrack-room with only a couple of punkahs which didn't cool the warm air but only stirred it. India was cholera, rabies, the misery of prickly heat, flood, fire and pestilence. India meant double guard on every sentry post north of Peshawar, or in Burma where the dacoits were led by the local Buddhist priests. Sex and drink were available – but you had to be prepared to risk catching the pox from the local girls or else go blind drinking the stuff which the locals produced.'

It was the teeming misery of India that affected Don Harding of the Royal Artillery deeply. He had gone East after the war began with Japan and like all the other new drafts was mentally unprepared for what he found:

'When we first set foot in Bombay, on 10 May 1942, the thing that struck us was the extreme poverty of so many of the people; dressed in rags and begging for a living. Thousands were just living in the streets and others in shelters made of palm fronds, bits of cardboard or wood – anything that would form a cover and sited on any bit of space available. Beggars were everywhere, with the most appalling disabilities, stumps for limbs, twisted bodies, blindness, etc., all displayed with beseeching cries for "baksheesh". Very sickening, especially seeing little children lying there with their begging-bowls – and nobody seemed to care. Sadly we soon got hardened to it all and were indifferent to their plight. There was little else we could do.'

If one saw past the misery at urban street and village level, India could be a romantic place. The late Trevor Marshall was a soldier who served in the pre-war days of the Raj and recalled the glory and the panoply of imperial power:

'The things I remember of India were the parades and the troubles. It goes without saying that India was stifling hot and that there were masses of people, far more than I had ever seen in one place together. The streets were packed with crowds of people by day as well as by night. I was serving with the Dorsets. Our regimental cap badge bore the motto "Primus in Indus", the first into India. When we, the British Army that is, left India it was our regiment, as the last to leave, who slow-marched under the arch at Bombay and on to the troopships. So we were the first and last in India. The British had been in India a long time, but we have never been given the credit for what we did there; irrigating the desert, giving them peace and justice and generally defending the country. I was only out East for a short time, but I remember that the military year in India began with a Proclamation Day Parade on 1 January. This was really what I think soldiering is all about. It was brilliant. The British in white drill and topees with puggarree and regimental flash. I felt sorry for the Jocks with their heavy kilts. The Indian

Army regiments were all in full dress – green tunics, scarlet tunics, blue tunics and turbans of all colours each regiment with its own special way of tying it. We paraded for the Proclamation Day Parade on Poona racecourse and the crowds had to be seen to be believed. The boxes in the grandstand were a mass of colour. Of course, most of the spectators were Whites; civil service wallahs, officers and their wives, I suppose. The rest of the year was marked with parades for almost every type of civilian or military brasshat from the Viceroy down to Provincial Governors. We Trooped our Colour and celebrated things like the King Emperor's Birthday, his accession to the Throne and the anniversary of his Coronation. I think that the parades were meant to keep us busy and to keep the Indians impressed.'

The Newmark brothers, whom we have met, had enlisted in order to go to India. John, the surviving twin, recalls their experiences:

'One day a list was posted on the battalion notice board detailing the men who had been drafted to India. My brother and I were among the first in the mad rush to see if our names had been included this time. Halfway down the list, in alphabetical order, we read, Private Nathan J., followed by Private Newberry S. and then, there it was, Private Newmark J., followed by Private Oldham B. But where was Private Newmark G? Why wasn't George on the list? We read it again and again but Private Newmark G. was missing from that list. There must be some mistake, we decided. How could they send one twin to Indian and not the other? We were both dumbfounded, dismayed beyond belief. Could this be a deliberate ploy to separate us once and for all.'

The two lodged protest after protest to higher authorities, all to no avail. John continues:

'One week before the troopships SS *Nevasa* sailed for India, the thought occurred to us that *King's Rules and Regulations,* which had helped us before, could possibly contain a paragraph, or section or sub-section which might help us again. We borrowed the volume from a friend who worked as a clerk in the Company Office and after much searching among the myriad rules and regulations found one particular sentence. We read it again to make sure we had it correct. This sentence stated quite clearly that an elder brother posted overseas could claim a younger to be posted also. We could not believe our luck. I was older than George, but because he had joined the army first the authorities had assumed that he was the elder twin! No wonder they were sending me to India. They thought me to be the younger. So when I boarded the SS *Nevasa,* together with a few hundred other troops for company, I was in a deeply contented frame of mind. True, George was not with me, but I was confident that we would be re-united before long.

'For the three-week long sea voyage I decided to volunteer to serve as batman to a young lieutenant who was also being posted to the 1st Battalion. In those days officers and other ranks rarely mixed in a social sense, but in the unusual circumstances on board ship *en route* to India, sailing into the unknown as it were, a degree of neighbourliness persuaded me to tell the officer my tale of woe concerning George. I did this just before the ship reached Port Said. "Would you have any idea, Sir", asked I, rounding off my story, "of the correct procedure for me to claim my twin brother and have him posted to India?"

"Leave it to me," replied my young officer. "I understand the position and I understand how you feel about it, so just leave it to me. I'll arrange for him to be on the next draft." 'The SS *Nevasa* docked in Bombay in January 1936. Our draft went by train to Secundarabad in the Deccan, from where we marched to Gough Barracks near Trimulgarry, a small village in the back of beyond, far removed from civilization, but for me it was not too far removed from heaven. I was in India. George arrived exactly one month later. I went to Secunderabad station to meet him, even though the station was out of bound to all troops. Precisely because of that I knew there would be nobody to charge me with breaking bounds and nobody on the new draft would be aware of it either. We fell in at the rear of the column for the march back to the barracks near Trimulgarry and I gave my brother an insight into army life in India.

'It's very much better and far easier than back in England," I explained, "mainly because nothing much happens after about 11 o'clock. By then it is far too hot to go on parade or do any work, so as soon as lunch is over everyone goes to bed!" "Goes to bed?" queried George. "Yes, everyone lies down on their beds under the mosquito nets and we all more or less do nothing. It's an afternoon siesta, really, and then about four o'clock when it begins to get a little cooler anyone who wants to plays football or something. In fact I consider soldiering out here is rather like a long drawn-out holiday. We do have parades and one thing and another in the mornings, of course, before it gets really hot, but in the afternoons it's into bed or out of barracks." "Out of barracks? What do you mean?" asked George. "Well, that's the unwritten rule which stipulates that nobody is allowed to mess around in the barracks when everyone else is resting. They don't want to be disturbed. If you don't want to rest, you have to clear out and disappear. I've been out a few times to look for birds and lizards and any other wildlife, but they also find it too hot so there's not much around in the heat of the day."

After digesting this news, George commented. "Well, I think we might go off occasionally. We've come all this way to India and don't want to waste every afternoon in bed." "Yes," I agreed. "We'll certainly go out occasionally, but I am fairly sure after a time you will be perfectly happy to go to bed like everyone else." As we continued marching I asked George whether he had brought his razor with him. "I've brought two. One for weekdays and one for Sundays," he quipped. "Well, you won't need either. Every morning an Indian comes round and shaves you. Furthermore, he shaves you in bed." "In bed?" asked an astonished George. "In bed," I repeated. "He shaves everybody every morning and you pay him a few annas a week, which is next to nothing. And that's not all. Somebody comes round every day with cha and wads." George interrupted. "What are cha and wads?" "Right. Cha is a cup of tea and wads are cakes. He comes round during break time in between parades or whatever's going on. He is known as the cha wallah." George considered this and began to think that India was a rest cure. "Oh, and there's another Indian who cleans and polishes your boots each morning. He sits on the verandah with about a dozen pairs of boots spread in a half circle around him and then puts a bit of polish on each boot in turn. Then he brushes each one and, finally, polishes them with a bit of cloth. Then he collects another dozen pairs and repeats the performance. Then there's the *durzi*, in other words the tailor and the dhobi who does all your washing; so it's all very pleasant having everyone doing all the chores!"

'We enjoyed service life in India and the months flew by. We were there, at last, proud to be serving with the Royal West Kent Regiment in an outpost of the British Empire. We found it hard to believe that our most cherished ambitions had been realized.'

Bags of Swank

Regimental Pride

The most important lesson in the Army's education of its soldiers was that of unit loyalty. Almost from his first day of service the recruit was told that he was serving in the finest regiment in the Army. In time that direction was even more sharply defined in an endeavour to convince him that he was in the finest company/squadron/battery of that regiment. This stress upon unit loyalty was calculated, unceasing and absolutely necessary. In a fighting unit each man had to know that he could depend upon his comrades doing their duty, just as they, in turn, relied upon him. Each formation had its sacred objects. In the heavy infantry the most important and revered artefacts were the Colours: the Sovereign's, symbolizing the unit's loyalty to the monarch, and the Regimental Colour, the focus of unit allegiance. Units that did not carry Colours had their own sacred objects or traditions which bound their members just as closely. In the Royal Artillery, for example, the guns evoked an emotion as deep as any devotion to a flag, and men sacrificed themselves to save the guns from falling into enemy hands. Such devotion as I have described, is an emotional thing. It cannot be measured, weighed or valued objectively. It is a feeling. The peacetime soldiers, both Regular and Territorial, those willing members of the introspective regimental tribe, felt this emotion and knew with absolute conviction that the things they held to be sacred were outward and visible signs of an inward and spiritual grace – the regimental spirit. Conscripts did not, to begin with, comprehend the mysteries of military honour as expressed in Standards, crests and badges and mocked as mumbo-jumbo or bullshit those things which they did not yet understand. Yet most knew what fervent loyalty meant for most had supported football and cricket teams in civilian life and maintained that support in barracks.

An example of how it is possible for a regimental tradition to be created, almost by accident, is that of a battle-cry first heard in Tunisia. 'During the first days of the Normandy campaign we heard our Airborne men shouting "Whohoa Mahommed", when they were about to attack the enemy. Just after I was wounded, the man in the next bed to me was from the Paras. I mentioned that battle-cry. He told me that it had been first used in North Africa. An airborne battalion in the Tunisian campaign was dug in near an Arab village. At some point during the day one of the Arab locals would have a shouted conversation in another village. The Paras soon noticed that almost all those shouted conversations began with 'Whohoa' and that Mahommed was the most popular name. The battalion took to shouting in that way to one another and eventually it was taken up by the Brigade and then by 1st Airborne Division when it fought in France.'

Roy Cooke, an Englishman serving with the 5th Seaforth Highlanders at El Alamein realized the inspirational nature of the pipes:

'Above all the din the sound of the pipes could clearly be heard and even an Englishman can feel proud to belong to a Scottish regiment when he hears the shrill, warlike sound of a pipe tune above all the racket around him. It sounded so incongruous, yet it was just what was needed to keep up one's spirits for what lay ahead.'

An example of pride of regiment is given by John Newmark:

'When I returned to the United Kingdom in 1940, from Malta, I went to OCTU and was commissioned in the Royal Warwickshire Regiment. I had, of course, applied for the Royal West Kents or the Indian Army, but apparently both were full up, so I had to be content with the Warwicks. At some point during 1943 or 1944, I was transferred to the Shropshire Light Infantry, very much against my will. Most of my platoon were transferred with me and we all refused to "dog trot" on parade. We kept to our regulation pace of 120 to the minute – or whatever it was. Furthermore, I refused to wear an SLI cap badge, keeping my Warwickshire cap badge up, despite my CO telling me to change it. One day Montgomery appeared on the scene and congratulated me on wearing the Warwicks' badge – his old regiment – and my CO avoided me, thereafter.'

A demonstration of unit pride was shown by the paratroops who had been captured at Arnhem. It will be appreciated that hutted prisoner-of-war camps are not the places, nor captivity the time, best suited to maintain the highest standard of turn-out. It must also be realized that men in captivity may degenerate and lose that sense of self-pride, unless the military spirit can be kept alive. The Paratroop RSM kept his camp on its toes and morale was high. In the last weeks of the war the camp was liberated by the Americans who were astonished at what met them. In other camps they had liberated indifferently, even casually dressed troops who had rushed to the gates in welcome. Not at the Para camp. On the gate stood an airborne soldier immaculately turned out – boots gleaming, brasses shining and red beret *comme il faut*. Inside the gate stood a Quarter Guard, just as immaculately turned-out, and waiting to welcome the American Army stood the Para RSM. He handed over the camp as if he were handing over a billet to an incoming unit; everything documented and in good order. It was a demonstration of pride of unit, that factor of morale which cannot be measured or weighed, but which has the power to raise the soldier to deeds he had not though it possible to achieve.

DISCIPLINE

Discipline is a regimen seldom lightly accepted. Those who are incapable of disciplining themselves are reluctant to have others impose it upon them. They resist the compulsion of discipline because its demands are associated with discomfort or inconvenience. Certain disciplines enclosed within the military framework, including cleanliness, punctuality and obedience, contribute to the making of a good soldier.

Sergeant Joseph Ramsden, a Regular with more than two decades as a soldier, recalled the recruits who came in as a result of conscription and those who had enlisted in pre-war days:

'Basically, there was no difference in physique between the two types of soldier, Regular or conscript, when they first joined up. Most were physically unfit, with poor muscle development. Proper feeding and regular exercise soon changed them into fit young men. There were many who had no idea of how to keep their person clean. The Army has one crime which it stamps on very heavily indeed – dirty flesh. I have known recruits who did not wash past their ears so that they had tide-marks on their necks. Others who thought that to have a regular bath would weaken them sexually. About one in four had never used a toothbrush and not a few had head lice. Most settled down and kept themselves clean, but there were always a few who would not wash regularly or thoroughly. They were taught a lesson by a means which although unofficial and frowned upon was still carried out. They were bathed in public on the square. The offender would be stripped and scrubbed using cold water and army issue soap. Once was enough for most, but there were a few persistent offenders thinking, perhaps, that they could gain their discharge using wilful dirtiness as the reason. This had happened in peacetime, when one could pick and choose recruits, but it could not be allowed to happen in wartime, and the conscripts who thought they could "work their ticket", as it was called, soon found that they could not. Punctuality was the most difficult lesson that the conscripts had to learn. It was not that they were wilfully lazy, just that as civilians time-keeping had not been as necessary as the Army insisted it was. One way to overcome persistent idleness was communal punishment. The whole hutful of men would be punished by extra drills or parades – and would be told the reason. The offender soon learned his lesson because his comrades would knock it into him. No soldier wants to be an outsider, to be cast out by his hut mates and eventually the backsliders came round and paraded on time.'

Obedience was the third lesson that the recruits needed to learn. It is a common accusation that barrack square drill was intended to produce automata. Thomas Rodney was called up for service in the Ordnance Corps during 1941:

'I could not understand all the screaming and shouting on the square in the UK. It struck me as absolutely unnecessary. In the middle of the Second World War, halfway through the 20th century, we were being drilled as if we were to take part in 19th-century battles. It was all so archaic and so pointless. As recruits we were taught foot drill, arms drill, musketry and bayonet fighting. Our unit was, in effect, a semi-civilian one and we would never be expected to fight. So all that moving about in double-time and time spent in bayonet drill was a waste. It seemed to me that the incessant shouting was intended to reduce thinking adults to unthinking robots.'

Such an accusation is not borne out by facts. The good soldier is one who by disciplined reaction can adapt to the changing circumstances on a battlefield, who can by thinking evaluate the situation and use his initiative. The unthinking or badly disciplined soldier, generally, soon becomes a casualty. There are known cases where soldiers under fire did not fall quickly to the ground as they had been trained to do, but looked for a dry spot on which to lie. Shrapnel and snipers wait for no man. On the battlefield there are only the quick and the dead and those who are not quick are soon dead. Only on the battlefield can the strength of discipline be proven. If it was lacking the unit crumbled and broke, with men moving to the rear without and, sometimes, against direct orders. There were instances when British soldiers had to be threatened with summary execution in order to keep them fighting. The instance of a battalion of 49th Division in Normandy shows how a unit with poor discipline goes to pieces.

On 30 June 1944, GHQ, acting upon recommendation, withdrew the battalion from the line and broke it up. The men were posted to other regiments of the Division. A confidential report by the battalion's commanding officer, who had been with the unit for only a few days, painted a picture of the neuroses which had infected his unit. He mentioned, in particular, self-inflicted wounds, hysteria, overreaction to shellfire and to casualties. In fairness to the battalion the CO pointed out that there had been 350 other-rank casualties in two weeks and that only twelve of the battalion's original officers were still with it, all of whom were junior. The original commanding officer and all the Company commanders had gone. One Company had lost all its officers. The CO, a Regular officer who realized the gravity of the report he was making, stated that the battalion was not fit to take its place in the line and recommended that it be broken up.

Frederick Jarvis of 46th Division recalls discipline reduced to a nonsense:

'In the Canal Zone there was an IRTD whose commanding officer was said to be raving mad. Annoyed at two hills which he could see from his office window he ordered parties of men to be sent out each day in an attempt to shovel away the offending hills and to reduce them to the level of the desert. Not that he was very pleased with the nature of the desert. Its surface was uneven and he wanted it level. To achieve this he ordered men to drag large, coconut-fibre PT mats across the surface. I was called for a guard at Geneifa camp. We were out in the desert along the shores of Lake Timsah into which the Suez Canal flows. There was nothing around for miles, except native villages and a detention camp. The IRTD mounted a pukka guard twice a week over the jailbirds, a guard as pukka as the ones for Buckingham Palace. It was inspired lunacy. Two days before the guard was to be mounted its members had to hand in one set of their Khaki Drill clothing. This was washed and so stiffly starched that the short trousers stood up by themselves. The KD shirt was less heavily starched but still felt like cardboard. The nick Wallahs scrubbed our webbing equipment with bleach and polished the brasses till they shone like burnished gold. We paraded in the IRTD and then boarded lorries which took us to the detention camp. At the guard tent our parade KD and equipment were laid out. We took off the unstarched KD in which we had arrived and laid it on our bunks. We were then dressed in the starched clothing. Each man had an orderly who helped him to dress and who put on his boots and equipment. One man had two mates on the orderly detail who actually carried him to his position in the ranks. He was after being Stick Man. Every guard detail has one extra man in case of sickness. That supernumerary does not have to mount guard and there is keen competition to become the supernumerary or Stick Man.

'On the parade square outside the detention camp we were inspected by lance-corporals, by full corporals, by lance-sergeants, full sergeants, Warrant Officers of all grades and then by the RSM. Now that we had been checked by the lower orders, it was the turn of the officers to inspect us. We were at attention for all these inspections, of course. Finally, the decision had to be made – who was to be the Stick Man. They actually measured the length of our hair – it had to be the length of a matchstick. Then the guard mounting began. Our first movements produced a series of minor explosions as the KD cracked when we moved. March past in slow and quick time – the whole, full ceremony – and all out in thousands of acres of nothing. This was not discipline. This was bull and totally unnecessary bull at that. All the soldiers in the IRTD – excluding the permanent staff – were veterans of battle. They did not need this sort of discipline. It served no purpose and it was bitterly resented.'

Jarvis, who had been evacuated to Egypt from Italy after being wounded on the River Volturno, also saw the conditions suffered by prisoners under detention:

'Each group had a task. One lot had to scour tin cans. A prisoner would fish rusty tins out of a standing water tank and hand them out as the "screw" directed. The group then sat out on the ground unspeaking and scrubbed the rust away using desert sand. Each prisoner seemed to have a quota of tins to be cleaned. When he had produced shiny tins he had to double over to the "screw" and present them. If "Staff" thought that they were not properly cleaned of rust he would issue extra tins – to prevent frivolous claims – I think it was called. At the end of the day the shiny tins were flung into the water tank and left to become rusty again. Another group, I think they were undergoing special punishment, had to manhandle cannon-balls. These were piled up in the shape of a low pyramid. At the word of command one ball would be carried at the run for about 100 yards and then placed in position. The prisoners spent their time demolishing pyramids of cannon-balls and then erecting them again. As an exercise in stupidity it can have had no equal.'

Many conscientious soldiers were upset at the lack of reason in military thought. One of these was Roy Cooke of the Seaforths, who went into action at El Alamein and served throughout the African, Sicilian and Italian campaigns:

'Talking of the so-called pettiness of British military discipline, I can give you a first-hand account of that. After having survived the Western Desert, Sicily and Italy, I was downgraded and transferred to the Royal Corps of Signals in 1945, Heaven knows why!!! The one and only time I suffered the indignity of "Jankers" was through trying to be conscientious and do my job properly. I had been detailed for fatigues in our billet, a seaside hotel and was trying to sweep a staircase that was in pitch darkness. There was an empty light fitting above and I, temporarily, borrowed a light bulb so as to see what I was doing. Before I knew it I was on a charge for removing (stealing??) government property. When my "case" came up I had to admit the charge, but was never given a chance to explain WHY I had removed the light bulb. So I did seven days' "spud bashing" as a reward.'

Essentials and Desirables

FOOD

Napoleon's statement that 'an Army marches on its stomach' is no empty cliché, for food is important to the soldier and is the subject about which he never ceases to complain. The creation of the Catering Corps early in the Second World War went a long way to ensuring that standards were constant and high, although they could not always be maintained on active service, particularly in the primitive conditions of the jungles of Burma. Of course, even the best cooks in the world have to be taught, and the REME unit with which Harold Field served was one of those selected to test the dishes which the ACC cooks prepared and served:

'The Catering Corps was training recruits to be cooks to send them to various regiments and we were the guinea pigs. In our platoon was a typical Cockney recruit who was forever cracking jokes. His name was Alf Norman and he came from Lambeth. One day a very keen Second Lieutenant was on day duty and came round asking if there were any complaints about the food. Up jumped Alf Norman. "What is it?" asked the officer. Norman replied "I have a mouse's head in my dinner with his ears sticking out." "Good God!" the officer said. "So you have. Bring your dinner, Norman, to the cookhouse." He had the Sergeant Cook and all the recruits lined up and didn't half dress them down. When he had finished he turned to Norman and said, "Would you like another dinner, Norman?" "No fear Sir," was the reply, "I might find his flipping body in it." Everybody burst out laughing and even the officer had to turn away and smile. It was an incident I shall never forget.'

The Army authorities, aware of the failure of the Commissariat in the Crimean campaign, had since that time striven for excellence and for a balanced diet. Before the Second World War nutrition experts tested, sampled, and then retested and resampled until they had produced a very flexible rations system for the British Army. These composite, or 'compo,' rations were of various types. The basic one, contained within a wooden box, held rations for fourteen men for one day, for seven men for a two-day period, or any permutation of seven. Under active service conditions biscuits were issued to replace bread, but these were not the jaw-cracking type of popular fiction. They had to be hard to withstand the handling they would suffer, but they were palatable. They were packed in hermetically sealed tins to protect them from infestation, a common problem on active service. The contents of a box of 'compo' might include tins of oleo margarine, sardines, bacon, jam, meat and vegetable stew, steak and kidney pudding, rice pudding, steamed treacle pudding or tinned fruit. There were tins of boiled sweets, bars of chocolate, small packets of condiments and sheets of toilet paper. From that variety of tins it was possible to produce meals suitable for breakfast, lunch and tea. A variant of the standard box was the high-altitude ration, high in protein, for use by mountain troops, and there were other variants for those fighting in abnormally difficult terrain. Aware of the difficulties of campaigning, the nutritions experts produced light and mobile 'one-man packs' with such exotica as cubes of compressed tea, sugar and milk, porridge in small slabs and dehydrated meat and vegetables.

'After one attack, I found the body of a soldier of the Lincolns or Leicesters, and alongside him two one-man packs. Shrapnel had torn these open and had smashed most of the tea/sugar/milk cubes. My unit had had a bashing and the rifle companies had withdrawn to a vineyard where we had dug in. I got a fire going from the canes holding up the grapes, took a little dixie from an abandoned tank and got a brew on. The tea tasted terrible – as weak as the proverbial gnat's; but it was wet and warm and it steadied us for a bit. Then we went back again into the attack and this time took the farmhouses which we had not been able to capture on the first time. We got them this time and in the courtyard of a farm we found empty champagne bottles with a rubber stamp saying "Reserved for the German Armed Forces". The Jerries did themselves proud. We had weak tea; they had champagne.'

It was perhaps in an endeavour to encomize on shipping space that led to the introduction of dehydrated food which was first seen in the Mediterranean Theatre of Operations during the autumn of 1944. Dehydrated beef mince, which came on to issue at about the same time, was acceptable and some soldiers had tasted dehydrated potatoes before the war. Dehydrated cabbage was terrible both in taste and appearance and dehydrated egg powder when reconstituted could only produce scrambled eggs – never the golden-yolk, fried eggs which accompanied chips – the Army's choicest dish. Another culinary horror appeared at the same time – soya-link sausages. They looked obscene – like grey, triangular, skinless turds – yet, inexplicably, there were some soldiers who relished them. Ron Howard found one such phenomenon:

'I was in a leave camp outside Rome just after the war ended. We had German prisoners as orderlies for lunch and tea but breakfast was a sort of buffet arrangement. To help yourself instead of having food dumped on the plate was a real revolution in catering. On the buffet table there were the usual things, bacon, eggs and fried bread and also soya links. The man in front of me ignored the bacon and eggs and took five soya links which he piled on to his plate and which he then ate with great enjoyment. His only answer, when I asked him why he had taken so many was, "Well I like them and nobody else seems to want them." It was widely rumoured that the staunch defence of the German Army in Italy was due to a belief that if they fell into our hands as prisoners they would be fed soya-links. It was their determination to avoid such a diet that kept them fighting to the very end.'

There was another dish which had been with the Army since the desert days and which was issued throughout the campaign in Italy. This was melon and lemon jam. This surprising combination of tastes produced a jam resembling

Polycell in appearance and flavour. The proportion of fruit used must have been one very large melon to one very small lemon, for there was no tang, no zest, no citric sharpness – just a blank, tasteless sweetness that would have defied identification had it not been for the label on the tin.

'In our unit we called it "Herzog's Revenge" and the story went round that the recipe for the jam had been invented in the last years of the Turkish control of Palestine. The Jews there at the time had made and sold a whole consignment to the Turks. When the Turks went and we came in, the Zionists still had warehouses packed with tins and flogged the lot to the British Army. That was the story. It was tasteless stuff but we didn't complain while the war was being fought in Africa. But when the war moved into Italy, we thought that there might be decent jam coming from the UK. There was not and we had M&L dished up at every tiffin. Of course we sent trucks into Alex to buy some of the luxuries we could not get up in the Blue and these included proper jam. But why should we have had to pay out for good jam? It was up to the QM Department to get it for the troops.'

In addition to dehydrated food and compo rations the Army in north-west Europe was issued with self-heating tins of food, but these were not popular. A far easier method of heating food was to tie tins around a vehicle exhaust. Within minutes the cans were boiling hot – ready to eat. Tank crews who carried luxury items such as primus stoves, in their vehicles could and did produce hot drinks inside the comfortable commodious Shermans. Most Royal Artillery units had similar equipment in their portees. Small wonder then, that to an infantryman a deserted or abandoned tank or portee was looked upon as an Aladdin's cave of goodies. Even the most strictly worded Army Orders could not stop the jackdaw behaviour of infantrymen when they came across such abundance.

When it was not possible to supply the forward troops with compo, or in conditions of siege as at Kohima and Imphal, the beleaguered garrisons fell back on the basic constituents of British Army diet: bully and biscuits. Some of the tins of bully bore a manufacturing date showing the contents to be 30 years old. It was an example of Army thrift. Another example of this was the Carnation milk issued at the end of the war. The cases of tinned milk had formed part of the cargo of a ship which had been sunk in Algiers harbour in 1942–3. The boxes had been recovered and the tins were eventually issued to married families in the army of occupation in Austria.

However much the soldiers of the British Army may have grumbled at the rations they received and the scale of issue, there is no doubt that compared with the other armies the British Service was well fed indeed. Certainly, German reports talk in the most glowing terms of the food supplies which were captured in the desert. In Italy, enemy patrols were often intercepted as they returned from raids on British roadside dumps, carrying on their backs boxes of compo ration. The Germans had taken to heart Rommel's desert directive, 'You want supplies? Go and take them from the British. They have enough.' The Americans, too, shivering in their gaberdine uniforms in the depths of winter in the Apennine mountains, and fed on little tins of corn-beef hash and Spam, would visit neighbouring British units hoping to effect an exchange of food. They, poor devils, did not get meat puddings.

To supply the most advanced units, particularly in Burma, air drops were needed. Aeroplanes, usually the reliable Douglas Dakota, would be loaded with boxes of rations, each fitted with a coloured parachute. The technique of airfreighting supplies was described by T. Payne:

'The air dropping was like the parable of the sower. It was accepted that some rations would be lost completely; either they would be inaccessible or else they would fall on Japanese positions. These were the ones which in the Bible were said to have fallen on stony ground or among thorns. But those which fell on our own men not only gave them the food they needed but assured them they were not forgotten. The aircraft was packed with boxes arranged in the order in which they had to be dispatched. The Dakota would groan as it raced along the runway and literally staggered into the air. I was always afraid it would not make it. The flight over the jungle was always bumpy and when we hit air pockets it was like going down in a very fast lift. We would be told when we were approaching the drop zone and when the lights came on two of us moved to the door of the Dakota. We fitted our harness and then took off the side door. A team of "shovers" pushed the packages towards the open doorway and we, the other dispatcher and I, kicked them out. It sounds easy but we were soon sweating with the strain. One experience that always frightened me was when the plane lurched or banked without warning. When that happened we dispatchers would fly out through the open doorway and into the air. Only the harness kept us safe and when the banking procedure was over the effect of the swing would bring us back inside the machine again, and we would hit all sorts of projecting bits of metal as we swung in. It was frightening, sick-making and painful. And we carried out such a run about every third day, sometimes more frequently, depending upon the situation on the ground.'

John Clark described not the food, but the 'bull' associated with the culinary arrangements in a camp.

'I was in the camp at Capodimonte, outside Naples. Towards the end of the war soldiers went home from this place on demobilization. One day a VIP paid an official visit. He was a Labour MP and was something to do with the War Office. It seems that somebody had written to the *Daily Mirror* complaining about the camp conditions. Well, the VIP came and walked into the first dining-room. There were table-cloths, flowers, cruets and all the sort of unusual things we never ever saw under normal conditions. Of course, he was surprised. No more than we were. Outside the hut he was shown in great detail the washing-up facilities and was introduced to every cook on the camp establishment. This was to give the permanent staff time to whip the cloths and flowers, etc., from the tables in the first dining-hall and to put them on the tables in the second dining-hall. At a given signal the MP was invited to go into the second dining-hall where the tables were now properly laid. It was a lovely exercise in eyewash.'

SEX

In the services there was one aspect of human behaviour to which all discussions turned to as inevitably as night follows day. This was sex, known in the Army as 'subject normal'. Talk could begin on any subject. At some point the argument would change direction and 'subject normal' would have replaced the topic originally under discussion. Of course, everyone is interested in sex, but in the peculiar conditions of service life sex was the inevitable topic. In a situation where men were forced to live for long periods in the closest companionship and with scant opportunity for a social life outside their own circle, sex talk was inescapable. It was more than that. It was all-absorbing and often the only subject which could be discussed without a violent argument ending in an invitation for someone to step outside and settle it. Barrack-room language included sexual words of unusual flexibility, capable of being used as nouns, adjectives and verbs; as punctuation or emphasis, capable of shocking with their brutality or of demonstrating the deepest feelings of comradeship. I remember one of my comrades during the campaign in northern Italy looking down at the dead body of his best mate and asking, 'What the ***** hell, did you ****-well go and get killed for, you ****.' It may not have been Shakespeare, but in those oaths there was as much tragedy and love as anything ever written by a poet.

Even formal instruction in the Army was illustrated with sexual innuendo or description by NCOs who were aware that such words reinforced the message. To explain that a correct map co-ordinate was obtained by first using the latitudinal and then the longitudinal measurements, our instructor said, 'Think of it like a woman. You have to get across her before you can get up her.' The 75 Grenade, an anti-tank device, was an especially good source of innuendo. The two halves of the fuze fitted one within the other and were protected against damp by a small rubber tube. On the grenade-firing range when the sensitive fuzes of the Mills bombs had to be fitted into the body of the bomb, there would always be one recruit who would cry out in anguish. 'I can't find the hole, Sergeant," to which the inevitable response was, 'You would if it had hair round it.'

Postings within the United Kingdom took the soldier to parts of the country where something as normally unremarkable as his accent might be considered by the local girls as sophisticated and he, by association, glamorous. Assisted with the power of the King's uniform and the glamour of the big city, and encouraged by the stories he had heard in the barrack-room the soldier would seek to find some outlet for his desires. He was usually to be frustrated by never achieving the full sexual act. The girl had her reputation to consider and was confined by precisely those restraints and attitudes from which military service had released the soldier. She, too, was the victim of social and family pressures. The great majority of the Army must have been chaste as a result, among other factors, of the social pressures to conform to the the contemporary strict moral code. Ex-Bombardier Millett of an HAA regiment stationed in Scotland wrote that the Army was:

'A fine introduction into monastic life with the emphasis on poverty, chastity and obedience. The soldier's poverty being created by rates of pay kept deliberately low in order to restrict him socially. The demand for total obedience resulted in the issuing of lunatic orders by men who had little idea of the consequences of carrying out those orders. The unnatural demand for chastity was enforced by locating men in wildernesses, deserts and jungles, sometimes for years at a time.'

Nòt all Bombardier Millet's statements are substantiated. When the British Expeditionary Force went to France at the outbreak of war the soldiers were introduced to continental habits and customs. They found, to their surprise, that there were local, municipally run and licensed brothels. The pay of the British soldiers, although low by British civilian standards, was nevertheless princely by comparison with the pay of the French poilu and brothels were quite cheap. Ladies of the town were also available in very large numbers and were cheaper, but they, being unlicensed and therefore, seldom medically inspected, were often infected with venereal disease. There was an alarming increase in the number of soldiers of the BEF reporting sick with the early symptoms of syphilis and gonorrhoea.

The Army was prepared and its reactions were predictable and understandable. It fought back with a campaign at two levels. The first of those was a combination of blackmail and financial loss. Those who contracted VD were classified as having a self-inflicted wound. There was no court-martial as there would have been in the case of a standard SIW, but all the soldier's pay and family allowances were stopped and the wife who asked why was told that her husband had a sexual disease. The fear of VD in those far-off days was not restricted to only the working class but ran through the whole of British society and manifested itself most publicly when the men of the Desert armies came back to Britain at the end of the campaign in Africa. Lady Astor suggested that those soldiers should be made to wear a yellow disc on their uniforms signifying that they had come from an infected region. Although there was an outcry at her words she was only echoing the sentiments of a great many others who felt themselves at risk from the returning veterans.

The other level at which the Army fought back was education aimed at giving the soldiers information on the diseases as well as inculcating a morbid fear of them. Propaganda campaigns conducted by unit medical officers used luridly coloured oil-cloth charts to show infected organs and the degenerative effect of the diseases upon the sufferers. The temporary result after every lecture was a decline in the number of diseased soldiers. When the rate rose again, the power of the cinema was used by the Army to produce and show films using actual medical case-histories to demonstrate the stages of the terrible diseases. The effect was again a drop in numbers; short term only, chiefly because the films being in black and white lacked psychological impact. They could not be related to one's own body. Not until colour films supplied by the American Army were shown, was the deterrent effect longer lasting although, of course, not permanent.

There came a time during the Second World War when it was accepted that soldiers needed a sexual outlet. The idea of brothels licensed by the Army was unacceptable to the Anglo-Saxon mind and indeed, Montgomery was credited, if that is the right word, with having closed down those in Egypt. If a habit cannot be broken or a desire curbed then every measure must be taken to direct it into safe channels. In that effort the American and British Armies, accepting that their soldiers would seek sex, set up PAC centres, the first of which were opened in Italy. In those cheerless little shacks a soldier about to set out on a sexual encounter signed a book and received a condom. On his return to the PAC centre he signed the book again. His penis was then washed in a mild disinfectant and a cream was squirted down into it. If the soldier contracted VD but could prove that he had visited the PAC, his allowances were not stopped and he was not treated as a case of self-inflicted wound.

So determined were the military authorities to contain promiscuity that the Military Police of the American and British Armies were given the unusual authority to arrest each other's soldiers. If they saw a serviceman whom they suspected of being drunk, it was assumed that he had had sexual intercourse and he would be taken promptly to a PAC centre.

'When I was in Naples in the spring of 1944, one of my mates was a New Zealander with a naturally unhealthy pallor which was accentuated by malaria and jaundice. In the Via Roma one morning he and I were stopped by two US military policemen who took his pallor to be a sign of intoxication. We were taken to the PAC and he was given the full treatment. Back in the street again and pretty soon two more policemen intercepted us and he and I went back under escort to the PAC. The treatment he received made him not only nervous but also unsteady on his feet – there was no tenderness on the part of the medical orderlies – and we were caught again before we had reached the NAAFI down near the San Carlo opera house. Back again to the PAC where the only question which the medical orderly could ask was, "How long have you been up the line then?" We caught a taxi back to our billets in Capodimonte rather than risk walking about in the streets full of suspicious policemen.'

The war-time armies serving in the Near and Middle East found no respectable women readily available for heterosexual exploits. In Egypt and Palestine where virginity was vital to a marriage and loss of it was a ground for divorce, no girl intending to marry would be seen with a soldier. The brothels in Egypt's main cities had been closed and the bulk of the Army was up the Blue.

'It was possible to find some sort of relief from women who hung around the great camps which lay alongside the Sweet Water canal and Lake Timsah. I had finished an early morning swim just near Geneifa and lay down for a rest and a smoke under some stunted palms. I heard the sound of a voice and found it was a shepherd trying to cadge a cigarette. Not until then did I realize that it was a girl, not so young any more, blind in one eye, quite grubby and very smelly. Despite all that when I realized it was a girl I really got in the mood. She was quite willing and I did it to her without any protection. Afterwards I called myself all the fools imaginable and sweated blood until the results of the tests came in and showed that I was not infected.'

There were, of course, British servicewomen and nurses serving in every theatre of war, but these were not generally available to the rank and file. The nurses were commissioned officers and the other-rank WRENS, ATS or WAAFS capitalized upon their scarcity value as white women. They were soon to complain once the war ended and the male soldiers in the armies of occupation found partners in every town or village in Europe or Japan. One of the Sunday newspapers at home carried reports of British girls being lonely in Germany and stuck behind barbed wire because it was not safe for them to be out alone. They were alone because none of the ordinary soldiers wanted them. The Tommies were all busy 'fraternizing' with the local girls.

'Fraternization' had been forbidden by Army Order for British soldiers when they first entered Austria and Germany. Fraternization could be defined as any contact between the locals and the military unless for an official reason. Reduced to its illogical absurdity just to say 'Good morning' might be considered as fraternization. It was ludicrous and the Order being unenforceable, was quickly lifted. Marriage, however, was still forbidden and this the authorities were determined to maintain. In time the demand by soldiers to be allowed to enjoy the comfort of the sacraments of their religion could not be denied and marriage applications were entertained. The Establishment did not give way without a struggle and placed a great many obstacles in the way of those who intended to marry 'foreign'. In Austria the General Officer Commanding, wrote in the soldiers' newspaper *Union Jack*, that 'Austrian girls would make silly wives'. The General did not reply to a letter that I sent to him asking how many Austrian wives he had had that he could make so sweeping a judgement. Unable to stem the flood of marriage applications the Army tried to deter the prospective brides by summoning them to interrogations by NCOs of the Field Security Sections where the girls were humiliated by being asked such questions as 'How many other soldiers did you sleep with before getting this one to propose?'

By 'losing' marriage applications, by posting men away from their units and by any number of other means the Army tried to control the flood. One soldier was posted from Austria to southern Italy. He stole a motor cycle and returned to his intended bride. The sentence at his court-martial for desertion and theft was seven years. He was one of many. Another soldier who fell in love with a girl from a brothel in Algiers was sent to a psychiatrist in a hospital in northern Palestine. The military authorities were nothing if not determined to stop the troops from enjoying the new-found peace. They had a difficult task for they were flying in the face of nature.

'I'll soldier no more!'

The imposition of Army discipline produced in many conscripted soldiers a revulsion which could only find its release in their deserting the service, determined never to return. Other discontented soldiers gave thought how they might capitalize upon the needs of demand and supply by exploiting the shortages which are an inseparable part of a war-time economy. By dealing on the black market they would enrich themselves as a reward for the sacrifices they had made. There were again others who on active service, out of fear, deliberately mutilated themselves or deserted from their units for short periods. In Army parlance there were euphemisms to cover the true nature of these deliberate crimes against KRs; the Army's code of laws. In the Mediterranean theatre of operations the term 'Trotters' Union' was applied to those who deserted and who intended never to return to military service. 'Duckers and weavers' were also deserters, but these intended to be away for only a short period after which they would give themselves up, be court-martialled and spend a period in a detention barracks as an alternative to front-line service. The term 'weaver' also covered those who were guilty of a self-inflicted wound. The euphemism 'colour scheme' was widely used to cover black market activities.

In a very amusing paper, the distinguished naval historian, Martin Brice, expressed the view that only in the service was a soldier considered an important individual:

'If a civilian tires of his job, has a row and walks out, what happens? In some enlightened firms a personnel officer may be sent to interview him. I suppose he could be sued for breach of contract, but nothing else is done to him. Nobody even cares if he deserts his family, and in any case, they may not miss him. But if a serviceman goes absent, deserts or mutinies he will be hunted by police and soldiers for the rest of his life, wherever he goes. If he is caught he will be forcibly dragged back, tried and punished. It will be made perfectly clear to him that because of his one personal transgression the whole fabric of military discipline will crumble and the entire war will be lost.'

DESERTERS

Those who deserted in the United Kingdom did not find it particularly hard to submerge themselves into the civilian world. If they were determined to desert the service forever, they seldom went back to their parents' home. Most parents would have refused to help them or might even have informed the authorities. In addition the civil and military police would be watching out for the deserter. He would not find it hard to buy a forged or stolen identity card and to start life again under a new name in a civilian occupation; there were a great many young male civilians to be seen in the United Kingdom.

Once overseas, to be a permanent deserter was more difficult but not impossible. The greatest difficulty lay with mastering the local language and customs. To procure false papers presented no problem for the bribery of officials was accepted as the norm. Short-term deserters on overseas service followed one of two roads. Most allowed their appearance to deteriorate by not shaving or cleaning their boots. Vigilant Redcaps would soon arrest them. A court-martial was the almost automatic next step followed by detention in a military prison. There was no fear of being condemned to death. Execution by firing-squad as a punishment for desertion had been abolished during the 1930s. The rigours of the 'glasshouse' might be preferred to the dangers of combat. The following accounts are by men who preferred not to be named, for obvious reasons.

'In the glasshouse we got three meals a day, a roof over our heads and safety. Up the line we slept in slits open to the pouring rain which fell most of the time in sunny Italy. Food didn't always get to the forward positions so we often went hungry and then, on top of everything else, there was the danger. Time in the nick was hard, but I had had a hard life in civvy street, so whatever the screws could fling at me was water off a duck's back. Some of the men doing time were well off in the moosh. They had got themselves some right khushti numbers: in the cookhouse as orderlies, in the Sergeant's Mess as waiters – a couple were said to have been bumboys to the screws. What did such nick wallahs want with remission of sentence? This was offered to those who had deserted from front-line units, in order to get them back up the line. After about six weeks the prisoner would be interviewed and told his case was under revision. On a second interview he would be offered remission of sentence if he returned to a front-line unit. At the end of the war in Europe this sort of offer was made in most nicks, in the UK and overseas, to bring the drafts for Burma up to strength. The attitude of most of the blokes doing time was that if we would not fight Jerry in Europe we were certainly not going to fight in a jungle against the Japs.'

As opposed to the deserter who attracted attention to himself by his untidy state, there were those who kept out of trouble in the major cities by having shiny boots, short hair and polished brasses, gambling that no Redcap would check a pukka-looking soldier. To maintain that immaculate military appearance was not easy but it could be done. The easiest way was to find a large transit camp and pretend to be a soldier being posted back to his unit. By this pretence there was food, a bed, a NAAFI whack and washing facilities. There was another sort of transit camp through which, so it was said, all the *serious* Trotters' Union members passed, that is those who were determined to desert the service for good while on active service overseas. R. Fairclough, RAOC:

'I was stationed in a Base Ordnance Depot outside Naples. I think the name of the place was Torre del Greco or Torre Annunziata. Our working day used to finish in good time to get our evening meal, be washed and dressed and in unit transport to the big NAAFI by the side of the Opera House in Naples. Our unit transport would drop us there and pick us up at 23.00 hrs. We would be back in our billet within half an hour, well before midnight. One evening Naples was swarming with Redcaps. I have never seen so many. They checked on every serviceman in the town, not once but all the time. Every military policeman who passed us stopped us and checked us. This kept on occurring for days until finally our unit issued us with a special pass. Apparently, all the permanent base units in Naples issued them. Later I found out what the fuss had been about. It seemed that a couple of sergeants or senior NCOs had joined Trotters' Union and had come into the city. Somehow they had commandeered a billet and got from somewhere proper documentation to make it seem they were officially established as a transit camp for "special units" and there were a great many such units operating in CMF – Popski's Private Army, the LRDG, the SAS, the SS [Special Service] and a great many others. Those NCO deserters knew or learned the ropes very quickly. It takes one to know one and they would chat to soldiers who they suspected to be deserters. It would take some time before the swaddy would admit this; he was afraid that these men might be from the SIB. When he was convinced he would go back to their so-called transit camp. As long as there was a pukka RP guard on the gate it all looked legal from the outside. Inside the Union members would organize thefts from individual soldiers – this used to be called "rolling a guy" – it is called mugging today. Some times a couple of "union members" would pretend to be military police and would flag a truck down which they knew to be carrying NAAFI goods. The union members lived the life of Reilly; high-jacking lorries, mugging. They were up to all sorts of tricks. They were on velvet. One of them, so the story goes, ran a string of girls in Rome. They worked the Colosseum and he used to do a twice weekly journey to collect the money and to dish out rewards and punishments. From what I heard that is how the Trotters' Union transit camp came unstuck. One of the girls became jealous and shopped the ponce. When he was interrogated he spilled the beans but when the SIB got to the Transit Camp only the guard on the gate was there. All the other "union members" were "out working". Very few of them were caught. The local Eytie civvies warned them. But for weeks there was intense pressure in and around Naples. Somehow the city was never the same again. You know how it is if you are pulled up by the police in this country. You sit in your car and wonder what you have done wrong. Going along the Via Roma after that police activity was like that; all the time you were rehearsing what you were going to say when they pulled you up.'

SELF-INFLICTED WOUNDS

To many the thoughts of deserters living in a sort of seedy luxury might be considered humorous. They might be seen as lovable chappies. They were not. Desertion meant abandoning one's comrades in the middle of a fight. Another way of letting down one's comrades was to become a casualty before the battle began. The enemy was seldom so obliging as to give a nice clean wound in a soft, fleshy part of one's anatomy. This had to be organized and the product of this organization was the self-inflicted wound. Such obvious crudities as shooting off the index or trigger finger or a bullet in the foot produced permanent mutilation. A nice clean wound, not too painful and with the minimum of mutilation, was the ideal.

'The only cases of self-inflicted wounds I saw were both in Africa. In one a sergeant loaded a Bren and put the catch to fire single rounds. Presently along came the Bren gunner, saw that the gun was cocked and pulled the trigger – thinking it to be empty and not knowing that the sergeant had put one up the spout. Down went the NCO with a bullet through his calf. I never saw him again. The next SIW was on Tripoli docks where we were waiting to embark for Salerno. One of our draft wrapped a couple of towels round his upper arm and his mate broke it with a blow from his rifle.'

The Black Market

Another group of military misfits were those who exploited the shortages brought about by war for their own gain. It may be hard for young readers to understand, but there was a time in Europe when money had little value and the worth of any commodity was expressed in goods – usually in cigarettes, chocolate or soap. Frederick James was in a transit camp at Benevento during Christmas 1944:

'We were under canvas and it was bitterly cold. A gypsy woman came into our tent and told us it was 10 cigarettes, two bars of chocolate or a couple of bars of soap. For a blanket you could have something really special. I didn't fancy her but a lot of the blokes in the tent did. A tent held 22 men. Men from other tents also came in and used her. When the supply of customers ran out, and she had been at it for a couple of hours almost non-stop, she whistled. In came a couple of kids and they piled together God knows how many bars of soap and chocolate. She begged a couple of empty cigarette tins and packed in the fags she had earned.'

That was the bottom end of the scale. At the top end a copious supply of NAAFI goods could purchase the things that would please a hungry Countess or dress an aspiring actress in silks bought up by unit truck from a big city. The black market or 'colour scheme' embraced every social class in the civilian world and every rank in the Army. At the highest level it was rationalized as being a *quid pro quo;* a gesture of thanks for a special favour. At the lowest level it was; 'Do you want, Johnny?' and a negotiated price in Craven A or Players cigarettes.

'I remember Gold Flake were considered too strong for continental tastes – too raw – and Senior Service or any American cigarettes were preferred. I suppose that somebody, somewhere, did smoke the cigarettes that were passed from hand to hand like money. The "colour scheme" died in Austria and Germany during 1948, I think it was, when those countries came off the rationing system. Good old Blighty kept rationing, and the black market that goes with it, until 1953, as evidenced by the Sidney Stanley scandal. We had lectures from unit officers about not dealing on the black market, but we found it hard to take them seriously when they were on the "colour scheme" themselves. About the middle of 1946, there was a move made to replace military officers with civilian officers of the Control Commission. I do not know who recruited that lot or how they came to be selected, but most of them were little short of being racketeers. They seemed to be above military and German civil law. They fiddled on a massive scale – not just fifty free issue cigarettes, but tons of coal taken across frontiers with forged papers, chiefly into Denmark where there was no shortage of food. Out would go the coal – back would come sides of pork, bacon, butter, eggs – all the things you could not get in Hamburg. Some "loot", as they termed it, was converted. Foreign stamps were ideal, being small and valuable; also favoured were small antiques. A lot of antique firearms passed to dealers in the UK. I was told of one British employee of the CCG who bought a castle with his "loot", but I doubt if any of them would have flown that high. A flat, certainly – a villa, perhaps, with the property deeds made out in the name of the harem piece who comforted our hard-working hero. The Yanks, so I heard, were worse than us, in the black market, but then their PXs handed out black-market goodies on a very generous scale. The Americans could buy anything.'

In some perverted way it was not considered really wrong to be a military criminal. And yet desertion from the line meant that those soldiers who stayed and fought had been abandoned. The desertion of every man from a fighting unit meant that his comrades carried an extra burden; each man who mutilated himself by a self-inflicted wound meant that there were fewer proper soldiers to fight the enemy. To be an operator in the black market was not clever and entrepreneurial; it meant the exploitation of the poor – the starving civilians – by the rich, the servicemen with cigarettes and soap. I suppose very few of those who dealt in the 'colour scheme' saw themselves in that light any more than those who deserted felt themselves to have betrayed their mates. It is very easy to be blind to one's own faults.

'CONCHIES'

The final group of dodgers were not military personnel. They had, in fact, never served; had never worn uniform. They were those who for conscientious reasons would not fight for their country. So far as the bulk of the Army was concerned those dodgers were despised because it was thought they concealed cowardice under the term conscience. Roger Cooper, formerly a sergeant in the RAC, was particularly bitter about them:

'Their consciences would not allow them to take part in the war effort. They wouldn't work in the ARP or in the factories producing weapons, for that would be supporting the war. But their consciences didn't stop them eating food which seamen brought in; seamen whose ships had run the gauntlet of U-boats, the Luftwaffe and mines. It didn't stop them, either, from driving cars, using petrol brought in by seamen who risked death or disfigurement on every trip. The worst ones were the dodging bastards who shot off to America as soon as the Blitz started and were looked up to in the States as representatives of the gallant British people. And those cowards bathed in the glory they were too yellow to fight for. There was one bishop who thought that it was wrong for us to bomb the Jerries, in the way that they had bombed the UK, Warsaw and France and all the other

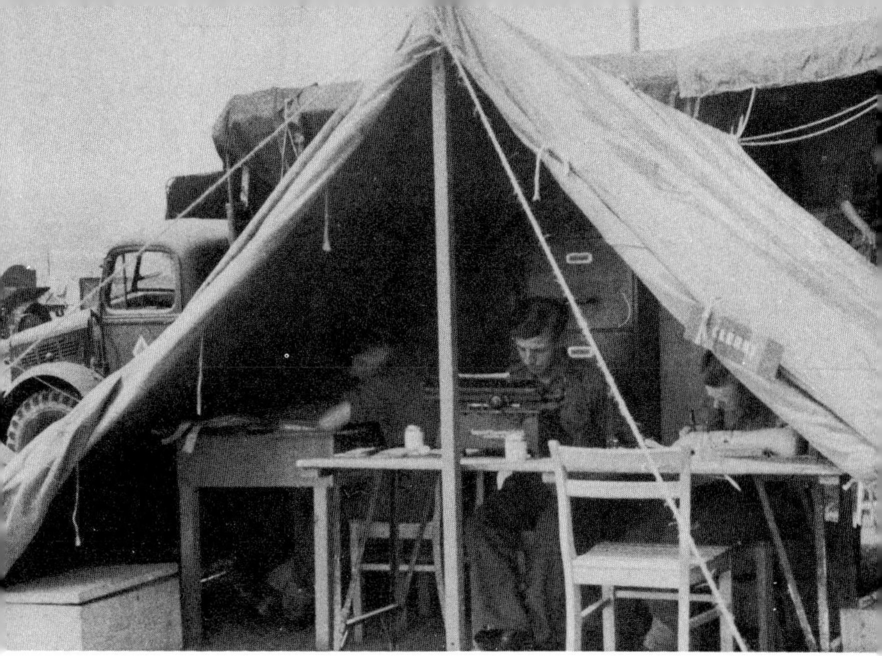

***Above:** An orderly room in the field somewhere in Germany at the end of the war. (P. T. Beaton)*

***Below:** A. G. Bell relaxing, as he says on the back of his picture, 'in Tripoli at last!'. (A. G. Bell)*

Left: *Danny Exley who fought in Italy and Greece with an infantry battalion of 4th British Division. His account of the battle for Cassino is included in this book. (Mrs Frances Exley)*

Right: *A group of Seaforth Highlanders pictured on the seafront at Port Said, Egypt, while on convalescent leave in May 1943. Roy Cooke is kneeling at the right; Andy Sutherland is kneeling at the left. The names of the other three Seaforths are now forgotten. (R. Cooke)*

Left: *C. W. Carpenter of 2nd Battalion, The Royal Norfolk Regiment. (C. W. Carpenter)*

Right: *Malcolm Armstrong (third left, front row) posing with his comrades in Schilberg Prisoner of War camp in Poland. (M. Armstrong)*

Left: *F. Farmborough of No. 4 Commando in 1943. Known as 'Shrapnel' to his comrades because of the number of times he was wounded on manoeuvres, he was wounded on D-Day while serving with the 1st Special Service Brigade. (F. Farmborough)*

Left: *Harold Field in Paris during December 1944. He enlisted in the RAOC and became one of the first men to be transferred to the newly formed REME. (H. Field)*

***Right:** Men from the 2nd Battalion, The Coldstream Guards, on 'street patrol' in Algiers, November 1942, prior to their unit moving up to Medjez-el-Bab. Pictured with 'Abdul' are, from left to right: Fitness, Craggs, and Smith. (Bill Fitness)*

***Right:** Joe Harris (standing, second from right) in a group pose many modern tourists will recognize. (J. Harris)*

Above: *Men from 141 RAC (The Buffs) during a pause in Operation 'Suffolk', 1943. Back row, left to right: Bennett, Bateman, Martin, Bovingdon. Middle row: Cheesman, Underwood, Wood, Moore, and Pearson. Front row: Staples, McColgan and Adams. (D. Hischier)*

Left: *Joyce, a Regular soldier with 29 years of service in the Royal Engineers, seen here in the Middle East. (Mr. and Mrs. R. A. Joyce)*

Above: *Baghdad, 1942. From left to right: Brockbank, Leacroft, Morgan, Joyce, Watson and Outram. (Mr. and Mrs. R. A. Joyce)*

Right: *The author, James Lucas, In Austria shortly after the war.*

Left: *This photograph was taken in December 1945 after Walter Mole had arrived in Australia for further treatment for some injuries sustained in the Pacific fighting. Taken at Bondi Beach, the back of the snap reads: 'Don't I look happy, so would anybody be, heatwave on and NO BEER – sold out!!'* (W. Mole)

Below: *A happy group aboard* Empress of Canada *bound for Singapore in October 1941. Walter Mole is on the far right in the second row from the front. His two comrades on the left of the front row were killed before Singapore fell.*

Right: *'Tishy' Parker in France, September 1939. A Regular soldier, 'Tishy' was taken prisoner near Calais in 1940. (T. Parker)*

Below: *A group of P.O.W.s in a camp in Poland, May 1941. 'Tishy' is shirtless in the front row. (T. Parker)*

Left: *Parker and others in 1940 at Roggenfeldt working camp in Poland, standing shoulder-to-shoulder with their German guards.*

Left: *A view of 'Tishy's' first working camp, 'Usch' in Poland, which, he writes, is 'not to be confused with Butlins'. (T. Parker)*

Right: *John Newmark in his tropical gear, Karachi, India. (J. Newmark)*

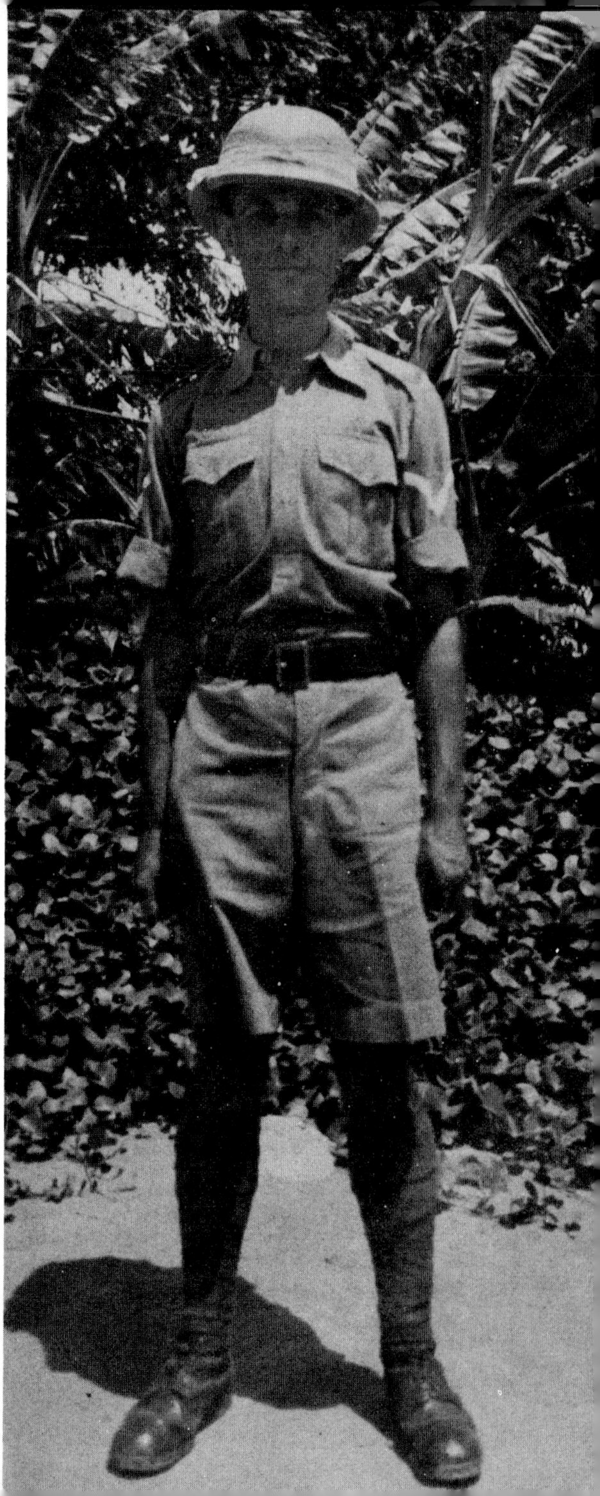

Above: *A Standing Patrol in Palestine shortly before the war. Note the cap badges have been removed.*

Left: *Alf Sampson, the soldier-cartoonist. He depicted his record of four years overseas service in the Middle and Far East in his own cartoons. (A. Sampson)*

Top right: *An example of Sampson's cartooning skill reveals some of the humour which existed amongst the ranks despite experiences that might encourage just the opposite. (A. Sampson)*

Right: *'B' Company of The 2nd Queen's Own Royal West Kent Regiment take a well earned tea break during their brigade training. (Bert Stubbings)*

***Above:** E. W. Stonard, at the front, smiling, with the BEF advance party landing at Cherbourg in January 1940. (E. W. Stonard)*

***Left:** This picture was taken in 1941 on a 'showing the flag' operation in Palestine just before departure to the Western Desert. The NCO is Bombardier E. W. Stonard; the officer is Lieutenant Watson, who was later killed in action at Gazala in 1942. (E. W. Stonard)*

***Right:** Major, later Colonel, G. B. Thatcher, D.S.O, of the Royal Artillery. (G. B. Thatcher)*

***Above:** A pen and ink sketch depicting life for a 3.7in anti-aircraft gun crew during the war in the desert. This drawing by Fergal Hearns was reproduced in Richard Doherty's excellent book* Wall of Steel. *Grateful acknowledgement is made for permission to use it here. (R. Doherty)*

***Left:** Bill Turner of The East Surrey Regiment at Colchester in Essex just prior to the outbreak of war. (W. Turner)* cities. It was alright for the Luftwaffe to destroy British cities and to kill British women and children, but it was wrong for us to do the same to them. It was people of that sort who stopped "Bomber" Harris becoming a Lord, like Monty and other commanders. There was an outcry after the abbey at Cassino was bombed. Those who shouted loudest hadn't been in a ruined house in Cassino with that abbey looking right down your throat.'

Combatants

Our Allies

No nation sets out to fight a war unsupported, but seeks to ensure that she has countries which will give her aid. She may require bases or war materials or, perhaps, just the reassurance of offers of assistance. Whatever the reason, a country at war needs allies. In 1939 Great Britain was able to maintain a large navy but only a small land force. Thus, the British Army was placed under foreign leaders. In 1939, the BEF, was commanded by a French General. When France was lost in 1940, the Army was free of foreign influence until December 1941. Within a year our new allies, the Americans, being superior in numbers and more lavishly equipped, demanded and were granted military control, firstly, in the western and then in almost every other theatre of operations. They first exercised this authority when French North Africa was invaded by an Anglo-American force in November 1942. Then, despite his lack of battle experience, Eisenhower was placed above Montgomery and Alexander who had successfully beaten the Axis forces at El Alamein. That battle was the swansong of the British Army fighting in an independent role. Henceforth it would be a junior partner under the overlordship of Americans. By a terrible paradox many British soldiers thought more highly of our enemies than of the Americans, whose aid in the war had sustained us and upon whose support we had depended in the darkest days of the war.

The French

At the end of June 1940, France, Britain's last remaining ally in the west, surrendered. As a result of her capitulation Britain stood alone but, paradoxically, this situation produced among the British people, not the fear or despair that might have been expected, but rather a feeling of relief based upon the fact that we had got rid of the foreigners who held us back. Allies, it was felt, were an encumberance, an inhibition to OUR way of doing things. Britain had sent out a fine little Army in 1939, and so far as the man in the street was concerned, because of the incompetence of French generalship our BEF had been shattered. Some of our best infantry divisions had been captured, including the 51st Highland, which had been included in the French surrender at St-Valéry to a German General named Erwin Rommel.

The Allied contingents now in exile in the United Kingdom were welcomed, initially, out of a British sense of compassion for what had happened to their countries. But as the post-Dunkirk euphoria evaporated, resentment of these foreigners grew and with it the prospect of conflict between the British and Allied soldiers. The government, aware of the danger that Allied Servicemen billeted near British Army units might be the unsuspecting agents in a confrontation, sought to avoid such unpleasantness by separating foreign and native detachments The Poles, a major contingent, were eventually sent to Scotland.

Bombardier Millett: 'Almost as soon as the Poles settled in there were stories of their sexual appetites. There were stories that in the grip of sexual passion they had been known to bite off the nipples of their girlfriends. Then, too, it was rumoured that those coming from the primitive areas of eastern Poland, were phenomenally equipped, even by Polish standards. It was rumoured that the Poles had been exiled to Scotland because they had created havoc in the mill towns of Lancashire which led to a very high birth rate among unmarried girls. Sexual jealousy had a bad effect upon our morale and we had lectures from our officers that we should not desert if we were worried about our wives. Compassionate leave would be granted to deserving cases. It seldom was. Such talks did little to reassure the Scottish men in the unit. Those who were married men or were going steady, as I was at the time, were petrified when they heard that foreign units had moved into their home town. We were well aware of the sexual threat; that we would be compared against the foreigners and might be found lacking.'

The armistice of 1940 split the French nation into those who, under the leadership of Charles de Gaulle were prepared to fight on, and those who accepted the terms of the surrender and served the government set up in Vichy. This deep divide was very evident when the Anglo-Americans landed in French North Africa in November 1942. The walls were plastered with posters showing the face of Marshal Pétain.

'It was not until March that I first saw [in Algiers] pro-Allied posters. These did not show de Gaulle but General Giraud who was being groomed by the Americans as a rival in the contest for leadership of Free France against de Gaulle whom the Americans thought to be a British puppet. Those posters that did not show Pétain did not, so far as I recall, show the faces of Roosevelt or Churchill but only quotations from their speeches. Not to put too fine a point on it the French did not like us. A great many of the civvies in Algeria told us we should have surrendered in 1940. Then the war would have been all over and finished.'

Conversely, there were French officers who worked for an Allied victory. One of those who made an outstanding demonstration of loyalty was General Le Clerc who marched his men from equatorial Africa to fight alongside British Eighth Army in the desert. His defence of Bir Hakim in May 1942 was one of the finest examples of courage and devotion to duty by any Allied army during the Second World War. The fighting ability of the French Army in North Africa could not be truly demonstrated because of their poor weapons and equipment, but during the Tunisian campaign the Americans began to re-equip the French and continued the process until the whole Army was completely refitted and supplied with US equipment. Among the many picturesque units of the French

Army in Italy were the mountain warriors known as the Goumiers. These men made a deep impression upon the British soldiers. Ronald Johnston, a driver in an RASC unit which was supplying Eighth Army recalled:

'In many mountain villages it was almost like being back in North Africa. Those places were crammed solid with native soldiers, their families and livestock. They were Goums, who were from North Africa. They were a frightening lot. I was used to the well-disciplined soldiers of the Indian Army. The Goums seemed to have no discipline. They were mostly tall and wiry. Most had fringe beards and stained teeth. It must have been something they ate, something similar to the betel-nut which is widely chewed in the East. They wore a long caftan of rough wool. Basic colour brown with very thin stripes of white or black. Often, but not always, a sort of turban, not like the Sikh one, but more a wide bandage around the head. They wore uniform under this caftan garment. The Jerries hated them. The Goums were quite vicious by our standards although probably not by their own local North African standards. They had no idea of the value of loot. One of my mates asked for a souvenir once. The Goums showed him combs and toothbrushes which they had taken from the enemy. They did not take anything like binoculars or pistols. We could not understand why they wanted combs and toothbrushes – such things had no value to us.'

When the French re-entered the war in 1943, Britain's leadership role had already been usurped by the Americans. It was they who had equipped the resurgent French Army and it was under US command that the French formations fought. In Normandy when Patton's Third Army broke out of the beachhead perimeter, French formations were on its order of battle and it was to Le Clerc and French 2nd Armoured Division that the honour fell of liberating Paris. Since the French fought chiefly with the Americans, the British Army had little experience of their Gallic allies during the campaign in north-west Europe. Relations were chiefly with the French civilians whose attitudes ranged from hostility, through resigned acceptance that the Tommies were back again, to the never to be forgotten joy of liberation. As examples of that first attitude, British troops in Normandy were often asked point-blank why they had brought the war to Normandy? The peasants told them that relations between themselves and the Germans had been good. The Boches had been very correct. They had paid, in cash, for everything they needed and a *modus vivendi* had operated. The British Army had brought artillery and air bombardments which had killed large numbers of cattle, smashed houses, flattened whole cities and brought about destruction on an unbelievable scale. The German occupation had meant a continuation of the normal way of life. Liberation had brought nothing but death and ruin.

The attitude of the French civilians in the cities towards girls who had fraternized with the Germans, disgusted many British soldiers.

'In one little town outside Lille, the locals paraded those poor girls, there were about twelve of them, and publicly humiliated them. A couple of girls were stripped to the waist; another had her skirt held up and her knickers removed so that the townspeople could see what it was the German Army had paid for. All of them had their hair shaved off and swastikas painted on their bald heads. Some of the lads wanted to stop it but our officer wouldn't let us. We didn't understand, he said. All we understood was that these women were being bullied by people who must all have collaborated with the Germans to some extent at some time or another.'

There were other French people who saw the men of British Army in a different light. Some battalions that had fought in the 1940 campaign returned to the same villages and towns during 1944, and were welcomed as heroes; as sons of France. It was to many a most emotional experience to be greeted by civilians who had been abandoned to four years of German occupation, but whose faith had always been that the Tommies would come back again. One citizen of Ypres told me that he regretted that it had not been the British Army, but the Poles, that had driven the Germans from the town in 1944. He thought that as an emotional gesture it ought to have been one of the units that had fought through Ypres in 1940, to whom the honour should have gone to liberate it in 1944.

AMERICANS

A major part of the British Army was already on overseas service before the Americans arrived in the United Kingdom and did not come home again until the bulk of the GIs had themselves been repatriated. The result was that much of what the Tommy knew about his new ally's behaviour in the United Kingdom was hearsay which he had to believe because he lacked personal knowledge. How much of what he learned at second-hand was untrue, ill-founded or just malicious is anybody's conjecture, but what he heard or read made him uneasy. There were stories of the attitude of the Americans towards women in the United Kingdom. Among the German propaganda leaflets fired into the British lines during the fighting in Italy was one which showed on the obverse a British Girl and a GI in what is called, 'a compromising situation'. The Government, deeply aware of the effect on British military morale of the influx of US troops, sought to reassure public opinion at home and the soldiers overseas, that the GIs were warm, generous and friendly. When the soldiers of the two allied armies first met, the Tommy was quick to realize that the GI on active service was often 'a very ordinary bloke.' Not so the ordinary British soldier in the United Kingdom. Try as he would he could not get to like his US ally and the feeling was mutual. This led to hostility and there was at least one murder of a British soldier by a GI in the United Kingdom.

Both at home and overseas it was chiefly the ignorance of the average American soldier which was the chief cause of concern. The GIs knew nothing of Britain or her empire. They were influenced by the fact that their country had once been part of that empire. Theirs was a profound naïvety at every level. A GI once assured one of my correspondents that the Cunard liner *Queen Mary,* on which the Americans had sailed to Europe, was a US ship because 'you Limeys could not build anything as good as that'. Through Hollywood films the citizens of America were, in British eyes, thought to be sophisticated and their conversations filled with quick-fire repartee. From the films it appeared they all lived in luxury houses surrounded by masses of gadgets to make life easy. The British soldier soon found that those people who lived in the big cities were a very small minority. The great mass of Americans were poorly educated peasants whose staple reading matter was children's comics. These hicks knew nothing of the outside world and cared less. Everything they encountered was compared to its US equivalent and found wanting. They firmly believed that America had discovered penicillin, had invented television and radar, had produced the first tanks and had won the Great War. What went on in the United Kingdom between the American soldiers and British women is the stuff of myth and legend. 'Any British girl could be had for a pair of nylons,' was a taunt which would guarantee a fight between American and British soldiers. German propagandists, aware of the potency of sexual jealousy, sought to create hostility between the Americans and the British soldiers overseas, just as they had sought to turn the French *poilu* against the Tommies in France in the first year of the war. The sexual threat was a powerful weapon and one that was exploited by the Germans to the full.

The one area which the German propagandists seem not to have explored in their attempts to undermine the morale of the American soldier was that of race. Yet that was one sector of American life which disquieted the British. There was not at that time the racial awareness in Britain that there is today. The coloured British were few in number and had been either generally accepted or else had learned to ignore bigotted racist remarks. White girls in this country saw all US troops as Americans – their colour was not an issue. What those girls did not realize was that it was deeply offensive to many GIs to see white girls in public with Negro soldiers. The outcome of that tension were race riots in several parts of the United Kingdom.

British military commanders were critical of the way in which American generals planned and executed a campaign. The ordinary British soldiers were scornful of the fighting qualities of their transatlantic allies. The first operation in which the two allies fought side by side was Operation 'Torch', the invasion of French North Africa. Not long after the landings a rumour swept through the British army in Tunisia that the US troops had expected to be greeted as liberators and had carried on their sleeves the Stars and Stripes to distinguish them from the British who were thought to be unpopular with the French. The US invaders were not met with open arms, but by sporadic firing which caused many of them to turn tail and run for the beaches. According to the rumours British infantry units were ordered to dress in American jackets and to make a success of the landing. The men of 78th British Infantry Division to whom the task was given tore off the American insignia before undertaking the assault which captured the area.

'It was naïve of the Americans to expect that they would meet no opposition. They were, after all, invading a neutral country and one which was not occupied by the enemy. Surely, they must have anticipated some hostile response from the local inhabitants.'

The rumours which had circulated after the Algiers landings became a bitter truth at Kasserine Pass in the early months of 1943. US tank forces struck through the mountain pass and were repelled by the Panzers. High ground which US II Corps had occupied without struggle in its advance was given up in a panic retreat and US tankmen abandoned undamaged vehicles. The British Guards

Brigade was sent to capture the mountain peaks from which the American infantry had pulled back. The Guards are particularly bitter about that operation. They had had earlier experiences of American inability to hold ground during December 1942, on Longstop Hill. During Christmas week the Guards had fought their way up the rocky slopes of Longstop. In places their battles against the German defenders had been hand-to-hand. The hill was then entrusted to an American unit which lost it in a matter of hours. The Guards were put back in again and recaptured the feature. Again it was handed over and again the American defenders lost it. Bitter weather prevented the now depleted Guards regiments from undertaking a third capture of the hill and by the time that good weather returned the Germans had turned Longstop into a fortress. It remained in German hands until the final weeks of the campaign when the 78th Division, the men of the Algiers landing, stormed and captured it.

Inexperience, some men of the British Airborne named it cowardice, was given as the reason for the shambles that opened the campaign against Sicily. Americans were piloting the aircraft towing the gliders holding British paratroops. British 1st Airborne Division was to drop over objectives inland from the invasion beaches. While the armada was still flying over the sea, miles away from the landing zone, a German Flak ship opened fire. Unnerved by the explosions many US pilots cast off the gliders leaving them to come down either in the sea or to crash-land on the beaches.

At the Salerno landing, US formations began to retreat back to the landing craft, a movement that was only halted when British units flung back the attacks of a Panzer division. At Salerno, too, the Guards relived the same bitter experience as at Longstop and Kasserine – and so it went on, so far as the British soldiers were concerned, throughout the whole Italian campaign, with them having to take over or recapture positions which the Yanks would not, or could not, hold.

During the campaign in north-west Europe the differences between the Allies resulted in many lost opportunities. British tank experts had produced a number of variants to standard vehicles. These 'funnies', grouped into 79th Armoured Division, included tanks mounting a large-calibred bombard intended to smash the enemy blockhouses and permanent defences on the landing beaches. Squadrons of such 'funnies' were offered to the US units which were to land on Omaha Beach where the principal obstruction was a high sea wall. In the event the US troops who tried to scale it were caught in the fire of German machine-guns and shot down in hundreds. The other US soldiers huddled on the narrow beach were slaughtered by German mortar and artillery fire. It was clear that not until the sea wall was breached could troops escape from the trap which was Omaha. Only the self-sacrifice of some US engineers in blowing a gap allowed other American units to advance off the beach and into open country. The arrogance of their military leaders in rejecting British specialist weapons was responsible for the carpet of American dead on the D-Day beaches and for the hundreds of bodies bobbing in the Channel tide.

And so the dismal story continued. Of the campaign in Italy halted by the deflection of troops and supplies away from a possible victory and into an unnecessary assault landing in southern France. Of the failure of the Allied High

Command to resolve a battle strategy; of the collapse of the Americans in the Ardennes and of the brutalities which accompanied their rapid advance through Germany in the spring of 1945. Of Patton gloating over the towns and villages which his army had destroyed during its drive. Of one US Armoured Division which took no German prisoners for a whole week, but shot, summarily, all those who surrendered. Of post-war court-martials which condemned to imprisonment German children found guilty of 'Wehrwolf' activities.

In Burma the men of the British Fourteenth Army were astonished to learn that an American unit in the jungle had mutinied and demanded to be sent home because it had completed the mission for which it had been recruited. It was certainly a most unusual army. The following compilation of accounts shows them in the way that they were seen by so many British soldiers.

'Their method of service was unusual. A division would enter the line and stay there for months on end. One division, either the 34th or 36th Infantry, spent over one hundred days and nights in action without relief. This must have had a serious effect upon morale. Our method of frequent rotation was much better.'

'As individuals they certainly had greater freedom to move about than we had. They were a highly mobile army; all of them could drive and they had access to transport to a degree which would have been impossible for an ordinary soldier in the British Army. They were also very well equipped and it seemed that they could lose equipment without a court-martial. Once, we relieved a US unit just south of the River Garigliano. Whoever had occupied the slit-trench I got into had left behind a carbine and ammunition, hand-grenades, whole cartons of cigarettes and ration packs. The CO of the outgoing US unit told our CO that it was a real hot spot with frequent and heavy barrages. There was a bit of stonking by Jerry; always punctual and always on the same targets. Unless the enemy had changed his firing pattern because we had come in, this place was an easy sector and not the hell-hole which the Yank made it out to be.'

'One of our armoured car patrols [in Normandy] heard the sound of small-arms fire coming through the bocage. Then we saw, preceded by another fusillade, the strangest of cavalcades. The "enemy" were Americans . . . about a Company strong. In the middle of their column and sitting like Buddha on a mound of kit in the back of a jeep was an officer chewing a large cigar and studying by its glowing ash a crumpled map folded to the size of a small pocket-book . . . casually glancing from his map to the shadowy outline of a tree, as if identifying a landmark he sprayed its topmost branches with a tommy-gun. "Snipers," he grunted. When he ran out of ammunition, someone else took up the running. The amount of ammunition carried by those Americans must have been prodigious, for long after they had scraped by our armoured cars we could still hear them firing at the tree tops.

'They were quite bloody-minded. They opened a super-fast highway for their supply trucks to bring petrol forward. This was called something like the Red Ball Highway. The truck drivers all seemed to be Negroes who drove with one foot out of the cab window. They all smoked fat cigars. God help anyone who got in their way when one of the convoys was moving up. They were just driven off the road.'

'Although we did not mix much with the black GIs we were surprised to learn how much the white Americans hated them. I was on temporary detached duty in Austria and was billeted for a couple of days in Salzburg. One night I saw a Negro soldier walking along arm in arm with a local girl. Suddenly, a jeep-load of US military police roared around the corner and drove up to the soldier. The "Snowdrops" jumped out and started bashing him with their long truncheons. For all I know he may have been a hard case; a wanted criminal. I don't know. As it was all I saw was that one Negro was being bashed into a pulp by six white MPs.'

'In Munich there was an exhibition of US soldiers' paintings and one painting in particular came in for lots of criticism and demands that it be withdrawn. It was labelled, I think, "Munich. Morning. 1945" and showed a blonde German girl lying exhausted on a bed while in the foreground a US Negro soldier was getting dressed.'

'The US Army put a Negro division into the line in northern Italy. As I understood it their senior officers down to battalion level were all white and no attempt was made to form a unit loyalty. The white officers were guilty, according to my informant [a black GI], of blatant racism and of making the most offensive remarks. Most of the white officers had not wanted to serve in the "nigger unit", and had had to be ordered to take up their appointments. They were very upset and felt that their careers had been blighted. So they took it out on the rank and file. This unit with a very low morale was attacked on New Year's Day by a German battle patrol. The Germans penetrated as far as divisional headquarters before they were challenged. It seemed that the soldiers of the Negro units through which the battle patrol had passed had all been drunk on duty.'

'The US attitude towards their coloured troops was shocking and yet their 442nd Regiment, made up of Japanese-Americans' was the best unit they had in Europe. You know the way things spread in the Army? Well, we heard that at least ten of the regiment had been recommended for their equivalent of the Victoria Cross, but that for political reasons it was felt that these should not be awarded. Although I never saw any soldier of the 442nd in action, from reports I heard it must have been a marvellous unit.'

'To me it came as no surprise to learn that so many black GIs deserted. The French, of course, have had black colonies for hundreds of years and treated the coloured GIs just as they would have treated a black Frenchman. This attitude upset a great many white soldiers in France who went about in gangs beating up Negro troops, whether they were with white girls or whether they were alone. It seemed to us that in some way the white soldiers felt that they had to maintain the "white boss – black slave" attitude that seemed still to exist in the States. There were stories that Ku Klux Klan chapters were set up in France.'

A more positive aspect of US/British relations at ordinary soldier level was the extraordinary generosity of the Americans:

'The contrast in attitudes between the American and British peoples towards their servicemen was never shown more clearly to me than in Algiers. The American PX, their equivalent of NAAFI, occupied a very large building about four or five storeys high. On the ground floor they served coffee and doughnuts –

free. At the reception desk they issued free tickets to their shows and these were first class. We had to queue up for our ENSA performances outside the theatre and after the war, certainly in Germany, you had to buy tickets for a performance. Our NAAFI was on the first floor of a house in a side street of Algiers. The only things sold were tea and bread and jam. There were no china cups so that the tea was served in the metal tins that had once contained fifty cigarettes. Handles had been soldered on the tins – these were our tea cups – fag tins.'

'The thing that surprised me most was the casual relationship between the doctors and patients in the hospital. When the MO made his rounds there was none of the bull found in RAMC hospitals. I heard one MO ask a man how he was feeling and when he received the reply that the soldier still didn't think himself fit, the MO told him he'd better stay in hospital for another couple of days. Every day a trolley came round with cigarettes and sweets. The first time it came round I said that I had lost my wallet because I did not want to be embarrassed if I didn't have enough money. I was told that everything was free. So were the coffee and doughnuts that came round twice a day. People came round with newspapers, magazines, reading material – all of it free issue. If you stopped a US unit to ask the way or to fill up with petrol or something, you were always asked in for a meal or given quarters for the night. Whatever time you arrived the cooks would always make some sort of meal – not like the unit cooks in the British Army.'

To many British soldiers the casual attitudes of the Americans was a sign of poor discipline which must lead inevitably to incompetence in battle. Yet this US attitude exactly paralleled the officer/man relationship evident in the British Dominion forces. It was possible in the armies of the younger nations for an officer's commission to be gained by men and women from a wider social circle than in the British Army. The strict, restrictive lines of class and/or education did not apply in the forces of the young nations and this resulted in a more casual relationship. It did not necessarily guarantee a reduction in or a loss of discipline – it was just a different approach to achieving this.

The British soldier envied much of what he saw available to the GI; his uniforms, rations, mobility, pay and opportunities, but considered the American soldier to be pig-ignorant and loudmouthed. Ready to exploit any opportunity to make money he most certainly was, but individually generous in a way that we could not match. And that incredible generosity was demonstrated at national level with the post-war Marshall Plan which did so much to restore war-ravaged Europe. They were a complex lot our American allies.

THE RED ARMY

Very few men of the British Army met the soldiers of our principal European ally, Russia. Those who did were the men who had served with British Ninth Army in Iraq and Iran. They had met the Russians in those Middle Eastern countries when Britain and the USSR occupied them in order to prevent pro-German governments from gaining power. The only other British soldiers to meet the Russians before the end of hostilities were those who had been prisoners-of-war in Poland, East Germany or in Czechoslovakia, and who at the war's end were footmarched westwards by the Germans. Those columns of prisoners were liberated by the speedy advance of the Red Army. The greatest number of men of the British Army who met the Russians did so after the war's end as members of the army of occupation in Germany and Austria, while others, in north-west Europe and in Italy, had actually fought against units of former Russian soldiers who had volunteered to fight with the German Army.

Michael Henshaw, who had been taken prisoner during the fighting on the Anzio beachhead, had good reason to remember his liberation by the Red Army. He had been one of the prisoners marching on a trek from a camp in Saxony and southwards across Czechoslovakia. One night the column halted in an area on the borders of Hungary and Austria.

'One morning in late April we noticed that the guards had left us. We found their uniforms and weapons. They must have changed into civvy clothes and deserted. Our officer told us to stay put. We should not go wandering off. If we left the column and it moved off again we would be without its protection. We all had hard tack saved from the Red Cross parcels and were prepared to wait a day or two. After all, if the guards had deserted then Allied troops must be near. Mid-morning of the second day the Russians arrived. I think our location had been reported by one of their cavalry patrols and the officer of the group which liberated us gave orders for us to remain where we were. It was dangerous to move about, he told us. The war was still on. The Germans were still in the area. So we stayed put. I was sitting down reading late that afternoon. A Red Army soldier, very drunk, came up and offered me a drink. I cannot drink alcohol because during my time as a POW I began to suffer from asthma and found that alcohol affected me. So I refused his offer and kept on refusing. Suddenly he took his rifle off his shoulder and smashed me in the face with the butt end. That blow smashed my jaw, broke my nose and knocked out most of my front teeth. I received no medical treatment from the Russians and our own RAMC men could only patch me up as best they could. I was unable to eat and could only manage things that did not have to be chewed. I lost weight as a result and I was already painfully thin from my time as a POW. I think it took two weeks before we were moved across Germany and into the British Zone and then flown home. Back in the UK there were operations to remove bone splinters and the bones which had begun to knit together had to be rebroken and reset. The doctors were not able to restore my face completely. The pain I felt from the time I was struck until the first treatment in the UK, was terrible although aspirin, the only medicine we had as prisoners, did keep the worst pains down to a dull ache. Bad weather sets off that ache, even now.'

What came across from the Red Army, and this impression is one shared by all who mentioned our Russian allies, was the coldness they displayed. They were frightening in their remoteness. If it was necessary for a Western soldier to enter the Soviet Zone there was always at the back of the mind the feeling that from the barrier pole, in Germany or Austria, with its mandatory red star and red flag and all the way to Vladivostock, it was all *their* territory. There was the worrying knowledge that in that vast area, their silent, grey world, it would be so easy to be lost forever. The feeling of coldness which was so apparent to the British soldiers was translated into feelings of absolute terror for the civilians of the lands through which the Soviet troops had passed or which they still occupied. Three years after the war's end at a performance in the Opera House in Graz in Austria the chatter of the audience before the orchestra tuned up, slowly died away. All eyes were turned towards a box in the dress circle. Three of the four occupants were British Army officers. The fourth was a middle-aged, bald-headed Russian officer whose cold eyes surveyed the audience. Under that impersonal stare the audience stopped talking. Those present were dominated by that one man. By the fear of what he represented, by the memory of what this part of eastern Austria had suffered in the final months of the war. The Red Army had been an instrument of frightening power and its representative was sitting in a box in the Opera House. The civilians were terrified – three years after the war's end.

One phenomenon which surprised the British soldiers was that there were fighting units on the German Army's order of battle composed almost entirely of former Red Army men. These Russians had been prisoners-of-war in Germany and had volunteered to fight in the Wehrmacht as an alternative to starving to death in prison-camps. These men had exchanged the iron discipline of the Red Army for that of the Germans, and had fought for their new masters with undeniable bravery, until their German officers and NCOs had been killed. Most of them then surrendered. They were very pragmatic in their approach. When they had first been taken prisoner they had given away details of their own army's defences and some had even led German patrols through gaps in Red Army minefields to attack their own units. When they fell into British hands in Normandy they were prepared to betray German positions to us and to lead our patrols against their former masters. Loyalty was a very flexible characteristic among the soldiers of our Russian ally.

'Nichevo' (it doesn't matter) was widely used to cover those sort of eventualities over which the ordinary Russian soldier had no control. In their zone of occupation if the Red Army sent out a civilian work detail and a couple of Germans escaped from it, then *Nichevo*. It was a simple matter to snatch a couple of bypassers from the pavement. The most important thing was that the number of people in the detail had to be correct. The Red Army had an outstanding ability to ignore the feelings of almost everybody. The soldiers had been told that Russia, single-handed, had won the war. Thus, according to Soviet propagandists the world and particularly the nations which had been occupied by the Germans owed the Russians a debt of gratitude. Whatever the Soviets needed, they could have. The world was there to serve them.

Corporal Samuels, formerly of an RASC Company of 46th Division:

'I was in the British Army in Austria and was *en route* to Vienna in a 15cwt. Also in the van was my driver, a former German soldier and a couple of Austrian people, civilian employees in my unit, who had business in Vienna. They preferred to come with us in our uncomfortable truck rather than go by train with all its dangers and delays. We had crossed the Semmering checkpoint and were approaching Wiener Neustadt. Just outside one village a Russian sentry stepped into the road, cocked his MP and pointed it at us. I told the driver to stop. The sentry walked up and asked; 'Wien?' [Vienna?] "Yes," I replied. He whistled loudly. Two officers came out of a house and without a word climbed into the back of our truck. The sentry waved us on. The Russian attitude was very much that we weren't so much allies who had helped to win the war, but that we were some sort of allied servants, there to do whatever the victors of the Red Army told us to do.'

There were factors which prevented the British soldiers from fully understanding their Red Army allies. The language difficulty was the first and most obvious one. Then, too, the British Army had not seen the Russians in action and could not properly judge them. Corporal Samuels' letter continued:

'There were newsreels showing the "glorious" Red Army in action, but all of us knew that newsreels showing battles and infantry attacks could be faked, so we did not believe camera evidence. Civilians who had experienced the Red Army as conquerors spoke of them as murderers. The soldiers would mutilate people. There were stories of deportation and of the violent rape of any girl over the age of about 11. We found it hard to believe such stories – very few of us at that time realized the degradation that rape means. And, also, we thought that those complaining civilians had been Nazis until the end of the war so they were prejudiced. None of us wanted to believe the stories of concentration camps. We couldn't believe that soldiers, like we were, could act like that or that the Russians could act as brutally as the civvies said they had. Well, we had been wrong about the Germans and the concentration camps. It was very likely that we were wrong about the Soviets and their atrocities.'

In Austria the mass of Eighth Army did not meet the Red Army until after the war's end, but before the two forces met rumours were current among the British divisions in the army of occupation of how in East Prussia the Soviets had taken one man of every rank from the mass of German soldiers who had surrendered. Those representatives were stood in front of the mass of POWs – and were then shot as a warning. Other rumours said that in Königsberg all the Volkssturm men had been slaughtered and in Saxony the atrocities were said to have been unusually brutal. Could such stories be believed of our gallant allies or were they the last efforts of Goebbels' propaganda machine to sow discord between the Soviets and ourselves? And then the British Army met them. Unsmiling, hard, cold men, soldiers of a vicious system that would not scruple to waste thousands of them in senseless attacks. Their discipline was unusual. Within a unit not only officers but also NCOs had to be saluted, but compliments were never – or seldom – paid to officers of other units. So much for the barrack-room lawyers who had said that saluting had been abolished in the Red Army.

There were inevitably confrontations and fights at troop level. One of these, in Vienna involving Red Army men and soldiers of the Argyll and Sutherland Highlanders, resulted in fatal stabbings. The British Army also carried out sweeps against Soviet deserters who, in both Austria and Germany, had turned to crime to support themselves. One of my correspondents, a former military policeman, was on the firing-squad that executed some of those convicted murderers. He has asked not to be named.

'In Hamburg, in those days, there were among the displaced persons going home a lot who decided to stay in Germany. They all lived from the large black market. Others turned to crime and violence. Groups of these would board passenger trains and during the journey would produce firearms and run through the carriages robbing the civilians. This practice is called "steaming" these days. Anyone who did not hand over their valuables was killed without mercy. Multiple rape was not uncommon. One gang was caught and tried for a number of particularly violent murders. Its leaders were sentenced to death by shooting. I was one of the firing-party. It was a very quick operation, done quickly to spare the condemned man's feelings. All they had to do was to walk out of a door in the prison courtyard, turn left and walk for four or five paces, turn and face us. There were other policemen on duty to act as escorts. There was none of the long-drawn-out agony you see in films. Once the men were in position with a circle of white paper over their heart, the squad was given the order, aimed and fired. We had already loaded our rifles, so there was none of the clicking of bolts that you read about. From the time they walked out of the door to the time they fell dead was less than two minutes. I don't believe there were all that many executions in the British Zone and we only shot the most criminal murderers. And remember this was in the first days of the occupation. In Austria, so I believe, the British forces hanged the criminals. I was told that Albert Pierrepoint [the British public hangman] was sent out to show the Austrians the quick British "drop" method. Apparently, the Austrian method of execution had been garrotting.'

Our Yugoslav allies were like the Red Army; a dour and humourless lot who thought that the world owed them honour and glory. Because their Army lacked the proper facilities, Yugoslav wounded were brought into British military hospitals in southern Italy. There they received treatment, food and clothing. According to my correspondents they were an ungracious lot who gave no thanks for anything they received. The fear of the Party informer, the fear of being reported for collaboration with the soldiers of the West, inhibited them from expressing their proper feelings. Ron Johnston, whose account of the Goums has already been given, met the wounded partisans in a hospital in southern Italy:

'There was no distinction between the sexes and that extended even to the ablutions. The first time I came across this was in the latrines dug in the hospital grounds. You know the sort of thing I mean – a wooden box with holes placed over a trench and screened by canvas attached to poles. I was sitting there one day reading some mail from home. Somebody sat down beside me. I turned round and found it was a girl. I tried explaining in Italian that this was a latrine for men but she either wouldn't or couldn't understand me. I was very embarrassed but she wasn't and over the following days I got used to the partisan girls sharing our lats and showers. They were a sad bunch and completely under the control of their commissar. If the *Union Jack* [the British forces newspaper] wanted photographs of partisan and British comradeship, the Jugs would pose and smile to order. Once the pictures had been taken they moved away unsmiling and unspeaking. The impression I got was they resented us.'

The Greeks had become our allies at about the same time as had the Yugoslavs and, like them, had endured years of German occupation. The return of the British Army was welcomed by the great majority of Greeks as liberation, but there were Communist groups determined to seize the country and convert it into a Russian satellite. The Americans saw British attempts to stop that take-over as evidence of British 'colonialism' and gave support to the Red guerrilla groups. It was one of the great tragedies of the war that British soldiers who had fought in three campaigns to liberate Europe were murdered by political fanatics of an allied nation in a bloody and bitter civil war. In a number of cases British soldiers who fell into the hands of the Reds were burned alive in a vain attempt to provoke reprisals by the Army.

To summarize the feelings of the British soldier for his allies, in those letters which mention our allies the Belgians are always described as our staunchest friends. This feeling may be a hangover from the First World War, but the Belgians and to only a lesser extent the Dutch, are referred to in glowing terms. The French are held to be a curious lot. The first French that the British met in 1944, when they returned to north-west Europe, were Normandy farmers who made no secret of the fact that they preferred the Germans to us. That feeling was not held by the people of northern France with whom the BEF of 1940, had had time to establish good relations. The pace of operations in 1944 did not allow the troops of the British Liberation Army to establish the same rapport, and although those of 1944 are critical, the men of the old BEF are unstinting in their praise of the friends they made in northern France in the earliest months of the Second World War. The farther east in Europe one went the cooler became the relationship and the tension between Western and Communist ethics made close relationships between the rank and file almost impossible. Language problems merely added to the sum total of barriers.

The Americans as our closest ally were the ones with whom the ordinary soldiers had the most contact. If one discards the envy that most British soldiers felt and which was, perhaps, the background to their accusation that the GI lacked fighting spirit, then what we see of the Americans is a great mass of generous, open-hearted soldiers who, if their attitudes occasionally jarred, illustrated Kipling's cop-out for the British Tommy, ' . . . and if sometimes our conduct isn't what your fancy paints – well single men in barracks, don't grow into plaster saints'. What was surprising about the Americans and ourselves was how much we had in common. Those things which linked us far exceeded in number and importance those which divided us.

Our Enemies

In one of his poems Rudyard Kipling voiced the sentiment of the fighting soldier towards his enemy by asking, 'What is the sense of hating those whom you are paid to kill?' He then went on to declare that he preferred to 'soon as not respect the man I fight'. It was a curious paradox that the British fighting soldier often felt more akin to his battlefield opponents than he did to his own Army or to his allies. The infantryman detested the artillery; the 'long range snipers' and accused them of blunders and incompetence when firing barrages. The gunners of the Royal Artillery countered those accusations and said that the infantry moved either too fast or too slow – charging with berserker ferocity through a carefully co-ordinated fire plan or else advancing so slowly behind the barrage that the enemy had time to emerge from his shattered positions to engage the attackers. Yet the German gunners were praised for their skill and ability even though these resulted in casualties to our own side.

The British infantry hated the armour, especially in those situations where the tanks were used as mobile pillboxes.

'The tanks would roll as far forward as our slit-trench line, fire off a few shots and then pull back. Ted [the enemy] once he recovered from the pot-shots, would open fire on where the tanks had been seen – right on our slit-trench line and we would be deluged in shit. Whenever we needed the tanks they buggered off to refuel or to carry out maintenance or something, and as for the gunners, they refused to believe that their guns fired short.'

The animosity which it might have been thought ought to be directed against the enemy was in fact heaped upon the other arms of service. The enemy was respected – at least the German enemy was. The Italians were considered to have had no chance to demonstrate their military ability for they were equipped with far worse weapons than even the British Army had. It was said that Italian tanks could be opened using the key of a sardine tin. The Japanese soldier was respected for his bravery in battle, his tenacity in attack and his powers of endurance. He was not underestimated by British fighting troops who realized that each Japanese fighting man had to be killed because the warrior code did not allow him to be taken prisoner.

THE GERMANS

The British soldier's respect for the German foe would not have been understood by civilians during the war. Even now, nearly half a century after the end of the conflict, most people still find it strange that British soldiers speak of their former enemies with deep respect. Another paradox is that the farther removed from the battle line a soldier was the more antagonistic he was to the Germans. There were cooks in Allied Forces Headquarters whose hatred of the Germans was pathological – yet they had never ever seen one. Conversely, I have met infantrymen and tankmen who had nothing but praise for the soldierly qualities of our former enemies against whom they had been fighting, in some instances, for many years.

One speaks as one finds. The Nazi fanatics who murdered their prisoners as the SS did in 1940 or in Normandy in 1944, were not considered by many British soldiers to be representative of the German Army. What the British soldier considered to be proper German soldiers were the skilled, hard-fighting, but fair men whom they met on battlefields in Europe and in Africa.

The German soldiers were good fighters who handled their weapons well – and their weapons were first class; many of them superior to those in our own service. Because they had a higher distribution of machine-pistols and faster-firing machine-guns which were capable of being used in a light or medium role, the Germans could put down a volume of fire which we could not match. Their attacks rode in on waves of bullets and the assaults of their enemies died in the criss-cross fire of their fast-firing MGs. Their tanks were better designed than ours and were continually upgunned so that they outranged our vehicles throughout the war. The German artillery had the 88mm gun, which served equally as well in anti-aircraft, anti-tank or field roles. The German Nebelwerfer projectors were frightening in the sound their shells made and in the destruction produced by their detonation. German rations were not to our taste but satisfied them. Like all soldiers the Germans wanted variety of diet and whenever they felt like a change or when supplies had failed to arrive, they penetrated Allied lines and helped themselves to what they wanted. Much of their perishable food came in tubes; butter, cheese and meat paste were the three principal ones. Biscuits (*Knackerbrot*) were foil-wrapped to keep them fresh and they had a lot of sardines. Day-to-day rations were produced in a wood-fired, wheeled, field cooker and man-portered into front-line positions. British Army cookers were fuelled by sump-oil and a forced draught and were more versatile than the high, chimneyed, German version. The German *Landser* had at least two years of disciplined training behind him when he joined the army. Most Germans were at home in the country, whereas most British soldiers were from cities and towns. The German military system was more flexible than the British. The speed with which they could form and deploy a battle group was impressive. In a retreat those who came back would be grouped at a collecting-point and were then sent back into action where they fought well under officers and NCOs whom they did not know. The strength of the British Army lay in the regimental allegiance; that of the German Army was to the nation.

THE ITALIANS

The Italian Army was armed for a war that did not take place. Had there been a major conflict in Europe in the first years of the 1930s, Mussolini's hosts would have been well equipped to fight it. By 1939, all the equipment of the Italian Army was obsolescent. When Italy entered the war in 1940, the infantry arm was being re-equipped and there were five different calibres of rifle in service. Much of the artillery dated from the Great War – some of it was made up of guns surrendered by the Austrians at the end of that war. The tanks were poor; underarmed and lightly armoured. British tankmen felt nothing but pity for their Italian opponents who went out to fight in what were mobile sardine-tins. The Italian soldier was as good a warrior as his poor equipment allowed him to be. When he was well led he was a formidable foe. It was our good fortune that his commanders did not lead him well. The men of the German Afrika Korps in the desert were disgusted to see the vast difference in living standards which existed in the Italian Army. The officers ate first and best. The NCOs ate next and what was left over went to the men. Small wonder that morale was poor among the ordinary troops. It was in the Blackshirt formations that the highest morale was to be found and to only a lesser degree in the *Bersaglieri* and armoured regiments.

During the war it was necessary to show the enemy soldiers in a bad light. Thus the Anglo-Americans nearly always depicted the Italians as heavily bemedalled cowards forever going on about pasta and vino. The image of the German soldiers which was presented to the western public was of blond-haired, sabre-scarred bullies all wearing enormous Iron Crosses. Or they were sadistic psychopaths murdering for the joy of killing or else, comic prison guards forever bamboozled by their quick-witted Anglo-American charges. The German soldier was seldom shown as a normal fighting man, subject to the joys and pressures endured by the ordinary warrior. It was imperative that he be not seen in civilian eyes as having any human virtues. Films and television programmes today project a new image of the German soldier of the Second World War. These productions no longer show the stereotyped and caricatured Nazi of the war and immediate post-war years, but depict German soldiers recognizable as normal human beings, even sympathetic. Very little, however, is known of our other principal enemy – the Japanese soldier. His image is still very much a stereotype.

JAPANESE

He was not, as the films portrayed him, a stunted, bespectacled, sub-human, more at home in the jungle than in an urban environment. The average soldier, 5 feet 3 inches tall and weighing 8½ stones, had as little experience of jungle conditions as had the Allied soldiers. It was his ability to adapt to those primitive conditions which was the key factor. To help him the ordinary Japanese soldier had qualities of stolidity and frugality which were improved by a long and strict military training. As a result he could carry an extraordinary amount of equipment and weapons for distances up to 20 miles each day. On active service his daily 4lb basic ration of food was not always supplied and he was expected to live off the land or from enemy stocks. Because of his natural frugality the Army needed few 'tail' units, allowing its greatest strength to be concentrated in its fighting formations of whom the infantry formed the greatest number. As a result of his training the Japanese soldier on the battlefield would and did attack with a ferocity unmatched by the soldiers of any other nation, advancing stolidly across the bodies of his fallen comrades, enduring wounds and sicknesses in the pursuit of victory. And when victory in attack did not come and he was forced on to the defensive, he was prepared to fight to the death.

Military training began very early, was very thorough and was aided by two factors; an intense loyalty to the Emperor and the literacy of the ordinary Japanese. In that latter respect 96 per cent could read, write and calculate and 50 per cent had learned English. Loyalty to the Emperor was absolute and the soldiers were taught that the disgrace of being defeated could only be atoned for by suicide. The idea of a battle to the last bullet was no empty concept in the Japanese Army. For them, to surrender represented so great a disgrace that a prisoner was considered to be a dead man. Believing that this concept must be accepted by all warriors, the Japanese treated their Allied prisoners-of-war as men who had forfeited their honour and who were, therefore, already dead. The prisoners were men upon whom any and all humiliations could be heaped; who could be worked literally to a physical death because they were already morally dead. The most chilling example of the Japanese code was shown when they executed an Australian serviceman who had been captured after carrying out a daring and successful mission. In the belief that the Australian had achieved the greatest glory in his life by carrying out the operation and that his imprisonment would represent an unbearable humiliation, he was beheaded.

The Japanese, as a race, have always shown themselves prepared to study and to learn from foreign military doctrines. The Army was no exception and its soldiers learned to 'go native'. They learned to live with and in the jungle and not to fight it. It was this ability which gave them the successes they achieved in the first years of the war in the Far East. Once the Allied soldiers had learned the lesson of using the jungle the belief of Japanese invincibility vanished. On active service the Japanese used ruses and strategems, shouting orders in English or calling out the names of soldiers which they had overheard. It was not unknown for individuals to be seen lying by the side of the road, covered with blood and apparently dead, to come suddenly to life and to fire into the backs of advancing Allied soldiers. Seriously wounded Japanese would wait with a grenade in their hands for a chance to kill an Allied stretcher-bearer who went to help them. The use of booby-traps planted under dead or even wounded soldiers was widespread. In the words of an American handbook on the Japanese forces, 'The variety of those devices (booby traps) is limited only by the commanders' or soldiers' imagination.'

Japanese equipment was basic, robust and unsophisticated. The artillery arm was particularly poorly served and it was only from the middle years of the war onwards that new gun types came on to issue. In the matter of tanks there were four principal types; the lightest of 5½ tons to a medium armoured fighting vehicle of 22 tons. Armour was not used in *Blitzkrieg* operations. Tanks had a chiefly infantry support role. The communications systems were poorly equipped with old-fashioned and cumbersome equipment. Of all the support arms of service, the most efficient were the engineers, whose men displayed considerable skill in construction as well as demolition. The ability of the Japanese sappers to construct field defences in the shortest period of time and using local materials was most impressive and their skill at siting and camouflaging those defences was especially high.

It was upon its infantry force that the Japanese Army depended for its victories and to which all other arms were subordinate. The military doctrine demanded sudden and swift offensive action to attack the enemy or to regain from him ground which had been lost. It was obedience to that doctrine which led to the successive waves of attacks which my correspondents recalled, and it was an offensive spirit which was maintained even in the final days of the war. One correspondent who served in a tank unit during the advance to Rangoon wrote of seeing individual Japanese soldiers attacking British vehicles with aircraft bombs clasped in their arms. This was not tank-busting on the German pattern, but self-sacrifice – suicide – the destruction of a tank and a five-man crew for the loss of a single Japanese soldier. Each tank destroyed represented a small victory.

The Japanese soldier was a formidable opponent; courageous in attack, staunch in defence, implacable and cunning – but neither a superman nor invincible. The British soldier beat him as he had beaten those other foes who had stood against him before and after the Second World War.

At War in North-West Europe

FRANCE AND FLANDERS, 1939-40

Following the outbreak of war the first elements of the BEF began their move to France and by 10 September the flow of stores and lines of communication troops was in full swing. Behind those service units came the fighting formations. W. Donovan:

'In my opinion that move was a fine example of British Army organization. It was clear that a great deal of planning had been carried out; routes reconnoitred, meal halts organized and halls for overnight sleeping prepared. Of course, that move by I Corps may have been a "showing the flag" exercise but it succeeded. Even as a soldier you have no idea of the power of the Army, of numbers, of equipment. Our BEF was all mechanized. There was not a single horse on our establishment. This was in contrast to the French Army. Later on, sometime in November 1939, I was on a parade which ended with British and French units marching past the saluting base. The French looked very much as they must have done in the Great War, the same uniforms and horse-drawn artillery. Our men wore the new battledress. As a military policeman on duty I was one of the few still wearing service dress. The only French units which impressed me were the Mountain Troops [Chasseurs Alpins]. They were very smart, very professional with bags of swank.'

The poor impression made by the French upon Bill Donovan was reflected in the opinion of Brooke, commanding British II Corps. He attended a parade to commemorate Armistice Day and wrote in his diary of the French Army:

'Men unshaven, horses ungroomed, clothing and saddlery that did not fit. Vehicles dirty and a complete lack of pride . . . the look in the men's faces, disgruntled and insubordinate . . . '

At 07.00 hrs on 20 May, the battalions of 170th Brigade were resting alongside the Arras–Cambrai road when German armour attacked the Durham Light Infantry. The Tyneside Scottish were at Neuville-Vitasse when news of the attack was received and the battalion was ordered to march to Ficheux. The rear Company was trapped by tanks in Neuville and overrun. At Mercatel other Panzer units struck the marching men and soft-skin vehicles. Despite being in a tactically unfavourable situation it is clear that the Tyneside Scottish put up a desperate resistance. As an example of the spirit of the battalion, it was reported that Provost-Sergeant Chambers was last seen alive trying to prise open the hatch cover of a Panzer with his bayonet. In the unequal battle against overwhelming odds, much of it against Rommel and his 7th Panzer Division, the 1st Battalion lost over a hundred men killed in action; about 1 in 7 of those who fought that day. One of the wounded was Malcolm Armstrong, with HQ Company:

'We marched south of Arras which was in flames at the time. We took to the 15cwt trucks and made our way to Ficheux. I was in the first lorry and we were all standing as we moved. Between Mercatel and Ficheux we had got to a farmhouse when machine-gun fire above our heads halted the lorry. Our truck pulled up suddenly and everyone jumped down on to the ground. In the truck where I had been, Private Todhunter was still sitting in the front. I told him to get out, but he did not do so and then I saw that a single bullet to his head had killed him. Our first casualty. As I turned round I could see a small tank approaching. We fixed bayonets in order to attack. At that moment I noticed that the tank gun was pointing straight at me! I think I escaped being killed then because the gun then swung in a different direction and one of my mates was killed. Together with Private Albert Foster (who was also killed that day) we advanced along the side of a farm as far as the stables. I was about to go inside when a bullet, or something like it, hit my rifle which flew out of my hands. I bent down to pick it up and that movement saved my life for the second time. When I reached a hedge that ran behind this building, I came across about ten of my mates who had been cut down by machine-gun fire. I quickly got down behind them and it was then that I was wounded by a mortar bomb. I immediately applied my first-aid dressing and as the Germans seemed to be everywhere the rest of us surrendered. I remember they led us along a column of tanks but as I was in considerable pain, everything became hazy in my mind. We were all interrogated then. Like most of the other wounded, I was placed on a stretcher. I then fainted through loss of blood and when I came to there were only two of us left. My companion asked for a drink. I was able to get to my feet in order to try to find a tap and I ran into two Germans. One of them put up his rifle to his shoulder and aimed at me. I had quite a job explaining to him that I was only looking for a drink of water. Later I was moved into a hospital at Cambrai and as I was unable to find any other men from my battalion could only presume that many had died of their wounds. I heard a rumour that our French liaison officer collaborated with the Germans. Perhaps he did, because the ambush was so perfect.'

Roy Cooke completes the story:

'There are sixty-two headstones of men from the 1st Battalion, The Tyneside Scottish at Bucaquoy Road, British War Cemetery at Ficheux, all dated 20 May, 1940. Private Albert Foster rests there, aged 21, but Todhunter may be one of the twenty-five unidentified. The name of the farm was "Ferme Fronier" and there is a plaque nearby which commemorates the sad events of that Monday morning in May 1940.'

The Allied armies were soon under such intense pressure from the Germans that withdrawal was the only option if they were to avoid encirclement and destruction. As some of the divisions of the British Expeditionary Force moved back through Belgium they crossed an area which was hallowed in British military history – the Ypres salient. Henri Braem was a young boy living in

Zillebeke, a small village between Ypres and Menin, when the British Army conducted its fighting retreat through Flanders in May 1940. Although this book is restricted to the memories of former soldiers I thought an exception should be made and that the story of Henri Braem should be included because it gives a new dimension: war through the eyes of a young civilian foreigner.

'The year 1940 was a milestone in my life for on 10 May, war broke out. Until that time it had been a strange situation for the British soldiers [in Northern France] as they hadn't had to fight . . . most of them got back to Great Britain during the week-ends and could spend a couple of days with their families at home. For that reason some people translated the initials BEF as BACK EVERY FRIDAY. Although they were at war with the Germans, they hadn't seen a German soldier. Behind our house my father had constructed a shelter of corrugated iron and had reinforced the top and side walls with earth. There were other shelters in the area [British and German ones which had been put up during the Great War]. These were concrete ones because we lived surrounded by WWI battlefields. On Sunday 26 May we went to church as usual and in the afternoon we heard shooting. "German rifle fire," said my father who recognized the dry sound from WWI. My parents decided to leave our village. We would leave as soon as possible and my parents collected some supplies and valuable possessions, locked all the doors and gave a last look at our beloved house. At 5 pm we set out carrying all our luggage and we young people found it really a pleasure because we didn't know the real truth of the danger hanging over our heads. We came across a Belgian armoured train on the Ypres-Roulers track, put there to stop the German advance on that sector. Eventually we reached the village of Poelkapelle which was packed with refugees like ourselves. During the 28th the Belgian Army capitulated. The people were very pleased because if the Germans had bombarded the village there would have been a massacre. On the 29th we saw the first German soldiers in Poelkapelle. We young boys were not accustomed to the grey colour of the tunics and that unusual helmet shape. The soldiers paid no attention to us as we made our way home. We saw lots of discarded equipment. Holes had been dug here and there. There were some trenches, or rather infantry holes [foxholes]. Several houses had been damaged by shellfire, and there were plenty of shellholes. Several cows, pigs and other animals had been killed and some had already begun to give out an awful smell. The front door of our house had been forced and all our food had been stolen. All the pots and pans had been used and food left inside them. An HE shell had destroyed our toilet and all our animals had gone. They had all escaped into the fields, but eventually we got them all back again.

'The first days back it was difficult to get accustomed to the new life; a life of occupation. People began to clear the traces left over from the previous week. We buried the fallen soldiers; British as well as German. One of the British belonged to 6th Battalion Seaforth Highlanders. His name was John MacManus and he was buried by my father and his cousin in the corner of the field along the roadside. John had been hit by a piece of shell and then hit again as he was dressing his wound. Our local carpenter put a wooden cross on his grave with his helmet on top. The cross bore his name and for us his grave symbolized the heavy fighting that had raged in the village. From post-war researches I have discovered that both the British 5th and 50th Divisions had been in our area. They had earlier been involved in the bitter fighting around Arras and began to arrive in the Zillebeke–Hollebecke–Houthem area of Ypres during 25/26 May. They were attacked during the afternoon of the 25th by elements of German Sixth Army, and the rifle fire which we had heard had been the first contact in our area between British recce patrols and the Germans. The British used the natural defence lines in our area. These were Hill 60 and Hill 62, the Ypres–Comines railway line and the canal line alongside it. The Zillebeke sector was defended by: 6th Seaforth Highlanders (17th Infantry Division of 5th Division) and the 4/5th Battalion The Green Howards (15th Brigade, 50th Division) on the left. The 2nd Royal Scots Fusiliers in the centre with 2nd Northamptons in reserve. On the right the 2nd Royal Inniskilling Fusiliers and 2nd Cameronians.

'The main German assault, on Monday 27 May, went in under a heavy barrage. The Germans advanced from Zillebeke village green and Hill 60 against the railway line. The British slaughtered them and each time the German attack was renewed the British shot them down from their good defensive positions. A Mr. Bauwen, who owns the café hardly 30 metres from the railway line, stayed there during the whole battle. From his reports it seemed that the British troops had been ordered to hold the enemy until at least 3 pm on 28 May. Although they were outnumbered, exhausted and without food they held to the last. Meanwhile on the 27th the remnants of 6th Seaforths and 2nd Royal Scots Fusiliers were overwhelmed. The survivors regrouped. The next morning, the 28th, the Germans opened a furious bombardment and attacked with fresh troops. Eventually, the British were forced back to the main road from Ypres to Warneton, and then to Voormezele where a dressing-station had been set up. They continued to withdraw and some may have been lucky enough to re-embark for Great Britain from the area between Dunkirk and La Panne. According to Major-General Franklyn, GOC 5th Division, the Divisions which held firm along the Ypres–Comines canal made it possible for the main body of the BEF to re-embark safely back to Great Britain. The fighting was very heavy and in my village of Zillebeke the 6th Seaforths lost 48 out of a total of 77 killed in action. Inside Zillebeke village the Germans lost 55, who were first buried on the spot, then exhumed and buried in Lommel.'

John Donovan of 2nd Royal Ulster Rifles:

'We were retreating through Belgium and in this town there was a hotel. I remember looking in the door and there was nobody there but a whole collection of musical instruments. Well, me being a musician and all that I dashed in and got a trumpet. I carried that trumpet all the way back to Dunkirk and brought it back with me. I still have it today and if the rightful owner would like it back I'll gladly return it. I suppose we looked on things like that as a soldier's prerogative. I can remember coming across an abandoned train full of NAAFI stores; cigarettes and things like that. A lot of the lads filled their pockets with stuff. Everybody thought that the Germans were going to get it anyway so nobody would worry about us taking it. Well, believe you me, somebody did, for not long after we had reformed in England we were all docked five bob for the stuff we had taken from the train and most of us had thrown the bloody stuff away. We got off the beach at Dunkirk in a small boat which we rowed ourselves. All the lads were shattered; no sleep, no proper food for nearly three weeks and it was all we could do to row the thing. Anyway there was this second lieutenant from some English crowd and he said that we might be at sea for a week or two weeks. I think he had dreams of going to America. Then he promised to take us all to the best hotel in London and stand us all the best meal when we got home. We might have been going round in circles when we heard this boat. It was a Navy patrol boat with a man at the front with a gun aimed at us. We asked where they were going, expecting to be told Dover or Folkestone or somewhere like that and they said "Dunkirk". We couldn't believe it; we had only left the place and here we were going back. I fell into a hazy doze and what woke me up was the boat being hit by shrapnel. We were in Dunkirk. It was awful, like a scene out of Dante's *Inferno*. People screaming in agony and flames. I wouldn't like to go to hell, for that's what that was. And the officer who was going to treat us all to a meal? We never saw him again after we landed in England.'

The Field Regiment with which Gunner Stonard served was part of the 50th Division, which had the dubious distinction of being designated 'motorized':

'Our role was to be a GHQ Reserve, ready to rush to any part of the battle that needed rapid reinforcement. The 50th was to spend the two or three weeks after the German attack, swanning backwards and forwards getting hopelessly enmeshed with the tens of thousands of refugees who blocked most of the route along which the BEF was ordered to move. The Battery arrived at a small village called Bailleul. Immediately in front of the gun position was a large bank of tall fir trees and a German cemetery of the 1914-18 war. On the opposite side of the field was a small British war cemetery. In that cemetery one of the Troop found the grave of a relative. So the first shots that E Troop fired were flanked by the dead of both sides of the last war. We were selected to take part in a counter-attack which was to be launched at Arras by a unit called "Frank Force", after its commander. The Battery came into action during the early hours of the morning of 21 May. Firing began in support of an infantry attack, then at various targets; mainly armoured units. We finally came out of action late in the afternoon and then carried on a long, slow withdrawal during the night. When the Regiment returned to England, exchanges of experiences with the infantry who had also taken part in the counter-attack revealed that the gunfire was quite effective. The German division involved was the 7th Panzer commanded by Rommel. The counter-attack advanced for nearly ten miles and captured four hundred enemy prisoners. General Le Q Martel's 50th Division was considered by the Germans to have been one of the most determined that had been encountered during the campaign. The German High Command gained the impression that the counter-attack had been launched by five divisions and that the BEF was much stronger than had been anticipated.'

The Regiment withdrew via Ypres with 150 Brigade and then to the Dunkirk area where it destroyed its guns.

'The battery withdrew into the corner of a field. All surplus equipment and vehicles were destroyed. The guns fired off the remaining ammunition except for two shells. The Troop decided to destroy their guns by the traditional method of "one down the spout and one in the breech". I volunteered to help destroy my gun, feeling that having spent the greatest part of the last six months polishing and cleaning it I was entitled to the dubious honour of blowing it up. The road to the embarkation port was bordered by fields containing hundreds of lorries, some burning, but most of them with their bonnets raised, the engines having been smashed with a sledge-hammer. The BEF marched in a disciplined order carrying what equipment and weapons they could. Some of the officers and NCOs carried rifles which they had found discarded. Some carried two.'

Stonard was one of several correspondents who recalled that while marching towards Dunkirk they had been sniped at, probably by Fifth Columnists. Bill Priest, who was also in the Dunkirk evacuation and who also recalled that his unit came under sniper fire, wrote that one sentry who complained that he had been shot at was told by an unsympathetic Regimental Sergeant Major, 'Well, you shouldn't have such a bloody ugly face.'

Stonard reached the outskirts of Dunkirk where:

'A sailor directed us towards the docks. There we saw a long queue being formed and joined the men as they shuffled their way along a wooden pier at the end of which was a destroyer. Looking around it was amazing to see that some of the soldiers were in full battle kit, carrying rifles. A closer scrutiny revealed them to be Guardsmen. Although obviously very tired they still managed to have that aloofness that is so distinctive of the Guards. That men should form a mile-long line, three abreast, patiently waiting for their turn to climb aboard a small boat, seemingly oblivious to the constant noise of gunfire and the exploding of bombs and yet maintain a degree of cheerfulness was the true "Dunkirk spirit"; a term now a part of the English vocabulary, often used in the wrong context.'

DUNKIRK

Gunner Evans, a Regular soldier in an AA regiment, was recalled to the Colours shortly before the outbreak of war and served in France during the 1940 campaign. During his time in the Dunkirk perimeter he was asked by his sergeant, 'Tich' Proctor to go with a group that was bringing back one of the guns which the regiment had abandoned near La Panne.

'The French infantry tried to stop our lorry shouting, "Boche", meaning that the Germans were only one and a half miles up the road. We found the gun and firing breechblock. When we got back to the beach out of the blue a young officer came up. He said, "I was on board a boat ready to go to England, but I saw you blokes having a go so I decided to join you." He was calm and cool and one of us. We had no instruments so he used his hands and experience to put us on target. We accounted for seven planes. At night we manned two Bren guns on a bridge up the road. When the beach was nearly clear [of troops waiting to be evacuated] we marched in single file round the back streets. We saw some terrible sights. In front of our eyes were field guns complete with gunner crews, some smiling. I didn't see any blood, but they were all dead. It must have been shell blast. The last couple of days was like hell let loose. On our way along the beach some soldiers were killed or wounded by our own ammo lorries set ablaze by German machine-gun fire or by bombing. We lay on the sand. Near me was a French sailor who was dead. His face was dark-blue. As I went farther along the beach I took cover in a wide tunnel which was filled with wounded. A ginger-headed medical officer was cutting one chap's leg off. Lots of chaps were groaning in pain. It was horrible. We finished up in Liverpool and I heard a man in a civvy suit go on about being dumped at Stoke-on-Trent. He was a soldier who had just picked up his clobber and gone home. I went back to the barracks, dumped all my kit in my valise and thumbed a lift. As I walked through Chatterley valley which led to the bottom of our street, I heard a woman shout to another woman, "That's one of Evans lads isn't it?" So I darted through an entry, up our back-yard, let myself in and sat on the sofa. There was only my dad in. After a bit he said, "OK son?" I said "Yes." He carried on cutting bread and then the penny dropped. He turned round, looked at me and said, "Hast bin in that bit of a do?" He meant Dunkirk.'

The fighting which Bill Priest described so vividly was that in which French and British rearguards held off the attacking Germans, thereby allowing the BEF and other French formations to be taken from the beaches at Dunkirk. One man who was taken off in one of the small boats was R. H. C. Wileman. Ex-Gunner Wileman enlisted into the Territorial Army on a six-year engagement in 1938, and joined a local unit, 57th Field Regiment. This was equipped with 25pdr guns. He recalled that upon being called to the Colours at the outbreak of war, his Brighton-based regiment was billeted in the Dome and the Corn Exchange for three weeks before being moved to Stoke sub Hamdon, in Somerset.

'Soon we were told off to embark for an unknown destination. We sailed from Southampton to Cherbourg, then travelled up country to Ypres in Belgium. A couple of days later we were told to fall back so we retreated to a place called Béthune, only to find that the Luftwaffe had paid a visit and there were many dead or dying people and animals. We moved farther back to Lyons. We used an old coffee warehouse but there were many Fifth Column spies in those days and again the German Air Force were soon dropping their scrap iron on us. We were then ordered to make for the coast and all went well until we reached the La Bassée Canal and it was there I somehow became separated from my regiment. I got mixed up with the Grenadier Guards who had been told to hold a bridge crossing the canal. As I was a Gunner and had no rifle I was speedily transferred to another RA unit. Then we got to Calais only to find that the German Army had encircled the area so we hurriedly moved to the Dunkirk area where we were ordered into a field and told to climb into the surrounding hedge which would act as camouflage. We were there for quite a time and to my horror I found that my Iron Ration had been stolen from me. By the time we were ordered down to the beaches I was feeling weak from lack of food, but still kept moving. I can still remember the Stuka dive-bombers. Even today I can visualize those cannon-shells whipping up the sand. I, for one, used the vehicles bogged down in the soft sand as a cover against them. Soon we were on the move again towards the water's edge to board some of the boats which had come from England to save us. I was one of the fortunate ones and marched along a jetty towards a ship which I boarded with great haste. I quickly went down into the hold not caring what the Germans did and must have fainted from hunger because when I came to, I was in a train which stopped at Salisbury station. I vaguely remember having a bun, an orange and an Army Field Card put into my hand and being told to tick off where necessary and to address it to my family so that they knew I was safe. Eventually, we reached Yeovil town station where we were loaded into ambulances and ferried to Hounstone army camp. I was there for a period of three weeks' convalescence after which I was given a medical examination and found to be unfit for further service overseas. My Regiment, which was part of 44th Division, was sent to Africa. Not many came back.'

Another Gunner who went to France with the first elements of the BEF, was Brian Thatcher, a Regular officer who, by the end of the war, was commanding his Regiment.

'When "in the line' [during the winter of 1939/40] (there was the whole of Belgium between us and the Germans), we found ourselves responsible for observation on I Corps front and were centred round the vicinity of Douai. After we had been "in the line" for some weeks, someone got the idea that we should be withdrawn, so back we went to the little village of Contay, some 10 miles from Amiens. It was a hard winter but we made ourselves pretty comfortable one way and another. We alternated between "the line" and "rest" preferring the latter because the country and surroundings were so much more pleasant. We were very "gas conscious" in those days with our bits of detecting paper – white, yellow and blue, which were alleged to produce pink spots on the approach of anything particularly horrid. When the gas scare was at its height the Colonel was very keen on surprise practices. One day, with a screech of brakes, he drew his staff car up and shouted "gas!" at the sentry outside the headquarters of a certain battery. The chap doubled off smartly as though to give the warning only to return with a 2-gallon tin of petrol. Early in May 1940, I was on leave in England when the Germans started to walk through Belgium. The adjutant was home on leave at the same time so we arranged to meet at Victoria station where, by the use of the loud-speaker, we rounded up a few other members of the regiment who were trying to get back. Against fairish odds we fought our way over to Boulogne and then on to Amiens. We were back with the regiment and involved in battle within 36 hours of having left England. I am afraid that my memories are very vague about the retreat via Dunkirk. We never quite knew in which direction we were fighting and all the time we seemed to be slipping quietly towards the coast. The weather was fine throughout and I remember sleeping the afternoon of my birthday (16 May) quietly in an orchard. Spirits were high and we were never short of anything to eat or drink for by this time we were living largely off the country. Comparatively early on in proceedings the regiment found itself in Dunkirk, the docks of which were still intact. The place was, of course, being bombed from time to time, but there were plenty of cellars in which to take shelter while we waited for some craft to convey us home.

'I wish I could remember the name of the ship in question. I do know that she was one of the little ferries which in peacetime used to function off the west coast of Scotland. Having destroyed everything of value except our instruments, binoculars, etc., which we took with us, we moved aboard in a very orderly manner quite worthy of the Guards, marching in single file up the gangways, later to be battened down below decks. I suppose if one had been less tired and fired with a little more imagination, one could have developed a bit of an anxiety complex shut up down there with the odd bomb falling around, but I know I had only two desires: one was to shave and the other was to sleep. The former I managed with a borrowed razor; the latter I accomplished on the floor, all the way to Dover where we landed. There is no doubt that the regiment enjoyed (hardly an appropriate word but it conveys my meaning) a pretty easy exit via Dunkirk. None of the mud of Flanders or unshaven faces for us. Quite apart from anything else, the Colonel would see to that and he ordered a best clothing parade twenty-four hours after having landed in England. This parade went off well with the exception of one incident. Behind the rear rank of my battery was spotted a tarpaulin lying on the ground, obviously concealing an object of some bulk. The unveiling ceremony revealed one of my ex-trumpeters, now a DR, asleep. Our regiment managed to land home pretty spick and span, but then we had had an easy passage. Even so, in my opinion, there was little excuse for some of the scruffiness we saw. Just about the first sign of demoralization is when a soldier ceases to shave – this I confirmed later on in the war. In any case it was a pity that the expression "Dunkirk Heroes" arose. I know that heroism went on round the perimeter and on the beaches, but the whole thing was a glorious defeat.'

One tragedy at sea, involving a heavy loss of life among British troops, and which is still commemorated annually, was the loss of the *Lancastria* in June 1940. R. A. Joyce, a Sergeant of the Royal Engineers, was on board the ship and his account described the event with characteristic British understatement.

'During the retreat from France, my RE unit, attached to the Advanced Air Striking Force, reached St. Nazaire. We got on board the *Lancastria* at approximately noon on Monday, 17 June, some of the very last to be packed in, so we ended up in the cabins on the boat deck. We managed to get a meal but the ship remained at anchor until about 4.00 pm, when there was the never-to-be-forgotten whine of dive-bombers. Being on the boat deck I quickly realised that there was no point hanging about as the boat was sinking by the bow and was going around and up. I climbed down a rope-ladder and then jumped 40 feet into the water. I swam for about two hours, gradually undressing to make things easier and luckily the water was warm. When I looked back I could see that the *Lancastria* had turned turtle and was covered with little figures singing *Roll out the barrel*, but soon even that stopped and the boat settled. I was picked up, together with hundreds of others, by a tramp steamer which made a dash across the Channel and landed us at Portsmouth where we were concentrated in Devonport Park and held incommunicado. No word of the sinking of the *Lancastria* reached the newspapers until well into July or even later.'

DIEPPE, 1942

On 19 August 1942, British and Canadian forces mounted an assault from England upon the French port of Dieppe. In the years that have passed since then, a great deal has been written about the sacrifice of 2nd Canadian Division and questions asked why the attack had to be made. The town of Dieppe, standing at the mouth of the river Arques, was known to be strongly garrisoned. Cliffs outside the town carried heavy guns to defend the port and to dominate it.

Dieppe's shingle beaches were backed by a high-walled promenade from which there were few exits. As a consequence, soldiers debarking on to the shingle would be held in a killing-ground unless they could force their way over the promenade wall and into the town.

What were the compelling reasons for sending those highly trained but as yet 'unblooded' Canadians into what was so obviously an unequal struggle? It would seem that several factors coincided. The Americans were demanding the opening of a Second Front to take pressure off the Russians, although it was obvious that they had no idea of what such an operation would involve. The British High Command was convinced that the Western Allies were still not strong enough, nor well enough equipped, to undertake a successful full-scale cross-Channel invasion of Hitler's Europe. The impatient Americans must be given a demonstration of just how difficult and bloody an invasion would be. In addition the British had a new tank that had to be tested under battle conditions together with tank landing craft of new patterns. They, too, had to be tested to see whether they would be suitable when the real invasion of France was made. The 2nd Canadian Infantry Division, supported by the new tanks, would prove whether an assault landing and the capture of a strongly defended port was feasible. It proved not to be.

More than 2,000 of the 5,000 Canadians who had set out to test Hitler's Europe were lost. Sixty-five per cent of the assaulting infantry battalions were casualties. Those losses demonstrated two things: *Festung Europa* was too strong to be invaded in 1942 or 1943. More preparation and more assault craft were essential as well as covering fire of fearsome power if the entrenched German defenders were to be destroyed.

Jack Brewin's account is one man's story of the Dieppe operation:

'This account is based on notes which I made about a week after the event when the Special Sea Service squad with which I was serving was given intensive training for a secret operation. At Fort Gomert our NCOs and officers joined us and we then paraded for Lord Louis Mountbatten who startled us with his informal approach, telling us to break ranks and to gather round him. The four special squads were first posted – mine to Sunderland and then ordered to the south coast. During the afternoon of 18 August, things really began to take shape as the jetty crowded with troops, for the most part Canadians, but also men of No. 3 Commando. These were all embarked directly on to landing craft. We left Newhaven about 0100 hours, on a very dark night with a swelling sea. We were under orders not to fire, even at suspicious targets. In the darkness of the night there were several near collisions between craft and we narrowly missed hitting an LCT. I have the impression now of being lonely in my position as gun-layer on No. 2 pompom. I was not afraid of events. I think none of us were, but we had time to think and to contemplate what might be in wait for us. We were all about 19 to 20 years of age and none of us had seen previous active service. About 03.00 hours the sky suddenly filled with tracer and it was obvious that some sort of attack was taking place. I know now that this event was the unfortunate chance meeting with a small German convoy, a meeting which contributed towards the terrible outcome of the operation. As dawn broke we had our first glimpse of a hostile shore, at that stage quite normal with some white cliffs and a town. Apart from some distant thuds there was nothing seemingly other than the commonplace. As the morning light grew I could see the magnitude of the operation. The foreshore was obliterated by many craft, the sea around us occupied by many ships. With the coming of full light the scene changed. The air was suddenly filled with aircraft and we fired madly at all of them. At this time we were about half a mile offshore and so occupied with our fire that what was happening on the beach escaped us. There appeared to be hundreds of planes swarming everywhere and identification was so difficult that we fired at everything which came near and when a plane was shot down we cheered and claimed responsibility. The RAF was that day operating Mustang fighters for the first time and resemblance of this aircraft to the German Me 109 was such that we most certainly shot one of these down.

'It was about 0830 hrs when our role changed. We steamed closer inshore and what we had already experienced under air attack was nothing to the holocaust which now presented itself. It is difficult to describe each separate detail of events. I even doubt that I ever could have done so. It now all seems to be one mixed impression of terror and nightmare. I can only try to describe that impression, *en bloc* so to speak. By this time the withdrawal was taking place and landing craft, mostly LCPs, were streaming from the beach filled beyond normal capacity with badly wounded men. My craft lay broadside to the beach and it seemed that every gun, light and heavy, was directed on us from the shore. I seemed rooted to the gun platform, possibly because I imagined the shield would give some protection. Tracer flew in all directions and a great piece of metal from the ship's side landed at my feet. I heard terrible screams all around me, the gun had jammed and wounded were being lifted aboard from the shore. The sights were ghastly. A Canadian minus an arm climbed aboard unaided calmly smoking a cigarette. I could not have believed such courage. Terribly mutilated bodies lay all around; the sea was full of débris and floating dead, tremendous noise and the air full of stinking smoke. The officer's mess-deck was being used as a sick-bay and the orderlies were almost throwing the wounded down to the surgeon. Almost as continuously the dead were being arranged on the deck. One of those Canadians was covered in a Union Jack which had been found inside his jacket. Surely not the reason for which it had been intended. I have no idea how long this terrible episode lasted, but orders were eventually given for our withdrawal and we were among the very last to leave. A heavy cloud of smoke enveloped the town; the beach was filled with immobilized tanks and landing craft. Our journey back was one of utter misery. The mess-deck was crowded with survivors and wounded lay around everywhere. A stench of mutilated humanity prevailed. I myself was in a state of utter shock. I had no knowledge of what our role had been. I knew even less of what, if anything, we had achieved. I suppose someone, somewhere, was able to make a pattern of the day's events. I couldn't. We arrived off Newhaven late at night and as the boom defence nets had been drawn and the harbour entry blocked had to remain outside all night. We entered port next morning and tied to the same jetty as that from which we had left some 30 hours before. Then we had been young and so immature. Now we felt older and full of terrible experience. The wounded were loaded into ambulances and the poor dead were hoisted ashore on large flat boards. A war correspondent came aboard and approached me. "What did you think of Dieppe?" he asked. "So that's where we have been," I replied. How ridiculous that must have sounded to him, but the name meant nothing to me. Hell has many different names.'

NORMANDY, 1944

Four years after it had left France as a result of the catastrophic débâcle of 1940, the British Army returned to north-west Europe via the D-Day landing beaches in June 1944. The personal stories of those who took part in the liberation of Europe begin with Jack Brewin's account of his part in the opening phases of the assault landings.

'On the night of 5 June 1944, we lay off Spithead surrounded by the "vehicles of war", grey battleships, heavy cruisers, sleek destroyers, the heavily laden sea transports and the multitudes of different types of landing craft. The night was cold and wet, the sea was swelly and inclined to be a bit choppy further out. We waited aware that final decisions were being taken, the time of estimation was about to cease and history was about to be made. I was by now accomplished in assault landings having been in on "Torch" [the invasion of French North Africa], in Pantelleria, Syracuse in Sicily and at Salerno in Italy. France was the next target. The LCI on which I served was American-built and designed to carry about 200 troops in three separate apartments. The craft had a speed of about 15 knots, but did not float on the water like the other assault landing craft, which were flat-bottomed, but cut through the water. As a result the ship was almost constantly awash on the upper deck. The troops did not like this type of vessel for they had first to clamber to the top deck and then descend steep narrow ramps on either side of the bows and hope that the water was not too deep from then on. All the previous landings I had taken part in had begun under some secrecy, but in southern England it was obvious that major landings were sure to take place. In fact I think that this tremendous concentration of troops was in itself a great morale builder. The actual victory was 50 per cent won before the first commencement of battle. I understand that as the troop convoys left Portsmouth civilians lined the coast cheering the departure, loud-hailers aboard some of the ships played military music and ships' sirens sounded, almost like the farewell that had been for troops off to fight some colonial war during the previous century. Morale has never been higher amongst troops of any nation. How did I feel as we left Spithead? I don't think that any of us felt fear for we had trained for this great operation and all felt confident that our leadership had been supreme. Then, there was great comfort in the vast numbers and the knowledge that great forces were on our side. The comfort also of one's comrades, although most were new to me. But they looked up to me with some respect due to my previous experience and that fact alone did much for my own morale. How could I disgrace myself when many of those around me looked to me for support. Most of us kept up our good spirits during those early hours. We were spoken to by our Troop Commander and at this point we were told that our destination was to be France; that and nothing more. We knew that 48 Commando was to land with us to perform a pincer movement in order to connect the groups separated by a beach unsuitable for landing on. We were told that ours was to be Sword Beach, Peter Sector, and we were assured that by the time we landed the fortifications would have been softened as a result of heavy air and sea bombardment.

'We were closely packed together, not just because of our numbers. Our equipment weighed individually above 90lb. I also carried a rifle and, as a signaller, had a radio transmitter weighing about 30lb to be shared between me and another of my comrades. Our task was to make contact with 48 Commando and French civilians. To ensure mobility we were to use folding bicycles which were stored in racks in the stern of the craft. I cannot now remember the hour we actually landed but it was certainly after dawn. A tremendous bombardment was taking place almost up to the time we were to land and always it has been a fear of being caught in one's own fire. I could see the sector we were to land on. Later I was to learn that we were far from our allotted place. A tremendous battle taking part on our right flank was, so I learned later, 48 Commando, which lost half its numbers in that fight. By now I was on the deck of the craft with the folded cycle as addition to my load while my signaller comrade was struggling with our transmitter. Then the disembark signal was given – I think it was probably a combination of flashing lights and sirens. The ramps were lowered and we surged towards the beach. We were still a long way from the beach when it finally stopped. I would have felt much better landing from a craft with wider ramps instead of the crazy, steep, ladder-like gangways fitted to our vessel.

'The beach was clearer now, despite the smoke and fog which enveloped it. I saw what appeared to be several large houses on some kind of promenade and then a vivid streak of tracer shell streamed out of the windows towards some object to the left of us. I recall being surprised that anything could have survived the barrage from the sea. This had now stopped. I was first down the portside ramp with my comrade immediately behind me. It was no dash ashore as Hollywood might portray. Instead I remember it as an agonizing stumble down the steep ramp under my heavy load. I jumped into the sea and immediately sank into deep water that came over my head, although thinking about it now it might have been the choppy sea that gave that impression. I scrambled eventually to the beach around the bows of the craft. The bicycle was beneath the waves but I still had all my equipment and rifle as I dashed up the beach to shelter behind some rocks. The rest of the Troop seemed to be some distance from me all lost in the gloom of the morning. The fire from the houses was joined with heavy mortar fire and big bursts which suggested artillery shells. There were a great many bodies strewn around the beach. At that stage they gave the impression of being soldiers other than my comrades. Some Beach Marshals and Redcaps were trying to organize exits from the beach. I looked for my signaller comrade but could see him no more. I found out later that he had been badly wounded on getting ashore. He had had the transmitter so our combined contribution was not to be. A sergeant of our Troop was gathering his men together and I joined him in an attempt to get a foothold to the right of the houses. My mind is very confused from that point. I remember perhaps thirty of us leaving behind a beach of great confusion and gathering in a field behind the houses. I remember also some Canadian soldiers who appeared to be in some confusion and leaderless.

'We were eventually joined by a lieutenant and about twenty Marines. He told us that the remainder of the Troop had now regrouped and had moved to the left against Lion-sur-Mer. We were to attack a large house or château which had been his original objective. The distance seemed a long one and the roads were strewn with German dead. We gained our objective, but the proposed link-up with 48 Commando was never achieved. A big counter-attack was supposed to be prepared by the Germans, but this never took place. In any case there was no strength left in 48 Commando and most never left the beach alive. During the actions of the next three days we took many prisoners. They seemed to be a mixture of asiatic-type Russians who had been recruited from POW camps as well as some young and frightened German boys. Many were suffering from shell-shock following the intense bombardment and I saw little to indicate the fanatical resistance that was to come further inland. It was at this time I was sent back to England with German prisoners and our own wounded, many from 48 Commando. I was treated with great care and consideration on my return to the barracks at Eastney; white bread, well-cooked food and white sheets and, most important of all, leave. I suppose we had achieved something on that day, but success is seldom witnessed by the ordinary soldier. That is for the planners and manipulators of the General Staff to enjoy. Victories are things we are told belong to us long after they have taken place.'

The extreme left of the Allied beachheads in Normandy rested on the River Orne. Airborne troops had landed to capture intact the important bridges across that river and had orders to hold these until relieved by Lord Lovat's Brigade. One of the soldiers taking part in the Commando Brigade's operation was Private Farmborough, who was wounded during the operation.

'We were part of the 1st Special Services Brigade, which comprised four separate Commando units, commanded by Brigadier The Lord Lovat. We were on the extreme left flank of the British Army and landed on Sword Beach at first light on 6 June 1944. The plan was that three of the Commando units went hell for leather to join up with the Airborne troops which had landed around the bridges on the River Orne and the Orne Canal and to hold those bridges at all costs. No. 4 Commando, of which I was a member, had to dash along the coast road, a distance of about a mile, to destroy and blow up a battery of big guns at Ouistreham on the mouth of the River Orne. Then we had to speed with the utmost alacrity to rejoin the brigade at the bridges a few miles inland. We had about 500 men, which included 60 French Commandos attached to us for this little episode. I myself never reached Ouistreham. I was shot on the way, I believe by an automatic weapon. I can't say what type because I never saw it. However, a couple of bullets made a mess of my left arm, shattering the bone in four places. I didn't realize how fortunate I had been until back in England some days later, when they took off my Mae West and found three more bullet lines running along the Mae West and completely missing me. Strange as it may seem, I didn't feel a thing when the bullets hit me and had no pain at all, but I was knocked to the ground. I did feel most annoyed because I was out of action. One of the lads picked up my Bren gun and off he went. You see, in circumstances like those there was no stopping to help the wounded. This we all knew. Luckily,

I was able to get behind a and dune and gradually made my way to the landing area, though not before I had nearly been run over by one of our tanks. The driver didn't see me and I had to roll out of the way a bit sharpish. I must have fainted because when I came to there were a couple of Medics beside me. They helped me back to a dressing-station by a pillbox. They couldn't do much except strap my arm across my body. I had the comfort of a stretcher and was lifted on to a DKW and ferried out to a hospital ship which sailed next day to Tilbury. I had some injections, but no other treatment until reaching England. They soon got me to hospital and started the repair business. Six months later, I left hospital, almost new.'

After the landing British Second Army, in accordance with Montgomery's strategy, attracted to itself the bulk of the German armour in Normandy and the fighting was hard and costly. Against the British perimeters were several SS Panzer Divisions whose staunch defence delayed the capture of Caen – a road communications centre which had been a D-Day objective. Brian Thatcher recalls:

'The month we spent before Caen was a pretty bloody one in more ways than one. Those who had fought in the 1914-18 War told me that the battles before Caen came up to anything they had ever experienced and I know that of the 212 casualties suffered by my regiment in the campaign in north-west Europe, at least seventy-five per cent were incurred during this month in Normandy.'

Among the many attempts which were made to destroy German opposition in the city were massive air raids, but these succeeded only in creating piles of rubble which served the defenders but impeded the attackers. Other ways had to be found if Caen was to fall. It was felt that if the city could be outflanked, the defenders, drawn chiefly from the 12th SS Division 'Hitler Youth', would be compelled to withdraw. In pursuit of his plan to bypass the obstruction, Montgomery ordered 7th Armoured Division, the élite formation which he had brought with him out of the desert, to drive south-east from Bayeux to Villers-Bocage. Once the 7th Armoured had reached and consolidated around that area the German position would be untenable. Albert Kingston served with one of the battalions of the Queen's Brigade which formed part of 7th Armoured.

'The Brigade had served in the African campaign as part of 7th Armoured. I did not get called up until late in 1942, so I didn't serve in the desert. My first action was in Normandy. We landed on 10 June, and I was surprised to see so little destruction. From BBC reports we all expected to see the place [Normandy] looking like the pictures of the Western Front – all mud and tree stumps. They tell me that Caen was a mess, but I never saw it so I cannot say. The countryside was very green with high hedges running along little roads. Some of the roads had hedges which were more than twelve-foot high and so thick you could not see through them. They were good defensive positions and the units that had been fighting in this sort of countryside deserve every credit. It must have been a real hell. There were lots of little cemeteries we passed as we moved up the line. Four or five graves in a group – an infantry Section perhaps, or a Sherman crew, because the place was littered with knocked out Shermans. And some of them stank. There was more than likely bodies still in them. So far as I remember from what we were told in 'O' groups, 7th Armoured was to capture a little town called Villers-Bocage. If it could do this it would have trapped the Jerries in Caen. They would have to pull out or be destroyed and if they pulled back we would have them on the run. Things turned out a bit different from what we were told was going to happen. The Jerry opposition was quite strong and it took us a couple of days to reach the little town which was our objective.'

For there to be an Allied breakout of the confining beachheads the mass of German armour available to OKW had to be prevented from reaching Normandy because each new Panzer Division arriving in the area made the Allied task more difficult. The build-up of German divisions had to be stopped or slowed down. On the German side the Panzer formations which had been fighting since D-Day needed to be relieved and reinforced. The replacement formations struggled to reach the battle line, and as each arrived it was committed immediately to action. The thrust from Bayeux by 7th Armoured was countered along the line Verrières–Tilly, by the newly arrived crack Panzer Lehr Division, whose opposition forced the British formation to seek alternative routes to the objective.

In the fluid situation which existed in the second week of June, possession of Villers-Bocage was vital to both sides. As the most important road centre to the south of Bayeux it was a key point. To ensure that it stayed in German hands OKW had sent forward 2nd Panzer Division, but until it arrived in force a stop-gap unit, 501 SS Heavy Tank Battalion, was put in to hold the ground through which 2nd Panzer would pass to the combat zone. On the British side, 7th Armoured Division, held up in front of Tilly, was probing to locate the left flank of Panzer Lehr Division. Once this had been turned the advance would be resumed towards the high ground which dominated Villers-Bocage. By 13 June, part of 22nd Brigade of 7th Armoured had worked its way round 2nd Panzer flank and begun its move towards Villers-Bocage. Orders were issued that once the little town had been reached, 4th County of London Yeomanry and 'A' Company of 1st Battalion, The Rifle Brigade, were to push on and to take Point 213, the high ground which lay about a mile to the north-east. By 09.00hrs the point unit of 22nd Armoured had reached the little town.

Albert Kingston:

'We were in the town centre, a little square and not much else. There were a few shops open, cafés I think, and we were just standing about waiting for orders when we heard the sound of gunfire coming from the road out of town. There seemed from the noise to be a big battle going on and presently we saw black clouds of smoke in the air. One of our soldiers said they were tanks blowing up. This did not sound so good as we had one of our armoured brigades on the road ahead. Then, all of a sudden our anti-tank platoons were ordered into action – to take post. The ammunition trucks were driven into side streets and all the rifle sections were told to take up positions in windows of houses on the "enemy" side of the village, as it was called. To be honest, I saw nothing of the battle which followed, although I was in it. My memories are of the noise and the solid shot that smashed through the walls of the room in which I and a group of other Queensmen were positioned. I suppose, when you are excited or frightened noise sounds louder in some way. Also the narrow streets seemed to hold the noise in so that it sounded really loud. There were several loud bangs which were our 6pdr anti-tank guns going off and then one very loud explosion. I learned later that this was a Bren-carrier of ammunition that went up. Then we heard tank tracks squeaking and squealing and these must have been Jerry's because the sound seemed to be coming from the "enemy" side. Then there was a whooshing sound and a sort of flashing light behind us in the room. We all turned round and there was a hole in the outside wall and another in the inside one. A solid shot had passed through the whole house – in one side and out the other. It had been an AP round, I suppose, from a Jerry tank. There was a lot of plaster dust in the air, but none of us had been hurt. We didn't think of it at the time, but if that shall had struck a couple of feet from where it did, all of us in that room would have been killed.

'The firing seemed to spread and I believe that Jerry infantry [Panzer Grenadiers] were working their way into the town. Then there was some more tank gun fire, some machine-gun fire and then dead silence. We all waited. Nothing happened for about ten minutes or more. Then an officer came up the stairs and told us to fall in outside. The street was a mess. Bricks and rubble all over the place. A couple of hundred yards up the road there was the biggest tank I had ever seen. It looked undamaged. One of our 6pdrs was lying on its side, just opposite our house. Up came the unit transport and we moved back up the road which we had been along first thing that morning.'

The battle in Villers-Bocage in which Albert Kingston had been engaged was one in which a single Tiger tank crew from the SS Heavy Tank Battalion had created a path of destruction. It had destroyed, according to British official histories, 25 tanks, fourteen half-tracks and fourteen Bren-gun carriers. The SS officer who carried out that destruction was SS Obersturmführer (Lieutenant) Michael Wittman, a veteran of the Eastern Front where his special ability had gained him one hundred and seventeen 'kills'.

From a vantage-point in woodland Wittmann had seen the 22nd Brigade advancing up the narrow road towards the crest of Point 213. Through his binoculars he saw that the British column had halted and that men were jumping down from the vehicles. The commanders of 4th CLY point squadron and the Rifle Brigade trucked infantry were holding an 'O' Group, a final briefing before making the last bound to take the hill. A fresh squadron of the CLY was ordered to take over duty as point unit. To make room for that squadron to pass, the tanks and half-tracks already on the narrow road were ordered to 'close up' and move tight against the bocage hedge at the side of the road. It was a tactical blunder. The road was not wide and with the vehicles closed up, nose to tail, they were immobile until the new point detachment had passed them. It was a tactical blunder which Wittmann was quick to appreciate and to exploit. Moving downhill out of the woods in which he had been concealed, he smashed the leading Cromwell with a single shot. Now that he had knocked out the lead tank the British were bottled-up. They could not advance, neither could they pull back except by reversing, nor could they fire at the Tiger as it cruised down the road firing round after round into the column. A succession of shots from his massive 88mm gun destroyed the vehicles of CLY and of the 8th Hussars which came up the road to challenge him and now, reinforced by the other tanks of his

Command and the Tigers of another SS Company, he drove towards Villers-Bocage.

In the narrow streets of that place, the 6pdr anti-tank guns of the Queens went into action. A shot fired by one of them blew off the track of Wittmann's Tiger and he and his crew were forced to abandon the vehicle. In the centre of the town the other Tigers came under such fire that they were forced to pull back. This was a retreat of short duration for the Panzer Lehr Division's units soon entered the battle and launched a pincer attack upon Villers-Bocage. The 7th Armoured Division withdrew out of the town and towards Tilly from which its formations had advanced that morning. Raymond Rolls is critical of the whole operation and of the weapons with which the units were issued:

'I was in the 7th Armoured Division, but not at Villers-Bocage. I heard about what had occurred there some time later and it only confirmed what many of us thought about the division's leadership. It must have been obvious to those in command that the 22nd Brigade was in enemy territory. We had been fighting for days and regimental histories make it clear we had got round the flank and were behind the German Panzer Lehr Division. Behind the enemy line implies that you are in his territory. Yet on a narrow road in enemy territory the CLY stop and then close up their vehicles nose to tail. Why didn't they do that in the main square of the town, where there would have been more room for one unit to pass the other. Some of the histories mention the PIAT mortar as if it had been the best anti-tank weapon in the world and not, as it really was, the worst. The German anti-tank projectiles were rocket-propelled. One, which was a single shot weapon, was called the *Panzerfaust*. One man operated that. Then there was the two-man weapon, the *Panzerschreck*. One man loaded the rocket and the second man fired it. Our PIAT was spring-loaded. It had to be cocked before firing the first round and the easiest way to cock it was standing upright with both feet fixed firmly on the shoulder piece. The spring's recoil, so it was said, would recock the weapon. If the PIAT misfired, it had to be recocked again. Imagine it! Standing up in view of the enemy to pull on a strong spring. The shell it fired was shaped like a turnip. It was fitted into a cutout section on the top side of the PIAT. The sights were primitive and the range was short; effectively, about 50 yards. When the turnip flew through the air it had to strike its target squarely. If the nose did not hit point on the target the bomb did not explode. I understand a graze fuze was fitted some time later, which meant in theory that the projectile should explode so long as any part of the fuze hit the target. I must admit that when a Piat grenade did explode a lot of damage was caused. I do not think it could penetrate the front armour of a Tiger tank, but it could smash through the side and rear armour. That stupid weapon, which had to be cocked while standing up; which had only a short range and was fitted with a useless fuze, was lauded as if it were the most brilliant anti-tank device in use in any army. I know that Fusilier Jefferson of the Lancashire Fusiliers of 78th Division won the Victoria Cross at Cassino for knocking out two enemy tanks. Being a cynic, I think it was the fact that he survived that particular engagement that earned him the Cross he so richly deserved. We had PIATs in use in north-west Europe, but the number of Panzers which were knocked out were very, very few indeed when one considers how many PIATs were in use.'

The Rhineland Campaign and Advance into Germany

Montgomery wanted to press on into Germany without delay. He planned to establish a bridgehead and outflank the Siegfried Line with an ambitious airborne drop combined with a rapid thrust by Second Army. The 1st Airborne Division (British) and 82nd and 101st Airborne Divisions (US) would seize bridges and strategic points, hold them until reinforced and thereby assist in forming a corridor which would end in a bridgehead on the Rhine from which Second Army could sweep on to the North German Plain. The subsequent Operation 'Market Garden' in mid-September 1944 failed badly but it did not deter Montgomery from persisting with his efforts to cross the great river barrier.

The planners at Supreme Headquarters chose to make the point of maximum effort on the sector held by Montgomery's 21st Army Group. In preparation for the crossing of the Rhine the most intensive geological research was undertaken and such details obtained as the speed of the river's current, the tidal movement and the height of the river's bank. For Operation 'Plunder', the code-name for the offensive, 21st Army Group would deploy three armies: First Canadian (eight divisions) on the left, Second British (eleven divisions including three armoured) in the centre and Ninth US (eleven divisions including three armoured) on the right flank. More than one and a quarter million men would be involved in the operation, of whom a quarter of a million would be in the first assault. For Second Army alone, the logistics problem was enormous and included the movement and storage of more than 30,000 tons of Engineer equipment, 28,000 tons of supplies and 60,000 tons of ammunition. The barrage on Second Army's assault sector, between Xanten and Rees, would fire 1,000 shells each minute for four hours.

Efforts to conceal the preparations reached a climax on 19 March, when an artificial smoke-screen was laid. A press report on this 60-mile long opaque curtain reads, in part:

'The greatest artificial wall of smoke, the longest and thickest in the history of warfare has been laid across the western bank of the Rhine to hide [our preparations] from German eyes. A mixture of oil and water is passed through a heated boiler and is pumped out through small exit holes. A white steam is produced. The smoke-screen is laid from an hour before first light to an hour after last light. As a further camouflage measure, dummy vehicles and guns were set up in the American Army's sectors and smoke-screens of lesser density laid. The local civilian population in those sectors were moved away, which seemed to confirm that the main assault would be made by the US Army.' Much of the preparations to 'lift' British Second Army men across the River Rhine suddenly became academic. The Americans had found and had crossed the Rhine on an unblown bridge at Remagen early in March and had gained another bridge south of Mainz later in that month. Montgomery continued to press ahead with his own plans which included not just crossing in boats but also an airborne drop behind the 'Berlin' bank of the river. Among the letters received which describe the crossing of the Rhine, were ones from T. Bridges, in an RASC unit, R. Maloney and A. Jenkins, both members of the Royal Artillery and extracts from them are reproduced below:

'We were told that the AGRA, which had the task of firing the barrage on our sector, had nearly a thousand targets on which there would be the heaviest concentrations of fire. There were, so far as I remember the figures, 54 confirmed and 70 possible German gun positions; over 40 observation posts, 50 or more headquarters areas, 36 depots, a number of enemy concentration areas and forward routes. All those thousand targets would be bombarded from 01.00hrs until 10.00hrs, according to a precise fire plan. At 21.00hrs the first waves of 51st Highland Division began to cross. The searchlight batteries behind our gun positions shone their beams on to the low cloud so as to produce a pale sort of glow that we called "Monty's Moonlight". We were given an almost continuous running commentary on what was happening. The German artillery fire was heavy but patchy, and there was little counter-battery fire by them. They concentrated more on the boats making the crossing and on the 51st Division's bridgeheads. There was a massive air raid on Wesel. A couple of hundred bombers went in. I read later in *Union Jack,* I think, that the RAF had dropped 1,100 tons of bombs in a couple of minutes, some of them being over 5 tons in weight. Wesel was flattened. In the words of a newspaper report, "The RAF gave a perfect demonstration of night-time, precision bombing." As a Gunner [LAA] I must say how proud I was of being in the Royal Artillery, particularly for the Rhine crossing. As you will know the Luftwaffe, the German Air Force, had not worried us much. From the first days of Normandy we had hardly seen them. By the time we had reached the Meuse [Maas] it was a rare thing to see them. They were said to have attacked and sunk ferries crossing to the far bank of the Rhine during the first crossings, and although we were on full alert at the time we did not go into action at all. When the airborne drop was made there were so many of our fighter planes in the sky escorting the Dakotas and the gliders that it would have been suicide for any German aircraft to attack them. So the LAA and the HAA had little to do. The thing that made me most proud was to see our 5.5s lined up. You must have read of guns standing wheel to wheel. Near us there was a whole regiment of 5.5s lined up just like that. There is a picture of it in the War Museum. That picture says it all. We did not have to worry about German air raids or their artillery fire so the guns are standing in the open and not a camouflage net in sight. No slit-trenches either and the guns are not dug in or have sandbag sangar walls. It is a picture of near victory; of our superiority. No wonder I am proud.'

An account of the Rhine crossing and the fighting on the 'Berlin' bank has been supplied by Lance-Corporal Bagshaw who was a Section commander in an infantry battalion of the 51st Higland Division:

'At the end of March 1945, 5th Battalion, The Seaforth Highlanders, with which I was serving, crossed the River Rhine. The enemy put down a very heavy barrage to try to prevent our crossing, but like all well-trained and seasoned veterans we carried on regardless of all his efforts to try and halt our advance. We were all determined to try to end the war as quickly as we could. I was a veteran of the battle of El Alamein and the Sicilian campaign, like so many men from the famous reformed 51st Highland Division, under Major-General Douglas (Big

Tam) Wimberley. One of the assault boats I was in reached the far side of the Rhine. We marched inland ready to meet enemy attacks, but all was clear. As we approached the town of Isselburg at night, it was alight like something from Dante's *Inferno.* I shall always remember that town as there was no sign of life and we ran quickly to reach the narrow bridge which was minus its wooden flooring. We clambered along the sides with enemy shells coming in close. It felt as if the shells were crawling along the ground toward us, such is one's imagination at night in a battle area. Incidentally, many of the assault boats were lost during the Rhine crossing. We finally formed up under our Company Commander who detailed his platoon commanders to do likewise to our Infantry Section commanders, of which I was one. In the far distance at night I could see a large house alight, with groups of our infantry crossing in front of it and the enemy in the basement of the house busily firing at them. Whilst we were advancing a German plane dropped several butterfly bombs on us. I spotted a shellhole and dived into it. Later on each Section formed up at its prospective defensive position. My Section had the task of holding the bridge that was nearest to my Company HQ. The unfortunate Section on the opposite bridge of the Astrang Canal embankment was in the pillbox nearest to Battalion HQ. We consolidated at approximately 12.30 am and on checking my Section, found that during the enemy shelling of our position, four of my Section had deserted into the night.

'At 2.30 am approx. some 200-odd Germans started to attack towards my Section on the far end of the two bridges, having succeeded in wiping out the other Section – minus the Section commander, who, I later heard had been out on the scrounge at the time. It was a pity that the other unfortunate lads were not out on the scrounge likewise, but such is war. One slip and we pay the extreme penalty for being caught off guard, as they did. My Bren-gunner, Pte Kavanagh, stood up in the middle of the canal bridge road and was firing at the enemy as they tried to rush us. His gun stopped, either due to an empty magazine or to a stoppage. I can't say which it was, and as he tried to remedy matters Jerry fired in his direction and he fell down, mortally wounded in the head. From where I was in my slit-trench opposite him I could see he was dead on hitting at the ground and at the time I was thankful that he wasn't lying down badly wounded yet still alive. I had seen this in many other cases during my various actions in the war. My aim was to make up for the loss of so reliable a comrade as he was to me in my role of Section leader. I had with me a German Schmeisser machine-pistol with two full magazines, which was much better than my Lee Enfield rifle. I discarded this minus its bolt, which I flung in another direction. I waited my time for the enemy to make another dash towards us and I told the last remaining member of my Section to be sure to keep his head down. At last they came towards us in the early dawn light. I fired a whole magazine into them and could hear their screams of pain. Just as I was getting my head down to reload the Schmeisser a machine-gun burst hit me in my left arm, right in the muscle, severing the bone and the radial nerve (as I learned later in hospital in England). I held on to my left wrist to try to ease the fracture and luckily it was all numb. At the same time I told my only companion, Pte George 'Boy' White, who was aged 18 then, to get out and over to Coy HQ which was behind us on the left of a field. He helped me to get out and said "Shall we go by the bridge road?" To this I replied, "No, into the water as the enemy will only shoot us in the back." I was glad to know that my mind was at the top of its form as I needed it badly to try and save both our lives. I didn't even consider how deep was the canal and if it had been too deep I would have drowned. Thank God, it was OK.

'We walked across a field towards a house which was surrounded with barbed wire that was too high for us to get over. This was our Coy HQ and I remember a stretcher-bearer there who was full of the German civilian's wine with the owner looking on dismally as he was drinking the place dry. On reaching this house I must have collapsed, due to loss of blood. I woke up to find myself lying on a double tier bunk. The stretcher-bearer, whose name I didn't know, had tied string or something similar around my arm as a makeshift tourniquet. He asked me about my Bren-gunner, who had been a friend of his. I told him the sad news and he wanted to go out and shoot every bloody Jerry on sight, until I told him I had made them pay for the death of my Bren-gunner. Later on I was taken out to a Bren carrier on a stretcher and our wireless set contacted the artillery to give us covering fire as Jerry was advancing into our area, having now crossed the empty bridges. We had tried so hard to defend those bridges to the last man, with the exception of the cowards of my Section who had deserted us in our hour of need, leaving us to die. On reaching the carrier our mortars were coming too close to where I was lying on my stretcher. With me was that wonderful Padre, Captain J. I. Simpson, MC, who was nicknamed "Ironside" by the men of the 5th Seaforths. He saw to it that I was moved back into the house, having covered me with his own body while the heavy mortaring lasted. I shall always be grateful to so fine and fearless a man. After some delay I was then taken out to an amphibious vehicle known as a "Duck". I was strapped down on top minus the tin hat that I had worn ever since Alamein and right through Sicily, Normandy and so to Germany. Up the road we went at about 60 mph, to the nearest Casualty Clearing Station where I found to my horror that I was the only British wounded. All the rest were Jerries lined up along the pathway and chock-a-block inside with a German Corporal medical orderly busily looking after his own wounded. Coming towards me was an RAMC doctor whom I recognized as being my old TA Medical Officer from when I served with the 2/7th Middlesex Regiment. The MO told me that he would give me some morphia to ease the pain and that I would be flown home after an operation at the main hospital.'

That operation was the first of six which H. J. Bagshaw underwent to save his shattered arm. As was usual in the Service, Lance-Corporal Bagshaw was reduced to the ranks due to his wounds. It was a strange reward to be penalized financially for having been wounded in the service of one's country.

Resistance stiffened along the front of 51st Highland Division as its battalions moved deeper into Germany. The Highlanders were up against the paratroopers of Schlemm's First Airborne Army, many of whom were veterans with years of battle experience. The Scottish infantry battalions were not supported by armour at that time because the ferries bringing the tanks across had been attacked by German aircraft and some had been sunk. The 51st came under fire from SPs firing from the centre of Rees. That town, unlike Wesel, had not been bombed and was a centre of fierce resistance until it was captured.

Winston Churchill reached the Rhine and witnessed the British Army's crossing. One contributor wrote that he had been told that the Prime Minister had urinated in the German river. "He had come a long way, had Churchill. In 1940, he had been made PM at the time of Dunkirk. It was our worst time. Now Britain was on the last lap. Germany would soon be defeated."

Field Marshal Brooke wrote in his memoirs; 'We found a very proud Montgomery, proud because he had set up his TAC HQ for the first time in Germany.' On the following day Churchill witnessed Operation 'Varsity', the air drop on the Berlin side of the Rhine. Brooke records that it was a glorious day and that they had a good view of the crossing between Xanten and Wesel: 'At about 10 am the skies filled with aircraft . . . which disappeared into fog on the eastern side . . . Then the first aircraft came back from the para drop with open doors and trailing ripcord lines . . . About an hour later wave after wave of gliders passed over our heads . . . Then we [now on the Berlin bank] went in two armoured vehicles via Xanten, Marienbaum and Hochwald to a small ridge to the south of Kalkar. Here we had a very good view of where the 51st Division had crossed.'

The *Sunday Express* reporter sent a dispatch on Operation 'Varsity' which included the words: 'It is 1 o'clock German Summer Time. We are flying at just over 1,000 feet. Looking eastwards so far as the eye can see Germany is shrouded in smoke and flames. What is happening all around us in the air, on the ground and on the water is like a futuristic painting of the Day of Judgement. And, indeed, for the Germans on the east bank of the Rhine this is the decisive battle, then this is a day in which every type of invasion is rolled into one. The sky is filled with transport machines, two-engined Dakotas, four-engined Halifaxes which stream across the sky in two columns. I saw the first wave of this aerial armada go in. A row of little dots left each aircraft. They suddenly became larger and then parachute canopies unfolded. In a moment a thousand soldiers were falling to earth . . . The flight in continues as the second wave approaches. Through the window of my observation plane I see the huge machines each towing two gliders on nylon ropes. These are the small American Waco gliders . . . Then follow the large British Horsa machines towed by Halifax bombers . . . They come in hundreds. Their tow ropes are cast off. They begin to descend circling and diving to find a landing place. To the North the next wave of gliders is landing. For miles the fields are covered with red and orange parachutes . . . The gliders carrying men or supplies take risks when they land. I see how some crash into hedges and fences, how some dive into the ground and others run into trees. Men leap from them and run into action.'

The *Daily Telegraph* reported: 'Within four hours we had gained all our objectives and had formed a bridgehead. There were camouflaged 88s in the fields loaded with incendiary shells. There were [German] machine-gun nests and infantry positions in the hedges, but the sight of our assault caused a panic flight.'

With the Allied armies now firmly established on the 'Berlin' bank of the Rhine, the advances began which would end the war in Europe. Churchill, and the British Army had, indeed, come a long way.

War in the Deserts of Africa

On 14 June 1940 Mussolini, the dictator of Fascist Italy, declared war on Great Britain. He gave his Generals in Africa orders to invade Egypt and to seize the Suez Canal. The first advance of the Italian Army, on 13 September, was brought to a halt by his hesitant commanders, after only 60 miles and there was little further action until 6 December, when Archibald Wavell launched a counter-blow. His offensive had been planned to be only a short, sharp jab for it seemed unlikely that a major assault could succeed by a British force which was outnumbered by ten to one. Boldness in war is often rewarded and Wavell's offensive flung back the Italian Army in total disorder. By early February 1941, it seemed likely that the thrusting drives by the British Army of the Nile would destroy the Fascist empire in Libya and Tripolitania. In an effort to bolster his flagging Italian ally, Hitler sent a German force to Tripoli and the arrival of Erwin Rommel and the Afrika Korps changed the situation dramatically. Rommel was able to halt Wavell's understrength and overstretched force. A German offensive during March 1941, drove back the British and fighting in the desert then swung backwards and forwards, one time in favour of the Germans and then to the advantage of the Eighth Army, as the British force was now named.

At the end of May 1942, Rommel resolved to pre-empt a new British offensive by launching an attack of his own. His plan would avoid a direct, frontal assault against the 'Gazala Line' as the British positions were called. That line was a series of 'boxes', each defended in Brigade strength by an all-arms group, and protected by extensive minefields. They were, in effect, contemporary versions of the British Square. Rommel's plan was for his German/Italian army to drive southwards, deep into the desert, to turn the landward flank of the Gazala Line and then strike northwards so as to come up behind the 'boxes'. Each of these would be attacked and destroyed in turn and then through the gaps which had been made his Panzers would drive towards Cairo and the Canal. His plan nearly succeeded and Eighth Army retreated in an undignified scramble towards Cairo and Alexandria in a flight that was thereafter known as 'The Gazala Gallop'. The Axis thrust towards the principal cities of Egypt failed to smash through British prepared positions at El Alamein for now it was the Axis forces that were overstretched and tired. Certainly, they were not strong enough to force the Alamein defences, only 60 miles or so from the Canal. There was then a lull in operations as both sides built up their strength for the decisive battle. In September there was an unsuccessful Axis attempt at Alam Halfa to repeat the success of the Gazala operation. When that offensive was destroyed Rommel strengthened his defences to meet the British assault which he knew would come in against him.

On 23 October, the guns of Eighth Army opened a barrage of First World War intensity. There were tank and infantry battles climaxing in a charge by 9th Armoured Brigade to crush an Axis gun line. This succeeded and by 5 November, the German and Italian forces were in full retreat. Three days later Anglo-American divisions landed in Algeria and had soon marched into Tunisia. Between Eighth Army in Libya and the Anglo-American forces in Tunisia the Axis armies were certain to be trapped. The end was never in doubt and although there was to be hard fighting before the campaign in Africa ended, end it did in an Allied victory on 13 May 1943. The entire German/Italian host passed into captivity. The Fascist empire in Africa was destroyed and the campaign had demonstrated that the Anglo-American Allies could plan together and fight together.

LIFE IN THE EIGHTH ARMY

Many of those who served in the 'old' Eighth Army in the desert recall with pleasure the time they spent there. They wrote of open skies, beautiful dawns, spectacular sunsets and the peace that was to be found up in the 'Blue'. Life was uncomplicated and basic – there was little that war could destroy nor too many people in danger of being killed – always excepting the enemy, who was looked upon almost with affection. Rommel was so popular with Eighth Army that an Order was issued, which in effect, forbade British soldiers to think kindly of him and the Afrika Korps. Roy Cooke served as an infantryman in 5th Battalion, 51st Highland Division, and his recollections of life in the desert are representative of most of the men who served in the old Eighth Army:

'What was day-to-day life like in the desert? Despite the ever-present possibility of hostile enemy action, on the whole life was a very healthy one. There was plenty of fresh air and sunshine and there were miles of absolutely nothing in every direction. If you were lucky enough to be stationed within sight of the Mediterranean you occasionally were able to go for a dip in the deep blue sea. Before the battle of El Alamein it was quite common for British troops to swim naked in the Med and to see a mile or two further to the west, men of Rommel's Afrika Korps doing exactly the same. At Alamein we had the single line Alexandria–Mersa Matruh railway which was later pushed on almost to Tobruk. From June to October 1942, Rommel made good use of this as far as he was able, despite constant RAF interference. About a mile nearer the coast there was the famous desert road, known in Libya as the Via Balbia. The Italians had been working on this in 1940, from the frontier at Capuzzo/Sollum towards Sidi Barrani via Buq-Buq. Then, between the coast road and the sea there were dazzling white sand dunes, whereas further inland the sand was more yellowish in colour. Before the battle of Alamein we lived in what were known as "boxes". These were areas that were surrounded by several coils of Dannert wire for all-round defence. Once inside these "boxes" our life was fairly uneventful, apart from the occasional unexpected Stuka raid. In fact, one of our locations was simply known as "Stuka valley". We slept in holes in the ground for protection against the shellfire, etc., and every morning and evening there was "stand-to" for a certain period. The nights were bitterly cold and if on the move Reveille was before dawn. We had to wash and shave in ice-cold water with our frozen fingers trying to hold an often blunt razor. Our food was very basic. Plenty of bully and hardtack Army biscuits and, of course, during the daytime it became extremely hot so that if a tin of bully were opened, the contents dried up very quickly. Nearly all our food was in tins; butter, bacon, sausages, cheese, potatoes, rice pudding and Australian tinned fruit. Rommel's men enjoyed this whenever they happened to capture one of our supply dumps. At times water was severely rationed and was often less than a gallon per day per man, for all purposes. On a very cold morning it was not unknown for men to drink half a mug of tea and to save the rest for hot shaving water. Further up in the desert the water was often brackish or very salt, with the result that a mug of tea with milk in it just curdled.

'There is a very famous photograph in the Imperial War Museum's photographic archives of two Eighth Army men standing beside a 3-tonner lorry which has a teapot painted on the door with the message, "When in doubt. Brew-up." Now the expression "brew-up" could have two meanings. One was when a tank caught fire, but it usually meant the time-honoured Eighth Army "tea ceremony". When on the move no self-respecting 3-tonner or 15cwt truck would think of setting off without its "brew can" dangling at the rear. Perhaps I ought to go into more detail. Jerry (our affectionate ?? name for our enemy), as always, was much better equipped than ourselves for war. We in Eighth Army had what were commonly known as "flimsies" to carry petrol. These were made at the Base in Egypt and as the word "flimsy" implies, the tins were made of very thin metal with a flimsy handle on top. The result was that more petrol was lost on the way than ever was poured into any petrol tank. Jerry, on the other hand, was superbly equipped with extremely robust large cans which have ever since been known by British and US troops simply as Jerricans. There were two distinct types: the most common ones being painted green and marked "Kraftstoff" and "Feuergefaehrlich" (Fuel; Inflammable). The other type had a big white cross painted on the side with the one word "Wasser" or "Trinkwasser". Needless to say, these Jerricans were much sought after by the Eighth Army. They each held about 5 gallons and it wasn't long before the Allies were making their own Jerricans, though needless to say, the German pattern was far superior to our imitation model. The German one had an ingenious catch which locked the can and allowed air to enter the can whilst it was being poured. The Allied model just had a round cap which was not nearly as efficient as the German one.

'To revert to the "tea making ceremony". When in convoy, whether on the coastal road or far out in the desert – commonly known as the Blue – there came a time when a halt was called and the cry "brew-up" was given. Previously a good fairly robust empty "flimsy" would have been selected and cut in half. One half would then be almost filled with sand and petrol was poured on top. The mixture was then stirred with a bayonet as if stirring up cement. Another flimsy half would be ready filled with water. A match would then be thrown into the sand-cum-petrol mixture and this would blaze merrily away. The other half, containing water, would then be placed sideways on top and as the water came to the boil, a handful of tea-leaves would be added. As soon as it was strong enough, mugs would be produced together with tinned milk and some sugar. Tea was the common Eighth Army "brew". Coffee was unheard of.

'Although day-to-day life "up the Blue" was on the whole very healthy, there were problems such as Gyppo Tummy, desert sores and, of course, the fly menace. Gyppo Tummy was quite common; a form of diarrhoea which often turned into dysentery. Desert sores were quite a problem, If you had a graze on an arm, finger, knee, etc., it was almost impossible to keep the sand out of it and in consequence it festered and became filled with pus. Flies were an absolute menace, especially before the El Alamein battle. The problem became absolutely impossible when trying to eat, for example, a piece of hardtack biscuit with jam or marmalade on it. It was almost as bad trying to drink a mug of tea. However many flies you killed or swatted, reinforcements would be on their way. I believe that Rommel's men in particular, suffered very badly from both Gyppo Tummy and flies. Also a flesh wound would soon become infested and swell up. I myself was slightly wounded at Alamein but carried on, only to be evacuated for that very reason. Hygiene was of the utmost importance in the desert, especially when we were static. Fresh latrines had to be dug and old ones filled in. Out in the Blue, when Mother Nature called, you just borrowed a shovel and went for a walk well away from the others. The Western Desert has often been compared with the sea, as far as navigation was concerned. When off the coastal road we always travelled in convoy, as at sea, with a navigating officer in the lead. At night it was very easy to become lost, even over a distance of 50 yards or so. Major-General Wimberley, GOC, 51st Highland Division, once spent hours in the dark trying to walk from one place to another. A compass bearing was essential.

'During Alamein and afterwards the British infantrymen often tried to capture a German MG 34 or 42, their quick-firing machine-gun, commonly known to us as Spandaus, so as to add considerably to our fire power. Sunsets and sunrises were spectacular in the Western Desert. One moment the sun was there and the very next moment it had sunk below the horizon. The opposite happened in the morning. You could literally see the sun shoot up from below the horizon. This had certain advantages and disadvantages, as in the early morning Rommel's men were dazzled by the early sunlight and in the evening it was the Eighth Army who had the sun in their eyes.'

Roy Cooke considered that the worst day of the Battle of El Alamein was 2 November:

'Having gained our objectives during Operation "Supercharge", [the second stage of the El Alamein offensive] we were forced to lie out in the open desert, unable to dig down more than a couple of inches as the ground was rock-hard. At dawn a mass of our Sherman tanks came through and over us – we had to watch it or we'd all be crushed alive – and the whole of that day was spent in the midst of a terrific tank battle at Tel el Aqqaqir. Rommel's Panzer Armee still had quite a few tanks available. I think that the greatest menace was his 88s and other anti-tank guns, as by the time sunset arrived you saw nothing but brewed-up tanks as far as one could see; both his and ours. Rommel was later to forecast that D-Day in Normandy would be the "longest day", but 2 November 1942 was without doubt MY longest day. I was expecting that fatal shell or mortar bomb at any second and was never so thankful in my life as when nightfall finally came.'

Another soldier of the 5th Seaforths who remembered that day was R. Stuart Wilson:

'I remember seeing Captain Farquhar Macrae, MC, our battalion medical officer, in a captured Jerry truck picking up both British and enemy wounded in the midst of a very heavy shelling and surrounded by 88mm air bursts. An ambulance he was driving was knocked out previously and it had wounded men on board. During the last big attack which resulted in our breakthrough, we were the most forward platoon in the entire battalion and when we were digging in after taking our objectives an Aussie soldier from 9th Division wandered into our positions and proceeded to dig-in with one of our lads. In the afternoon of that day (2 November) Jerry put down a number of very heavy "stonks" on top of us. One shell landed almost in the slit-trench dug by the Seaforth and the Aussie. One of them was killed outright and the other had some dreadful wounds and died soon afterwards. I shall always remember his awful screams. The strange thing about this was that both the Seaforth and the Aussie had the same name. Later on our Platoon Sergeant was killed, just behind me.'

Roy Cooke remembers how well dug-in were Rommel's Panzers:

'We saw several sloping holes which had previously held hull-down Panzers. When his army finally withdrew we stayed behind for a day or two then followed up the famous desert highway, the Via Balbia, in three-tonner trucks passing other three-tonners coming back the other way, crammed with Rommel's men who had surrendered. They all wore the Afrika Korps long-peaked caps and tropical uniforms with lace-up boots. Then on past the famous white mosque at Sidi abd el Rahman, which was reputed to have been Rommel's HQ during the battle of Alamein, and on to Fuka with masses of smashed Luftwaffe fighter planes on the airfield. We bypassed Mersa Matruh and all along the highway were many burnt-out Italian trucks, both Army and Italian Air Force, also some Italian tanks which were sometimes referred to as "mobile coffins" as they were pretty well useless. We finally halted at Mersa Brega, as Rommel had decided to make a stand at El Agheila.'

It was at Mersa Brega that Roy, who had served with 'I' Section of his Battalion, was posted to 'B' Company to bring it up to strength:

'One night I was selected to join a recce patrol and we emptied our pockets beforehand so as not to help Jerry in the event of capture or death. We set out as it was getting dark under a platoon officer who was a very keen type. He detailed me to be the "Get-away man", which meant that should we run into trouble, an ambush, etc., my job was to try to get back in order to say what had happened. It was a very still night and as we were quite close to the sea we would clearly hear the waves breaking on the shore. It was quite dark and we could barely see anything. Suddenly we came across a steep slope and our platoon commander motioned for us to stay at the bottom of the slope while he silently crept up to the top. This we did and he very soon came down again. He made it clear that we were to withdraw without delay. Later on he was able to tell us that he had peeped over the top of the slope only to see that Jerry was just a few yards on the other side. We had been very lucky not to have been spotted. Later we found somewhere to spend the rest of the night as our officer decided to await daybreak before attempting to re-enter our lines, just in case we happened to be mistaken for the enemy. Later on we were badly held up just beyond Homs, at a place called Corradini. Here the 90th Light Division ambushed us. We called it "The battle of the Hills" and our ultimate objective was nicknamed "Edinburgh Castle", as it looked just like it in the darkness. We put in a pre-dawn attack and had many casualties. I was one of them and was evacuated down the line from one CCS to another before being taken out by tender to a hospital ship at Benghazi and finishing up at Alexandria in a very comfortable hospital.'

A. G. Bell was with an artillery regiment and recalled the winter campaign of 1941 as seen by a gunner:

'This was the start of what was called the "Second Push". We set off up the desert road as far as Mersah Matruh and then turned south on to the track which led eventually 200 miles away to the oasis of Siwa. As soon as we got on to the Siwa track we fanned out into what was called "Desert Formation", several columns wide and with about 100 yards between vehicles in all directions. After three days we joined 1st South African Division which we were to support. We took our positions in this formation and the entire division moved forward in desert formation, a most fantastic sight. Thousands of vehicles as far as the eye could see in every direction, and disappearing into the heat haze and looking as though they were driving in the sky, all keeping their station 100 yards apart, all travelling on the same compass bearing, each with its little plume of dust behind it. The guns were in the centre, Bren-carriers in front, the soft vehicles further back and all around the outside the OPs and the armoured scout cars. And so we travelled first south then eventually west, through the wire and finally turned north in what was to become the classical desert manoeuvre of a hook round the lightly held southern enemy flank. During the afternoon the guns dropped into action. The sun had already set and the light was fading fast, but the OP ACK of the other Troop went forward with his Troop Commander to make contact with a squadron of tanks. They got to what they thought was the correct map reference and dismounted to check, spreading the map out on the bonnet. The squadron of tanks was there alright, but the voices calling "come here" didn't sound very English and the Troop Commander ordered the driver to keep the engine running as he didn't like the situation. Eventually one of the soldiers in the tanks gave the game away by shouting "Avanti". Immediately, everybody leapt on board and the truck belted away taking slit-trenches and other obstacles in its stride and came racing back to the guns which then fired their first rounds, hopefully, at the Itie tanks. This was the kind of confusion which was to become the regular pattern for the whole of the rest of that part of the campaign.'

The Gazala Battles: Summer 1942

By the summer of 1942, the Germans had taken over the direction of the war in Africa. There was, nominally, an Italian Commander-in-Chief, but the *de facto* leader was Erwin Rommel, the Desert Fox, who had arrived in the Italian colonies during February 1941, and who had stamped his image immediately on the fighting. Aware that the Eighth Army was about to launch an offensive against him, he pre-empted that assault by an offensive against what was known as the Gazala position. Rommel's plan was to turn Eighth Army's flank, come up behind the main body and strike it in the back. Rommel made his move on 26 May 1942. There followed days of hard and wasteful fighting for both sides, but then on 12 June, Eighth Army suffered a disaster. Rommel's two Panzer Divisions acting in concert, smashed the British armoured reserve in what became known as the "Battle of the Cauldron". When that day of combat ended Eighth Army's strength had been reduced to just 70 'runners'. The Cauldron was not only a disaster for the British armour; both the infantry and the artillery also suffered grievously. The destruction of 3rd battery of 28th Field Regiment is described by Captain R. A. Doyle, in a piece he wrote for his unit publication, *This was your Regiment*:

'I remember that day as clearly as if it were yesterday. A Sunday paper of 7 June was headlined "Fury rages in Devil's cauldron", but this fell short of reality. I was there with the 3rd Field Battery, RA and it was the last day there was a 3rd Field Battery for us. Clearest of all I recollect the sound of German solid shot, whirring through the air in their strange throbbing ricochets, perhaps because these signalled the new day's coming and portended its finale. We huddled behind the guns, half a mile east of the Tamar Ridge where, yesterday, the attacking armoured brigades and our infantry had been hardly dealt with by Panzers and 88s. At nightfall the weary Crusader tanks clattered their way rearwards through our defensive positions. The guns of D Troop fanned out in an arc facing west and by each gun and in the Command Post, artillerymen crouched in shallow rocky trenches at best only a few feet deep in this iron rock, where tools and hands were battered and bruised in wresting a few inches extra from mother earth; to whom many of us were soon to return. High-explosives we were accustomed to, both in giving and receiving, but there was something uncanny about these heavy bolts of steel flashing down on us from a crest, hazy and laden with dust and smoke so that we could not see to retaliate. We sat in our holes. For an hour death thudded among us. One [shell] crunched down in front of me and came jerking, trundling and rolling up to where I sat by the gun position signaller. I put out my cautious hand and the burning warmth of the still hot metal seared my finger. A solid shot would thrash in one's face like a burst tomato.

'But it was fire and high-explosive which drew first blood. Shells dropped to burst graciously and harmlessly with their bright flash, spume of sulphurous smoke and lively crack, but they drew nearer and became dangerous. One of our ammunition trucks was hit and the energy of a hundred shells was dissipated in brilliant pyrotechnics. To the south and south-east many vehicles were now on fire, fingers and pillars of blue-black smoke eddying upwards in a motionless air, a familiar sight to desert soldiers. And still the shellfire increased. I walked over to No. 1 gun to have a chat to the sergeant for a few minutes. A yard or so in front of me the Troop Commander returned from a useless observation post and scanned the crest with binoculars from a meagre slit-trench. Over at No. 4 gun some of the detachment were starting to disperse the long, brass, cordite-filled cartridge cases so that all could not be hit together. The Battery Commander and two other officers were nearby. The Major stood on top of the limber amongst the flying metal in an effort to pierce the haze; then the blow fell. There was no gradual merging of life with death; they coincided instantanteously. A snapping roar and a huge sheet of flame pulled all eyes to No. 4 gun. An enemy shell had dropped right on the cartridges of cordite and had exploded. The ferocious heat of the flame instantly roasted to death the gunner bending over them and his comrade was pierced through the neck by a sliver of steel. I rushed across to meet a young soldier still brave and cheerful, reeling away with gory wounds in his head and body and half-helped, half-carried him to an RHQ truck, just in the rear. I can still see now the bloody knots of flesh and steel driven into his skull. As I returned to the scene the two officers were being loaded into a truck, the one pale and unconscious beneath a blanket, the other with thighs smashed to pulp. The Major, wounded, having been taken off, was hit again before he reached the Aid Post. Of these none lived. A signaller had a hunk of flesh knocked out of his back and the gun's bombardier, his officers and comrades decimated in a second, was dazed. A few paces to the right the driver of our Bren-Carrier was wounded in the foot so we placed him for safety inside a knocked-out tank. The day was not a few hours old and so far we had not fired a single round, yet death was already whittling deep.

'Hardly had the wounded left when a senior officer drove into our position and barked an order, "Pull out immediately to your old position and engage tanks." Within seconds the tractors were up from the nearby wagon lines and as I hung on to the door and framework of the first to move off, I experienced a strange mixture of exhilaration, excitement and calmness as the roaring tractor raced the few hundred yards to action. Within seconds we had unhooked the gun, swung it around on its metal firing platform and, as the other guns came in on the left, our first shot, fired over open sights, crashed out. About half a mile away lay a small group of Rommel's tanks, two Mk IIs and a Mk IV. At that range the odds were on the side of the Panzers as they lay at the extreme range of effective field gun range and presenting the smallest and thickest part of their epidermis; the front. They fired back with their 75mm guns at men protected intermittently only by the thin steel of the gun shield. When we had fired three rounds there was a deafening explosion and I felt my face blasted and riddled. For a fraction of a second I thought I was shattered. I clapped both hands to my skin and brought them away again stained with blood and grit. I worked the muscles of my face but miraculously felt unhurt. A German shell had burst directly under the shield, puncturing the nearside tyre and slicing steel rashers from the firing platform. The layer collapsed in his seat with a faint groan, the base of his spine and the top of his buttocks a bloody exposed mass of red flesh slashed raw. My face had been splattered by gobbets of pulverized tissue. Two minutes earlier he had rubbed his hands with glee at the prospect of action; now he was dead and in an amazing way had shielded me from the blast as I stood on the left of the trail a couple of feet behind him. Beside him the ammunition gunner dropped lifeless. I don't know what killed him as I could see no mark. The loader was hit in the wrist and a little Scotsman, the last gunner, went deaf as a door post. With a lance-bombardier I dragged the two bodies clear of the gun. As I bent over to grip the layer's ankles he gave a death grunt. As the body slid backwards over the sand it left behind a large shining slice of liver glistening with drops of blood. I kicked sand over it so that the others would not see. These happenings all occurred within seconds and in a fraction of the time it takes to tell. The Panzers were still firing.

'A signaller leapt forward and with the lance-bombardier we got the gun firing again. One laying, one loading and myself ramming the shells into the breech and slipping outside the shield to observe the shots. Then we changed and I layed and fired. We were all quite mad, swearing and cursing the Germans for what they had done to our comrades. One gun versus one tank and we were all oblivious to all else; E Troop was pulling in on our right, more tanks and enemy guns on the ridge. All we saw was the front of one stationary tank. I let the air out of the other tyre to level the gun and its movements on the wheels became sluggish. To make matters worse the extractors, which are used to expel the hot and expanded cartridge cases from the breach, cracked and slid over the lips of the case. Each time this happened the signaller had to rush round me to the front of the gun and throw the rammer down the muzzle to knock the case out of the breech. The ground was hard and dusty and the teeth of the firing platform failed to bite the earth. Each time we fired, a cloud of sand was raised and the whole gun slithered back about six inches. Once or twice the trail was brought up against the layer's body and I had to drag it clear. Suddenly, the firing died down. The action seemed to have lasted hours but it was probably more like ten minutes. Our adversaries still squatted quiet and motionless in the same position, damaged, out of ammunition or just not wanting to come in any nearer. There was a long lull after the storm during which we licked our wounds. Half a mile to the north lay a crest of German tanks. We had no tanks and hardly any infantry left. Our casualties in gunners was already high. We scraped away at the ground trying to protect ourselves, but digging was impossibly hard. At the best we got down six inches so we placed the broken body of the layer in the rude and shallow grave and scraped back the earth over him. His best friend, the signaller, made a rough cross from a piece of wood and pencilled on his name. The other body, lying motionless nearby, was covered with a blanket. We said no prayers and removed no identity discs; we ourselves were still too close to death. The Germans were masters of the high ground and had perfect observation on us. More and more tanks assembled in that threatening arc. Through binoculars I could see a few of the crews come out of the tanks for a smoke and a breather. All we could do was to sit and wait for them to come in. None of us expected to see the day out but nobody seemed unduly worried.

'A few Bofors guns pulled in to our right rear. Away to the left were a couple of anti-tank two-pounders. Here and there were Indians in weapon pits; Brens against 75mm guns in armour. On rising ground to the east our other Troop had come into action. Solitary vehicles moved around on the flanks, probing for a getaway. The Germans scorned to fire a shot. The Troop Commander, observing from a point just behind me, shouted "Tank Alert". As the Panzers moved in we leaped to the guns and opened fire. Within seconds a hellish battle developed. A quick side glance showed E Troop shooting it out with tanks closing in on them. Those advancing on my Troop eased into a fold of ground and, halting, poured in a hail of shells and bullets. At the same time the German artillery opened up and they had our range to a yard. At intervals of a few seconds there was a rushing roar, followed by a black smoking crash as the shells burst in the air about thirty feet above our heads. These were quite terrifying and distracted our attention from the bullets hissing past the gun shield. At each crash we crouched down and then went on firing. It was indeed a devil's cauldron of flame, explosion, heat, cordite, fumes, fire and death. We had fired a dozen rounds when there was a wild crashing rush over the gun and with dazed shock I saw a stream of blood pouring from a channel gouged across my wrist, soaking shirt and shorts and spattering on to my boots. I thought a main artery was severed and turned to the Troop Commander for a field dressing. Even today I can still hear myself saying queerly, "They got me, Joe." As I walked towards him another rush of blood came from my thigh where a jagged piece of metal, ricocheting upwards from the trail drove itself into my flesh above the knee. I felt no real pain, just shocked a bit and thought I was bleeding to death. The little Scotsman was hit in the arm. There were no bandages left so Joe tied my wrist up in a brown silk handkerchief. The Panzers at last crushed the guns and the few survivors were defenceless. As I was helped towards the collecting post for wounded, I passed a tragic sight. A troop of four guns laid out in action, breeches still open, trails littered about with cartridge cases, silent as a grave. At No. 2 gun a corpse, white and naked save for a pair of boots, was draped like a gruesome pinwheel over the right gun wheel, head and arms hanging to the ground. This was the symbol of our defeat. Four regiments of field artillery were decimated on this day. My Troop was one of the many which died thus; without fame or mention, but simply in the line of duty.'

Another soldier of the 28th was Bombardier J. P. Blackmore, who served with E Sub Section of 1st (Blazers) Battery of that Regiment:

'My story begins on the night of 5 June 1942. We were artillery support to 5th Indian Division forming the Knightsbridge Box, and for six days we had fought and held the box. We had now been told to expect strong tank attacks from first light. We stood-to an hour before dawn, this being the normal practice through the whole Army. At about 10 o'clock when we were trying to make a brew of tea, what remained of some of the tank crews and anti-tank gunners came through our position, most of them on foot and all looking rather grim. At about midday what remained of the infantry withdrew through our position. The order came "Tank alert" and with it the order to destroy all sights on the gun, less the telescopes. All personal documents, letters, photographs and pay books were to be immediately burned. We laid our gun roughly in the centre of our allotted anti-tank zone. It was now a matter of team work if we were to fight and survive. I set a thousand yards on the telescope and laid on the far escarpment. We waited and weren't kept waiting long. The first enemy tanks nosed their way slowly over the escarpment, paused and then seemed to slide down the other side one by one. I laid on as many as three tanks at once through my telescope and it was agony to keep my hand from the firing lever. Before we fired one round we had a direct hit on the limber. We were hit again, this time on the front of the recuperator, followed by another hit on the axle which blew the gun wheel off. This was rather surprising because that was where the Major was sitting in the layer's seat. The gun wheel sort of slowly rolled away and laid down, and I must have watched it fascinated. The next thing I knew was the Major on his feet shouting "It's every man for himself."

'We attended to our wounded and made them as comfortable as possible. In the meantime the enemy were occupying our positions. The nearest tank from us was about eight yards. I remember looking at it spellbound. I can see the number painted on its side today as I did then – 78. The tank commander spared us a glance, but the follow-up infantry took more interest. One of the German NCOs started giving us instructions or orders. None of us could speak German and he couldn't speak English. It was standstill until from out of the blue appeared a German officer who could speak reasonably good English. He said that the wounded would be attended to as soon as possible and that all those who could walk should evacuate themselves from the battle area immediately and pointed the direction in which we were to march. As best we could, with the walking wounded, we struggled our way through the German positions, infantry, anti-tank guns digging in, right down into the Cauldron itself. There appeared to be a German Brigade headquarters close by. In the distance was seen coming towards the HQ several German vehicles. They drew to a halt and as the dust cleared everyone around the HQ seemed to shoot up as if they had been given an injection. I took a close look at the person who was gripping the handrails of a half-track and leaning forward there could be no mistake, the cause of all our troubles, General Rommel himself. With him, was his staff, a half-track, a wireless truck, a couple of queer things like Volkswagen and an eight-wheeled armoured car. The commander of the brigade that we were close to gave the Nazi salute and Rommel returned it with a salute to the peak of his cap. Everyone looked at him as if he was God. He wasn't tall. He appeared to be squat and his uniform wasn't hard to describe. The German officer's cap and what appeared rather funny, a pair of British anti-gas goggles around the top. What we could see of him was covered with a leather overcoat and dangling from his neck what looked like a cross. He seemed to give his orders in a quick guttural voice and now and again a wave of his hand. In a few minutes it was all over. Heels clicked, salutes were given and Rommel and his staff were already in a cloud of dust. I think it dawned on us for the first time that we were POWs. I think we must have met it with mixed feelings; happy that we were still alive and for us the war was over.'

In fact Bombardier Blackmore's war was far from over. Some days later, after incredible adventures, he managed to escape back to the British lines.

Tank Attack in the Desert

Such was the confidence of the Axis commanders in those heady days of June and July 1942, that Mussolini flew to Tripoli intending to lead the Victory Parade through Cairo and Alexandria mounted on a white stallion. It was a vain journey. The attacks of Panzerarmee Afrika were halted at a series of prepared defences called the Alamein Line. The pursuit battle had so exhausted the enemy forces that they would not be able to fight their way through the British positions until they had recouped their strength.

Throughout July Eighth Army attacked at various points along the Alamein Line and their assaults were met by Axis counter-attacks just as thrusts by the Italian/German units were repulsed by the British and Dominions Army. The fighting was to gain tactically important ridges and the tank battles which were a feature of the bitter struggles wore down the Axis strength. On 21 July 1942, the Afrika Korps, the core of Panzerarmee, had only 42 'runners' and the strength of the Italian tank force was 30 vehicles. Although there were a further one hundred German machines under repair, the Eighth Army had in 1st Armoured Division alone, no fewer than 170 'runners' and with the newly arrived 23rd Armoured Brigade there were another 150. The tide of battle was turning in favour of Auchinleck's army.

On one fateful day in July, that British advantage in numbers was reduced when the armour made a stupid blunder. Not that this particular instance was seen as anything new or exceptional by the infantry who felt that blunders were what the tank regiments seemed always to make. Mutual hostility existed between the armour and the Foot amounting almost to a hatred. R. Cooper, 50th (Tyne Tees) Division:

'There was a feeling among the infantry units of Eighth Army that whenever our tanks were needed they were never there. We felt let down by them. At the height of a battle our tanks would suddenly roar away leaving us defenceless against the Panzers. If we had known then, as we know now, that they were going to refuel or to load up with ammunition or that they were regrouping, we would have understood. As it was nobody told us anything and all we knew was that our tanks were dashing away trailing clouds of dust and that presently along would come Rommel's boys.'

John Bucknall, who had been in the desert since the first battles, was on duty on the day of the armoured blunder:

'Our tank people never seemed to learn. Time after time Rommel would entice the regiments on to a line of dug in 88s. Our tank commanders seemed unable to grasp this tactic. One thing was certain when fighting Jerry; one mistake and you were dead. On 22 or 23 July, I am not certain which day it was, I was on duty in Cairo HQ, when a staff officer came out of the Signals Office looking as white as a sheet. Really ghastly. The word soon spread. We had lost an entire armoured brigade in a couple of hours. Only later did I learn that the 23rd Armoured Brigade, fresh out of Blighty, had gone in at the charge to support the New Zealander's attack.'

The New Zealand Division had been ordered to take Ruweisat Ridge which lies about halfway between El Alamein station in the north and the impassable Qattara Depression in the south. Whoever held Ruweisat was in the dominant position. In the bitter fighting to take it, the New Zealand Division lost 700 men and it was during the battle that 23rd Armoured Brigade was committed to 'lift' the New Zealanders on to the objective. John Bucknall:

'The 23rd Brigade had been in the Middle East for only ten or so days. They hadn't had a chance to get their knees brown. Why that unit was ever chosen to make the attack, Heaven alone knows. I have heard it said that the Prime

Minister insisted they be put straight into battle. He didn't or wouldn't realize that it is not just the climate to which you have to become accustomed. You have to learn the desert, and the 23rd hadn't. They did not know about terrain or about the Jerries, and that inexperienced brigade was put in to support the Kiwis in a crucial operation. According to what I heard, and what I have read since confirms what I heard, the regiments charged, just as they would have made a cavalry attack. They had no idea of wireless procedures and because of that they couldn't be told that immediately ahead of them was an unswept minefield. Within minutes the charge had been brought to a halt as tanks blew up one after the other and as the tanks in the second line tried to pass those which had already been blown up, they too ran over mines and were destroyed. The leading regiments lost fourteen tanks in about as many minutes and not one of them had fired a shot because there was no enemy to be seen. The charge had halted in the middle of that minefield and nobody knew it, but the tanks were halted almost under the muzzles of a German anti-tank gun line. As usual, Jerry's positions were well sited, well dug-in and well camouflaged. His gunners had a sitting target. A whole brigade of Valentine tanks, more than a hundred of them, immobile, within range and bewildered by what happened.'

'Then the Jerry anti-tank guns opened up and while they were in action the 88s, which had been hidden behind a ridge, came forward and formed line. On either flank of the gun line the Panzers formed up and under that combined barrage the 23rd Brigade was cut to pieces. In post-battle reports, so I heard, the officers of the brigade complained that the Germans had fired on tank crews making their way to the rear after their vehicles had been knocked out. Those officers were still mentally on schemes on Salisbury Plain. The brigade had begun its "Charge of the Light Brigade" attack at about 8 in the morning. By midday it had been destroyed. It had advanced no farther than five miles. Only eleven Valentines got out from that shambles.'

In addition to the 99 tanks lost with 23rd Armoured Brigade, Eighth Army had suffered other casualties that day. A total of 131 machines; 40 per cent of its total strength had been wiped out. Truly could the planners at Eighth Army write on 27 July 1942, in an Appreciation of the situation in the Western Desert, 'None of the formations of Eighth Army is sufficiently well trained for offensive operations. The Army needs either a reinforcement of trained formations or a quiet period in which to train.' It got both when Montgomery took over Eighth Army. He insisted upon, and was given, reinforcements and time to train them. The result was the Battle of El Alamein; the last victory by an independent British Army during the war.

El Alamein: November 1942

The ex-soldier's view of the Battle of El Alamein is coloured by the arm of service to which he belonged. To the tankmen it was the charge by 9th Armoured Brigade across the Axis gun lines which broke the enemy. The infantry and the sappers consider their mine-lifting activities and attacks as the most important considerations. The gunners believe that it was the barrages they fired which destroyed the morale of the German and Italian troops. A. G. Bell, who served in an artillery regiment, gives lectures to local Territorial Army on his wartime service, part of which was spent in the desert.

'The build-up of troops, vehicles and equipment [in the summer of 1942] created a great air of expectancy and when Churchill made a surprise visit to the front we knew that great things were afoot. At last, on the morning of 23 October, my officer came around with General Montgomery's latest order of the day and said that in fact tonight was the night. He said that if we cared to go over to his dug-out, which was on higher ground, at about 9 o'clock that evening we should have a good view of the start of the battle. The full moon was up as I walked across to Captain Monk's dug-out. There was sporadic firing up and down the line so as to give Jerry the impression that this was just like any other night. By 9.30 p.m. there was total silence. We sat in deathly silence as the minutes ticked away and then at twenty to ten all hell was let loose. No less than 1,500 guns on that 10-mile front opened up simultaneously and continued pouring shells on selected targets for ten minutes. There was another ten minutes' silence to allow the guns to be re-layed. Then they spoke out again, this time in a creeping barrage behind which the infantry were to advance. All the details were explained to us so that we could appreciate what was going on. Clouds of dust were expected which might cause confusion, so for the artillery a number of searchlights were switched on pointing vertically to act as aiming-points. For the infantry who might lose direction the Bofors guns were to fire a burst of tracer shells every five minutes on fixed bearings. Gaps were to be created in the minefields by flail tanks which would be followed by Engineers with mine-detectors and behind them more Engineers with iron posts and white tape to mark the cleared routes. In due course the infantry advanced and on the Highland Division's sector the troops were led in by regimental pipers.'

In the Mountains of Tunisia, 1942-3

The Anglo-American landings in French North Africa brought their forces behind Rommel's desert army. It is true that in November 1942, the Allied formations in Algeria and Tunisia were few in number and more than a thousand miles from the desert. But the Anglo-American forces would grow in strength and would then begin to drive down upon the Axis hosts. Between the Allies in Tunisia and Eighth Army in the desert, the German/Italian Panzerarmee would be destroyed. Hitler's response was to rush in troops, principally airborne detachments, who created and held a bridgehead perimeter. The story of the war in Tunisia from November 1942 until May 1943, is of German attempts to hold that bridgehead and of Allied attempts to smash it and, thereby, to bottle-up the Axis forces. The German troops who landed at Tunis airport on 9 November flung out fighting patrols which raced for and seized the dominant high ground to the west of Tunis. Medjez el Bab was the key to the campaign, but just outside that little town rose a high and isolated mountain peak which the British knew as 'Longstop'. The Germans called it 'Christmas Mountain' because of the battle which is described by E. W. Fitness, of 2nd Battalion, Coldstream Guards.

'In the last week of December 1942, we felt that something big was afoot. The Company Commander's conference ended our speculation. We were to attack after nightfall on 23 December. The enemy was to be cleared from the hill that had faced us so grimly since we had moved into Medjez el Bab two weeks earlier. When we had achieved this a tank thrust was to be made towards Tunis. That hill was known as "Longstop". The battle plan was simple. The Guards were to take Longstop and on the morning of 24 December they were to be relieved by American troops. Tanks could then thrust forward towards Tebourba and Tunis with supporting infantry. Reports on the opposition were sketchy, but it seemed that the German troops were well dug-in and were receiving reinforcements. Our Company's [2nd Company] line of advance was by way of a thin strip of woodland running parallel to a railway line. Our objective, The Halt, was a stopping-place on this line just beyond the enemy-held reverse slopes of Longstop. The 23rd December was not unlike the previous days – cold, wet and miserable. The Company moved off with our Platoon [No. 11] last of all. We were all carrying a heavy weight of extra ammunition and rations and progress was slow. The moon cast eerie shadows as we passed burnt-out vehicles, evidence of a previous battle. Occasional bursts of machine-gun fire came from Longstop. We made our approach, waiting for our artillery barrage which was to open up just before the attack. It started and we hoped that the whining shells, passing overhead, were pinpointing their targets. It was not long before the Germans began to reply, and the angry snarl of their Spandau machine-guns told us that our forward companies were meeting stiff opposition. Very lights illuminated the scene and mortar shells began to land nearby. The woodland was thinning out, giving only minimum cover, but our platoon was ordered to push through the two leading platoons and get to The Halt as soon as possible.

'Ironic comments were made as we advanced. "Don't let the train go," and "You won't need a ticket," mingled with cries for stretcher-bearers. Our platoon was now reaching the end of the woodland, using what little cover the few remaining trees and undergrowth offered. In the distance, we could see our objective, a small building at the side of the railway line. We were heartened to see figures silhouetted on the skyline immediately to our left, as we knew these must be the forward platoons of our other companies. Our platoon was still intact as we reached the last fifty yards of the woodland. We edged forward; only a few yards separated us from The Halt. Violent explosions suddenly tore the ground. Flashes of blue light blinded us and the air was full of pieces of metal. Explosion followed explosion. It was impossible to tell what had happened. We hugged the ground as the explosions continued. Machine-gun fire pinpointed us. Through it there were cries for help. Most of the platoon had been hit. Again the ground was wrenched by explosions. At last we understood. We had walked into a minefield. The Germans, masters as they were at defensive tactics, had anticipated that the woodland could be used by an attacking force under cover of darkness. Their plan had worked well. By calling to each other we knew there were a few man capable of carrying on to the objective, but it was unnerving to realize that after only a few seconds most of our platoon were no longer in the battle. The remainder pressed forward, our Bren-guns sounding sluggish in reply to the rapid fire of the Spandaus. We reached The Halt. Then, together with the other two platoons, fought on to a point about fifty yards beyond The Halt and started the difficult task of digging-in before dawn. Fire from machine-guns enveloped us from our flank and front. Tracer bullets carved a pattern in the sky. The noise of vehicles to the rear of the German positions indicated that they were receiving reinforcements. Some of these were seen on the skyline, but quick bursts from our Brens dispersed them. We each managed to scoop out some form of slit-trench. Camouflage was out of the question. Roughly five yards apart we were positioned between the railway line and Longstop. The small building behind us made it easy for effective range-finding by the enemy mortars. We began to wonder if the Americans could relieve us. If we were not relieved our numbers were too few to last long against counter-attack. Our ammunition was low and our position would be ruthlessly exposed at the break of dawn.

'Enemy machine-gun fire became intense. Mortar bombs fell amongst us and the Germans were able to gauge our position. We fired back endeavouring at the same time to conserve our dwindling ammunition. A few of the enemy managed to creep to within a short distance of our position, but they were quickly dealt with by hand-grenades and rifle fire. Then the increased volume of fire sweeping over us confirmed that the enemy had been reinforced and had succeeded in working round our flanks. Mortar bombs fell around us and we were pinned down in our exposed positions. The incessant croaking of bullfrogs played on our nerves. Then dawn began to break and we realized that we could not expect to be relieved. No troops could advance over the flat, open country behind us without running the gauntlet of murderous machine-gun fire and concentrated mortar barrages. Suddenly it became quieter on Longstop. We hoped that this meant the exchange had in fact taken place and that the Americans were firmly established. Our own position seemed hopeless. Further casualties had reduced our numbers and we were no longer in contact with the battalion. A runner managed to get close to The Halt and shouted to us to move to the woodland as soon as possible.'

Although E. Fitness's account does not mention it, a US formation had in fact relieved the 2nd Coldstream Guards. The platoons of No. 2 Company had been so isolated that they could not be relieved by the incoming Americans. Meanwhile, the men of his platoon were looking for a way to reach the woodland in accordance with orders.

'Our one hope of doing this seemed by way of the railway cutting running from The Halt into the German lines. This was pitted with mortar holes and covered with severed telegraph wires and smashed telegraph poles. It did offer some cover if we could first cross the open ground. The Germans had anticipated this and were using a machine-gun on fixed lines to sweep the cutting. Daylight came. Our position was desperate. We were outnumbered by the enemy who was firing on us from three sides while at our backs was the minefield. A number of us reached the bottom of the railway cutting. The Germans had seen us and their gunfire was intense, tearing into the earth around us. Heavy rain added to our discomfort. We hugged the ground moving slowly, inch by inch. A few of us reached The Halt, our movements being impeded by wiring. Again we hugged the ground, moving slowly, intending to skirt the area of the minefield. One of our number was trapped in the German wire entanglements which were strewn in front of us. It took us some time to free him and then, slowly, still harried by the fire of the machine-guns, we made what we hoped would be a safe deviation around the minefield. Our chief need at this stage was to get one of our survivors to the nearest Field Dressing Station. He was suffering intensely as the result of bullet wounds and severe shock. After what seemed an eternity, we arrived at the FDS, feeling very tired, dirty and dazed. We handed over our colleague and were then informed that the battalion was reforming at a farm some distance away. Wearily we set off to rejoin it. We were soon halted. Two German aircraft were doing a strafing run. We dived off the rough track into some stunted bushes, escaping a hail of machine-gun bullets. A shot from a nearby Bofors AA gun scored a hit and to our delight one plane came down in an adjoining field.

'We were too tired to talk, although our minds were full of thoughts of comrades whom we knew would fight no more battles. We wondered how the remainder of the battalion had fared. The rain stopped and the sky became clearer. Eventually we reached the farm. Exhausted, we sank down on the side of a small stream waiting for blankets to arrive. The rain started again. Very heavily this time. Our blankets arrived – wet and soggy. A flurry of activity around the Company Commander's area made us wonder what was to happen next. The news was not long in coming. The position on Longstop had deteriorated rapidly and we were to return immediately to make a counter-attack.'

The Americans who had relieved the Coldstreams had been struck by a German counter-attack before they had settled in and had been flung back.

'Considerable ground had been lost and every effort was to be made to wrest the lost territory back from the enemy. We were too tired to think objectively of what this meant. We left our wet blankets, collected fresh ammunition and started off again. We reached Chassart, roughly a mile from Longstop and formed up. Three Companies were to make a frontal attack and the remaining platoons were to be responsible for carrying ammunition and other supplies. For the second time in less than twenty-four hours we set off towards Longstop. The heavy rain had soaked well into the ground and every step taken through the heavily churned-up mud was a demanding physical effort. We reached the American defence line. Very little was said as we passed through, apart from repeated comments that it was "Hell up there". Heavy rain and mist obscured most of the hated Longstop. Machine-gun fire crackled as our companies split into formation and worked towards the top. Soon the air was filled with bullets, mortar bombs and shells. The Germans had recaptured the crest of the mountain and were fully prepared for our coming. Fighting continued, sometimes at close quarters as we struggled upwards. Casualties were heavy as we sought to move from one exposed spot to another, all the time trying to gain a few more yards. Darkness fell and the all-revealing Very lights illuminated the bitter scene. We began again the feverish efforts to dig-in and to hold the ground we had regained. Throughout the night vehicles were heard behind the enemy lines. Once more they had pushed up reinforcements. The whine of German mortar bombs continued as our positions were bombarded frequently. An uneasy daylight began to break through and the enemy's fire stepped-up in intensity. What appeared to be armoured cars had worked up part of the slope on our right flank and added the weight of their fire power to that which raked us from above. This was war. The infantryman's war. No glamour, just simply a grim, deadly battle where boys quickly became veterans. Many would die. We scrambled from boulder to boulder in our efforts to escape the withering fire of the Spandaus. At the same time we inched towards the mist-shrouded crest, becoming fewer in number as the enemy's efforts took toll of our decimated but proud battalion. This was a Christmas we would never forget. "Peace on earth, goodwill to all men," seemed a long way off on Christmas Day, 1942.'

East of Medjez el Bab, in the spring of 1943, the 4th British Division went into action for the first time in Africa. The aim of the offensive was to drive the German paratroops from hills they occupied around Peter's Corner on the Medjez–Tunis road. With those positions in British hands the final offensive could begin. It was due to open on 23 April 1943, but the strong and experienced Fallschirmjaeger launched a pre-emptive attack. Their operation struck the 2nd Duke of Cornwall's Light Infantry. A very dear friend, the late Joe Harris, described that action:

'We were very unlucky in that it was our first major action in Tunisia. From the time that we moved towards the front, we had always occupied positions won by other units, being in a sense, follow-up troops. The intention was plain. We were being quietly broken to active service life so we had the usual stand-tos, patrols and small wiring-parties. Around our company positions there were several unburied dogs stinking like hell and crawling with maggots. Quite nasty. Some of us were detailed to cover the dead animals with earth. This was not an easy task as the soil was only a few inches deep. Below that were huge rocks and boulders. Still, we did manage finally to cover the smelly carcasses.

'We were relieved in those positions by a unit from the 1st Division and then we moved to a place between Medjez el Bab and Peter's Corner. The positions we were now holding were called "The Basin" because the area was a number of low hills surrounding a low-lying piece of ground. At 'O' Group our Platoon Commander told us that Jerry was just over two miles away to the east and holding some low features around Peter's Corner. He also told us that the Jerries were all fanatical Nazi paratroops from the Hermann Goering Division. They must have known that we were fresh in the line, having just relieved the Loyals. I think it might have been the Arabs that told them we were new troops. They passed between our lines and the Germans as freely as anything. The first night we were in the line, 20 April, we stood-to as usual at last light but were not ordered to stand down. Instead our Section Corporal told us that the Hermann Goerings were expected to attack us that night. So far as I remember it was just before midnight when the firing started. Out in the dark open ground in front of our positions there was a lot of Spandau fire and explosions. There were carrier-parties from the RA out in front of our positions, out there dumping shells for the big attack. Those carrier-parties were being guarded by sections from one of our platoons. From that firing it was obvious that those out in no man's land were being attacked by Jerry fighting patrols. From the volume of fire it was clear that our men were fighting back with a will. Then, quite suddenly, it was all quiet on the plain. Then a lot of flashes were seen from the enemy area and crash, crash, crash; his stonk started.

'Under that stonk the Hermann Goerings attacked us. Even though shells were falling all around us we did not duck below the parapet of our slit-trenches, but remained with our rifles or Bren-guns pressed into our shoulders waiting for the order to fire. In between the intervals in the barrage we could hear the sound of tank engines and I learned later that one of the platoons was attacked by flame-throwing tanks or by a flame-thrower – I can't remember which. It was a strange night. There were bursts of fire all round us; some close at hand and others farther away. This firing would start quite suddenly, continue for some minutes and then stop. Then it would begin somewhere else. And all the time Jerry was stonking us with mortars as well as with artillery shells. Those mortars were deadly. You couldn't hear them coming like you could hear a shell. The first thing you knew was a blinding flash of light and then an explosion. Jerry's Spandaus seemed to be all around us making us feel that we were surrounded on all sides. Our battalion was supposed to have Vickers machine-guns in support, but I don't remember hearing them firing. As we lay there with our elbows on the trench parapet looking out into the dark, I thought several times that I could see shapes but without the order to fire, you didn't dare open up. Once the order was given we would fire fifteen rounds rapid for a couple of minutes. This brought a quick response from the Germans. Their mortars would switch target and would drop their bombs on our trench line. They were ranging and aiming at the flashes from our rifles and from the Bren. It went on like that all through the night. At one time we seemed to be running out of ammunition, but the A Echelon men came up with fresh bandoliers so that we could carry on firing. I also remember the different coloured flares that Jerry fired. Red and green mostly, but also white ones. When these white ones burst high up in the sky it was like daylight for a couple of minutes. One of them lit up a German group as it was trudging up the hill towards the Company on our left. We caught that group in enfilade fire, but the light died before we could get them all.

'In this, our first fight in North Africa, we lost over a hundred men; killed, wounded or missing. Not all of them were killed during the German attack. Some, who had been on escort to the artillery carrying-parties, were caught in a minefield by a Jerry battle patrol. Our battalion had been unlucky. We lay right in the path of the German attack and its whole weight fell on us. They had wanted to take the high ground from us, but had not succeeded and had retreated back to Peter's Corner.'

John Mitton, formerly of the RTR, described the anecdote he sent in as amusing, for he had tried to impart that, 'We were at the time green and naïve civilians playing at being soldiers' when he was first 'shot over'. His story continues:

'After three years' training in England without hearing a shot fired in anger, the powers that be had finally decided that we were required abroad and, fresh from Blighty, here we were in Tunisia. So far the war had passed us by and as we were carried by tank transporters towards the front it was just like being on an exercise back in England. We just sat and enjoyed the February sun as we were carried along. Leaving Le Kef, we now proceeded on tracks towards El Arrousa over ground that was very reminiscent of our last training area, the South Downs, just behind Worthing. On this particular morning after a long night drive, the sun was now up, the road lay straight ahead, when the order came to disperse off the road, camouflage, maintainance, etc. The tank commander took me off the road to the right into a natural hollow some 100 yards from the Troop Leader who, for some reason best known to himself, had remained where he had stopped on the roadside verge. He stood out uncamouflaged and silhouetted. The rest of the squadron had gone to ground and were not visible.

'Having duly camouflaged, maintenance was next. During the night's run both tracks had stretched and had to be tightened, so with Mick the gunner, who was also the crew's aircraft recognition expert, we were working away under the cam net between the horns at the front of the tank. As we both worked on the bolts of the idler wheel, I saw out of the corner of my eye a movement to the right up and over the road. Two planes in tandem, engines throttled back, were cruising just above the road coming across our front. As they came nearer I said to Mick, more out of curiosity than anything else, "What are they, Mick?" He took a long look and said "Spitfires." I said, "What, with black crosses?" The two Messerschmitt 109s, with their black crosses prominently displayed on the fuselage, passed over the Troop Leader's tank and continuing down the road, climbed and turned in the distance. Now they were coming back on full throttle just above the road. Mick and I watched in silence. The first bore down on its target; a burst of black smoke from the underbelly then a split second later the noise of a long machine-gun burst and the scream of the engines which was repeated as the second plane came in to repeat the exercise. We ran. Fearing the worst, not knowing what to expect, mentally stunned by what we had seen, the whole episode could not have been more than a couple of minutes' duration. We both rounded the rear of the vehicle, fearing the worst only to find the crew sat at breakfast a couple of yards from the tank side. And there between them and the vehicle was a deep rutted gulley of ground, churned up by both planes' gunfire which had passed between them. No one hit, tank untouched, but a very shocked crew. The war had finally found us. Up till now playing soldiers had been enjoyable, but when the other side started using live ammunition it was not funny any more. They could have killed us. By the end of the month all of us would have been blooded in action and learning the hard way.'

War in Sicily and Italy

Sicily is remembered by many of my correspondents as being a Europeanized version of Italy's North African provinces. The one difference was that in Sicily there were no Arabs, more white women – most of whom were unapproachable – and a feeling that we were now, at long last, beginning to win the war. The general theme of most accounts of Sicily is the failure of American pilots to put down our airborne troops over the correct targets, the tenacity of the German defence around the Primasole bridge and the battle for Centuripe. From correspondence it is clear that in many ways the Eighth Army was still, mentally, in Africa.

The peculiarities of dress which had marked out the Eighth Army soldiers were retained in Sicily and by the time the army was in Italy the oddities of dress had become eccentric as if to emphasize that the wearer was one of the 'originals' of Eighth Army. R. G. Bell was kind enough to supply me with an extract from 7th Medium Regiment's History:

'In the matter of dress, the campaigns in the desert and in North Africa had created a very casual attitude among most units of the Eighth Army towards personal turnout. Officers offended with their corduroys and coloured scarves, other ranks largely by their stage of undress. It was fashionable to serve the guns stripped to the waist, and quite properly in such a climate, but the habit grew even away from the guns and in Sicily it included such additional unconventional items as "captured" civilian straw hats, cloth caps or "toppers". On one occasion, it must be recorded, a somewhat amusing incident (which caused mild repercussions) happened to a certain Troop of 27/28 Battery. The Troop, led by the GPO in his truck, was advancing to a forward position in action; the four guns towed by the 7th Medium special brand of Matadors with their sawn-off tops, open to the sky, containing the usual loads of ammunition, gun stores, etc., the odd chicken or other livestock, with the gun detachments lying around on top of all, almost naked and wearing a varied type of headgear, none of which had come from the Quartermaster's Store! Down the road towards the Troop drove the Corps Commander's car with the Corps Commander (General Sir Oliver Leese) and the CCRA, who had been up visiting one of the OPs. General Leese, recognizing the regimental sign, which was very well known to him, must have been rather surprised (or was he?) on approaching the leading Matador to see it driven by a bronzed body, naked to the waist, wearing a bowler hat of civilian pattern and with pipe in mouth. However, the General raised his own peaked cap in civilian fashion to the driver, who responded by removing his pipe and lifting his bowler in salute. It is hoped that honour was satisfied on both sides, but in closing this record it must be added that a letter (NOT from the General) was received by RHQ within 24 hours, stressing the point that as the Regiment was now fighting in a civilized country, the matter of dress . . . etc., etc., etc.'

The Eighth Army had, of course, been in the desert for years and that time 'up the Blue' had had its effect. In a country where much of the fighting took place in open desert, there had been no need to worry about damage to cultural buildings and the few civilians living in the area managed to remove themselves from the battlefield well in advance, so that the concern about non-military casualties did not arise. Under such conditions it was hardly surprising that there was non-military influence most of which manifested itself in the matter of dress. The Eighth had fought for years in the desert. By comparison, its sister army, the First, entered and completed its service in Africa within six months. It had had no time to become eccentric in the way that Eighth Army had, and when the two armies met it was a shock to them both. The First wondered just who were these scruffy gypsies while the Eighth were astonished at the military formality which was still very evident and which its own units had abandoned years earlier.

A photograph taken at the conclusion of the campaign in Sicily shows Montgomery standing on a headland looking towards Italy. That country would be the next objective. Sicily had been only a stepping-stone to the invasion of Europe. The invasion of Europe would only be accomplished when the first Allied soldiers debarked on the shores of Italy. At the highest levels of command in Britain and America, it had been anticipated that two Allied armies, the US Fifth and the British Eighth, would advance quickly up the length of the Italian peninsula. The intention of opening this Second Front in Europe would be to draw German forces away from Russia; the First Front. A second consideration would be to gain airfields from which Allied bombers could raid the oilfields of Roumania as well as other economic targets in the Balkans. The third advantage which would be gained would be the political one – the liberation of Rome, making the cradle of Christianity the first European capital to be freed from the Germans. As the first units of US Fifth Army headed towards the invasion beaches of Salerno the news was broadcast that the Italians had surrendered. As Ron Bullen wrote in his history of 2/7th Battalion, The Queen's Royal Regiment:

'It might have been armistice night. The Italians had capitulated and, somehow, the news had spread like lightning. The Brigade Commander records: "I had a nasty moment when I heard on the evening of D minus 1 that Italy had signed an armistice, because I thought the troops might think they were on an easy wicket and run into a packet of trouble. I had a personal signal made to all ships to the effect that it was the Boche we were fighting anyhow and not the Italians." '

Other units did not have so wise a commander. H. Rawlinson, an infantryman:

'You can well imagine what effect such an announcement had on us. As far as we were concerned half the war was over. The Jerries would surely follow the Italian lead and pack it in. Then there would be only the Japs to finish off. When we touched down near Battipaglia [9 September] the reception we got from the Germans surprised us. Some of our lads thought that the German units could not

Right: *This photograph of Arnold Watson, RASC, was taken in Alor Star, Malaya 1941, before the Japanese invasion. (J. Wyatt)*

Below: *A unit of Royal Artillery from Singapore, pictured in Ceylon. (A. Watson)*

Left: *G. Webb, a Regular soldier in the Grenadier Guards, saw service in Tunisia and Italy. He was wounded on Monte Battaglia. (G. Webb)*

Below: *The ruins atop Monte Battaglia following the fierce combat to capture the heights. (G. Webb)*

Right: *The Monte Battaglia area in 1988. The ridge to the right (not in picture) extended north-west from the castle and was occupied by Nos. 1 and 2 Companies. The building on the partly wooden hill in the centre was the tactical H.Q.; the one in the valley was where 75 P.O.W.s were taken after the attack. The ridge on the left was the causeway from Castel del Rio and was occupied by Welsh Guards.*

Below right: *This hymn sheet was expected to serve, and did for many, as an inspiration shortly before going into battle. (G. Webb)*

FIRST ARMY SIGN

IELD Representing our country - ne set in the midst of the sea,a sure safe refuge - a land,shaped like a ,which has stood us in good stead all the long pages of our history. The f our strength to-day. "Breathes a man with soul so dead,who never to f hath said,'This is my own,my native

USADERS CROSS The symbol by which shall know the ideals and princip- r which we stand. No sacrifice being eat in the cause of freedom. For can be higher than the hope expre- y that symbol - persecution,oppress- d terror banished,and replaced by ian peace and toleration. No one can the intention of those who serve and The Cross.

WN SWORD Long ago a Christian r gave us an example of the cause ich the sword should be drawn. This e we of First Army endeavour to . St George drew his sword and dest- a dragon which had enslaved a nation. eavour to destroy a dragon which has in Europe which would enslave the world. We cannot sheath our sword our task be thoroughly finished.

A prayer for final victory

Almighty God,Who art set in the throne that judgest rig judge our cause we beseech Thee,and if we seek only that which is agreeable to Thy will,grant to us both victory in this war and grace,in the day of victory,to seek no selfis ends,but only the advancement of Thy kingdom among men; through Jesus Christ our Lord. Amen.

A dedication of ourselves to the tasks that still lie ahead.

Teach us,good Lord,to serve Thee as Thou deservest;to give and not to count the cost;to fight and not to heed the wounds;to toil and not to seek for rest;to labour and not to ask for any reward,save that of knowing that we do Thy will;through Jesus Christ our Lord. Amen.

HYMN

Lord of our life,and God of our salvation,
Star of our night,and Hope of every nation,
Hear and receive Thy Church's supplication,
Lord God Almighty.

See round Thine ark the hungry billows curling;
See how Thy foes their banners are unfurling;
Lord,while their darts envenom'd they are hurling,
Thou canst preserve us.

Lord,Thou canst help when earthly armour faileth,
Lord,Thou canst save when deadly sin assaileth,
Lord,o'er Thy Church nor death nor hell prevaileth;
Grant us Thy peace Lord.

Grant us Thy help till foes are backward driven,
Grant them Thy truth,that they may be forgiven,
Grant peace on earth,and,after we have striven,
Peace in Thy heaven.

(Sung to the tune of A&M 214)

ADDRESS

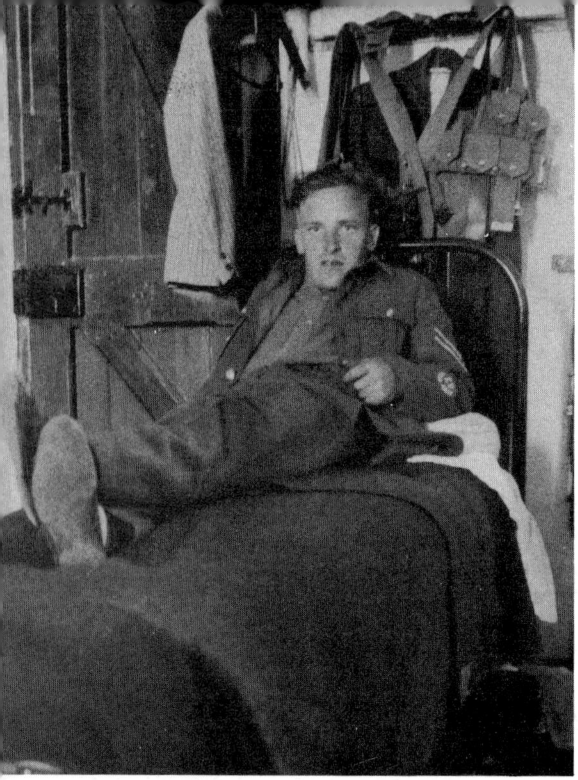

Left: *Bert Stubbings relaxing on his cot at St Andrews Barracks, Malta. (Bert Stubbings)*

Below: *Two British soldiers who have just escaped from the enemy share a cigarette with men of The 16/5 Lancers as the Eigth Army advance continues. The two escapees are Lance-Corporal George Dobson of The Durham Light Infantry and Hector Bowman of The Scots Guards.*

Right: *'When in doubt, brew up.' This was the Army's solution to every problem.*

Below right: *In the absence of actual battle shots, Army photographers often posed their subjects. This picture purports to show Germans surrending at the Fuka Pass in the Western Desert in 1942.*

WHEN IN
DOUBT.
BREW-UP.

Above: *Lieutenant-Colonel R. Dawson of No. 4 Commando gives a last-minute briefing to some of his men as they prepare for the D-Day landings on 6 June 1944.*

Top right: *An '88' and its half-track, knocked out during the German retreat from El Alamein.*

Right: *Vessels packed with men of the BEF who had been evacuated from France and Flanders arrive at a port on the southern coast of England in 1940.*

***Above:** The aftermath of the battle of El Alamein, November 1942. The wounded of 51st (Highland) Division lie in the open air awaiting treatment.*

***Left:** A piper of the Highland Division plays-in the crew of a Bren gun carrier as they return from patrol in the Western Desert.*

***Top right:** Winston Churchill inspecting the mortar platoon of battalion headquarters, Seaforth Highlanders (Caithness and Sutherland) in Egypt, 1942.*

***Right:** A platoon of Royal West Kent Regiment, 132 Brigade, 44th Infantry Division, moving forward to the start line for an attack in the desert, September 1942.*

The DERBY ~ 19
HORSE
JOCKEY
GLINT
D. SMITH
14-1
C. RICHARDS
16-1
LORD BOBS
G. LITTLEWOOD
33-1
8-1
14-1
7-2
H. RICHARDS
10-1
A. WRAGG
12-1
3-1
G. RICHARDS
EVENS
J. SIME
20-1
10-1
10-1
10-1
33-1
6-1
6-4
10-1
10-1
EXCELLENCY
C. ELLIOTT
2-1
F. RUTTER
ERVESCENCE
16-1
4-1
M. BEARY
33-1
8-1
20-1
5-1

WEEK

Left: *There may have been a war on, but it did not stand in the way of a Derby Day sweepstake. The board shown here was at TAC H.Q. of 2nd Armoured Brigade, Creully, Normandy, in June 1944.*

Below left: *Another posed picture for home consumption. This shot taken near Roubaix, northern France, in the late autumn of 1939, is intended to show a group of Royal West Kents happily making music while one of their number keeps watch on a trench parapet.*

Above: *The Welsh Guards march past at the conclusion of a ceremony held in northern France at which General Gamelin (second from the left) awarded the Legion of Honour to Lord Gort (right) and General Ironside (far left).*

Below: *A group of men belonging to the 4th Lincolns who were cut of by the Germans at Steinkjer during the invasion of Norway in 1940. The troops marched 56 miles across snow-covered mountains in order to reach British lines.*

Left: *A Priest gun crew preparing to attack Ngazun village en route to Meiktila, Burma.*

Bottom left: *A 3in mortar crew in action during the fierce battle near Singu on the Irrawaddy bridgehead, one of the toughest contests in the Burma war.*

Below: *A patrol of The Buffs of 26th Brigade advance cautiously through Burmese jungle country on the northern approaches to the Japanese-held town of Myitson.*

Left: **Left:** *Fusilier Jefferson of The Lancashire Fusiliers, 78th Division, was awarded the Victoria Cross for destroying a German tank with the short-range PIAT mortar, thereby breaking up an enemy tank attack at Cassino in Italy 1944.*

Above: *One of the features of the fighting in Cassino was the use of snipers. This picture shows a Grenadier Guards sniper in the ruins of a house in the town.*

Below: *British troops coming ashore in Sicily, July 1943.*

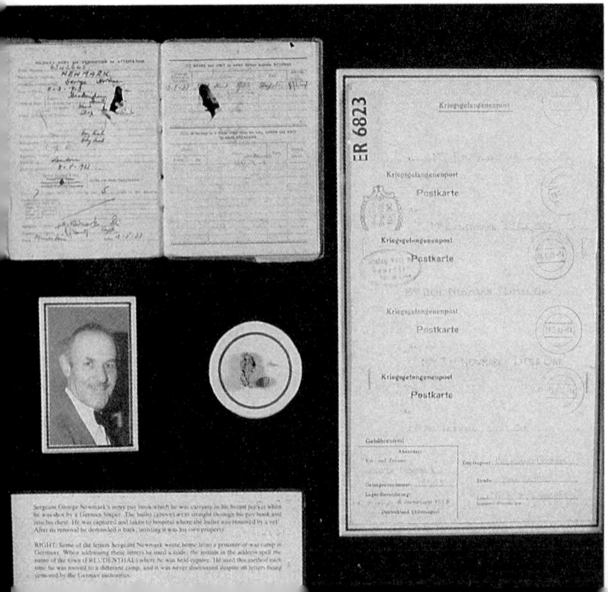

Above: *Scottish troops, led by their piper, march inland from the beaches of Sicily.*

Left: *George Newmark was wounded during the fighting in France, May 1940. A bullet passed through his AB 64 and penetrated deep into his chest. This photograph shows the bullet-torn document, the bullet which was removed from George's chest and a letter sent by him from the prisoner of war camp. (Courtesy of V. Moss, Curator of the Redoubt Museum, Eastbourne)* have heard the news that the war was over, but then when the 88s came in and the Tiger tanks started attacking, as they did several days later, it was plain that the Jerries had no intention of packing it in at all, but that they were fighting like hell to drive us into the sea.'

CASSINO

The staunch German resistance at Salerno was an indication of how determined the enemy was to hold Italy. It was evident that the intention was to delay – if possible to halt indefinitely – the Allied northward advance at every river line and every mountain range, and the Germans built defences to strengthen positions already naturally strong. One such area was at Cassino, a small town to the south of Rome. At that place lies the Liri river valley, a narrow strip of land between the mountains and the sea. No advance could be made towards Rome without passing through the valley and to reach its mouth the town of Cassino had first to be taken. That town lay at the foot of Monte Cassino on whose summit stood the world-famous Benedictine abbey. In order to reach the town of Cassino Fifth Army would have to advance over a wide and open plain under the eyes of German observers on the mountains behind Cassino town. The attacking troops would have to cross the fast flowing River Rapido, capture the town and force the Liri valley, before they could debouch out of the hills and advance upon Rome. It is the fighting to achieve these objectives which makes up the story of the four battles for Cassino.

The first of these offensives opened on 17 January, with a thrust across the River Garigliano by a British Corps which formed part of Fifth Army. Then two US divisions were committed in an operation so badly planned and so incompetently handled that a disastrous outcome was inevitable. Later in January, in an attempt to strike into the back of the German divisions holding Cassino and to split the defence there, the Allies made an unsuccessful amphibious assault at Anzio/Nettuno. The American infantry losses in the first battle of Cassino were shocking, but the attacks were ordered to be continued. To support the US forces, three divisions of Eighth Army were brought across the width of the Italian peninsula and put into the fight. Their attacks, which opened on 12 February 1944, mark the opening of the second battle – made notorious by the bombing of the monastery on 18 February, which was carried out because it was believed the Germans were using the building as an observation post. Another aerial bombardment was made on 15 March, and was followed by an artillery barrage, during which nearly 200,000 shells were fired into the town. The Eighth Army infantry and armour who fought in this, the third battle of Cassino, had as little success as had the earlier offensives. The fourth and final battle opened on 11 May, with a barrage fired by 1,600 guns. Six days later and the troops of the French Expeditionary Corps had reached a point in the mountains behind the German positions. The defenders of Cassino, chiefly the paratroop battalions of the Luftwaffe's 1st Airborne Division, had been outflanked and would have to withdraw. On 18 May, Polish troops raised their national flag over the ruins of the Abbey. The town fell to British divisions, chiefly 4th and 78th Infantry, whose accompanying armour smashed through the Liri valley and on to the flat ground leading towards Rome. At Anzio/Nettuno, the beachhead had been contained by German troops that included 4th Para Division. The British forces that had captured Cassino linked hands with the Anglo/US forces striking out of the Anzio beachhead and the drive upon the Italian capital began.

On 5 June 1944, the first troops of the Allied armies entered the Eternal City. The first major political objective of the campaign had been achieved. By a bitter twist the importance of the first climacteric of the Italian campaign was eclipsed within a single day, when on 6 June, the Allies landed in Normandy. The sacrifice of the four battles of Cassino was ignored in favour of the news from France, but those losses had been heavy and nearly 350,000 men of the Anglo-American forces had been killed, wounded or were missing. Among the battles of the Second World War, there were few in which the infantry suffered as grievously as their forefathers had in the trenches of the Great War. Stalingrad and Cassino were two battles in which it was not unusual for soldiers of the opposing sides to share the ruins of the same house. The fighting in Cassino was often hand to hand and bodies lay unburied, rotting in the rain of the Italian winter. On the German side the units detailed to carry out the terrible task of bringing in the dead had to tie scarves soaked in eau de Cologne round their faces and around the nostrils of the horses carrying the dead against the stench of decay and decomposition. One of the most bizarre sights to be seen in Cassino was the pair of German Army jackboots which stood on the platform of the railway station. Out of the tops of those boots projected glistening white shin bones. This may have been the most bizarre sight, but to Fred Majdalaney the most poignant one was the row of little boots sticking out from under British Army blankets. These marked the Gurkha dead for the Gurkhas being small in stature, had small feet. The rows of little boots was a sight which moved Majdalaney, a hard-bitten journalist and veteran of the Tunisian campaign, to unashamed tears. Cassino was an infantryman's Calvary – a bloody and bitter agony. George Webb served there with the 3rd Battalion, The Grenadier Guards, and although he concludes his story by saying it was a quiet sector, the reader can judge for himself what this meant.

'No. 9 Section of No. 3 Platoon, No. 1 Company, relieved some regiment, I forget which one, and we took over a cellar of a house on the south side of Cassino. The house had been razed to the ground. We were separated from the Germans of General Heidrich's 1st Parachute Division, by a river bank and our positions were some 400/500 yards apart. We observed German movements by telescope, similar to submarine periscopes, and I suppose the Germans did the same when observing our positions. One afternoon we had the order to remove all tracer rounds from the Bren-gun magazines and that at about 11pm that night we were to fire on a certain target on a fixed line. Half a dozen blankets were soaked in water so as to diminish any muzzle flash from the Bren. In our Section we had a very good soldier, but he was a little on the dim side. I was a lance-corporal and second-in-command of a Section, with a sergeant as the section commander. When the order to fire was given – in a count-down from Company headquarters – a blaze of tracer was fired from our Bren-gun. It was thought that the man responsible was the dim-witted one. Seconds after the incident the Company Commander came on the field telephone and the air was blue. I am sure the sergeant would have been relieved of his stripes had that been possible at the time. Among the other things our Company Commander said was that we were sure to be shelled because the tracer would have given our position away. Sure enough, within three minutes or so we had a hell of a stonk. After it had finished I suddenly thought of the two sentries who were positioned in an abri outside the cellar. When I reached them, one Guardsman just sat there with his rifle between his knees like a waxwork model in Madame Tussaud's. The other Guardsman seemed too numb to say anything. When we examined the first sentry some time later it was found that a piece of shrapnel, no bigger than a little fingernail, had pierced his great coat and had gone straight through his body. You could hardly see where the shrapnel had penetrated. The next thing was to get him back to the RAP at first light. Now the Germans were not very particular about the Red Cross flag and had been known to fire on stretcher-bearer parties, even though these were displaying the Red Cross flag. So consequently, I had a devil of a job getting a volunteer to accompany me to carry the stretcher bearing Nobby's body to the RAP, which was some 400/500 yards away. I did eventually get a volunteer and we ran and walked with the stretcher. We were not fired on and the MO pronounced Nobby as being dead. It subsequently transpired that the barrage that had fallen on us after the tracer bullets incident had not been German retaliation but by a quirk of fate it was some American 4.5 howitzers whose shells were falling short. According to our regimental history " . . . the battalion was not called up to attack nor to resist attack nor even to patrol . . . " What was unnerving was the fact that smoke shells by day and by night were fired by the RA and at night when the empty canisters fell on to the rubble outside our cellar it seemed as if someone was advancing on our positions. This resulted at times in our standing-to for long periods with our fingers on the triggers, so to speak. We were also in Cassino when the American Fortresses bombed the abbey. This was as terrifying for us as it was for the Germans.'

Nearly every unit of Fifth and Eighth Armies was involved in the struggle for Cassino. It was one of the few battles involving the Western Allies in which conditions were similar to those that had obtained in France and Flanders during the First World War. Conditions in the stricken city were so appalling that battalions had to be rotated frequently. In the late spring of 1944, 4th British Division, which had been all but broken-up after the campaign in Tunisia, was reinforced, reactivated, brought to Italy and in time entered the battle for Cassino. Danny Exley was an NCO in one of the infantry battalions of 12th Brigade:

'For the fourth and final battle of Cassino we were put in the picture properly. We would be in the big push which was to be carried out by US Fifth Army and British Eighth Army, of which our division, 4th Infantry, was a part. Eighth Army was given the task of attacking and capturing the town of Cassino and Monastery Hill. Once that hill was taken the battle would be over because it dominated the whole battle area. Every move made by the Allied armies was watched by the eyes of the enemy on Monastery Hill. We were told that the battle would commence at 11pm, with the greatest barrage since Alamein. Two thousand guns would be used to smash into the German lines and God help those who were on the receiving end. At Zero Hour all hell broke loose as the massed guns of Eighth Army opened up. It shook us with fear and fright and we were behind the gun lines. God knows how Jerry felt. Was he ready for this lot and would he stand and fight? Until it was our turn to enter the battle all we could do was to sit down and wait. At dawn we moved forward to the assembly area just behind the forward gun line. After a few hours, information began to filter through; nothing definite, mostly rumour, but things did not seem to be going so well. A slight bridgehead had been established and the only way to get to the weak forces in that bridgehead was to get a Bailey Bridge erected as quickly as possible. So far the work of the REs had been held up by heavy enemy shellfire and sniping and their casualties had been quite heavy. But the bridge had to be erected at all costs. As the day passed it was clear that the Germans were standing their ground and had not started falling back on our sector. Still we had no bridge across the river although the Sappers were working under extreme conditions. God help the men in the bridgehead. We knew they must be looking over their shoulders, sweating and cursing and saying, "Where are those 12 Brigade bastards who are to relieve us?" They had been holding the bridgehead for nearly 24 hours and must have become desperate by this time. By the following morning the bridge had been built for the cost of fifteen Sappers killed in action and 57 wounded.

'The first armour to cross Amazon bridge was 17/21st Lancers following behind the infantry who had crossed over into the bridgehead. The 12th Brigade was now moving fast. The Black Watch and the Royal Fusiliers were soon over and Jerry began to leave his positions and fall back. By noon it was our turn to cross which we were to do mounted on tanks. I was on the lead tank with our platoon officer. After ten minutes' drive we could see that the bridge was still under fire. As we came close to it ready to turn on to it we came under fire from a Jerry machine-gunner. The tank stopped for some reason making us a sitting target. Our platoon officer was hit right across his legs. He fell off and crawled to a crater, gave me the thumbs-up signal and made himself comfortable to await the stretcher-bearers. We never saw him again. He had joined us only that morning as a replacement. We never even knew his name. We jumped off the tanks and raced across the bridge dodging the fire as best we could. The bridge was littered with dead and wounded. Men were lying on stretchers waiting to be evacuated. Some wounded men were attending to the more seriously wounded. Bodies wrapped in blankets were being removed for burial. The bridge was also littered with vehicles, some of which were burning. Once the rifle Companies were clear of the bridge they advanced towards their objectives. On our way we had to move up a track. We had to keep to one side to let the walking wounded pass on their way to the rear area. We pushed on and got the better of the snipers. Some were killed, but most of them had a field day, picking off our comrades all day. When they had no more ammunition they just broke their cover and put their hands up. Some were shot down where they stood. They had fought like soldiers. Now they died like soldiers. We took our objective. Jerry was well dug-in and his positions were well sited. We winkled him out and took over his trenches ready to receive the shelling and mortar fire which would come in once his troops were clear of the position. Within an hour we got it alright and it lasted on and off over a period of a couple of hours. First he tried his heavy mortars, then he sent over his airbursts; the ones which did most damage. These shells explode above the target and shrapnel rains down into the trenches and positions.

'After the barrage stopped, Sherman tanks arrived to give us protection in case we got counter-attacked. Then Vickers guns came up, again to give strength to our position. By the evening we were well entrenched and ready to resist any attack. The bridgehead was small but reinforcements were pouring over the bridge and every hour we were getting a stronger hold of the ground we had taken. It became dark and it seemed to us we would not be moving tonight. Our only orders were to watch our front and be ready to hold and to fight off any attack the enemy might make. It was a long night and although we were all tired we could only snatch a few minutes sleep. As it began to get light we received orders to advance and take another objective. We moved forward at 5.00am and a mist came down. We took no notice of it at first, but after a while we could not see a few yards in front of us. The tanks stopped but we were ordered to keep going forward on a compass bearing. The tanks started to crawl forward again. We had the worry of them crushing us. In the end we let them get in front with a couple of our men in front of them to guide them while the rest of us followed up behind – following the noise. There was no contact with anybody on the left or right. All of a sudden the mist began to clear and the Monastery came into view towering over us. The German OPs would have a field-day. We were caught out in the open. We spread out as quick as we could and moved forward. It was then that Jerry put in his counter-attack. We hit the ground and started to fight him off. We were surrounded and our Company Commander shouted to us to kill as many Jerries as we could. This was the moment we had been waiting for. We had a real battle but we could not move forward and had to start digging-in. Jerry was holding us. When the enemy infantry stopped firing, over came his heavy mortar fire followed up by shellfire. Then we got the airbursts. Things quietened a bit. He must have fell back on to another prepared position. At six that evening we received orders to cut the road which was his only escape route out of Cassino. This task was to take another four days of hard and bitter fighting and reports that "everything was going to plan" did not seem true to us. We did not seem to be moving. Our casualties were very heavy indeed and the shelling and mortaring seemed to increase.

'As we left our slit-trenches to form up in extended order, some of our comrades never moved. They were the aftermath of the heavy shelling and mortaring which had been belting down for the best part of eight hours. Those sights never did us any good even if the dead soldiers were German. Us who survived knew that any second we could be like them if your luck runs out. We spread out and faced our front. We were to advance on a battalion front. We were waiting for the RAF fighters to strafe the enemy positions and then our guns were to soften up the opposition with a barrage. Some of the shells from the barrage dropped short, killing and wounding officers and men waiting to advance. We moved forward cautiously with fixed bayonets. Jerry was not far away. Ahead we could see a road which we had to capture and cross. We had advanced about a thousand yards with no contact when all of a sudden two or three machine-guns opened up just 50 yards away. It was too late to take cover. Men fell like ninepins. We destroyed the machine-gun posts, crossed the road and carried the advance into open country. By now Jerry opposition in some places was beginning to crack, but on our sector the enemy made us fight for every bit of ground. Then it was clear that the fighting for Cassino was ending and on the morning of 18 May the Monastery and town fell to Eighth Army. On 20 May we turned our backs on Cassino. It was over, but none of us could forget the bloodshed and it still remains imprinted in our thoughts.'

THE GOTHIC LINE

With the fall of Cassino the liberation of Rome followed quickly and on 4 June the Allies entered the city. This splendid piece of news was eclipsed two days later by the announcement that a successful invasion of Normandy had been accomplished. Thereafter, the campaign in Italy took a secondary place in the minds of the British public. North of Rome the Allied armies took up their former formation, with Fifth Army on the Tyrrhenian side and Eighth Army on the Adriatic, and pushed their way forward. During September they struck the German defences of the Gothic Line. The troops of British 56th Division were told that the timetable for the offensive was "Two days to reach Bologna, four days to reach Venice and a week to reach Vienna.' They were also told, according to Thomas Weller, that the Germans had three divisions facing Eighth Army:

'Those three divisions were short of everything. One had only a limited supply of ammunition for its three machine-guns, a second had no rations to issue and the third German division had only one gun and that was drawn by oxen. There were some Eighth Army soldiers who believed it all. We had with us gunners from LAA regiments who had been guarding Alex and Cairo since 1941. Their units were broken up and they were posted lock, stock and barrel into infantry regiments. They believed the rubbish that the IO told them. Mind you, he was only repeating what he had been told at Brigade or Division and was duty-bound to pass it on. Well if Jerry had only one gun and that was drawn by oxen, then we reckon that poor bastard animal must have been mated with a greyhound because that so-called one gun was firing along a battle front that reached from Rimini and well into the mountains.'

Donald Featherstone served with 51st RTR in Italy:

'Some of the unit's toughest fighting (including eleven assault river-crossings in three weeks) took place in the Gothic Line on the Adriatic coast of Italy in the autumn of 1944, although it began on a note of comedy. To conceal the movement of armour from the Florence front, the unit's tanks went by transporters by night while the men were driven across in trucks, their tell-tale black berets hidden in packs and each man wearing some form of wide-brimmed soft-felt hat from a hat factory captured at Montevarchi. Although a chronological blur, the Gothic Line still paints a vivid picture in the writer's mind of slit-trenches dug in the shelter of lines of vines where grapes could be had by merely stretching out the hand, at least until we learned painfully that this same salubrious vegetation could set off the proximity fuzes of the 88mm shells fired at us on a flat trajectory, converting them into airbursts. Our camp site below Gemmano or was it Coriano Ridge was soon vacated because of the stench of Canadian dead unable to be moved from the minefield. It was here that I acquired the moon-shaped scar that still adorns my right elbow, when a sudden mortar stonk caused a general dive into slit-trenches. Mine was already occupied by a snake so, turning in midair like an Olympic diver, I flew into Sergeant Stan Saville's trench and his steel-tipped boot heel caught my arm and opened it up.

'We lost a lot of good men. One of our drivers could not escape from his Sherman because the depressed barrel of the 75mm gun would not allow the lid of the escape hatch to be opened to its full extent. And Lieutenant Neale's Churchill, knocked out in midstream when crossing the River Ronco, blocking the crossing, was later drawn by war artist Eric Kennington and for many years was commemorated annually as an In Memoriam notice in the *Daily Telegraph.* In the incessant rain of that time we took our chance outside the slit-trenches which quickly became ponds. And the mountain village of Camerino from which the ground dropped away to leave the world stretching before the eye, echoed flatly with artillery fire that flickered colourfully at night. It was here that the RSM was doing a line with a black-garbed widow, a poor, fat lady, who rarely spoke, but gazed uncomprehendingly at these loud-talking, guffawing men from another planet. Then there was the mad dawn dash by the tanks across Forli airfield. When the town was entered it was said that the departing Germans left an Italian partisan hanging from each of the tall lamp-posts in the town square. One of them was a woman. At least that's what I seem to recall, but it was 45 years ago, wasn't it.'

John Mitton, MM, describes an incident in November 1944, as Eighth Army advanced towards Forli:

'In typical British Army fashion, after I returned to the regiment, from a six-weeks' driving and maintenance instructors' course, my OC told me he had a job for me. Radio Op in the regiment's Tactical HQ, driving a scout car and maintaining liaison between the tanks and the infantry. Talk about a round peg in a square hole. One morning we crossed over a river. A few hundred yards in from the crossing-point, our B Echelon vehicles were under fire from Spandaus on fixed lines. We turned left into a farmyard where TAC HQ was located. The infantry FDL was about half a mile from us. There was a brooding, uncanny silence even though there was a great deal of activity and excitement, particularly when the Spandaus fired. Stupidly, we selected as bed spaces in TAC HQ's farmhouse, that part of the room which was in the direct line of fire of those guns. They opened up from time to time, the bursts ricocheting off the wall by the door and then whining away through the trees. It was quite indiscriminate fire. If we wanted to go out we had to wait until the burst had stopped, then open the door, run like hell and hope he didn't fire again until you had made the corner. Sometimes you were lucky – sometimes not. The heavy rain flooded the rivers and swept the bridges away. We of A Squadron and the infantry ahead of us were cut off. One dark night I was detailed to go up to Casa Bordi and deliver a message to the OC. The driver of the infantry Bren carrier drove flat out into the wall of darkness. Half a mile on we were stopped and challenged by a vague figure who suddenly materialized from nowhere. To the left I could make out

Casa Bordi. The rain had stopped and an occasional coloured German flare rose into the sky and lines of Spandau fire lanced across the fields. We drove across a second field; finally the farm building loomed up ahead, there was a low challenge and then we went inside the house. The building was full of infantry who were sat against the walls resting, looking dirty, tired and in need of rest. Outside was a Sherman with a neat hole punched through the gear box, put there by a German fighting patrol with a *Panzerfaust.* There was another unexploded Panzerfaust stuck in the upstairs curtain frill. Shortly before we arrived the house had been attacked but this had been beaten off and three prisoners taken. Because I would be going back to TAC HQ I was told to take them with me. The prisoners looked very young, about 15 years old, frightened, dejected and a little ludicrous with their long field-grey overcoats down to their ankles. What had happened, I wondered, to the great German Army; the ones who had been in the Afrika Korps; big, blond and arrogant? I don't know who was the most scared, I or the prisoners.

'But before I could take them back I had to deliver the message to the OC. To the right there was the faint silhouette of a Churchill, closed down, engine switched off but with a faint light coming from the turret whose cupola was open. I climbed up the outside and looked down inside the turret. The Commander was standing on the floor of the turret looking at his maps when I tapped him on the head. I thought at that moment I had given him heart failure. With headphones on, intent on reading his map, to be tapped on the head when you least expect it, especially when surrounded by the enemy isn't exactly good for the nerves. Tearing his headphones off Major Powditch asked what the ********* hell was I doing there and to clear off as it wasn't safe. I felt safer than he did as he was in a steel box, blind, hearing over the 19 Set of Tigers in the immediate area and unable to do anything but sit there in the turret, cold and with the rain trickling down his neck. I passed my message, made my way back to the infantry carrier, met up with the SSM and the prisoners and then away we roared, down the road and into the farmyard of TAC HQ. It was only then that we found the SSM had been left behind at the FDL. He was not amused and said so in no uncertain terms when he finally arrived back on foot. The rest is history. The bridges were rebuilt, Forli airfield was attacked and taken and we moved into the centre of the town, where on the first morning, after a good night's sleep in the Post Office, we were blown out of bed by a German SP gun.'

The speedy reaction of the German High Command in Italy brought sufficient German divisions into the line to hold Eighth Army. The British hope of driving up the old Roman road from Rimini to Bologna and then via Venice through the Lubljana gap into Austria and on to Vienna, died when heavy fighting for the first objectives of the offensive upset the timetable of the offensive. The hope of reaching Bologna within two days faded and it was not until 6 months later that the city finally fell. As in all offensives there were accusations of cowardice. The 1st Armoured Division was hated because one of its regiments refused to go in at Tavoleto in support of the Gurkhas. It was a disgrace that was never lived down. Later in the offensive and deeper into the mountains, George Webb of the Grenadier Guards sent an account of a reconnaissance patrol at Imola. The sober narrative conceals the strain and danger of such a mission:

'After a bout of leave [left out of battle] I was summoned by the Commander of No. 2 Company and told I was to take a reconnaissance patrol to recce a position held by the Germans and about two miles or so in front of our positions. The Major told me that he had already sent three or four patrols out, but these had returned with no worthwhile information. He took me on to a mountain peak and we observed the German positions through binoculars. I was given instructions that by no means were we to engage the enemy, but to try and ascertain the strength of their forces in that particular area. I was told to choose my men, preferably those who would volunteer, but only to take two. I had no difficulty in obtaining the services of one Guardsman – a cheeky Cockney. The other man I asked was a lance-corporal and he too volunteered. On reporting to the Major I was told that I could not take the lance-corporal as the Company was short of NCOs. I then made the choice of a young Guardsman, who had recently been transferred from the Brigade Intelligence unit and who could speak German. I told him that he would be in the middle of the patrol, so it was up to him to identify any Germans that we might bump into and to tell me what they were saying. I took a compass bearing on the German positions and we set off about 21.00hrs, through atrocious mountain shrubbery. After about 20 minutes we crossed a mountain stream and as we were crossing I slipped and dropped the compass. I retrieved it but it was muddy and not of much use. Casually I asked the men, "What shall we do now?" wondering whether or not they would like to carry on and not march on a possibly faulty bearing. I was given a blunt reply of, "You are the Sergeant. It's up to you." "Right," I said, "You wait here. I will go back to the start-line and get a new compass bearing. Then we will go on from there."

'This I did. In the course of events we had to rest frequently, because it was almost like going on all fours as we made our way up the mountain. On one particular occasion, after a short rest, as I rose from my sitting position I saw a form rise up in front of me, and only about three or four yards away. My Tommy-gun was pointing downwards and I thought for all the world that my time had come. But instead, nothing happened. It was a mountain goat or sheep, but the silhouette appeared to be that much like a human being. I was quite sure it was a German but vastly relieved when the form ran away.

'On we went and I was overjoyed when I came to the actual spot where we believed the Germans to be. No one seemed to be about and it was in my mind to see if I could locate an Italian farm and see if there was anything that we could scrounge. All of a sudden I heard a voice – "Is that you, Tommy?" Immediately I thought that we had hit the wrong place and that British troops were occupying the place. The next thought was that it might have been one of my Guardsmen speaking to the other, because the Cockney was called Tommy. Before I could react all hell let loose. Schmeissers, and either grenades or mortar bombs exploded all around us. We were under orders not to engage the enemy, so I called the men together and was about to beat a hasty retreat when one of the two – the lad who could speak German – shouted out, "Get down! get down!" and dropped to his knees. I said, "No, we are getting out," but he wouldn't budge. I pulled him by the shirt collar six or seven yards and he yelled, "Leave me, leave me!" Unfortunately, that is what I did, because of the intensity of the German fire. As we made our way back to the battalion positions I heard that poor lad crying out something like "Mercy! Mercy!" It was clear to me that he had been hit by a grenade or something and the more he shouted the more the Germans poured their fire upon him. When I reported to the Major that I had lost one man and that there was at least a "Platoon strength" of Germans on that position, he said, "You will have to report to the commanding officer." When I saw the CO and told him how sorry I was to have lost a man, I can remember his exact words. He said to me "Sergeant Webb, this is war." I am led to believe that nothing was ever heard of the man we lost, from that day to this. He was listed as missing and having died of wounds. He is not buried anywhere, but his name appears on a plinth in the Commonwealth War Graves cemetery at Cassino.'

'Monte Battaglia is more than 2,000 feet high. It stands, an isolated feature, high up in the mountain heights south of Bologna. It is not many miles from Firenzuola and nearer still is a little town called Castel del Rio. It is unlikely that you will find it on any maps available in England. Yet it is one of those places which the last war will make unforgettable to some men; and those men are the Grenadiers of 3rd Battalion, and the Welsh Guards. The battalions took over the area from the Americans late in October 1944. Four miles away from the ruined castle which surmounts the hill, all mechanical transport had to be left and from that point everything was brought forward on mule back. In places one could only reach the summit by clinging to ropes. The clay slopes were as slippery as a glacier. Our positions formed a salient projecting into the German positions and were under observation from three sides. Monte Battaglia was a key point which the Germans were trying hard to recapture. For days while the Guards were on this height it rained incessantly. On other days the mountains were shrouded in thick mist. Life in the slit-trenches, half filled with water and lashed by driving rain can well be imagined. Add to this the incessant shell and mortar fire, day and night, filth, excrement and the stench of unburied corpses of German and American dead, and you get a picture of a virtual hell on earth. Our positions lay at the junction of a long earthern causeway, only wide enough to carry a single track and pin-pointed by enemy mortars. That track was used by 150 mules and 100 men of the ration-parties, night after night. The surface soon became knee-deep mud and a stretcher party needed about 3½ hours to reach the nearest point from where a jeep could drive.

'In the worst spot they had known since Cassino, the Guardsmen hung on grimly. Then, one dark night, doubtless judging that days of continuous bombardment must have shattered the defenders, the Germans attacked in force. The Guardsmen let them come in. There was confusion as the first Germans fell over the trip-wires and then all hell broke loose. For men who for six days or more had been pinned in their slit-trenches there was no need to cry "Up Guards and at 'em!" They were in and among the enemy before the Germans realized just what a hornets' nest they had struck. When the battle was over the Guardsmen had taken nearly one hundred prisoners and the remaining Germans who had launched the attack were lying dead on the hillside. They did not attack the position again.'

F. Richmond:

'The onset of winter – "whoever called it sunny Italy had never been there" – first reduced and then halted full-scale military operations by both the US Fifth and British Eighth Armies although aggressive patrolling continued. Rivers barring the Allied advances were in full spate; there was a lot of snow, almost incessant rain and a great deal of misery. It had been a long and wearing campaign. We began it wildly optimistic [at Salerno on 9 September] believing that the war was over. After D-Day in France, Italy became a backwater and so few reinforcements were coming from home that units had to be broken up. They broke up one of the brigades of my division [56th London] and replaced it with a Gurkha brigade. It had been a long slog up the length of Italy and against the grain of the country. Now we faced our second winter – our second Christmas in Italy. Speaking for myself I remember only two highspots in the last months of 1944. One was seeing Dave and Joe O'Gorman – the comedians. The second, and nicer memory, was when Gabrielle Brun (I think I've spelt her name right) came to a transit camp where I was and put on an impromptu show for the blokes who were confined to camp awaiting transport up the line. I shall never forget seeing that lovely girl, standing on a table and belting out a whole succession of songs and all without a band or even a piano. She was marvellous.'

THE LAST PUSH AND INTO AUSTRIA

Nineteen months after the Allied armies had landed in Italy, to begin what had been anticipated would be a rapid advance up the peninsula, they were at last approaching the River Po. There remained only a few more mountains to take and then the Allies would be on the flat Lombardy plain. How often had the Allied infantry been given the reassurance, "This is the last ridge", when they received orders for an attack. Those who looked at maps realized that the oft-repeated promise might at last be true for beyond the last peaks really did lie a plain. But they saw, too, and with despair, that once they had crossed the Po and had thrust across the plain of Lombardy, there lay before them the Alps, into whose protection German Army Group 'C', defending Italy, would withdraw to defend the Fatherland. To fight a war in the Alps against the men who had turned Monte Cassino into a hell, was a chilling prospect. The 78th Division was one of the few formations that did not lose its fighting edge. Perhaps because it lost so many men and had to receive so many replacements, that its combat units always contained 'fresh' men led by experienced commanders. One of those new men, the fresh blood to infuse the 78th, was Robert Hayward. He joined 5th Buffs in time for the final battle in Italy and fought his first action with that battalion.

'We finally arrived at a camp near Forli, just behind the front, close enough to hear the guns and to realize you weren't dreaming. It was on the evening of 8 April 1945, as we were queuing with our mess-tins for the evening meal, that the guns opened up and kept up the barrage all that night. We knew that the attack across the River Senio and on to the Po was on. That night we were driven up to a small village and joined our battalion. My mate and I were posted to a platoon which had taken over a house with the occupants living upstairs. The men in the platoon had fought all through the North African campaign and up into Italy. They looked at us and asked if we had come straight from school, how old we were and what was our demob group number? When we said "60" they laughed. They were in "24," "25" and "26" groups for release. Next morning, after being issued with two bandoliers of ammunition, two grenades, an entrenching tool and hardtack rations, we boarded troop transport lorries and crossed the Senio over a small bridge. We headed towards the front. It was a lovely spring day, the sun was shining and we arrived at a point where the trucks could go no farther. Looking out of the truck we saw our first dead British soldier. He was dressed exactly the way I was, which gave me a scarey feeling in the pit of my stomach. We grouped behind the guns that were still pounding away at the enemy positions. Some time during the afternoon our platoon officer told us to gather round and with a map in front of him explained what our objective was. We were brigaded with the Argylls and the West Kents. It worked out that two battalions were in the Line and one was held in reserve. That night we passed through the Argylls and I shall always remember the Jocks saying "good luck" to us as we passed them. We marched in single file along the road, passing by dead horses lying stiff on the ground. Fire and tracer bullets seemed to be coming from all directions. We had a Churchill tank to keep us company and at one stage my mate and I had to crawl round the side of the vehicle so that it was between us and the gunfire. There was firing everywhere and German prisoners with their hands on their heads were being marched to a place behind the line.

'This went on all night and my mate, Sid Allen, and I could have dropped on the spot and gone sound to sleep where we were. Our platoon officer kept paying us a visit to see how we were. Also the platoon sergeant who was really concerned about us. I remember he kept singing *Melancholy Baby* most of the time. We never did reach our objective that night. This was a small bridge. Instead we finished up in some sort of orchard. At dawn we were told where to dig our slit-trenches. Ours was in the front line of trenches and there was another line behind us. We managed to hide our Churchill tank. Sid Allen and I got the names "Digger One" and "Digger Two" because we finished our trench the fastest of the lot. By the time we had finished digging it was daylight and the sun was shining. We were told to keep quiet so as not to give our position away. We took turns in looking out of our trench and things were reasonably quiet. On one occasion we saw a German patrol and I remember that one of them wore a shiny black steel helmet. About noon we opened a tin of M & V stew and ate that between us with some hardtack biscuits, which almost broke your teeth biting through them. The Germans were in position half a mile in front of us in a wood and during the afternoon our CO ordered rocket-firing Typhoons to blast their positions. The few houses that were about all had big white sheets hanging from their windows.

'Not until 6 in the evening were we relieved by a Canadian tank unit which came amongst us and opened up with everything they had before moving forward towards the enemy line. We got out of our trenches for the first time since dawn and it was nice to get the circulation back. I never knew how many Germans were in front of us until I saw them coming back with the Canadians. I nearly had a fit.

Some were even riding on the tanks. It wasn't until we found a place in a field to sleep that we were informed we had been cut off throughout the whole day. Hence the reason we were ordered to keep quiet and to let the German patrol pass by without firing on it. I couldn't have slept more soundly if anyone had given me a Mickey Finn. The next morning our Section was given the job of carrying out a daylight patrol, led by Corporal Barnett. We hugged the woods that had been alive with Jerries the previous day and except for meeting some Italian partisans wearing red scarves, and some Italian people trying to get back to their homes, plus a few false alarms, things were pretty quiet. I was really pleased to get back to our platoon and to see my mate again.

'During the rest of the day the rocket-firing Typhoons were really giving the Jerries a pasting. It was hard for us greenhorns to relax. We were all tense and excited, whereas the old soldiers were resting and even having a nap. However, we paid for it that night because we could hardly keep our eyes open. That night was almost a repeat of the previous one; advancing along the road. This time we could see the German slit-trenches and our troops fired into them although they appeared empty. The Germans had marked these trenches with a pole sticking up with a lump of straw or grass tied around the top, which I found very strange. This time, before dawn, we dug-in at the side of a country lane and seemed to be on our own. I was pleased when the platoon officer crept up to us to tell us that there would be a "stonk" in a few moments and to keep our heads down because it was ours and there were some Jerries nearby who needed to be cleared out. When the stonk happened it was too close for comfort and we were praying that no shells would fall short. Among the loud bangs you could hear the Italians in their houses screaming all the time and we were glad when the guns ceased. That morning I received a letter – the first one – as I sat on the side of my trench I was amazed that the army knew where I was. We rested that day and had a hot meal. Afterwards, a mobile bath lorry arrived. This had about twelve shower heads. At the entrance you took off all your clothes, discarded your dirty underwear and walked in. If you got one of the first six units you had a good shower. But gradually the water would peter out and at the end [shower head] you would be lucky to get a few drips. Then out of the other end to put on clean fresh clothes.

'About this time Jerry had left a lot of propaganda leaflets behind. One sticks in my mind. It was about seven inches long by four inches wide and on the front was an attractive Italian signorina carrying a basket of flowers and fruit with the River Po in the background. On the reverse side was a skeleton holding in one hand an American steel helmet and in the other a British one with the words "We are waiting for you". It also showed the details of how fast the river flowed, the widest and narrowest parts and the best places to cross, etc. I had this fear of crossing the river because I was not a swimmer and with all the gear we had to carry the situation didn't seem all that rosy. Lorries brought up little, collapsible boats made from wood and canvas. You stood inside them and pulled up the sides, wedging them with wooden struts. We rested for a few days and then one afternoon we lined up for rations and ammunition. We knew we were going back in. You could see the look on the faces of the men, knowing that the war was nearly over. Some had seen years of action. They didn't want to cop it now. As we lined up to march out that night one of the boys who carried a radio pack overheard that the Jerries had surrendered in Italy. The date was 2 May 1945; four days earlier than in Germany. What a relief.

'We crossed the Po on a pontoon bridge then, in convoy, made our way towards the Alps. The chalk and dust that came off the roads made us all look like ghosts. Our platoon stopped at a little railway track and that night we lit a huge bonfire, like a beacon, so that the Germans could come marching in to surrender. It was funny hearing them marching towards us knowing that a day or so earlier you were killing each other. They were unable to surrender during the day because the Italian partisans were stopping them doing so. Trips were made to places where the Germans were, to rescue them from the partisans. There were weapons everywhere, discarded by the surrendering Germans.

'A day or so later we were again loaded on to lorries and made our way to the Austrian border. It was a long and tiring journey and the road twisted up and around the sides of mountains seeming to go on forever. Then we started the descent which took us over the frontier. We took over the first village (Mauthen), and occupied the only hotel. This had previously been in the hands of the Germans. We cleared out all the clothes they had left in the wardrobes and took great pleasure in taking a photo of Adolf Hitler off the wall and putting it on a fire. It was great to have a roof over our head and a good bed to sleep in. It took a while for the villagers to come out of their houses because we were the first enemy troops they had seen. We had orders not to fraternize with them. The first few days were spent cleaning up the hotel, smartening ourselves up, blancoing our gear white and spit and polishing our boots. The officers put their pips back on and sergeants and corporals put up their stripes. The war in Europe was now over. The occupying forces had a mammoth task of sorting out thousands of displaced persons. I wish I could have finished my army service there, but in September I was posted to Greece.'

War in the Far East

THE FIRST CAMPAIGN IN BURMA AND MALAYA

In December 1941, the Empire of Japan opened a war against America and Great Britain. In a swift blaze of conquest Japan flung back both opponents and by February 1942 the British Army in Burma and Malaya was being forced to retreat by an enemy who, striking through the jungles, had caught it off-balance.

British Far Eastern defence plans had been predicated upon an enemy seaborne assault upon the large cities of Britain's far eastern Empire. It had been considered militarily impossible for large bodies of enemy troops to move through the jungle which covered Burma and Malaya. Although the Japanese were as unfamiliar with the jungle as were our own soldiers, they quickly learned to live in the conditions encountered there. They did not see the jungle as a barrier between them and Britain's Asian cities, but rather as a covered approach towards those objectives. Consequently they moved large bodies of troops through the jungle by splitting them into small parties, using whatever transport was available. Not being dependant for supplies upon a long and tortuous line of communication, the Japanese troops advanced quickly and came up behind the British prepared positions defending the coastal towns.

The Japanese strategic plan against Britain was to capture India through Ceylon and/or Burma. The Ceylon thrust was not developed; the campaign in Burma depended upon the struggle by both sides; the Japanese to enter the sub-continent through the 'gateways,' Imphal and Kohima, and the British to prevent this. The high-tide of Japanese Imperial effort turned at those two small villages and once these offensives had been foiled, Slim's Fourteenth Army – the forgotten Army – began to force the Japanese Army out of Burma and then to go on to reconquer the territories which had been lost in the first flush of Nipponese Imperialism. When the full force of the Japanese assault fell upon the British Army in Burma, forces were brought from other theatres of operation to hold back the enemy thrusts. One unit rushed from the desert fighting was 7th Armoured Brigade. At first it was ordered to help defend Singapore, but by the time the brigade arrived in the Far East the city had fallen. The following account of armoured actions around Rangoon is taken from *The Tank*, with kind permission of the Editor:

'The Brigade numbered 114 Stuarts; 10 in Brigade Headquarters and 52 each in the 7th Queen's Own Hussars and 2nd Battalion Royal Tank Regiment.

On 21 February 1942, it began to unload at Rangoon and spent the first few days in Burma preparing itself for the battles to come. Meantime the Japs were driving west from Thailand and the Burma Corps was already hard pressed on the Sittang River, east of Rangoon. The 2nd Royal Tanks were the first to be blooded and standing patrols found the oncoming Japs at intervals along the west bank of the Sittang. The Burma Corps came streaming back and soon the 2nd RTR was fighting a very confused and bitter action. One tank was knocked out by a Jap mortar when it was running at 30mph on a tarmac road. Japs were nowhere to be seen, yet the tanks were fired on from all directions. The Browning machine-guns took their toll and later many Japs were killed as they came unsuspectingly upon the standing patrols. Meantime 7th Hussars had accounted for five Jap tanks, which were all knocked out by the 37mm guns, at a range of 400 yards. The 37mm shot went through them all very easily taking with them pieces of Japanese. The only other tanks which were encountered were Stuarts which had been captured earlier. The Armoured Brigade was ordered to delay the Japanese drive on Rangoon, but those instructions were countermanded by General Alexander who based the defence around Mandalay – a move which gave Field Marshal Wavell time to organize the defence of India. There followed a series of actions against Japanese infiltration parties as the Burma Army retreated slowly northwards. At Prome, the largest roadblock of all, 7th Hussars lost 10 Stuarts after 48 hours' fighting. Many of the crews who had to bale out were not seen again because the Japs were waiting for them with bayonets. There were scores of Japs killed here and many snipers hung dead in the palm tree tops where they had tied themselves. One officer's tank was knocked out and he was captured by the Japanese during the night. Tied hand and foot to a roadblock, he managed to escape when the British 25pdrs opened up on it.

'The Japanese infiltration parties detailed to make roadblocks were generally armed with either light mortars or automatic rifles. They used petrol bombs against the tanks. Quick to seize the initiative, they would creep up close enough to the tanks to lob in hand-grenades and to fire at the visors. During all this time the tanks had little respite and drivers would leave the leaguers at first light knowing that a long day's fighting lay ahead and that through the night they would have to withdraw to the next stand. But the worst stroke of fortune was yet to come. Whereas the road from India met the Chindwin River at Kalevo, the road from Burma met the Chindwin six miles farther south. Thus, when the tank crews arrived at the river they had to destroy all the equipment they had so carefully maintained throughout the campaign. The Brigade was ordered to march out and reach the Indian frontier as best they could. In some cases the men marched for over a week and their fitness was proved since not a single man was lost during the retreat on foot.'

John Wyatt of 2nd Battalion, The East Surrey Regiment, was one of those who had been fighting against the Japanese from the first days of the war:

'Ourselves, that is the East Surreys, the Leicestershires and the Argylls, were the first white troops in action against a superior enemy. Our first battle was at Jitra which the Japs had no difficulty in taking as we had very little air support and no tanks . . . We fell back withdrawing and fighting and put up a stiff resistance at Gurun which stopped the Japs for about three days. We had been in action for two weeks and found ourselves at Gurun. At about 4 one morning we heard the Jap [tank] column. We were told by the officer in charge, "Last man, last round." We smoked our last cigarettes and said goodbye to each other. Dawn was just breaking when the Japs broke through. All hell let loose. Three aircraft came over and there were bombs all around us. All we could do as we crouched there was to wait for one to hit us. The planes flew off and four tanks rumbled up the road and gave our positions hell. They flung everything at us. All of a sudden we heard a shout, "Run for it lads!" and we ran and that was the last I saw of the officer. I shall never forget him as we ran past him, pistol in hand, holding off the advancing Japs while we got away. We also left another East Surrey propped against a tree. He had been hit in the ankle, a water-bottle and rifle was left by his side. I dread to think what the Japs did to him when they found him. He must have had a lonely death. We waded through about a mile of paddyfields, reached the safety of the jungle and then set out to find the British lines. We tramped about twenty miles, or so it seemed, and reached safety about 5 o'clock that night. Then for sleep, food, clean clothes and a shave, for we had lost everything. Most of the battalion reached safety, but a lot of chaps are still missing – some of my friends, too.

'We marched to Johore where we were cut off and where a miniature Dunkirk took place. There were about 400 of us, now known as the British Battalion because the casualties had been so heavy to the East Surreys and Leicesters that we had had to be amalgamated. We were taken off right under the noses of the searching Jap troops by two gunboats, the *Dragonfly* and *Firefly*. They took us to Singapore. After a brief rest we went into action when the Japs crossed the causeway. I was hit in the shoulder by Jap mortar fire at Bukit Timah racecourse, rescued by Chinese guerrillas and taken to Alexandra hospital where I survived the massacre by Japs who had gone beserk and so passed into captivity.'

The confusion of those first days is reflected in Sidney Sheldrick's account, which described the convoy in which he sailed as containing:

'The most unlucky bunch of soldiers in World War 2. The large convoy had sailed from the UK on the very day that the Japs bombed Pearl Harbor and we became the convoy that nobody wanted and what was more terrible, we were the convoy that nobody knew what to do with. Winston Churchill decided that as a token gesture to the Dutch we would be landed on Java. Sadly our 8,000-odd total of soldiers contained no infantry or tank units. All the soldiers were either RAOC, RASC, light or heavy anti-aircraft regiments. Few had seen action at all.'

Gunner Evans, whom we first met at Dunkirk, then went on to Far Eastern service with his anti-aircraft regiment which set up its guns on the golf course at Kuala Lumpur.

'The day before the fall of Singapore we were ordered to the docks to try to get away in two boats. We loaded the guns on board; half on one boat, half on the other. The Japs were knocking the hell out of the docks. My wife's name saved my life. We were going up the gangplank on one ship when Jock Liddle stopped dead nearly causing me to fall off into the briny. "Digger," he said, "Look there." On top of the funnel of the second ship was my wife's name, *Iris*. "Come on," said Jock. "She'll look after us." The reason why we left Singapore was to protect a secret aerodrome in Sumatra. We landed in Palembang, then moved inland into the jungle. The next morning there was a trial run on the guns. Then about half-past nine the chap on spotting duty shouted, "Planes approaching!" The chap on the UB2 shouted, "They're dropping parashooters!" So we loaded shrapnel and fired on them. You could see them doubling up as the shrapnel pierced their bodies. When it quietened down the lads wanted their breakfast. You had to go to an open piece of ground, so the lads volunteered me to go. Off I went, made some buckets of tea and started the bacon. When I looked up there were three painted soldiers, just like the doll ones you buy in a box. They were Jap paratroops. So I just dived [into the river] and swam to the gun pits. We fired into the jungle where I last saw them. We decided to go and see what damage the shrapnel had done. Tommie Gill put the only Bren-gun we had on to my shoulder and fired it from there. Two lads with the only two rifles we had fired at the first lot of bushes. One chap said, there's something a back of this bush. He kept poking about with his rifle. Then he fired. A Jap squealed and died. We went farther into the jungle but all we saw was Jap paras hanging in the trees.

'The pilots of the secret fighter drome were doomed. We had orders to destroy our gun as we had no more ammunition and get across the Palembang River. A lorry took some of our group halfway to the river and then went back for the remainder. They passed us heading towards the river, but *en route* the lorry was ambushed and they were killed. We lost four more going to their aid. One of our gun lorry drivers, Allen, a Geordie lad, took the Bren-gun from the officer, placed it on his hip like a gangster and went in. He was stunned for a bit by a hand-grenade, but he got up shouting "You yellow bastards!" and wiped out the four remaining paratroops. We found a steam train, but had no driver until out of the blue came two British sailors. Their boat had been sunk by the Japs. They told me, "Tell your mates to get mounted. We'll drive it." We were well on our way when the train stopped and an officer came along. The Japs had dropped a second batch of paras on an Australian bomber drome and he wanted volunteers. I was detailed to go, but would have volunteered anyroad, because we were like a close-knit family. I still think back how artillery lads, not trained in jungle warfare, took on the finest jungle fighters in the world. Some of our lads were Glasgow tram drivers, Irish lorry drivers, Geordie dock workers, Welsh and Yorkshire coal miners and office workers, also two butchers. I'd go through hell with them. They joked about everything and if we were moving from one place to another the Welsh lads would start them all singing. We set off towards the aerodrome; one rifle between eleven men, hoping to be armed by the Australian air force. When we got there all the bombers were on fire. We set up guards while the rest of us washed our feet. We had not had our boots off for days. What a shock I had when I took my sock down. My feet were all blue. I thought of gangrene. One of my mates said, "It's allright, Digger, its the dye out of your boots through going through the swamps." Next morning we tried to get in touch with the Aussies. We found a few of them tied to trees. When we were resting one of the lads came running up to the officer telling him that some more Japanese paras had been seen in an open clearing. The officer told me to sort them out. No rifle, no arms at all. Off I went. Orders are orders.

'I got to the clearing and stood there with my arms crossed fascinated as I watched a dozen Jap paras moving towards the bomber drome which was all ablaze. They just ignored me. Whether they thought I was a native or whether they were trained to go for their target, I do not know. I could see their eyes looking at me. What I can't understand is why I was not frightened. We boarded the train again and finished up at a sea port, Osthaaven, facing Java. Our Major volunteered us for anti-paratroop fighters for the Dutch in Java. So we sailed across to Batavia. We went by train to the other end of Java. We didn't have much food so some of the lads went hunting. They brought in mountain goats – like donkeys with twisted horns. It took Arthur Barnet, a skilled butcher, twenty minutes to kill them. They were really tough. One morning I woke up and there were Mongolian guards. So I told the lads, be careful as we were surrounded. They took us to a prison camp just outside Batavia which was already occupied by Americans, Aussies and Indians. We were prisoners-of-war of the Japanese.'

THE FIGHTING IN SINGAPORE

Impressions of conditions in Singapore and the fighting for the city were given by a great many former soldiers, and from their accounts I have selected that of C. W. Carpenter of the Norfolks, to describe the confusion of the fighting and the bewilderment of surrender. What follows is only part of his much longer typescript.

'December 29th, 1941. We sailed from Mombassa and as the shore faded from view we were told our ultimate destination; Singapore!! Well we wanted action, by golly we had got ourselves a real beauty. The latest news was bad; the situation was really serious. The Yellow Peril was advancing rapidly on all fronts sweeping away all opposition. Murdering, raping, looting as they advanced and worst of all taking no prisoners of war. We were told that an officer and a sergeant from the Intelligence Corps were to give us a lecture on what they had learned from behind the Japanese lines and show us some of the arms and equipment they had captured. The officer told us that we should have not trouble in pushing the Japs right back where they had come from. He said the Japs were terribly short of modern arms, equipment and supplies. The sergeant was backing up the officer's statements by showing us the various guns and equipment. Some of it must have been issued in the Boer War. He went on to say that the Japs were shortsighted and were so scared of darkness that they would not move at night. The lecture finished on a happy note. We were confident that in no time at all we should have pushed the Japs back to where they belonged and taught them a lesson. January 16th, 1942. The sound of smallarms fire was heard in the distance. The enemy was not far away. Runners came back from the forward Companies to say that one of our scouting patrols had run into a heavy force of Japs and had suffered heavy casualties. Men were coming back wounded and bewildered. From the reports they gave we realized that we were up against a very cunning enemy. Our men were being shot down and our lads could see nothing to fire back at. During the night large parties of Japs had got in behind us. They had used boats to land behind us and as we had not got even a rowing-boat they had no trouble at all. The Japs were fanatics. Death was an honour to them. I have seen one of our light machine-gun sections, consisting of about four Bren-guns, firing their guns until they were literally too hot to handle, surrounded by piles of dead Japs and still they have come forward shouting their blood-curdling scream of *Banzai!* and overrun the gun position.

'January 29th, 1942. A conference was called for all senior officers. The news our CO gave us was grave. Japanese forces were only twenty miles away and were overrunning our defences. It had been decided to withdraw from Malaya and make a stand at Singapore. So the battle for Malaya was over, but the Japs had had a taste of British stubbornness and fighting qualities. All our forward troops had been in constant action for the past four to five weeks against the cream of the Imperial Japanese Guard. The withdrawal began and our troops came through our lines. Tired men, disillusioned men, but not beaten men. The withdrawal from the mainland of all the Allied troops was now complete. Australian troops on the island gave the rearguard troops covering fire. The rearguard action was fought by one of the toughest and bravest regiments in the British Army, the Argyll and Sutherland Highlanders. With bagpipes playing, kilts swinging, one would have thought that they were on a drill square somewhere in Blighty. What a glorious sight they were. The won not only the respect of us all on the island but the enemy as well. An Australian Major [whose infantry unit Carpenter joined] told us the situation on the island was desperate, water was so short it was being rationed. The death rate was high, disease was spreading, bodies of the dead and carcasses of animals were rotting everywhere. There would be no question of surrender; evacuation was impossible. The Japanese Army Commander was still demanding an unconditional surrender. Our Army Commander was still adamant. "No surrender at any price." The whole Commonwealth force was behind him to a man. After the last round had been fired it would be hand-to-hand fighting with fixed bayonets. Saturday, February 14th, 1942. The light was beginning to fade. We all wondered what would happen tomorrow. While our guns were firing we were still active. I know that if it had been left to the troops we should never have surrendered. The streets would have been piled high with our dead and wounded. The end came abruptly when the civilian authorities approached the military commander and pleaded for a surrender.'

The rapid advance of the Japanese Army into Burma and Malaya struck and split the hastily formed British front and forced the defenders back. The confusion that existed in the British colonial territories in those early days of the Far Eastern campaign has been recalled by many correspondents and is shown here in the experiences of Arnold Watson. He was a Private soldier in the RASC, who reached Singapore on 28 November 1941. War with Japan had not yet broken out. Nine days after Watson's arrival the Japanese struck at Pearl Harbor. In the fury of the enemy assault, Kuala Lumpur fell and Arnold Watson's unit, which was in the city, was split up. He moved to Malacca where he joined another RASC detachment until that city fell, in its turn. His letter touches upon the highlights of those days.

'We went down-country from Malacca to Johore and at Baharu we helped to take the wounded from hospital to a waiting Red Cross ship in Singapore. We worked until the Japanese air raids stopped us. The ship, packed with wounded, left the port during an air raid. Back in the city some hospitals still had wounded men and, of course, casualties were coming in the whole time. There were no more hospital ships to take them away. The nursing sisters and doctors refused to leave the wounded men and stayed with them until the Japanese Army arrived. We RASC men reported to a camp at Bukit Timah Road and were sent to a naval base in search of food. Our first foray succeeded, but when we went a second time we could not reach the depot. Japanese tanks barred the way. It was very clear that the city must soon fall. The order was given that all equipment which could be used by the enemy was to be destroyed. This meant all arms and all forms of transport. Lorries and motor cycles were the obvious ones and we set about making them useless. One sad task at this time was to have to shoot the horses on the Singapore race track, so that the Japanese could not use them.

'By this time the evacuation of British women and children was in full swing and our unit helped to embark Service wives and families. This was a terrible time. The Japanese air force had command of the air and bombed transports just outside the harbour, sinking most of them, with a great loss of life. The general deterioration of the military situation meant that while some formations were arriving in the dying city others had been ordered to leave it. Those fragments of units that had been smashed during the retreat were evacuated while fresh units were coming in from the liner *Empress of Asia*. Those "unblooded" units were too few to halt the Japanese drive and when the city fell some battalions marched almost from the ship and into prison camp.

'When Singapore city was surrendered some of us went to Blakang Mati island, so small that you could virtually walk round it. We found out that the Japs had already landed there, so one night about twenty of us left in a small boat. The intention was to sail to some British-held point. Nobody wanted to become a prisoner of the Japanese. During our short voyage we picked a couple of airmen out of the water. They were lying exhausted in a dinghy and when we found them they were very far gone. Neither of them had the energy to speak and both died the next morning. Our sense of humour did not leave us during this very hazardous trip. I was sitting as look-out in the front of our dinghy looking through a pair of binoculars. I saw a boat and asked what flag it was flying. I pretended not to know that a white flag with a red circle on it was, of course, the Japanese flag. It was flying on an enemy gunboat which was checking the river traffic. We would not have been able to pass the control-point in our dinghy so we beached it and headed inland. We were lucky enough to find an old bus which took us down-country. When we next came to the sea there was a British ship the *Danie* on which we sailed to Java. Even there we were not safe and a group of ninety of us, led by Captain Johnson of the RASC, who had led us in our first invasion, took over the *Uchang*. This was a flat-bottomed, wooden river boat and in that craft we sailed out and straight into a naval battle. While we were sailing through the fighting a Japanese submarine surfaced alongside us. We were lucky. We had two flags with us; our own White Ensign and the Japanese one. We flew the Jap flag when their submarine surfaced and it submerged again without checking us. For the duration of the three-weeks' voyage I was the cook, serving up chiefly rice and bully beef. Eventually we landed in Ceylon and for a short time I was with an Indian Base Ordnance workshops in Colombo.'

When HMSS *Prince of Wales* and *Repulse* were sunk, the possibility of a Japanese strike through Ceylon became a probability. To counter that threat, reinforcements were rushed from India and among them was the 114th Field Regiment Royal Artillery. Don Harding:

'The Japanese invation did not take place, but tragedy struck the regiment. They took away our beloved 25pdrs and gave us 3inch mortars. We were now the 114th Jungle Field Regiment – RA with peashooters. After our training period in Ceylon we went to a place called Ranchi in Assam, where the 20th Indian Division was formed. We moved to the railhead at Dimapur, thence by road to Imphal and on to the Manipur–Burma border. There we were in various areas supporting infantry units and the regiment was now split into three batteries. Each battery consisted of a further two troops. So you can see that whereas before we were more or less together as a regiment, now we were spread through the division in small groups and it was only during the few rest periods that we were together again.'

Don Harding was sent on a course and his letter recalling his return to the unit at Witok begins in a way that will be familiar to most soldiers:

'I had hardly unpacked my kit before I was assigned as OP wireless op on a detachment of mortars in support of 4/10 Gurkhas on Hilltop 2007, overlooking the River Chindwin. My particular unit or Troop was of two mortar sections each of four mortars. Each section would support an infantry Company from within that Company's perimeter. The mortar fire was directed from an OP by an officer supported by a specialist and a signaller (me) who was in contact with the mortar position by line telephone and/or radio. We came under heavy attack from the Japs but held the position. It was during this action that Ron Biggs was killed and Jack Price wounded by a mortar bomb which exploded on the parapet of the slit-trench they were manning. We were eventually relieved by another section, but they had to pull back sharply on a night evacuation. The Japs were, by now, attacking on all fronts and we returned to Witok and another Jap attack. Then came the withdrawal along the Tamu road to Palel and then to a position which we had to hold to stop the Japs advancing on Imphal. That was a place that the Japs had to take if their "march on India was to succeed". By this time Kohima was under siege and our main supply line to India, the Manipur road, was cut. Our positions were known as "Crete", "Scraggy", "Malta" and "Gibraltar". There we took the brunt of the heavy Japanese night assaults to take Imphal. Endless nights of shelling by Jap 105mms, until about 1am, then wave after wave of infantry attacks. Our mortars had a devastating effect on those attacks, but still the Jap infantry came forward. Our men would blaze away from their slit-trenches and so it would go on until just before dawn when their attacks would cease. There would then be a brief respite during the daylight hours, except for spasmodic sniping. Then the same all over again the next night, and so on, night after night. One night, after the shelling stopped, everything went deadly quiet. Then we heard the ominous rour of tank engines approaching "Scraggy". We thought it was our lot until the lead tank was hit by shellfire. It blocked the road and stopped any further tank advance.

'The Jap offensive was finally broken. Their supply lines, always over-extended, ceased to function and the final blow, the start of the monsoon season, helped to halt their operations. We were able to take a well-earned leave and enjoy a period of rest in Calcutta. At Wenjong we got our 25pdrs back; at last becoming proper Gunners again. We fought our way to the Irrawaddy River, crossing the mile-wide stream on makeshift rafts at dead of night. On the road to Meiktila we received an Intelligence report that a Japanese division was pushing south on the west bank of the Irrawaddy, but that some units had crossed over and were coming down a road on the east bank, running parallel to the river. An ambush was set up by an Indian unit (Frontier Force Rifles) with our 25pdrs and 5in Medium batteries in support. Our OP party was a shallow slit-trench on the forward perimeter right next to the road. The guns were ranged in on the road and then it was a case of waiting. Night fell and for a few hours all was quiet. Suddenly out of the darkness thundered a truck. It smashed right through the ambush, but the second one was halted by smallarms fire and grenades. It stopped in the middle of the position. The convoy of lorries behind it halted and the guns opened up, bang on target. Then came the biggest fireworks display I have ever seen. The trucks were carrying ammunition. Shells were exploding and smallarms ammunition was crackling away like jumping jacks and the whole place was lit up. I was trying to contact the OP on the radio, but the static interference was too bad to make contact. At the same time we were trying to keep our heads down and also keep our eyes peeled for wandering Japs. Suddenly out of the smoke a figure appeared. Bill Bridger let rip with his Sten and killed a Jap practically on top of us. The rest of the night was spent waiting to see if the Japs would attack. But all was quiet in that respect. When dawn broke we were able to see the havoc wrought by our guns. The convoy had been destroyed and about a hundred Japs were killed. From Mandalay we pushed south towards Rangoon with skirmishes all the way. The Japanese were in retreat, but far from beaten. Every soldier fought to the death and few prisoners were taken. I was taken sick before we reached Rangoon and, much to my disappointment, by the time I had recovered the war was over.'

VICTORY IN THE FAR EAST

The last days of the reconquest of Burma were recalled by Tony Pellet, who had served in the same artillery regiment as Don Harding:

'It was July, we were well into the monsoons which meant that a great deal of time it was raining "cats and dogs". For us the war had now passed by, except for one Troop of guns which had been sent to Pegu to assist in dealing with the Japs who were trying to get out. The talk now was of going home to "Blighty" – repatriation had started for those who had been overseas 3½ years or thereabouts and all those who had come out with the Regiment in 1942 (which was most) qualified for this. The talk was true, but the Regiment had to stay and go on to French Indo-China (now Vietnam). We, the old hands, could not go until our replacements turned up. They did and were all much younger than us. A lot had come from the 12th Army Group and had been in the invasion of Europe. They were not very happy about the prospect of fighting the Japs, having had to deal with the Nazis, but there it was. Someone had to do it. We old hands were told to get our kit ready and hand our weapons in, then be prepared to move out. We were leaving to be transferred to a holding-unit known as 12th FRU. After all these years the name still registers, still with dismal memories. One of the places best forgotten, but somehow never quite. It turned out to be a collection of tents in the middle of nowhere just outside Rangoon. We arrived to be met by some Infantry NCOs who did not seem to be expecting us. They certainly knew nothing about a horde of Gunners asking when was the boat going to be ready to take them home. The Infantry NCOs started to treat us as though we were newly arrived white-kneed rookies, ready to go into action. This did not amuse us and I think secretly we were a little scared. Was it possible that if we didn't do something positive we might find ourselves going through the sausage-machine and posted to some Infantry mob bound for Singapore, or worse still left to rot in Burma? It was worrying. Feelings got worse when we were segregated from our own senior NCOs, and the infantry's main preoccupation was to make the camp safe against Burmese dacoits. We were very amused. It was hardly likely that having met the Japs we were concerned about a few Burmans who might have bows and arrows. In the end a state of mutiny existed, something that shot and shell, rain, half-rations and no beer had never reduced us to before. One day nearly all the Gunners were put on a charge for some trifling reason. They dropped that because there were too many to deal with. We felt like breaking out, but somehow we didn't. I suppose the remains of our self-discipline prevailed and in any case there was nowhere to go. Somehow our senior NCOs got to hear of this and they managed to get through the red tape and make a complaint to the CO of the camp. The result was that we were moved to another part of the camp and our own NCOs took charge. Of course, we responded and there were no problems or misunderstandings.

'It was while we were here that the "Bomb" was dropped and the war ended. We were stuck in this camp with one bottle of beer to celebrate a victory to which we had contributed in no small way. As far as the "Bomb" was concerned most of us did not moralize over it. At the time it was considered by many that it no doubt saved thousands of Allied lives. Those, for example, who had to retake Malaya and occupy Japan and all those who were living under wretched conditions as POWs. It is probably true that their lives were saved. At about this time there was a spot of unrest among the British troops in Rangoon, the bulk of whom were awaiting repatriation. But it seemed to be going very slow, somewhere the pipeline was getting blocked. We were told it was a shortage of shipping. The result was that the lads were getting upset and in one or two cases, though it wasn't mutiny, things happened that were very close to it. Lord Louis Mountbatten and General Bill Slim came back to Rangoon to sort things out and the steam was taken out of the situation. There is no mention of this in the Official History of the War in South-East Asia – but it did happen.

'At last came the day to leave; as usual, at the crack of dawn we piled into trucks to take us down to the docks [and] the ship *Felix Rousell,* lying in the

Rangoon River. We boarded. No one smiled, no one cheered. All looked somewhat dazed as though it was not true. We were actually getting on a ship and going home to Blighty. The war, a way of life for six years, was over – or nearly over – for us. We could not take it in.

'One morning it was very foggy and apart from the cries of the sea birds all was quiet. We were hove-to off the Liverpool Bar, at the entrance to the River Mersey, waiting to go into Liverpool. The tale going round the ship was that there might be delays. There was a strike in the docks at Liverpool and we might not get off that day. The troops were not amused. We had lads with us who had been POWs under the Japs. What a welcome home for them! We went down the river and waited for the dockyard hands to tie us up. Meanwhile there was much shouting from the troops and caustic remarks directed at the dockers. We only wanted to be tied up and to get ashore. We didn't need their help. All our belongings were carried on our backs. After a long-winded discussion the dockers agreed to do whatever they had to do and the gangplanks were lowered. A band was playing; someone made a speech (we didn't take much notice of) and then we started going ashore, the POWs leading off, which I expect was only fair . . . Then slowly the Hastings train (from Charing Cross) backed in and we got in. In two hours we would all be home again. Hastings where it had started for us on Friday 1 September 1939. We were on our way home. The Great Adventure was all over and we could start being normal human beings again.'

The Rewards of Soldiering

Death

The first dead men seen on the battlefield did not bring the violent shock that is portrayed in films. Death in many forms was not unfamiliar to the working-class man of the Second World War. Infant mortality and a catalogue of fatal illnesses took away relatives, friends and neighbours and it was the custom for the corpse to be laid out in a coffin in the house. Dead bodies – in civvie street, better arranged and presented, but nevertheless dead bodies, were a normal feature of life. The dead on battlefields often bore no disfiguring wounds so that they appeared to be asleep.

'In one attack we passed over ground which another Company had already crossed. Lying flat on his back with a knee drawn up was one of my mates – "Pop". We called him that because to us 19-year-olds he seemed so old. He was probably about 30. He looked so natural. The only thing missing was his ground sheet. Pop never lay on the grass without one. He was paler than usual, but he lay there quite peacefully with only the blood on his chest and stomach to show where he had been hit. All those things I registered in two or three paces. I felt no terrible sadness at that time, although now, forty years on, I still remember him and can see him on that Italian hillside on a warm, autumn morning.'

The fresh-killed dead were one thing. Those that lay unburied and open to the elements were frightening in their grotesque, inflated obscenity as the following accounts show. F. Shaw:

'We were advancing along a road. It had been raining for days and the ditches were filled with water. My Section Corporal and I were leading the platoon. We both saw this movement in a ditch on the right side of the road and both realized it was a Jerry crouched down with his back towards us. We both fired and hit him. When we reached him it was clear he had been dead for days and had been crouched in that water-filled ditch for all that time. He was blue-green in colour, horribly bloated and his scalp was peeling off in one place. I don't know how the Corporal felt, but I was ashamed that I had fired at a man already dead. He was the worst sight I ever saw during the war.'

J. Cartwright, RTR:

'On a ridge outside San Savino, near Rimini, there was a Jerry spreadeagled on the road, with another sprawled backwards in a hedge. The one on the road was absolutely flat. Tanks had run over him and his squashed body was like something you see in cartoon films. Clouds of bluebottles were all over him – not many on the man in the hedge and they flew off when the officer and I went through his pockets for documents. I could not read German, but the officer told me that the man in the hedge came from Sudetenland in Czechoslovakia and the entries in his Army book confirmed that he was in the 29th Panzer Grenadier Division.'

Robert Fleming, RAMC:

'One of the worst duties I had was to take the bodies out of tanks which had been recovered from the battlefields. The "brewed-up" ones were worst. We usually tied scarves around our mouths and noses, more to stop germs than anything else. It was no easy task getting the bodies out. They fell apart. Some had been incinerated down to their boots. The things we were looking for were identity discs. They were almost indestructible. It was a rotten job sifting through the rubbish on the bottom of a tank searching for a couple of identity tags, but it was necessary and someone had to do it."

Henry Saunders, Infantry:

'The worst parade in the war was the roll-call after an attack. If you have had a pasting you are still a bit jumpy. The roll-call brought back all that you had been through. It was usually held on the morning after you came out of the line. We would then be paraded and once you were all together you realized how many had gone. The CSM would call us to attention for the officer and then he would read out the roll. Those on parade would respond to their names. When there was no response the questions would begin. "Did anyone see him fall? Was he wounded? Where and how badly? Was he killed? How? Where?" The Company clerk would take down the details and so the parade would go on until everybody was accounted for. Sometimes parties of us would be detailed to walk across the attack area looking for any mates that were missing and who couldn't be accounted for on the roll-call parade. We also had to help the Pioneer platoon collect any arms and equipment in our attack sector. There was always piles of it.'

Paradoxically, the longer the time spent on active service, the more upsetting were the battlefield sights; the fallen and the wounded. One did not become more accustomed to them. The opposite was true – they affected the soldier more. It was, perhaps, the realization that his luck was draining away. There was an awful inevitability at the back of every fighting soldier's mind. He had only to look round the circle of his comrades to see how few there remained of those who had sailed out with the unit for overseas service. Each day of battle cost men. Each group of men who became casualties would include a veteran. It was, thus, only a question of time before one's own turn came and one would feature in that heart-breaking roll-call parade described above.

MUTILATION

To be wounded was not the dramatic affair seen on TV or in the films. Many did not realize at first they had been hit. Others, unaware of the seriousness of their wounding, tried to carry on with their duty. One such was the late Bunny Warren, a Regular soldier. He had excelled at most sports, particularly swimming. He went to France with the BEF in 1939. On the fighting retreat to

Dunkirk he was hit in the side by a tank shell and sustained wounds that might have finished a less fit man. He recovered consciousness on the open beach and realized that he would have to make arrangements of his own if he was to avoid being left behind. Warren walked into the sea and began to swim. In later years he recalled that he knew no more until he woke up in Mount Vernon hospital, eight days later. Declared medically unfit for service, his pension amounted to a few shillings each week; a derisory amount which was only increased some forty-five years after his wounding. Another man who overcame the pain of his wounds was ex-Sergeant Frank Lovett, MM. He was wounded in an attack upon Stoppiace in Italy. George Webb, from whom I received the story, wrote that Sergeant Lovett was badly wounded in the stomach. According to eyewitnesses half of it was shot away. The Sergeant reached for his small pack, removed his face towel and placed it over his wounds, waiting calmly until the stretcher-bearers came and carried him to the RAP.

George Webb was wounded on Monte Battaglia in October 1944.

'I can well remember there were the ruins of a castle at the top of Battaglia. When we passed by to get to our positions we had literally to walk over the dead American soldiers who lay adjacent to the ruins. The stench was quite unbelievable. The Americans had not dug-in like the British Tommies. All they had done was to scrape out foxholes which were totally inadequate against the relentless and accurate German shelling. No. 3 Company was moving forward and one of my men stepped on a mine. I didn't know at the time that it was a mine. We were in the last section of the Company and my first thought was that we had been ambushed by Germans. I can remember seeing, out of the corner of my eye, a white, blue and red flame. I turned round with my Tommy-gun at the ready. The Nos. 1 and 2 on the Bren in my section had been blown to pieces. Another chap was shouting for help. He had a leg blown off and the rest of the section had dispersed. I learned later that the man who had lost his leg was the one who had set off the mine. I looked down at my denims and saw that the left side was all torn. I put my hand inside the hole where the gaiters had held the denims in place. It was as if I had dipped my hand into a bowl of hot creamy custard. When I got back to the RAP a piece of my thigh was also missing. It looked to me as if someone had come along with an axe and had put a U-shaped cut into my thigh. What worried me at the time was that I did not have a lance-corporal as 2 i/c of the section. I had to delegate a senior Guardsman who, unfortunately, was a bit bomb-happy.'

F. Farmborough was wounded several times, twice while undergoing training:

'In 1941 I left the infantry after volunteering for the Commandos. After intensive training I was posted to No. 4 Commando. Often we would go out on practice exercises, nearly always using live ammunition. Before the green beret was introduced we used to wear cap-comforters and on a number of times I had mine taken off by shrapnel from the mortars. As you can imagine I was known as "shrapnel". In 1942, I got a chunk through my right knee and in 1943, another chunk through my right elbow. In 1944, we were on our way to Normandy and one of the lads was trying to run a book on who would get it first. But as we pointed out, whoever did get it first wouldn't collect. So instead we had a kitty and cut the cards. Sure enough, I won and my mates weren't surprised. I collected a fist-full of occupation money which I promptly lost at cards. But I fooled them really, because although I did cop it on D-Day, it wasn't by shrapnel. I copped a couple of bullets instead.'

John Logue of the RASC:

'The first time I was wounded was in Sicily. When we were taking the DUKWs out and in from the supply ships we usually had a Pioneer Corps bloke with us to hold the DUKW steady against the ship while they were lowering the stuff into it. Anyway, we were on our way back to the beach when this bloke says to me, "Paddy, there's water coming in." I knew I could get down into the bottom of the DUKW and get the pump fixed to get the water pumped out, but your man couldn't drive the DUKW. So I had to show him how to keep it on a steady course; it had a steering wheel just like a lorry. When he was settled behind the wheel I got down into the bilges. I don't know how long I was there, it was ages anyway, but the first thing I knew was the thump as the DUKW hit what I thought first of all was a rock but which turned out to be a spike on the beach; one of those big anti-invasion spikes. There was a big hole torn in her so we had to get out and start walking up the beach. We could see nobody, but I thought we were bound to be close to our own people. Then I heard a strange sound and I knew he had stepped on a mine. I tried to push him out of the way but it was too late; the mine had popped up and exploded. He was hurt; there was a lot of blood and I started to carry him. After a while I saw an officer, one of the beach landing organization blokes. He asked us how we had got there and I told him. I told him the Pioneer Corps lad was pretty badly hurt. The officer said, "You are hurt, too," and when I said no, he told me I had a wound in my thigh. We had walked through a minefield, he said, and it was a miracle we hadn't been killed! About an hour later I knew I had been hurt when my leg started to stiffen up. I was evacuated back to North Africa and by the time I came back to my unit we were ready for Salerno. I was wounded a second time at Anzio. We had gone in on 22 January, and had a couple of our blokes killed on the way in by mines. These were Italian mines in a wooden box and the detectors couldn't pick them up so the Engineers had to prod the beach with bayonets to find them. It was on 9 March that I was wounded. I had just finished my shift and parked up my DUKW. My relief said to me, "Paddy, you've got a puncture." I told him I'd give him a hand to repair it and as I climbed up the ribs on the side of the DUKW a shell burst above me and something hit me in the leg. I just dropped down off the DUKW. After a while an ambulance arrived and I was put on a stretcher and was slid into the ambulance, just like sliding a drawer into one of the old bread vans. So there I was lying with my head up towards the driver's cab when the ambulance was hit by a shell. It landed at the front and the next thing we knew the vehicle was on fire. I thought to myself, "Paddy, this is it," for the driver was on his own and he was running round the back of the ambulance screaming for help, but there were three of us inside who couldn't even help ourselves, let alone him. I was put in a hospital on the beachhead. The beachhead wasn't very big and everywhere in it was being shelled, including the hospital. It was hit while I was there and I thought, "Paddy, Hitler's out to get you." On the way down to Naples on a hospital ship one of the nurses came over and turned me on my side and told me to look out of the porthole. There was Vesuvius blowing its top all this smoke and flame and ash flying everywhere. I can tell you I was certain that somebody was out to get me and if it wasn't Hitler, then it was a great big volcano.'

CAPTIVITY

Another possible consequence of war was captivity. Much has been written of the horror of being taken prisoner by the Japanese and those who served in the Far East recall their determination not to be taken alive. As Don Harding wrote:

'Our main fear was to be captured by them as the only outcome would be a slow and painful death after interrogation. So even in the most critical situation surrender wasn't even considered.'

This chapter includes accounts of some of the brutalities, humiliations and degradations suffered by just a few of those thousands of British soldiers who became slaves in the Far East. The intention to murder them all in the event of a Japanese reverse was only prevented by dropping the atomic bomb which took Japan out of the war and thereby saved the lives of other British soldiers who would have been killed fighting on the soil of mainland Japan.

In respect of the Germans and Italians it was believed that if the newly taken British prisoner survived the first five minutes of captivity he could expect to reach a prison camp. The condition in which he arrived might vary, but arrive he would. Jeffrey Holland was captured during the battle of Leros in November 1943 and taken by ship to Pireaus.

'Upon our arrival the British column was marched through Athens, watched by a sympathetic crowd of Athenians. The intrepid Captain Olivey, LRDG, stepped out of the line of march and merged into the crowd; for the rest of us two weeks in a transit prison. At the railroad station lines of boxcars, festooned with barbed wire stood ready, doors open, into which were herded groups of forty prisoners. Each man was provided with a three-day ration; a hunk of grey bread. The doors were slammed shut and bolted from the outside. The train pulled out. For fifteen days and nights the prison train clanked its way through Greece, Yugoslavia, Bulgaria and Hungary. Arriving at the station in Budapest, after a journey of twelve days, the troops received one half-inch of potato soup in their mess-tins. The journey resumed. Three days later a ring of lights – Stalag VIIA, Moosburg, Germany. The doors to the boxcars were flung open and the lice-ridden, emaciated troops merged from a month of hunger and privation and staggered into the cold dawn. It was Christmas Eve, 1943.'

That there were exceptions to the thesis that to survive the first five minutes of captivity ensured arrival in a prison camp we have seen from the tragedy of the Norfolks in France in 1940. Much depended upon the unit making the capture and its morale. Generally, the better the regiment the better the treatment. Inevitably, each German who spoke English would say at some point, "For you the war is over," and this could lead into a dialogue during which he would claim that we Anglo-Saxons had no business to be fighting each other: "What do you want with Latins or Slavs?" It is very likely that the Jerries had variants of that line to tell their French, American and Russian prisoners.

For you the war is over, did not really apply to British office prisoners who were expected to make escape attempts. Other ranks worked and could be employed in a great variety of jobs. Very few were on the land. There was no 'peasant' tradition in Britain and most prisoners were given duties in factories, down mines and on the railways. In whatever field the soldiers were employed it gave them a chance to carry on, as one correspondent put it, 'buggering up the German war effort'. The extent to which one carried out small acts of disruption was determined by the attitude of the German employers and guards towards the prisoners. A good employer might only be given a very minor go-slow operation. Those who were brutal were given the full disruptive treatment. Jeffrey Holland recalls:

'We were quite Bolshie by 1943. By 1944 we could get away with murder – given the right circumstances. We knew that they were going to lose the war and they knew it too."

It is true that a lot depended upon the period of the war. In the first years of their conquest some Germans were often brutal and arrogant. As the military situation deteriorated British soldiers took more and more chances to sabotage the enemy war effort. Escape was seldom possible for other ranks for they lacked the skilled committees which ran the officers' efforts, but some did get away. There is one man who, so it is said, having escaped from a camp at Wolfsburg in Austria, gave himself up voluntarily. He had intended to reach Yugoslavia – only a handful of miles away – but had stopped to talk to some Russian women who had been recruited by the Germans to work on the land. Those ladies had had no sexual comforting for some time, and what began for him as a short sexual interlude became a terror from which he only escaped by surrendering to the local gendarmerie. Truly life as a POW was no picnic!

Tishy Parker's account of life as a prisoner was philosophical in tone:

'Very few people indeed would realize the implications of becoming a prisoner-of-war. Those who have gone through such an experience fully understand what goes through one's mind, especially during the first few days of captivity. The whole basis of finding yourself behind barbed wire, often happening through circumstances beyond your control, makes you think at that time, "Why me?" Then after a few days it registers. It means being cut off from home, friends, family, relatives. No more meeting people you know, or celebrating birthdays or anniversaries. You can't even make plans for the future. If you were in a normal prison for some crime you would have a certain sentence with a chance of remission. But a POW does not know when, or even if, he will be released. I suppose, in some respects, it was just as well you don't know, as the possibility of existing for five years behind barbed wire could mean you losing your reason – which many did. Just think what it is like. Every step you take from the time you get up off the straw bed, to when you return, you are followed everywhere. Endless roll-calls. No baths. No sanitation. Lice, fleas, sores, boils. You name it; we had it. We worked out in all weathers: rain, sleet, snow, freezing winds as only Poland and east Prussia could serve up. Working on roads, railways, canals, farms; all part of our day-to-day jobs. It was sometimes possible to remain in the main camps, but I preferred to go out on working-parties rather than stagnate by walking round the wire all day long. I suppose that we [the British] were lucky inasmuch that we were covered by the Geneva Convention, which gave us protection, up to a point. That did not mean that you wouldn't be shot, or receive a donation from the butt end of a guard's rifle. More so, if he was in a bad mood, or he had had news from home that his town had been bombed the previous day.

'Having worked alongside Russian POWs in east Prussia, I do admit that they had a far harder time than we did, with no Red Cross parcels or anything from home. In fact they were entirely disowned by their government. Our position was governed by events. If everything was going smoothly for Jerry you got what you were entitled to. If it wasn't that was your hard luck. You got no Red Cross parcels. This may seem no hardship, but to work an eleven hour day on 'Jerries' Menu' was cutting it a bit fine and was pretty grim. We were allowed one-fifth of a loaf per day, which was equivalent to about a 1½-inch thick slice from a small Hovis, together with a litre of soup. As the bulk of German food was ersatz, you never really knew what you were eating. People might wonder how we did survive for five years. You had no idea how long the war would last so you took it day by day and at every opportunity made the guards' lives as awkward as possible. As you may know, most Germans are very methodical in their habits, so we set about upsetting their routines and putting them out of their stride. If we were working on the railways, at the end of the day's work we would manage to put some pick-axes, shovels and crow-bars on the lines which meant they were chopped in half. When we were working on a building site with Polish workmen, when any excavation was made we would fling in anything (tools or equipment) we could lay our hands on and with split-second timing the Poles would follow up with barrow-loads of wet concrete.

'It would take some considerable time to relate every incident and happening over a period of five years; some tragic, some laughable. But to get through five long years as a POW you needed to have a strong sense of humour.'

The long-term effects of POW life are evident in the attitudes and behaviour of many ex-prisoners. Compulsive hoarding is just one symptom and deep bouts of depression are another. Thomas Burden, who was taken during the 1940 campaign, is a victim to the latter.

'The first months as a prisoner-of-war were terrible and even now I still have days when I get depressed thinking about the years I lost out of my life. Once things settled down and the Red Cross parcels came through then the situation got a bit better. This was now late in 1940 and the Germans were cock-a-hoop. They had won the war. They said it was only a question of time before they invaded and Britain would be beaten. We suffered when London was bombed and the Jerries gloated over it. But we consoled ourselves with no news from home being good news. Mind you we sweated when the post came up and the handwriting on the envelope wasn't the one you were expecting. We were all afraid that bad news would come in a strange handwriting. Anyway, by the end of 1940, we had had enough cabbage soup to last a couple of lifetimes and did not want any more. With the Red Cross parcels arriving regularly we could have a change of diet. We knew we would not starve – but we wouldn't get very fat either. I was in a number of camps, mostly in Silesia and Poland. In some the camp staff were real swine. Sometimes, as a punishment, so they said, but really out of sheer spite and jealousy, they would open all the tins in the parcels so that the perishable contents had to be eaten before they went off. We soon got round that though. When it happened we would take the tins with us when we left to go on outside work. There was another POW camp alongside ours holding foreign soldiers. We would tell them to be alongside the wire at a certain time and then we would lob over our damaged tins into their compound. It drove the Germans mad but it helped to feed the other prisoners, some of whom were very badly off. The German treatment of the Russians was downright inhuman. Some of our work details passed close by the wire of the Russian laager. We would throw across to them things like German ration bread and hardtack. Those poor devils got nothing from home not even letters, but then I reckon that even if Stalin had allowed parcels to be sent the Germans would not have distributed them. They really hated the Russians.'

A great many former prisoners of the Japanese supplied anecdotes. Their stories of courage moved me so deeply that I found it hard not to include them all verbatim and unabridged. That, of course, was not possible, but from the catalogue of sad and bitter memories recalling degradation and almost daily beatings, I have selected extracts from several accounts. The first of these is the story of Bill Turner, a Regular soldier of 2nd Battalion, The East Surrey Regiment. This has been selected as representative of the daily life in a camp on the Burma railway:

'The working day started at 06.00hrs every morning and then when you got outside to line up for your first meal of the day the line was about 100 yards long. Try and imagine this. You are starving, it is raining cats and dogs, you are standing there with your tin plate or something and when you get to the front of the queue all you get is a little dried fish and milktin of rice. The morning is as black as Newgate's knocker and as soon as you get your little bit of eats you move over to form another queue in case any food is left over. You are standing there bareheaded, a little bit of rag tied around your vital parts and nothing on your feet. You have had no wash, but what you have got is a great big dirty beard, but hardly any hair on your head. Smothered in sores and racked with fever you can't stop going to the toilet. Lice- and crab-ridden, and all this just to start with and you still have to go out to work. The work on this part of the railway was pure murder and slavery at its highest. The Japanese guards and engineers were pure bred ********. Absolute swine. On our first morning we were ordered to collect tools; a great big 14lb coke-hammer, cold chisels of all sizes, bamboo baskets and chunkels for digging. You had ten minutes for a break all day and when you got back to camp it was just as black as when you left it in the morning. Sometimes you worked 19 hours. In fact anything between 14 and 18 hours was quite normal. You worked until they told you to stop and that was it. To top it all, it was the monsoon season. One day I got detailed to go with another party up the line. We had to chop down bleeding great trees and then to carry them to a certain area. When we had brought them to the collecting-point the Japanese used elephants to drag them away. After two or three hours of carrying the trees your shoulder started to bleed. We were sent back to the main camp. When we arrived the place itself looked just like a graveyard. A stench was everywhere and I said to some bloke, "What's the smell?" and he said that cholera had broken out. One of my mates showed me where the cholera sick were. That was a sight I shall always remember because the lads in there didn't look human. The Japs were getting annoyed because the numbers on the working-party were getting smaller and smaller for the reason that illness in the camp was taking its toll. The death rate was about 70 per cent. We all had to work even if we were sick. If the Jap medical officer said you had to work then that was it. What our Medical Officer said didn't stand a chance. The outcome was that you had fellows with dysentery, malaria, beri-beri, ulcers, malnutrition, all working like slaves and actually dying trying to lift a hammer or trying to lift baskets full of wet earth, digging in the heat and humidity, plus hardly any food. So far as the Japs were concerned if you died lifting one basket of dirt they were satisfied.'

Many of the accounts I received told stories of men who carried out sabotage of Jap-baiting, knowing full well the risks they were taking. Arthur Penn, a Bombardier of the 5th Searchlight Regiment of the Royal Artillery, had a friend, Mac, with whom he was ordered to cut steps in a rocky ridge. As a result of one piece of baiting the guard charged at Mac, who side-stepped: "Foaming at the mouth the Nip started to bash Mac with his rifle butt. The defiant Scotsman could control himself no longer. He picked up the hammer and smashed the nip's rifle as it came towards him. There was a sickening thud as Mac brought the hammer down on the Nip's head. Shouting at the top of his voice Mac then charged at the nearest Nip and felled him with a blow to the throat before dropping dead, filled with rifle bullets."

At various times during the war in the Far East the Japanese shipped prisoners to the mainland in convoys which, towards the end of hostilities, had to run the gauntlet of US submarines. Walter G. Mole, of the RASC, had spent two years of hell on the notorious Thailand railway before he was returned to Singapore for onward trans-shipment.

'Late in 1944, I was told that I had been selected for a party destined for Japan. On arrival at the Singapore docks we were pushed up the ship gangways. I saw our quarters. Hundreds of men were being forced into the hold of the ship where tiers of platforms, just like shelves, had been fixed up. As I reached the entrance to go down the narrow steps, the stench from the perspiring human cargo below was unbearable. Despite the terrible conditions we had encountered during our POW days, we never lacked discipline and through previous experience we knew just how to get organized and did not give way to despair, whatever the odds.

'We discovered that there were twenty-odd ships in the convoy and our ship was one of the largest. We had been at sea for seven days and as dusk fell our convoy was attacked by Allied submarines. We were ordered below and the Nips stood guard at the entrance. As each depth-charge exploded it was like a clap of thunder echoing through the hold and each time it felt as though the ship had been struck. All through this terrible ordeal there was still an air of calmness and, true to British tradition, nobody panicked. For the next few nights we went through the same ordeal and the convoy was now reduced to five ships. We knew our turn was to come and dreaded the nights. When the guns above us started to fire again everyone's mind must have been on that narrow staircase; our only means of escape. Our lads queuing on the stairway to use the latrines gave us a report on the action taking place and when we were told that another ship was ablaze it was now received with mixed feelings. There was an uncanny silence. Each time the guns fired someone had the presence of mind to call out not to panic and order was maintained.'

The ship was hit while Private Mole was on deck on his way to the latrines:

'I soon realized the terrible position. There were hundreds of our men down below and they had to be got out without panic. An officer calmly called down the stairs and told them they could all come up and get some fresh air. Meanwhile me and some of the other lads were throwing batons and rafts overboard. I decided it was time for me to leave and one of my pals found a rope that was tied to the rail and hanging over the side. It was a very long drop and the rope was only about six feet long. As I hung there in midair I could feel my friend climbing over me (on his way down the rope), so I just let go. I swam like mad. I heard voices and thank God they were English. It was three of our chaps clinging to a raft about four feet square. After an hour or so our raft drifted into another that was much bigger, but crowded with POWs. About thirty yards from us was an upturned lifeboat crowded with Nip officers still with their swords and briefcases. A prettier sight I hadn't seen for years. Our boys were getting in good spirits now and some of the rude remarks that were shouted out to the Japs were nobody's business and to cheer them up we sang to them *Sons of the Sea* and *Rule Britannia!* Several hours later a tanker was spotted and as it sailed towards us suddenly it was a sheet of flame and when the smoke disappeared it had vanished. Some more smoke turned out to be a couple of Jap destroyers. They picked up all the Japanese survivors but some of our men who had swum alongside and tried to scale the rope-ladder were thrown back into the water. Two Nips with daggers started stabbing at our boys. We could hear firing and I was told that the Nips on a destroyer were shooting at us in the water. The shooting stopped and then the Nips invited us to come aboard, but knowing what bastards they were we were reluctant to do so. After about fifty of us had been crowded to the extreme front of the ship an alarm was given and the Nips all rushed to action stations and made off. All the food we had was a bucket of rice dished out in our greasy hands and when evening came we were so cold that we huddled together like a load of monkeys. The next morning we arrived at the port of Hainan.'

As the war situation deteriorated the Japanese seemed to become more brutal. American bombers were now raiding the mainland islands on a round-the-clock basis. Tom Evans, who was working in a pit, remembered the raid whose aftermath showed the high morale of the British prisoners:

'One night the raid was so bad that the new commandant asked our senior officer if his men would help save the camp. We agreed because we wanted to see if the bombers were making a good job. Our man who was acting as lookout shouted that the bombers had destroyed the mine. We all cheered as we thought, no more pit work. Next morning four prisoners and a guard were sent to collect the rice rations from down the village. We loaded our hand truck. Then we saw the women and children had no rice because the bombers had destroyed it. We felt sorry and dished ours out to them. When we got back to the camp and told the British officers and men, they agreed with what we had done. The Japs were spellbound. The commandant could speak perfect English paraded us and praised us for what we had done, putting women and children in front of ourselves and for saving the camp. The commandant said, I have always admired the British as a very brave people. As he was saying this a Japanese sergeant came on parade, all nice and clean. The commandant grabbed him and said, "Look at these Britishers, all black and tired through saving the camp. How is it you are so clean?" One day the US bombers came over dropping leaflets. We got one off one of the Japanese miners who translated it. It said "We have split the atom. If you don't surrender we shall drop the bombs!" A few days after this we came up from the [new] mine; and there it was – a miracle mushroom. The Jap guards said it [radiation sickness] was a disease. We agreed but we knowed different. One miner [Japanese] who had done soldiering and was a Christian came to us, put his arms around us and said, "War is finished. You have won." The villagers were round the camp like flies asking for food and cigarettes, offering their young daughters. The lads gave them food and cigs, feeling sorry for them and knowing we were going home. Eventually the camp was liberated and the prisoners sent telegrams home announcing that they were well and safe and *en route* back to the United Kingdom. A lot of the lads had received telegrams saying their wives had married again or had had babies by other men. You couldn't blame them as we were posted as missing believed killed for two years. I was one of the lucky ones. My wife had faith in my coming back. Its a good job she did because it took at least twelve years to get over it [being a prisoner of the Japanese].

As the war neared its end Walter Mole recalled:

'The Japs seemed to be getting more aggressive with us and found any excuse to give us a beating. This must have been around the time the atom bombs were dropped and some of the men were made to dig trenches around the camp and about five feet deep. Nobody knew why at the time. Soon afterwards we saw aircraft for the first time and the guards said that all POWs would be executed. Whether those trenches were to be our graves we never ever knew. They were never used as air raid shelters.'

That the Japanese intended to murder the prisoners in their hands was no idle rumour but was substantiated by documents at the war's end. It is the belief of the former prisoners that only the swift ending of the war by the dropping of the atomic bombs prevented a bloodbath.

The news that the war had ended was given to Bill Turner via the Thai driver of a steam-roller. That man had passed the information to some prisoners who then listened to the illegal wireless set that had been constructed in the camp out of odds and ends.

'I couldn't believe it and the first thing I heard was Ann Shelton singing. That night I couldn't sleep. In the morning we thought we would have to go to work but we had to go back to our huts. Then a British officer came in and said that the war was over. We had a church service out there in the open, just a Cross made out of an ordinary piece of wood. Your religion didn't matter. We were all one, Protestants, Catholics, Jews – they were all there. The British officer got us together and said that although the war was now over, we were not to go out as some Japs that had been coming down from Burma were just up the road and that they wouldn't hesitate to shoot the lot of us. We were also told to stay in our huts because aeroplanes were going to drop some containers with medical supplies and clothing. One fellow in his excitement dashed out to grab one of the containers and got hit straight on the head. What a way to go after all the terrible things he had gone through. One of the containers, when it was opened contained medical aids for use in brothels. It must have been a joke by some person with a great sense of humour. On the subject of brothels . . down the road there was a small village and one of the lads suggested to go down there and see what he could find. Our mate hadn't been in more than five minutes and out he came at the run and believe me I didn't stay there. When we stopped I asked him what all that was about and he said because he didn't have any money. I don't know where he got the strength from after all we had been through. The next day in strolled the fellow we had seen driving the steam-roller and he had the rank of Major plus the fact that he had with him about thirty Chinese women guerrillas, all with grenades and smallarms. He told us that we would soon be going home.'

When Walter Mole left Tokyo to go home he experienced one of the most emotional moments of his life.

'All the biggest battleships and aircraft carriers in the world were assembled there and as our ships passed, every craft from submarine to battleship had their crews manning the decks, sounding their sirens and giving three cheers as we passed. We cheered them back and some started to sing *Rule Britannia.* To me this was the end of the nightmare.'

List of Contributors

Jacky Allen
Malcolm Armstrong
H. J. Bagshaw
A. G. Bell
J. P. Blackmore
H. Braem
Jack Brewin
Martin Brice
T. Bridges
John Bucknall
Ronald Bullen
Thomas Burden
C. W. Carpenter
J. Cartwright
John Clark
Roy Cooke
Roger Cooper
John Donovan
William Donovan
R. A. Doyle
John Eardley
'Nobby' Esplin
Thomas Evans
Daniel Exley
R. Fairclough
F. Farmborough
Donald Featherstone
Harold Field
E. W. Fitness
Robert Fleming
Donald Harding
Joseph Harris
H. Hagley
Robert Hayward
Michael Henshaw
D. Hischier
Jeffrey Holland
Ronald Howard
Henry Jackson
Frederick James
Frederick Jarvis
A. Jenkins
Ronald Johnston
R. A. Joyce
Jack Kelly
Albert Kingston
John Logue
Frank Lovett
R. Maloney
Anthony Marshall
Trevor Marshall
J. Millet
John Mitton
Walter G. Mole
Charles Morrison
John Newark
Tishy Parker
Trevor Parnacott
T. Payne
Anthony Pellet
Arthur Pellet
Arthur Penn
H. Penrose
Arthur Pickford
William Priest
Joseph Ramsden
H. Rawlinson
F. Richmond
Charles Ridley
Thomas Rodney
Raymond Roys
J. Rowlands
H. Samuels
Henry Saunders
F. Shaw
Sidney Sheldrick
L. Smith
Samuel Staples
E. W. Stonard
R. Stuart Wilson
Albert Stubbings
William Summers
J. Talbot
Brian Thatcher
William Turner
Arnold Watson
George Webb
Thomas Weller
R. H. C. Wileman
A. Withey
John Wyatt

Index